FIFTH EDITION

BUSINESS INFORMATION SYSTEMS

AN INTRODUCTION

FIFTH EDITION

BUSINESS INFORMATION SYSTEMS

AN INTRODUCTION

David Kroenke
Richard Hatch

Mitchell McGRAW-HILL
New York St. Louis San Francisco Auckland Bogotá Caracas Hamburg
Lisbon London Madrid Mexico Milan Montreal New Delhi Paris
San Juan São Paulo Singapore Sydney Tokyo Toronto Watsonville

About the Cover

The authors of *Business Information Systems, Fifth Edition,* define business information systems in terms of five components: hardware, programs/software, data, procedures, and people. The pentagon on the cover symbolizes this Five-Component Model. This timeless model has served as a unifying framework throughout the text since it was introduced by the authors in the First Edition in 1981.

Mitchell **McGRAW-HILL**
Watsonville, CA 95076

BUSINESS INFORMATION SYSTEMS: AN INTRODUCTION, 5th Edition

2 3 4 5 6 7 8 9 0 VH VH 9 0 9 8 7 6 5 4 3

ISBN 0-07-035871-0

Sponsoring editor: Erika Berg
Editorial assistant: Jennifer Gilliland
Technical reviewer: Miles Ulrich, Waldata
Director of production: Jane Somers
Project manager: Greg Hubit, Bookworks
Interior designer: The Book Company, Wendy Calmenson
Cover designer: John Edeen
Compositor: Harrison Typesetting, Inc.
Printer and binder: Von Hoffman Press

Library of Congress Card Catalog No. 92-64039

When ordering this title, use ISBN 0-07-112987-1

Brief Contents

Complete Contents

PART I

PART V

SPECIAL TOPICS 442

MODULE A History of Information Systems 444

Preface to the Instructor

Business Information Systems: An Introduction, Fifth Edition, is designed for a business-oriented introductory information systems course that prepares business students to use information technology efficiently and effectively in their careers.

Our Primary Goal

This fifth edition of **Business Information Systems** focuses on fundamental concepts, concepts that will endure the changes in information technology that users confront daily. Specifically, this book prepares students to answer the following key questions:

1. What are the components of an information system?
2. What are the basic levels of information systems?
3. How are information systems developed?
4. How can computers help us increase productivity?
5. How can information systems facilitate management and decision making?

Here's how **Business Information Systems** answers these questions.

1. What are the components of an information system?

As in every edition of **Business Information Systems, information systems are defined in terms of hardware, programs, data, procedures, and people.** In any computer-based information system, these five components interact to satisfy information needs.

Many books share this definition. But only **Business Information Systems** uses this definition throughout the text as a unifying framework—in Chapter 2 to present the fundamentals of information systems, in Chapter 3 to describe the components of personal information systems, and in Chapters 8 and 9 to describe the components of shared information systems.

Whenever students encounter a new type of system, they will know to ask: What type of hardware is required? What programs? How is the data organized? Which procedures will be required? Who will be needed to support the system? This *five-component framework provides a durable structure for teachers to organize their lectures and for students to organize their learning.*

2. What are the basic levels of information systems?

Personal information systems versus shared information systems. Only **Business Information Systems** clearly differentiates these systems. Since personal systems seem more relevant and of greater interest to the average business student, they are covered first, in Part II. Shared systems follow, in Part III. Thus, we *meet students at their level of expectation, then expand the discussion to satisfy the rest of our expectations.*

3. How are information systems developed?

This course is often the only information systems course required of business students. It may be their sole opportunity to learn how systems are developed. At the same time, users have become increasingly involved in this process with the boom in end-user computing. However, users' *roles and responsibilities and the development methodology followed depend on the complexity of the business needs and the desired system.*

Only **Business Information Systems** recognizes the need for varied development methodologies. **Chapter 7 introduces prototyping, most appropriate for developing personal information systems.** Here, users assume primary responsibility for development. Then **Chapter 11 introduces the more in-depth systems development life cycle (SDLC) and computer-assisted software engineering (CASE), more appropriate for shared systems.** Once again users are actively involved in the process, if only to ensure their information needs are satisfied by the new system.

4. How can computers help us increase productivity?

Chapters 4, 5, and 6 focus on the concepts underlying the business applications of word processing, spreadsheets, and personal databases. These chapters don't demonstrate specific keystrokes, which would be quickly dated. Instead they *illustrate useful techniques for exploiting software functionality and for building effective business applications.*

These chapters benefit most from our use of brief, real-world vignettes to simulate the business environment where productivity tools are used. Users of the past four editions have told us *the vignettes enable their students to envision the types of problems and information needs they'll face in business.* They add interest and motivate students to develop effective applications.

5. How can information systems facilitate management and decision making?

In addition to improving their own productivity, students will need to know how to facilitate management. Information has emerged as an organizational resource—much like capital. *To be competitive, students must be prepared to quickly recognize and assess opportunities to use information technology to strengthen the organization's competitive position.*

Chapter 12 illustrates how effective systems can enhance managerial decision making. Organizational information systems are defined in terms of the five components: hardware, programs, data, procedures, and people.

Building on the Strengths of Prior Editions

Reviewers of the previous edition endorsed our overall structure for the reasons just described. In addition, our reviewers offered a number of useful suggestions which resulted in the changes summarized in Figure I.

Change Requested	Example of Response	Benefit
Use five-component framework *only* where appropriate	Chapter 2 and chapters introducing Part II (3) and Part III (8) are organized around this framework.	Demonstrates how hardware, programs, data, procedures, and people *interact* in a system.
Delineate text structure more clearly	Part II on personal information systems; Part III on shared systems.	Introduces concepts *in context* of appropriate level of system.
Differentiate systems development processes	Chapter 7 describes how users develop personal systems using prototyping; Chapter 11 describes the more structured systems development life cycle for shared systems and introduces CASE.	Increased practicality; reflects how systems are developed *in reality.*
Emphasize concepts over keystrokes	Chapter 4, 5, and 6 now emphasize the concepts underlying how to use software effectively rather than specific keys to press.	Students learn *timeless* concepts for exploiting software functionality *transferrable* to any package.
Centralize coverage of related topics	Reorganize Part III; consolidate coverage of data communications (9) and shared database processing (10). MIS is consolidated in Chapter 12.	Easier for students to relate pieces, and reference later.
Reduce technical load in Chapter 2	Redistribute parts of Chapter 2; some material integrated into Chapter 3.	Enhances *continuity* of presentation.
Update information technology	Increase coverage of prototyping, CASE, downsizing, outsourcing, client-server processing, line MIS, RISC computers, groupware, GUIs, etc.	The more *current* the text, the more *competitive* your students.
Add coverage of ethics and international issues	Add section on international information systems to Chapter 9; ethics to Chapter 12.	Heightens students' sensitivity to issues of increasing concern in business.
Integrate real world vignettes	Vignettes illustrate key concepts throughout the text.	*Simulates real-world* environment for students lacking business experience, reinforces concepts in context.
Enhance text design	Brand new interior design, including 4-color photos and illustrations.	Increases student interest, motivates learning.

FIGURE I Changes in *Business Information Systems: An Introduction*, Fifth Edition

Comprehensive Support Package

A variety of supporting materials is available to adopters of this text, including:

- **Application software tutorials** More than 30 lab modules can be mixed and matched to support this text and meet your specific lab objectives. Ask your local Mitchell McGraw-Hill representative for a current listing.
- **Student Study Guide**, by Diana Stark. Each lesson includes Highlights, Objectives, Knowledge Review (in fill-in-the-blank, multiple-choice, and true/false formats), Case Study Review, and Recommended Readings. Over the past four editions, this popular supplement has been ordered by over 50% of adopters of the text.
- **Instructor's Manual**, by David Kroenke and Richard Hatch. Includes lecture outlines, a summary of changes to ease the transition from the fourth to the fifth edition, teaching tips, and answers to review questions.
- Color **transparencies** and black-and-white masters.
- **Test Bank**, printed and on disk with computer test generator.
- Twelve documentary-style, broadcast-quality **videotapes**.
- **Electronic Computer Glossary**

If you would like information and costs on the application software tutorials, Study Guide, color transparencies, videotapes, and Electronic Computer Glossary, please contact your Mitchell McGraw-Hill sales representative

Acknowledgments

Thanks to the many people who assisted in the development of this text. First, we are grateful for the support and guidance of Erika Berg, who has been editor of this text for many years. We also appreciate the hard work of Jane Somers, Director of Production; Greg Hubit, Production Manager; Jennifer Gilliland, Editorial Assistant; John Ambrose, Marketing Manager; and Kristine Johnson, Marketing Assistant.

In addition we'd like to thank our reviewers for their helpful comments and suggestions:

Linda Anderson, Clackamas Community College
Gary Armstrong, Shippensburg University
Fred Augustine, Stetson University
Robert Behling, Bryant College
Eli Boyd Cohen, Bradley University
Caroline Curtis, Lorain County Community College
Annette Easton, San Diego State University
Terry Evans, Jackson State Community College

Barry Floyd, California Polytechnic State University,
San Luis Obispo
Robert Grauer, Miami University
Stephen Haag, University of Texas, Arlington
Bernard Han, Washington State University
C. Brian Honess, University of South Carolina, Columbia
Peter Irwin, Richland College
Constance Knapp, Pace University
Kenneth Kozar, University of Colorado, Boulder
Rose Laird, Northern Virginia Community College, Annandale
Verlene Leeburg, Leeburg & Associates
Metta Ongkasuwan, California State University, Sacramento
R. K. Raja, University of Texas, Arlington
John Schillak, University of Wisconsin, Eau Claire
Leonard Schwab, California State University, Hayward
Fred Scott, Broward Community College
Vincent Skudrna, Baruch College
Jill Smith, University of Denver
Norman Sondak, San Diego State University
Margaret Thomas, Ohio University
Miles Ulrich, WalData
Janet Urlab, Sinclair Commuity College
Tim Vaughn, University of Northern Iowa
David Whitney, San Francisco State University

David Kroenke
Richard Hatch

ABOUT THE AUTHORS

David Kroenke has more than 25 years of experience as a practitioner in information systems. David has authored seven books for information systems curricula. He is a popular speaker at ISECON, ICIS, and the National Computer Educator's Institute, and each spring for the past 12 years has participated in Interface's Computer Currency Seminar series.

Richard Hatch has taught business information systems and business communications for over 25 years at the University of Illinois at Urbana, Western Michigan University, and San Diego State University. Dick's clear understanding of student needs complements David's practical, real-world knowledge of how information systems are developed and used in business.

FIFTH EDITION

BUSINESS INFORMATION SYSTEMS

AN INTRODUCTION

PART ONE

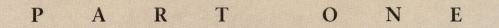

FOUNDATIONS OF BUSINESS INFORMATION SYSTEMS

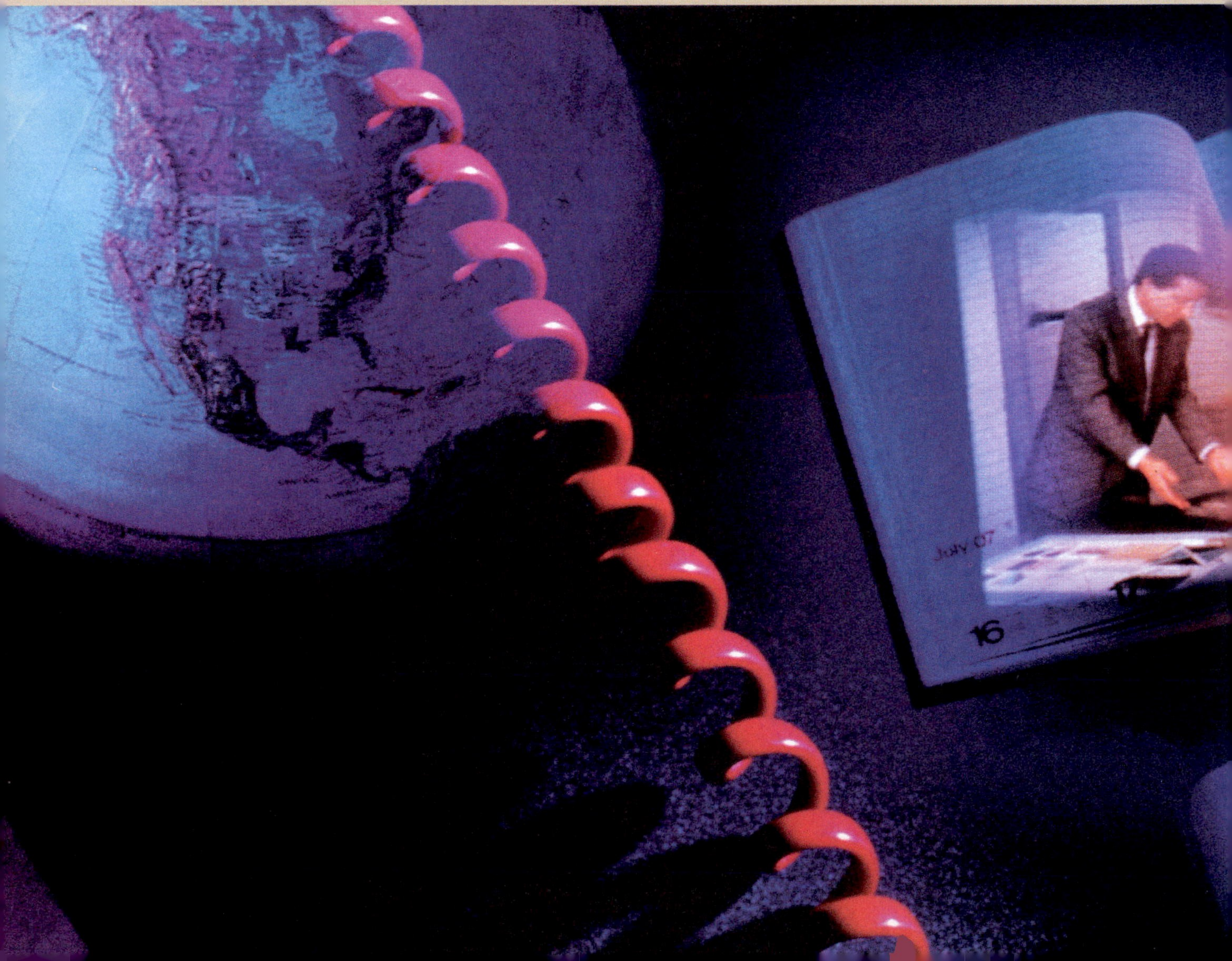

In Part One, you will learn the basics about business information systems. You will see that people use business information systems to make better business decisions and increase their productivity.

Throughout this text, you will discover how you can put information systems to work for you. Chapter 1 considers what business information systems are and how they contribute to the decision-making process. In addition, you will see examples of several kinds of working business information systems and begin to learn how they work.

In Chapter 2 you will learn about the five components that make up every business information system. Besides equipment and programs, the system includes several things. It includes data that must be collected, entered, and stored. It includes people, who must be trained to use, develop, and operate the system effectively. It includes written procedures that every system user, developer, and operator must follow to make the system function.

As you study these first foundation chapters, think about the information systems you have already encountered, such as the system that issues monthly telephone bills or the system your school uses for class registration. How does what you learn from this book relate to computer systems such as these?

CHAPTER 1

Introduction to Business Information Systems

This is not a computer text. It does not focus on computer hardware, nor is it primarily concerned with computer software. This is not a book on how to run a microcomputer or produce spreadsheets using Excel or Lotus 1-2-3. It is certainly not a book on designing and writing programs in a language like BASIC. There are books devoted to these subjects, but this is not one of them.

Rather, this is a book about business. It is a book about businesspeople, about business organizations, and about the use of information in attaining the goals and objectives of those people and organizations. It is a book about business information systems—what they do, what they consist of, and how people develop them.

In short, this is a book about your business career and about how you will use computer technology to become a better decision maker and a more productive worker. To do this, you need to learn about business information systems, which include not only computers and programs, but also data, procedures, and people. You need to know why information systems are important, what their components are, and how you can make them work for you and your company.

CHAPTER OUTLINE

BUSINESS INFORMATIONS SYSTEMS ARE IMPORTANT

Although mastering this book requires no prior knowledge of computers, we recognize that you may have some experience with personal computers, which are sometimes called PCs. You may have used them to write high school or college term papers, and you may already have worked with spreadsheets and personal databases.

However, there is a lot more to business information systems than using personal computers for term papers and spreadsheets. What happens with word processing on a personal computer is far different from what happens, for example, with the computerized inventory system at General Dynamics Corporation. Consider the differences.

Information Systems Include Personal Information Systems and Shared Information Systems

There are two major categories of business information systems. When you use a personal computer to write a report, you are using a **personal information system**, one that has only a single user. From beginning to end of your report, you are the only participant.

The inventory information system at General Dynamics Corporation is a **shared information system**. Shared information systems are much more complicated than personal information systems. Not only are the equipment and programs more complicated, but (more importantly) the interpersonal relationships required to work effectively with the system are also much more complex. For example, a shared system not only has multiple users but also has additional participants who design and develop the system, operate it for the users, and receive the benefits of its operation. As a result, many people with widely differing interests must work together effectively to make the system successful.

This book will first add to your knowledge of personal information systems in Part Two, then it will help you become an informed user of shared information systems in Part Three.

Information systems have many uses in businesses. The next few sections provide some illustrative examples—a small survey of the kinds of things computers do in business. In these examples, you may encounter a few unfamiliar terms. It is not necessary to fully understand them now; they will be explained later in the book. In the final chapter of this book, you will learn about all the major types of business information systems.

Increasing Foot Traffic at Jefferson Hardware

Lola Jefferson owns and operates a small, neighborhood hardware store. She has been in business for nearly 50 years and has remained competitive with major chains by offering personalized attention and service to customers. Lola has a warm, engaging personality and is a cornerstone of her neighborhood.

For her small space, Lola has an enormous inventory. There is almost no hardware item that she does not carry. She has irons, tablecloths, power saw blades, screws, bolts, washers, brooms, cleaning agents, paint, garden tools and supplies, and so on. Lola has arranged her inventory so that it is nearly impossible for someone to leave her store without wanting to buy something. Thus, the key to her business success is getting people in the door.

To increase foot traffic, Lola uses a desktop publishing (DTP) system to produce a quarterly newsletter that provides practical advice and tips on gardening, home maintenance, and minor repairs. A typical issue contains articles that create a demand for her plant and bulb stock, fertilizers, insecticides, gardening tools, and lawn mowers. Lola enjoys writing the articles for the newsletter, and her gregarious personality shows through in her work. The newsletter is an important way for her to stay in contact with her customers and to encourage them to visit her hardware store. Her formula for success must work, because Lola also owns the entire city block and all of the buildings on it.

Lola's DTP system is a personal information system. Its word processing, graphics, and DTP programs run on a personal computer. Lola is the system's only user. With advice from knowledgeable friends, she selected the components, purchased and assembled them, and devised her own procedures for using them effectively. Personal information systems are the subject of Part Two of this book. Chapter 4 describes the use of word processing, graphics, and DTP programs.

Tracking Boat Slip Reservations at Bull Harbor Marina

Here's another example of a personal information system. This one is used at Bull Harbor Marina to keep track of boat slip reservations. The marina's operator is John O'Reilly, a retired police officer. Several years ago, he and his wife, Mary, purchased Bull Harbor, which is located in a remote harbor on the Alaskan coast. The business includes a fuel dock, a small repair facility, a coffee shop, several boat slips, and some rental cottages. When John and Mary purchased the marina, it was in run-down condition, and business was slow.

The O'Reillys observed, however, that Bull Harbor was well located to serve not only fishermen, but also local farmers and ranchers who commuted to their properties by boat. Further, in the summer, there was substantial recreational boat traffic from both Canada and the mainland.

During a three-year period, the O'Reillys rebuilt and refurbished the restaurant and the cabins. They upgraded the restaurant food to excellent, and it attracted many new customers. Business increased dramatically—to more than double the couple's initial three-year projection.

Bull Harbor's boat slips were frequently fully occupied on summer nights. At the beginning, the O'Reillys kept track of boat slip reservations by writing them on pieces of paper and hanging these on a nail near the cash register. However, since the nearest alternative marina was several hours away, boat owners who had made reservations were understandably upset if they arrived only to find all the slips occupied. This happened on several occasions.

John O'Reilly had been a ham radio operator in the 1950s, and he had been intrigued by personal computers. He built an early model microcomputer and recently had been using a Macintosh for word processing. Since Bull Harbor had telephone service, John used it to join an on-line service to stay in touch with the outside world. Using the forums in the service, John learned about several database packages that he could run on his personal computer. He purchased the software and developed a reservation-tracking system for the boat slips and the cottages. He used the on-line forums to obtain advice and assistance when problems developed.

John's personal information system includes PC, personal database and communications programs, data about the reservations that he processes, and procedures that he follows in using the system. Chapter 6 describes personal database programs and how people use them. Chapter 9 describes data communications, including the simple system that John uses to communicate with the on-line service.

Keeping Accounts at Midwest Restaurant Supply

Some systems serve more than one user. These systems are called shared information systems. Here's an example.

Midwest Restaurant Supply Company sells, leases, and services restaurant supply equipment, including major kitchen appliances such as ranges and ovens; kitchen supplies; and service items such as glassware and linens. Midwest had been using a personal computer to do its accounting, but soon outgrew that system. The problem was that the accounting effort required for leased equipment was so time-consuming that, to meet government-imposed deadlines, several people needed to work on the system concurrently.

To meet this requirement, Midwest purchased several personal computers and connected them with a local area network (LAN). Using this system, several people could work at the same time. To create the system, Midwest installed the hardware, obtained operating system software to manage the LAN and upgraded its single-user accounting software to provide support for multiple users.

Initially, Midwest was displeased with the results. For one thing, during the first month, the equipment frequently failed. The problem was eventually traced to a faulty LAN adapter card. It was not difficult to correct the problem once it was identified, but considerable time was required to identify it.

Additionally, Midwest found that there were problems in having multiple users. Sometimes work done by one person would interfere with work being done by others. To solve this problem, the company developed procedures to better coordinate its work. In some cases, these procedures required employees to adjust their activities in ways that they did not like.

Still, once the problems were worked out, the shared system enabled Midwest to accomplish its required work within the required schedule.

Because shared information systems are far more complex than personal information systems, Midwest's initial problems are not unusual. Designing and building a shared information system—even a small one—is a very complicated task. Shared information systems are the topic of Part Three of this book.

Inventing New Games at ZVG

Zoom Video Games (ZVG) illustrates another type of shared information system. ZVG invents video game concepts, creates prototypes of the games, and sells the concept and the prototypes to major game manufacturers. To develop game concepts, ZVG uses a group conferencing facility.

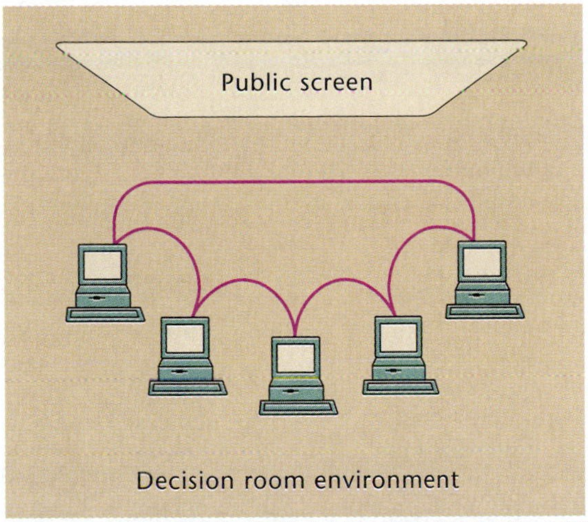

FIGURE 1-1
Equipment in a Group Conferencing Facility
The group conferencing facility provides communicating personal computers, along with a public screen where each participant's contributions are displayed for reaction and comment.

ZVG first identifies key ideas for a video game and then invites customers, salespeople, product marketing people, and managers to attend a five-day session and explore the nature and implications of their key ideas. The sessions are held in a group conferencing facility that ZVG leases from a local consulting company.

The group conferencing room (see Figure 1-1) consists of a series of desks, each equipped with a personal computer that is linked to all of the other personal computers in the room. The participants in a meeting can communicate in writing via computer. They can also communicate via a group bulletin board.

Before a meeting, a professional group facilitator meets with ZVG management to determine the desired meeting outcomes. Then the facilitator selects one or more group processes from a library of applications. Examples of applications include idea exploration, brainstorming, consensus building, and so forth. A week-long meeting is broken into a series of sessions. For each session, the facilitator explains the purpose of the session, describes the use of the group conferencing software application to be used, and initiates discussion. Participants then key in comments on the topic, and these comments are posted to a group viewing screen so they can be read by other participants. Usually, ZVG chooses to allow all comments to be made anonymously.

ZVG uses group conferencing because it allows all members to participate in a meeting without the danger that any one person will dominate the conversation. Also, some of the best game ideas are created by people who are shy and unlikely to make comments in a more public forum. Since comments are anonymous, participants feel freer to offer ideas that might seem silly or outlandish. Since some of the best video concepts arise from exactly those kinds of comments, ZVG wants to provide a safe environment for their expression.

The group conferencing system at ZVG is a shared information system. Its purpose is to enhance communication among people. Such systems are discussed in Chapter 8.

INCREASING YOUR PERSONAL PRODUCTIVITY

Box 1.1

Ubiquitous Computing: The Third Computing Revolution

In the first computing revolution, the ratio of people to computers was N-to-1. In the second revolution, personal computers insisted the ratio be 1-to-1— one person, one computer. In the third revolution, we are exploring the impact of having computers everywhere, many per person, 1-to-N.

A prerequisite of ubiquity is that computers be cheap. Making them smaller also helps, and we see the progression down from mainframes, minicomputers, desktop personal computers, portables, laptops, notebooks, palmtops, and so on. Supporting this progression have been such exciting new technologies as flat-panel displays, low-power semiconductors, and long-life batteries. And today we talk about pen-based computing—because keyboards are too big to carry around—and wireless networking, because you'd look funny dragging a very long cable behind you all the time.

Of course, as computing becomes really ubiquitous, we may not have to carry our computers around anymore. Wherever we go, computers will already be there. Or, to put it another way, future computers may be more like beds than clothes. When we travel we often carry our own clothes, but we expect to find beds waiting for us in our hotels.

Now, what if each of us always carried a very small computer pinned to our shirt, and a wireless network to keep us in constant touch as we move about our office buildings?

These badges can be a whole new technology for identifying people. For example, you walk up to a door, and the door, identifying who you are from your badge broadcast, unlocks and opens up. I bet you guessed this one and can think of a thousand related applications.

Also, these badges enable a range of applications for finding one another. For example, if you want to talk to someone, you look at your workstation to see where they are and who they are with, and then maybe dial the number of the phone in that room; no more telephone tag, no more wandering around buildings from one empty office to another.

And the badges can be used to help people remember. For example, after a full day of work, you can get a minute-by-minute printout of where you have been and with whom. Researchers have been experimenting with having these badges assist video cameras to record a person's entire day, day after day. Later the individual can go back to recall any of a large number of small things that might otherwise be lost.

Selling Credit Accounts at Consolidated Department Stores

Some shared systems are extremely large and complex. The system used to sell credit accounts at Consolidated Department Stores is an example. Consolidated operates major department stores throughout the United States and Canada. The stores sell men's, women's, and children's clothing; household goods; major appliances; jewelry; cosmetics; tools; auto supplies; and a host of other goods. Consolidated accepts major credit cards such as VISA and MasterCard and also issues its own credit card. In fact, the credit card business is a major profit center for the company.

Because customer credit is profitable, salespeople are given incentives to sell new charge accounts. To increase the likelihood that customers will want to open new accounts, Consolidated has developed a sophisticated system to provide immediate, on-the-sales-floor credit decisions.

Consider this scene: A customer is making a large purchase—a refrigerator—and is presenting a bank credit card. The salesperson points out the advantages of using Consolidated's card. If the customer agrees, the salesperson places a long-distance call to the corporation's international credit department and initiates the credit application. The customer is then given the telephone. The credit clerk asks several questions regarding income, home ownership, mortgage payments, and so on, and enters the answers into a computerized information system.

Then, through sophisticated data communications, the information system initiates an on-line credit check with a national credit bureau. Based on data from the customer and the credit bureau, the system first determines whether to approve the new account and then determines a credit limit. If credit is approved, the account is opened, and an account number is issued on the spot. The entire process adds less than three minutes to the processing of the sale.

Consolidated has over two hundred stores in North America. Hundreds of credit applications can be in progress in the same centralized credit information system at the same moment. The information system involves very sophisticated data communications among dozens of large mainframe computers.

INFORMATION: A VALUABLE RESOURCE

These examples share common elements. For example, each example involves the use of computing in a business. More importantly, as your study of this book will show, each example involves the processing of information.

Information is an odd concept. All of us seem to understand what the word *information* means. Yet, when we are pressed, we find the word difficult to define. We seem to know when have information or need it, but defining the term itself is difficult. This section considers several definitions of information and describes the characteristics of good information.

To clarify what we mean by information, we must differentiate it from *data*. For example, in a payroll system, one data value represents the simple fact that Harold Jensen worked 31.6 hours last week; another data value represents the fact that Denise Yamada worked 42.7 hours; and so on. Figure 1-2 illustrates this data. If 3,017 hourly employees worked last week, we have 3,017 data values, each representing a single fact. Unfortunately for the person who needs to know exactly what happened last week, a list of 3,017 names, with hours worked, is not very helpful. That person needs information.

What Is Information?

There are many different definitions of the term **information.** For example, here is one: *Information is knowledge derived from data.* **Data**, in turn, is defined as *recorded facts or figures*. An example of data is a list comprised

Employee Name	Employee SS#	Hours
Jensen, Harold	241-09-3434	31.6
Yamada, Denise	552-48-2837	42.7
Lightner, Theodore	182-64-4833	38.4
Himmel, Lawrence	825-17-8730	45.0
Hedgecock, Roger	638-43-9283	40.0

FIGURE 1-2

Data: Number of Hours Worked by Each Employee This data is collected by an hourly wage payroll system.

of employee names and number of hours each worked last week. For a supervisor, information may be the percentage of last week's labor costs that were paid in overtime, a value calculated from each work crew's data.

Another definition of information is this: *data placed within a context.* For example, the data that a work crew produced 93 standard units of output at an electronics company last week becomes information when its context is provided: the supervisor's quota is 72 units. The information is that she has succeeded spectacularly.

Other definitions of information involve *uncertainty reduction*. Although these definitions originated in the highly technical field of electronic-signal processing, the basic concept is applicable to business management. According to these definitions, if a manager must select a course of action from among a great many alternatives, the odds of making a correct choice are small. However, when information permits the manager to eliminate some alternatives, the odds of choosing correctly improve. Thus, information reduces the manager's uncertainty about the set of choices that ought to be considered.

Yet another definition that will be helpful to us was set out by the social scientist Gregory Bateson. He defined information as "a difference that makes a difference."[1] This definition turns out to be surprisingly robust. It reflects much of what people mean when they say they would like to have information.

Consider a budgeting situation. Why do organizations have budgets, and why do they keep track of expenses and compare them to budgets? The answer is that they are looking for differences in expenditures that make a difference to the department or to the enterprise.

Or, why might a company maintain an inventory control information system? Such systems exist to determine when an item needs to be ordered or whether items are being stocked and used at an acceptable rate. These reasons are differences that make a difference.

What Makes Information Valuable?

Not all information statements are equal. Some are better than others. In your career, you will be presented with thousands of information statements. Since you will rely on those statements, you need to be able to as-

[1]Gregory Bateson, *Steps to an Ecology of Mind* (New York: Ballantine, 1978), p. 271.

ACME ELECTRONICS CORPORATION

Overtime Report by Assembly Crew **Week of 04/29/94**

	LABOR COST				
Supervisor	*Total*	*Regular*	*Overtime*	*% Overtime*	
Falani, R.	$4,094.48	$3,971.37	$123.11	3.1	
Nikol, U.	3,626.10	3,608.06	18.04	.5	Low
Prescia, Y.	7,266.95	6,977.39	289.56	4.0	
Schott, L.	6,936.13	6,470.27	492.47	7.1	High
Wittmer, G.	6,452.70	6,101.10	351.60	5.4	

FIGURE 1-3 **Weekly Overtime Report**
This report is distributed weekly to evaluate work crew supervisors' performance with respect to the company's overtime standard.

sess their quality. Here we will discuss criteria and characteristics of good information.

First, information must be *pertinent*. The information statements must relate to the business at hand and to the matters that are important to the person who has requested the information. Information should help the person deal, in some way, with the issues in his or her world.

Second, information must be *timely*. It must be available when needed. If a media buyer needs to make a commitment on advertising by October 1, survey results that are available on September 15 are far more valuable than those that arrive on October 15.

Third, information must be *accurate*. If the report in Figure 1-3 has substantial errors—perhaps a mistake was made in processing and the report actually represents data about a different production plant—then these statements will obviously be misleading and harmful.

In some cases, however, accuracy is not so cut-and-dried. Information accuracy often depends on context. For example, people expect information statements about current and past periods to be more accurate than predictions of the future. If the year-end shareholders' report states that a total earnings of $315,687.00 was disbursed to 267,878 shares of record for a per-share earning of $1.18, people expect those numbers to be accurate.

On the other hand, if that same report indicates that next year's earnings will be $415,000 and it turns out that those earnings are $411,000, nobody will be very upset. In fact, everyone will probably be delighted. People apply different criteria for accuracy, depending on the information statement and its intended use.

In addition to pertinence, timeliness, and accuracy, good information also *reduces uncertainty*. Good information involves differences that *make a difference*. Another way of saying this is that good information contains an *element of surprise*. It contains something the person did not know. Characteristics of good information are listed in Figure 1-4.

Good information is:

- ▶ Pertinent
- ▶ Timely
- ▶ Accurate
- ▶ Able to reduce someone's uncertainty

FIGURE 1-4
The Characteristics of Good Information

INFORMATION SYSTEMS CAN IMPROVE DECISION MAKING

The decision-making process begins when someone determines that a problem exists. A problem is a difference between *what is* and *what ought to be.* When a problem is discovered, someone must determine what action to take. In making that determination, the person may have information about the current situation and about the characteristics of the desired situation, which are often termed *goals* or *standards*. Standards are typically set by the management of the organization. In deciding what to do, the decision maker uses information about the problem, the current situation, and the organization's standards. Figure 1-5 illustrates this process.

Figure 1-6 lists the four ways that information systems improve decision making: (1) They help identify problems; (2) they provide information about the current situation; (3) they provide information about standards; and (4) they facilitate communication among co-workers. Consider the following situation.

Improving Inventory Decisions at City Appliance Company

Twenty-three years ago, when City Appliance Company was founded, keeping track of inventory was no problem. The single store was small, and you could see all the stock from nearly anywhere in the room. Deciding whether you had a refrigerator to sell was easy. If it was in the store and not marked "Sold," you could safely sell it.

Ten years ago, with five stores, a large warehouse, and nearly 50 employees, things were considerably more complicated. Suppose that a salesperson at the Main Street store had just sold the only Model 91 electric dryer in the warehouse and that another customer at the store on Johnson Street wanted to buy that same model. The salesperson checked the in-

FIGURE 1-5
The Decision-Making Process

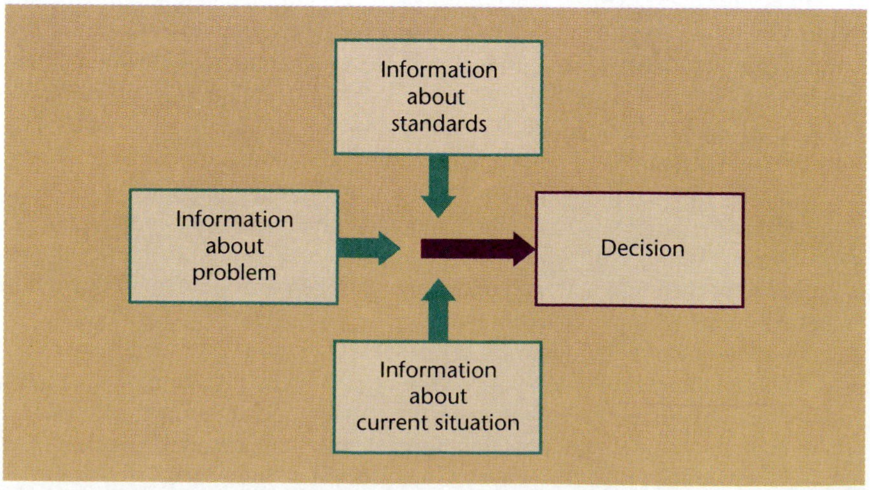

Information systems

- ▶ Help identify problems
- ▶ Provide information about the current situation
- ▶ Provide information about standards
- ▶ Facilitate communication among co-workers

FIGURE 1-6
Information Systems Support Decision Making

ventory book that was assembled at the warehouse overnight and delivered to all five stores this morning. He decided that the unit was available; he wrote up the order; and he took the customer's money.

Of course when the customer arrived at the warehouse to find no dryer waiting, he was pretty mad. It happened a lot, and the long-term ill will was costing the appliance company business. Under this system, deciding whether you had a refrigerator to sell was difficult, especially late in the day, and wrong decisions—like selling a refrigerator when none was available—were common.

Today's system is a big improvement. Here is how it works. When a salesperson at the Main Street store has a customer for a Model 91 dryer, she goes to the computer terminal in her store and enters the code to check inventory on that model. The terminal is connected to the computer in the warehouse. Figure 1-7 shows a sample inventory display. If a Model 91 is available, she enters the customer's name and other sales data, and the inventory master file is immediately updated to show that unit as sold. When any other salesperson checks inventory, even a few seconds later, that unit will not appear as available. Deciding whether she has a refrigerator to sell has become easy; and, as a bonus, the system helps her do her paperwork. After updating inventory, the system prints a customer receipt

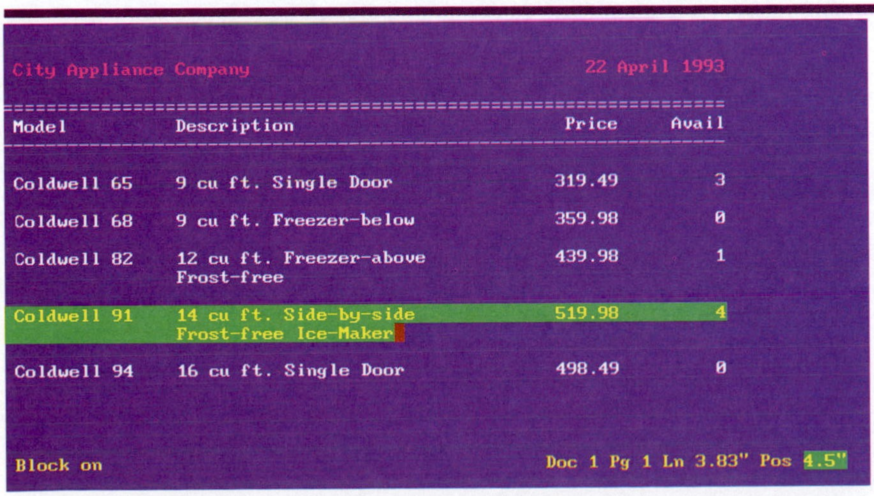
City Appliance Company 22 April 1993

Model	Description	Price	Avail
Coldwell 65	9 cu ft. Single Door	319.49	3
Coldwell 68	9 cu ft. Freezer-below	359.98	0
Coldwell 82	12 cu ft. Freezer-above Frost-free	439.98	1
Coldwell 91	14 cu ft. Side-by-side Frost-free Ice-Maker	519.98	4
Coldwell 94	16 cu ft. Single Door	498.49	0

Block on Doc 1 Pg 1 Ln 3.83" Pos 4.5"

FIGURE 1-7
Inventory Display Screen
When a salesperson checks inventory, this report appears on the terminal screen, listing the number of units available by brand and model number. To enter a customer's order for a unit, the salesperson presses the F10 key to display an order-entry screen.

Box 1.2

INCREASING YOUR PERSONAL PRODUCTIVITY

Read a Good PowerBook Lately?

The hard-cover book is a pretty venerable piece of technology. The letters on the page are descended from movable type pioneered by Johannes Gutenburg in the 1400s. The paper is not all that different from papyrus used by the Pharaohs. Books today may be written with word processors, but they are still printed in ink, bound with thread and delivered essentially by hand.

Computer enthusiasts have long predicted that the digital revolution would soon liberate the word from the printed page and put it directly on the screen. In the past decade, hundreds of reference books—including such well-known titles as Bartlett's *Familiar Quotations* and Roget's *Thesaurus*—have appeared in electronic form. But when it comes to literature, the electronic-publishing movement has run into resistance from both readers and publishers. As inevitable as the paperless book may seem, neither group could quite imagine sitting down to read one of the classics on a computer.

Nevertheless, software and hardware packages are being developed to this end. One type of software displays the text on clean white pages that replicate the design of the hardback rather than using the scrolling strings of text so familiar to computer users. A touch of a button turns the page or allows the reader to flip back and forth. Users can dog-ear the corner of a page to mark their place, or attach an electronic paper clip for easy reference. Passages can be underscored or marked on the side, and there are generous margins for putting down notes.

The computer also brings benefits not offered by ordinary books: a backlit screen that permits reading in a darkened bedroom without disturbing a spouse, the option of enlarging the type to reduce eye strain, the ability to copy passages onto a "notebook" page, and a search feature that displays occurrences of any chosen word, name or phrase. This last option could prove handy for, say, recalling the identity of an obscure Dostoyevsky character who suddenly reappears after 100 pages.

One software company has even designed a notebook-size reading device that could be loaded with digitized books from a cash machine-type dispenser that would serve as an electronic library. By eliminating distribution and warehousing costs, Booklink's backers think they can make classics available for as little as $1 or $2 a title.

But will readers give up the feel of paper and the smell of ink for a machine whose batteries have to be recharged every three hours?

Ultimately, it may be the economics of publishing, not the aesthetics, that determine what shape literature will take.

and warehouse pickup slip on the printer in the store, completing the transaction.

Ten years ago, the technology to permit instant access to absolutely current inventory data was too expensive to be cost-effective at City Appliance. Since then, the cost of computer technology has been substantially reduced, so today's improved system actually costs far less than the old system did.

Harold "Bud" Morgan is the owner of City Appliance Company. Once a month, Bud **downloads** data on sales by each salesperson, transferring the data from the company's computer into an electronic spreadsheet application on his personal computer. Using the spreadsheet, Bud can analyze these sales figures and produce the report shown in Figure 1-8. The information in such reports helps Bud make personnel decisions.

City Appliance Salesperson	Hours	No. Sales	Sales Analysis Amt. Sales	No./.Hour	Amt./Hour	Week of 04/23/94 Amt./Sale
MAIN STREET STORE						
Seymour, J.	39	119	21,443.79	3.1	549.84	180.20
Zachmann, W.	27	64	17,294.90	2.4	640.55	270.23
Katt, S.	33	51	9,093.23	1.5	275.55	178.30
Gibson, S.	29	82	24,841.77	2.8	856.61	302.95
Store Total	128	316	72,673.69	2.5	567.76	299.98
Johnson Street Store						
Alsop, S.	43	96	27,448.80	2.2	638.34	285.93
Cringley, R.	36	47	6,738.31	1.3	187.18	143.37
Machrone, B.	34	82	31,837.66	2.4	936.40	388.26
Dvorak, J.	43	50	6,245.87	1.2	145.25	124.92
Store Total	156	275	72,270.64	1.8	463.27	262.80

FIGURE 1-8

Electronic Spreadsheet Report

This report, created by an electronic spreadsheet application on Bud Morgan's personal computer, is an example of the output created by a personal information system.

Information Systems Help to Identify Problems

Information systems often help businesspeople determine that a problem exists—that some action needs to be taken. For example, the inventory system at City Appliance flags items that need to be reordered, signaling to department managers that action is needed.

Information Systems Provide Current Facts

In addition, information systems show exactly what is currently happening—where we stand at this moment. Typical information system output is composed of a variety of reports that meet the needs of various employees for information about the company's—or their own—recent performance. For example, salespeople at City Appliance can step up to a terminal and determine whether the company has a Model T51 microwave oven in stock. Similarly, supervisors at an electronics company can receive a report at any time during the workday, to see exactly how much of their quota has been completed to that point (see Figure 1-9).

Information Systems Communicate Goals and Standards

Further, information systems communicate company standards about what is supposed to be happening. Built into many reports is information about company standards—for example, indicators to flag performance that is outside the standard. Some systems provide reports, called *exception*

FIGURE 1-9
Factory Floor Data Terminal Workers in the factory can step up to a computer terminal and receive information that is necessary to their jobs.

reports, that list only cases falling outside the standard. For example, at City Appliance, department managers receive a report of inventory items that are completely out of stock, on the assumption that they may wish to telephone suppliers to request immediate shipment.

Information Systems Facilitate Interpersonal Communication

Finally, information systems facilitate communication among groups of businesspeople who share responsibility for decision making. Although many decisions are made by individuals, some decisions are made by groups of people who must coordinate their individual expertise and interests by meeting together and thrashing out a decision. Information systems frequently provide such groups with a common body of information to be considered. In addition, information systems are increasingly used as communication channels during decision making, reducing the amount of time that busy people must spend in face-to-face meetings (see Figure 1-10).

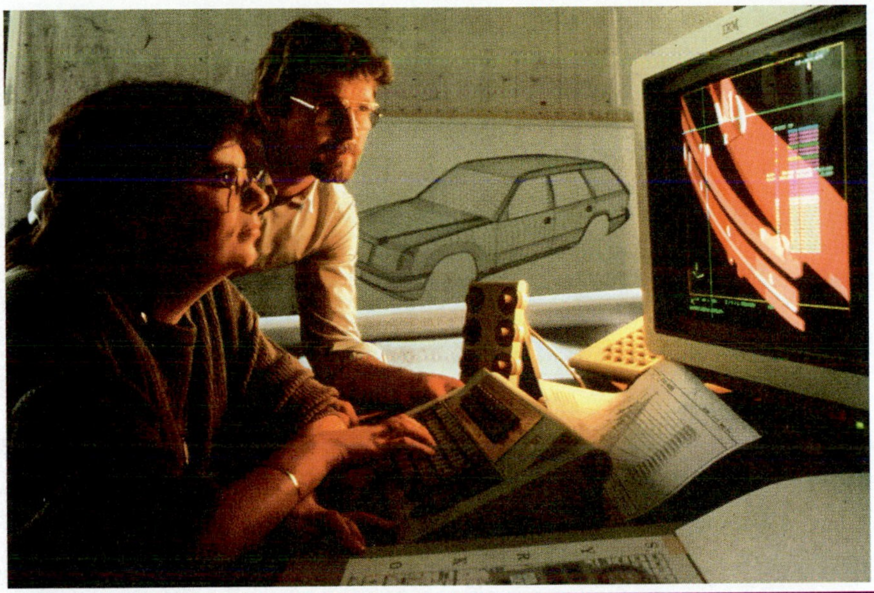

FIGURE 1-10

Creating Product Designs by Computer

This computer-aided design (CAD) system helps product designers to create new products. The resulting printed drawings assist decision makers in determining the final product specifications.

COMPUTERS ENHANCE BUSINESS INFORMATION SYSTEMS

The key functions of an information system can sometimes be performed without the use of a computer. That is, if the amount of data is small enough, you may be able to use a **manual information system**, which records data on paper forms by hand. A checkbook record keeping system is a good example of a manual system, as Figure 1-11 illustrates. The check register that comes with your printed checks provides an effective system for tracking checking accounts. Most personal computer owners use this register, rather than a computerized checkbook-balancing system. Thus, a computer is not always required in an information system.

At the same time, we must recognize that computers enhance our processing abilities so much that most business information systems actually do include computers. For the remainder of this text, we will generally assume that information systems are computer-based.

To further understand these implications, let us consider what computers can do. See Figure 1-12.

Computers Can Calculate

First, computers can *calculate*—perform arithmetic and mathematical operations. For example, to calculate the amount of a paycheck, a computer multiplies an employee's rate of pay times the number of hours worked, giving gross pay. Then it multiplies this value times a factor, giving the

RECORD ALL CHARGES OR CREDITS THAT AFFECT YOUR ACCOUNT

NUMBER	DATE	DESCRIPTION OF TRANSACTION	PAYMENT/DEBIT (−)	√ T	FEE (IF ANY) (−)	DEPOSIT/CREDIT (+)	BALANCE $
			$		$	$	

FIGURE 1-11

Manual Information System The manual check register that comes with printed checks supports a simple, efficient manual information system.

amount of federal withholding tax. The computer repeats this process for other amounts to be withheld and deducted. Finally it subtracts these amounts from gross pay, giving net pay (the amount of the paycheck).

Computers Can Store and Retrieve Data

Second, computers can *store and retrieve data*. For example, in a payroll system, the computer stores data about work hours for each employee who works in a given week. In addition, the computer stores a permanent record of each employee's name and address, Social Security number, pay rate, tax withholding rate, deduction categories, and so on.

Computers Can Communicate

Third, computers can *communicate information and data*. Part of this communication is between computer and computer, as different computers share in an information system's processing or as different information systems exchange results. Another part of the communication is between people and computers, as people enter data into computerized systems and receive reports produced by computerized systems. A final part of the communication is that between one person and another, as aided by the computer. For example, when a businessperson uses a computerized word processing system to write a report, the computer becomes part of the communication link. If the person also uses computerized electronic mail to deliver the report to the recipient's office, then the computer's communication capability is being used even further.

Computers enhance business information systems in all these ways. But computers don't solve problems. People do. Without people like you to take the initiative in developing and managing systems, none of these benefits will occur.

Computers Can
- Calculate
- Store and retrieve data
- Communicate

FIGURE 1-12
What Computers Can Do

THE GOALS OF THIS BOOK

The goal of this book is to help you learn the things that you, as a businessperson, need to know about information systems. To do this, the book is organized around four key themes. The book's organization is illustrated in Figure 1–13.

First, the book uses a consistent set of *five components of business information systems*: hardware, programs, data, procedures, and people. Chapter 2 introduces each of these components. Many other chapters throughout the book are also organized around these components.

Second, the book divides business information systems into two major categories—*personal information systems* and *shared information systems*. Part Two describes personal information systems, and Part Three describes shared information systems.

Third, for each type of system described, the book shows *how people develop such systems*. Chapter 7 shows how people develop personal information systems with prototyping, and Chapter 11 shows how shared systems are developed using widely accepted systems development life cycle (SDLC) concepts.

Fourth, the book describes the strategies used by large corporations to create information and provide it to decision makers at all levels. These strategies, called *management information systems*, are described in Chapter 12.

Summary

Business information systems include both personal information systems and shared information systems. Shared systems are far more complex in technical details, and they require the cooperation of different people with varying interests and goals.

Data is recorded facts or figures. Information is knowledge derived from data. It is data placed within a context. It is a difference that makes a difference. To be useful, information should be pertinent, timely, accurate, and capable of reducing the decision maker's uncertainty.

When a problem is discovered, a decision maker applies information about the problem, information about the current situation, and information about company standards. Information systems can provide these kinds of information. In addition, they can facilitate interpersonal communication among decision makers.

Although manual information systems are fairly common, computers enhance our processing capabilities. Most information systems considered in this book include computers. In information systems, computers can calculate, they can store and retrieve data, and they can communicate. The communication can be computer to computer, computer to person, and person to person with computer support.

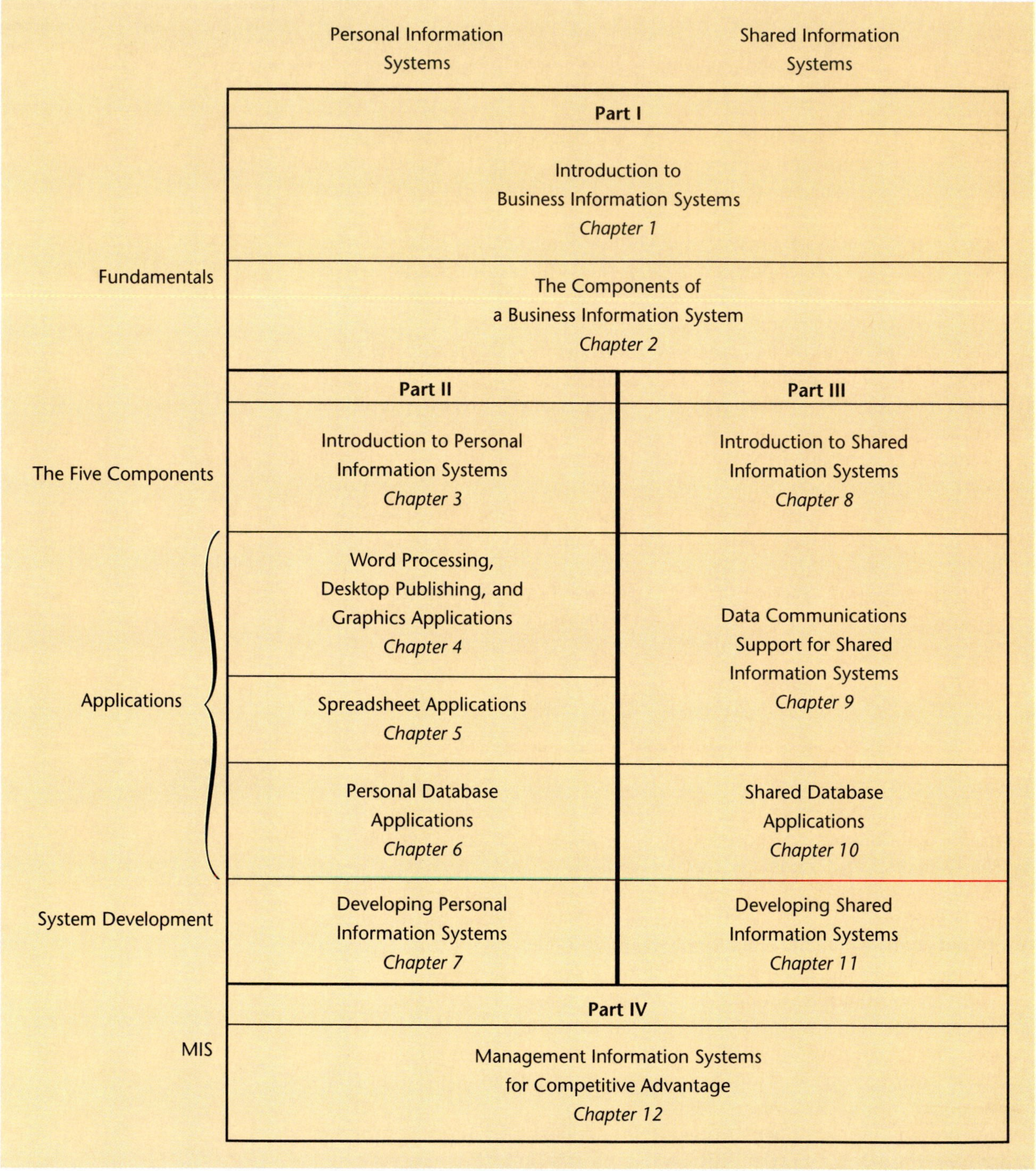
Personal Information Systems
Shared Information Systems
Fundamentals
The Five Components
Applications
System Development
MIS
Part I
Introduction to Business Information Systems
Chapter 1
The Components of a Business Information System
Chapter 2
Part II
Introduction to Personal Information Systems
Chapter 3
Word Processing, Desktop Publishing, and Graphics Applications
Chapter 4
Spreadsheet Applications
Chapter 5
Personal Database Applications
Chapter 6
Developing Personal Information Systems
Chapter 7
Part III
Introduction to Shared Information Systems
Chapter 8
Data Communications Support for Shared Information Systems
Chapter 9
Shared Database Applications
Chapter 10
Developing Shared Information Systems
Chapter 11
Part IV
Management Information Systems for Competitive Advantage
Chapter 12

FIGURE 1-13 How This Book Is Organized

Key Terms

personal information system
shared information system
reducing uncertainty
information
data
download
manual information system

Review Questions

1. What is the primary topic of this book?
2. In addition to computers and programs, what are the other components of business information systems?
3. What are the two major categories of business information systems?
4. Name at least three ways in which shared information systems are more complex than personal information systems.
5. What is the goal of the personal information system at Jefferson Hardware?
6. What is the goal of the personal information system at Bull Harbor Marina?
7. What kind of change was made in the business information system at Midwest Restaurant Supply?
8. Describe two problems that arose because of the change in the information system at Midwest Restaurant Supply.
9. What was the goal of using a group conferencing system at ZVG?
10. Name two advantages of computerized group conferencing over standard business meeting procedures for the purposes of ZVG.
11. What is the goal of the computerized credit application procedure at Consolidated Department Stores?
12. Should the credit application system at Consolidated Department Stores be considered a personal information system or a shared information system?
13. Give two definitions of information.
14. Define data.
15. What are the four characteristics of good information?
16. What is a problem?
17. Name four ways in which business information systems can improve decision making.
18. Characterize the differences among the inventory systems at City Appliance 23 years ago, 10 years ago, and today.
19. Ten years ago, why did City Appliance use an inventory system that created serious problems?
20. What is an exception report?
21. Name at least one information system that does not involve the use of a computer.
22. Name three capabilities of computers that are used in business information systems.

Discussion Questions

A. Do you agree that a knowledge of computers and programs is insufficient for you to take full advantage of computer technology in your business career? If not, why not? If so, what other knowledge do you think you will need?

B. Describe some differences between the personal information system that you may have used to write term papers and a large shared information system such as the inventory system at General Dynamics Corporation. Can you name at least six differences in addition to the fact that one is a personal system and the other is a shared system?

C. Do you agree that a list of names and hours worked is a poor source of information to a decision maker who must plan for tomorrow's labor supply? If not, why not? If so, what kinds of operations—specific calculations—could be used to convert that data into useful decision-making information? Describe at least three kinds of decisions that could be aided, and indicate, for each, the operations that would be needed to provide useful information.

D. Assuming you had easy access to a personal computer, would you prefer to maintain checking account records by a manual system or a computerized system? Name at least two advantages and two disadvantages of each method.

MINICASE

A High-Tech Rx for Profits

Here's a trick question: Which retail giant has a name starting with *Wal*, a no-nonsense, middle-America sort of appeal, and 17 straight years of record sales and earnings? Warning: The top man at this company does *not* drive a pickup, hunt birds, or call himself Sam.

The correct answer is Wal*green*, the largest drugstore chain in the U.S. and one of the longest-running successes in retailing. Recession and debt have cashiered many venerable merchants, but Walgreen, based in Deerfield, Illinois, is flush with cash. It has 1,678 stores in 29 states and Puerto Rico and plans to add 1,300 more by the end of the decade. Says Gary Vineberg, a security analyst at Dean Witter Reynolds: "This is a terrific company, very focused, very well run, and very well financed."

Like Sam Walton's Wal-Mart, Walgreen thrives by paying attention to customers, sticking to a simple business plan, and investing heavily in technology. . . . In a generally low-tech industry, it is leagues ahead of rivals in the use of computers, scanners, and satellites. . . .

The major money-spinner at Walgreen is the pharmacy. Sales of prescription drugs have increased at a double-digit clip for 48 consecutive quarters and now account for 38% of total revenues. Two big reasons: the aging of America—the average 60-year-old fills twice as many prescriptions per year as the average 30-year-old—and the rapid inflation of drug prices.

But Walgreen's prescription profits are being squeezed, mostly by insurance companies, HMOs, and state Medicaid programs. These third-party payers, which account for about half of Walgreen's prescription business, now force pharmacies to offer volume discounts. The upshot, says President Daniel Jorndt, who like Cork Walgreen was trained as a pharmacist, is that "we have to be more aggressive in controlling costs."

That means using technology to boost productivity, an area where Walgreen already excels. The company was one of the first drugstore chains to link all its pharmacies electronically to third-party payment plans, eliminating the need for pharmacists and customers to fill out time-consuming claim forms. . . .

The company's big investment in technology has a direct impact on customers. Intercom, the chain's satellite communications network, ties every pharmacy to a mainframe computer in Des Plaines, Illinois. When Clarence Jones, a Tampa businessman, takes a trip, he knows he can get a refill of his blood pressure medication at any Walgreens in the country. How much is service like that worth? "I'm such a loyal Walgreens customer that I won't buy the medicine at the Phar-Mor across the street, even though it's $5 cheaper."

Questions

1. Describe two reasons why customers like Jones are willing to pay more for a prescription drug at Walgreens than at another store.
2. Consider the following statement: "When a customer purchases a prescription from Walgreens, they are buying not just the prescription, but also information." Explain how this statement applies when Jones buys his prescription in Denver.
3. According to this article, Walgreens' pharmacies are directly linked by computer system to insurance and other third-party payers. What benefits accrue to Walgreens because of this connection? What benefits accrue to the third-party payers? What benefits accrue to the customers?
4. How does the linkage between Walgreens and the third-party payers create a competitive advantage for Walgreens?

CHAPTER 2

The Components of a Business Information System

CHAPTER OUTLINE

This is the first of three chapters that discuss the five components of a business information system: hardware, programs, data, procedures, and people. This chapter describes concepts that pertain to all types of business information systems. The following chapter, Chapter 3, begins Part Two of the book by concentrating on personal information systems and their five components. Later, at the beginning of Part Three, Chapters 8 and 9 concentrate on shared information systems and their five components.

Throughout this book you will learn how business information systems can help you work more effectively. Business information systems vary in size, features, capabilities, and price. They can be used by individuals and by groups of people. They are used in thousands of applications. Yet, despite all these variations, all business information systems share five common components. These components provide a framework that you can use to examine any business information system, no matter how big or small, simple or complex. This framework is called the *five-component model*.

THE FIVE-COMPONENT MODEL

A system is a collection of components that interact to achieve some goal. A **business information system**, as Figure 2-1 illustrates, is a collection of components, usually including a computer, that interact to satisfy some business information-processing need. For example, some business information systems manage inventory, some issue invoices, some compute taxes, and so forth.

Many businesspeople incorrectly believe that a business information system is merely a computer—with perhaps a few programs—and that, if

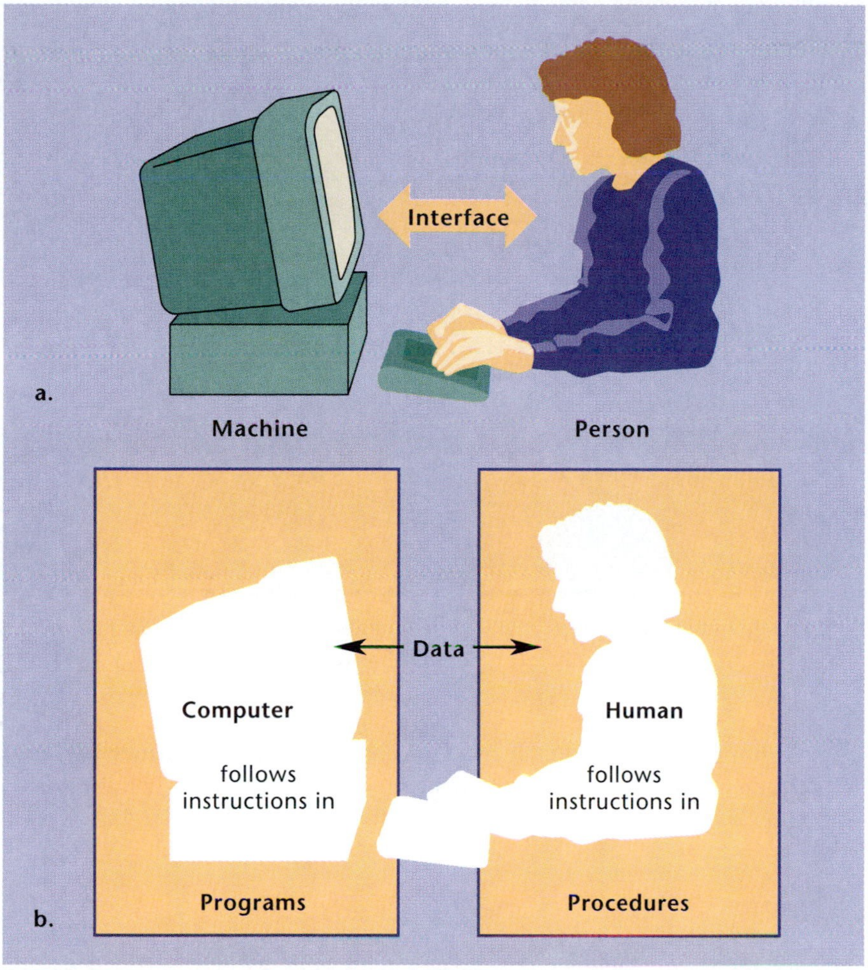

FIGURE 2-1

Five Components of a Business Information System

a. Information system components include both human and computer elements.
b. The five components of a business information system.

they simply buy a computer, all their business problems will be solved. Actually, the computer is only one of five components of a business information system. The other four components are important and often more expensive than the computer, and integrating all five components into a working system can be a challenging task.

The five components of a business information system are hardware, programs, data, procedures, and people. If any component is poorly designed or badly managed, then the business needs that the system was supposed to satisfy cannot be met.

Hardware

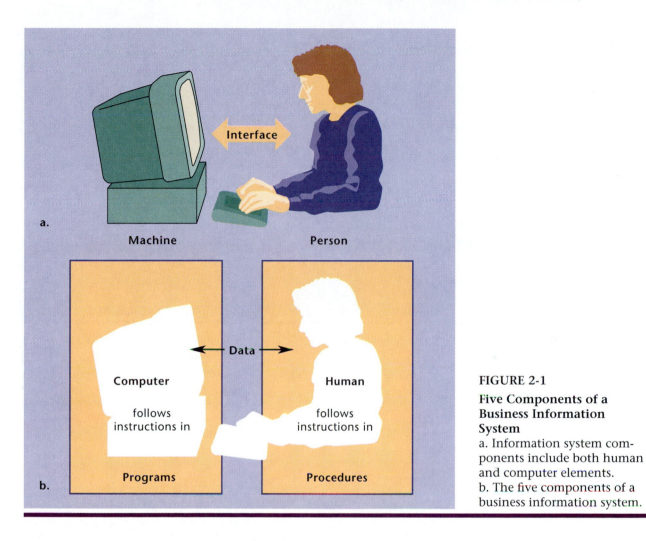

The most obvious component of a business information system is **hardware**, usually computer equipment. In a manual system, the hardware could consist of pencils and filing cabinets. As you can see in Figure 2-2,

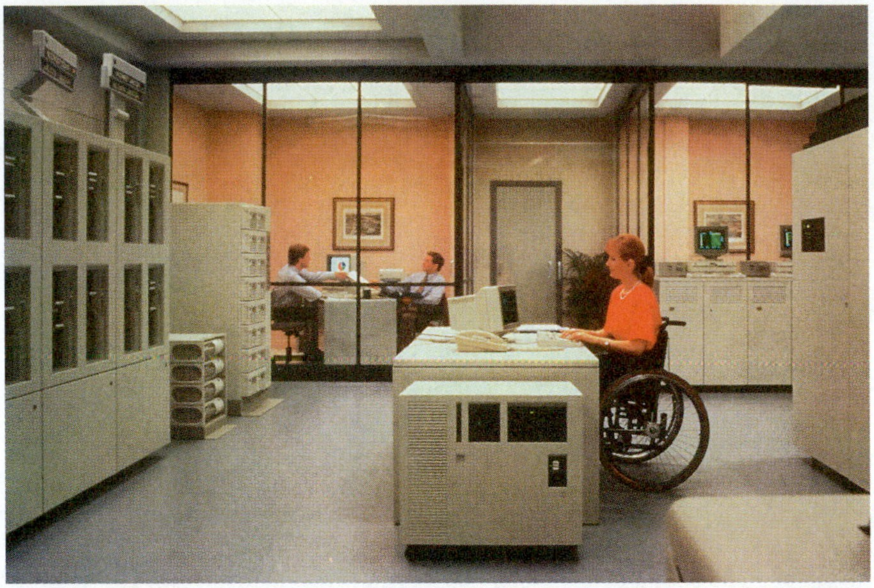

FIGURE 2-2
Mainframe Computer
In a mainframe computer room, cabling and cooling lines are mounted under the floor, and the operator sits at a console with screen and keyboard.

the equipment used in a major company can be very large (and expensive). The hardware used in a small office to meet the needs of only a single person is considerably smaller and less expensive, as shown in Figure 2-3.

Programs

The second component of a business information system is its **programs**, or instructions to the computer. Most computers are general-purpose information processing machines, which means that they can perform fundamental operations like adding, subtracting, and comparing, but that they are not especially designed for any particular purpose. For one application, a computer may create payroll checks. For another application, the same computer may prepare customer invoices. For another, it may summarize last week's production figures for the company's top executives. For yet another, it may design airplane engines. To perform each task, the computer must follow a particular sequence of instructions—a program. Figure 2-4 shows an example computer program.

Data

The third component of a business information system is **data**. Data is the thousands of raw facts that go into a computer to be processed or stored for later retrieval. Hardware, programs, and data work together to produce **information**, or useful knowledge derived from these raw facts.

Complete and correct data is essential for the successful operation of a business information system. Computers are fast, but by themselves,

FIGURE 2-3
Personal Computer
A business professional scans output produced on the personal computer on his desk.

```
100 REM This program converts temperatures
110 REM in Fahrenheit to centigrade
120 PRINT "Enter a temperature in Fahrenheit degrees";
130 INPUT F
140 LET C = (F - 32) * 5 / 9
150 PRINT "The centigrade equivalent of "; F;
160 PRINT "Fahrenheit is "; C
170 END
```

FIGURE 2-4
Example Computer Program in BASIC

they do not solve business problems. With incorrect or incomplete input, they will work diligently and produce gibberish for output. "Garbage in, garbage out" is an old, but appropriate, saying in the computer business.

Procedures

The last two components of a business information system—procedures and people—go hand in hand. **Procedures** are instructions to people on the use and operation of a system. Procedures explain to people how to operate the computer hardware. They describe what programs to run, what data to use, and what to do with the results. Procedures also describe how to correct errors and what to do when the system fails, or **crashes**.

People

People who possess the required skills bring together the other four components and integrate the information system into the business environment. Skilled people are needed to develop business information systems, operate them, enter data, and use the results to make decisions.

HARDWARE

In most business information systems, the hardware is computer hardware. A computer is an electrically connected configuration of five types of devices. The heart of the configuration is the *central processing unit*. Attached to it are *main memory*, *input devices*, *output devices*, and *storage devices* (see Figure 2-5).

The Central Processing Unit

The **central processing unit** (also known as the **CPU**, or, simply, the **processor**) interprets and carries out program instructions, and communicates with other devices.

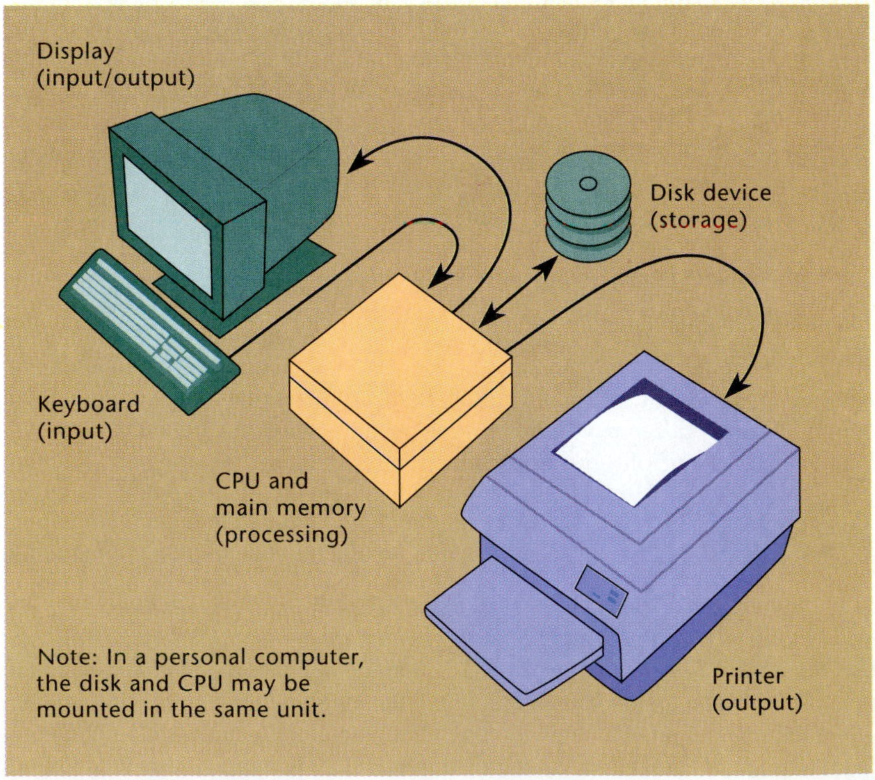

FIGURE 2-5

Schematic of a Typical Computer Hardware System
A typical hardware system includes CPU and main memory, and input, output, and storage components.

The CPU consists of a **control unit** and an **arithmetic-logic unit (ALU)** (see Figure 2-6). The control unit interprets program instructions and communicates with the input, output, and storage devices attached to the CPU. The ALU performs arithmetic and logic operations (such as comparisons) when the control unit tells it to do so.

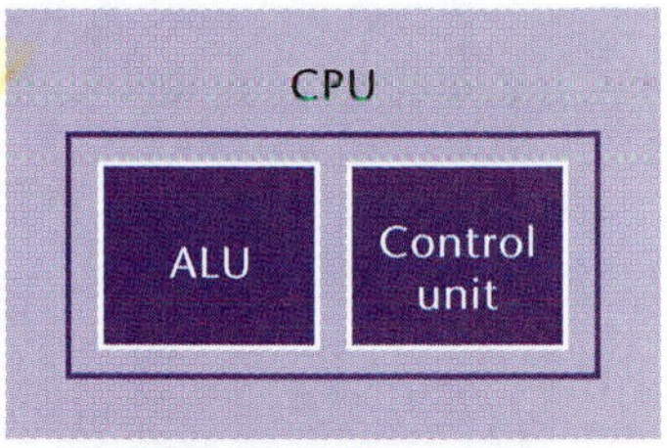

FIGURE 2-6

The CPU

The CPU includes the ALU and the control unit.

Just a few years ago, CPUs could be sharply divided into four sizes—*supercomputers*, *mainframe computers*, *minicomputers*, and *microcomputers*—differentiated by computing power, physical size, and cost (see Figure 2-7). However, recently the costs of processor and memory chips have dropped dramatically, and their capacities and speeds have rapidly increased. As a result, the differences in cost and power among today's computers are less clear. In general, microcomputers are usually small enough to fit on a desktop and, though they may have as much raw computing power as some mainframes, they are typically configured to meet the computing needs of a single user. In contrast, mainframe CPUs are usually housed in floor-standing cabinets and require elaborate cooling systems and under-floor cabling. They are configured to meet the needs of many concurrent users who need to share access to the same programs and data. Minicomputers, as in Figure 2-8, are intermediate in size and cost. Supercomputers, the world's most powerful systems (see Figure 2-9), are highly specialized machines for scientific and engineering computation.

Main Memory

Main memory holds the data to be processed, the program instructions to be executed, and the program results waiting to be issued. Both data and program instructions must be in main memory before processing can proceed. Main memory is also called *temporary storage*, because data and programs are temporarily stored there during processing. The size of a computer's main memory is measured in **bytes**. In simplest terms, a byte is the amount of memory required to store one letter or digit.

Input Devices

Input devices translate data from people-understandable form into computer-understandable form. All data must be represented as binary 1s

FIGURE 2-7 Characteristics of Mainframe Computers, Minicomputers, and Microcomputers, as of 1993

Type	Application	Speed	Memory Size	Number of Concurrent Users
Mainframe	Organizational	10–100+ MIPS	32–500MB	Hundreds
Minicomputer	Workgroup, small organizational	4–40+ MIPS	24–250MB	Dozens
Microcomputer	Personal computing	2–40+ MIPS	0.5–20+MB	One (dozens in LAN)

FIGURE 2-8

Minicomputer

Minicomputers capable of supporting both local terminals and remote terminals are traditionally smaller, less expensive, less powerful, and less demanding of special cooling and electrical supplies than are mainframe computers.

FIGURE 2-9

Supercomputer

This Cray Y-MP is an example of today's most powerful computers for engineering and scientific applications. Supercomputers of the next generation may fit on a desktop.

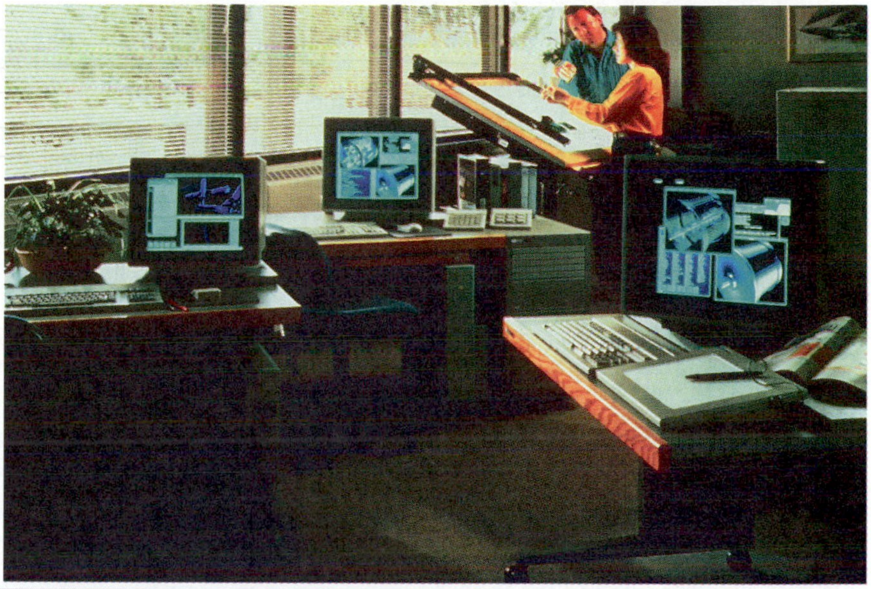

FIGURE 2-10

Engineering Workstation The engineering workstation is a computer with high-resolution graphics display and specialized input devices used by designers to create engineering specifications and drawings.

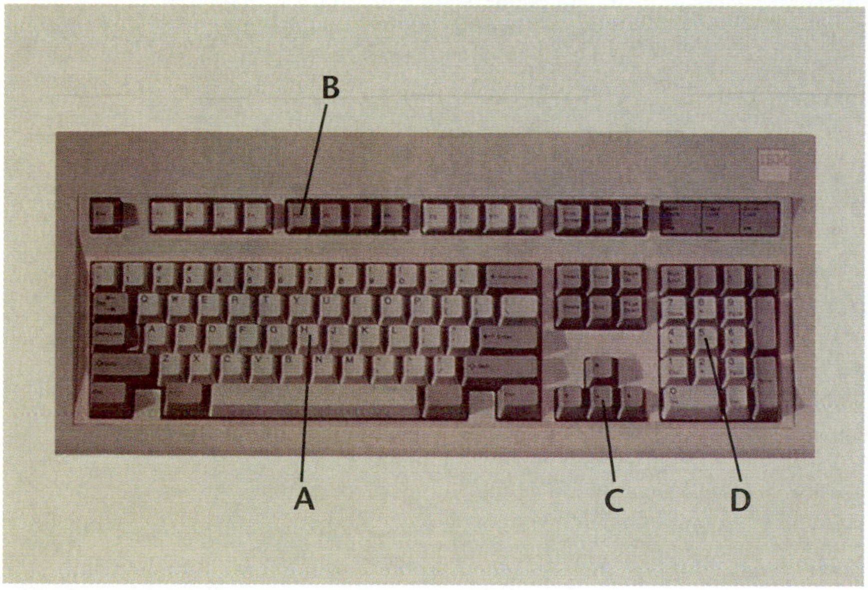

FIGURE 2-11

Computer Keyboard The areas of a typical computer keyboard layout include (*A*) alphanumeric keys, (*B*) function keys used for entering programmed commands, (*C*) cursor movement keys for moving the cursor on the screen, and (*D*) numeric keypad for rapid entry of numeric data.

and 0s inside the computer. The most common input device is the keyboard. Today, the use of various alternative input devices is dramatically increasing.

The Keyboard The most widely used input device is the general-purpose *keyboard*, typically containing alphanumeric keys, function keys, cursor movement keys, and numeric keypad (see Figure 2-11). A computer user

INCREASING YOUR PERSONAL PRODUCTIVITY

Box 2.1

Buying Smart: Picking a Personal Laser

When you're buying a low-end laser printer, you can't expect to get all the fancy fonts and speedy, sophisticated paper handling you'd find in more expensive printers. But even when you're spending less than $1000, you should demand a lot.

Output Quality Because most laser printers have 300-dot-per-inch resolution, almost all deliver reasonably sharp text. A few of them get the *jaggies*—the stair-stepping pattern you sometimes notice on the curves of letters—and *shadowing*—the blurring of characters by faint outlines of themselves. Also, many low-end printers have problems with graphics output: They often produce streaks in solid areas of black or gray and apply toner unevenly.

Performance Print speeds vary widely from printer to printer and from print job to print job. Check out the speeds for the kind of work you do, whether it be straightforward word processing, spreadsheets, or complex desktop publishing jobs.

Price The whole point of personal laser printers is their low price—shop around and you'll find some great deals. Remember, however, to add in the cost of consumables to your budget: These printers will require a new toner cartridge every couple thousand pages.

Service and Support Because printers are mechanical beasties with plenty of moving parts that can break, solid service and support are essential. When it comes to repairs, look for on-site service from the manufacturer.

Design and Construction Convenience is the best measure of good design. With this in mind, it should have small footprints, low weights, and integrated toner-drum assemblies that aren't a mess to change. You'll also want understandable front-panel controls.

Font/Graphics Options Most of these printers do a fine job with typical office correspondence. They come with an adequate supply of resident bit-mapped fonts. If the resident fonts aren't enough for you, you can either add a font cartridge or download soft fonts. Look for printers that take HP-compatible font cartridges, because they give you access to a wide range of fonts and emulations from both HP and third-party vendors. If you're stuck with just one vendor's cartridges, you won't have the same range of options.

Paper Handling Personal printers don't need as sophisticated paper handling as a network machine does. But even on a personal printer, a large paper tray means you spend less time running to the supply cabinet for another ream of bond. Look for printers with adjustable trays that can accommodate more exotic paper sizes. If you print a lot of letters and your printer has the option of dual bins, you might consider buying a second tray so you can load letterhead in one bin, envelopes in the other, and then switch between them.

enters data by typing it on the keyboard. However, because it is a slow, costly, and error-prone process, data entry through general-purpose keyboards is being partially replaced by various other methods of capturing data electronically.

Alternative Input Devices Alternative input devices include special-purpose keyboards, scanning devices, touch-tone input devices, and voice recognition devices.

Special-purpose keyboards include those found in the **point-of-sale (POS) terminals** that have replaced cash registers in many stores and fast-

FIGURE 2-12

Special-Purpose Keyboard This keyboard on a POS terminal in a fast-food restaurant has keys labeled by product rather than by amount of money as with traditional cash register keys. When a customer orders a hamburger, the clerk presses the "one hamburger" key. An attached computer interprets this input and creates a receipt showing items and amounts charged.

food restaurants (see Figure 2-12). They are called point-of-sale terminals because transaction data is entered at the point of sale to the customer, helping the company to keep records current.

Scanning devices Scanning devices, or **scanners**, are cameras that translate images on a page into codes for computer processing. Scanning devices eliminate the manual conversion of source data into digital format by keyboard data entry. Specialized scanners are used for various types of source documents. The **mark-sense reader** scans a page like the one in Figure 2-13 and detects pencil marks. An **optical character reader (OCR)** scans a document and interprets symbols as numbers or letters of the alphabet. OCRs are used in some department stores, where the clerk passes a pistol-shaped scanner over the price tag, and the OCR interprets the letters and numbers on the tag (see Figure 2-14). To eliminate ambiguity between similar characters, a special type font is used. The **laser bar-code scanner**, as in Figure 2-15, is familiar to anyone who shops in a major grocery store chain. The **Universal Product Code (UPC)**, which this unit scans, is printed on everything sold in supermarkets—from soup to nuts and from clothing to record albums.

When you press a key on a touch-tone telephone, the keypad generates a specific audio tone. A **touch-tone input device** detects that tone, permitting data entry by telephone.

Voice recognition devices These are not widely used today, but they hold the promise of very convenient computer input—by simply speaking. Voice recognition technology is still in the development stage.

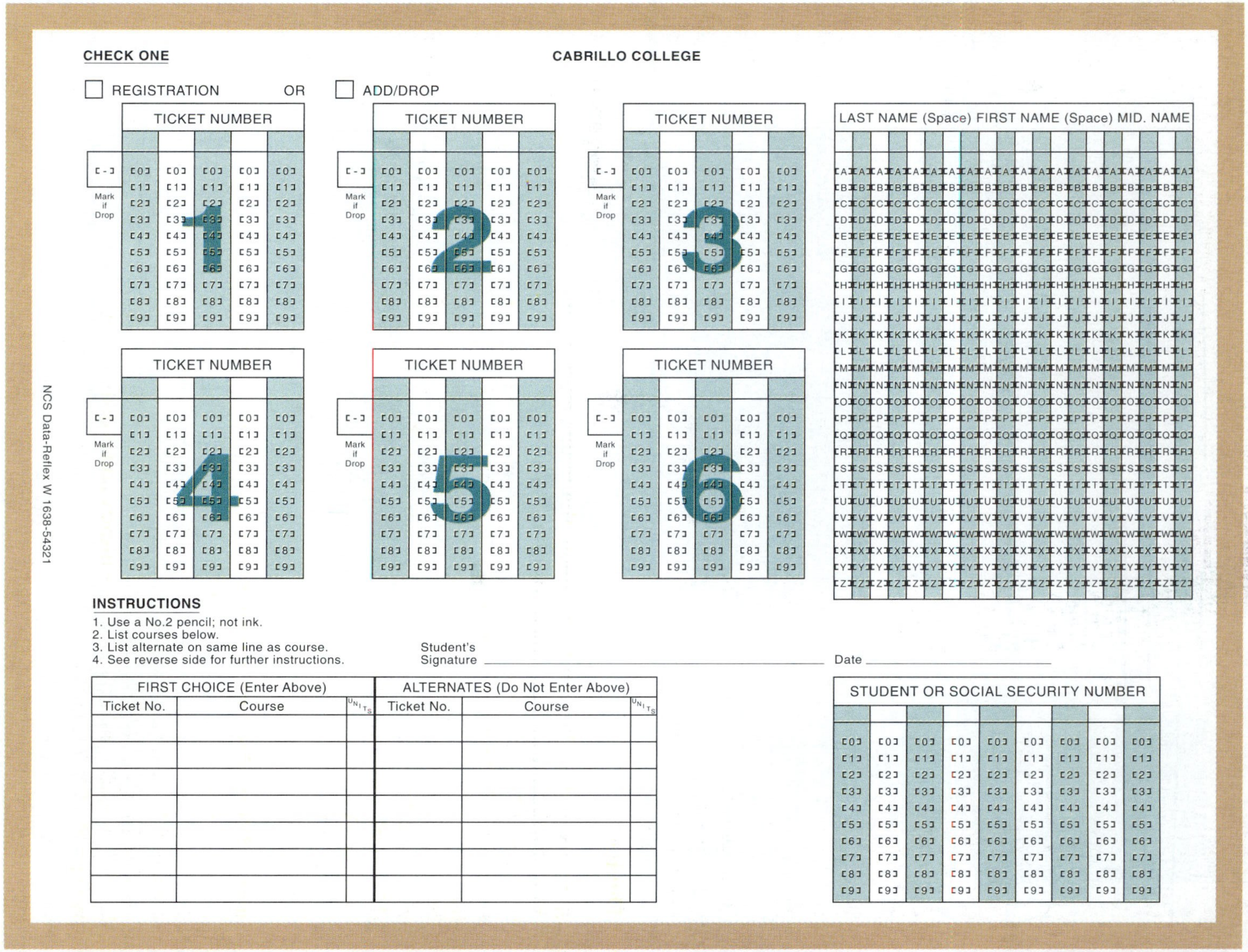
CHECK ONE

CABRILLO COLLEGE

☐ REGISTRATION OR ☐ ADD/DROP

TICKET NUMBER (×6, numbered 1–6), each with [-] Mark if Drop and columns [0] [1] [2] [3] [4] [5] [6] [7] [8] [9]

LAST NAME (Space) FIRST NAME (Space) MID. NAME

[A] [B] [C] [D] [E] [F] [G] [H] [I] [J] [K] [L] [M] [N] [O] [P] [Q] [R] [S] [T] [U] [V] [W] [X] [Y] [Z]

INSTRUCTIONS
1. Use a No.2 pencil; not ink.
2. List courses below.
3. List alternate on same line as course.
4. See reverse side for further instructions.

Student's Signature ____________ Date ____________

FIRST CHOICE (Enter Above)			ALTERNATES (Do Not Enter Above)		
Ticket No.	Course	UNITS	Ticket No.	Course	UNITS

STUDENT OR SOCIAL SECURITY NUMBER

[0] [1] [2] [3] [4] [5] [6] [7] [8] [9]

NCS Data-Reflex W 1638-54321

FIGURE 2-13 Mark-Sense Form
Mark-sense readers can translate the marks on this student registration form into computerized data for processing.

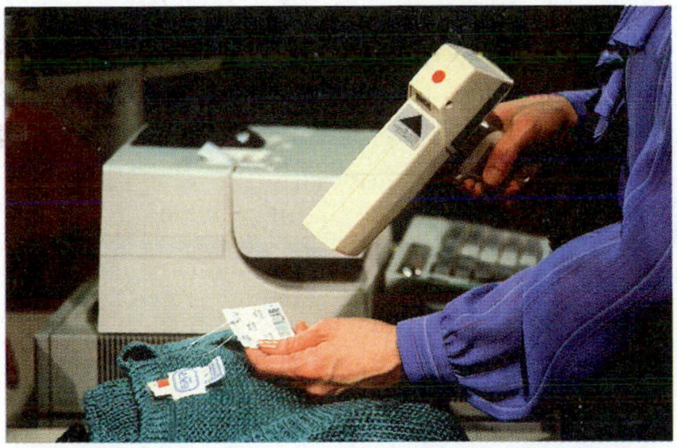

FIGURE 2-14

A POS Terminal in a Retail Store
By scanning a bar code on the price tag attached to each product, the sales clerk is ensuring that correct data is used during the transaction and also in tracking the store's inventory for purposes of planning.

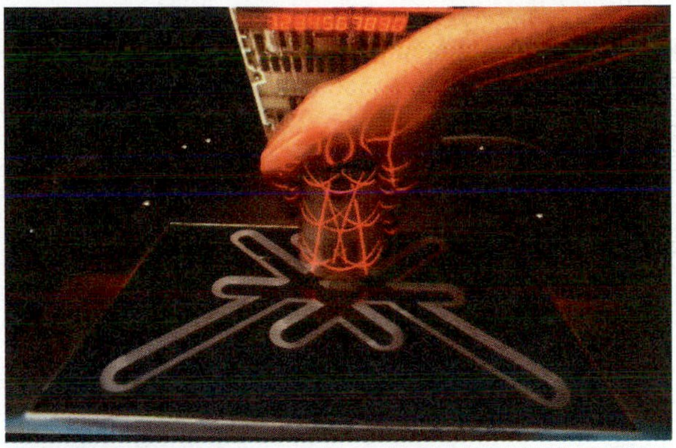

FIGURE 2-15

Grocery Store Bar-Code Scanner
By passing each item over a laser bar-code scanner, the clerk is letting the store compile customer bills and keep inventory with an accuracy never before possible.

Output Devices

Processing occurs in the CPU, but to be useful, the results must be presented in human-readable format, which is the purpose of **output devices**. Output devices translate data from computer-understandable form into human-understandable form. They include soft copy devices and hard copy devices.

Soft Copy Output Devices **Soft copy** is computer output on a **display screen**, which is also sometimes called a **computer monitor** or a **video display terminal (VDT)** (see Figure 2-16). Various video technologies are employed to produce soft copy, but they all accomplish essentially the same thing: They display output (numbers, text, graphs, and pictures) on a screen.

The most widely used technology for display screens, as for television screens, is the **cathode-ray tube (CRT)**. A CRT uses an electronic gun to shoot beams at the back of the screen, creating tiny points of light. Each point is called a *picture element*, or **pixel**. Patterns of light and dark pixels create a visible image, as Figure 2-17 shows.

Resolution refers to the sharpness of the display and is determined by the density of pixels. The higher the number of pixels per inch, the sharper the image, as in Figure 2-18.

Screens can display either monochrome images or color images. Monochrome displays show one color against a contrasting background—for example, green on black or amber on black. Color displays are not so limited. Depending on the sophistication of the equipment, a color screen can display thousands of shades of color.

FIGURE 2-16
VDTs Connected to a Minicomputer
VDTs provide text and graphic output from the processing of this minicomputer.

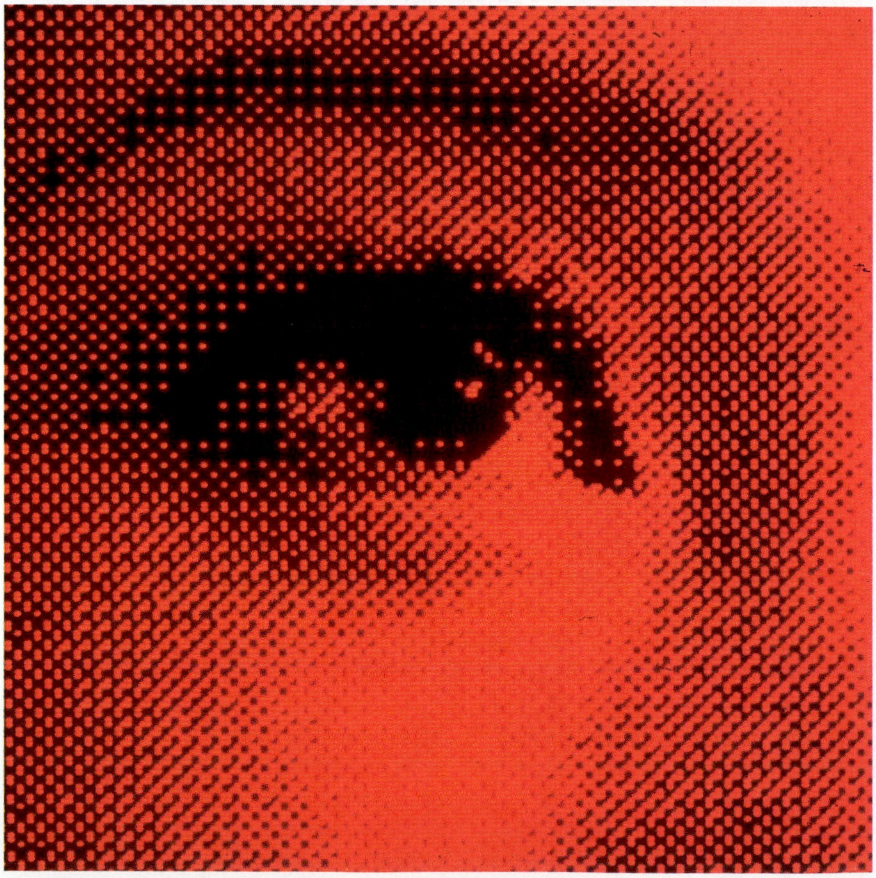

FIGURE 2-17
Pixels
A screen display is composed of many pixels of different colors and intensities.

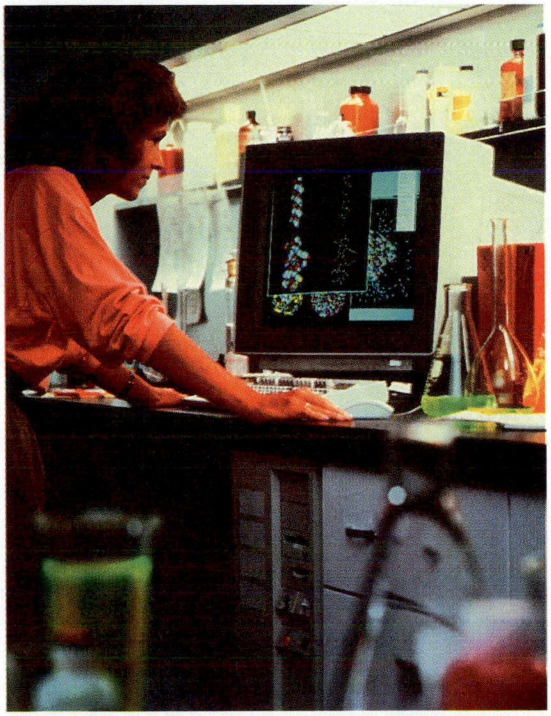

FIGURE 2-18
A Very-High-Resolution Video Display
The display provided by this engineering workstation has much higher resolution than do most personal computer displays.

Hard Copy Output Devices **Hard copy** is computer output on paper. Devices that produce hard copy include printers and plotters.

Printers record information on paper in a variety of ways. There are three major ways of categorizing printers: (1) impact versus nonimpact printers; (2) character versus line versus page printers; and (3) dot matrix versus formed-character printers.

The first way of categorizing printers includes *impact versus nonimpact* printers. In impact printers, a metal die is struck against an inked ribbon, which then strikes the surface of the paper and transfers ink to the paper (see Figure 2-19). Nonimpact printers, as the name suggests, do not involve such impact. Most use xerographic technology, as in office copiers. Such printers are called **laser printers**. Others, called **ink-jet printers**, shoot tiny droplets of ink onto the paper.

The second way of categorizing printers includes *character versus line versus page* printers. **Character printers**, like the small dot matrix printers commonly used with personal computers (as in Figure 2-20), create one printed character at a time serially across the printed line. **Line printers**, such as those commonly used with mainframe computers (see Figure 2-21), create an entire line of output in one operation. Line printers usually produce output much faster than character printers. **Page printers**, such as laser printers (see Figure 2-22), create an entire page at a time, much as an office copier does. The fastest printers in existence are the advanced laser page printers used with some mainframe computers.

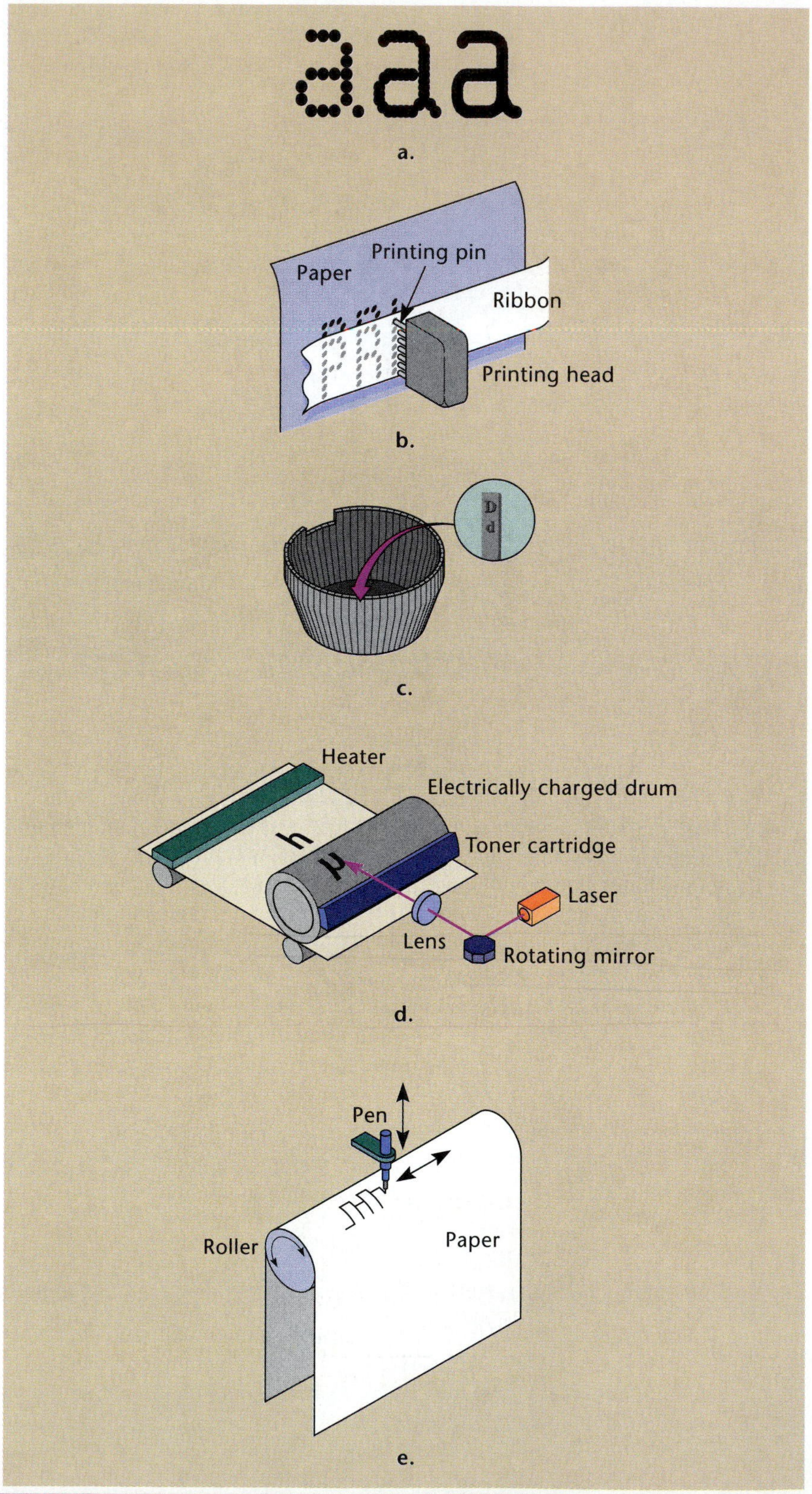

FIGURE 2-19

Ways of Creating Printed Output

a. Dot-matrix output consists of a series of dots.
b. The dots are made by a print head that uses small pins to strike the ribbon against the paper.
c. Formed-character printing uses a die in the shape of a letter to strike the ribbon against the paper.
d. A laser printer shares much of its technology with an office copier.
e. A plotter uses a pen to draw lines on paper.

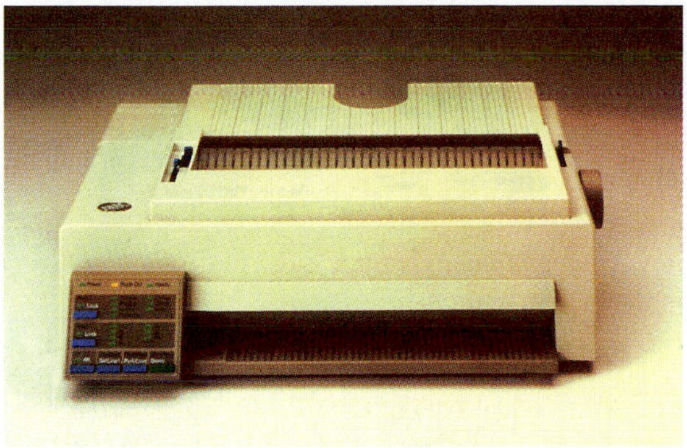

FIGURE 2-20

Dot-Matrix Printer

The dot matrix printer is inexpensive to purchase and operate. Its speed and print quality are modest, and its operation is inherently noisy in an office or study environment.

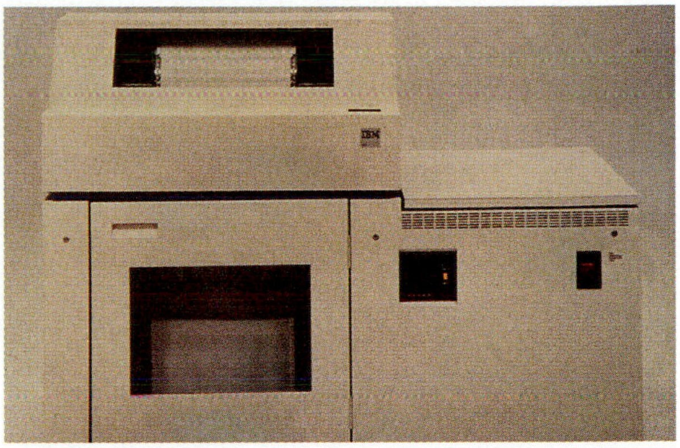

FIGURE 2-21

Line Printer

A line printer connected to a minicomputer or a mainframe computer produces high-speed output of text material.

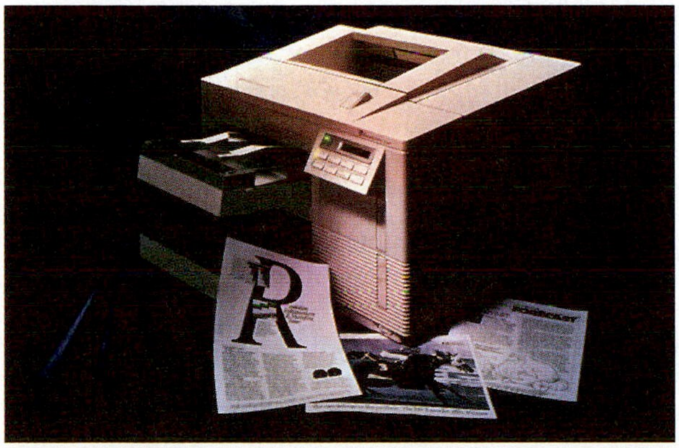

FIGURE 2-22

Desktop Laser Printer

The laser printer uses technology similar to the office copier. Instead of creating its image from the light reflected from a paper original, it uses a laser beam to paint an image that is then fixed onto a page of output.

The final way of categorizing printers includes *dot matrix versus formed-character* printers. The **dot matrix printer** forms characters from many tiny dots, each made by striking a pin into an inked ribbon and the paper. Laser printers also create output in the form of tiny dots, but their very high resolution, typically 300 dots per inch or more in each direction, makes the resulting image very sharp. The **formed-character printer** strikes a metal die in the shape of the character onto the inked ribbon and the paper.

Plotters use computer-controlled pens to produce hard copy by drawing lines on the paper to form letters, numbers, and other symbols, as well as graphical output such as diagrams, charts, and maps (see Figure

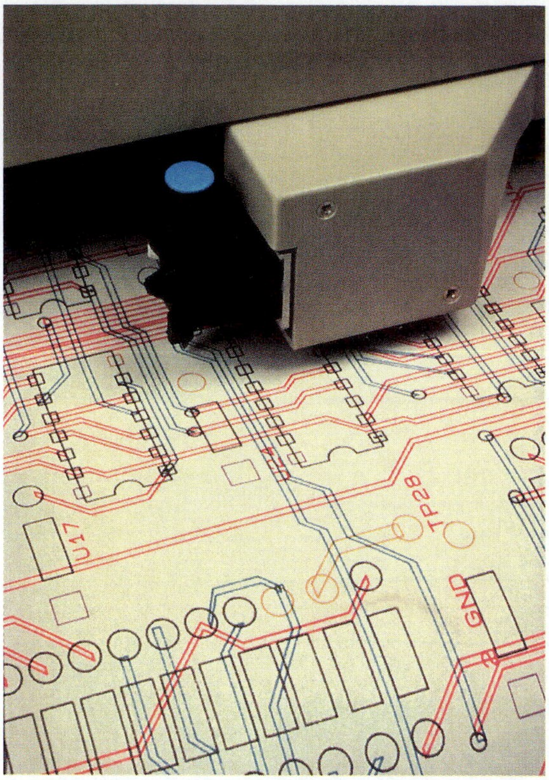

FIGURE 2-23
Plotter
A plotter creates output by moving pens around over the surface of the paper.

2-23). They are used especially to create line drawings such as engineering drawings.

Storage Devices

Computers use two kinds of memory systems. Main memory contains data and programs for immediate processing. **Storage devices** provide long-term storage for data and programs. Main memory is much more costly than the equivalent amount of storage, so computer systems include only enough main memory to contain the data and programs that must be processed concurrently. Storage space is provided for all the data and programs that will be processed at various times.

Most storage devices record data and programs as magnetized spots on a thin film of a medium that can be magnetized. Such storage media can be reused. That is, when stored data or programs become obsolete, other data or programs can be recorded over them. The recordings remain until they are erased or until something else overwrites them.

The most commonly used storage devices are magnetic disk and magnetic tape.

Magnetic Disk The **magnetic disks** that store data are coated with a brown iron-based compound that can be magnetized. One disk, or several

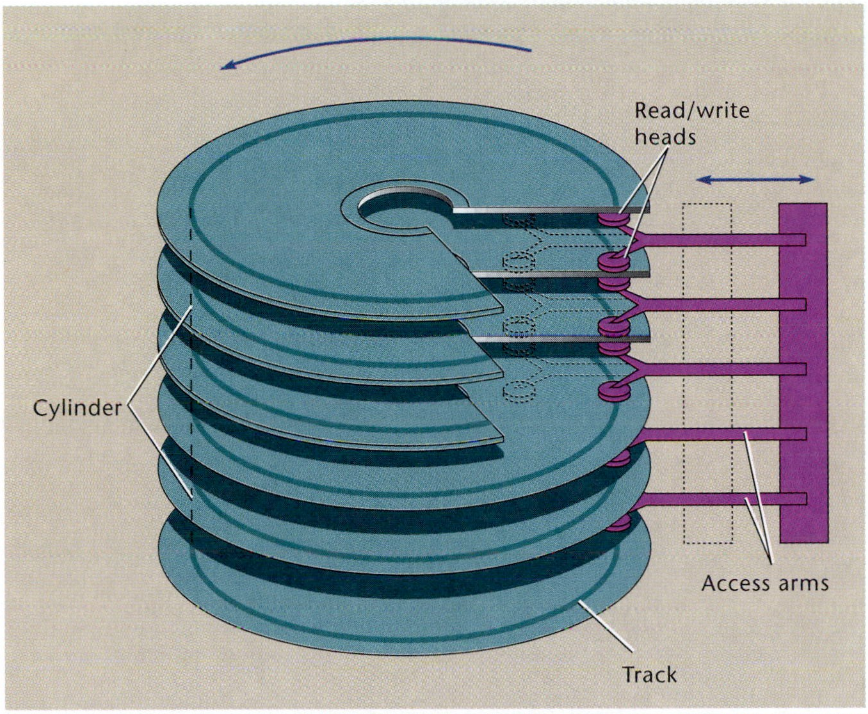

FIGURE 2-24
Multiple-Disk Hard Disk Drive
As the disks rotate, the read/write heads on the access arms sweep over a single track on each disk. Since the access arms move together, all the read/write heads are synchronized on the same track.

disks attached to a central hub, are enclosed in a disk drive, which rotates the disks at high speed (see Figure 2-24). Read/write heads attached to access arms read or record information as magnetic spots representing 1s and 0s in concentric **tracks**. Since each track may hold many thousands of bytes of information, tracks are divided into arcs called **sectors** for easier management, as Figure 2-25 shows. Each sector typically holds about 500 to 1,000 bytes, depending on the design of the particular disk drive.

Magnetic Tape Once used as the primary storage medium, **magnetic tape** (see Figure 2-26) is now used mainly for permanently storing records, called archives, and for making **backups**—copies of data and programs stored on disk. Backups are made in anticipation of accidental data loss. For example, if a read/write head in a disk drive malfunctioned—called a *head crash,* fortunately an unusual occurrence—some or all of the data on the disk in that drive could be destroyed. However, you could recover from this potential disaster by repairing the drive, then restoring the lost data to the new disk from backup copies.

A tape drive is a **sequential access** device, and a disk drive is a **direct access** device. That means data recorded on magnetic tape can only be accessed in exactly the order in which it is recorded, in contrast to data on magnetic disk, which can be accessed by moving directly to a specific sector. Therefore, to retrieve a specific piece of data from a magnetic tape, the

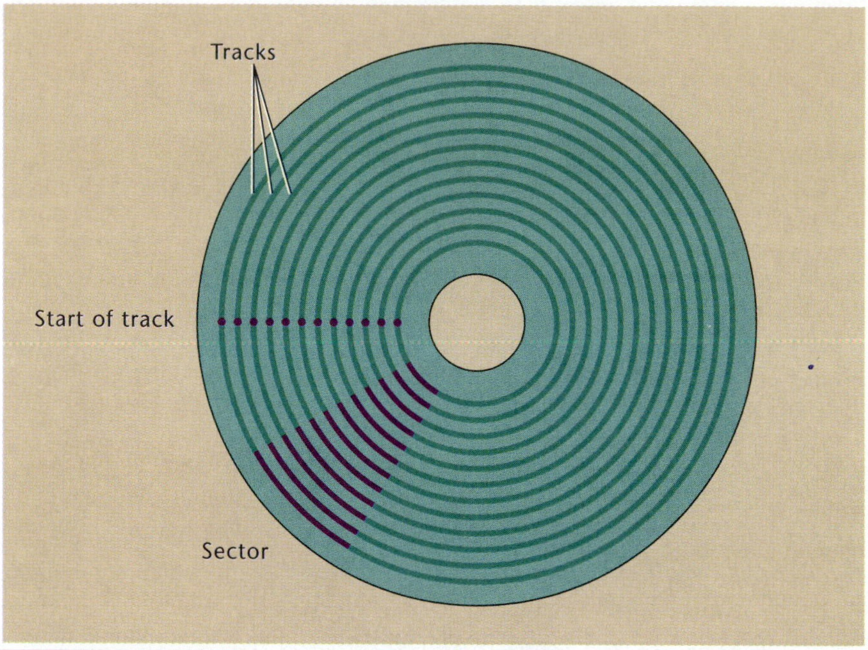

FIGURE 2-25

Tracks and Sectors on a Magnetic Disk

To access data on a magnetic disk, the access arm must move the read/write head to the proper track, then the disk must rotate until the proper sector passes under the read/write head.

FIGURE 2-26

Using Magnetic Tapes

These magnetic tapes in their cases have been selected for mounting on the tape drives for processing.

computer must read through all of the preceding data values on the tape until it arrives at that item. Since, in normal processing, data may be needed in an unpredictable order (depending on the sequence of transactions that happen to be entered into the computer), tape is not well suited as a medium for storing active data.

PROGRAMS

A computer is a *general-purpose machine*. At one moment, it can be a payroll machine; at another, an inventory machine; at still another, a machine to monitor the heartbeat of a patient in intensive care. The component that makes a computer perform a particular task is the **program**, a set of instructions to the computer. Computer equipment is called *hardware* because it is tangible; programs are called **software** because they are not.

There are two types of programs: system programs and application programs. **System programs** operate the computer equipment and establish the general computing environment. **Application programs** solve specific user problems or satisfy specific user needs.

System Programs

System programs exist to provide general computing services to anyone who wants to use the computer. We will discuss four types of system programs: operating systems, utilities, language translators, and communications programs (see Figure 2-27).

Operating Systems An **operating system** is a program (or set of programs) that coordinates the execution of all other programs. It is the system's traffic cop. The operating system, rather than the hardware, gives your system a distinctive look and feel—its own way of interacting with you.

When a computer is powered on, the first thing it does is give control to the operating system. The operating system takes over and remains active in main memory until the computer is shut off. The portion of main memory not used by the operating system is used by application programs and data.

The operating system assists application programs by performing basic input-output (I/O) operations. For example, the operating system handles the technical details of output, such as displaying words and numbers on a computer screen. Similarly, when an application program needs data from a disk, it asks the operating system to handle the details. The operating system determines where the data is located on the disk and issues commands to the disk drive to retrieve it. To support disk I/O, the operating system maintains disk catalogs. A catalog, or directory, as it is sometimes called, records who created the data, when it was created, when it was last processed, and exactly where it is stored on the disk.

Most large computer operating systems (and many personal systems) support **multitasking**. That is, they allow several application programs to be loaded into the CPU at once for execution. In large computers, the operating system may be given a list of the programs to be run during a particular period and the resources—access to printer, disk drives, and the like—required by each. The operating system determines when each

- ▶ Operating systems
- ▶ Utilities
- ▶ Language translators
- ▶ Communications software

FIGURE 2-27
System Programs

Fabricating a Chip: The Heart of a Computer

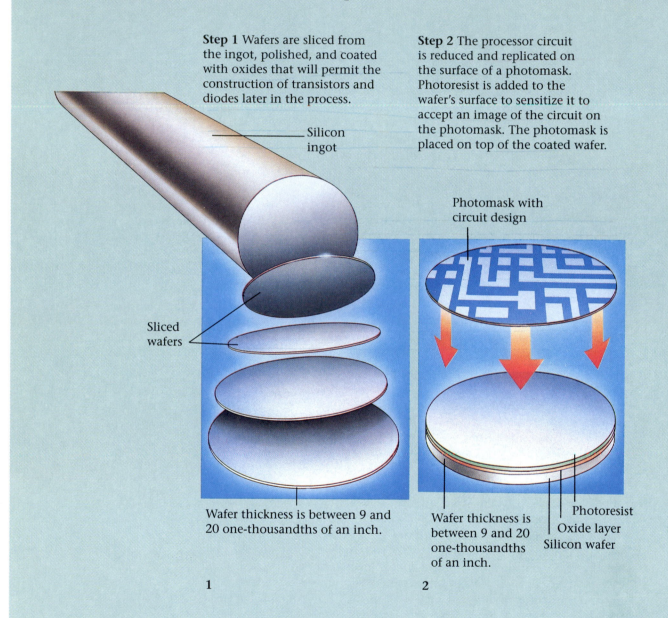

Step 1 Wafers are sliced from the ingot, polished, and coated with oxides that will permit the construction of transistors and diodes later in the process.

Step 2 The processor circuit is reduced and replicated on the surface of a photomask. Photoresist is added to the wafer's surface to sensitize it to accept an image of the circuit on the photomask. The photomask is placed on top of the coated wafer.

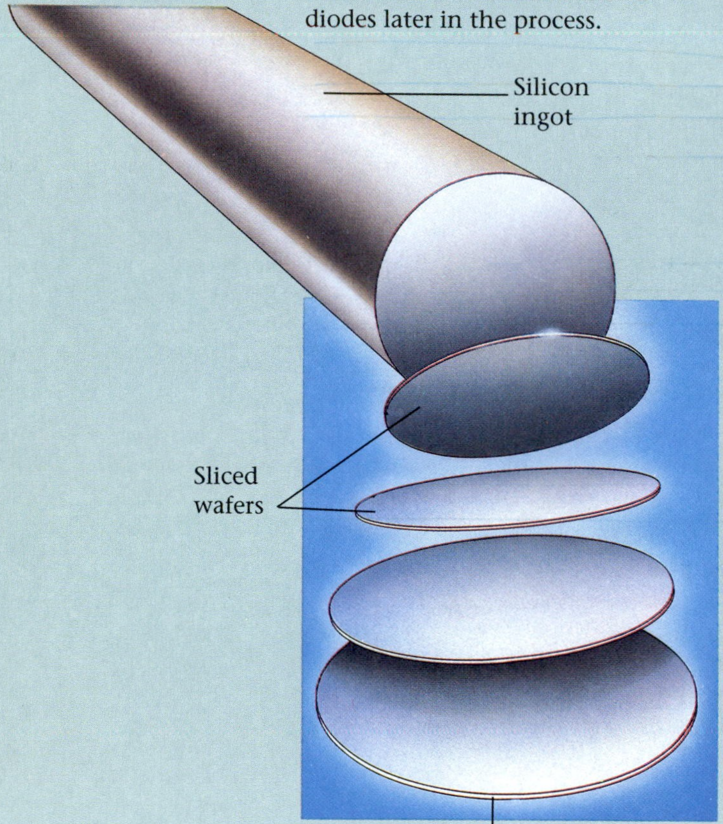

1

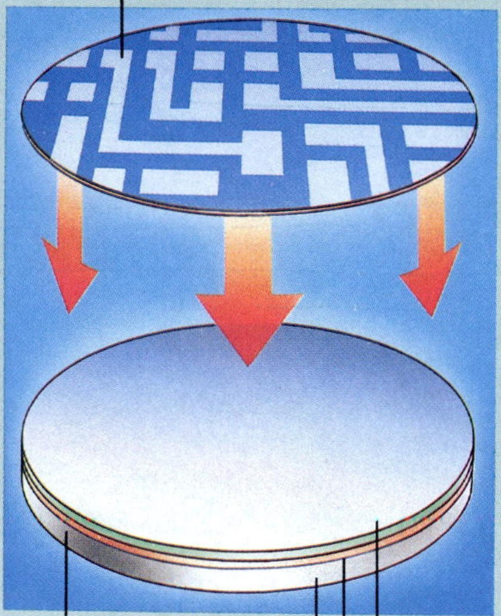

2

Box 2.2

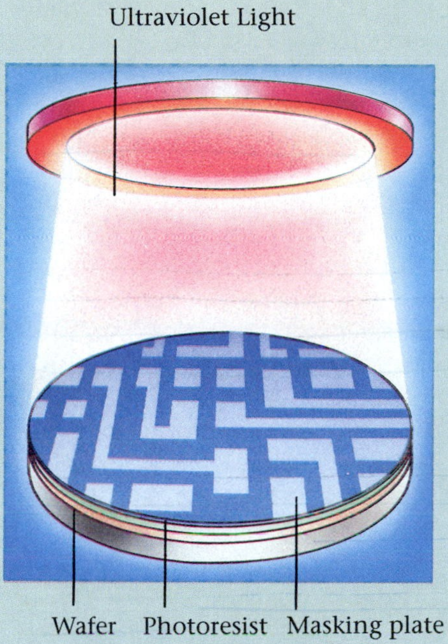

3

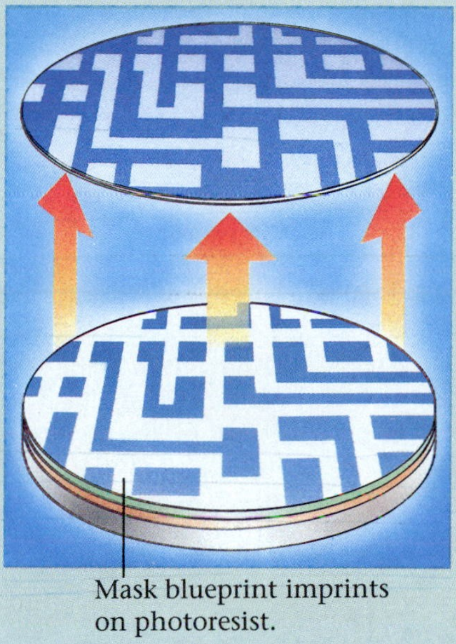

4

Step 3 The wafer is exposed to light and an image of the circuit is transferred in a process similar to that used for everyday photographic film.

Step 4 The photomask is removed and the wafer is exposed to acids and other chemicals. These etch the circuit in areas where the photomask has been printed.

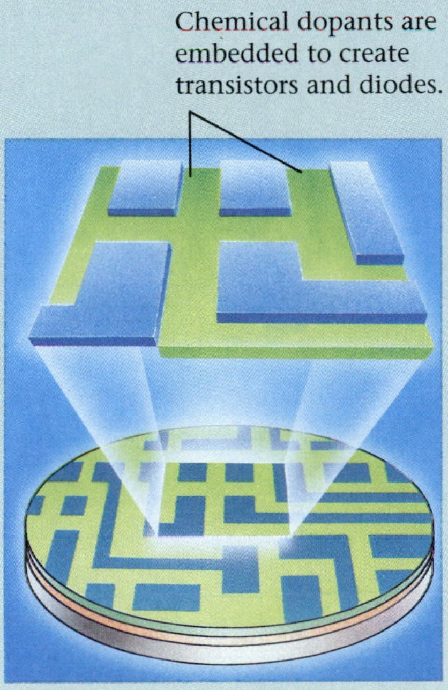

Chemical dopants are embedded to create transistors and diodes.

5

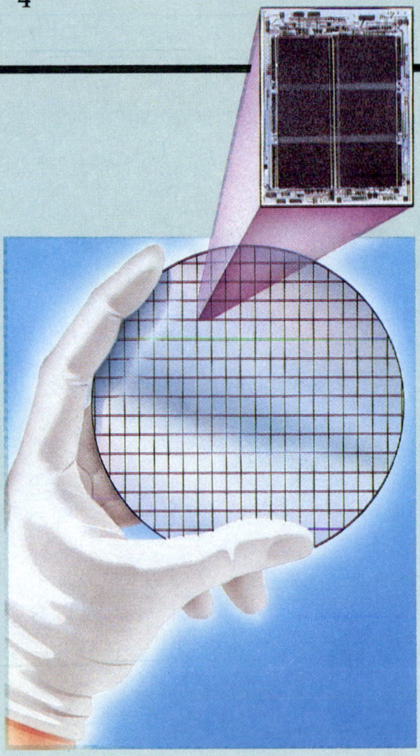

6

Step 5 Ions of boron, phosphorus, and arsenic (the dopants) are implanted in the wafer to create transistors, diodes, and other components.

Step 6 A finished wafer is examined under a microscope and with other techniques. Defective wafers are discarded.

Steps 3 through 6 may be repeated a dozen or more times to build up layers of circuits.

program will be run to minimize contention for these resources at any one time.

In multitasking, the operating system gives each loaded application program a portion of the CPU's time. For instance, if five programs vie for CPU time, the operating system lets the first one use the CPU for, say, one-tenth of a second—perhaps a million operations—then lets the second program use the CPU, and so forth. Eventually the first program gets another chance to execute, as do the others. Spreading the limited CPU resources this way is called **time slicing**.

In addition, the CPU could often be forced to wait while a program's relatively slow I/O operations are performed. The CPU executes instructions at a phenomenal rate—perhaps ten million instructions per second. If it must wait while the user types input, for example, it would have to wait through nearly a million instructions between keystrokes, even from the fastest typists. To avoid this, the operating system watches for times when the CPU is merely waiting for input or output—when the CPU is **I/O bound**—and it immediately switches the CPU over to another program.

In personal information systems, commonly used operating systems are DOS, System 7, and OS/2. In shared information systems, commonly used operating systems are UNIX, VMS, and MVS.

Utilities The second type of system program is the **utility**. A utility program satisfies a common need such as file management. For example, utilities exist that perform the following functions:

- Backing up an entire database onto tape or disk
- Converting a file from one format to another
- Printing the contents of a disk file
- Preparing a new disk for use
- Renaming a file
- Deleting a group of files
- Sorting a group of records

These and other common routines are used so frequently that they must work as efficiently as possible. Some of the most expert programmers build careers around optimizing routines like these. For both mainframe computers and personal computers, utilities can be obtained from the operating system vendor and from third parties—companies other than your company and the computer company.

Language Translators

A computer can execute programs only when they are in **machine language**—strings of 1s and 0s like this: 1101101110011100. But writing programs in machine language is an error-prone and tedious process. As a result, programs are written in programming languages, which are codes that people understand more easily. For example, here are two instructions in a language called COmmon Business-Oriented Language (**COBOL**):

```
MOVE "0056" TO PAY-CODE.
MULTIPLY HOURS TIMES PAY-RATE GIVING GROSS-PAY.
```

The first instruction directs the computer to place the value 0056 in the memory space predefined as PAY-CODE. The second instruction causes the computer to calculate an employee's gross pay, using data values stored in memory spaces predefined as HOURS and PAY-RATE.

Compilers are language translation programs that translate program code such as this COBOL code (called **source code**) into binary machine instructions (called **object code**). A separate compiler is needed for each programming language that is used on a particular computer.

At any given time, about a thousand different computer languages are in use for various purposes. Of these, only about a dozen have become commercially important. As a future businessperson, you need to know about the four programming languages that are most widely used in business.

Programmers use the first three—COBOL, C, and BASIC—to develop applications. COBOL is the oldest, most widely used language for developing programs in shared business information systems. C is used to develop commercial microcomputer programs, such as word processors and spreadsheets. Beginners All-Purpose Symbolic Instruction Code (**BASIC**) was designed to teach people the rudiments of programming. Early versions of BASIC were not useful for commercial programming. Recently, a number of vendors, most notably Microsoft, have revised BASIC to make it a sophisticated and powerful language.

The fourth important language, Structured Query Language, or **SQL** (pronounced "sequel"), is the one you are most likely to use yourself. SQL is widely used to retrieve data from a database.

Communications Programs **Communications programs** let computers talk to one another, a surprisingly complex activity. When communication takes place, a program in the sending computer is needed to package the message, address it to a destination computer, and send it on its way. Communications software in the receiving computer accepts the message, unpackages it, verifies that it was received in good condition, and acknowledges, through a return message, that it was received. Some communications programs control the fairly straightforward dialogue between two computers. Others control the complex communications among an entire network of up to thousands of computers. Data communications, including communications programs, is the subject of Chapter 9.

Application Programs

Application programs apply technology to help you solve your business problems. They tell you to whom to send bills this month, how much money you have left in the household account, which salespeople will receive bonuses this week, and so on. Application programs can be purchased ready-made (packaged programs), or they can be custom developed.

Packaged Application Programs Packaged application programs are purchased, ready to use, from a commercial vendor. Packaged applications have several advantages. First, they are immediately available, so development time is minimal. Second, ready-made programs are less expensive than are custom-made programs. Third, products that have been around for a while have been thoroughly tested and are probably very reliable.

One risk of using packaged application programs is that the developer could go out of business. The developer usually provides customer service; program improvements (for example, to accommodate capabilities of newer hardware); and, to some extent, training. If the developer is suddenly no longer available, then you no longer have customer support. However, if you choose popular packages from reputable developers, you can minimize this risk.

Packaged application programs deal with business problems that are common to many users. Depending on the nature of the problem, it may be common to many different types of users—lots of businesses of all kinds use electronic spreadsheet programs to do budgets. Or it may be common to many users of the same type—most retail stores use some sort of computer-based inventory-control system. Consequently, packaged application software has two possible markets: the horizontal market and the vertical market.

Horizontal market programs provide general business functions to a variety of users (see Figure 2-28). Some widely used business applications include accounts receivable, accounts payable, general ledger, and payroll

FIGURE 2-28
Characteristics of Horizontal Market Application Programs

- General business functions
- Read computer magazines for information about these programs
- Benefits:
  - Minimum development time
  - Cheaper than custom-developed programs
- Risks:
  - Vendor could go out of business

FIGURE 2-29
Characteristics of Vertical Market Application Programs

- Industry-specific functions
- Read industry literature for information about these programs
- Benefits:
  - Minimum development time
  - Close fit to user needs
  - Cheaper than custom-developed programs
- Risks:
  - Vendor could go out of business
  - Might not be a perfect requirements fit

- Developed by programmer using traditional programming language
- Lengthy and expensive development process
- Risks:
  - High expense
  - Skilled personnel requirements
- Benefits:
  - User requirements satisfied perfectly

FIGURE 2-30
Characteristics of Traditional Custom-Developed Programs

functions. Other horizontal market software includes personal productivity software such as electronic spreadsheet programs, word processing programs, and graphics software. All of these programs provide general business tools that can be employed in many industries.

On the other hand, **vertical market programs** provide industry-specific functions to one type of user (see Figure 2-29). For example, a software developer might write a package of programs to be used in a dentist's office that includes features such as appointment scheduling, consultation-summary writing, and insurance processing. Dentists of all types have needs like these. Designed properly—and with provisions for minor tailoring for each user—one package can be sold to many users within the same industry. However, since each dentist's office has slightly differing requirements, some modification is usually needed. As a result, vertical market programs are often provided in a package that includes program, modifications, installation, training, and other consulting services.

Custom-Developed Application Programs Custom-developed application programs are developed by computer professionals on behalf of one company (see Figure 2-30). To accomplish this, the developer must identify specific user requirements, then build and test computer programs that will satisfy the requirements. It is a long, tedious, risky, and expensive process. Custom development is necessary in those instances where no software already exists to address the user's needs.

Some companies have staffs of computer programmers, analysts, and other technicians to custom develop software. Other users hire contractors or consultants to develop applications. In either case, the job is labor intensive. Because the application is custom tailored, it can be used only in that organization. Consequently, that company must bear all the development costs. For example, let us contrast custom developing an accounting package with purchasing one ready-made. Assume each program costs $100,000 to develop. The entire cost of the custom-developed application is borne by the company that developed it. The cost of developing the packaged software, however, is shared by each of perhaps 500 companies that will purchase it.

Despite the high cost of custom-developed software, it has one major benefit: It can fit the user's requirements like a glove. And sometimes, a perfect fit is required regardless of cost. Just as a suit bought off the rack never fits as well as a tailored one, packaged application programs seldom satisfy every user requirement. But just as your budget or willingness to compromise may lead you to buy most of your wardrobe ready-made, so most users find the convenience, price, and availability of packaged software reason enough to compromise on some of their requirements.

Conclusion If another alternative exists, do not custom develop programs. The costs are very high, and the corresponding benefits seldom merit the expenditure. As a user, you will probably never develop programs, at least not with the traditional method of writing code in a programming language. You might develop some applications using the application-development software described in Part Two. For the most part, however, software already exists to meet ordinary business needs. Take advantage of such packaged software, and you will have more time and money to devote to your business.

DATA

The representations of facts that go into an information system are called *data*. In this section we examine how data is represented in the computer.

The basic building block for representing computer data is called a **bit**. The term *bit* is an abbreviation for *binary digit*, the single 0 or 1 from which binary numbers are constructed.

Bits are used to represent computer data because they are easily represented with electronic components (see Figure 2–31). Bits are recorded in various ways, depending on the computer device. In the CPU, for instance, a bit is recorded as a direction of flow of electricity or as a voltage, or no

FIGURE 2-31 **Bits and Electronic Switches**
Bits are represented by things that have two states, such as on and off. For example, we can say that when a switch is on, it represents a 1. When it is off, it represents a 0. This panel of light switches represents the bit pattern 1101. Each of the millions of transistors inside a computer is an electronic switch that can switch between the 1 state and the 0 state.

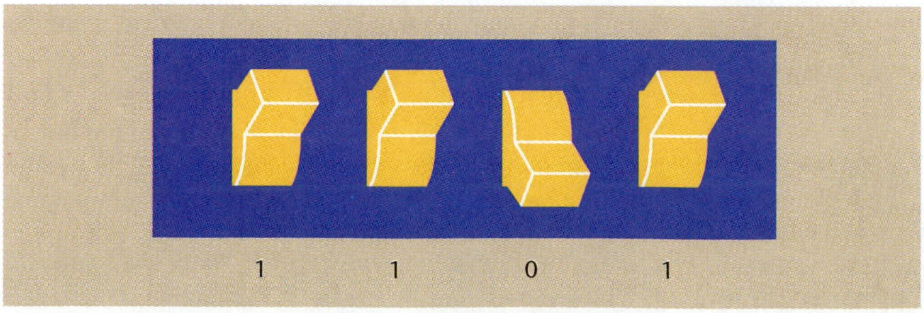

voltage, at a particular location. On magnetic media such as tape or disk, a bit is recorded as a direction of magnetization: One direction indicates a 1, and the other direction indicates a 0.

Bits are used to represent both numeric data and alphanumeric data.

Decimal	Binary
0	0
1	1
2	10
3	11
4	100
5	101
6	110
7	111
8	1000
16	10000
32	100000
64	1000000
100	1100100
120	1111000
128	10000000
256	100000000
1024	10000000000

FIGURE 2-32
Binary Equivalents of Selected Decimal Values

Numeric Data

Numeric values are represented either as their equivalents in the binary number system or as sequences of alphanumeric characters (see "Alphanumeric Data," below). Binary equivalents of some common decimal values are shown in Figure 2–32. Note that the number 1111000 in binary means exactly the same thing as the number 120 in decimal; only their appearance is different. When you count 120 match sticks, you can represent the result equally accurately in either notation. Decimal notation is considerably easier for humans to use, just as binary notation is better suited to data representation inside the computer.

Alphanumeric Data

Extended Binary Coded Decimal Interchange Code, or **EBCDIC** (pronounced "eb-sa-dick"), and American Standard Code for Information Interchange, or **ASCII** (pronounced "as-key"), are the two most widely used codes for alphanumeric data. Each code uses patterns of bits to represent letters *A* to *Z*, digits 0 to 9, and special symbols, such as #, &, {, and %. For example, the pattern 11000001 might represent an *A*; the pattern 11000010, a *B*; and so forth. Figure 2–33 gives both codes. The two codes were developed at a time when data was seldom transferred between types of computers, so there was no reason to standardize on a single code. Thus, it is a matter of historical accident that the computer industry today is saddled with the problem of two incompatible codes.

Neither a human nor a computer can determine, by inspecting a pattern of bits, whether it represents numeric data, alphanumeric codes, or even program instructions. For example, if a processing program mistakenly tries to process some program instructions as though they were alphanumeric data codes, only the unexpectedness of the results may reveal the error—and the results, though incorrect, may not look unusual enough to attract attention. To avoid such errors, the programmer who creates each processing program must ensure that it keeps track of the method of representation used with each set of data.

Data Hierarchy

Data in business information systems forms a hierarchy of bits, bytes, fields, records, files, and databases, as Figure 2–34 illustrates.

As described above, a group of bits in a particular pattern may represent a character, such as Q or 5. Although almost synonymous, the terms *character* and *byte* usually are used in different contexts. When describing data such as a customer's name, we might say it is 25 *characters* long. But

Character	ASCII-8	EBCDIC
A	0100 0001	1100 0001
B	0100 0010	1100 0010
C	0100 0011	1100 0011
D	0100 0100	1100 0100
E	0100 0101	1100 0101
F	0100 0110	1100 0110
G	0100 0111	1100 0111
H	0100 1000	1100 1000
I	0100 1001	1100 1001
J	0100 1010	1101 0001
K	0100 1011	1101 0010
L	0100 1100	1101 0011
M	0100 1101	1101 0100
N	0100 1110	1101 0101
O	0100 1111	1101 0110
P	0101 0000	1101 0111
Q	0101 0001	1101 1000
R	0101 0010	1101 1001
S	0101 0011	1110 0010
T	0101 0100	1110 0011
U	0101 0101	1110 0100
V	0101 0110	1110 0101
W	0101 0111	1110 0110
X	0101 1000	1110 0111
Y	0101 1001	1110 1000
Z	0101 1010	1110 1001
0	0011 0000	1111 0000
1	0011 0001	1111 0001
2	0011 0010	1111 0010
3	0011 0011	1111 0011
4	0011 0100	1111 0100
5	0011 0101	1111 0101
6	0011 0110	1111 0110
7	0011 0111	1111 0111
8	0011 1000	1111 1000
9	0011 1001	1111 1001

FIGURE 2-33
EBCDIC and ASCII Codes

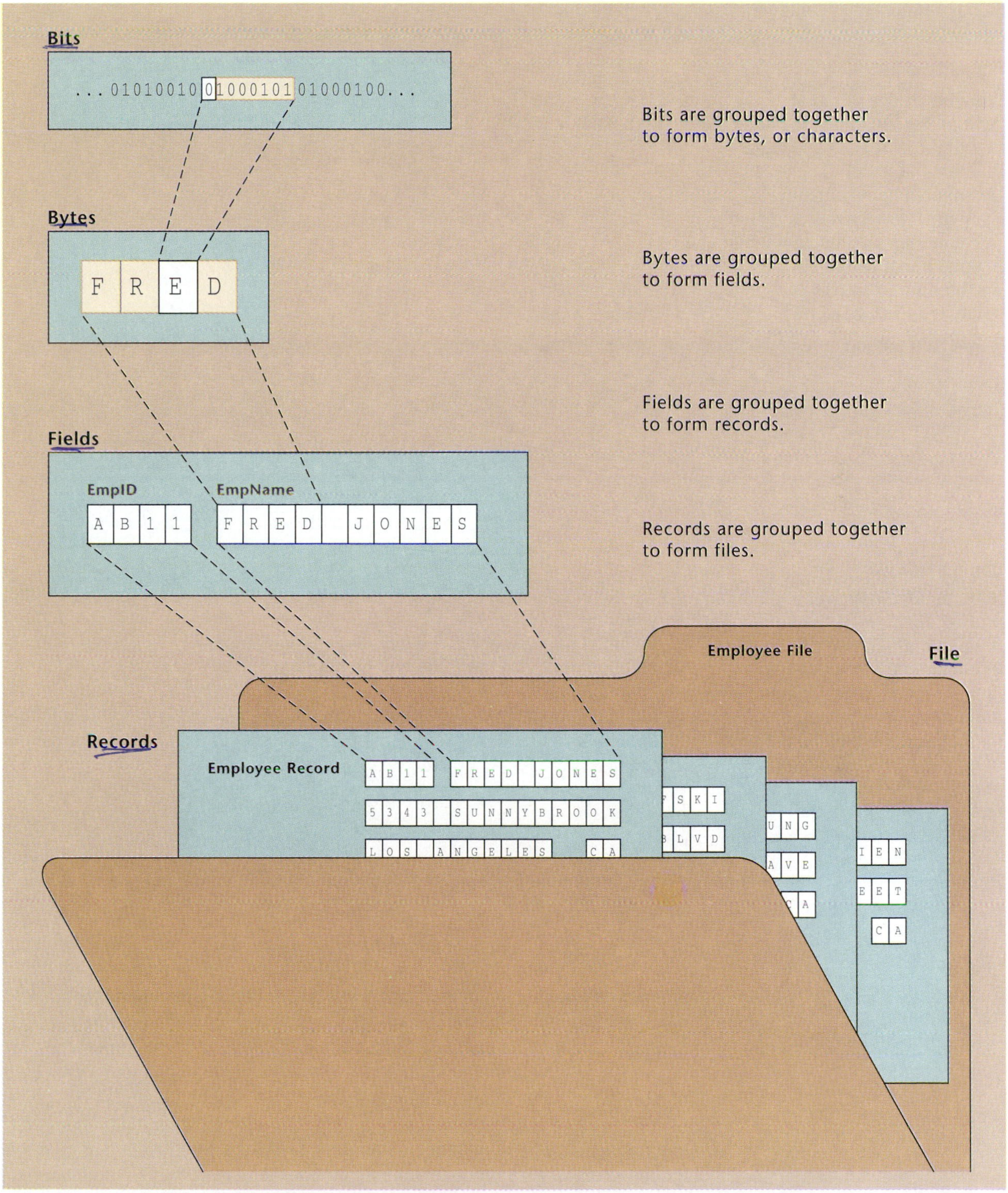

FIGURE 2-34 **The Hierarchy of Data**
Data in business information systems forms a hierarchy of bits, bytes, fields, records, and files.

FIGURE 2-35

Format of the Student Status Record

A student status record with this format might be used in a university's administrative system. The numbers across the top refer to character positions or columns. They are in the figure just for reference. If an image of this record was printed, the student number would appear in positions 1 through 9; the name would appear in positions 10 through 29; and so on.

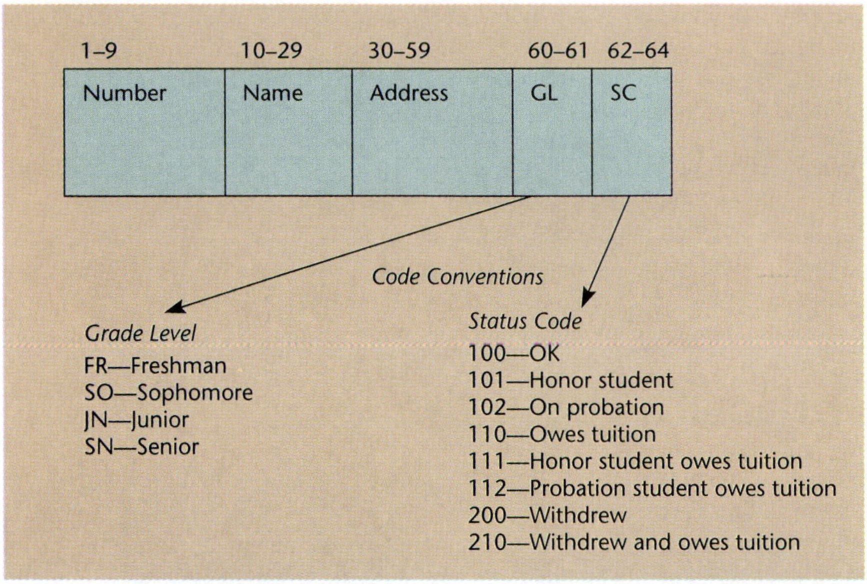

FIGURE 2-36

Part of the Student Status File

The student status file contains a record for each student, with all records formatted alike. These are the first five records in the file. Notice the hierarchy of data as illustrated: A file is a group of records; a record is a group of fields; and a field is a group of characters.

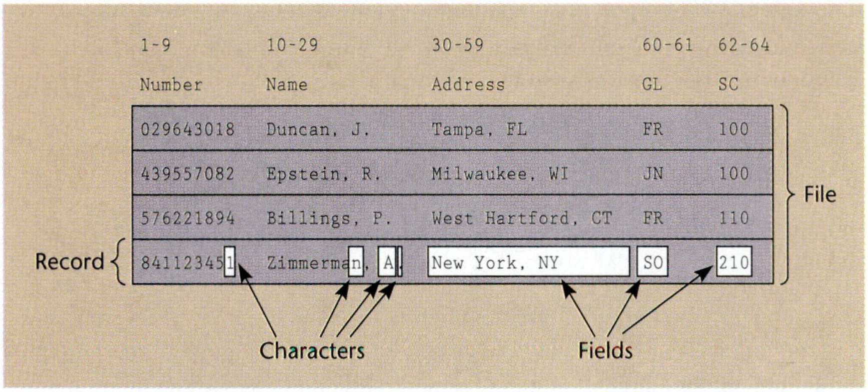

when describing amounts of memory or storage, we might say that a certain computer's memory holds 4 million *bytes* of data, or that the Customer Name field requires 25 *bytes* of storage. When programmers use the term *byte*, they mean the amount of memory required to store 8 bits, no matter what type of data is stored there.

A group of related characters is called a **field**. Fields usually have logical meanings. They represent some item of data, some fact. Thus, the 5 or 9 characters in a zip code are the Zip Code field, and the 9 characters in a Social Security number are the Social Security Number field.

A collection of related fields is called a **record**. A collection of fields about a student, for example, is called the student status record, as described in Figure 2-35. Fields are commonly fixed in size, so a field needs to be as long as the longest possible entry. Thus, in the student status record, the name Susan Nguyen would use only 13 positions of the allowable 20 positions in the Name field. The rest would be filled with spaces. The name Pauline Papadopolous would just fit. A name longer than 20 characters would be *truncated*, or chopped off, to fit in the defined space.

A collection of related records is called a **file.** All student status records together might be called the *student status file*, as shown in Figure 2-36. The schedule file might contain all of the class schedule records.

A collection of related files is called a **database.** In a database, each file is called a **table**, with rows corresponding to records and columns corresponding to fields. Figure 2-36 illustrates the terminology: *Characters* are grouped into *fields*; fields are grouped into *records*; related records are grouped into a *file*, and related files are grouped into a database.

PEOPLE

The remaining components of a business information system—people and procedures—are closely related. First, we will describe the roles that people play in information systems, then we will consider the kinds of procedures that they follow.

The fourth component of a business information system is *people* who possess key skills and training. Four types of people are involved: system clientele, system users, operations people, and systems development people (systems analysts and programmers).

Clientele

System clientele are the people who ultimately benefit from a system, although they may not directly interact with it (see Figure 2-37). As a student at a school, you are a client of a class enrollment system, a grade-posting system, a billing system, and many others.

Sometimes system clientele do interact with a system—for example, the bank customer who uses an automatic teller machine. Because such people receive absolutely no formal training, procedures for using the system must be explicit and unambiguous. Initially, the teller machine's miniature screen contains one instruction: Insert bank card. A drawing above the slot shows how to orient the card for insertion. The next instruction is equally direct: Enter personal identification number. In fact, at any time, only one simple instruction is displayed on the screen. Only after that instruction is successfully completed does the system prompt the client/user with another instruction. One step at a time, the system leads the client/user through the procedure to perform the desired banking transaction (see Figure 2-38).

FIGURE 2-37
System Clientele and System Users
The users of this bank information system, who are tellers, are entering data on behalf of the system's clientele, bank customers.

FIGURE 2-38
Automated Teller Machine
The network of automated teller machines and their associated processing systems extends around the world.

Users

System users have expertise in some business specialty, and they use the information system as a tool to do their jobs. Users are the people who interact with the computer directly. Typically, they either enter data to be processed or order output in the form of screen displays or reports. Many users—and the number grows each day—employ personal information systems on personal computers as part of their job. Part Two of this book addresses personal information systems.

Personnel	Training Requirements
Systems developers	Communication skills Business fundamentals and principles Programming languages Software packages Computer hardware Computer technology Project management
Operations personnel	Computer operations Failure recovery Business information systems operations Preventive maintenance Operations staff supervision
Users	Input preparation Output interpretation Duties and responsibilities Forthcoming changes to systems

FIGURE 2-39
Examples of Training Needs of Systems Personnel

The need for trained users is so obvious that it is often overlooked (see Figure 2-39). When users do not receive adequate training, system implementation is delayed until they learn by experience—a slow and costly process. They often use the system ineffectively or inefficiently. They may take two hours to accomplish a task that would take only a few minutes if done properly.

Users have a right to be trained during system development, either by systems development people or by other professional trainers. As a future user, you should insist on proper training. Plan your budget and schedule the cost and time for training programs.

Operations People

Operations people (operators) run the computer. They need to know how to start the computer, how to stop it, and how to run the programs. They also need to know how to operate equipment like printers and disk drives. When the computer fails, operations people need to know what to do to minimize the damage, and they need to know how to restart the computer. This is true of the operator in a large mainframe installation. It is equally true for the user of a personal information system, who also plays the role of operator.

In a well-run mainframe-based data processing center, most processing is done according to a schedule. In addition, everything the operators need to know about running a system is documented. Therefore, neither developers nor users need to be in the computer room. To enforce this measure, many companies control access to the computer room with security systems that allow access only to operations people.

Operators of mainframe-based processing centers need to know how to run computer systems, but they do not need in-depth knowledge of computing technology, nor do they even need knowledge of how the computer works. Consequently, operations people usually have less technical knowledge than system developers do. A typical computer operator has three to six months of formal training, followed by about the same amount of on-the-job training (see Figure 2-39).

Systems Development People

Systems development involves two major types of skills. The first type is found in systems analysts, systems designers, and consultants, who help users specify system requirements and design systems. The second type is found in programmers, who write the programs used in systems.

To do their jobs properly, systems development people need to know the latest in computer technology. Training is thus a recurring need (see Figure 2-39).

Systems Analysts and Consultants When a system is being developed, **systems analysts** and **consultants** interview users and, with them, determine the requirements for the new system. In addition, they—or specialists titled systems designers—design information systems to satisfy the users' requirements. Systems analysts are staff members in a company, whereas consultants are usually independent, self-employed persons with similar skills, who contract to provide specific services. When developing a personal information system, the system owner often hires a consultant to play the role of the systems analyst.

Good systems analysts possess a rare combination of skills. They must be good at communicating with people. They must understand at least one business specialty. And they must know computer technology. The same skills should be found in a skilled consultant. As a user, you will probably have occasion to work with both analysts and consultants.

Programmers Systems analysts specify system requirements and determine what types of programs will be needed to meet those requirements. **Programmers** design the details of the individual programs and then write the programs. Programmers do not need to be as good as analysts in dealing with people, nor do they need to know business as well. However, they must know more about computer technology. Specifically, a programmer needs to know one or more programming languages, various data storage techniques, and technical details of computing.

After a system is implemented, it is likely to need further changes over time. Such changes are called **system maintenance**. Maintenance might

FIGURE 2-40

Business Information Systems Are Used Worldwide Like computer hardware, business information systems are very similar the world over, especially in large companies.

be done by development people, or it might be done by a group of technicians who specialize in maintenance. Changes might be needed in any of the five components.

PROCEDURES

Consider this situation. At Central University, George arrived at the registrar's office at the appointed time to register for classes. When he submitted his class request form and the data was entered into the information system, George was told that the college thought he owed money. Although George knew he had paid all his fees, the registrar clerk would not allow him to register until his account was resolved. So he went to the finance office. The finance office agreed with George—he owed no money. They did not know what to do, so they sent him to the computer center. The computer center told him they could not change his records and sent him back to finance. In desperation, George went to his advisor, who was sympathetic but unable to help. George went back to his room wondering if college was worth the hassle.

Why is George having this problem? Obviously an error has been made, but why can't it be corrected? Is the hardware incapable of changing George's record? No. Can programs be written to change the errant data? Certainly. George has a problem because of lack of procedures. No one knows what to do.

The Need for Procedures

Procedures are instructions to people on how to use an information system. Without planned procedures, people will develop their own methods of working with the system. These methods seldom meet all needs, as

	Normal Processing	Failure-Recovery Processing
Users		
Operators		

FIGURE 2-41
Categories of Procedures for a Business Information System

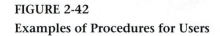

Normal Operating Procedures	Failure Recovery Procedures
Activating of system features	Error correction
Data entry	Processing during system crash
Screen interpretation	Resumption of processing after system is restored
Report interpretation	Identification of emergency contacts
Duties and responsibilities	

FIGURE 2-42
Examples of Procedures for Users

George's experience demonstrated. Like other aspects of information systems, procedures require effective management to obtain good results.

As Figure 2-41 shows, the critical categories of procedures to be developed for each business information system are user procedures for normal processing, user procedures for failure recovery, operator procedures for normal processing, and operator procedures for failure recovery. In addition to these system-specific procedures, companies have general procedures relating to information systems, such as procedures for systems developers.

User Procedures for Normal Processing System users need to know how to employ the information system under normal conditions. They need to know how to activate each available function, how to enter data, and how to interpret the results. Users also need to know any special responsibilities they have. For example, bank tellers need to know whether they should correct an incorrect deposit slip or return it to the customer (see Figure 2-42).

User Procedures for Failure Recovery In addition to normal operating procedures, users need to know how to correct certain types of errors that may occur. They need to know what to do if the system becomes inoperable—whether there are manual procedures to follow, or whether they should hang a "Gone fishing" sign on the office door until the system is up again. When the system is returned to normal, what does the user do—start from the beginning or resume where the work was interrupted? Procedures answer these and other questions that users may have regarding the system. Finally, when all else fails, the user needs to know who to contact. A list of emergency telephone numbers can prove very helpful to an anxious or frustrated user.

Normal Operating Procedures	Failure Recovery Procedures
Authorization of input persons	System crash
Input format	Communications failure
Job schedules	Equipment failure
Output destinations	Restoration of data from backups
Backup procedures	
Mechanics for running jobs—tapes to use, forms to mount, etc.	

FIGURE 2-43
Examples of Procedures for Operators

- Requirements definition methods
- System design standards
- Program writing and testing standards
- New systems implementation methods

FIGURE 2-44
Examples of Procedures for Developers

Operator Procedures for Normal Operations As you can see from Figure 2-43, under normal conditions operators need to know who is authorized to make entries, what entries to expect, how often to run jobs, where output goes, how often to make backups, and so forth. Operators also need to know the mechanics of running jobs, such as which tapes and disks are to be read and what sort of paper should be used in each printer.

Operator Procedures for Failure Recovery Operators also need to know what to do in case of any system failure. They need to know how to restore the system quickly and correctly to its proper status when it crashes (stops in midstream); when communications failures occur (for instance, when a terminal is suddenly unable to send data over the communications network); when equipment fails (for example, when a disk drive or a printer malfunctions); or when a database is rendered unusable and must be restored from backups. Other failures for which procedures are needed can occur—this is hardly an exhaustive list.

Procedures for Developers Systems developers need procedures that specify a standard way of building business information systems. These procedures, often called *development standards*, explain how to determine requirements, how to develop system designs, how to write and test programs, and how to implement new systems (see Figure 2-44). Later in this course you will learn a standard way of doing systems development.

Development procedures are very important. Some companies have hundreds of systems analysts and programmers working on projects that might take years to complete and cost hundreds of thousands or even millions of dollars. Development standards help keep projects on track, enable easier communication among project members, and provide a record of what has been and needs to be done in the event a team member leaves the project team.

Procedure Documentation

Procedures are ineffective if they are lost or forgotten. Consequently, they must be documented. **Documentation** includes written procedures, which should be evaluated by concerned personnel and approved by management. Documentation is extremely important, not only as a way to preserve procedures, but also as a way of ensuring that procedures are complete and comprehensible. Most large computer installations have two volumes of documentation for each system: one for users and one for operators.

Summary

A business information system is a collection of components, usually including a computer, that interact to satisfy some business information-processing need. The five components of a business information system are hardware, programs, data, procedures, and people.

In most business information systems, the hardware consists of a computer. A computer is comprised of five types of devices. First, the CPU interprets and carries out program instructions and communicates with the other devices. It consists of a control unit and an ALU. Until recently, CPUs could be sharply divided into four sizes: supercomputer, mainframe computer, minicomputer, and microcomputer. However, technological advances have increased the power of all computers, and there are no longer sharp and clear differences among types. Second, the main memory holds data and instructions during processing. Third, the input devices translate data from people-understandable form into computer-understandable form. The general-purpose keyboard is the most common input device. However, since keyboard data entry is slow, costly, and error-prone, alternative input devices are increasingly used. Fourth, output devices translate data from computer-understandable form to human-understandable form. The most commonly used output devices are display screens and printers. The major ways of categorizing printers are as follows: impact versus nonimpact; character versus line versus page; and dot matrix versus formed-character. Fifth, storage devices provide long-term storage for data and programs used by a computer. Magnetic disk is the primary storage medium for most business computers. Magnetic tape storage is used for archives and backups. Tape drives are sequential access devices, and disk drives are direct access devices.

Programs include system programs and application programs. System programs consist of operating system, utilities, language translators, and communications programs. The operating system takes control when the computer is turned on, and it remains active at all times. It handles I/O for application programs and may support multitasking. Utilities provide commonly needed support functions such as file management. Language translators let humans write programs in human-understandable codes and then translate those codes into computer machine language for execution. Four widely used programming languages are COBOL, C, BASIC, and SQL. Communications programs support data communications.

Application programs can be purchased as commercial packages, or they can be custom developed. Commercial packages can be horizontal or vertical market programs. Programs should be custom-developed only when suitable commercial programs are not available.

Both numeric data and alphanumeric data are stored as bits in a computer system. EBCDIC and ASCII codes are used for alphanumeric data. Data in business information systems forms a hierarchy of bits, bytes, fields, records, files, and databases.

The people in a business information system take on the roles of clientele, users, operations people, and systems development people—including the systems analysts and consultants who help users determine system requirements—and programmers—who design and write programs.

Procedures are instructions to people in the use of the system. Procedures for each business information system should include user procedures for normal processing, user procedures for failure recovery, operator procedures for normal processing, and operator procedures for failure recovery. In addition, companies need general information systems procedures, such as procedures for systems developers. To be useful, procedures should be documented.

Key Terms

business information system
hardware
program
data
information
procedure
crash
central processing unit (CPU)
processor
control unit
arithmetic-logic unit (ALU)
main memory
byte
input device
special-purpose keyboard
point-of-sale (POS) terminal
scanning device (scanner)
mark-sense reader
optical character reader (OCR)
laser bar-code scanner
Universal Product Code (UPC)
touch-tone input device
voice recognition device
output device
soft copy
display screen
computer monitor
video display terminal (VDT)
cathode-ray tube (CRT)
pixel
resolution
hard copy
laser printer
ink-jet printer
character printer
line printer
page printer
dot matrix printer
formed-character printer
plotter
storage device
magnetic disk
track
sector

magnetic tape
backup
sequential access
direct access
program
software
system program
application program
operating system
multitasking
time slicing
I/O bound
utility
machine language
COBOL
compiler
source code
object code
C
BASIC
SQL
communications program
horizontal market program
vertical market program
bit
EBCDIC
ASCII
field
record
file
database
table
system clientele
system users
operations people (operators)
systems analyst
consultant
programmer
system maintenance
documentation

Review Questions

1. What are the five components of a business information system?
2. What is a business information system?
3. Which component of a business information system consists of instructions to a computer?
4. What component of a business information system consists of instructions to people?
5. Describe each component of a CPU.
6. Why is it no longer particularly useful to differentiate sharply among mainframe computers, minicomputers, and microcomputers?
7. What unit is used to measure amounts of main memory?
8. Describe the translation performed by input units. That is, they translate from what to what?
9. Name the most widely used input device.
10. Why is the general-purpose keyboard being replaced by alternative input devices?
11. Name three types of scanning devices.
12. What does a touch-tone input device do?
13. What translation do output devices perform?
14. Differentiate between soft copy and hard copy.
15. Give two other names for a video display screen.
16. Explain the connection between pixels and resolution.

17. How does an impact printer create an image on a page?
18. Name two types of nonimpact printers.
19. Differentiate among character printers, line printers, and page printers.
20. How does a dot matrix printer create an image on a page?
21. Why does laser printer output usually look better than dot matrix printer output?
22. How does a formed-character printer create an image on a page?
23. What type of output is best suited to the use of a plotter?
24. Differentiate between the purpose of main memory and the purpose of storage.
25. How is data recorded on storage media?
26. What are the most commonly used storage devices?
27. In a disk drive, describe the purpose of read/write heads, access arms, tracks, and sectors.
28. What are archives and backups, and how do they relate to magnetic tape storage?
29. Differentiate between sequential access and direct access.
30. Why is tape poorly suited as a storage medium for active data?
31. Differentiate between system programs and application programs.
32. What is an operating system?
33. How do the terms *time slicing* and *I/O bound* relate to multitasking in an operating system?
34. Describe at least six functions performed by utility system programs.
35. Why is programming in a language like COBOL preferable to programming in machine language?
36. How are the terms, *compiler*, *source code*, and *object code* related to language translation?
37. Describe the key characteristics of COBOL, C, BASIC, and SQL programming languages.
38. Describe the advantages and disadvantages of packaged application programs.
39. Give examples of horizontal market programs and examples of vertical market programs.
40. Describe the advantages and disadvantages of custom-developed application programs.
41. Why are bits used to represent computer data?
42. Name two codes used to represent computerized alphanumeric data.
43. Name and describe the relationships among the elements of the data hierarchy in business information systems?
44. What are the four types of people who are involved in business information systems?
45. Why is user training important?
46. What background and training does a computer operator for a mainframe computer center need?
47. Compare and contrast the skills that are needed by systems analysts and programmers.
48. Describe system maintenance.

49. Name the four critical categories of procedures that should be developed for each business information system.

Discussion Questions

A. What do we mean when we say that most computers are general-purpose information-processing machines? Are there limitations in the types of information-processing tasks that a computer can do? (For example, can you think of any information-processing task that a computer could not do?) See if you can name half-a-dozen information-processing machines that are *not* general-purpose machines.

B. For each of the five components of an information system, describe types of problems that would occur if that element were poorly designed, badly managed, or inadequate to its task.

C. Compare two computers of different size—for example, a microcomputer and a minicomputer. Concentrate especially on the differences in programs between the two systems. For example, what capabilities are provided by the operating system of the minicomputer but not the microcomputer? Are there capabilities provided by the operating system of the microcomputer that are not available in the minicomputer? What application programs are most commonly executed on the microcomputer? On the minicomputer? If possible, interview the manager of the larger computer for the necessary information.

D. Identify the nearest supercomputer center to your college campus. Ascertain from personnel at your college's computer center whether people at your school can submit computations to the supercomputer center if they need to do so. What sorts of tasks would be suitable?

E. Develop a list of as many alternative input devices as possible. Begin with those in this chapter, and extend the list by talking to computer-using friends and teachers and looking in current books and computer magazines in the library. If possible, visit a computer store to add to your list.

F. List the hardware components of a computer system on campus—for example, your own (or a classmate's) system, a school administrative system, the computer lab, or computers used for research. Classify each device according to the categories of input, processing, storage, output, and communications. Identify the manufacturer and model of each unit. For example, the system may have a Hewlett-Packard DeskJet printer. Compare your list with that of another student.

G. Investigate programming languages in your school library. From textbooks or technical manuals, photocopy sample programs in at least three programming languages.

H. Interview a computer user: a businessperson, a school administrator, or a working graduate. What has been the person's experience with custom-developed software? What has been the person's experience with packaged software? Does the person agree with the assertion that, whenever possible, packaged programs are preferable to custom-developed ones? Why or why not?

I. For your school's course registration system, describe the people component of the system. Who are the clientele? Who are the users? Who are the operators? Who are the systems development people? If possible, interview a knowledgeable administrator to obtain additional information about each category of people. Be prepared to explain what you mean by each category. Report your findings.

MINICASE

McKesson Cuts Costs with Wireless Scanner

Warehouse workers at McKesson Co. have the ultimate "busy hands, busy eyes job." Their job is to fill customer orders with the correct quantity and brand of products from more than 20,000 units of aspirin, shampoo, and hairbrushes, so orders can be shipped overnight.

Previously, warehouse workers did this manually with a paper list, clipboard, and pencil; they filled their "tote boxes" with the ordered goods, according to customer specifications.

Now, however, workers have a state-of-the-art system that has improved their productivity and eliminated skyrocketing costs associated with the manual process of filling orders.

The main challenge to getting warehouse and order-fulfillment jobs done quickly and efficiently is overcoming human error. "The single biggest problem is one of inappropriate shipments to customers," says Doug Hoover of Electronic Data Systems (EDS).

EDS worked with McKesson to develop an automated approach to warehouse and distribution functions. Previously, it wasn't uncommon for a worker to place the wrong item—or the wrong quantity of an item—in a tote. Unfortunately, the mistake wouldn't be discovered until the shipment reached the customer.

The costs associated with mispicked orders were staggering. Because of transportation costs and inventory issues, the cost of correcting mispicks ran around $80 per mistake—which is about seven times higher than the cost of filling a customer's order correctly the first time.

Hoover says it was clear from the start that the solution would not be traditional computer or bar-coding technology. "These workers need to have their hands free in order to reach up to shelves and retrieve items.". . . Portable bar-coding laser scan technology has helped the distribution industry tremendously, Hoover says. But in a warehouse, where employees need both hands free, the little scanning "hand gun" used by supermarket and drugstore workers simply wouldn't work.

EDS worked with Symbol Technologies Inc. to develop a new system, called AcuMax. . . . With it, workers wear a scanner glove that is activated simply by pointing an index finger at the appropriate bar code.

On their arms, workers wear small computer screens that display the customer order list, along with exact shelf locations. When workers go to the shelf, they scan the bar code on the shelf to confirm the pick and ensure that the correct quantity has been selected.

McKesson has tested the AcuMax system at its distribution center in Spokane, Washington. Improper shipments have been cut dramatically in the first two months of the project. Initial figures estimate that errors have been cut fifty percent. . . .

One key aspect to making AcuMax a success: EDS and Symbol Technologies were designing new hardware and software and warehouse workers at McKesson were involved in the design and prototyping phase of the new project.

Charles Williams is a picker and order filler at the McKesson distribution center in Spokane and a user of the system. He was also heavily involved in the testing and the prototyping of the hardware and software.

Williams says productivity has vastly improved over the clipboard days; he expects it to increase even further. . . . In fact, Williams has become the "top picker" at the Spokane warehouse. The reason? Williams is a Nintendo fanatic. "His eye-hand coordination is well developed, and he has turned into our most productive picker," says Bruce Russell, McKesson Vice-president.

Questions

1. This article focuses on the hardware and program components of the AcuMax system. Name three other system components and describe what you think would be the important characteristics of each.
2. According to this article, what advantage accrued to McKesson because it custom developed the hardware and programs? Although disadvantages of custom development are not mentioned, they do exist. List and describe some disadvantages.
3. Charles Williams is supposed to be an excellent user of the new system because he is "a Nintendo fanatic." Do you believe this statement? Why or why not?
4. Suppose that Walgreens (Minicase, Chapter 1) buys drug products from McKesson. Describe potential advantages to both companies by linking their information systems together. What challenges would need to be overcome to create such a system?

P A R T T W O

PERSONAL INFORMATION SYSTEMS

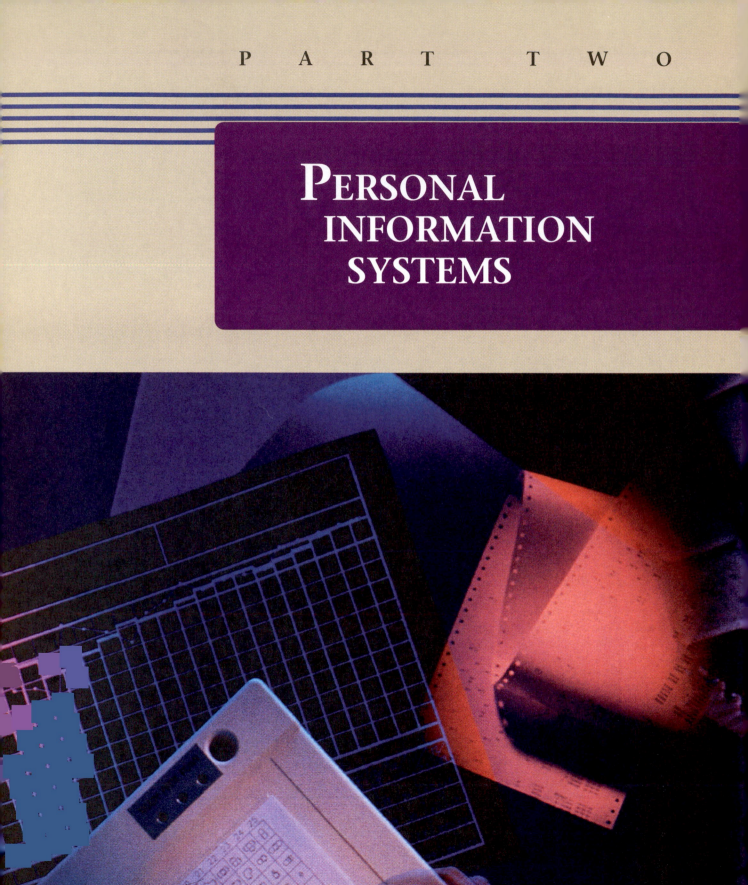

During the 1980s, personal computers brought a new level of productivity to business users. Large computer systems had always been expensive to buy, use, and maintain. Their use by a single individual was almost never cost- effective. When personal computers appeared, near the beginning of the decade, the way people did business was forever changed. Today, the personal computer is cheap and conveniently small, and a growing pool of inexpensive software is available. Personal computers are now standard business equipment in companies of all sizes.

In Part Two you will learn about personal information systems. Chapter 3 builds on the five-component model you learned about in Chapter 2, by defining the unique characteristics of a personal information system. As a user, you will almost certainly be specifying the components of a personal information system within the next several years, either for yourself or for your company. The material in this chapter will be directly applicable to that task.

In Chapter 1, we saw that the major functions of a computer in a business information system were calculation, data storage and retrieval, and communication. These capabilities are mirrored in the main categories of personal application software, which is discussed in Chapters 4, 5, and 6. Chapter 4 describes how communication support programs—word processors, graphics programs, and DTP programs—help you communicate your ideas. Chapter 5 discusses electronic spreadsheet programs, which specialize in the calculation function. Chapter 6 discusses personal database systems, which specialize in data storage and retrieval.

Chapter 7 shows how to use these tools to develop your own applications. You will see that prototyping, the development method described here, is a natural, efficient way of creating applications that meet your needs. Most importantly, you will learn how you fit into the process, as system owner and primary user.

As you study the material in Part Two, think about how these tools could be used in your own academic or business situation. How could you use them? How might your employer use them? Also think about business situations in which personal information systems might *not* be practical or appropriate. It is important to realize not only the power of personal information systems, but also their limitations.

CHAPTER 3

Introduction to Personal Information Systems

This is the second chapter about the five components of a business information system. This chapter is concerned with the five components of a *personal* information system. It builds on the material in Chapter 2, which introduced the basic concepts of the five components.

In this chapter, you will learn how personal information systems are unique. Can you begin identifying their characteristics in the following example?

EXAMPLE: MAINTAINING AN EQUIPMENT INVENTORY

The burglary revealed the problem. The morning after it happened, the entire accounting department was in chaos. File drawers were dumped out on the floor. Desks were shoved around the rooms. Cabinets were looted. Several PCs were missing, and no one knew what else. When the police arrived, they wanted a list of the missing items: names, model numbers, serial numbers, and so on. The good news was that the office inventory file was intact. The bad news was that no one had paid much attention to it over the past several years, so it contained little of the information the police needed.

When the police left, the boss called Merlene into his office. "Here's a job for you," he said, "even though this is only your third day in the department. The office equipment inventory is a mess. I need you to straighten it out."

When she looked inside the file folder, Merlene saw the problem. The first item was a scrap of paper with a handwritten note: "Metal desk, Henson's office, 1987." The second item was an invoice for a copy machine purchased in 1985 (which she couldn't find in the office). The third item was a list dated 1985 showing the configurations of three PCs that had since been replaced.

Looking around the office, workrooms, and storerooms, Merlene noticed that most equipment items were numbered. She learned that the numbers were applied by the receiving department when each item arrived. The receiving department had records showing all numbers and descriptions, but their records did not show when the items were transferred to another department or taken out of service. Still, they provided a good starting point, combined with a thorough room-by-room inventory that Merlene conducted herself.

To improve the inventory's usability, Merlene decided to use a personal database program named Q&A on her PC, since she had worked with such a program in college. After several weeks of collecting data in her spare time, she created a database and entered about two-dozen test records. Then she created the formats for the two major reports that the system should produce: a listing by inventory number and a listing by office location. As she created these reports, Merlene realized that some adjustments to the database structure were needed, so she made them. When she showed the sample reports to her boss, he suggested further modifications. Merlene also made those.

By this time, Merlene's regular duties were taking most of her time, so her boss authorized hiring a temporary clerical worker to come in and enter the inventory data, under Merlene's supervision.

The first results from the project came almost immediately. Receiving department records showed that two VCRs had been allocated to the accounting department 18 months ago. People in the department could remember using them in presentations and during training sessions. However, neither was to be found. Merlene reported them as missing.

Since PCs are often the target of burglars, data security was definitely an issue with this system. If the PC containing the inventory was stolen, the inventory itself would be lost. Therefore, Merlene developed a procedure for backing up the inventory system each time it was updated. Backup floppy disks contained not only the data, but also the programs required to process it.

In operation, the system was simple. From day to day, Merlene collected notes about inventory changes in a file folder. Once a quarter, she entered the data into the system. She soon realized that in the three months between sessions, she was forgetting important steps in the processing. Therefore, she spent several hours creating written procedures for the following quarterly update tasks: taking inventory, adding new equipment, recording disposal of equipment, handling disparities, and backing up the system. She also created a written procedure for recreating the entire system from the backup in case the primary copy on her PC could not be accessed.

Less than a year later, Merlene was promoted to another job, and a new person took over the equipment inventory. Since the written procedures were easy to follow, the new person had no difficulty keeping the system working.

As Merlene's experiences show, **personal information systems** are used by individuals to help them do their jobs more effectively. The most

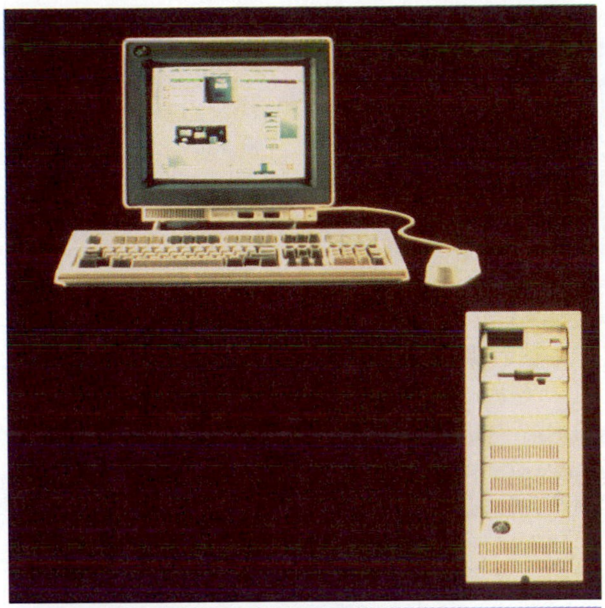

FIGURE 3-1

IBM Personal Computer

This IBM PS/2 personal computer uses the tower design, in which the case is vertical, often on the floor. Keyboard and display screen are placed on a desktop nearby.

FIGURE 3-2

Macintosh Personal Computer

This Macintosh II computer has an optional monochromatic portrait display capable of displaying an entire page in black print on a white background. Macintosh computer displays and printers are designed so an image on the printed page will be exactly the same size as the image on the display.

common kinds of personal information systems involve the use of word processing systems, electronic spreadsheets, and personal database management systems (DBMSs). Personal information systems help us to store and analyze information and to communicate more effectively.

More than 60 million personal computers have been sold since IBM introduced the IBM Personal Computer in 1981. The majority of these are used by individuals in businesses as tools to help uncover problems, analyze possible solutions, store and process data, and communicate ideas effectively.

BENEFITS OF PERSONAL INFORMATION SYSTEMS

A key advantage of a personal information system is that it is personal—it is under your control. You can use its tools in the ways you find most productive. You can collect and store the data you want to have available, and you can store it in the form that makes it most useful to you. Once you know how to use the system's tools, you can process as you think best, without having to convince others to write or modify their programs for your benefit. Your personal information systems are yours.

At the same time, personal information systems in many settings must serve interests beyond your own. Consider the following uses for personal information systems:

- A small Italian restaurant owner uses a personal information system to keep accounts and do the payroll.
- An engineer in an architectural firm uses a personal information system to analyze stresses on roof structures.
- A high school teacher uses a personal information system to manage a stock portfolio and keep accounts for rental properties.
- A lawyer uses a personal information system to create legal documents and maintain client billing records.
- A marketing manager uses a personal information system to analyze the results of advertising campaigns.
- A surgeon uses a personal information system to produce correspondence.
- A salesperson has purchased hardware and programs and developed an information system to plan sales calls and cover her sales territory efficiently.

Some of these information systems are entirely personal, such as the surgeon's correspondence system and the high school teacher's portfolio management system. These systems serve only the interests of their user.

Other information systems are used by entrepreneurs in the operation of small businesses. These systems are influenced by the needs of the business and by the reporting requirements of the Internal Revenue Service. Systems used in the practice of a profession, such as the one used by the lawyer in the above list, are similarly influenced by the needs of the practice.

Systems used in large companies (the engineer's structural analysis system and the marketing manager's advertising analysis system) are heavily influenced by the needs and requirements of the organization. For example, the organization may specify hardware and programs to be used and place limitations on the processing that can be done.

If we take these influences into account, however, the key characteristic of a personal information system is that a single person takes responsibility for determining the requirements, then designing, creating, and using the system. Even if you ask a friend or hire a consultant to help, the responsibility is yours.

Of course, this is also a major disadvantage of a personal information system—your own limitations of knowledge and experience may limit the effectiveness of the system. In addition, the system can only process data that you have access to, so its data may be less complete and current than you might wish.

Like any business information system, a personal information system has five components: hardware, programs, data, procedures, and trained people.

HARDWARE

The heart of a personal information system is a **microcomputer** (also called a **personal computer**, or **PC**). Like any other computer, it consists of CPU, main memory, input devices, output devices, and storage devices. Figure 3-3 shows the components of a typical PC.

The CPU

A microcomputer's CPU consists of a **microprocessor**, which includes ALU and control unit, along with some support circuitry, on a single silicon chip (see Figure 3-4). The two families of microprocessors most commonly used in personal computers today are the Intel family and the Motorola family, described in Figure 3-5.

Because of continuous technological improvements, the number of transistors contained in chips such as these has doubled, on the average, about every 30 months since they were first used in the early 1960s. With the increased capacity comes significantly increased processing power, which is sometimes measured in **MIPS**, millions of instructions per second. It is misleading to compare dissimilar CPUs by measuring MIPS, since the results are not always comparable and various measurement methods give different results. Still, a CPU's MIPS rating gives some idea of its processing power. Figure 3-6 shows how the power of the Intel chip family has increased.

FIGURE 3-3

Components of a Personal Computer

Inside a personal computer are printed circuit boards, disk drives, and a power supply. The keyboard, screen, and printer are attached by plug-in cables.

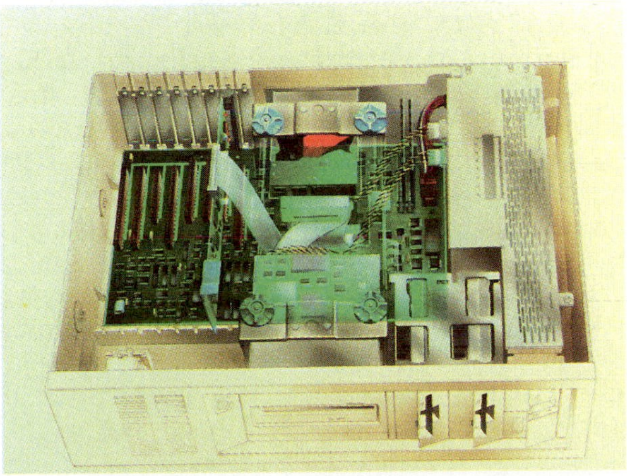

FIGURE 3-4

Design for a Microprocessor

An engineer lays out the design of a microprocessor for study.

Word Size	Intel	Motorola
8 bits	8088 *PC-XT*	68000 *Mac Classic*
	(80186) *(little used)*	(68010) *(little used)*
16 bits	80286 *PC-AT*	68020 *Mac LC*
32 bits	80386 *386 PCs*	68030 *Mac II*
	80486 *486 PCs*	68040 *Mac Quadra*
	80586	68050

FIGURE 3-5

Intel and Motorola Families of Microprocessors

Processor	Speed	MIPS
8088	5 MHz	.7
80286	8 MHz	1.2
80386	25 MHz	8.5
80486	33 MHz	27.0

FIGURE 3-6

MIPS Ratings of PC Microprocessors

Two characteristics of a microprocessor relate directly to its relative power: word size and cycle speed. You can assume that a processor with larger word size and higher cycle speed is more powerful than one with smaller word size and lower cycle speed.

Word size measures the amount of data that a computer can process in a single step. Word size is measured in bits. For example, a 32-bit processor retrieves data from main memory 32 bits at a time, transports the data to the ALU through a 32-bit channel, and performs arithmetic 32 bits at a time. As Figure 3-7 shows, a 32-bit processor can add two values totaling greater than $40 million in a single step, large enough to encompass most business accounting needs. By comparison, a 16-bit processor would require twice as long to perform such an addition, since it would have to compute the result in parts. Some microprocessors use a hybrid word size. For example, the 80386SX processor does arithmetic 32 bits at a time, but it transports data from main memory through a 16-bit channel, which reduces its overall speed.

The second microprocessor characteristic related to its power is cycle speed, measured in **megahertz (MHz)**, or millions of cycles per second. A single computer instruction requires more than one cycle for completion, and different instructions require different numbers of cycles. Therefore, cycle speed and MIPS are only indirectly related, but higher cycle speeds indicate greater power. The earliest IBM PC had a cycle speed of 4.7 MHz. Typical speeds of current 80386 and 80486 microprocessors are 25 MHz and 33 MHz, with speeds twice as fast predicted soon.

Both the current families of microprocessors use complex instruction set computer (**CISC**) technology. CISC computers are designed to use a large set of relatively complex instructions. Today, an alternative approach to computer design is reduced instruction set computer (**RISC**) technology. RISC microprocessors use a much smaller set of simpler instructions. To

Word Size in Bits	Stored Value
8	$2.55
16	$655.35
32	$42,949,672.95

This table shows the largest positive number that can be stored in various word sizes.

Decimal	Binary
255	11111111
+ 1	1
256	100000000 (a 9-bit value)

If we add 1 to binary 255 (equivalent to $2.55 above), the result will overflow an 8-bit storage place—that is, it will be too large to fit in the space.

FIGURE 3-7
How Large a Number Will Fit?

complete a given task, today's CISC personal computers require fewer steps, but each step is more complex. Tomorrow's RISC personal computers, now being designed, require more steps, but each step is much simpler. The result is that RISC computers are usually much faster overall.

Note, however, that the time required for a computer to complete a task depends on other factors in addition to the machine's computational power. The most important additional factor is its speed in storing and retrieving data on a hard disk. Another factor is the speed of its video display. Therefore, CPU power is only one factor in a computer's overall performance.

Main Memory

The memory chips that make up a microcomputer's main memory include **random-access memory (RAM)** and **read-only memory (ROM)**.

RAM is the standard memory. The capacity of RAM chips doubles, on the average, each 30 months or so, as does the capacity of microprocessors. (The capacity of each memory chip is measured in bits, even though the capacity of memory as a whole is usually measured in bytes.) Current RAM chips, like those in Figure 3-8, can each hold 1 million bits (1 megabit) of data. Nine chips are required to hold 1 megabyte (MB)—8 chips for the data itself and 1 more to hold additional data essential to memory error detection. Increasingly, today, 4-megabit chips are coming into use, and 16-megabit chips are on the horizon. The price of a memory chip remains nearly constant, despite the great increase in capacity, so memory prices as a whole have decreased tremendously. Today, the amount of memory used in a microcomputer—typically 1MB to 8MB—contributes very little to its overall cost.

FIGURE 3-8

1 Megabit RAM Chips
A single memory chip stores 1 million data bits. Nine chips comprise 1MB of RAM.

FIGURE 3-9

16K Memory Board from 1972 PC
All the chips on this memory board from a 1972 personal computer provide 16K of memory. By contrast, nine chips today provide 1MB of memory—more than 60,000 times as much!

In the early days of microcomputers, even a small amount of main memory required dozens of chips, each of which had to be installed into the computer, as Figure 3-9 shows. Their cost made up much of the price of the computer. The required space was substantial, and additional printed circuit boards were often required, an added cost. Today's nine-chip main memories have reduced costs and complexity significantly.

RAM is **volatile**—when the power goes off, the contents of RAM are lost. If a computer's initial start-up instructions were in RAM, they would be lost every time you turned off the computer. Nonvolatile ROM, however, can contain such instructions permanently. Both start-up routines and certain other operating system routines are stored in ROM in most of today's microcomputers. The remainder of the operating system is usually stored on disk storage, which is also nonvolatile.

The microprocessor and at least part of a computer's main memory are typically mounted on a single, printed circuit board called the **motherboard**, shown in Figure 3-11. In addition, the motherboard usually has **expansion slots** permitting the user to plug in add-on circuit boards such as those illustrated in Figure 3-12. These boards may contain additional memory; hardware to support various screen displays, printers, and storage devices; and other specialized hardware. Finally, the motherboard, or sometimes a plug-in circuit board, contains one or more **parallel ports** and **serial ports**. Parallel ports include circuitry and plugs for connecting printers. Serial ports include circuitry and plugs for connecting other devices, such as an external modem (see Figure 3-13).

FIGURE 3-10

A Semiconductor Chip
An individual semiconductor chip like this 4MB memory chip is about the size of your smallest fingernail. The plastic package that contains it is much larger, mostly to provide a firm foundation for the connection to its socket.

FIGURE 3-11

PC Motherboard
On this Macintosh motherboard are microprocessor, various supporting chips, main memory chips, and slots for add-in circuit boards.

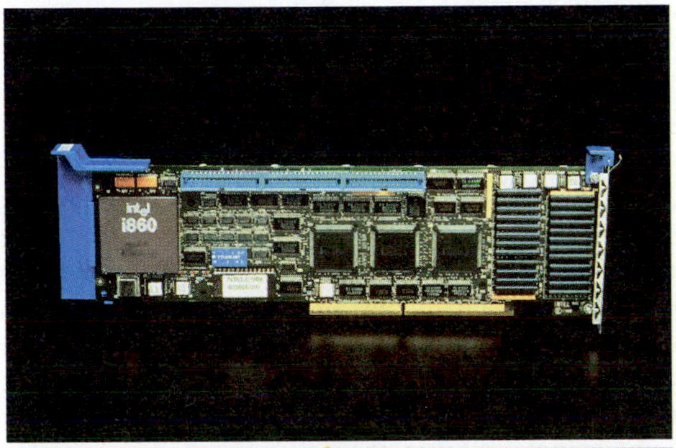

FIGURE 3-12

An Add-On Circuit Board
Circuit boards plug into slots on the motherboard. Boards like this add specialized input and display capabilities, added memory, and other functions.

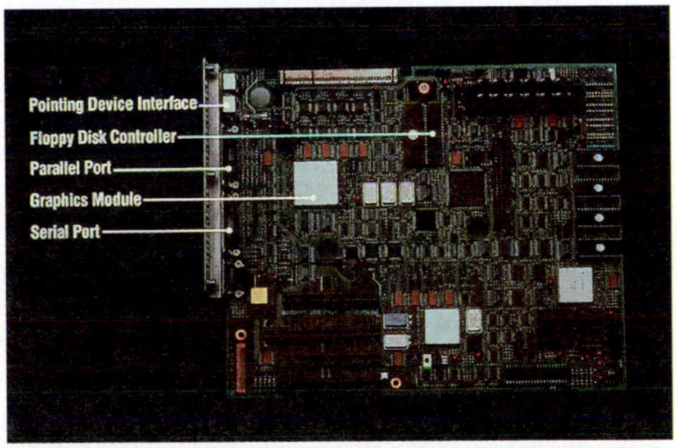

FIGURE 3-13

I/O Components on a PC Motherboard
This IBM PS/2 motherboard includes circuitry and connectors for a parallel port, a serial port, a mouse, and a graphics display. It also includes circuitry to control floppy disk drives.

INCREASING YOUR PERSONAL PRODUCTIVITY — **Box 3.1**

How to Test a Used Computer

Pre-owned computers can be tested in a matter of hours, following procedures Alexander Randall V, cofounder of Boston Computer Exchange, recommends in, *Alex Randall's Used Computer Handbook* (Microsoft Press, 1990). Some examples:

- Open the box. A layer of dust would be discouraging.
- Power-up from a floppy disk in the A drive. If the system fails, its floppy-disk controller card, floppy-disk drive, or motherboard may be defective.
- Try booting up from the hard disk. A failure suggests the hard disk has been improperly formatted or is missing essential start-up files, the hard-disk controller card is defective, or the motherboard is defective.
- Check the memory. Make sure the amount of RAM displayed on the monitor after the initial memory check jibes with what it's supposed to have.
- Format a floppy disk. If the format fails, try a fresh disk. Successive failures suggest the drive is defective.
- Try copying files from one drive to another. Repeated failures indicate a defective drive. If you're successful, run a disk comparison to make sure the files were copied accurately.
- Examine the monitor. Turn up the brightness and contrast controls to check for phosphor "burns." Determine if characters are out of proportion. Make sure the image doesn't waver.
- Check the keyboard. Do the characters on the screen match each character on the keyboard? Test the cable by gently tugging on it.
- Don't ignore the fan. "If, when you turn the computer on or off, the fan sounds like a helicopter, it's probably ailing," says Randall. It can be replaced, but it may have damaged the heat-sensitive electronics inside.

Input Devices

As with other computers, the most common microcomputer input device is the keyboard, which was discussed in the previous chapter. In addition to the keyboard, many microcomputers include a **mouse** as an input device, as Figure 3-14 illustrates. A mouse on the table is connected to a pointer or to some other symbol on the screen by software routines. If you move the mouse, say, forward on the table, the arrow moves correspondingly up on the screen, as Figure 3-15 illustrates. To use a mouse to select a command, move the mouse until the arrow on the screen points at a symbol representing the command you want. Then press a button on the mouse to make the selection. This sequence of actions is called **point and click.** The mouse can also be used with graphics software to create graphic images on the screen.

An alternative point-and-click device is the **trackball**, as shown in Figure 3-16. The user manipulates the device by rolling a ball with the fingers rather than rolling the mouse around on the tabletop.

A **digital scanner** can transfer a graphic image from paper into computer memory. Relatively inexpensive hand-held scanners, like the one shown in Figure 3-17, can input small sections of images at a time. Larger page scanners can input page-sized images in one pass. Even if the images

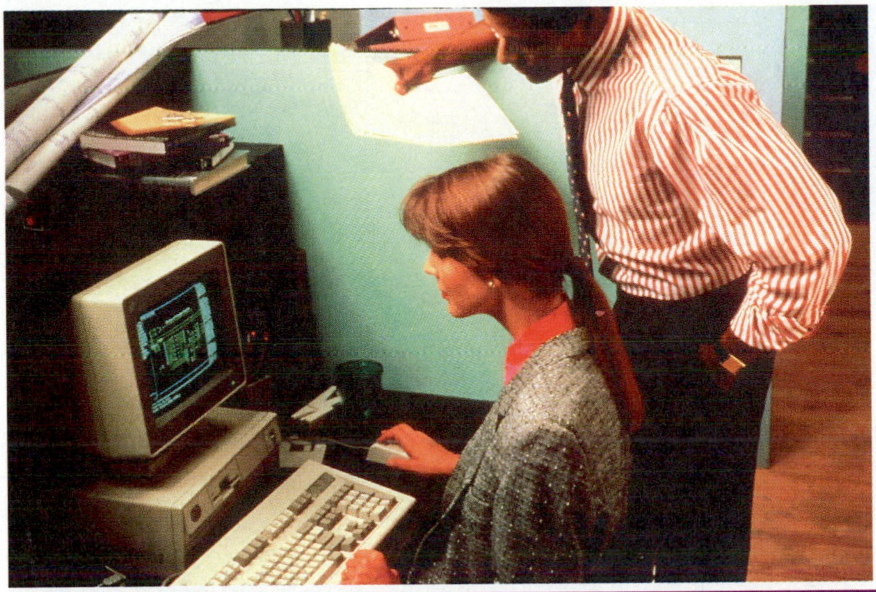

FIGURE 3-14
Data Entry with Keyboard and Mouse
The operator of this personal computer has her right hand on a mouse that she is using in data entry.

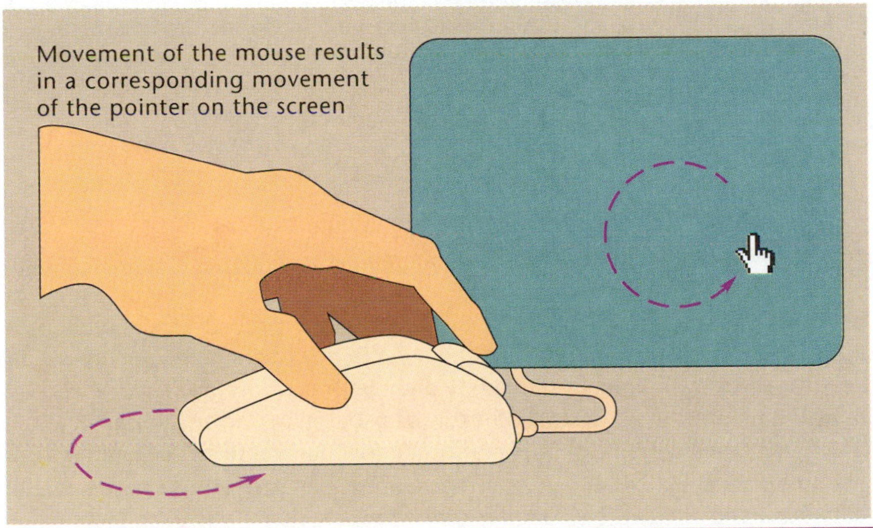
Movement of the mouse results in a corresponding movement of the pointer on the screen

FIGURE 3-15
Mouse Input Device
Movement of the mouse results in a corresponding movement of the pointer on the screen.

are of text—words and sentences—the images in memory are represented simply as patterns of dots. To convert scanned images of text into character codes for text processing, the memory image is processed by **optical character recognition** software.

Output Devices

As we saw earlier, the most common output devices are the screen display and the printer.

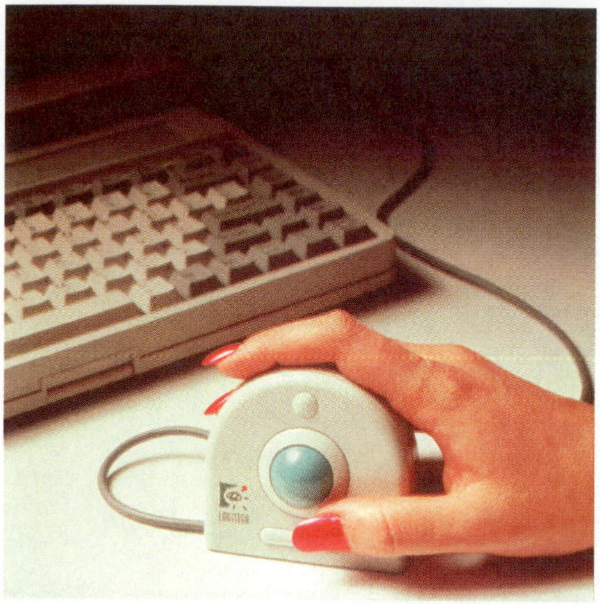

FIGURE 3-16
Trackball
The trackball is an alternative to the mouse.

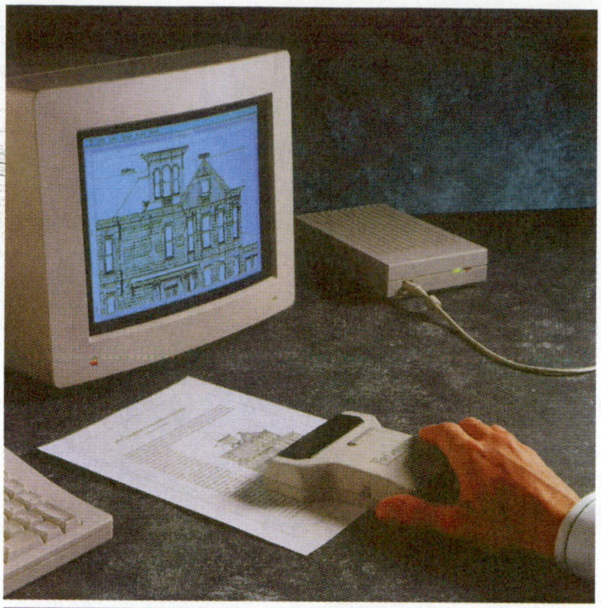

FIGURE 3-17
Hand-Held Scanner
This hand-held scanner can be used to digitize a small graphic piece in a single pass, or it can be moved back and forth over a larger piece to create the complete image in memory.

Screen Displays Microcomputer screen display hardware is divided into two groups: character displays and graphics displays. In a **character display** such as the one in Figure 3-18, the screen is typically divided into 24 lines of 80 characters each, making a total of 1,920 character positions. In each position, a single character corresponding to an ASCII code can be displayed. Lines and boxes can be created from combinations of ASCII codes, but the graphics possibilities are extremely limited. The advantage of the character display is that it is inexpensive, requiring simple screen hardware and relatively little memory or processing power.

By contrast, **graphics displays**, in which each screen dot is individually controlled, require much more sophisticated hardware, much more memory, and much greater processing power. The impressive result is illustrated in Figure 3-19. Fortunately, since the early days of microcomputers, the cost of displays, memory, and processing power has been falling rapidly. Today, graphics displays such as the commonly used video graphics array (**VGA**) display are very common. In the VGA display, each screen pixel in an array 640 dots wide and 480 dots high can be assigned 1 of 256 different colors. Many manufacturers offer *super VGA* hardware providing more pixels and more different display colors. Figure 3-20 summarizes today's commonly used display systems.

FIGURE 3-18
Character-Based Display
A character-based display can show text, but its graphics capabilities are extremely limited.

FIGURE 3-19
Graphics Display
This graphics display is typical of today's high-resolution screen displays.

	Resolution	Colors
Monochromatic	(1)	1
Hercules graphics	720 × 348	1
CGA	640 × 200	16
VGA	640 × 480	256
Super VGA	800 × 600	256
Mac (dpi)	72	(2)

(1) 24 × 80 character positions, no graphics.
(2) 1, 16, or 256, depending on video adapter.

FIGURE 3-20
Video Display Systems

Printers Printers used with microcomputers are usually dot matrix printers or laser printers. Dot matrix printers are the least expensive of the personal computer printers. They can produce up to about one to two pages of text per minute, considerably less if graphics output is needed. Output is of relatively low resolution. If you inspect the output of a 9-pin dot matrix printer closely, you will clearly see the separate dots making up the

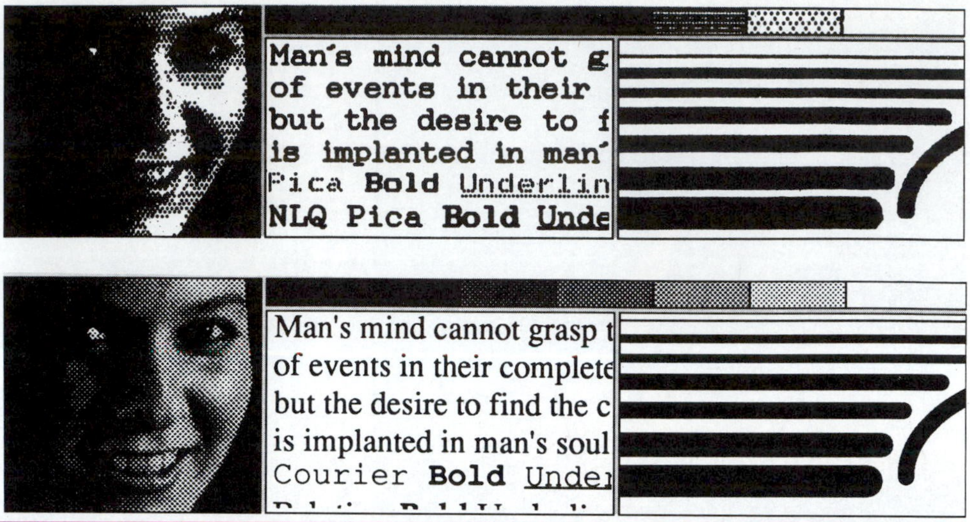

FIGURE 3-21 **Dot Matrix Printer Output versus Laser Printer Output**
When you compare relatively high-quality dot matrix printer output to standard desktop laser printer output, the difference is striking.

characters. A more expensive 24-pin dot matrix printer has more elements in its print head and they are more closely spaced, so its output has higher resolution. If a dot matrix printer is capable of graphics output, the resolution is typically a coarse 72 dots per inch, as Figure 3-21 shows. Dot matrix printers use impact technology and can be quite noisy in an office setting, though some are marketed as being relatively quiet.

A laser printer is more expensive to purchase and operate than a dot matrix printer, but its output quality is significantly higher, and it operates nearly silently. Its 300 dot-per-inch resolution provides attractive text output and fairly high-quality graphics. Laser printers with higher resolution, often 1000 dots per inch, are available for use with DTP systems. The output of these machines can be used as masters for high-quality printing.

A third less common option is the ink-jet printer, which offers near–laser-quality output at dot matrix–level initial price. Output is much slower than that of a laser printer, and operating costs are higher than with either laser printers or dot matrix printers.

Storage Devices

The storage devices used with microcomputers are hard disk drives and floppy disk drives.

Hard Disk Drives The main storage system used in a personal information system is the hard disk drive. Few microcomputers used for business rely entirely on floppy disk drives for storage. Hard disk drives provide nearly instantaneous access to all the programs and data that the typical

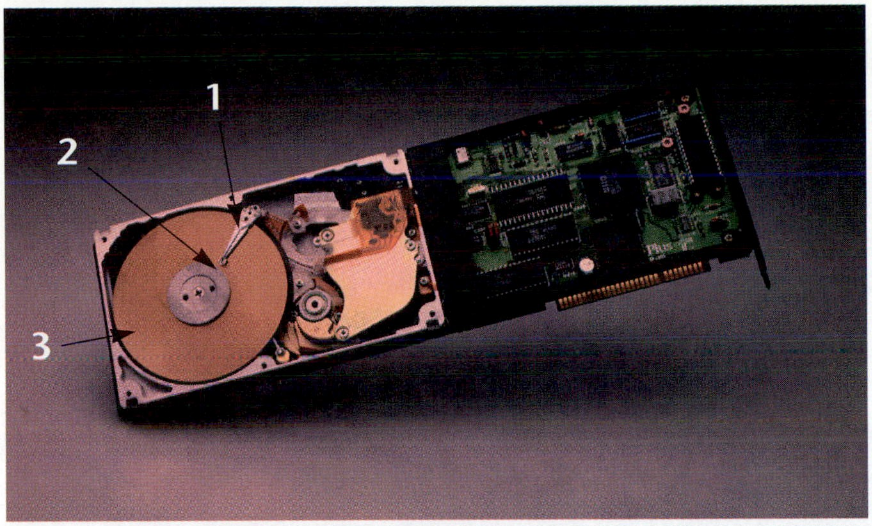

FIGURE 3-22 **Steps in Accessing Data on a Disk**
To access data on a disk, the access arm (1) must move the read/write head (2) to the proper track; and the disk (3) must rotate until the proper sector passes under the read/write head.

personal information system uses. Floppy disks have limited capacity, so a single program typically requires more than one floppy disk of storage space. In addition, access is much slower than with hard disks. The cost of a hard disk may add less than $300 to the price of an inexpensive microcomputer system, making hard disks very cost-effective additions.

Microcomputer hard disk drives are rated for both capacity and speed. Capacities range from about 40MB to several hundred MB. Capacity of 40MB may seem like a lot of disk storage. It is equivalent to about 20,000 pages of text. However, today's easy-to-use graphical software, described below, requires a great deal of storage. A graphical operating system and two or three applications can completely fill 40MB, leaving little room for data.

Speed ratings indicate the average number of **milliseconds** (thousandths of a second) required to access a particular data item. To read data from the disk, the disk drive must first move the access arm until the read/write head is positioned above the correct track. Then it must wait until the disk rotates the correct sector into position. The steps are illustrated in Figure 3-22. The time required for each of these steps is dependent on the chance starting positions of disk and read/write head, so the result is expressed as an average of a large number of trials. Average access times of 40 milliseconds are considered relatively slow today, whereas average access times near 10 milliseconds are considered very fast.

Floppy Disk Drives Although hard disk drives are used for everyday program and data storage in personal information systems, floppy disk drives are needed too. They are used to load new programs onto hard disks, trans-

FIGURE 3-23
Compatibility of Common Floppy Disk Formats with Standard Disk Drives

	Disk Size				
	$5\frac{1}{4}$-Inch		$3\frac{1}{2}$-Inch		
Drive Size	360K	1.2MB	720K	1.4MB	MAC
$5\frac{1}{4}$ inch, 360K	Yes	No	No	No	No
$5\frac{1}{4}$ inch, 1.2MB	(1)	Yes	No	No	No
$3\frac{1}{2}$ inch, 720K	No	No	Yes	No	(2)
$3\frac{1}{2}$ inch, 1.4MB	No	No	Yes	Yes	(2)
$3\frac{1}{2}$ inch, Mac Superdrive	No	No	(2)	(2)	Yes

(1) Problems may occur if the disk must subsequently be used in a 360K drive.
(2) Compatible with the use of an optional software package.

fer data among computers, and provide backup storage of data and programs in case of hard disk failure.

Five floppy disk formats are commonly used with microcomputers in business information systems. Figure 3-23 shows which formats are compatible. The $3\frac{1}{2}$-inch floppy disk is rapidly becoming standard for personal information systems.

An advantage of floppy disks is the increased security provided because they can easily be locked away. Anyone who has access to the computer itself can gain access to its hard disk's data and programs. For example, co-workers can gain access to private material when an office is empty, such as during lunch hour and staff meetings. Similarly, competitors can easily engage in industrial espionage, simply by obtaining access to the office at night or over weekends. Because the floppy disk is removable, it can be physically locked up to discourage snooping.

Removable Mass Storage Devices Some storage devices with the capacity of hard disk drives have removable disks. In some cases, these devices are designed like hard disk drives, except that the disk and some other components are packaged in a removable cartridge. In other cases, the design is more like a floppy disk drive modified to allow greater capacity. Removable disk systems have the high capacity of hard disks and the security advantage of floppy disks. They are more expensive than comparable hard disk drives.

Communications Devices

To enable a microcomputer to communicate with other computers, a **modem** is often used to connect the microcomputer to the telephone line. Some modems are *internal*, consisting of a printed circuit board that plugs into a motherboard slot. Others are *external*, connecting through a cable to the microcomputer's serial port (see Figure 3-24). The use of a modem requires communications software in addition to the modem hardware.

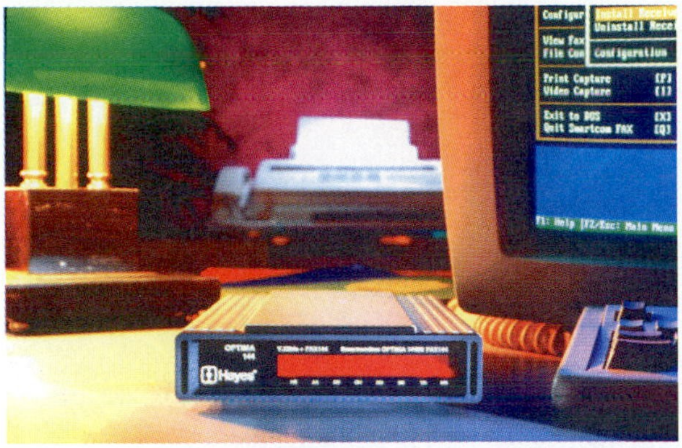

FIGURE 3-24 **Modems**
a. An external modem must be connected to a serial port by cable. *b.* An internal modem plugs into a slot on the motherboard.

Some modems also provide **facsimile (fax)** capability. Normally, a fax machine is a separate device that scans the images (text and graphics) on a sheet of paper and sends a coded signal through telephone lines to allow another fax machine to reproduce the images. A fax modem lets the computer compose images in memory without actually printing them on paper and sends a coded signal to let another fax machine produce the corresponding printout. In effect, it provides remote printing capability.

To enable a group of microcomputer users to share data and programs, a network may connect computers to a shared hard disk, high-quality printers, or other devices. To facilitate the connection, each microcomputer needs a plug-in **network interface card** with circuitry to manage the communications. Use of a network also requires networking software. These components are described further in Chapter 9.

PROGRAMS

A working microcomputer needs both system software and application software. A key decision that must be made in selecting microcomputer software is whether the operating system and applications will be *character-based* or will provide a **graphic user interface (GUI)**, as Figure 3-25 illustrates. Using a character-based operating system, the user enters system commands by typing them at a command prompt. Within programs, the user enters commands by selecting from a menu of choices, by typing commands, or by pressing special keys that are associated with command actions, although some character-based programs provide a point-and-click menu system. With a GUI, the user enters commands by

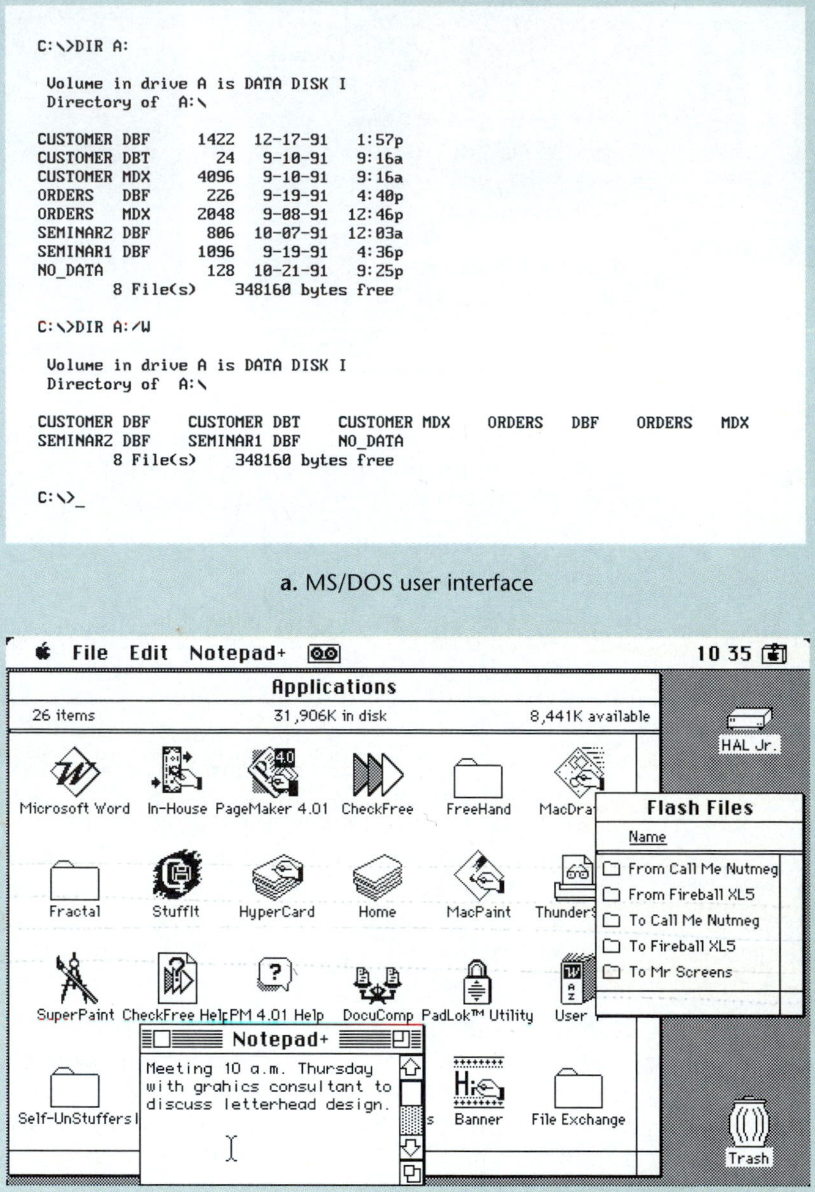

a. MS/DOS user interface

b. Macintosh user interface

FIGURE 3-25

Comparison of Character-Based Interface and GUI The DOS character-based user interface displays a directory of the files on a floppy disk. The corresponding GUI display on a Macintosh shows icons representing the files and folder icons.

pointing and clicking with a mouse. To run a program, the user points at the program's **icon** (a small pictorial symbol) and clicks the mouse. To enter commands within a GUI program, the user similarly manipulates the mouse.

A GUI and the versions of programs that work with it are relatively easy to learn to use. Commands are often the same or similar from program to program, easing the learning process. In addition, the most sophisticated versions of programs will tend to be GUI versions in the future. On the other hand, a very high-powered CPU is required to create and manipulate the GUI display, in addition to the power required to do the needed processing. Many useful programs remain available for character-based operating systems, and a character-based system works well with a lower-power microprocessor and a smaller hard disk system. Therefore, the choice may depend somewhat on the user's budget.

System Software

The operating systems widely used with microcomputers are DOS, GUIs, and UNIX.

DOS The most widely used operating system for microcomputers is **DOS,** *disk operating system,* sometimes marketed as MS-DOS or PC-DOS. DOS is a character-based operating system developed by Microsoft Corporation. It is a *single-user, single-tasking* operating system, meaning that it can support only one user at a time, running only one program at a time. To run it, the user must learn a small command vocabulary, along with the conventions used to name files and subdivisions of the hard disk. To simplify matters for the user, a **shell** can be loaded to let the user choose commands from a menu. Some shells provide a point-and-click interface.

DOS limits the amount of memory that a program can access. In 1980 (about the time DOS was designed) the standard amount of memory in a personal computer was 64 kilobytes (K), and the designers did not expect that anyone would spend the substantial amount of money required to put any more than 1MB into a microcomputer. Consequently, DOS was designed to manage up to 1MB of memory, of which 360K is reserved for operating system use. As a result, application programs and data under DOS cannot take up more than 640K of memory.

Today, program designers see the 640K limitation as constricting. The cost of 1MB of memory is low, and most new microcomputers have more than 1MB. Programs have been given new functions, better on-line help systems, and improved user interfaces. They have quickly expanded, to require increasing amounts of memory. To surmount the 640K limitation, DOS modifications called *extensions* have been devised to let DOS manage much larger amounts of memory, and some program designers have created programs that can take advantage of this additional memory.

GUIs GUIs are not limited to 640K of memory. In addition to their graphical screen displays and their use of point and click, GUIs provide context switching, windowing, and multitasking.

Context Switching Since several MB of memory may be available, a user can load several programs into memory at once and switch back and forth between the programs. For example, a sales manager creating a sales presentation could load her word processor, to compose the text of the presentation; her spreadsheet, to create the tables and graphs for display; and her

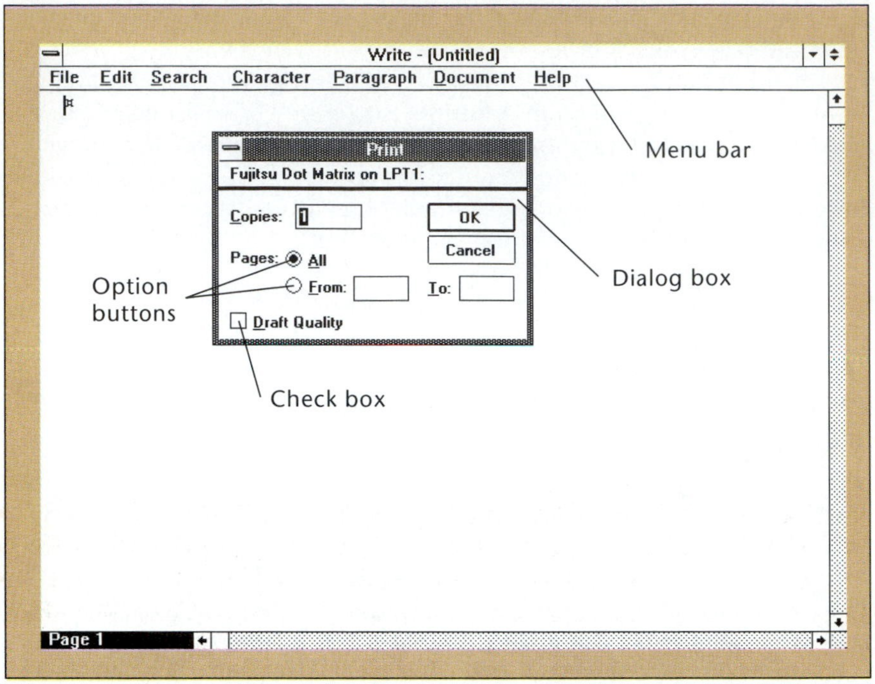

FIGURE 3-26

Example of GUI
From one program to another, you see a similar menu bar at the top of the screen and dialog boxes for such functions as printing, opening files, and saving files.

graphics program, to create overhead transparency slides. As she was composing text, she could quickly switch to the spreadsheet to check figures. When a section of text was complete, she could switch to her graphics program to create the corresponding slide. Each change would be instantaneous; she would not have to wait for the program to be loaded. This use of a microcomputer is called **context switching**.

Windowing A **windowing** system makes more than one program visible on the screen at the same time, with each program in its own subdivision of the screen, called a *window*, as Figure 3-27 illustrates. One window is in the foreground, containing the active program. All other windows are in the background and at least partly visible but inactive. To make certain figures in her spreadsheet available as she composes text for her presentation, the sales manager might switch to her spreadsheet—that is, bring it into the foreground window—and position those figures near the top of the screen. Then she could switch back to her word processor, positioning its window near the bottom of the screen to leave the spreadsheet figures visible. Some windowing systems let the user electronically copy data from one window to another.

Multitasking **Multitasking** means having two or more application programs in memory at one time, as in context switching and windowing systems. However, in multitasking, all the programs in memory are concurrently sharing the use of the CPU—that is, they are all running at the same

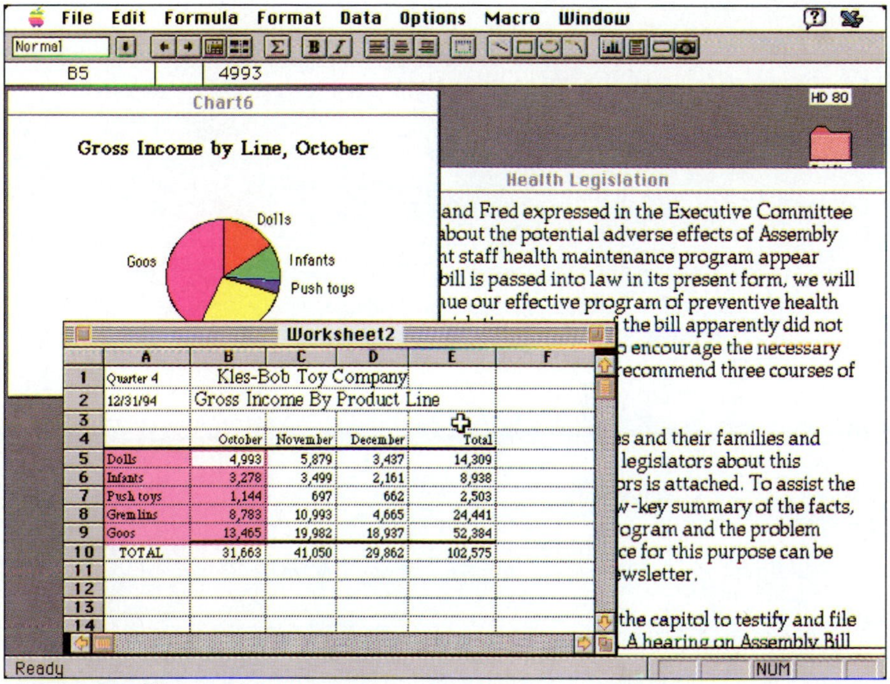

FIGURE 3-27
Screen Windows
Several tasks are in progress on this Macintosh at the same time, each in its own window. The user can move nearly instantly among word processor, spreadsheet, file copy, and communications program simply by moving the pointer into the appropriate window.

time, using the time-slicing system described in the previous chapter. The difference between the background program and the foreground program is that only the foreground program can receive input from the keyboard or the mouse.

The most widely used approach to multitasking on microcomputers today is provided by the product, Microsoft **Windows**, which is a sophisticated extension to DOS that adds memory management beyond the 1MB DOS limit, GUI, windowing, and multitasking. Although Windows can run versions of programs designed for DOS, its full capabilities are realized in programs specifically designed for Windows. Such programs can do useful work even when running in the background, and they can exchange data even when incompatible data formats would normally prevent such exchanges. For example, text from a word processing program can be inserted as patterns of dots into a graphics processing program, and graphics images can be transferred into the word processing program and positioned for display and printing.

IBM's **OS/2**, which is a complete operating system—used instead of DOS, not as an extension—is a more capable implementation of a multitasking system. It provides for management of large memories and for GUI, windowing, and multitasking. It can run programs designed for DOS and Windows, in addition to programs created especially for OS/2.

System 7 is the operating system used on the Apple Macintosh computer. The designers of System 7 and its predecessors concentrated espe-

INCREASING YOUR PERSONAL PRODUCTIVITY

The New Vocabulary of the PC

We are in a transition period as far as the PC is concerned, moving from the past of DOS and real mode into the future of some new (and as yet uncrowned) operating system and protected mode. Along the way, users can expect to encounter some alien ideas and concepts. To understand why the transition is taking place and how everything works, you should be aware of the following concepts:

Expanded Memory Expanded memory is a work-around solution to the DOS memory crunch. The Expanded Memory Specification (EMS) is a hardware and software standard that allows DOS programs to access extra memory in all PCs. It is supplied by a combination of hardware and software in 8088/8086 and 80286 systems, but it requires only software in 386-family computers.

Extended Memory Any memory in a 286- or 386-level PC above the 1-megabyte limit of the original PC's 8088 CPU is called extended memory. This memory is usable only when the microprocessor is in its protected mode (which the 8088/8086 is incapable of). DOS isn't a protected-mode operating system. Operating systems such as OS/2 and Windows gobble up all that extended memory and exploit the protected mode of the microprocessor.

Conventional Memory This is the term applied to the basic 640K of memory DOS uses to run all its programs. The 640K figure was derived somewhat arbitrarily. IBM almost decreed that memory above 512K was earmarked for the video display, BIOS, and future expansion, but it moved the line higher to 640K. Memory between the 640K and 1 Megabyte lines is called upper memory.

Future operating systems will blow away the 640K barrier. Indeed, most Windows and OS/2 applications don't care how much memory you have; as long as you have enough to boot the operating system, the programs should run. Adding more memory, though, may improve performance significantly.

Real Mode This refers to the native operating mode of the 8088/8086 CPU. The 286- and 386-level microprocessors' native operating mode is protected mode, which gives them access to more memory and uses the microprocessor at full strength. But the 286 and 386 can also run in real mode, where they behave just like the old 8088/8086, only faster.

Protected Mode This is the native operating mode of 286- and 386-level CPUs. In this mode, all the stops are pulled out; the microprocessor can access all its memory in 16- and 32-bit chunks.

The protected mode gets its name from the extra control the microprocessor can exert over programs and their use of memory. Areas of memory can be "roped off," preventing applications from stealing each other's resources. Under DOS, a real-mode operating system, programs assume they run the whole boat and grab resources without checking to see if other programs are

cially on the GUI, and the Macintosh GUI is generally considered the model for others, such as Windows and OS/2. Although the Macintosh hardware is different from other microcomputers, most data and many programs from DOS systems can be transferred to the Macintosh by using third-party translation and emulation programs. Macintosh hardware and software are well suited to graphics applications such as DTP.

UNIX Yet another approach to multitasking is provided by the UNIX operating system, designed by Bell Labs as a shared, multitasking operating

Box 3.2

using them. That's difficult if not impossible in protected mode.

Virtual-86 Mode Often called the V86 mode, this is a special mode of the 386 CPU. Unlike the 80286, which has a single real mode, you can run a 386 in dozens of real modes. Essentially, a single 386 can act like several 8086 computers, each of them running concurrently in full multitasking glory.

DOS Extender A DOS extender is a programming technique. The extender allows an application to run in protected mode under DOS. It shifts the CPU up from real mode to protected mode when the program starts. When the program accesses DOS, everything downshifts into real mode, then upshifts back to protected mode when DOS access is complete. The problem with the DOS extender, as with expanded memory, is that it is a work-around and not a full solution.

File Allocation Table DOS' method of storing and keeping track of files on a disk is referred to as the File Allocation Table (FAT) file system. It's a map that DOS uses to store and retrieve files on disk. The FAT's map also shows available and used disk space.

HPFS. OS/2 can use any file system it wants, thanks to its installable file system (IFS) architecture. Two choices available are the FAT file system, used by DOS, and the High Performance File System (HPFS). You can mix and match each and select one at boot time, thanks to OS/2's Dual Boot option.

Multitasking This is the capability of the operating system to juggle more than one program at a time. Unlike task switching, whereby users switch between different programs that run only one at a time, multitasking lets you work in one program while other programs continue to do work (perhaps creating a lengthy report or downloading a file).

Of course, you can only attend to one program at a time. This means that the programs you aren't using—but are still running—are kept "in the background." The program you are currently using becomes the "foreground" application.

Multithreaded A communications program could have three threads running: one that waits for characters to be received, another that monitors the keyboard, and a third that displays information. This is more efficient than running multiple tasks because it doesn't require the overhead of an operating-system context switch.

Interprocess Communications This is the capability of programs to share information. At the most basic level, consists of cutting and pasting information between two programs. Above ranks the "live" paste, in which information shared between two documents is updated whenever one of the documents is modified. This is referred to as Dynamic Data Exchange (DDE).

In advanced DDE, programs can send messages as well as data to other programs running locally or remotely. Beyond DDE is Object Linking and Embedding (OLE), which lets one program borrow the specialized capabilities of another program loaded on the machine (say, advanced chart creation) rather than having to implement that capability redundantly.

system for use on minicomputers. As processing power and memory capacity of microcomputers has increased, UNIX has been adapted for personal computers. Since UNIX is relatively expensive, it has been adopted primarily for its extremely powerful system-sharing capability. It is especially well suited to applications where users are already familiar with UNIX through the use of minicomputers. UNIX has become the standard operating system on *workstations*—computers that fall between microcomputers and minicomputers in power and are primarily used in engineering applications (see Figure 3-28).

FIGURE 3-28
A Workstation Using the UNIX Operating System
The extended graphics and math-processing capability of a workstation using the UNIX operating system make it suitable for engineering design applications.

Utility Programs DOS includes a number of utility programs for tasks such as editing text files (EDLIN and EDIT), printing text files on a printer (PRINT), comparing the contents of two floppy disks (DISKCOMP), and displaying directories and subdirectories on a hard disk (TREE). Other operating systems include similar utilities.

Third-party vendors market a wide variety of additional utilities. Here are three examples:

- The **DOS shell** replaces the DOS command line with a menu of options. The user can select a command from the menu or run a program by selecting it from a displayed directory listing.
- The **backup utility** replaces the DOS BACKUP module by automating the copying of hard disk contents to floppy disks or another medium. It also automates the restoration of files from the backup copy.
- The **file unerase utility** can often restore a file that has been erroneously erased from a disk. It often includes additional modules to restore a disk that has been erroneously reformatted (which erases disk contents) and to repair other disk problems.

Some utility programs are marketed as **shareware**. Such programs may be freely copied, so you may test them without obligation to pay first. If you continue to use the program beyond a brief test, you are required to mail payment to the author. Shareware programs are distributed through community **bulletin board** computer systems and on-line **information utility** systems such as CompuServe and America Online. These systems also frequently offer on-line discussion forums and electronic mail.

Application Software

An **application** is a program that processes information directly for the user, meeting the user's needs. Applications use the features and functions of system programs and hardware. Certain application programs are especially widely used. They are word processing programs, DTP programs, graphics programs, electronic spreadsheet programs, and personal DBMSs.

Word processing programs are used to enter and edit text: memos, letters, term papers, newsletter articles, and so on. Graphics programs are used to create graphs, line drawings, pictures, and other illustrative material. DTP programs combine text and graphics into complete publications such as newsletters, catalogs, brochures, annual reports, magazines, and books. For example, this book was produced using word processing, graphics, and DTP programs. These programs are explained in Chapter 4.

Electronic spreadsheet programs are used to record and analyze numbers. Typical spreadsheet uses include creating and analyzing budgets, estimating future costs, and performing other routine numerical calculations. Most spreadsheet programs can create graphs and printed reports to help the user communicate the results of the analysis. Electronic spreadsheet programs are explained in Chapter 5.

Personal DBMSs specialize in data storage and retrieval. Their uses include maintaining customer and client lists, inventories, test results, and the like. Personal DBMSs can create printed reports to help the user communicate the output. Some personal DBMSs include a programming language, which can be used to create complete, sophisticated small business accounting systems. These systems are explained in Chapter 6.

DATA

Some key issues of data in personal information systems relate to data files and directories in disk storage, data security, and data compatibility.

Data Files and Directories

Data is stored on disk in directories containing files. To use such a system effectively, you should develop a consistent pattern for naming files, and you should also develop a directory structure that helps you work efficiently.

Naming Files Consistently In DOS, **file names** consist of a series of up to 8 characters followed by a period and a **file extension** of 1 to 3 characters. The general format is NNNNNNNN.EEE, where *N* represents a character in the file's name and *EEE* represents the file's extension.

To identify the program that created a file, many applications use standard file extensions. Lotus 1-2-3, for example, applies the extension

Extension	Product	Description
bmp	Paintbrush	Bitmap
cal	Calendar	Data
cbt	Many products	Computer-based training data file
crd	Cardfile	Data
db	Paradox	Database file
dbf	dBASE	Database file
doc	Word for Windows	Document
doc	MultiMate	Document
dot	Word for Windows	Document template
dll	Windows 3.0	Dynamic link library
pcx	Paintbrush	Data
pm3	PageMaker 3.0	Data for version 3.0
pt3	PageMaker 3.0	Template for version 3.0
pm4	PageMaker 4.0	Data for version 4.0
pt4	PageMaker 4.0	Template for version 4.0
rbf	R:base	Database file
txt	Notepad	Data
wk1	Lotus 1-2-3	Spreadsheet
wri	Write	Document
xls	Excel	Spreadsheet
xlc	Excel	Chart
xlm	Excel	Macro

FIGURE 3-29

Typical File Extensions for DOS and Windows Applications

WK1 to all spreadsheet files. Thus, when you see a file with the name VR72M9XG.WK1, you know that the file was probably created by Lotus 1-2-3. Figure 3-29 shows some standard file extensions used by applications running under MS-DOS and Windows.

Some applications, such as the word processor XyWrite, do not append an extension to the files they save. For such programs, it is good practice to develop a standard extension of your own so you know which program created the file.

The first eight characters of the file name are usually left for the user to determine. It is good practice to develop your own standards for this part of the file name. For example, you might decide to prefix all word processing letters with the letter *L* followed by the date of the letter. The file name L121192.DOC would then represent the letter you saved on December 11, 1992 using Word for Windows. Similarly, you could decide to prefix all memos with the letter *M,* and so forth.

Using File Directories Efficiently All the operating systems described in this chapter support hierarchical **file directories**. This means that files

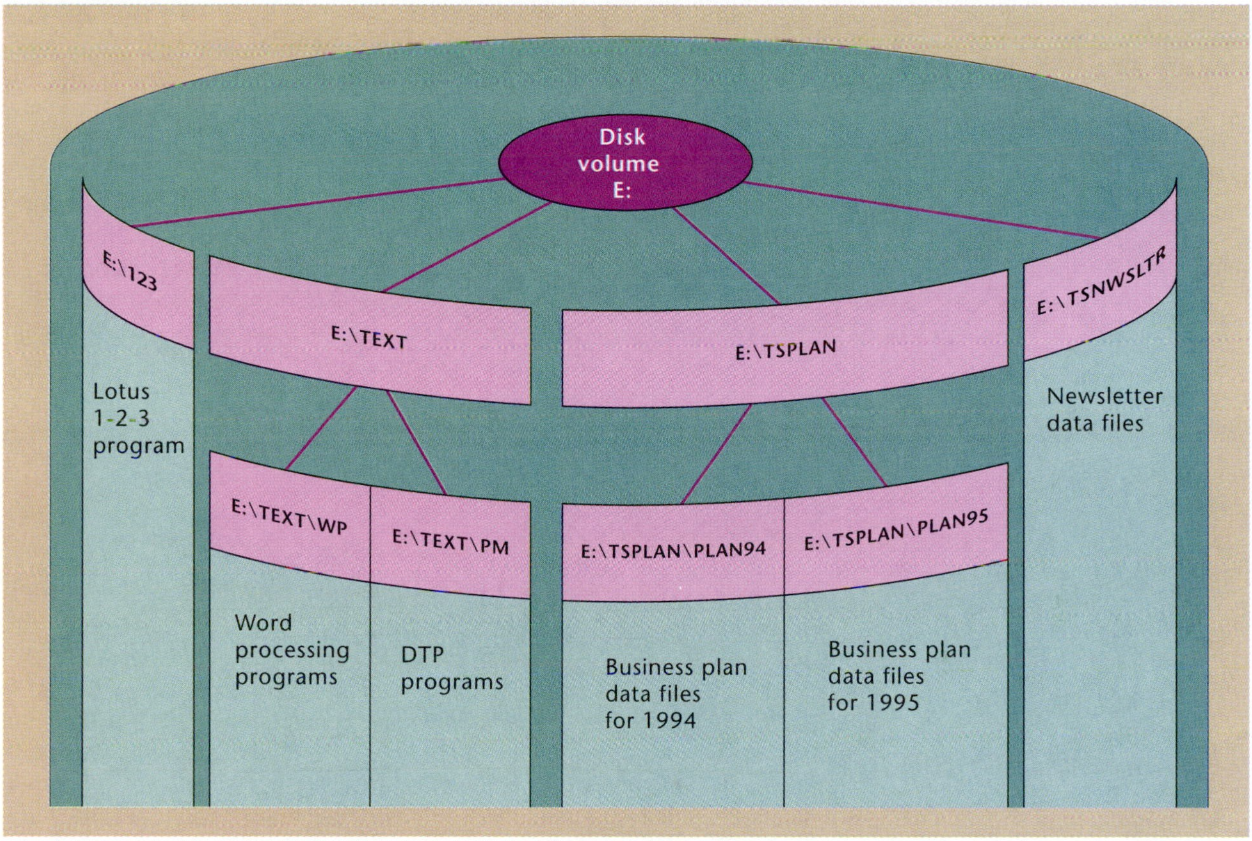

FIGURE 3-30 Directories and Subdirectories on a Hard Disk

can be grouped in chunks arranged hierarchically, like a family tree. For example, Figure 3-30 shows a hierarchy created to store business plans and newsletters and the programs that create them on a disk drive.

Disk drives are identified by a letter followed by a colon, such as A:. In a typical DOS system, drives A: and B: are floppy disk drives, and drive C: is a hard disk. If a system has more than one hard disk, the disks are labeled consecutively in alphabetical order beginning with C:.

In Figure 3-30, drive E: has four major directories. As shown from left to right, the directories contain Lotus 1-2-3 programs, text processing programs, business plan data files, and newsletter data files, respectively. Two of these directories have subdirectories. The first directory, E:\TEXT, contains the subdirectory E:\TEXT\WP, which holds word processing programs, and the subdirectory E:\TEXT\PM, which holds DTP programs. The second directory, E:\TSPLAN, contains the subdirectories E:\TSPLAN\PLAN94 and E:\TSPLAN\PLAN95 that have, respectively, the 1994 plan data and the 1995 plan data.

In designing such a system, the user could place all spreadsheet files, programs, and data in one directory, all word processing programs and data in another, and so on. Alternatively, the user could put all word processing program files in a directory, all spreadsheet program files in a directory, and all data files in a series of directories organized by project or subject. The user in Figure 3-30, like many experienced users, adopted the second method. Mixing programs and data files in the same directory makes the data files hard to spot. In addition, many users feel that dividing data files by project is more natural than dividing them by the program that created them—it makes the files easier to find.

Careful planning of directories can save considerable confusion, error, and reworking. It may not seem too important to you as a student, but when you become a frequent user of personal information systems in your job, you will find that you quickly generate many files that can become a confusing mess. The easiest way to solve this problem is to avoid it by careful planning at the onset.

Protecting Your Data

In designing systems, you should give attention to the problem of protecting your data from its two main threats: accidental destruction and unauthorized snooping. Protecting data from accidental destruction involves developing effective backup procedures and then actually following them. Backup is one of the most widely recognized needs—and one of the least met—in personal information systems. Be sure you regularly back up your work.

The second threat is unauthorized snooping. Since the data on a personal computer's hard disk is almost as accessible as data on paper, you should consider the consequences of snooping. Most offices are accessible to snooping when their occupants are in meetings, out to lunch, or otherwise away from the desk. If the data must be protected from snoopers, then three major options are available: (1) locking the computer; (2) storing the data on removable media, which can be removed and locked up; and (3) using software methods of locking the data files or the entire hard disk to make them inaccessible to others.

The simplest method of discouraging snoopers is to lock the computer itself. Most computers today include a key lock as standard equipment, and locking the computer may discourage most casual nosiness. However, technically skilled snoopers can evade the locking systems used on most computers, and you should not depend on the computer lock to stop someone who is very determined.

A more dependable method of ensuring confidentiality is maintaining data files on removable media—floppy disks or removable hard disks—and locking up the media when the files are not being used. Remember that the value of such protection is lost unless (1) the removable medium is locked up at every moment except when it is directly being used and (2) the disks are backed up regularly, just as files on internal hard disks should be.

The third method of protection is using special software to lock the specific data files or the entire hard disk against outsiders. To lock a file, a software package is used to **encrypt** it—translate it into unreadable form. Before it can be used again, it will have to be *decrypted* (retranslated), which may be somewhat time-consuming. To lock an entire hard disk, software may modify the operating system so it does not recognize the disk's presence except when the software enables it. Both encryption and disk locking require the user to remember a password to gain access. If you forget the password, the data is lost forever.

Data Compatibility

Data compatibility, the ability to transfer data without external translation from one program to another, can be a major problem in developing personal information systems. Each time a designer develops specifications for a new word processor or for a database program, the temptation is strong to design a brand new data format. If a designer dreams up a better way of representing, in the computer, the fact that certain word processing text is to be underlined, boldfaced, or indented, then the word processing package may actually work more efficiently or be easier to use.

But the result is that the files produced by each word processor and spreadsheet program are in a different form, and that these files are not automatically interchangeable. To respond to this problem, program vendors often include routines to translate data from other popular programs. In addition, there is a thriving market for third-party translation packages to convert data from one format to another.

Today, standard formats are beginning to evolve, and someday such translations may no longer be necessary. But for now, if you develop a personal information system and you need to share data among various packages, be sure their data is compatible—or translatable—before you buy software.

PROCEDURES

In shared systems, it is obvious that procedures are vital. The need for procedures is often not so obvious in a single-user system. However, the single user may not be the only person who depends on his or her system's output. If the system fails, other people will not receive its output, which they may need to do their jobs, too. In addition, someone else will nearly always need to learn to use the system eventually, such as when the original user is promoted to another job.

Every personal computer user should document standard procedures, if only to make life easier. Notice, in Figure 3-31, that users of personal information systems, like users of shared systems, need procedures both for normal processing and for failure recovery. You should document those procedures in a notebook that you keep on your desk. Notes like these

Normal Processing	Failure Recovery
Format for file names	Undeleting of lost files
Format for disk labels	Restoring of lost data from backups
New storage media preparation	Phone numbers for computer store's service department and software vendors' customer service departments
File and database backup	
Directories and subdirectories	
Loading of new software	
Changing of AUTOEXEC.BAT file	

FIGURE 3-31
Examples of Procedures for Personal Information Systems

prove very helpful, especially when you perform a task infrequently. For example, if you have a documented procedure for backing up your database, producing a pie chart, and typing an envelope, then you do not have to dig through computer manuals every time to remind yourself how to do it. Documentation is also vital for anyone else who needs to learn your system.

PEOPLE

People are an important component of business information systems. This section discusses people in the context of the roles they play and the training they need.

Roles

The roles described in Chapter 2 for the people component all exist in personal information systems: developer, operator, clientele, and user. However, in a personal information system, the user/owner may fill several of these roles or all of them.

The operator of a personal information system is invariably the user. After all, a personal information system is, by definition, a system used by an individual. The user also reads and interprets the output and enjoys the benefits of the system, thus performing the role of clientele, although many personal systems have other clientele in addition.

The role of system developer may or may not be played by the user. In a large corporation with an MIS department, one or several professional system developers might design and build a user's personal information

FIGURE 3-32
Packaged Software Documentation
The box containing this PC program contains floppy disks and several thick books of documentation.

system. Another option is for the user to hire a consultant to do one or more of the system-development steps.

A third option, for those users who have the time, interest, and skills, is to develop their own personal information systems. Because a personal computer system can easily cost $5,000 or more, such a project should not be undertaken lightly. You, or any user, should know what you are doing before spending that kind of money. We will discuss an approach to systems development in Chapter 7.

Training

Using a personal information system effectively requires training. You need to understand how each application works, how to use the system in order to achieve the maximum benefit from it, and how to add new applications to your existing system. You can learn about your system, and about the productivity software you run on it, from a variety of sources.

First, nearly every piece of computer equipment and every software package comes with **documentation**. Figure 3-32 shows an example. You should familiarize yourself with the documentation to understand how the reference material is organized. This will help you to look up information as you need it. Packaged software, such as an electronic spreadsheet or graphics package, also usually comes with a **tutorial program**. Such **computer-based training (CBT)** systems can help you get started quickly by introducing you to the basic operation and features of the software. You should, of course, run the tutorial program for any new software you acquire.

Second, almost all popular software packages eventually become the subject of books. Take a trip to your local, big chain bookstore. You will find dozens of titles in the computer section, many of them how-to guides for application software. Much valuable information can be found in such texts, but their quality varies, so you should seek advice from friends and experts. If you go shopping when you have a specific question, you can compare the usefulness of various books in answering it.

Third, for those who learn more effectively in a classroom, courses may be offered through local colleges or universities. In addition, computer stores and computer consultants may offer courses.

Training is an investment, just as hardware and programs are. You may spend $5,000 on hardware and software that you hope will help increase your productivity by, say, 40 percent (resulting in more income). It is probably cost-effective, then, to budget an additional $750 on training that will enable you to achieve your goal.

Summary

Personal information systems put processing power under the direct control of individual businesspersons.

Personal computer hardware is based on a microprocessor. Its processing power, measured in MIPS, is influenced by its word size and cycle speed. Main memory consists of RAM and nonvolatile ROM. Input devices include keyboard, mouse, and scanner. Output devices are character and graphics screen displays and dot matrix and laser printers. Storage devices include hard disk drives and floppy disk drives. Communication devices include modems and network interface cards.

System software is either character-based, such as DOS and UNIX, or based on a GUI, such as Windows, OS/2, and System 7. All but DOS provide some level of multitasking. Some utility programs are included with operating systems, and others are available from third-party vendors. Application software includes word processing programs, DTP programs, graphics programs, electronic spreadsheet programs, and personal DBMSs.

Data is stored in files in hierarchical directories. It should be protected against accidental destruction and unauthorized snooping. Data compatibility is a continuing problem.

Personal information system procedures for normal processing and failure recovery are vitally important.

The personal system user is also the system operator and sometimes, additionally, the system developer. Company computer professionals or outside consultants may serve as system developers. User training is essential.

Key Terms

personal information system
microcomputer
personal computer (PC)
microprocessor
MIPS
word size
megahertz (MHz)
CISC
RISC
random-access memory (RAM)
read-only memory (ROM)
volatile
motherboard
expansion slot

parallel port
serial port
mouse
point and click
trackball
digital scanner
optical character recognition
character display
graphics display
VGA
millisecond
modem
facsimile (fax)
network interface card
graphic user interface (GUI)
icon
DOS
shell
context switching
windowing
multitasking
Windows
OS/2
UNIX
System 7
DOS shell
backup utility
file unerase utility
shareware
bulletin board
information utility
application
file name
file extension
file directory
encrypt
data compatibility
documentation
tutorial program
computer-based training (CBT)

Review Questions

1. Name the key advantage of a personal information system.
2. When personal information systems are developed within large organizations, list two limitations that the organization may place on the user's freedom to develop exactly the system that is needed.
3. List the five hardware components of a personal information system.
4. Describe a microprocessor.
5. What are the two families of microprocessors most commonly used in personal computers today?
6. Describe the rate at which microprocessor technology improves.
7. Name a commonly used measure of computer processing power.
8. Describe the relationships between word size, cycle speed, and computer power.
9. Compare CISC computers with RISC computers.
10. What is the most important factor, other than CPU power, in the overall performance of a computer?
11. Name the two types of memory chips that make up a microcomputer's main memory.
12. In today's technology, how many memory chips are required to contain 1MB of main memory?
13. What is the typical amount of main memory in microcomputers today?
14. Define volatility as it applies to main memory.
15. Why is ROM useful in personal computers?

16. Describe the connection between the motherboard and the expansion slots.
17. Name four input devices commonly used with personal information systems.
18. What is point and click?
19. Describe the relationship between digital scanner and optical character recognition software.
20. Name the two most common output devices.
21. Differentiate between the character display and the graphics display.
22. Name the two types of printers most commonly used with personal information systems.
23. Compare the 9-pin dot matrix printer with the 24-pin dot matrix printer.
24. What is the most important factor that would lead a user to employ a dot matrix printer in a personal information system?
25. Describe the advantages and disadvantages of laser printers in personal information systems.
26. What are the advantages and disadvantages of ink-jet printers in personal information systems?
27. Indicate the steps required when a hard disk accesses a particular data item.
28. What hard disk access speeds would be considered relatively slow and relatively fast today?
29. Describe the problems that would arise if either a hard disk drive or a floppy disk drive was missing from a personal information system.
30. Describe the advantages and disadvantages of removable mass-storage devices.
31. Name the two communications devices commonly used in personal information systems.
32. What is fax?
33. Differentiate between character-based operating systems and GUI-based operating systems in the way a user enters the command to run a particular program.
34. What is the most widely used operating system for microcomputers?
35. Why is the 640K limitation on the size of programs and data under DOS a problem today?
36. Differentiate among context switching, windowing, and multitasking.
37. List four multitasking operating systems commonly used in personal information systems.
38. Name four utility programs that are included with DOS and three widely used utility programs that are marketed separately from DOS.
39. What are shareware programs, and where can they be obtained?
40. List at least two typical uses of each of the five application programs most widely used in personal information systems.
41. What are the rules for naming files in DOS?
42. Describe what is meant by hierarchical directories.
43. What are the two main threats to data security in personal information systems?

44. Name three ways to protect your data from unauthorized snooping.
45. What are two categories of procedures that every personal information system should have?
46. Name three roles played by people in a personal information system.
47. List three types of people who may play the role of system developer for a personal information system.
48. Describe three sources of training for personal information systems.

Discussion Questions

A. Describe the types of limitations that may exist in some settings on the user's complete freedom to create personal information systems exactly as he or she wishes. Do some limitations apply in all cases? Devise a series of at least four or five examples, other than those in the book, showing typical situations that place limitations on the personal computer user's freedom.

B. If you were configuring a personal information system of your own, would you choose a $3\frac{1}{2}$-inch or a $5\frac{1}{4}$-inch diskette drive? What factors should be considered in making the choice? Defend your decision.

C. Consider the selection of a printer for a personal information system. What factors should be considered? Describe the purpose and environment of one particular example of a personal information system, and indicate the reasoning you would use in selecting a printer for that system.

D. In comparing character-based programs with GUI-based programs, what are the factors that would lead you to select one or the other? Are there circumstances in which a character-based program could be preferable even when budget is not a factor? If not, why not? If so, give at least two examples.

E. Experiment with the user interfaces of at least two different operating systems that are available to you, and describe the differences. Examples include DOS, Windows, GEOS (an alternative character-based user interface for DOS computers), OS/2, Macintosh System 7, UNIX, and VMS (the operating system on the VAX minicomputer). In your comparison, describe for each (1) how the user obtains a listing of the programs and the data files on the computer's hard disk; (2) how the user runs a program; and (3) how the user selects particular program functions within a program run. What other differences can you observe? Why do you prefer one over the other?

F. A young entrepreneur was negotiating with the owner of a florist shop who wanted to sell the business—shop, inventory, computer, client accounts, everything. The two were having trouble agreeing on a price for the computer system. The hardware was adequate, and the previous owner had had a consultant custom-tailor an accounting package for him. The problem was that no documentation had been written for the system (that is, no written procedures), and the consultant had left the area. The owner insisted that the software was simple enough to run without documentation and wanted $15,000 for it—half the price it had cost to develop. The prospective buyer was wary of the claim. What would you do?

G. Find as many sources of training in your area as you can for the following software: Lotus 1-2-3; Excel; Ventura Publisher or PageMaker; dBase III+; dBase IV.

USER'S GUIDE: HOW TO SELECT YOUR OWN PERSONAL COMPUTER SYSTEM

The ideal way to buy a computer system is to discuss your needs with a computer expert—not just with someone who happens to own a computer, but with a real expert. Then take the expert along with you to a computer store. However, if you do not know a computer expert well enough to ask for advice, here are the questions that the authors ask when we assist our friends and an idea of the kind of advice we give.

GUI-Based System versus Character-Based System

The first question you need to answer is whether you need a GUI-based system or a character-based system. In making this decision, you can let your budget serve as your guide. The trend today is toward GUI systems based on Windows or on the Mac operating system, which are easier to learn and use than character-based systems. New versions of major software packages today typically require a GUI. A character-based DOS system that requires you to learn and type commands is somewhat more challenging to learn and use, though millions of users have mastered DOS. A DOS-based system is normally technically simpler and less expensive, but it makes greater demands on the user. The main reason for considering a DOS system would be strict budget limitations.

GUI-Based System: IBM-Compatible versus Apple Macintosh

If your budget can handle a GUI-based system, then you must choose between an IBM-compatible system and an Apple Macintosh system. The Mac designers are generally credited with the more advanced GUI, and as a result, the Mac is considered easier to learn and use. All major categories of software, as described in Part Two of this book, are available for the Mac, and Mac software is recognized for leadership in the field of DTP. On the other hand, IBM-compatible computers can be configured more flexibly to meet specific requirements, and a wider variety of specialized software is available. An IBM-compatible system with a Windows or an OS/2 GUI may be nearly as easy to learn and use as a Mac. In many businesses, including most large corporations, IBM-compatible computers are standard, and experience with IBM-compatible hardware and software may be useful in your career.

Configuring a System

In this section, we will consider suitable specifications for three systems: (1) a character-based system using DOS on an economical IBM-compatible machine, which we will call the DOS system; (2) a GUI-based system using DOS and Windows on an IBM-compatible machine, which we will call the Windows system; and (3) a GUI-based system using the Macintosh operating system on an Apple machine, which we will call the Mac system. For each system, we will consider choice of processors, amounts of main memory and auxiliary storage, display adapter, ports and expansion slots, printer, and programs.

Processor A DOS system should contain either an 80286 or 80386 processor. While the 80286 system is normally less expensive, the risk is that future versions of major software packages may not be compatible with it, though today's versions typically are. The 80386 processor (or a less expensive variant named 80386SX) is faster and more likely to be compatible with future software.

As you analyze your needs, compatibility with future software may or may not be very important. Although the working life of a computer may be ten years or more, PC technology changes so quickly that much more useful systems at attractive prices are likely to become available sooner. As a result, computers are commonly replaced after a working life of three to five years. The software you purchase with the original system may meet your needs completely for that period. By the time you are ready to upgrade software, you may be ready to upgrade the hardware too.

Since a GUI requires more processing power, a Windows system's processor should be at least a 25MHz, 80386 processor, and you should consider the faster 80486 processor.

To receive the full benefit of the Mac system, with its ease of use, you should consider a Macintosh II model based on the Motorola 68030 processor.

Main Memory and Storage In a DOS system, 2MB of main memory will meet most users' needs. The minimum hard disk size today is typically 40MB, which is sufficient to contain several application programs and their data files.

In a Windows or a Mac system, the minimum amount of main memory should be 4MB, and up to 8MB would be worthwhile. Since programs and supporting data files for graphics software are much larger, the hard disk should be at least 80MB with average access time of 15 milliseconds or less.

In all three systems, at least one floppy disk drive should be included for adding new programs and data and for backing up the hard disk contents. On a Mac system, the disk drive should be the so-called SuperDrive, which is capable (with the necessary software) of accessing data on IBM-format disks.

Display Most IBM-compatible systems today include VGA display adapters and compatible monitors. In a DOS system on an extremely limited budget, the much-lower-resolution color graphics array (CGA) display adapter and monitor may be available less expensively. The VGA system is generally considered quite preferable and is required for a Windows system. In fact, you may wish to consider the so-called super VGA adapter, which provides more attractive display and operates faster than the standard VGA system. Display speed is a limiting factor in the apparent speed of operation of a GUI-based system, so an improvement in this area can be quite noticeable.

For a Mac system, the high-resolution color display meets a wide variety of application needs effectively. The standard color display offers a less accurate representation of colored materials. A *portrait display* capable of showing an entire typed page at once may be useful for some applications.

Ports and Expansion Slots IBM-compatible systems should include at least one parallel port (for attaching a printer) and one serial port (for attaching an external modem or a mouse). To allow for future expansion, your system should provide at least one or two additional expansion slots beyond those required for the initial configuration. A Windows system requires a mouse.

Suitable ports and expansion slots are included in Mac computers, as is a mouse.

Printer On a low-budget DOS system, consider an inexpensive dot matrix printer, which may have sufficient output quality to meet your needs. You should compare the printout quality of several dot matrix printers and at least one laser printer before making your choice. A laser printer provides considerably higher quality, more flexibility, and faster output at a higher cost both for original purchase and for operation. Ink-jet printers offer high-quality output at a relatively low price, though they are much slower than laser printers and cost more to operate.

A GUI-based system needs a laser printer. You should compare features and prices of several laser printers before making your selection. Not all laser printers can make full use of the Mac's graphics, so you should receive assurance of full compatibility before you select a particular printer.

Programs Programs that should be purchased with your system include the most recent version of the operating system (plus Windows for the Windows system) and at least a word processor for term papers and correspondence. You may also consider an electronic spreadsheet package and a database package. So-called integrated software packages combine simple word processing, electronic spreadsheet, and database capability into a single product that may meet most of your software needs as a student, though as a businessperson, you may prefer more sophisticated separate packages, as described in Part Two of this book. Student versions of many software packages are often available quite economically through college bookstores.

Where to Buy a Computer

Three sources of computers should be considered: (1) local retail computer stores; (2) mail order sources; and (3) college bookstores.

In considering local retail computer stores, you should compare prices and solicit the advice of computer-knowledgeable associates. Some service-oriented computer stores cater to the needs of businesspeople, who often

FIGURE 3-33 PC Ad

want a considerable amount of costly help in selecting products and getting started. These stores discount their products very little. As a student, you may need much less of this expensive help, since you may receive the support of fellow students and teachers, and so you may prefer to seek out stores with heavily discounted prices.

Mail order companies advertise in *PC Magazine, PC World, MacUser, Mac World,* and other similar magazines. Prices are often heavily discounted. If you do not live near a large city where there are discount computer stores, mail order is an attractive alternative.

Some college bookstores often offer very attractive discounts on both hardware and software. You may want to check your bookstore's prices first, as a standard of comparison for other vendors.

Whatever your source, consider its willingness and ability to correct problems in case any part of the system you purchase does not operate correctly. Rigorous testing of electronic components is expensive, and it is one of the areas in which discount marketers cut corners. As a result, one or more components of your system may need replacement under the warranty, and you need assurance that your source can and will make such replacements. In such a case, a local store may be convenient to deal with.

Since many retail computer companies are short-lived, the company may go out of business before your system is completely working. Buying your system with a bank credit card obligates the bank to credit your account for the amount of the loss if your seller does not support its guarantee.

Testing Your New System

Since your system may not have been tested thoroughly before the sale, test it immediately after the purchase. To test the system, set it up and ensure that it initially works, obtaining replacements for parts that do not appear to work. Then let it run without interruption—do not turn it off—for twenty-four hours a day for at least a week. This is called *burning in* the system. A system that is working correctly at the end of such a test is reasonably likely to continue working correctly for some time.

MINICASE

Microsoft Nails Some Pirates

When the Microsoft Corporation unveiled its updated MS-DOS 5 software operating system last June, it was confident that it had devised a way to thwart the loss of $1 billion a year from software piracy. Its packaging contains two one-of-a-kind holograms, one a circular image on the package box and the other a rectangular image pasted inside on the product manual, viewable through a window on the box. The multidimensional images bear the company's name or the MS-DOS logo and tell consumers that the product is the real McCoy.

Microsoft pamphlets said the holograms are "virtually impossible" to reproduce and "raise the counterfeiting barrier to a level previously unattempted in the software industry." Yet within two weeks of the introduction, a Taiwanese counterfeiter commissioned a holographer in China to copy and produce the holograms. Over the next half-dozen months, Microsoft's counterattack took it to Taiwan, Japan, Hong Kong and Melbourne. The idea was to track down the counterfeiters, mostly without the aid of foreign governments. Ultimately, the company helped bust a major Asian counterfeiting ring that may have produced up to $150 million worth of the company's hottest products.

In the meantime, the company is trying to get the fakes off the market, an endeavor made difficult "because we still don't know the extent of what is out there," said David Curtis, head of international law and corporate affairs at Microsoft. So far, goods have been seized in the United States, Germany, Canada, Singapore, Hong Kong, Taiwan, and en route to Venezuela. The company is attempting to get a search warrant to seize goods in Melbourne shipped from Taiwan.

The software industry loses up to $14 billion a year to piracy, including illegal copying by dealers, corporations and individual users. Fakes are so common in Taiwan that Microsoft estimates that only 20 percent of the software used there is legally obtained. About 90 percent of all counterfeiting worldwide comes from Taiwan. . . .

This spring, China agreed to strengthen its copyright laws rather than face United States trade sanction. In late April, Carla Hill, the United States Trade Representative, identified Taiwan, India and Thailand under the special 301 provisions of the Trade Act of 1974.

The 301 provisions call for identifying trading partners that deny adequate and effective protection for intellectual property. The Government can take action if disputes are not resolved. China is one of 22 countries that have been placed on a special "priority watch" list.

Questions

1. This article mentions "illegal copying by dealers, corporations and individual users." Define what you think constitutes *illegal copying.*
2. If you steal your friend's bicycle, then he or she no longer has a bicycle to ride. If, however, you steal a copy of your friend's operating system, he or she still has a copy to use. Are the two thefts somehow different? Suppose you steal a copy of your company's customer list. Your company still has its list. Have you stolen anything? If so, what?
3. Assume that this article is correct in saying that 80 percent of software used in Taiwan is illegally obtained. Suppose you manage a small Taiwan business. If you pay for legal copies of software, you will be at a competitive disadvantage with most other companies. What would you do? Is the theft of software somehow more ethical in Taiwan than it is in, say, Denver?
4. The article mentions activities in the U.S., Germany, Canada, Singapore, Hong Kong, Taiwan, Venezuela, and mainland China. Clearly, values, mores, and cultures are vastly different among these countries. To what extent is it appropriate for a U.S.-based company to expect its values and mores to be accepted in so many different countries and cultures? Or, is this question irrelevant since users of a product supposedly accept the terms of the license agreement when they install the product on their computer?

CHAPTER 4

Word Processing, Graphics, and Desktop Publishing Applications

CHAPTER OUTLINE

This chapter discusses applications that help people communicate effectively: word processing applications, graphics applications, and desktop publishing (DTP) applications. These applications are all focused on the task of producing documents such as letters, memos, reports, term papers, brochures, newsletters, and display materials (the kind shown during oral presentations). Most businesspeople spend a significant portion of their time creating such documents. Making skillful use of communication tools can pay great dividends.

DOCUMENTS: TEXT AND ART

Documents are composed of two major elements: text and art. **Text** consists of words, sentences, and paragraphs. **Art** is everything else that can appear in a document: lines, boxes, pictures, drawings, charts, and other graphic elements (see Figure 4-1). To create text, you use a word processing application. If a document consists entirely of text, you may create it, format it, and produce it using only a word processing application. To create art, you use a graphics application. If a document consists entirely of art, you may create it, format it, and produce it using only a graphics application. To combine text and art into a single document and to make use of its sophisticated formatting capabilities, you use a DTP application.

Recently, the line between word processing applications and DTP applications has grown fuzzy. The more sophisticated word processors include many functions previously available only in graphics and DTP programs. As a result, your word processing program may let you perform some functions described below under graphics and DTP.

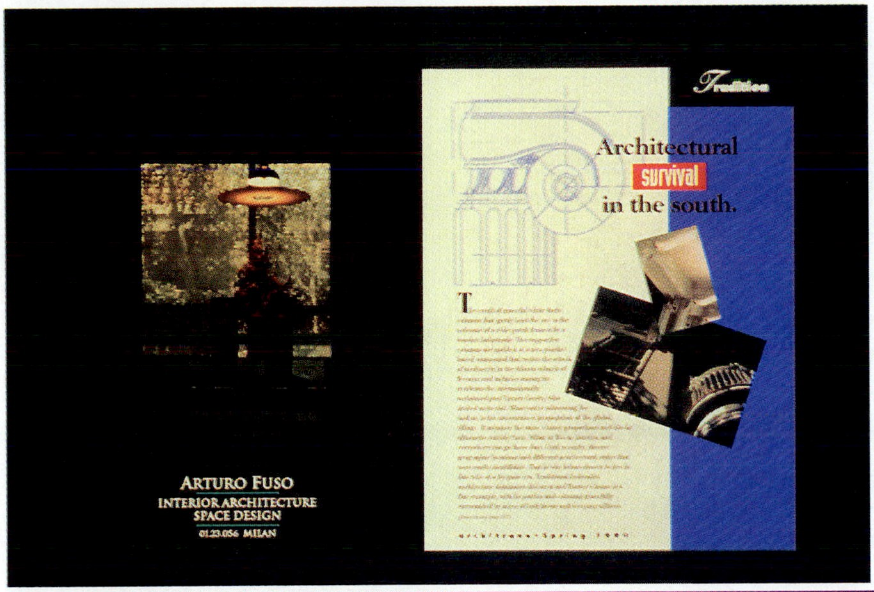

FIGURE 4-1

Text and Art

This document includes the two major elements in a document: text and art.

CREATING TEXT WITH WORD PROCESSING

Word processing programs such as WordPerfect and Microsoft Word eliminate much of the tedious manual labor that was once required to produce good-looking letters, memos, reports, term papers, and documents. They do this by automating many details. For example, the production of an error-free business letter once required that the letter be rekeyed from beginning to end several times, even for small changes. Word processing lets you enter text once and then make any required changes without having to retype. Only the new phrases and the corrections must be keyed. Thus, their major benefit is to eliminate the need to retype text that has already been keyed in.

Word processing also lets people who do not type well produce clean looking memos and reports. The secretaries who used to type final drafts of documents were highly skilled typists, and they could type line after line of material without making a single error. Word processing lets you correct errors easily and quickly, so you need not try to enter your material without making an error.

Finally, word processing lets you separate the various tasks involved in producing documents so you can do one (or a few) at a time. You do not have to try to think about phrasing, page layout, spelling, and paragraph indention all at the same time. As a result, even if you only produce reports and term papers occasionally, you can create professional-looking, error-free results.

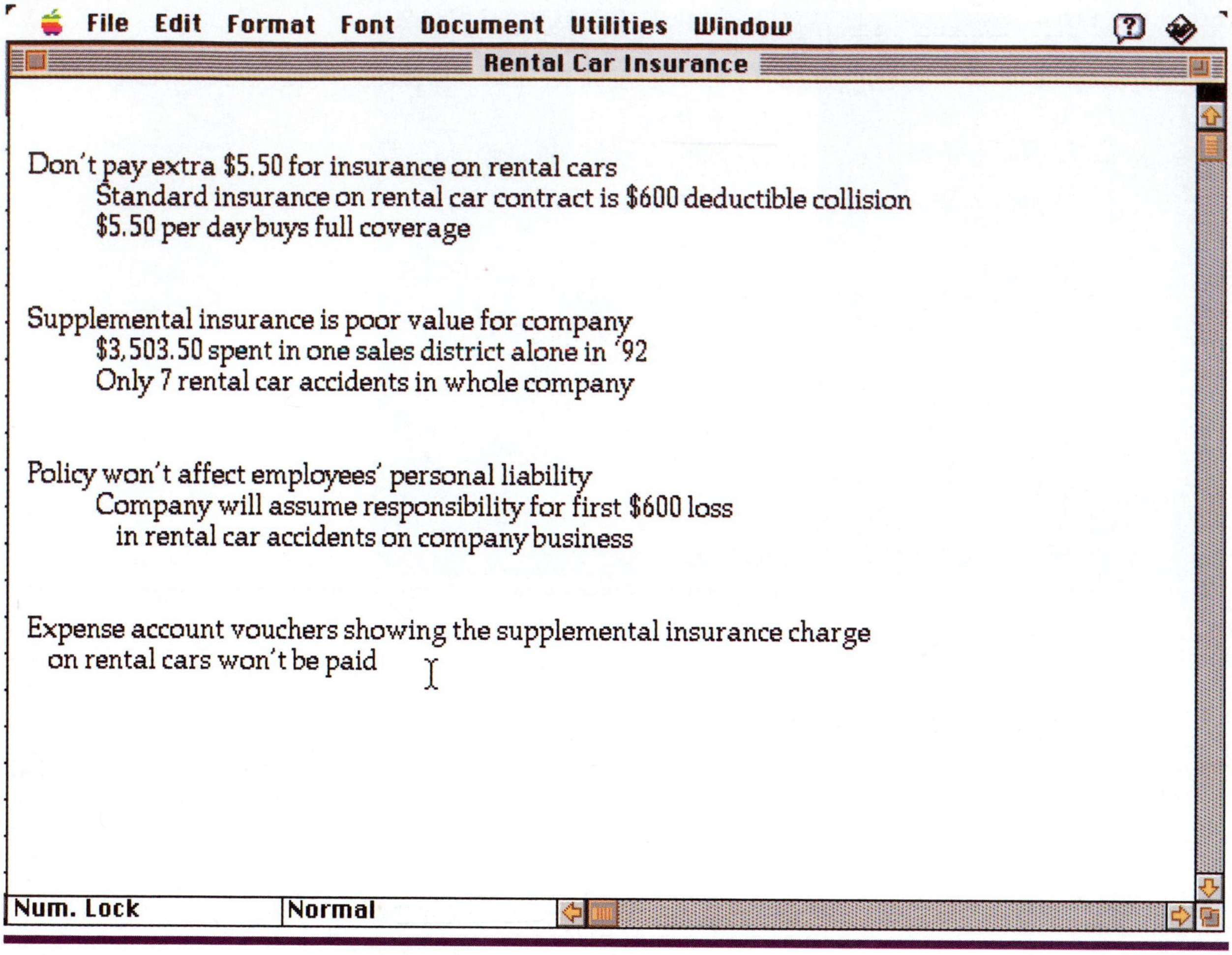
File Edit Format Font Document Utilities Window
Rental Car Insurance
Don't pay extra $5.50 for insurance on rental cars
Standard insurance on rental car contract is $600 deductible collision
$5.50 per day buys full coverage
Supplemental insurance is poor value for company
$3,503.50 spent in one sales district alone in '92
Only 7 rental car accidents in whole company
Policy won't affect employees' personal liability
Company will assume responsibility for first $600 loss
in rental car accidents on company business
Expense account vouchers showing the supplemental insurance charge
on rental cars won't be paid
Num. Lock
Normal

FIGURE 4-2

Planning a Message with a Word Processor
One way of planning a message is to make notes using the word processor.

Before word processing systems were available, most managers were supported by staffs of secretaries and clerk-typists who produced documents from dictation or from handwritten drafts. Today, many managers produce most of their documents themselves, relying on clerical support only for long or complicated reports.

Experienced writers often approach the task of producing a document as a series of predictable steps: planning, drafting, editing, formatting, and production or printing. Word processing can facilitate each of these steps.

Planning Your Communication

In the planning stage, the writer tentatively determines the sequence of topics to be covered in the document. For simple documents, most writers plan in their heads. As documents get more complicated, however, it is useful to work on paper—or on the screen. The word processor itself can be used in such planning, as Figure 4-2 shows.

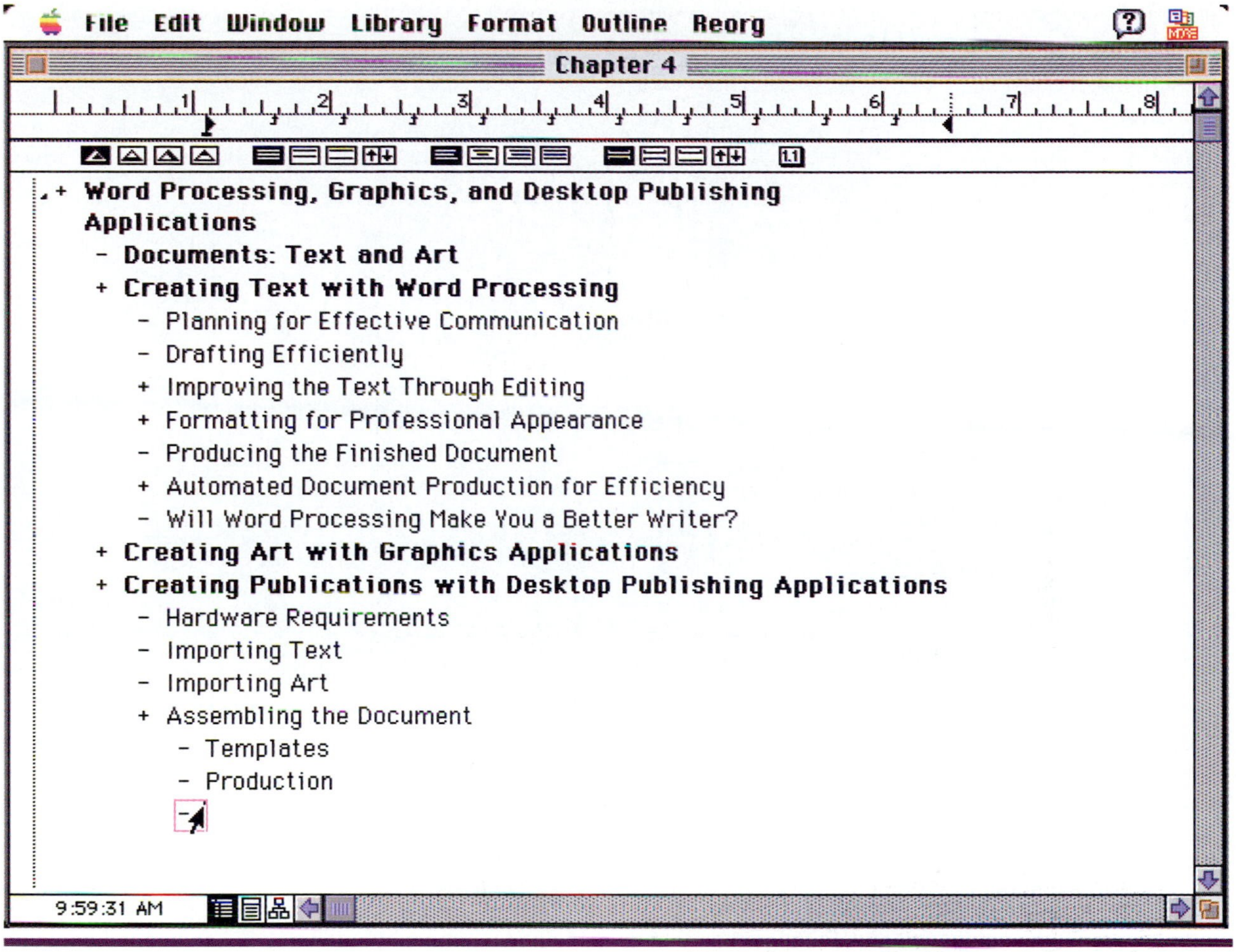

FIGURE 4-3

Planning a Message with an Outlining Program

For complicated documents such as term papers and reports, the outlining capability of many word processing packages is helpful (see Figure 4-3). In outline mode, you can type a series of brief entries, in a hierarchical format, as topics and subtopics. Then you can move topics around (each time automatically carrying all the subtopics along) until you have each point in correct sequence. If necessary, you can even promote a subtopic so it becomes a main topic, or vice versa. When the outline is complete, you can either print it and use the hard copy as a guide in your writing, or you can simply move the outline onto the standard word processing screen and begin filling in text, using the topics as headings.

Drafting Your Ideas

The writer's goal in the drafting stage is to get a version of the text recorded quickly. Although some people prefer to fix errors and polish phrasings as they go along, most experienced writers prefer to draft quickly without

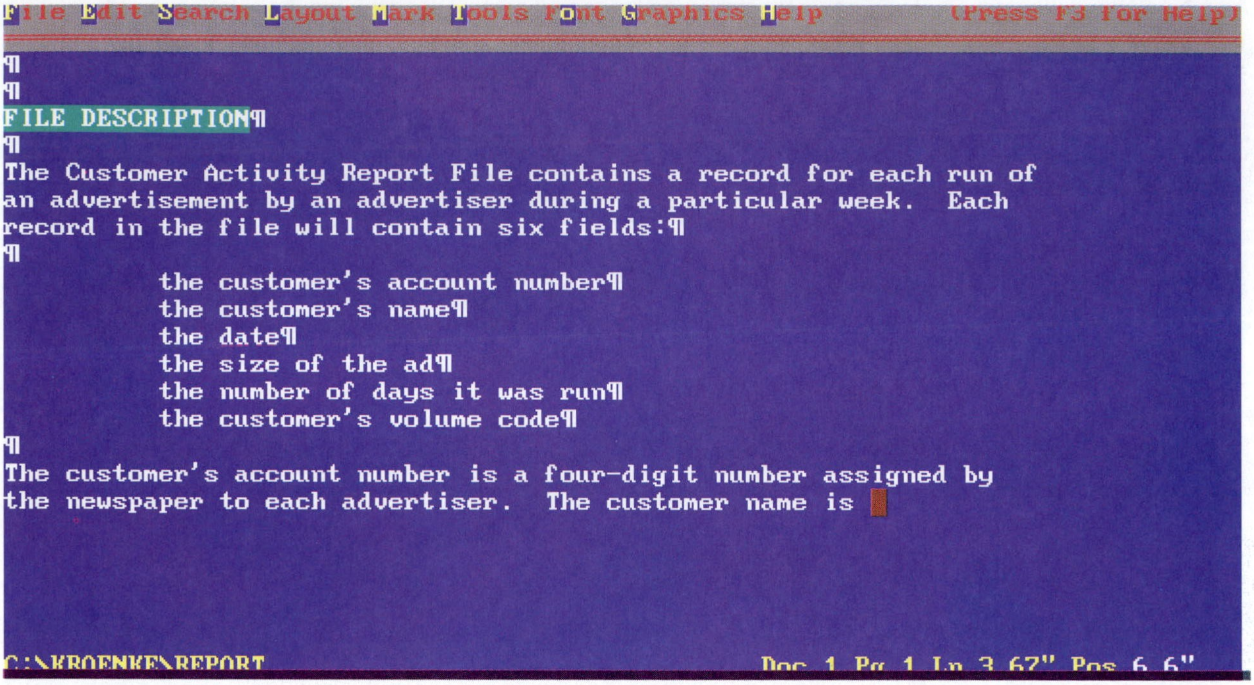

FIGURE 4-4

Entering Text in a Word Processing Application With word wrap, you can type to the end of a paragraph before you have to press Return. (The small ¶ symbols at the ends of lines on the screen shows where the user pressed Return.) The program divides text into lines automatically.

stopping. By working rapidly, they benefit from the same pace of thinking that they use in speaking, which they do comfortably and skillfully.

As you enter your draft, the **word wrap** feature of your word processor automatically breaks each line between words near the right edge of the screen so you need to press Return only at the end of each paragraph (see Figure 4-4). If you later insert or delete text or change the page margins, every affected line is automatically adjusted.

Being able to draft documents at the keyboard rather than with pencil and paper is a very useful skill. Most business messages must be produced quickly under pressure, and keyboard drafting is much faster than paper-and-pencil drafting. If you practice by drafting school papers at the keyboard, you will soon be working confidently in this mode.

Editing Your Text

Editing is making changes to correct errors and improve the text of the document. It is a normal and necessary part of the writing process, not an extra step that is useful only to poor writers. One mark of a good writer, in fact, is that he or she edits carefully. You should expect to spend some time editing in the normal course of nearly all writing.

Editing functions work somewhat differently, depending on whether the word processor's display is character-based or uses a GUI such as Windows, Macintosh, or OS/2. Where these differences arise, the following sections identify them.

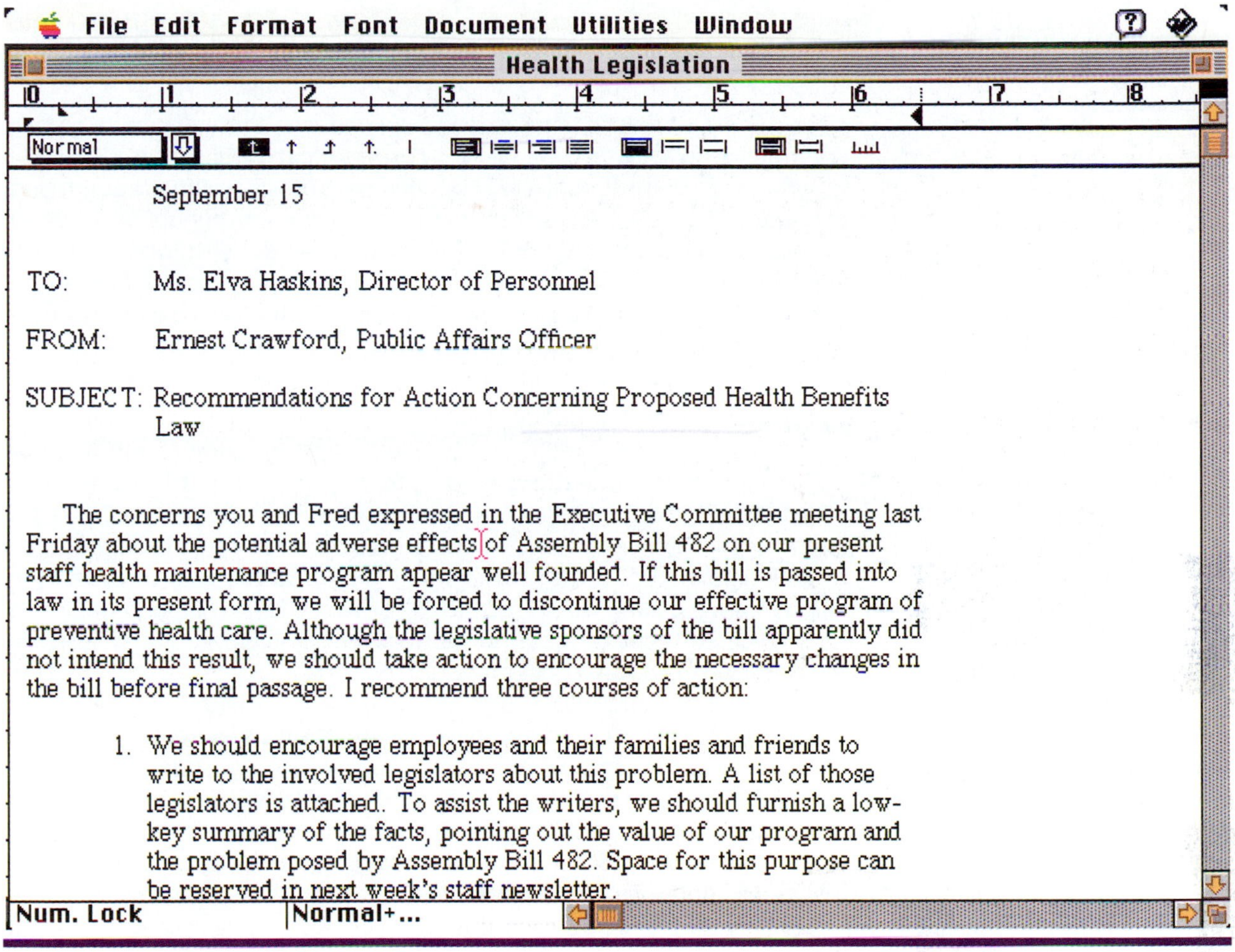
File Edit Format Font Document Utilities Window
Health Legislation
Normal
September 15
TO: Ms. Elva Haskins, Director of Personnel
FROM: Ernest Crawford, Public Affairs Officer
SUBJECT: Recommendations for Action Concerning Proposed Health Benefits Law
The concerns you and Fred expressed in the Executive Committee meeting last Friday about the potential adverse effects of Assembly Bill 482 on our present staff health maintenance program appear well founded. If this bill is passed into law in its present form, we will be forced to discontinue our effective program of preventive health care. Although the legislative sponsors of the bill apparently did not intend this result, we should take action to encourage the necessary changes in the bill before final passage. I recommend three courses of action:
1. We should encourage employees and their families and friends to write to the involved legislators about this problem. A list of those legislators is attached. To assist the writers, we should furnish a low-key summary of the facts, pointing out the value of our program and the problem posed by Assembly Bill 482. Space for this purpose can be reserved in next week's staff newsletter.
Num. Lock
Normal+...

FIGURE 4-5

Editing in a GUI Environment

A GUI system uses the I-beam as a pointer in text. To edit, locate the I-beam between two characters on the screen.

Simple Editing In a character-based word processor such as most DOS word processing packages, you make small changes by locating the cursor on a character. Then you type the text to be inserted to the left of that character (in insert mode) or type a new character to replace it (in overstrike mode). In many systems, you press the *Ins* key to change from insert to overstrike mode, then press the Ins key again to change back. (By pressing the Ins key repeatedly, you **toggle** between insert and overstrike modes.) Insert mode is the **default** mode, meaning that it is in effect when the program starts and remains in effect until you change it.

Under a GUI, you manipulate the mouse to locate the **I-beam** between two characters and then type to insert new characters there. (The I-beam, illustrated in Figure 4-5, is a pointer used to mark a text position in GUI systems.) To replace one or more characters, hold a mouse button down while you sweep the I-beam over the characters to be replaced (highlighting them), then type the replacement text. In a GUI system, the image shown on the screen is often an exact duplicate of the printout that will result. This feature, illustrated in Figure 4-6, is called **WYSIWYG** (pronounced *"whizzy-wig,"* meaning *"what you see is what you get"*).

Using the Electronic Thesaurus A *thesaurus* is a reference tool to help you find the exact word you need. To use an **electronic thesaurus** (which is part of many word processing systems), you must specify a word in your text and invoke the thesaurus. The thesaurus then displays a list of words similar to the word on the screen. For example, the writer of the text in Figure 4-7 could reconsider the word *review* by placing the cursor on that word and invoking the thesaurus. To substitute a suggested word from the thesaurus, the writer highlights it and presses Return.

Using Search and Replace To make a similar change in many places, most word processors provide a *search and replace* function to automate the task. For example, in drafting a report to your boss, you might refer to an associate as "Fred," since you and your boss know Fred personally. If you later discover that some text from your report will be incorporated into a formal report to the company's board of directors, you may want to change every instance of "Fred" to "Mr. Sarkesian," as Figure 4-8 shows. The search and replace function can make such a change nearly instantaneously, even in a large document.

The search and replace function must be used with care—it is often ruefully called the "search and destroy" function by experienced writers. For example, if you mistakenly use it to replace every instance of *cat* in the text with *rat*, the words *catch*, *delicate*, and *scathing* will be changed to *ratch*, *delirate*, and *srathing*. Unfortunately, search and replace cannot be used to undo the damage, since replacing every *rat* with *cat* will also change *separate*, *rather*, and *accurate* incorrectly.

Using Undo Many word processors provide an **undo** function, which restores your text to the way it was before your most recent action. For example, if you accidentally delete a line of text, pressing the *Undo* key may restore it. The most sophisticated word processors provide a *multilevel Undo* function that lets you restore earlier deletions in addition to the most recent one. Having the Undo function available in your word processor lets you work more confidently, knowing that if you make a mistake, you can set things right again.

Block Editing *Block editing* involves manipulating a marked block of text as a unit. A block can be as little as a few characters or as much as some pages of text. When the block has been marked, it can be deleted, copied (so it appears in more than one place), or moved (deleted from its old position and inserted elsewhere). In a character-based word processor, you mark blocks by locating the cursor at the beginning of the material you wish to block, entering a command to mark that point, moving to the end of the block, and entering another command. In a GUI-based word processor, you move the I-beam to the beginning of the block, press a mouse button, and hold it down while you sweep the I-beam to the end of the block.

FIGURE 4-6
WYSIWYG
As you can see, the Macintosh GUI screen display is showing exactly the same image of this newsletter as the printout has provided.

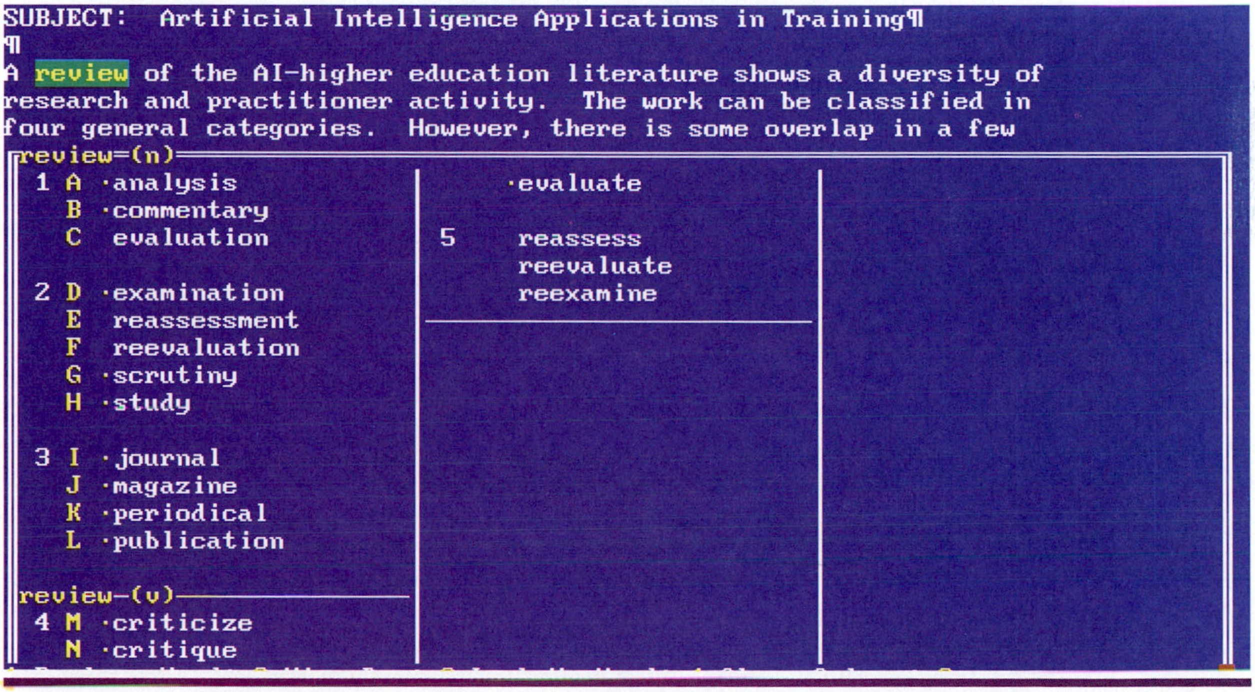

FIGURE 4-7 **Thesaurus**
To use the thesaurus, place the cursor on a word and give the command to look the word up. The thesaurus module displays other similar words. If you press Return, the highlighted word in the list is substituted for the word you looked up.

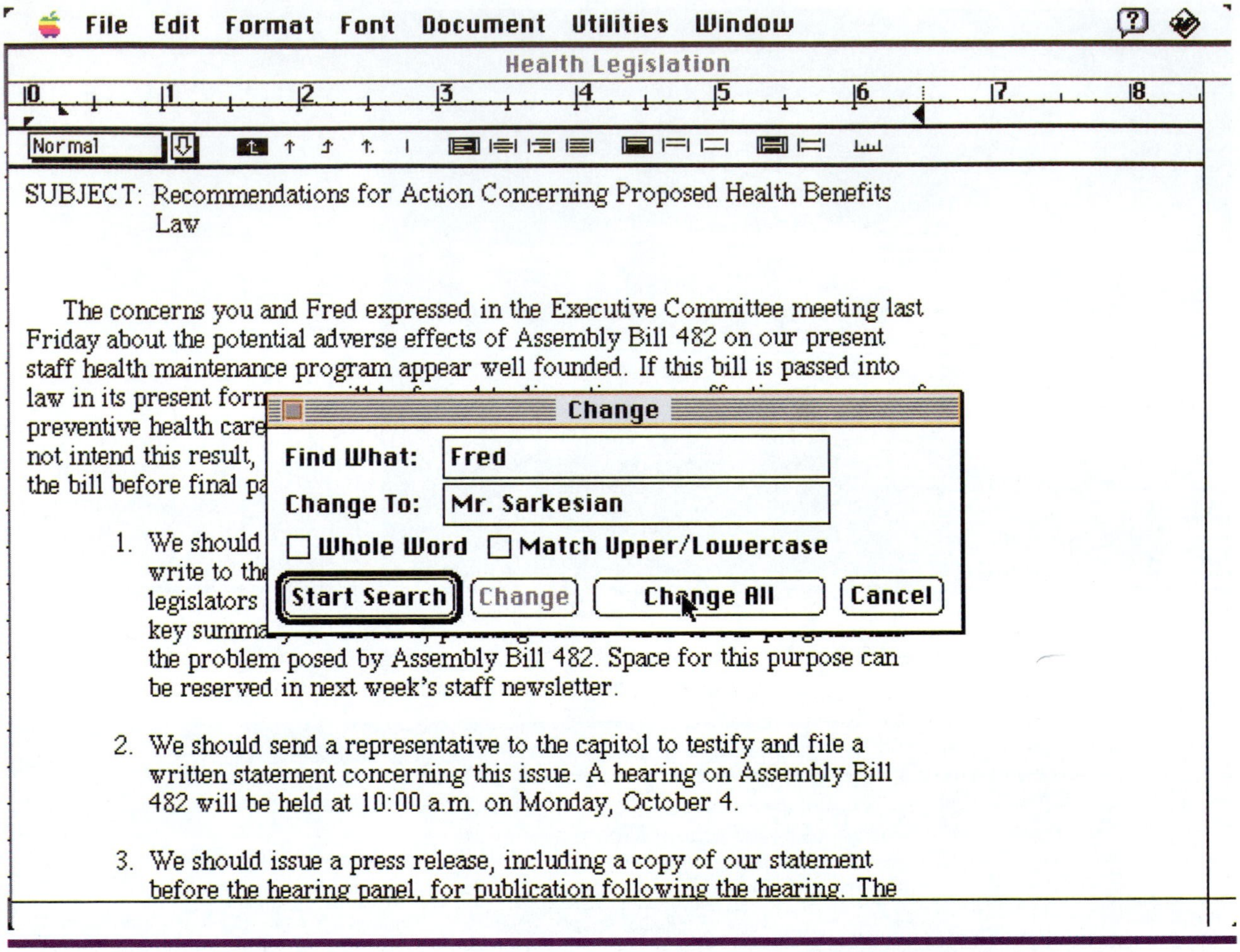

FIGURE 4-8

Search and Replace
When the user clicks on "Change All," the search and replace function will change every occurrence of "Fred" to "Mr. Sarkesian."

A block, once marked, is usually highlighted on the screen. Figure 4-9 shows block editing on a GUI-based word processor.

Once the block is marked, you may be able to designate a special format for that material, change all the letters to capitals, and make other changes. For example, many word processing systems use a **cut-and-paste** feature to manipulate marked blocks. The *Cut* command deletes the block from the display and records it in a *clipboard*. Then the *Paste* command is used to insert the material from the clipboard into a new text position.

Experienced writers first arrange major text elements—sections, paragraphs, and sentences—into final order before they spend much time polishing individual words and phrases. Graceful phrasings in one sentence often depend on the flow of ideas in the previous few sentences, so any time spent editing phrases may be wasted if sentences are subsequently reordered. When editing, work from the large to the small.

Using a Grammar and Style Checker Some word processors include modules to check for grammatical errors and poor writing style. Add-on

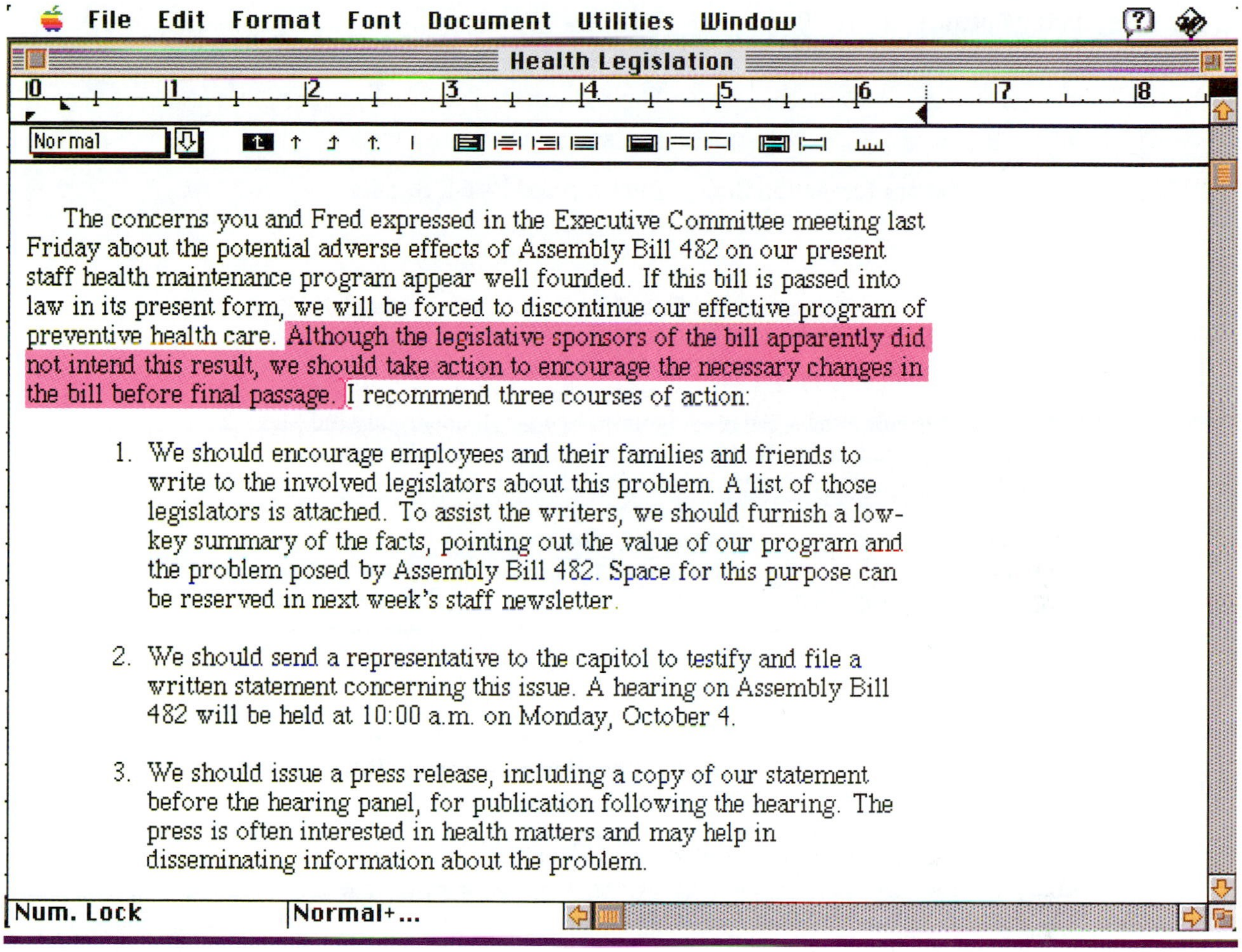
File Edit Format Font Document Utilities Window
Health Legislation
Normal
The concerns you and Fred expressed in the Executive Committee meeting last Friday about the potential adverse effects of Assembly Bill 482 on our present staff health maintenance program appear well founded. If this bill is passed into law in its present form, we will be forced to discontinue our effective program of preventive health care. Although the legislative sponsors of the bill apparently did not intend this result, we should take action to encourage the necessary changes in the bill before final passage. I recommend three courses of action:
1. We should encourage employees and their families and friends to write to the involved legislators about this problem. A list of those legislators is attached. To assist the writers, we should furnish a low-key summary of the facts, pointing out the value of our program and the problem posed by Assembly Bill 482. Space for this purpose can be reserved in next week's staff newsletter.
2. We should send a representative to the capitol to testify and file a written statement concerning this issue. A hearing on Assembly Bill 482 will be held at 10:00 a.m. on Monday, October 4.
3. We should issue a press release, including a copy of our statement before the hearing panel, for publication following the hearing. The press is often interested in health matters and may help in disseminating information about the problem.
Num. Lock
Normal+...

FIGURE 4-9

Block Editing
To mark a block in a GUI word processor, hold down the mouse button while you sweep the I-beam from beginning to end of the block.

grammar and style checkers are available from third-party vendors, too. These systems can be very useful, even though they are less capable than an expert human proofreader. They can identify some types of grammatical errors much of the time, such as subject-verb disagreement and run-on sentences. They can also point out phrases in your writing that are often misused, giving you a chance to reconsider. On the other hand, if your document passes a check with a grammar and style checker, that hardly guarantees that it is free of all types of grammatical errors.

Today, grammar and style checkers are rapidly improving. However, a completely reliable grammar and style checker will have to understand human language, and the problem of making a computer understand human language has proven very difficult to solve.

Using a Spelling Checker As a final editing step, most writers invoke their word processing system's **spelling checker**. This module goes through the text, word by word, looking up each word in a *dictionary* of correctly spelled words. If the word is not found in the dictionary (which

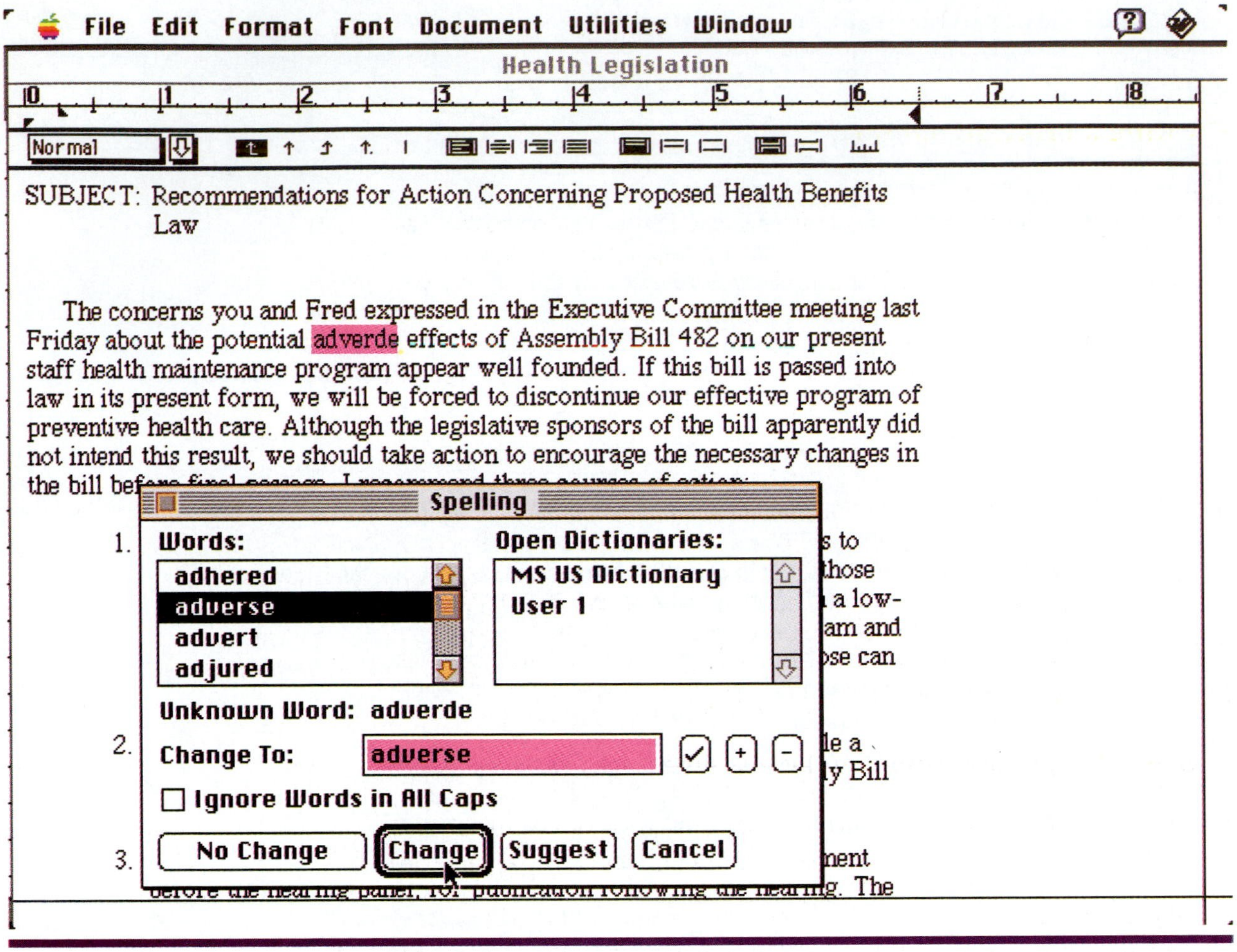
File Edit Format Font Document Utilities Window
Health Legislation
Normal
SUBJECT: Recommendations for Action Concerning Proposed Health Benefits Law
The concerns you and Fred expressed in the Executive Committee meeting last Friday about the potential adverde effects of Assembly Bill 482 on our present staff health maintenance program appear well founded. If this bill is passed into law in its present form, we will be forced to discontinue our effective program of preventive health care. Although the legislative sponsors of the bill apparently did not intend this result, we should take action to encourage the necessary changes in the bill bef
Spelling
Words:
adhered
adverse
advert
adjured
Open Dictionaries:
MS US Dictionary
User 1
Unknown Word: adverde
Change To:
adverse
Ignore Words in All Caps
No Change
Change
Suggest
Cancel

FIGURE 4-10

Using a Spelling Checker
The spelling checker suggests possible correct spellings for a word not found in its dictionary.

may include upwards of 100,000 words), then the module informs you that the word may be misspelled. Many spelling checkers can suggest correctly spelled words, offering to substitute one of those into your text, as Figure 4-10 shows.

Although spelling checkers are helpful in correcting many spelling errors, they do not guarantee that every word in your document will be correctly spelled. If you accidentally type the word *war* as *raw*, the spelling checker will accept it as correct, even though any human reader of English would recognize it as an error. The spelling check verifies only that the word appears in the dictionary. The human recognizes what the word is supposed to mean and sees the error.

In addition, the spelling checker will incorrectly identify as misspelled names of people and technical terms not found in the spelling checker dictionary. Most checkers let you add such words to a supplementary personal dictionary.

Because of these problems, it is still necessary for you to proofread your document after using the spelling checker.

Creating a Professional Image

The **format** of a document specifies its appearance on the printed page and the screen. Format includes margin size, line spacing, type size and style, paragraph indention, headers and footers, and special styles such as underlining and boldface type. The more expensive and sophisticated word processing systems are especially rich in formatting options.

In most documents, certain format characteristics are specified as **default** settings—standard for the entire document. For example, margins may be set at 1 inch on each side, top and bottom; the first line of each paragraph may be set for automatic indention of ½ inch; and the font may be set as 12-point Times Roman. Then, for exceptional situations, such as quoted material that must be double-indented, additional specifications can be added that affect only that material. (We will discuss these formatting characteristics later in this section.)

Although most writers partially format documents in the drafting stage, the fine-tuning should be done only after the editing is completed. The editing process can then concentrate on perfecting words and phrasings without the distraction of constantly adjusting the format.

Alignment and Justification In placing lines on a page, you should normally align at the left margin, making it straight. Occasionally, as for headings and titles, you may want to *center* lines of text. For special purposes, you may even want to right-align text, so the right margin is straight and the left margin is ragged.

If you want both margins to be aligned, as in the text of this book, then the program must **justify** each line by adding space to equalize line lengths (see Figure 4-11). Depending on the capabilities of the printer, the system may be able to add tiny spaces between each letter to equalize, or it may have to add larger increments only between words. If the printer and the program can handle it, adding tiny spaces between letters looks much better.

Typography Basics The creation and use of type is an art form. Although all of us read type every day, most of us are unaware of the large number of variations in type. However, with today's laser printer technology and word processing capabilities, even the most routine interoffice memo is expected to look like a professionally typeset document. People's expectations have become very high. As a result, you need at least the rudiments of typography to do your job successfully.

Typefaces The term **typeface** refers to the general style and appearance of type. Examples of several different typefaces are shown in Figure 4-12. The two general categories of typefaces are sans serif and serif. (*Sans* is the French word for without, and serifs are the cross-strokes that appear on many letters in serif typefaces.) **Sans serif** typefaces do not have complex

The company will provide free blood pressure tests for all employees who wish to participate during work hours on September 13 and 14 in the outdoor lunch area behind the Administration Building.

a. Left-aligned

Hypertension, or high blood pressure, is a serious condition that increases the risk of heart disease and other illnesses, but it's readily controlled under the care of your own physician. The test is quick and entirely painless.

b. Right-aligned

Supervisors and department heads will be scheduling release time for employees who wish to participate.

c. Centered

This screening is voluntary, and you're under no obligation to be tested. Results will be communicated to you immediately. No record of your test will be kept by the company.

d. Justified

FIGURE 4-11
Alignment and Justification Options

This is an example of Times

This is an example of Helvetica

This is an example of Palatino

`This is an example of Courier`

FIGURE 4-12
Examples of Typefaces

curves, flourishes, and cross-strokes, and they provide a cleaner, more contemporary appearance. Common sans serif typefaces are Helvetica and Monaco. **Serif** typefaces have embellishments and cross-strokes, and they have a classical, traditional look. Common serif typefaces are Times and Garamond. In general, serif typefaces are considered easier to read, though the degree to which this is true depends on the particular typeface.

Type varies in size, and it is measured in **points**. One point equals $^1/_{72}$ of an inch, so 6-point type is $^1/_8$-inch high and very small; 72-point type is 1-inch high and quite large. Since letters and other characters vary in height, not all characters in 72-point type are 1-inch high, and you should take the size in points as a relative indicator. Most books, magazines, and newspapers are set in 9- or 10-point type. Newsletters are often set with 11-point type. Figure 4-13 shows examples of 48-point Times and Helvetica.

Type also varies in *style* and *weight*. Examples of style are Roman, italic, bold, and small capitals as shown in Figure 4-14. The weight of the type refers, in general, to the appearance of thickness—bold type is heavier. Ad-

E

Recently

48-point Times—a serif typeface

E

Recently

48-point Helvetica—a sans serif typeface

FIGURE 4-13
Examples of Serif and Sans Serif Typefaces

Palatino Roman
Palatino Bold
Palatino Italic
Palatino Bold Italic
PALATINO SMALL CAPITALS

FIGURE 4-14
Examples of Type Styles

ditionally, many typefaces are designed in several weight versions. For example, Helvetica is available in regular, medium, and heavy weights.

All of the size, style, and weight variations of a particular typeface make up a **type family**. Common type families are Helvetica, Times, Garamond, Avant Garde, and New Century Schoolbook. One member of a type family, such as 10-point Times Bold Italic, is called a **font**. For example, this paragraph is set in $9\frac{1}{2}$-point Stone Serif type. The header at the top of this page is set in $8\frac{1}{2}$-point Stone Sans type. The caption on Figure 4-14 is set in 9-point Stone Serif type. Each is a separate font.

Type Spacing The amount of vertical space between lines of type is called **leading** (pronounced "ledding," referring to the metal strips that typesetters used to insert between lines of metal type for spacing). Leading is controlled by specifying the height of the line that contains the letters. A common specification is to set the leading 2 points larger than the text character. Thus, a 10-point type would be set in a 12-point line, a specification sometimes called 10 on 12, or 10/12. This specification allows for 2 points of space between lines. Several examples of leading possibilities are shown in Figure 4-15.

The amount of horizontal space between letters is determined by the designer of the typeface. In **monospace fonts** such as *Courier* and others that mimic typewriting, each letter is the same width. In **proportional fonts**, some letters, such as *W*, are much wider than others, such as *i*. Representing proportional fonts accurately on the screen as you work requires

The amount of space between lines of type is referred to as *leading* (pronounced "led-ding"). It is controlled by specifying the width of the line that contains the letters. A 10-point type can be set in a 12-point line, a specification sometimes called 10 on 12, or 10/12. This specification allows for 2 points of space between lines. Several examples of leading possibilities are shown here. The DTP program can determine the

a. 10/12 leading

The amount of space between lines of type is referred to as *leading* (pronounced "led-ding"). It is controlled by specifying the width of the line that contains the letters. A 10-point type can be set in a 12-point line, a specification sometimes called 10 on 12, or 10/12. This specification allows for 2 points of space between lines. Several examples of leading possibilities are shown here. The DTP program can determine the amount of leading, a feature called *auto leading*, or the user can specify the leading to create publications with different visual appearances.

b. 10/9 leading

The amount of space between lines of type is referred to as *leading* (pronounced "led-ding"). It is controlled by specifying the width of the line that contains the letters. A 10-point type can be set in a 12-point line, a specification sometimes called 10 on 12, or 10/12. This specification allows for 2 points of

c. 10/18 leading

FIGURE 4-15 Leading Variations

a GUI-based word processor, and printing them accurately requires a sophisticated printer such as a laser printer.

Many business messages are formatted to look like typewritten documents, with monospace font, two spaces after the punctuation at the end of a sentence, and straight quotation marks (' and ") found on the typewriter keyboard. Today, users are increasingly formatting messages to look more like printed documents, with proportional fonts, single spacing after the punctuation at the end of a sentence, and "curly" quotation marks (‘ and ’ or “ and ”). In printed text, straight quotes are used only to signify feet and inches and minutes and seconds. Figure 4-16 shows the differences.

The standard spacing between proportionally spaced letters can appear awkward with some combinations of letters, especially in the large type used for headings. For example, the combination of the letters *W* and *A*, when set in large type, can result in a space between the letters that appears too large, as Figure 4-17 illustrates. When this occurs, your word processor may allow **kerning**, which moves the left edge of the *A* nearer to the right edge of the *W*.

Figure 4-18 presents a number of recommendations for type usage published by the Aldus Corporation.

Headers and Footers Headers and footers consist of specified text automatically placed at the top or bottom of every page. For example, pages in this textbook have a running head indicating part and chapter titles and

```
     I'd like more information about the model
program for forms design that you mentioned in
your recent article entitled "Forms for the Fu-
ture," in Management and Administration Magazine.
Since I was recently given responsibility for
studying the more than 1,300 standard forms my
company uses, ranging from order forms and job ap-
plications to standard computer printout formats,
I'm very interested in your conclusions.  It's of
course very expensive to print and store this many
forms, and any justifiable reduction in this number
would be welcome.
```

I'd like more information about the model program for forms design that you mentioned in your recent article entitled "Forms for the Future," in *Management and Administration Magazine*. Since I was recently given responsibility for studying the more than 1,300 standard forms my company uses, ranging from order forms and job applications to standard computer printout formats, I'm very interested in your conclusions. It's of course very expensive to print and store this many forms, and any justifiable reduction in this number would be welcome.

FIGURE 4-16
Typewritten versus Printed Styles
Typewritten style uses monospace font, two spaces between sentences, and straight quotation marks. Printed style uses proportional font, one space between sentences, and "curly" quotation marks.

MILWAUKEE
MILWAUKEE

FIGURE 4-17
Kerning
The normal spacing between *W* and *A* seems too large because of the shapes of the letters. Kerning moves these two letters closer together for a more professional appearance.

page number. Some programs can put one header on even-numbered (left-hand) pages and another on odd-numbered (right-hand) pages, as in this book. Footers are often used to put page numbers at page bottom. Headers and footers are usually specified once, typically at the beginning of the document. Some programs, however, permit different headers and footers to be used in different parts of the document.

Columns In printing lists such as data records, you may need to format in rows and columns, as in a spreadsheet. This is called the **text table** format. In older word processing programs, it is called **tab columns** because the columns are created by using the tab key (see Figure 4-19). **Snake columns** are found in newspapers, newsletters, and magazines, where a

The following recommendations were published in Ronnie Shusshan and Don Wright, *Desktop Publishing by Design* (Redmond, WA: Microsoft Press, 1989):

- Match typeface to application. (For example, don't use thin and light typeface for a heavy equipment manufacturer.)
- Choose serif typefaces when presenting a lot of text, since these typefaces are generally easier to read.
- Do not use too many typefaces. In most publications, two will do.
- Use compatible and distinctly different typefaces together. (Helvetica and Times are a good combination.)
- Reserve italics, bold, other styles for titles, captions, and headings.
- Use small capitals for acronyms.

FIGURE 4-18
Recommendations for Type Usage

page may contain several columns of text. The text fills the first column to the bottom, then snakes up and fills the second, and so forth. To create snake columns, you simply specify how many columns you want and how much blank space to leave between them.

Style Sheets Many word processors let you save a formatting specification separately from any specific document, so it can be applied conveniently to a subsequent document. Such specifications are called **style sheets.** In addition to specifying such things as margins and tab settings, a style sheet may contain sets of special-purpose specifications for parts such as headings and quoted materials. For example, the heading specification may designate no paragraph indention, bold type font two points larger than standard text, and so forth. To apply such a special style, the user simply selects the affected text as a block and issues the appropriate style sheet command.

5

Printing Your Document

The final step in creating a document is printing it. Typical capabilities include (1) printing all of a document or only certain pages; (2) printing more than one copy; and (3) printing one document while continuing to edit another. In a document with automatic page numbering, some word processors let you print with a starting page number other than 1, as you may want to do if you print a document in sections.

The interface between program and printer is a program module called a **printer driver**. Each specific model of printer requires a different set of signals to make it print with certain spacings or in particular styles. The printer driver is matched to your particular printer, so it sends the signals that your printer needs. When you change printers, you must install a new printer driver from the set provided with your word processor or printer.

When you finish with a document (and periodically as you work on it), you should save a copy on disk. Later, you can retrieve it for reference

	Normal Operations	Failure Recovery
Procedures for Users	How to activate each function How to enter data How to interpret results Special responsibilities	How to correct certain types of errors What to do if the system becomes inoperable What to do when the system returns to normal Whom to contact in emergency (list of telephone numbers)
Procedures for Operators	Who is authorized to make entries What entries to expect How often to run jobs Where output goes How often to make backups Which tapes and disks are to be read What sort of paper should be in printer	How to detect when failure has occurred How to detect what type of failure has occurred How to restore the system quickly to its proper status for each type of failure

a. Text tables or tab columns print material consisting of rows and columns.

User Procedures for Normal Processing System users need to know how to employ the information system under normal conditions. They need to know how to activate each available function, how to enter data, and how to interpret the results. Users also need to know any special responsibilities they have; for example, bank tellers need to know whether they should correct an incorrect deposit slip or return it to the customer (see Figure 2-42).

User Procedures for Failure Recovery In addition to normal operating procedures, users need to know how to correct certain types of errors that may occur. They need to know what to do if the system becomes inoperable—whether there are manual procedures to follow, or whether they should hang a "Gone Fishing" sign on the office door until the system is up again. When the system is returned to normal, what does the user do—start from the beginning or resume where the work was interrupted? Procedures answer these and other questions that users may have regarding the system. Finally, when all else fails, the user needs to know who to contact. A list of emergency telephone numbers can prove very helpful to an anxious or frustrated user.

Operator Procedures for Normal Operations As you can see from Figure 2-43, under normal conditions operators need to know who is authorized to make entries, what entries to expect, how often to run jobs, where output goes, how often to make backups, and so forth. Operators also need to know the mechanics of running jobs, such as which tapes and disks are to be read and what sort of paper should be in each printer.

Operator Procedures for Failure Recovery Operators also need to know what to do in case of any system failure. They need to know how to restore the system quickly and correctly to its proper status when it crashes (stops in midstream), when communications failures occur (for instance, when a terminal is suddenly unable to send data over the communications network), when equipment fails (for example, when a disk drive or printer malfunctions), or when a database is rendered unusable and must be restored from backups. Other failures for which procedures are needed can occur—this is hardly an exhaustive list.

b. Snake columns print continuous text that extends past the end of a single column.

FIGURE 4-19 Columns

INCREASING YOUR PERSONAL PRODUCTIVITY

Buying Smart: A Clear Window on Word Processing

Because the best of today's Windows word processors can serve as a control center for all your work, making the right choice can be key. Ease of use plus editing and formatting tools should be your highest priorities, with customization and automation, graphics handling, and performance close behind.

Ease of Use Look for logical, well-conceived menus that group related commands and easy keyboard shortcuts. In a Windows word processor, effective use of the mouse is vital. Also, you'll learn a new program faster if it includes an interactive tutorial and provides help making the transition for your old word processor.

Editing These packages should offer the ease of Windows text-editing tools, including quick cut and paste, search-and-replace tools, fast text selection for block operations, and undo commands. The ability to move text with your mouse is a plus. Your program should be able to edit more than one document at a time, and should let you edit your report in magnified and reduced-size views that show the exact page layout. Other advanced editing tools fall into three categories:

Writing aids Context-based spelling checkers, grammar checkers, and a thesaurus.

Long-document options The capability to generate a table of contents and an index is a minimum requirement. You should look for automatic cross-referencing and a master document feature that allows you to assemble a document from smaller sections. Automatic footnotes and endnotes and equation editors are essential for academic and financial users.

Group editing tools Document comparison and revision-tracking tools monitor changes and help keep complex documents current. Document summary features maintain editing and revision records and allow quick file location using keywords to identify files.

Formatting You'll need a complete set of text, paragraph, and page-formatting tools to do the job today. Multiple columns with the capability to create columns with different widths are a must, and you'll need quick font selection and text formatting. Full support of scalable fonts, either printer-based or using font-scaling software such as Adobe Type Manager or FaceLift is a must. You'll also need the capability to import and ex-

or further work. Some word processors can import stored files containing the formatting commands of other word processors or other types of programs, making the necessary conversions automatically. If people who share work use different word processing systems, this capability is important.

Automating Document Production Using Mail Merge and Boilerplate

Many word processing programs automate the production of some documents. For example, mail merge systems efficiently produce personalized form letters. Even more sophisticated document production systems let a

Box 4.1

port files from other word processors while keeping basic formatting in place. For desktop published documents, you'll want kerning (letterspacing) and tracking (wordspacing) controls, plus the ability to link two or more frames with automatic text flow between them—especially handy for newsletter stories that continue on another page.

Performance Speed is always important, but all these programs work at a good pace as long as you have a 20-MHz 386 CPU or faster. If you want to start a print job and then get back to work on another document or application, look for a program such as AmiPro that has its own print utility.

Customization and Automation The capability to create macros by recording keystrokes is a must, but some users will also want to edit more advanced macros with a complete macro language. Corporate users will enjoy a program that can make automated templates, which create preformatted documents that prompt users.

If you ever send mass mailings with personalized letters, you'll want competent mail-merge tools.

Because Windows is a multitasking environment, you'll want links to other applications so you can work without constantly switching programs.

If you'd rather create worksheets with your word processor, all these programs include easy-to-use table editors.

Graphics Your program should be able to import all the popular graphics formats, and with built-in drawing and charting tools, you won't have to jump to another application to create or edit images and graphs.

Since all these programs offer framing tools for text and graphics, look for a program that lets you position, scale, and move frames without accessing a dialog box. If you need very precise layouts, you'll want to have snap-to grids on screen.

Service and Support Service policies vary greatly from product to product, but you should at least insist on unlimited free support. Toll-free telephone numbers and extended hours are a real plus. If you use on-line services, check for support forums. Finally, fax support can eliminate the possibility of busy signals and holding patterns.

user efficiently build complicated documents from boilerplate, which is explained below.

Mail Merge It is often useful to send the same message to a series of people. For example, an auto manufacturer may need to notify car owners that free modifications are available to correct a newly discovered problem. Or, a sales representative may want to send holiday greetings to a group of customers. Or, a direct mail advertiser may want to send news of a special offer to potential purchasers. In each case, the same text needs to be merged with a series of personalized headings, one for each recipient.

To create such letters, you first create the form text, marking the blanks where the individualized entries are to be inserted. Then you create a sep-

FIGURE 4-20
Word Processing Output
Most business documents are produced by word processing applications.

arate list of the individualized entries. This list often comes out of a database. When you print, the two lists are merged to produce the set of complete letters. Figure 4-21 shows the components of a mail-merged letter.

Producing Documents from Boilerplate At a major breakfast cereal company, one department handles complaints from customers. Although occasional complaints are unique and require a completely personal response, many complaints are frequently repeated. (For example, since breakfast cereal compacts in the box during shipping, many customers complain about partially filled boxes.) If each complaint were simple—on one point—then the company could develop a separate, complete message for each problem. But real complaints often involve several points, so the message system must be more flexible. Thus, the company has created and polished a series of **boilerplate** paragraphs, like those in Figure 4-22, that express precisely what the company wants to say in response to particular situations. A clerk reads a complaint letter; determines which issues are raised; considers the sequence of boilerplate paragraphs that would make an appropriate response (adding a custom-written paragraph or two if needed); and orders a letter with that sequence. The document production system creates the letter and prepares it for mailing. Similarly, in legal offices, many standard parts of legal documents such as contracts, wills, and trust documents are created from boilerplate paragraphs.

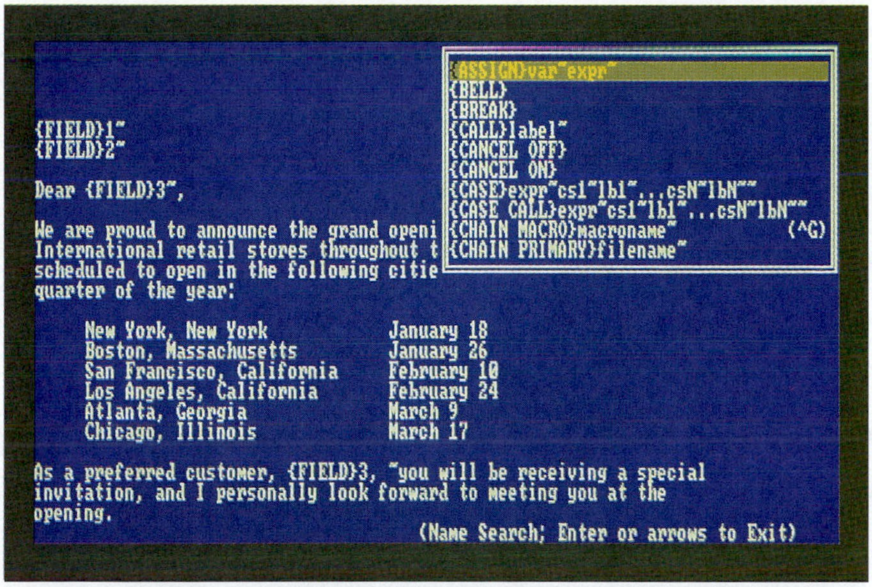

a.

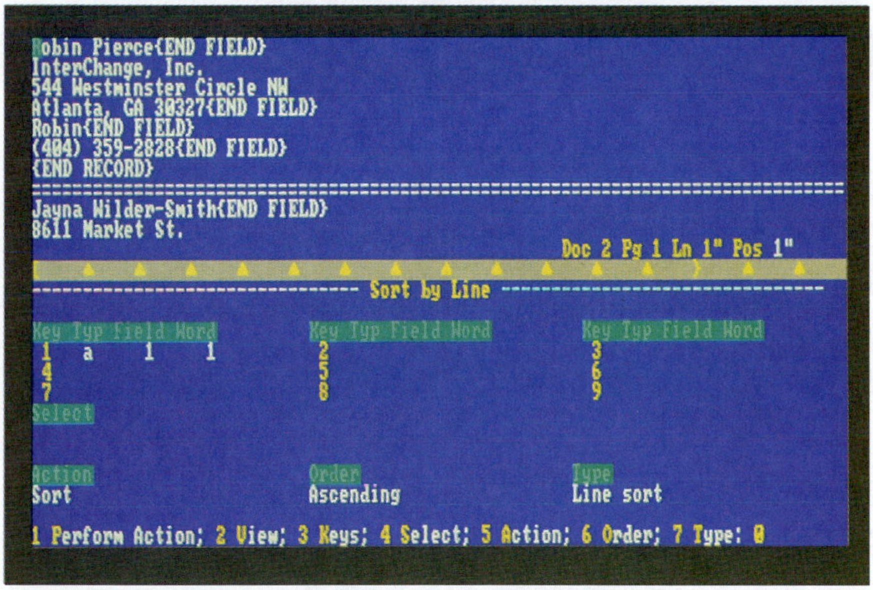

b.

FIGURE 4-21

Mail Merge

Mail merge combines a form letter with blanks to be filled in (*a*) and the data to be filled into the blanks (*b*) to make a complete letter.

Will Word Processing Make You a Better Writer?

Word processor advertising sometimes implies that a word processor can improve your writing. Of course, a word processor cannot make you a great writer, but it may be able to provide some help. For most people, better writing comes when they take time after drafting a message to think about it, improve phrasings, revise transitions—in other words, to edit thought-

Paragraph 128

The machine that fills boxes of cereal is designed to fill every box full to the top. An inspector checks each box before it is sealed to be sure it is completely filled. Then the box is weighed to make sure it contains the amount of cereal, by weight, that is indicated on the box. As the cereal travels from our factory to you, however, normal handling—bumping and jostling—may pack it down so the box has space at the top. This is normal and does not affect the amount of cereal in the box.

Paragraph 136

After cereal boxes have been filled, and again when they are put into large cartons for shipping to your store, the packaging is carefully inspected to be sure it is intact. Even small nicks in any package would cause the inspector to reject it, and you would never see it. When the carton reaches your store and an employee there opens it with a knife to put the packages on the shelf, the package may be accidentally damaged. If you find another damaged package on the supermarket shelf, please bring it to the attention of your supermarket manager.

Paragraph 214

We appreciate your letter. Your comments are carefully considered by Consolidated Cereals management. Your suggestions are helpful in making our products better meet your needs. We hope you will write again in the future.

FIGURE 4-22
Boilerplate Paragraphs
To produce a letter, a clerk selects a series of paragraphs by number, adding the recipient's address and any custom-written material.

FIGURE 4-23
Producing Legal Documents
Boilerplate is used routinely in producing standard legal documents.

fully. Back when editing meant rekeying the entire document, people were reluctant to revise. With word processing, editing is so easy that you may find yourself actually doing it more. The result may well be better documents.

CREATING ART WITH GRAPHICS

Graphics applications are used to create art—pictures, drawings, charts, and the like. Art emphasizes and illustrates the ideas in your document.

There are two kinds of art: line art and continuous-tone art. **Line art** consists of simple lines, usually of a single color on a background: divider lines between columns, line drawings, bar and pie charts, and so forth. Line art is often created by using a *computerized drawing program* that provides tools for this purpose, or by a spreadsheet program. DTP systems also provide simple tools for creating line art. **Continuous-tone art** is made up of pixels (dots) in many shades of gray. Continuous-tone art is often created by using a *computerized paint program*, which lets you manipulate the individual pixels that make up the image. Photographs and other continuous-tone art are often entered into the computer via a digital scanner and processed by a paint program.

A whole series of types of programs has been created to help you create graphics images, each specializing in a particular type of graphic output. This section considers four types of graphics programs: presentation graphics applications, paint applications, draw applications, and computer-aided design applications.

Presentation Graphics Applications

Presentation graphics applications—such as Harvard Graphics, PowerPoint, and Persuasion—specialize in producing the kinds of graphic images that are displayed during oral presentations: charts, graphs, and lists of topics or key points. Figure 4-24 shows examples of charts produced by a presentation graphics program. These programs were created partly to overcome the graphics limitations of traditional character-based electronic spreadsheets, but they have since developed into an application on their own. They provide more flexibility in creating charts and graphs than do traditional spreadsheet programs, and they let you combine elements very flexibly and add notes and comments where you want them. Electronic spreadsheet programs have improved their graphing capabilities recently, especially those that run under a GUI, and this competition has spurred creators of presentation graphics programs to provide even more flexible capabilities in their applications.

Presentation graphics applications also provide templates for **word charts**, the slides of key points that presenters often project on a screen

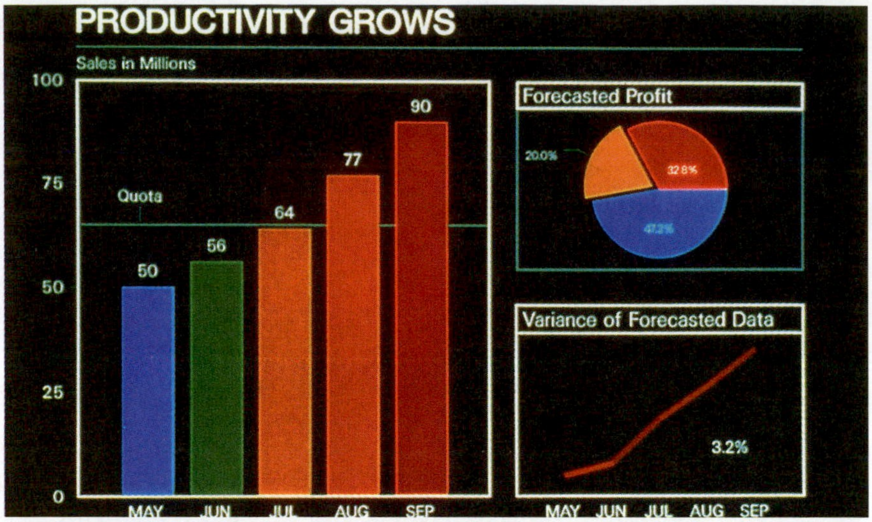

FIGURE 4-24

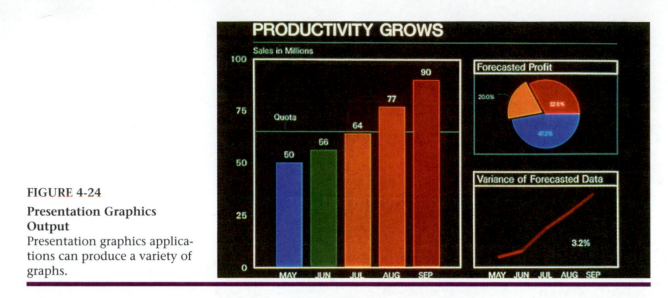

Presentation Graphics Output

Presentation graphics applications can produce a variety of graphs.

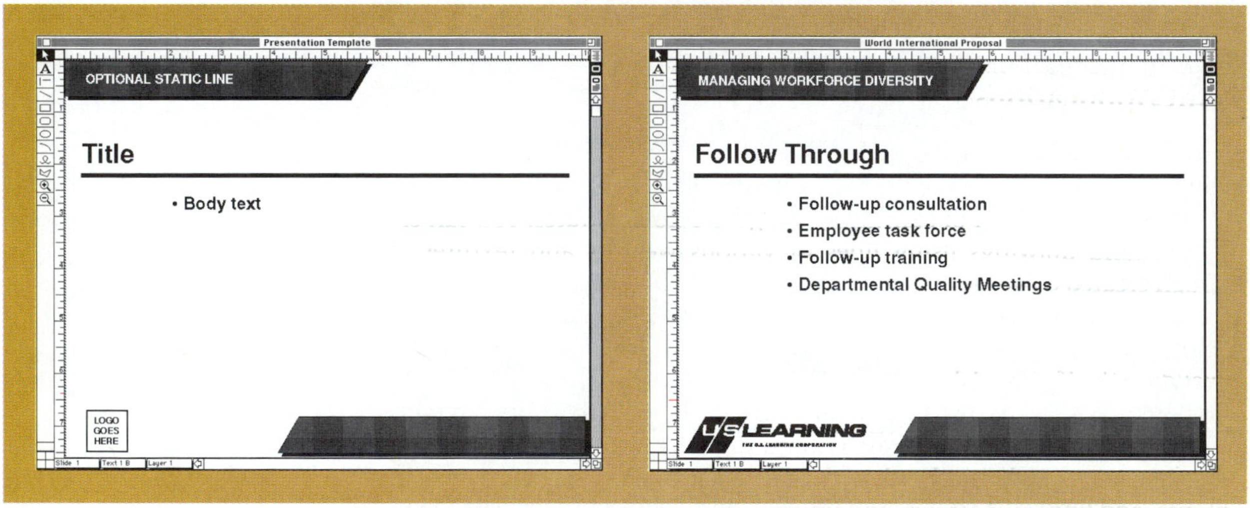

FIGURE 4-25 **Word Charts**

These word charts show how the use of graphic elements can provide a consistent image throughout a series of slides.

while they talk. An advantage of using a presentation graphics program to create such slides is that visual elements such as company logos and symbols can be consistently applied, giving a visual unity to the presentation, as Figure 4-25 shows. The more sophisticated GUI word processing programs and spreadsheets provide capabilities that are comparable to those of presentation graphics applications.

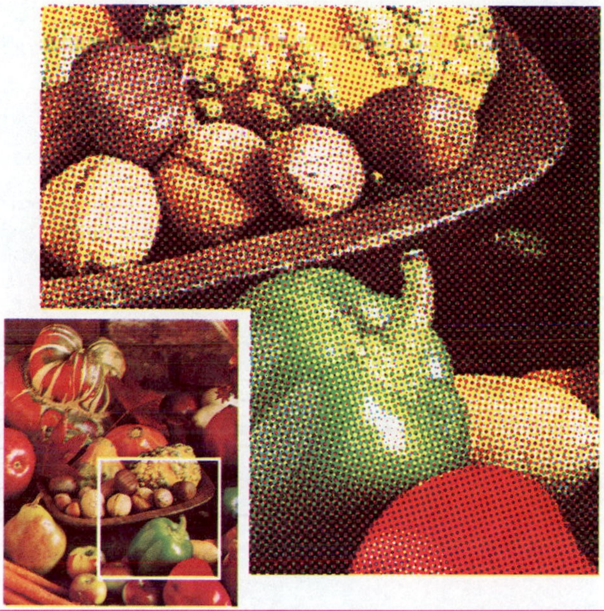

FIGURE 4-26
Continuous-Tone Art
Four-color process magnified dot pattern.

Paint Applications

Paint applications—such as Superpaint and MacPaint—specialize in manipulating the individual pixels in a graphic piece to produce continuous-tone art with the flavor of paintings, as Figure 4-26 illustrates. You can create freehand drawings using lines of various weights and textures, as though created by various kinds of pens, brushes, and even airbrushes. You can fill specified areas with patterns and textures, and you can create new patterns. You can **zoom** to magnify sections of a piece to manipulate each pixel directly, if you wish.

Because of their ability to manipulate pixels directly, paint programs are also used to modify images that are digitally scanned, such as photographs. You can change borders, deemphasize or eliminate unwanted elements, add lines and arrows, and improve the usefulness of the image for your purposes. You can also add lettering in various styles, sizes, and weights.

In paint applications, the unit to be manipulated is the pixel, whereas in draw applications (described next), the unit to be manipulated is the *object*, consisting of a line, a geometric shape, or a series of letters.

Draw Applications

Draw applications—such as CorelDraw, DrawPerfect, and MacDraw—specialize in producing line art, especially line drawings consisting of geometric shapes. Figure 4-28 shows examples. Each element in a drawing is a separate object that can be enlarged, reduced, reshaped, and manipulated in a variety of ways. When elements overlap, you can specify which

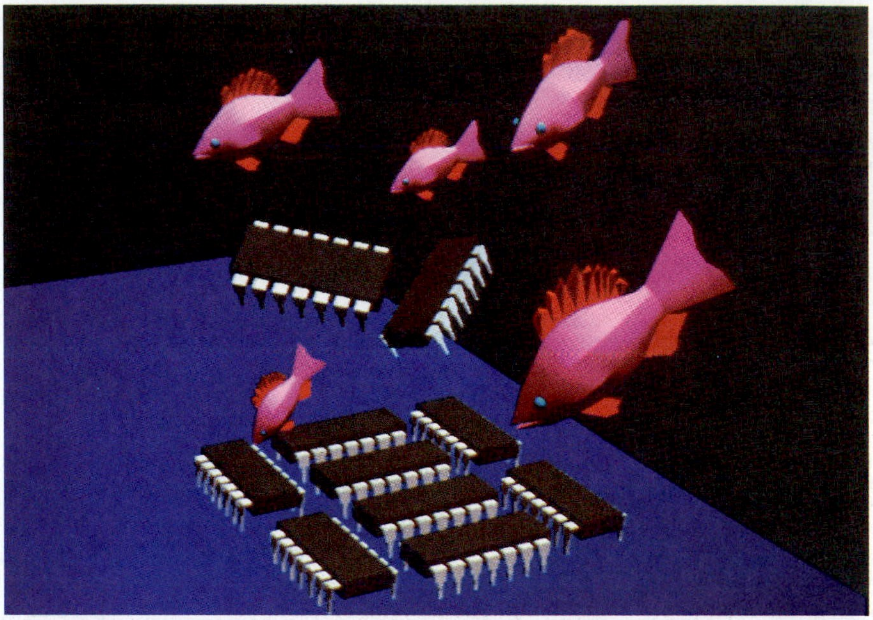

FIGURE 4-27
Fish and Chips
This art is produced by a paint program.

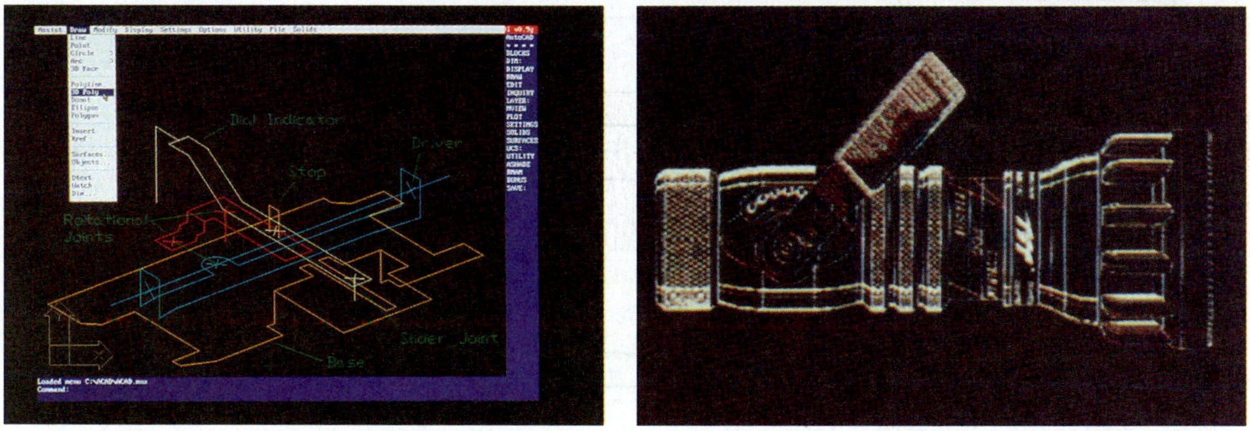

a. Line art can consist of fairly simple geometrical shapes, as in this schematic drawing of an industrial process.

b. Line art can also consist of very complex drawings constructed from many basic shapes, as in this conceptual design for a camera lens.

FIGURE 4-28 Line Art

element is on top and which is below, and you can also specify whether the top element is opaque or transparent (that is, whether you wish to let the lower element show through). You can group elements and manipulate them as single objects. You can include lettering in various styles, sizes, and weights. Draw programs are useful for diagrams, company logos, symbols, and many other kinds of line drawings.

Box 4.2

INCREASING YOUR PERSONAL PRODUCTIVITY

How to Improve Computer Communication

Scenario #1: "Oh no, I'm not busy, not at all," she said lightly, motioning me into her office.

Scenario #2: " Oh no, I'm not busy, not at all," she said sarcastically. I could almost see the obstacles hanging from her words as she slammed her office door in my face.

Tone of voice and body language can be as important as the words we use. Computer-to-computer communication, however, is limited to what we can keyboard. This limitation can cause misunderstandings, sometimes serious ones.

Over the last few years an interesting solution has evolved among users of electronic mail and bulletin board systems. They employ a series of symbols to supplement the written word. These symbols are sometimes called "Smileys," since they are based on the ubiquitous smiling face drawing, placed sideways. Here are some examples:

Symbol	Meaning
:) or :-)	smile; happy
:(or :-(	frown; sad
;) or ;-)	wink; shyness; sarcasm
;-0	surprise; shock; boredom
:*	kiss

Smileys also can be supplemented by abbreviations. Some of these also express emotions, while others are merely a form of shorthand.

Abbreviation	Meaning
AFK	away from the keyboard
BAK	back at keyboard
B4	before
CUL8R	see you later
<g>	grin
ILU	I love you
NBD	no big deal
ROFL	rolling on the floor laughing
IMHO	in my humble opinion

These are only a sampling, and more turn up all the time. Watch for them, adopt them, and invent your own. Using them will improve your computer communication, and mark you as a full-fledged E-mail or BBS aficionado.

CAD Applications

Computer-aided design (CAD) applications—such as AutoCAD—are highly advanced and specialized draw programs used in creating engineering drawings (see Figure 4-29). Today's CAD systems not only aid in creating drawings, but they also help engineers analyze the resulting designs, as Figure 4-30 shows. CAD applications are often combined with **computer-aided manufacturing (CAM)** applications, making combined *CAD/CAM* applications. In such an application, drawings for a machine part are converted directly into instructions to machine tools to create the part under computer control. The output from CAD applications is often generated on a plotter.

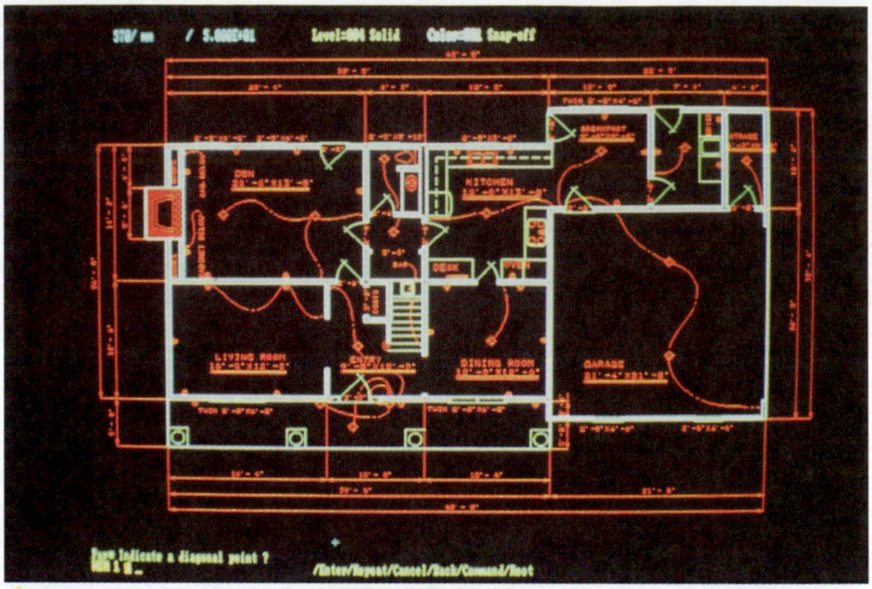

FIGURE 4-29
Computer-Assisted Design
This floor plan for a building has been designed through the use of a CAD system.

FIGURE 4-30 **Analyzing a Design**
This CAD system is being used to analyze the design of a tunnel.

COMBINING TEXT AND ART WITH DTP

Desktop publishing (DTP) programs—such as PageMaker and Ventura Publisher—provide tools to do the sophisticated formatting that graphic designers have done manually in the past. DTP programs let a user combine text and art into a finished publication-quality document, as you can see in Figure 4-31. DTP software lets professional designers produce publications at a fraction of the cost and time of manual production methods. Today, documents such as brochures, newsletters, fliers, annual reports, company newspapers, magazines, and even books are commonly produced by DTP. It also lets amateurs produce simple publications that would have required professional designers in the past.

As the formatting capabilities of today's word processing systems improve, they increasingly provide features previously available only in DTP. In fact, today's most sophisticated word processors include nearly all the formatting capabilities of some of the simpler DTP systems. For many users, a good word processor may provide all the DTP power they need. A DTP program is challenging and time-consuming to learn. For simple applications, the learning investment may not be worthwhile.

Hardware Requirements

DTP places strong demands on computer hardware. To work effectively, you will need a GUI running either on a Mac II or on at least an 80386-

FIGURE 4-31
Using DTP
With DTP, business professionals can prepare high-quality publications on their own.

FIGURE 4-32

Text and Art
DTP combines text and art.

based PC with a minimum 8MB of memory. A laser printer is required for output. As new versions of DTP applications are developed, they are likely to require even more powerful and expensive hardware.

Importing Text

The text for DTP applications is usually prepared with a word processor to take advantage of the word processor's editing capability. Then it is imported to the DTP document, along with whatever formatting may have been done, such as underlining. Imported text is entered into predefined columns and aligned and justified according to the user's instructions. Columns can be defined very flexibly—aligned vertically; slanted on one or both sides; or even shaped irregularly (for example to fit around a drawing or picture, as in Figure 4-33). To make text fit, the leading or white space can be adjusted.

For ease of reading, designers avoid allowing the first line of a paragraph to fall as the last line in a column (an **orphan**) or the last line of a paragraph to fall as the first line of a column (a **widow**). DTP software automatically detects and resolves such problems by shifting lines and adjusting leading.

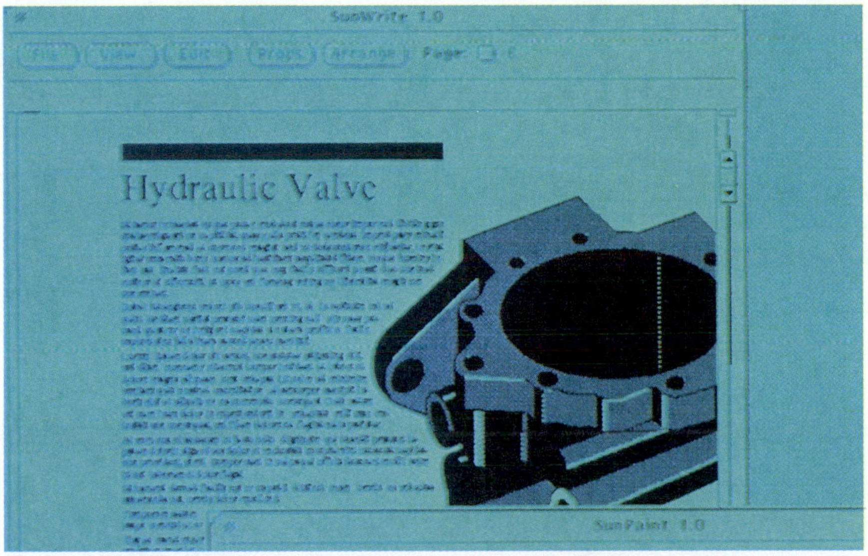

FIGURE 4-33
Column Shapes
DTP programs can automatically fit text around irregularly shaped art.

Importing Art

In graphic design for publication, art is everything other than text: lines, textures, drawings, company logos, and photographs. Although a DTP system usually provides simple drawing capability, most art is imported after being developed and processed by more specialized programs.

Many vendors offer collections of **clip art**—general-purpose graphics often reflecting common business themes, seasonal and holiday themes, and so forth. A wide variety of clip art is available inexpensively, which is very helpful to users who must produce monthly newsletters and other publications that can be enhanced by such graphics (see Figure 4-34).

When a graphic has been imported into a DTP system, it can be *sized* to fit into its appointed place by shrinking or expanding, or it can be **cropped** to fit by cutting off the edges. If necessary, it can be *rotated* to a particular angle and placed into position. If two graphic elements overlap, one can be designated to hide parts of the other, or the two may be combined, as though one partially shows through the other.

Assembling the Document

When the text and art elements are all at hand, the user lays out the document a page at a time. Although the DTP system provides powerful tools, page layout requires knowledge of graphics principles, skill, and keen artistic sense. A criticism of DTP is that it puts powerful design tools into the hands of users who lack the background to employ them effectively. The result is often unattractive publications. Some simple principles, such as those in Figure 4-35, can be helpful in getting started. Although amateurs

FIGURE 4-34 **Clip Art**

sometimes create good designs, graphic designers are still needed when the results must look professional.

Templates As you can tell from this discussion, a good design involves the complex interplay of many different factors. Unless you have a natural bent for design or plenty of time to experiment, you might want to use a **design template**. Such a template is sample design that has been created for a particular use such as a newsletter or a report. Generally, a template specifies typefaces and type sizes and styles to be used for various elements of the design such as title, headings, and text body. The template also shows where to place art and graphics for a balanced look.

To communicate a consistent image, an organization may adopt a set of templates using the same basic elements and graphic devices, as you can see in Figure 4-36. Templates are available from several sources. All DTP program vendors provide or sell templates for common kinds of publications. In addition, many books provide sample designs.

- Layout should match the purpose of the publication.
- For multicolumn layout, select type and column width to allow about 40 characters per column.
- Use plenty of white space—too much is better than too little.
- Balance the design for facing pages in a two-page layout.
- Use contrast of white space and graphics to achieve balance.
- When locating graphics, the edges of the graphics should line up with each other or with something else, such as a heading.
- Outline graphics with thin, not thick, lines.
- Justify text for formal, traditional look. Use left-aligned text for informal or contemporary look.
- Eliminate widows and orphans.

FIGURE 4-35
Recommendations for Page Layout

Production When the layout is complete, it may be printed on a laser printer and then duplicated on a copier. The 300-dot-per-inch resolution of the typical desktop laser printer gives sufficient resolution for many purposes, such as local church newsletters, interoffice mailings, and the like. When top quality is needed, the completed layout may be transmitted electronically to a **typesetting machine**, a printer that produces output at 1000 dots per inch or higher, equivalent to the best magazines and books. If multicolor output is needed, the DTP system can produce a **color separation**, a copy for each color to serve as the master for printing that color onto the page. Figure 4-37 illustrates this process.

Summary

Documents consist of text and art. Text is created with a word processing application. Art is created with a graphics application. Publications containing both text and art are formatted with a DTP application.

The steps used in creating a document with word processing are as follows: planning, drafting, editing, formatting, and production. Planning notes can be created in word processing or in an outlining system. Drafting should be done quickly at the keyboard. Editing includes the use of electronic thesaurus, search and replace function, undo function, block editing commands, grammar and style checker, and spelling checker. Formatting includes alignment and justification, type font selection, headers and footers, columns, and use of style sheets. Production involves printing and saving. Word processing programs facilitate the automatic production of documents through mail merge and use of boilerplate paragraphs.

Graphics applications include presentation graphics, paint graphics, draw graphics, and CAD graphics.

DTP applications combine text and art into pages of a publication. Purchased design templates assist beginners in developing attractive page layouts.

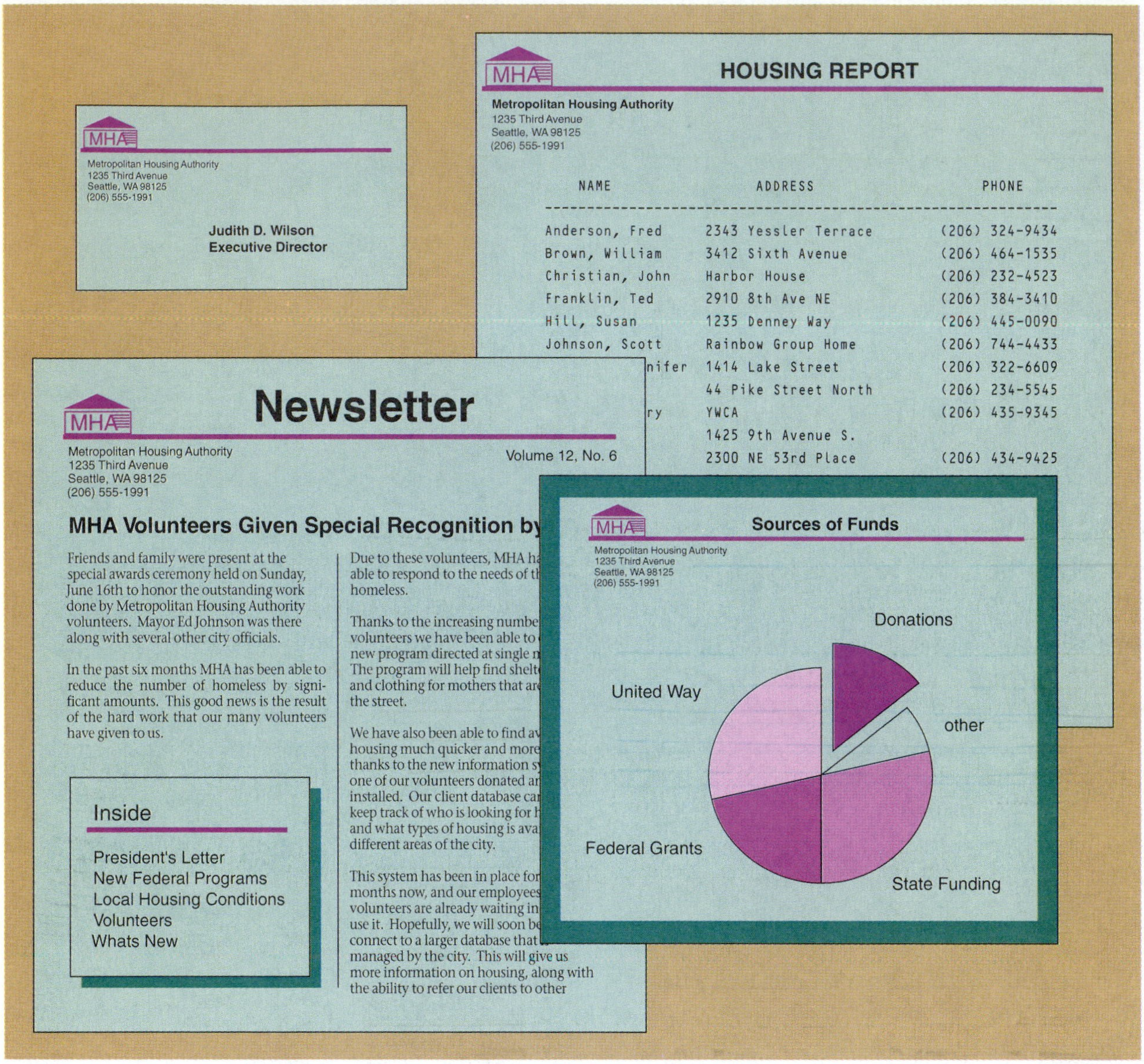

FIGURE 4-36 Consistent Design Used for Several Types of Documents

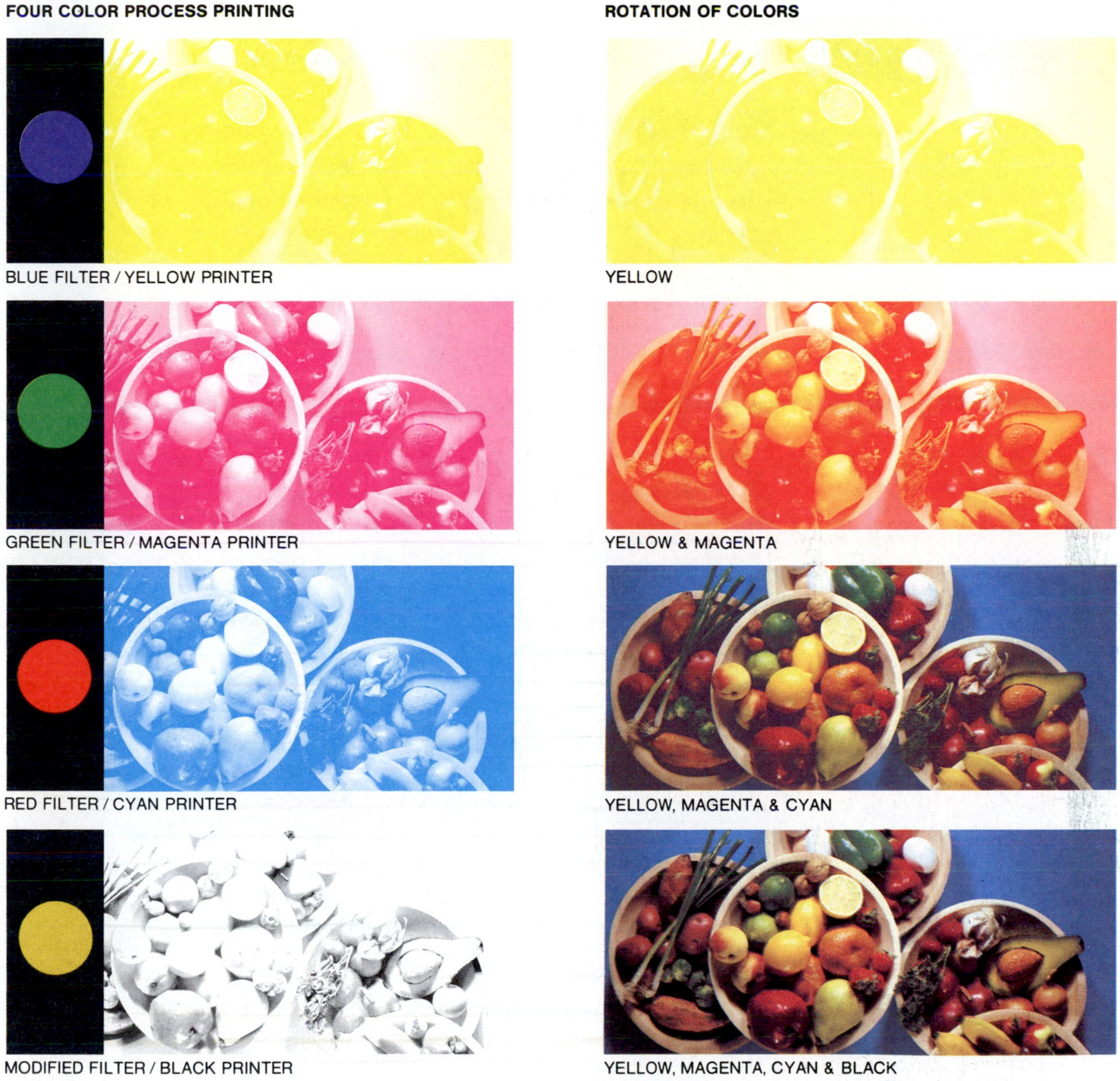

FIGURE 4-37 **Color Separation**
To print four-color art, a separate master copy is needed for the image of each color. This set of masters is called a color separation.

Key Terms

text
art
word wrap
toggle
default
I-beam
WYSIWYG
electronic thesaurus
undo
cut and paste
spelling checker
format
default
justify
typeface
sans serif
serif
point
type family
font
leading
monospace font
proportional font
kerning
text table
tab column
snake column
style sheet
printer driver
boilerplate
line art
continuous-tone art
presentation graphics
word chart
paint
zoom
draw
computer-aided design (CAD)
computer-aided manufacturing (CAM)
desktop publishing (DTP)
orphan
widow
clip art
crop
design template
typesetting machine
color separation

Review Questions

1. What are the two major elements that comprise documents?
2. Name the application used to create text.
3. Name the application used to create art.
4. Describe the manual labor required to create documents before computerized word processing systems became available.
5. Give three advantages of word processing over manual methods of producing documents.
6. List the five steps often followed by experienced writers in producing a document.
7. Describe the capabilities of the outlining module included in some word processors.
8. Why is it useful to draft text quickly?
9. For making small changes in text, differentiate between the method used in character-based word processors and the method used in GUI word processors.

10. Describe the use of an electronic thesaurus.
11. What does a search and replace function do?
12. For marking a block of text, differentiate between the method used in character-based word processors and the method used in GUI word processors.
13. Describe the steps in the cut-and-paste process.
14. Why does the use of a grammar and style checker not guarantee good grammar and style in a document?
15. Why does the use of a spelling checker not guarantee correct spelling of words in a document?
16. List at least six elements of a document's format.
17. Name three common alignments for the text in documents.
18. Differentiate between sans serif typefaces and serif typefaces.
19. What size type is usually used for text in books, magazines, and newspapers?
20. Name four styles of type and three weights of type.
21. Differentiate between a type family and a font; name at least three examples of each.
22. How are monospace fonts different from proportional fonts?
23. Describe the formatting differences between typewritten documents and printed documents.
24. Give at least two examples of pairs of consecutive letters whose appearance could be improved by kerning.
25. Differentiate between text tables (sometimes called tab columns) and snake columns.
26. List at least six elements that may be specified in a style sheet.
27. Identify at least four capabilities of word processing programs related to printing documents.
28. Describe the uses of the mail merge function and boilerplate paragraphs.
29. Differentiate between line art and continuous-tone art.
30. Describe the uses of presentation graphics applications, paint applications, and draw applications.
31. What is CAD/CAM used for?
32. Describe the major purposes of DTP programs.
33. List the minimum hardware requirements of a DTP system.
34. In defining columns to be filled by a DTP program with imported text, what variations in column format can be defined?
35. Differentiate between sizing, cropping, and rotating art that has been imported into a DTP program.
36. Describe the use of a design template in DTP.
37. Explain the differences in production equipment and operations between producing a simple, single-color newsletter for departmental use and producing a high-quality, four-color brochure to be distributed to major stockholders.

Discussion Questions

A. Is it true that business managers and executives no longer need staffs of clerical support employees because computerized word processing systems let them create their own documents? Defend your answer.

B. If the goal of drafting text is to get a first draft created as quickly as possible, describe the most suitable drafting method you can think of. Consider paper-and-pencil drafting versus working at a computer keyboard; working from outline or notes versus working from a mental plan; and other factors. The plan you devise should actually be practical for your own use. Do you intend to try this method?

C. Summarize the major differences between character-based word processing programs and GUI-based word processing programs. Which type do you think you would prefer? Why?

D. If computers can someday understand and transcribe human speech correctly, what differences do you think this will make in the functioning of word processing systems? An obvious difference, for example, is that a user can orally dictate the text of a message instead of having to enter it through a keyboard. Can you think of other likely differences? Do you think oral input will make word processing more efficient? Do you think it will improve the quality of word processing output? Defend your conclusions.

MINICASE

Scanning the Past

You need only glance through the advertisements in any computer magazine to understand how much electronic clip art is available to the desktop publisher. The amount and variety can satisfy many needs, but there may come a time when you want something different. In that case, you might want to collect your own clip art. If you have access to a scanner or are able to rent time on one in your neighborhood copy shop, you can find a virtually unlimited supply of clip art in older printed work.

Before the photograph came to dominate our visual life, drawn line reigned supreme. Each advance in printing, from carved woodblocks to steel engravings to lithographs, enabled images of progressively greater detail and subtlety to reach ever-greater audiences. The advent of photography halted this development, and now most of the best line drawing that ever graced a page are found in older books, magazines, newspapers, maps, and a host of other sources. The potential supply is so vast that we will concentrate here on just black and white line art. . . .

Before we begin looking, we should cover some of the legal and ethical ground rules governing the use of printed imagery. Unless you created the image you want to scan, or hired someone else to do it, the art will have been created by another person, and may be subject to copyright law.

Besides protecting written work, copyright law also protects pictorial and graphic work, whether created by an individual who owns it, or created for hire and owned by whoever paid for it. Copyright also protects anonymous work, which is the status of much illustration and decoration in printed works. Copyright law permits the reuse of portions of copyrighted material under certain circumstances—primarily when it is being used for nonprofit, educational purposes—but the simplest rule of thumb is that work older than 75 years can generally be reproduced without penalty. Be sure, how-

ever, that the image you intend to scan is not trademarked and is not being taken from a reprint. (In the latter case, copyright protects the reprint but not the original from which it is derived, if that's more than 75 years old.)

These are some of the legal conditions regarding printed imagery, but there are also ethical considerations. If a photograph is altered so that its content is changed, is it truthful? Joseph Stalin was a master at airbrushing figures out of history, but it's not a course most of us ought to follow. There is also such a thing as a visual joke, but if the intent of the alteration is subterfuge rather than humor, then an important ethic has been violated.

So where do you go to find all this stuff? A good place to start is an antiquarian or rare bookshop. If you ask the bookseller to show you something with old drawings, he will likely take down some lovely, leather-bound volume filled with exquisite engravings and elegant print, whose beauty and cost will take your breath away. . . .

Before shelling out a fortune for something like this, however, it would be prudent to browse around the shop first, paying special attention to the engravings and prints hanging matted and framed on the walls and grouped in folders. Many of these will have come from old books that long ago disintegrated or were broken apart and their illustrations saved. . . .

Another rich source is old maps. Empty seas gave artists room to create elaborate legends or send ornate carracks plowing through foamy seas accompanied by spouting sea serpents and saluted by mermaids. An imaginative cartographer might embellish his land masses with treasure cities, one-legged men, Amazons, unicorns rampant, and chimeras dire. As knowledge increased, maps became more accurate but hardly less beautiful. . . .

Questions

1. Explain why it is likely that some of the best illustrations will be found in sources published prior to the 20th century. Summarize the copyright rules that govern the uses of scanned images.
2. As the author of this article implies, with today's scanners, sophisticated image manipulation software, and DTP products, it is possible to eliminate portions of images and to add and combine images. Suppose that you have been given scanned images of candid photos of employees and families at your company's annual picnic and that you are using those images to publish a company newsletter. Describe an alternation or combination of photos that you think would be both ethical and appropriate. Describe an alternation or combination of photos that you think would be ethical but inappropriate. Describe an alternation or combination of photos that you think would be unethical. Justify your decisions.

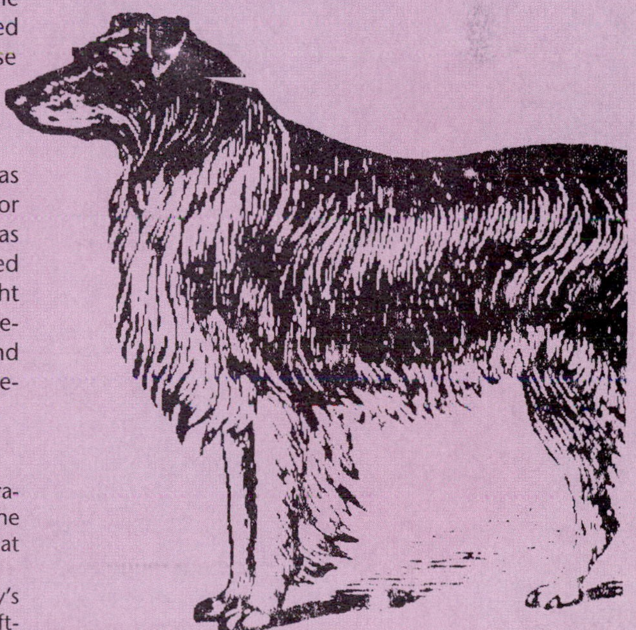

(Continued)

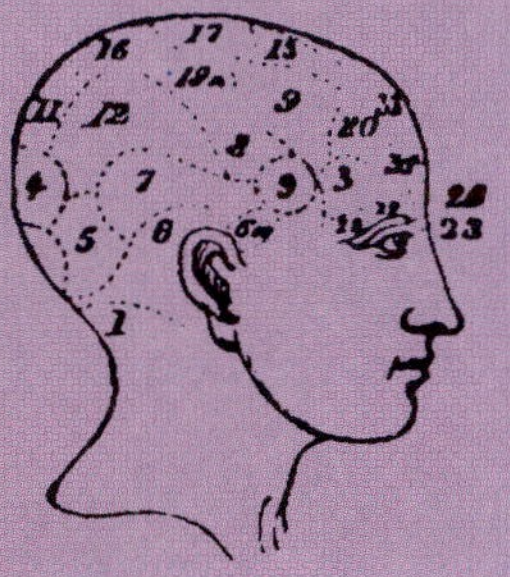

3. Suppose that you inherit your grandfather's modest collection of old books. All of the books have been well cared for and are in excellent condition. You learn that the market value of the collection is about $600. You also learn, however, that if you break the books up into separate pages and sell the pages separately, the illustrations in the books would be worth $1,500. Is it legal to tear up the books in this fashion? Is it ethical? Is it appropriate? What would you do with the books?

   Suppose the value of the collection is about $600, but the value of the pages, sold separately, would be $15,000. Would any of your answers change? If so, explain why.
4. Scanning and image manipulation technology is in its infancy. In the future, very-high-quality color images and alternations will be possible. What influence do you think such technology will have on the prices of museum-quality art? To the prices of lesser-known art? To business prospects for artists? To business prospects for art distributors?

Where the Art Came From

All engravings reproduced in this story were scanned on a Hewlett Packard ScanJet as TIFF files. We cleaned up spots and smudges in Aldus Digital Darkroom, and then imported them into PageMaker. Here are the sources, prices, and file sizes of the incidental engravings.

Snail (41K), head (67K), leaf (56K), snowshoe (8K), and dog (139K): from *Webster's High School Dictionary* (New York: G. & C. Merriam Co., 1892). We paid $1.75 for the book at a library sale; it contains some 800 illustrations.

C H A P T E R 5

Spreadsheet Applications

Tom had worked out all the details. He knew just how much money the new building to house his software consulting company was going to cost, and the spreadsheet told the story. He knew the cost of the land and how much it would take to develop it: road, sewer, water, gas line, and so forth. He had a beautiful design, and his consultant had developed the materials list—including prices, sales tax, delivery charges, and discounts—right down to the last nail. Tom was on a tight budget, so he scheduled work according to his finances. He arranged for a loan and immediately began repaying it through monthly payments. He anticipated a nice project bonus from a client this year that would serve as a cushion if unanticipated expenses arose. If everything went according to plan, he would be able to meet his payments to the bank, the general contractor, the subcontractors, and the lumber supply store.

Things did not go as Tom had planned, however. After the site had been prepared and the foundation excavated, the general contractor got tied up on another job, and the schedule had to be pushed back by three months. When this happened, Tom discovered that the prices of some of the materials were going up. Since he had no place to store the materials, he was afraid he would have to buy them three months later at the higher prices. What effect would this have on his overall budget? Would it be cheaper, he wondered, to rent storage space at $1,000 per month and buy materials at the lower price? Tom would have to recalculate the prices and total everything up again. That would take hours. Or would it?

Tom was using an electronic spreadsheet program. He changed some figures on the computer screen and instantly saw the new totals. In Figure 5-1 you can see the part of Tom's spreadsheet that summarizes some of his material costs, both before and after the price change. (His entire spreadsheet is actually much larger.) Aha! It would actually be cheaper to buy now and pay $3,000 for storage.

CHAPTER OUTLINE

	A	B	C	D	E
1	MATERIALS				
2	LUMBER				
3		Board feet	Type	Cost/Ft.	Total
4		6,000	2 x 4	1.25	7,500.00
5		4,000	2 x 6	2.30	9,200.00
6		15,000	3/4" ext plywood	0.70	10,500.00
7	INSULATION				
8		Unit	Type	Cost/Unit	Total
9		180	Roll 16" R23 Kraft	12.00	2,160.00
10		50	Roll 16" R16	8.50	425.00
11		200	Lb. loose fiberglass	0.28	56.00
12	FASTENERS				
13		Unit	Type	Cost/Unit	Total
14		100	#10d common	3.40	340.00
15		20	#8d finish	4.20	84.00
16		50	#6d roofing	6.15	307.50
17		50	Box #8 wood	3.00	150.00
18		20	Box #4 wood	2.75	55.00
19		540	Joist hanger	0.18	97.20
20					
21	TOTAL				30,874.70
22					
23					
24					

a. Tom's figures before price changes.

FIGURE 5-1 **Part of Tom's Spreadsheet**
This is a section of the spreadsheet Tom created to plan the cost of his new building.

Tom decided he would need to take out a short-term loan to cover the new expense. He would pay off the loan when he got his bonus. How much would that loan cost in interest? He needed to add that to the cost of storage. Would it still be cheaper? Again, Tom entered new figures into the electronic spreadsheet and immediately saw the answers. Although he was not happy about this change in events, he was happy that he could get right to the problem and not waste time refiguring everything with a calculator.

Price Changes

	A	B	C	D	E
1	MATERIALS				
2	LUMBER				
3		Board feet	Type	Cost/Ft.	Total
4		6,000	2 x 4	1.65	9,900.00
5		4,000	2 x 6	2.45	9,800.00
6		15,000	3/4" ext plywood	0.95	14,250.00
7	INSULATION				
8		Unit	Type	Cost/Unit	Total
9		180	Roll 16" R23 Kraft	12.00	2,160.00
10		50	Roll 16" R16	8.50	425.00
11		200	Lb. loose fiberglass	0.28	56.00
12	FASTENERS				
13		Unit	Type	Cost/Unit	Total
14		100	#10d common	3.57	357.00
15		20	#8d finish	4.41	88.20
16		50	#6d roofing	6.45	322.50
17		50	Box #8 wood	3.00	150.00
18		20	Box #4 wood	2.75	55.00
19		540	Joist hanger	0.18	97.20
20					
21	TOTAL				37,660.90
22			Price		
23			Changes		
24					

b. Tom's figures after price changes.

THE ELECTRONIC SPREADSHEET: A MULTIPURPOSE TOOL

As we have seen, the major functions of a computer in a business information system are calculation, data storage and retrieval, and communication. Electronic spreadsheet programs specialize in the calculation function. In addition, they help communicate results, and they provide elementary support for simple data storage and retrieval.

Elliot Bay Electronics
First Quarter Summary

		JAN	FEB	MAR	1st QTR TOTAL	
1	SALES					
2						
3	St. Louis	18000	7605	12953	38558	
4	Portland	21600	14900	6500	43000	
5	Appleton	11750	8800	17040	37590	
6						
7	TOTAL SALES	51350	31305	36493	119148	
8						
9	EXPENSES					
10						
11	Advertising	5000	2000	2000	9000	
12	Salaries	11200	11200	11200	33600	
13	Bonuses	650	1000	1300	2950	
14	Travel & Entertain.	8400	8000	8600	25000	
15						
16	TOTAL EXPENSES	25250	22200	23100	70550	
17						
18						
19	NET BEFORE TAXES	26100	9105	13393	48598	
20						

FIGURE 5-2 **Paper Spreadsheet**
Electronic spreadsheets are modeled on the paper spreadsheets that are traditional in accounting and financial analysis.

The first electronic spreadsheet program, VisiCalc, was sold in 1979. Since then, millions of electronic spreadsheet programs, such as Lotus 1-2-3, Excel, Quattro Pro, and VisiCalc, have been purchased for use on personal computers. Electronic spreadsheet programs are one of the most widely used personal computer applications. With prices ranging from under $100 to over $500, hundreds of millions of dollars have been spent on these programs. Why are electronic spreadsheets so popular?

An **electronic spreadsheet** program enables a user like Tom to manipulate numerical data quickly and easily in tabular format. The electronic spreadsheet is an automated version of the ledger paper used by accountants. Figure 5-2 shows an example of a manual, or paper, spreadsheet. The manual spreadsheet is simple in its concept and in its design. It consists of rows and columns in which data—usually numbers—is written and summarized. The electronic spreadsheet is equally simple, both in concept and design. It is far more powerful, however, than the paper version.

What Is a Spreadsheet?

The spreadsheet illustrated on ledger paper in Figure 5-2 is a typical one. Here, each **column** represents a time period: a month or the entire quarter. Each **row** in this case represents a source of sales income or an expense. Rows are totaled (under the heading 1st Qtr Total), and columns are totaled (beside the heading Net Before Taxes at the bottom of the page). Thus, many details about this company's financial status have been captured on a single page—for example, the income from each source for each month; the income from each source for the first quarter; the expenses for each month; the total income for the entire period; and the net income (income minus expenses) for each month and for the quarter. This kind of financial information is important to businesspeople in large and small companies alike.

An Electronic Spreadsheet Is Automated

Now examine the electronic spreadsheet in Figure 5-3. It uses the same format and presents the same data that appears in Figure 5-2. Parts of the spreadsheet have been labeled, though they would not appear that way on a computer screen. Notice that the electronic spreadsheet is also made up of rows and columns.

The intersection of a row and a column is called a **cell**. Each cell has an **address**. The address is defined by that cell's row and column, which are called its **coordinates**. Columns are identified with letters (*A* to *Z* for the first 26 columns, then *AA*, *AB*, and so forth), and the rows are numbered. Thus, A1 is the address of the cell in the first column, first row, and D16 is the address of the cell in the fourth column (D), 16th row.

Electronic spreadsheet programs offer some very interesting and powerful features. Among these features are the ability to represent calculations by formulas, automatic recalculation, large size, and graphics capabilities.

Formulas and Automatic Recalculation By far the most powerful aspect of electronic spreadsheet programs is that you can define **formulas** in the spreadsheet, making the computer automatically do specified calculations. To learn how this works, take a sheet of paper and manually follow this example.

By agreeing to buy the materials for his new building from one lumberyard, Tom has negotiated a 5 percent discount. He would like to add that discount to his spreadsheet, along with the 8 percent state sales tax.

	A	B	C	D	E
1		JAN	FEB	MAR	TOTAL
2	SALES				
3	St. Louis	18,000	7,605	12,953	38,558
4	Portland	21,600	14,900	6,500	43,000
5	Appleton	11,750	8,800	17,040	37,590
6					
7	TOTAL SALES	51,350	31,305	36,493	119,148
8					
9	EXPENSES				
10	Advertising	5,000	2,000	2,000	9,000
11	Salaries	11,200	11,200	11,200	33,600
12	Bonuses	650	1,000	1,300	2,950
13	T & E	8,400	8,000	8,600	25,000
14					
15	TOTAL EXPENSES	25,250	22,200	23,100	70,550

FIGURE 5-3 **Electronic Spreadsheet**
This is an electronic spreadsheet to meet the same needs as the paper spreadsheet in Figure 5-2.

FIGURE 5-4
The Spreadsheet as an Analytical Tool
The electronic spreadsheet is a fundamental analytical tool in business.

	A	B	C	D	E	F	G	H
1						Discounted	Sales	Item
2	MATERIALS	Units	Type	Cost/Unit	Discount	Price	Tax	Total
3	LUMBER (Board feet)							
4		6,000	2 x 4	1.65				
5		4,000	2 x 6	2.45				
6		15,000	3/4" ext plywood	0.95				
7	INSULATION							
8		180	Roll 16" R23 Kraft	12.00				
9		50	Roll 16" R16	8.50				
10		200	Lb. loose fiberglass	0.28				
11	FASTENERS							
12		100	#10d common	3.57				
13		20	#8d finish	4.41				
14		50	#6d roofing	6.45				
15		50	Box #8 wood	3.00				
16		20	Box #4 wood	2.75				
17		540	Joist hanger	0.18				
18								
19						TOTAL COST		

FIGURE 5-5 Spreadsheet Form
To increase the value of his spreadsheet, Tom has added columns to account for the 5 percent discount that he has negotiated and the 8 percent state sales tax.

He has added columns for these values, as shown in Figure 5-5. We have filled in some of the figures. Now you fill in the columns headed Discount (assume a 5 percent rate), Discounted Price, Sales Tax, and Item Total. When the lines for each item are complete, fill in the Total Cost.

Notice the process you follow. For each item, first multiply the cost per unit by the number of units ordered. This gives you the nondiscounted price (which is not written on the spreadsheet). Then multiply the nondiscounted price by .05 to get the discount. Subtracting the discount from the nondiscounted price gives the discounted price. Then multiply the discounted price by .08 to compute the sales tax. The item total is equal to the discounted price plus the sales tax. The total cost is equal to the sum of all the item totals.

With a calculator and some patience, this process can be done manually, as we just saw. But think how tedious it would be if there were, say, 50 items. And what happens if, just as you complete the work, the state suddenly raises the sales tax to 8.5 percent? Now you have to refigure everything.

Let's see how an electronic spreadsheet would help. First, we will look at the basic calculations you would do. Then we will see how easily you can make changes, when necessary, and get updated answers quickly.

Figure 5-6 shows the expanded spreadsheet. The cost per unit for board feet of 2 by 4 lumber is at D4, and the number of board feet ordered is at B4. Since the discount rate is 5 percent, the discount for 2 by 4 lumber (cell E4), is given by this formula:

```
E4 = (B4 * D4) * .05
```

(The asterisk [*] means multiplication.) The discounted price (F4) is computed this way:

```
F4 = (B4 * D4) - E4
```

That is, the discounted price equals the nondiscounted price minus the discount. Similarly, the sales tax is computed using this formula:

```
G4 = F4 * .08
```

That is, the sales tax equals the discounted price times 8 percent. Finally, the item total is computed:

```
H4 = F4 + G4
```

Using that row as an example, fill in the formulas for rows 5 through 17.

	A	B	C	D	E	F	G	H
1						Discounted	Sales	Item
2	MATERIALS	Units	Type	Cost/Unit	Discount	Price	Tax	Total
3	LUMBER (Board feet)							
4		6,000	2 x 4	1.65	=B4*D4*0.05	=B4*D4-E4	=F4*0.08	=F4+G4
5		4,000	2 x 6	2.45				
6		15,000	3/4" ext plywood	0.95				
7	INSULATION							
8		180	Roll 16" R23 Kraft	12.00				
9		50	Roll 16" R16	8.50				
10		200	Lb. loose fiberglass	0.28				
11	FASTENERS							
12		100	#10d common	3.57				
13		20	#8d finish	4.41				
14		50	#6d roofing	6.45				
15		50	Box #8 wood	3.00				
16		20	Box #4 wood	2.75				
17		540	Joist hanger	0.18				
18								
19						TOTAL COST		

FIGURE 5-6 **Tom's Spreadsheet**
When these formulas are added to Tom's spreadsheet, it will do its job.

Notice the pattern that developed. Each row of formulas used the same relative structure. For example, to compute the discount for any row, multiply the product of the two cells to the left by .05. Patterns like these occur so frequently in spreadsheets that electronic spreadsheet programs let you write formulas in one row, then copy the formulas to other rows. Thus, you could enter just the formulas for row 4, then quickly copy them into rows 6, 7, and so on. This feature is even more impressive when you are dealing with a larger number of rows. And the same technique can be used to copy columns of formulas. This feature makes developing the spreadsheet relatively easy.

Now consider the formula for computing the total cost in cell H19. The total cost is the sum of all the item totals. We can write the formula in two ways. We can name each addend, or we can describe a range—that is, a contiguous group of cells. In this case the range is from H4 through H17. Here are the alternatives:

```
H19 = H4 + H5 + H6 + H8 + H9 + H10 + H12 + H13 + H14
      + H15 + H16 + H17 or
H19 = SUM(H4:H17)
```

The first alternative uses a simple algebraic expression. However, if there were, say, 50 rows to be summed, the first alternative would not be feasible. Entering a formula with 50 addresses without error would be nearly impossible. The second alternative uses an electronic spreadsheet feature called a **function,** a built-in mathematical formula. The Excel symbol SUM indicates the sum function. Other spreadsheet programs might use different symbols, such as @SUM or %SUM.

At this point, you have seen an example of entering formulas into the spreadsheet. But the real power of an electronic spreadsheet becomes apparent when changes to values or to formulas need to be made. When values change—say the price of 2 by 4 lumber goes up to $1.75 per board foot—you need only type the new price over the old one. The spreadsheet program **automatically recalculates** every entry on the page affected by the change. Similarly, if a formula changes—say the sales tax is raised to 8.5 percent—then all you need to do is enter a new formula into cell G4 and copy it into cells G5 through G17. All the affected figures on the spreadsheet are automatically recalculated with the new data. Formulas and automatic recalculation are extremely powerful advantages of electronic spreadsheets.

Larger Size One difference between a paper spreadsheet and its electronic counterpart is size—that is, the number of columns and rows the spreadsheet can contain. Whereas a paper spreadsheet's size is limited by the dimensions of the paper, an electronic spreadsheet has much larger dimensions. For example, most electronic spreadsheets can contain thousands of rows. Of course, the entire spreadsheet cannot fit onto a computer screen at once, so at any given time you see only a piece of the entire form. This piece is called a **window** (see Figure 5-7), and you can position it on the form anywhere you want.

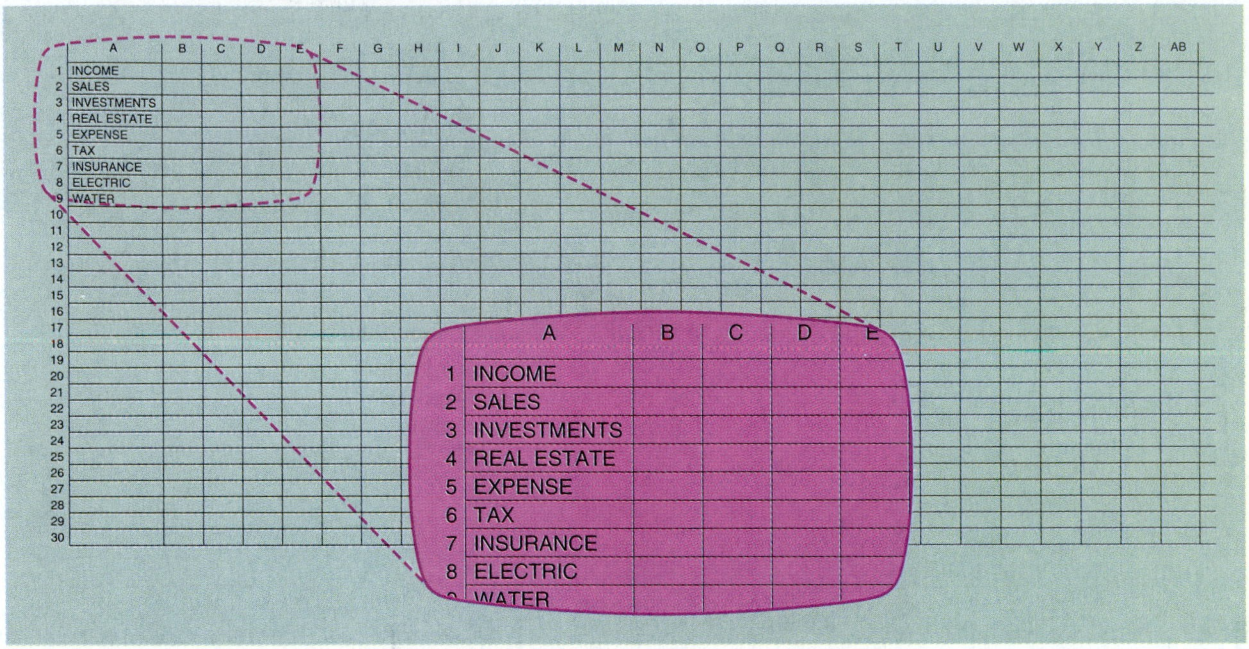

FIGURE 5-7 **Screen Window**
The display is a window into a much larger spreadsheet.

When working with a large spreadsheet, it might be helpful to view two parts of the spreadsheet at the same time. For example, you might want to see how the total is affected when one or several of the spreadsheet's components are changed. Some electronic spreadsheet programs provide a **split screen** feature in which each half of the computer screen is a window displaying a different part of the spreadsheet. Figure 5-8*a* shows the part of the spreadsheet that fits on one screen. The totals, however, are located in row 16, which does not fit on the same screen. Figure 5-8*b* shows how the split screen feature works. In one part of the screen the user sees rows 1 through 5. In the other part of the screen, the user sees rows 14 through 16. When the user changes figures in the top window, any effects on the totals can be observed instantly in the lower window. Screens that are split vertically work in a similar way.

Why Use Spreadsheets in Business?

Electronic spreadsheets are used for many purposes in which manipulating numbers in rows and columns helps to solve business problems. Three common kinds of applications are numerical summaries, financial models and simulations, and record keeping. Each is discussed below.

Businesspeople use spreadsheets not only to help them generate information, but also to help them communicate their findings to others.

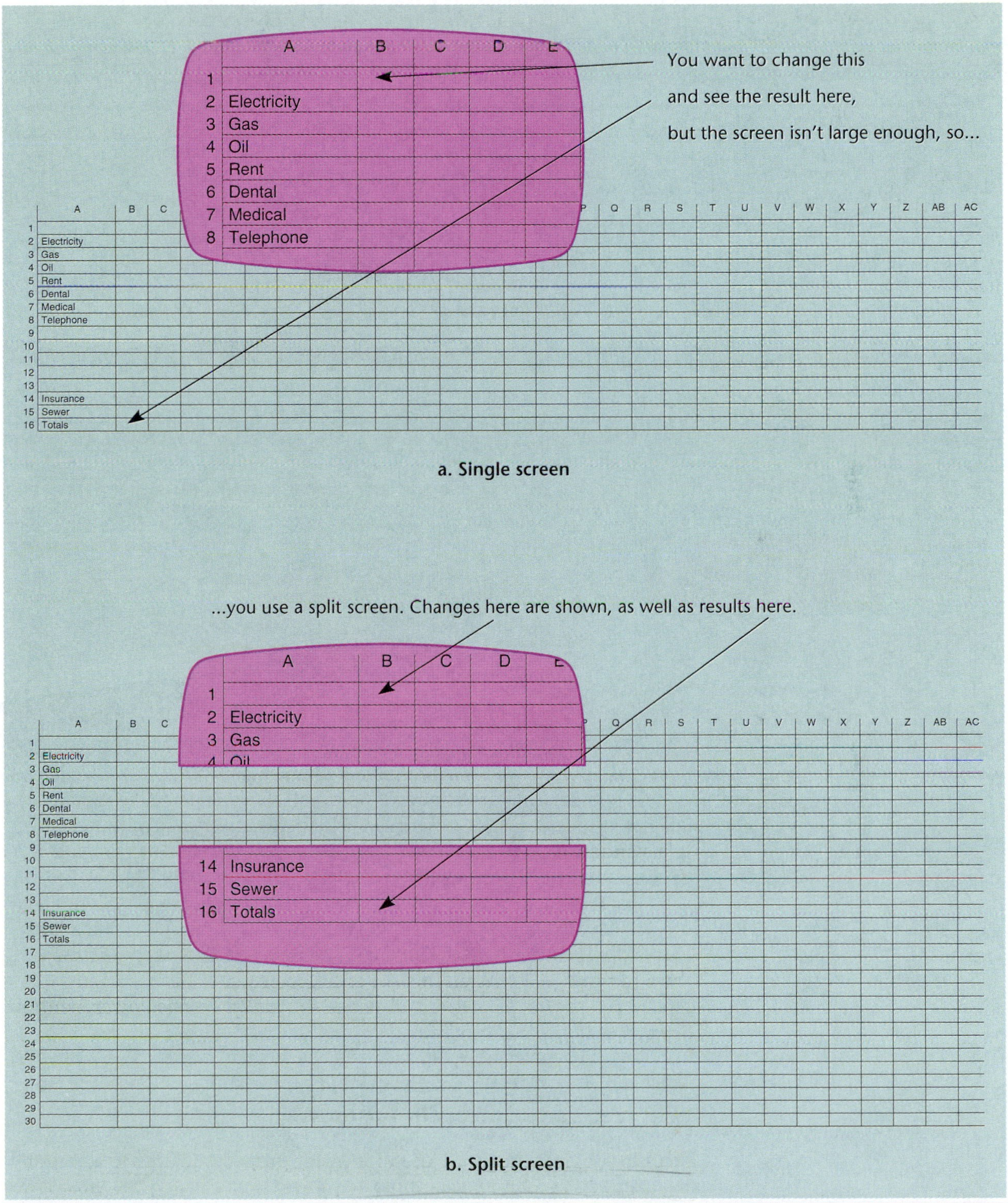

FIGURE 5-8 **Split Screen**
The split screen feature lets a user see two or more sections of a spreadsheet on the same display.

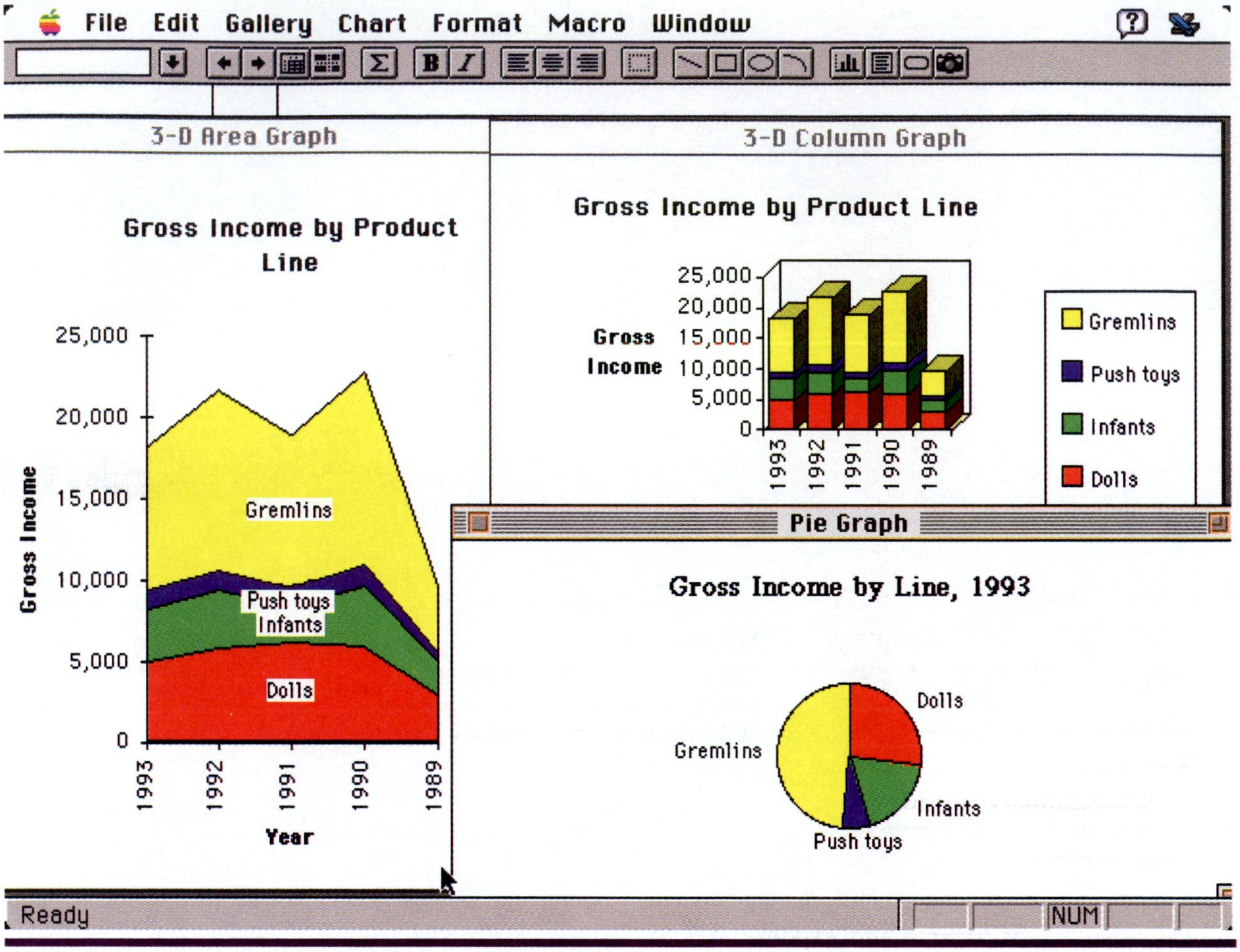

FIGURE 5-9 **Presentation Graphics**
These graphs were produced by an electronic spreadsheet program from spreadsheet data.

Thus, the communication function is basic to nearly all spreadsheet applications. Spreadsheet programs include many tools, including graphics capabilities, to help the user communicate results clearly and professionally (see Figure 5-9).

As you become more familiar with electronic spreadsheets and business problems, more types of spreadsheet applications will become apparent to you. The electronic spreadsheet program is a multipurpose tool.

Numerical Summaries In numerical summaries, such as budgets and expense lists, an electronic spreadsheet computes totals, averages, and other values. These applications are simple and straightforward. They simply record financial facts that the user enters. Calculations allow various subtotals and totals to be quickly determined and displayed. Examples include a summary of one student's college expenses (see Figure 5-10)

Summary of Yearly College Expenses	
Tuition	2,800
Books	400
Supplies	150
Lab/Studio fees	200
Student activity fees	250
Living Expenses	
Apartment rent	2,700
Food/Other	1,800
Phone	500
Entertainment	900
Car Expenses	
Insurance	1,000
Gas/Oil	600
Parking	50
Total	11,350

FIGURE 5-10

Numerical Summary Spreadsheet
This spreadsheet shows a summary of college expenses.

Ski Club			
Income		**Expenses**	
Membership dues	1,500	Trips	
Event fees	1,200	Buses	1,180
Student activity	500	Lodging	1,200
Trust fund	200	Trail fees & lift tickets	400
Ski-a-thon	125	Insurance	1,000
Car Wash	200	Flyers	25
Total	3,725	Postage	100
		Phone	100
		Total	4,005
		Ending Balance for Year	(280)

FIGURE 5-11

Numerical Summary Spreadsheet
This spreadsheet shows a summary of a ski club's income and expenses.

and a statement of income and expenses for the campus ski club (see Figure 5-11).

Financial Models and Simulation In financial modeling applications, such as sales forecasting, the user tests various business assumptions by entering them into a spreadsheet and seeing how changes are reflected in the results. Making the changes to test various assumptions is quick and easy.

A model **simulates** the relationships between things in the real business world. In other words, the results of changes in the values used in a model should be similar to the results of those changes if they were made in the real world. A **financial model** describes the relationships among various monetary aspects, such as income sources and amounts, cost centers, and payroll and other expenditures. Thus, a spreadsheet can contain a model of the company's finances.

By altering variables, the user effectively answers what-if questions. Often such simulation involves calculations that are more complex than simple summaries. For instance, a spreadsheet program can be used to determine the return on an investment such as a 12-month certificate of deposit, as illustrated in Figure 5-12. The user can vary both the initial deposit (in the example it is $1,000) and the interest rate (in this case, it is 10.5 percent).

Twelve-Month Certificate of Deposit

Deposit	1,000
Rate	0.105

Month	Value
1	1,008.75
2	1,017.58
3	1,026.48
4	1,035.46
5	1,044.52
6	1,053.66
7	1,062.88
8	1,072.18
9	1,081.56
10	1,091.03
11	1,100.57
12	1,110.20

FIGURE 5-12

A Financial Model Spreadsheet

This financial model can help answer what-if questions about return on a 12-month certificate of deposit.

Another example of a financial model is loan analysis. For example, consider a company that plans to finance the construction of a $200-million assembly plant. The company will probably consider several variables, including how much of the $200 million it will borrow, the time period over which it will pay off the loan, and the rate at which the loans will be financed. To assist in the decision-making process, the company's financial planners build several financial models, each reflecting one possible scenario. Results are compared to determine which is most favorable.

On a smaller scale, a college graduate who has worked for a couple of years and saved money for the down payment on a new car might want to consider how much money to borrow for a car loan and what the terms of the loan might be. One factor she considers is that interest rates for short-term loans are usually lower than those for longer-term ones. But a short-term loan will have a higher monthly payment.

A comparison of two different loan structures appears in Figure 5-14. The user enters principal, interest rate, and number of monthly payments. Then the spreadsheet program computes both the amount of monthly payment on the loan and the amount of total interest that will be paid over the life of the loan. Like the company financing a multimillion-dollar construction project, our car buyer needs these financial models (and maybe others) to help her decide which scenario best suits her financial situation. Finding these answers with a calculator is possible, but, again, it is time-consuming and prone to error. Using a spreadsheet program, only a few seconds are required to compare an 8½ percent, 12-month loan with a 13½ percent, 24-month loan. And with just a few more keystrokes, our car buyer could see the results of borrowing more (or less) money.

FIGURE 5-13

Financial Modeling in Action

When companies invest in new facilities, they create financial models with spreadsheets to answer what-if questions.

Cost of a Loan

Principal			4,000.00
Interest Rate			8.50
Number of Monthly Payments			12
Monthly Payment			348.88

Pmt. No.	Interest	Principal	New Balance
0			4,000.00
1	28.33	320.55	3,679.45
2	26.06	322.82	3,356.64
3	23.78	325.10	3,031.53
4	21.47	327.41	2,704.13
5	19.15	329.73	2,374.40
6	16.82	332.06	2,042.34
7	14.47	334.41	1,707.93
8	12.10	336.78	1,371.14
9	9.71	339.17	1,031.98
10	7.31	341.57	690.40
11	4.89	343.99	346.42
12	2.45	346.43	0.00

FIGURE 5-14a

Financial Model Spreadsheet
This spreadsheet can help answer questions about the cost of a loan.

Cost of a Loan

Principal			4,000.00
Interest Rate			13.50
Number of Monthly Payments			24
Monthly Payment			119.11

Pmt. No.	Interest	Principal	New Balance
0			4,000.00
1	45.00	146.11	3,853.89
2	43.36	147.75	3,706.14
3	41.69	149.42	3,556.72
4	40.01	151.10	3,405.62
5	38.31	152.80	3,252.83
6	36.59	154.52	3,098.31
7	34.86	156.25	2,942.06
8	33.10	158.01	2,784.05
9	31.32	159.79	2,624.26
10	29.52	161.59	2,462.67
11	27.71	163.40	2,299.26
12	25.87	165.24	2,134.02
13	24.01	167.10	1,966.92
14	22.13	168.98	1,797.94
15	20.23	170.88	1,627.05
16	18.30	172.81	1,454.25
17	16.36	174.75	1,279.50
18	14.39	176.72	1,102.78
19	12.41	178.70	924.08
20	10.40	180.71	743.36
21	8.36	182.75	560.62
22	6.31	184.80	375.81
23	4.23	186.88	188.93
24	2.13	188.98	0.00

FIGURE 5-14b

Record Keeping In record-keeping applications, the user stores data records in spreadsheet rows, with each column representing a field. For example, a table of employee personnel records can be stored, retrieved, and manipulated with an electronic spreadsheet program. Figure 5-15 shows such a spreadsheet.

Hermel Die Casting—Personnel Information

	Hourly Rate	Date Hired	Insurance Plan	Vacation Days	Sick Days	Department
Harder, T. Ried	13.00	04/17/53	C-83	337	53	Sales
Knurr, Edweena	14.18	09/29/87	HMO	65	16	Production
Larsonn, Lamona	15.72	07/30/74	C-99	119	83	Administration
Voge, H. Ross	11.36	08/18/84	C-07	11	8	Maintenance

FIGURE 5-15 **A Record-Keeping Spreadsheet**
This spreadsheet stores personnel data.

Calculations can be performed on the data. For example, we could determine the annual base pay for each employee (assuming, say, a 40-hour work week) by multiplying the hourly rate by 40 hours by 52 weeks. In addition to performing calculations, many electronic spreadsheet packages provide functions that help the user search the table for records that meet certain criteria. For instance, the program could find all employees who were hired before 1975 or all employees who earn more than $20 per hour.

Although the ability to search a spreadsheet can be useful, DBMSs (which will be described in Chapter 6) are designed specifically to provide secure storage and rapid retrieval, especially for large numbers of records. Consequently, a user who needs those abilities would probably create and maintain the data using a DBMS and then would **import** pertinent data from the database to the spreadsheet program for analysis. Importing files means using data produced by another program. With this approach, the user employs the best tool for each task: an electronic spreadsheet for financial analysis by means of cell formulas and DBMS software for secure data storage and retrieval.

A Word of Caution Like any other tool, the electronic spreadsheet can be misused; consequently, using this powerful software is not without some risk. Before the age of the electronic spreadsheet, some business decisions were made on instinct alone. Now, with electronic spreadsheets, users can rely more on financial facts. Building very complex financial models is relatively easy, and comparing many different scenarios can help people make sound decisions. Used carefully, an electronic spreadsheet can help increase profitability.

One problem is that users can forget that they are manipulating a model and not the real company. A financial model is just numbers inside a computer, merely an electronic image of a real company or even of an imagined one. Spurred by the excitement of playing with the numbers, users can forget that a company is more than numbers—it also includes people, corporate image and mission, corporate and individual values and ethics, and many other intangibles. Decisions that affect a company should often be supported by facts from a computer, but not to the exclusion of other factors.

Box 5.1

INCREASING YOUR PERSONAL PRODUCTIVITY

Tips for Better Spreadsheets

There is no one way to design a spreadsheet. But some tips collected from a variety of users, industry observers, and instructors can be helpful in simplifying design and eliminating errors.

- **Isolate Variables** Group the key parameters that will be frequently changed in one area of the spreadsheet. Have all references to that variable address that single cell. This simplifies changes, reduces errors, and makes the spreadsheet more readable.
- **Focus on Key Ratios** Plan the spreadsheet around those parameters that you believe drive your business. Those will be the values you'll want to manipulate or on which you'll want to see the impact of manipulating other values.
- **Use English** English is a wonderful language. Use it freely. It may take a few extra keystrokes to type "West Coast Sales" than "WCS" but the spreadsheet will be much easier to use and read, both for yourself and for anyone else with whom you share the matrix.
- **Keep It Simple** Mammoth equations are difficult to understand. Errors in using them are hard to trace and their logic is difficult to decipher. Break equations up by using intermediate variables.
- **Use Modules** An entire spreadsheet doesn't have to be built at once. Create a working spreadsheet for one then copy that to other sections of the spreadsheet. Finding errors in logic is easier in the smaller subsections.
- **Use Hash Totals** Spreadsheets created with paper and pencil invariably add numbers both horizontally and vertically across columns to doublecheck accuracy. The same approach can be of assistance for spreadsheets created with software.
- **Check Equations** It is easy to assume that anything printed out by a computer is infallible, but spreadsheets are only as accurate as the logic, and the typing, that created the equations. Check them carefully and recheck them.
- **Save Models** The value of saving copies of spreadsheets goes beyond the requirement for backup in case of disk failure or damage. As changes are made in the model it becomes ever more complex, and retracing your steps can become extremely difficult. Save copies of the model at each step, particularly if the spreadsheet is shared with other individuals who will be modifying it themselves.
- **Build in Checks** Use If statements, macros, comparisons with known ratios—anything you can think of to build in checks and safeguards against errors in either data entry or logic.
- **Have Fun** Lastly, remember that using personal computers is fun. In concentrating on the productivity enhancing power of computers, it is easy to forget this fact.

A second problem is that computers have a tendency to legitimize things. You will realize after taking this course that the output from an electronic spreadsheet program (or from any other program) is only as accurate and realistic as the formulas and input entered by the user. But some people do not realize that. It is easy to present true and accurate figures with an electronic spreadsheet. It is just as easy to present incorrect, incomplete, or misleading information with a spreadsheet. The problem here is a societal one—we tend to believe that what the computer tells us is true, especially when the results are printed into a professional-looking report.

As a result, we must take extra care to question the spreadsheet author about the source of his or her input, the formulas used, and the assumptions made. Computer printouts look so authoritative that we often accept them with complacency. We must instead question their authority.

INSIDE AN ELECTRONIC SPREADSHEET

In this text, our presentation of electronic spreadsheets applies to all electronic spreadsheet products. Furthermore, electronic spreadsheet programs provide enough material to fill several textbooks (in fact, many exist). In this single chapter, we focus on basic spreadsheet concepts. When you become experienced in the use of a spreadsheet product, you will be in a good position to explore other features that the product offers.

Spreadsheet programs come in three basic types. The first type is comprised of character-based spreadsheets that run under DOS, such as Lotus 1-2-3, Release 2.2. These programs offer about the same computational ability as the other categories but less sophisticated formatting of screen displays and printouts. The second type of spreadsheet program is comprised of graphic-based spreadsheets that run under DOS, such as Lotus 1-2-3, Release 2.3 and Quattro Pro. These programs provide the capability of selecting among various typefaces and type sizes, including placing lines and textures on a worksheet and locating graphs within the worksheet. The programs use the mouse for command selection, if a mouse is available, though they can also accept keyboard command entry. The third category of spreadsheets is comprised of GUI-based programs that run under Windows, OS/2, and Macintosh System 7. These programs include Excel, Resolve, and special GUI versions of Lotus 1-2-3. These programs offer capabilities comparable to graphics-based programs, but their command structure conforms to the standards of a GUI, making them particularly easy to learn to use.

The Spreadsheet Screen

When you load an electronic spreadsheet program, you will see a screen like the one shown in Figure 5-16. Part of the spreadsheet appears on the screen starting in cell A1, called the **home position**. At the top of the screen is a special area used by the spreadsheet program to give you information, accept your input, and display processing options available to you. This area is called the **control panel**.

The **cursor** is a highlighted rectangle that indicates where you can enter data. The cell at the cursor location is called the **current cell**. You can move the cursor to any position on the spreadsheet by pressing the Arrow keys (Up, Down, Left, Right), pressing other keys, or moving the mouse. Most electronic spreadsheet programs allow you to place the cursor at a specific cell location by using a command called Go To. When you

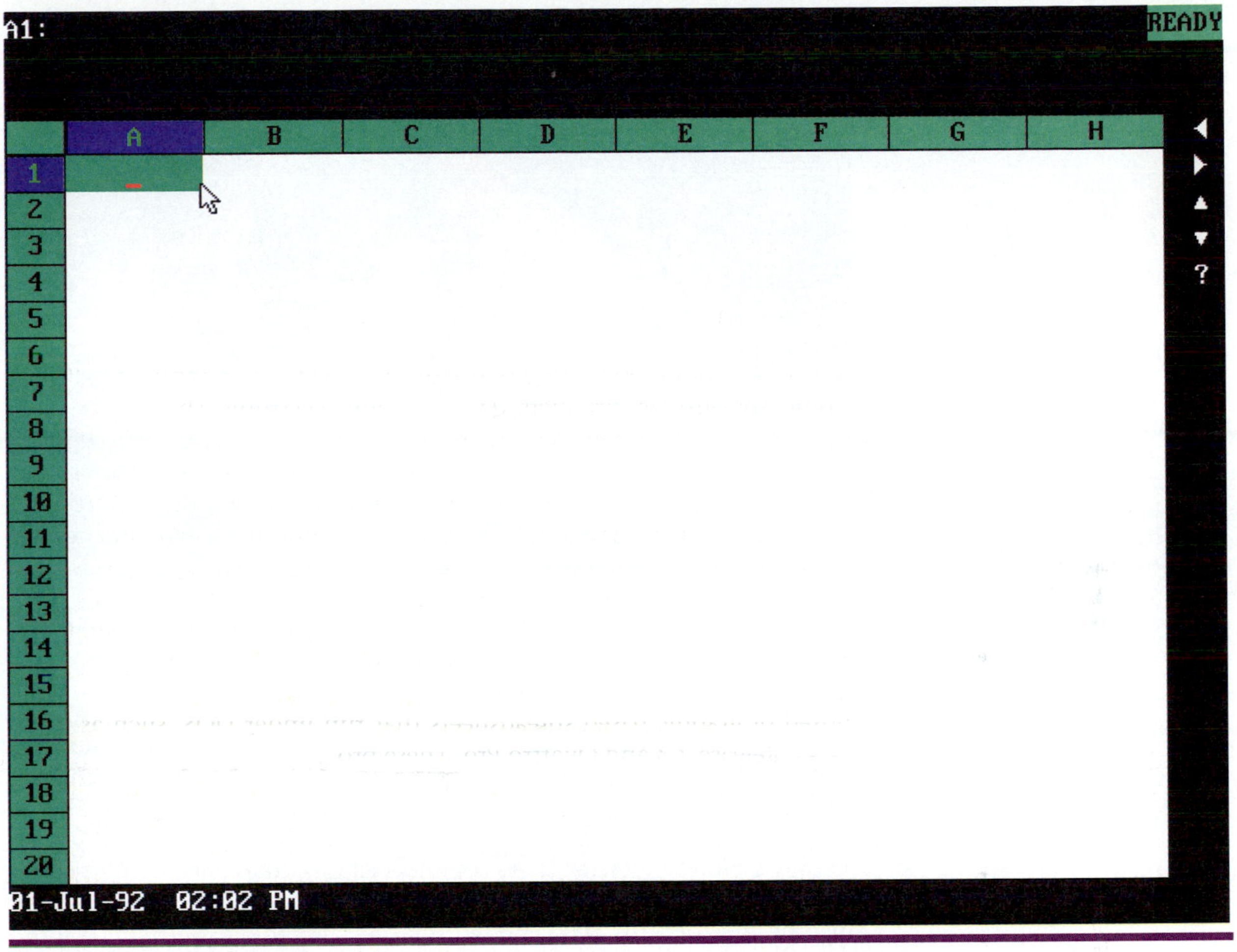

FIGURE 5-16 Spreadsheet Screen
Before any entries are made, the electronic spreadsheet screen looks like this.

invoke the Go To command, the program prompts you to enter a cell address for where you want to position the cursor.

Cell Entries

The most fundamental operation in a spreadsheet program is entering a value into a cell. With the cursor on a cell, you can enter either alphanumeric data or numeric data. An alphanumeric entry, or **label**, is brief text used to identify row or column contents. Alphanumeric entries are not used in calculations. A numeric entry can be either a number (sometimes called a **constant**) or a formula. When you type a label or a number, you see that value displayed in the cell. When you type a formula, you see the formula displayed in the control panel, but in the cell itself you see the value derived by the formula.

FIGURE 5-17

Spreadsheets Must Communicate Effectively

When the calculations are completed, spreadsheets are used to communicate the results to others.

Alphanumeric Data Alphanumeric data consists of labels that you enter to identify row or column contents for the user. These labels communicate the meaning of your figures much better than the bare row and column coordinates provided by the electronic spreadsheet program. You should use clear labels, avoiding abbreviations or codes wherever possible. "Sales Tax" is a more understandable column heading than "Slstx." All spreadsheet programs allow you to adjust the width of a column, so consider making the columns wide enough to accommodate meaningful column titles and row labels. If the data itself is narrow, consider dividing the column heading into two lines to make it meaningful in a small space.

Alphanumeric data is not used in calculations, and its formatting works somewhat differently from that of numeric data. Therefore, the spreadsheet program must determine which cells contain alphanumeric data. It does this by examining the first character of the entry. If that character is numeric, then the program treats the data as numeric; otherwise, the program treats it as alphanumeric. Characters considered numeric are the digits 0 through 9, the decimal point, the plus or minus sign, and the characters used in formulas, such as the parenthesis, the equal sign, and the at sign (@).

This system works well unless a label begins with a numeric character, such as the column heading *1994*, which will normally be treated as numeric. In such cases, the spreadsheet program provides a method of forcing the program to recognize the entry as a label. For example, the user of Lotus 1-2-3 can begin the entry with a quote character, which serves this purpose.

Numeric Data Numeric data consists of numbers and formulas. Entering numeric data into a spreadsheet is a two-step process. The first step is to enter the value itself. The second step is to specify its display format.

When you enter a number, type only its value: numeric digits, decimal point, and minus sign, if needed. Do not use dollar signs, commas, or any other punctuation.

When you enter a formula, you may include numbers, cell addresses, operators, and built-in functions. Numbers are entered as described above. When a cell address is included, the value displayed in that cell is used in the calculation. Operators include the following: + (addition); – (subtraction); * (multiplication); / (division); ^ (exponentiation); and others. Built-in functions include statistical manipulations such as finding the sum, average, count, and standard deviation of a range of values. Common financial functions are also available, such as calculating the future value of an annuity or the mortgage payment per period. Even if you do not yet understand exactly what each function does, it is important to know that many useful calculations are predefined in the spreadsheet program, ready for you to use. Figure 5-18 shows examples of spreadsheet formulas.

FIGURE 5-18 **Spreadsheet Formulas**
The results of a set of sample formulas are shown.

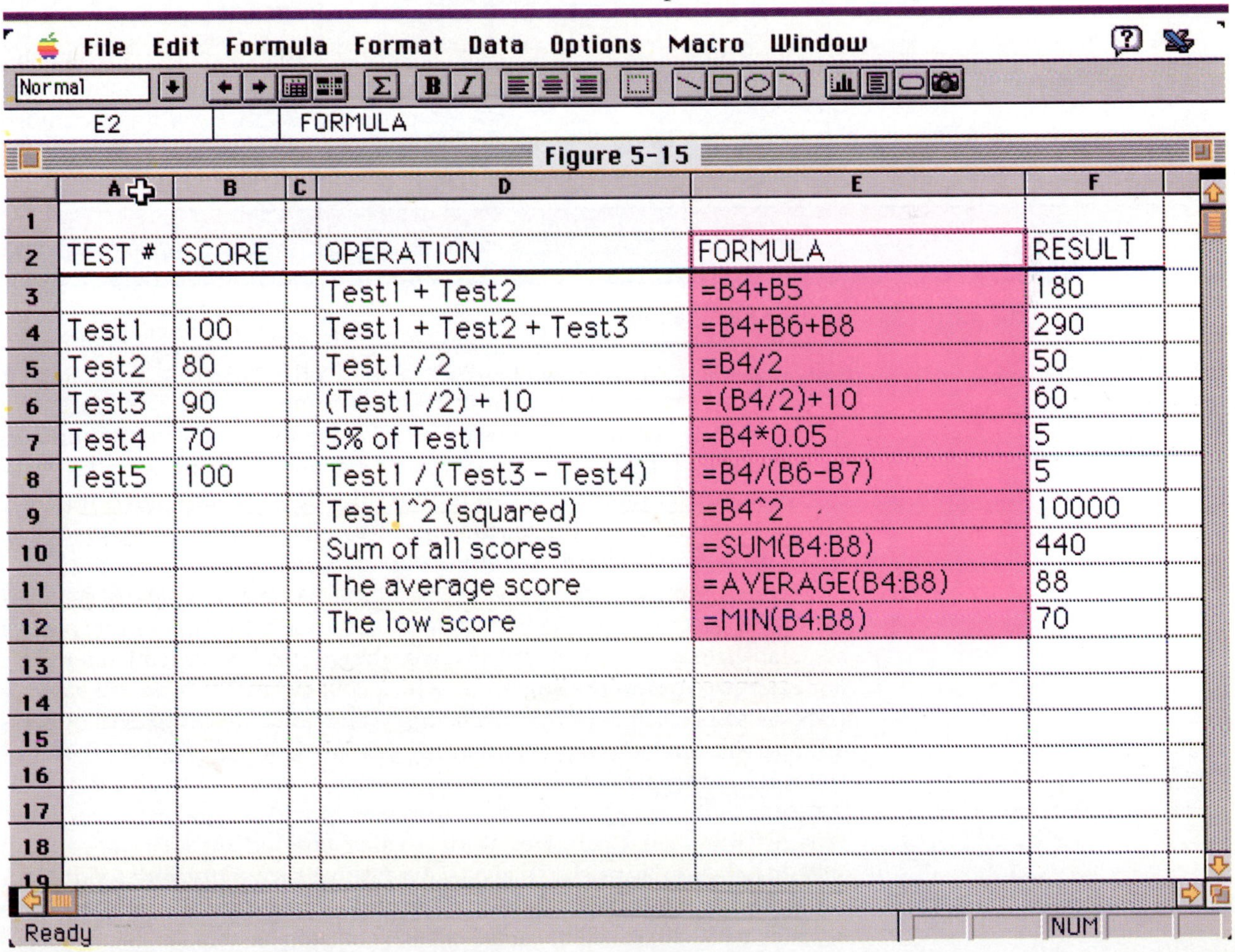

	A	B	C	D	E	F
1						
2	TEST #	SCORE		OPERATION	FORMULA	RESULT
3				Test1 + Test2	=B4+B5	180
4	Test1	100		Test1 + Test2 + Test3	=B4+B6+B8	290
5	Test2	80		Test1 / 2	=B4/2	50
6	Test3	90		(Test1 /2) + 10	=(B4/2)+10	60
7	Test4	70		5% of Test1	=B4*0.05	5
8	Test5	100		Test1 / (Test3 - Test4)	=B4/(B6-B7)	5
9				Test1^2 (squared)	=B4^2	10000
10				Sum of all scores	=SUM(B4:B8)	440
11				The average score	=AVERAGE(B4:B8)	88
12				The low score	=MIN(B4:B8)	70

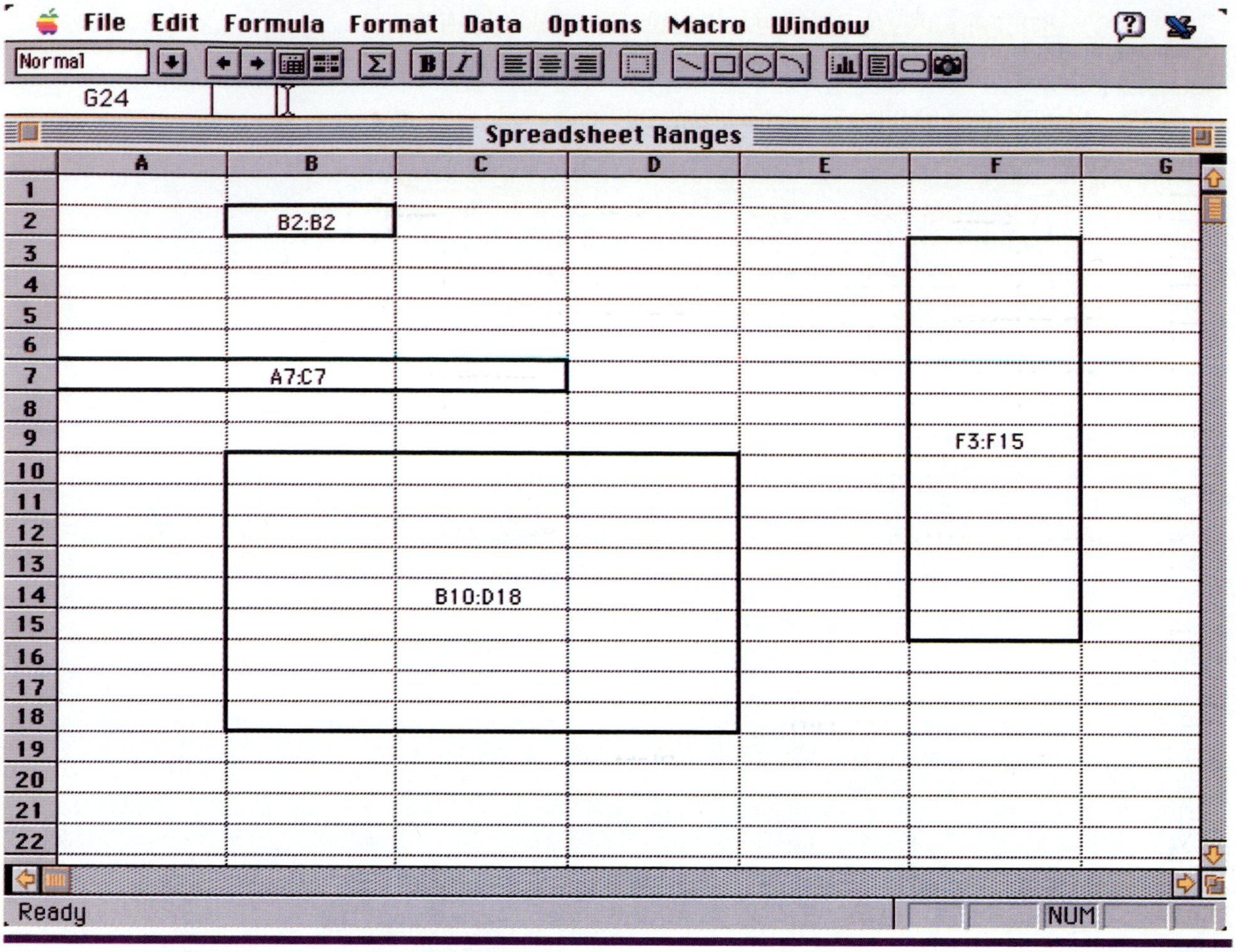

FIGURE 5-19 **Spreadsheet Ranges**
As a shortcut, spreadsheet programs let users refer to blocks of cells by using the range notation, as shown here.

When the contents of a cell is a formula, the cell's display shows the formula's value. To see the formula, put the cursor on the cell and look in the control panel, where the formula appears.

Many functions act on a series of values. For example, the SUM function adds a set of values. When these values appear in consecutive cells of a spreadsheet, we use a shortcut way of designating them, called a **range**. For example, to sum the values in cells L7, L8, L9, and L10, we use the formula SUM(L7:L10), with *L7:L10* being a range of cells. Similarly, B5:C7 is a range that includes cells B5, B6, B7, C5, C6, and C7. Figure 5-19 illustrates this concept.

Formatting Cell Contents With a value entered into a cell, you can specify how you want it displayed. Spreadsheet programs offer a variety of numeric **display formats**. For instance, you might want the figures in one column to be displayed as integers, with commas inserted every three po-

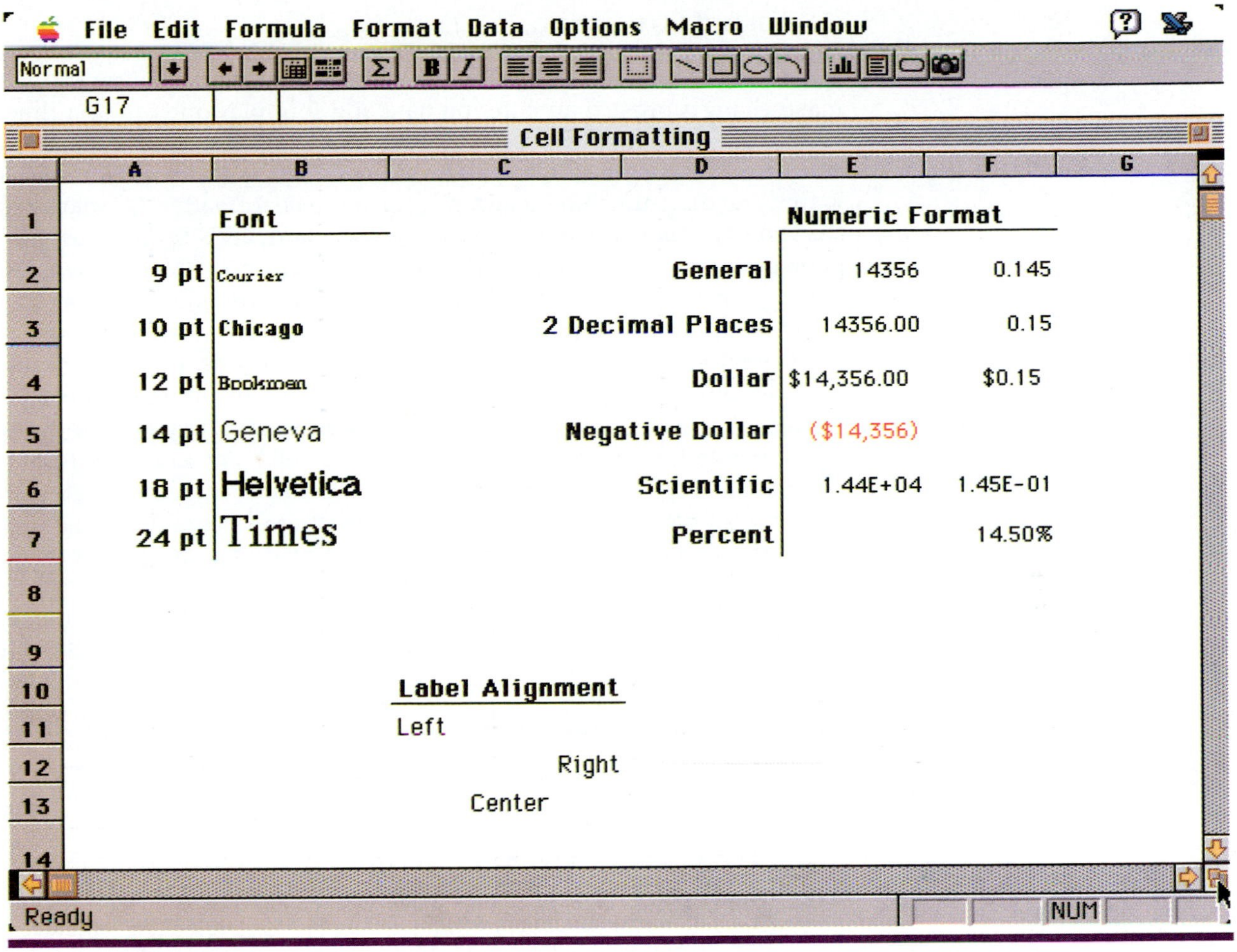

FIGURE 5-20 **Cell Formatting**
Factors that may be affected by cell formatting include numeric format, label alignment, typeface, type size, type style, and various graphic effects.

sitions (1,234,567). You might want the figures in another column displayed in currency format—that is, with leading dollar sign, commas in appropriate places, and two digits to the right of the decimal point ($1,234,567.89). Many other numeric formats are available. Select one for each cell to make the spreadsheet's meaning as clear as possible to the reader.

Formatting for alphanumeric data includes **justification**, which determines whether the label is displayed at the left end of the cell, centered, or displayed at the right end of the cell.

If a spreadsheet provides a graphic rather than a character-based display, you can specify typeface, type size, and type style of the displayed type. In addition, you may be able to specify the placement of lines, boxes, shading, color, and other graphic devices to enhance the appearance and clarity of the spreadsheet on the screen and in print. Figure 5-20 illustrates some formatting variations.

Command Structure

Spreadsheet programs are built around a set of commands that let you make changes other than entering data and formulas one cell at a time. For example, commands let you do the following things: save a spreadsheet to disk, copy cell contents from one location to another, create a graph, and determine how a group of cells is to be formatted. To spare you the task of memorizing the dozens of specific commands, spreadsheet program designers group related commands together into a menu. When you select a command from the menu, you are often presented with further choices until finally you get to the precise command you want.

Common commands can be categorized by purpose into four groups: housekeeping, editing, formatting, and additional capabilities. Figure 5-21 shows commands commonly provided in spreadsheet programs.

Many commands operate on a range of cells. For example, format commands are often applied to a range of cells rather than to a single cell. Similarly, in creating sums at the bottom of a series of columns, the user writes the sum formula once, then uses a command to copy that formula to a range of cells across the bottom of the columns.

In some spreadsheets, certain ranges are used repeatedly. For example, the range containing the output section of a spreadsheet may be printed often. Another part of the spreadsheet may contain data records that are frequently sorted. Ranges that are used frequently can be given **range names**, making them easy to specify. The range name becomes simply another way of specifying that range. The names, SORTRANGE and PRINTRANGE, once defined, can be used in formulas and commands just like ranges normally specified.

Printing a Spreadsheet

Several options are available for printing a spreadsheet. A small spreadsheet can be printed on a page measuring 8½-by-11 inches. That approach is fine if the spreadsheet fits in that space. If the spreadsheet is just a little too big, you can change the type to a smaller size or (in a character-based program) print it using **condensed print**, making all the letters and numbers smaller so they will fit on the page.

If a spreadsheet is too large to fit on a single, printed page, the spreadsheet program will first print the top-left page, then the page to its right, and so on. When the pages containing the topmost rows have been printed, the program begins printing the pages containing the second set of rows, working left to right, then printing the third page, and so on, until the printout is completed. If you wish, you can tape or paste the sheets together to make a complete printed display.

As we will soon see, many large spreadsheets are divided into sections, with one section designed to show the results. Often, the results section is designed with page boundaries in mind, so the results are printed on a single page or on a series of pages, each of which is designed to communicate its message clearly and professionally. For example, you might design the output so the part of the spreadsheet that summarizes the first year's bud-

HOUSEKEEPING

Save/Retrieve	Save and retrieve worksheet Save worksheet under new title
Print	Determine which cells are to be printed Determine page size and other printout characteristics Print Print to file
Range name	Specify names for particular cells or ranges
Protection	Determine which cells are protected from contents change Activate protection for protected cells
Macro	Record a macro from user entries Display a list of defined macros Run a macro

EDITING

Copy/Move	Copy cell contents from one location to another Move cell contents, deleting from original location Cut and paste
Find/Replace	Seek cells with specified contents Replace with other contents when found
Erase/Clear	Blank entire worksheet Clear a range of cells
Insert/Delete	Insert or delete rows or columns or specific cells
Go to	Move the cursor to a particular location

FORMATTING

Format	Determine numeric display format Determine label alignment within cell Select font, size, style Select cell borders and background patterns Apply to specified cells or entire worksheet
Cell size	Specify column width and row height
Recalculation	Determine whether formulas are recalculated after each data entry or only when specified
Titles	Lock cells containing column headings and row labels into position on the screen, so scrolling the screen window does not remove them Lock cells containing column headings and row labels so they remain in position relative to the cells they label when the window is moved

ADDITIONAL CAPABILITIES

Graph	Create and display a graph Select graph type Specify title, axis labels, and legends Specify graph format
Database	Sort selected range of cells based on contents of one or more columns Identify or extract rows that meet specified criteria Fill a range of cells with a specified sequence of values Create a data table

FIGURE 5-21
Spreadsheet Commands

get fits on one page; the second year's budget, on another page; and so on, for all the years described in your spreadsheet. A separate page might contain a summary of the yearly totals and the grand totals. This set of documents is easy to photocopy and easy to comprehend because each page contains a cohesive chunk of information.

In all of the techniques mentioned above, the spreadsheet is printed as displayed on the computer screen. This means that derived values appear in all cells that contain formulas. However, spreadsheet programs can also print the formulas themselves. Figure 5-22 illustrates these two methods of printing. Printing the cell contents lets you make a hard copy record of all your formulas. In fact, whenever you develop a spreadsheet application, you should print your formulas as part of your documentation.

Macros

A **macro** is a computer program written in the language of a spreadsheet program. It consists of a series of spreadsheet entries like the entries you would type or enter by mouse to perform some function. To create a macro, enter a representation of the series of entries into spreadsheet cells, then give a name to the cells. Thereafter you can invoke the macro by its name.

Macros are particularly useful in situations where you find yourself repeatedly making the same sequence of entries. For example, suppose you are developing a spreadsheet to serve as a computerized check register for your personal checking account. Each time you write a check or make a deposit, you create a new record in the register for that transaction. To reconcile your register with the bank statement that you receive monthly, you must sort your entries into the order used in the bank statement: (1) deposits and charges other than numbered checks, in order by date; and (2) numbered checks, in order by check number. The commands for this sort are not difficult, but they involve several steps that could be hard to remember from month to month. If you write them into a macro, then you must only remember the name of the macro each month when the sort must be done. When you invoke the macro, it executes the entries just as though you had entered them yourself.

Templates

Not only can macros simplify the entry of often-repeated sequences, but they can also help structure a spreadsheet for use by others. If you have a friend who needs a computerized check register, for example, you can remove the specific data about this month's checks from your spreadsheet, but leave intact all column headings, formulas, cell formatting, and macros. (Formulas automatically calculate a current balance for each entry. Formatting includes specification of date format and dollar value format for appropriate columns.) Such a skeleton spreadsheet is called a **template**. You can give your friend this template on a disk, and each month he can use it to begin a new check register, as you do.

MATERIALS	Units	Type	Cost/Unit	Discount	Discounted Price	Sales Tax	Item Total
LUMBER (Board feet)							
	6,000	2 x 4	1.65	495.00	9,405.00	752.04	10,157.40
	4,000	2 x 6	2.45	490.00	9,310.00	744.80	10,054.80
	15,000	3/4" ext plywood	0.95	712.50	13,537.50	1,083.00	14,620.50
INSULATION							
	180	Roll 16" R23 Kraft	12.00	108.00	2,052.00	164.16	2,216.16
	50	Roll 16" R16	8.50	21.25	403.75	32.30	436.05
	200	Lb. loose fiberglass	0.28	2.80	53.20	4.26	57.46
FASTENERS							
	100	#10d common	3.57	17.85	339.15	27.13	366.28
	20	#8d finish	4.41	4.41	83.79	6.70	90.49
	50	#6d roofing	6.45	16.13	306.38	24.51	330.89
	50	Box #8 wood	3.00	7.50	142.50	11.40	153.90
	20	Box #4 wood	2.75	2.75	52.25	4.18	56.43
	540	Joist hanger	0.18	4.86	92.34	7.39	99.73
						TOTAL COST	38,640.08

MATERIALS	Units	Type	Cost/Unit	Discount	Discounted Price	Sales Tax	Item Total
LUMBER (Board feet)							
	6,000	2 x 4	1.65	=B4*D4*0.05	=B4*D4-E4	=F4*0.08	=F4+G4
	4,000	2 x 6	2.45	=B5*D5*0.05	=B5*D5-E5	=F5*0.08	=F5+G5
	15,000	3/4" ext plywood	0.95	=B6*D6*0.05	=B6*D6-E6	=F6*0.08	=F6+G6
INSULATION							
	180	Roll 16" R23 Kraft	12.00	=B8*D8*0.05	=B8*D8-E8	=F8*0.08	=F8+G8
	50	Roll 16" R16	8.50	=B9*D9*0.05	=B9*D9-E9	=F9*0.08	=F9+G9
	200	Lb. loose fiberglass	0.28	=B10*D10*0.05	=B10*D10-E10	=F10*0.08	=F10+G10
FASTENERS							
	100	#10d common	3.57	=B12*D12*0.05	=B12*D12-E12	=F12*0.08	=F12+G12
	20	#8d finish	4.41	=B13*D13*0.05	=B13*D13-E13	=F13*0.08	=F13+G13
	50	#6d roofing	6.45	=B14*D14*0.05	=B14*D14-E14	=F14*0.08	=F14+G14
	50	Box #8 wood	3.00	=B15*D15*0.05	=B15*D15-E15	=F15*0.08	=F15+G15
	20	Box #4 wood	2.75	=B16*D16*0.05	=B16*D16-E16	=F16*0.08	=F16+G16
	540	Joist hanger	0.18	=B17*D17*0.05	=B17*D17-E17	=F17*0.08	=F17+G17
						TOTAL COST	=SUM (H4:H17)

FIGURE 5-22 Printing Display Values or Cell Contents
Printing cell contents documents a spreadsheet's formulas. You may need to widen cells to let the full width of all formulas show.

INCREASING YOUR PERSONAL PRODUCTIVITY

Box 5.2

Lies, Damned Lies, and Statistics

Graphics programs accurately chart the numbers you feed them. But are the numbers really right? In too many cases, there are out-and-out errors in the data, such as a sloppily handwritten 5 misread as an 8, 46 mistyped as 64, or the wrong formula (summing cells C2 through C14 instead of C2 through C13). Subtler and more insidious errors result from the unthinking application of accurate numbers.

Of all the misleading statistics that quickly find their way into graphs and charts, those involving the time value of money rank at the top. If your house increased 240 percent in appraised value in the past 10 years, don't forget that life in these United States costs significantly more than it did 10 years ago.

Comparisons involving people, goods and services, and territory should be adjusted logically, too. If you're charting the number of lawyers, the magnitude of defense expenditures, or the volume of crop production by state, it's no surprise that California, New York, and Texas would rank near the top because they're so big. Fairer comparisons might involve data adjusted per 100,000 residents or per 1,000 square miles. If you're studying total sales and profits per division, look at sales per employee in addition to total sales.

Anyone doing business abroad should chart data both in dollars and in the currencies of foreign trading partners. That might help explain why overseas sales are on a roller coaster while domestic sales are rock-steady. Try the numbers with and without an inflation deflator or some other common divisor. Do likewise for charts involving population or sales.

Usually, factoring the effects of inflation makes for a less dramatic and more accurate graph. Ignoring them makes your position look either much worse or much better than it is—which may be just what you intended to do, anyway. Just do it with your eyes open.

When your friend loads your template, the first screen he sees might contain instructions for invoking a set of macros. To enter data on the spreadsheet's data entry screen, the screen tells him, he must press a certain key combination. To print the resulting report, he must press another; and so on. Such macro-driven spreadsheets are especially useful when computer beginners must use spreadsheets. In fact, a spreadsheet can be so completely automated by macros that the user need not know any spreadsheet commands at all.

Consolidation and Linking

In a large corporation, budgeting is often done department by department, using procedures designed by the finance department. Often, the procedures involve using a budgeting spreadsheet template that is provided to each department. Workers in the department enter values representing their proposed budget, including salaries, office expenses, travel expenses, and many other categories. The predefined formulas in the template show totals by category and other summary results.

When every department has completed its budget spreadsheet, central budget planners can quickly consolidate the many spreadsheets into division and company totals. Since the value for, say, travel expenses, is in the same cell of each department's spreadsheet, the consolidated spreadsheet is easily created by summing corresponding values on the various spreadsheets into a single summary spreadsheet. Today's spreadsheet programs provide facilities for such consolidation.

Similar facilities can link individual cells on different spreadsheets. For example, if a corporate marketing department uses a spreadsheet to make periodic sales forecasts, other departments can use their numbers by linking cells in their spreadsheets directly to the sales forecast spreadsheet. When the market department revises its sales forecast, then each linked spreadsheet will be updated to the latest values. As a result, everyone's forecasts of various aspects of future performance can be constructed on the same foundation of data. The techniques used to share access to the sales forecast spreadsheet are described in Part Three of this book.

Presentation Graphics

Spreadsheet programs offer a powerful **presentation graphics** feature. Presentation graphics are charts, often used during oral presentations, that summarize quantitative information visually. Examples include pie graphs, bar graphs, and line graphs.

Graphs are communication devices. So when you are deciding on a type of graph, consider the concepts you want your graph to convey to the reader. A line graph shows performance over a period of time. For example, the line graph in Figure 5-23 shows how a die casting company's performance has varied over a four-year period. The graph tells us that sales of zinc castings and tool work have held fairly steady and that sales of aluminum castings have increased.

In contrast, a bar graph and a pie graph both show the relative contribution made by various factors. Look at the same product sales data illustrated as a bar graph (see Figure 5-24). In this diagram, you can more easily see the relative contribution made by each product type during each year.

Now look at the pie graph in Figure 5-25. This pie graph (showing only the 1994 sales) even more dramatically illustrates how each product contributed to the 1994 total. Each wedge of the pie represents the portion of total sales made in a product line.

Having selected the type of graph, you can use various spreadsheet commands to define title, axis labels, and legend (Figure 5-23) and data range. The data ranges indicate the spreadsheet locations at which the program will find the data values it is supposed to graph.

When you have defined all the graph components, you can view the graph on the computer screen, print it on paper, or save it for future use. When you update the spreadsheet values that are graphed, the graph is automatically updated. The particulars of graphing depend on the electronic spreadsheet product you are using.

	A	B	C	D	E	F
1			Sales By Product Line			
2			Hermel Die Casting, Inc.			
3						
4		1991	1992	1993	1994	
5	Zinc Castings	473,668	478,294	383,449	430,501	
6	Aluminum Castings	293,840	253,495	405,944	324,856	
7	Tool Work	70,559	73,449	41,258	81,882	
8		838,067	805,238	830,651	837,239	
9						
10						
14						

a. **Sales by product line at Hermel Die Casting.**

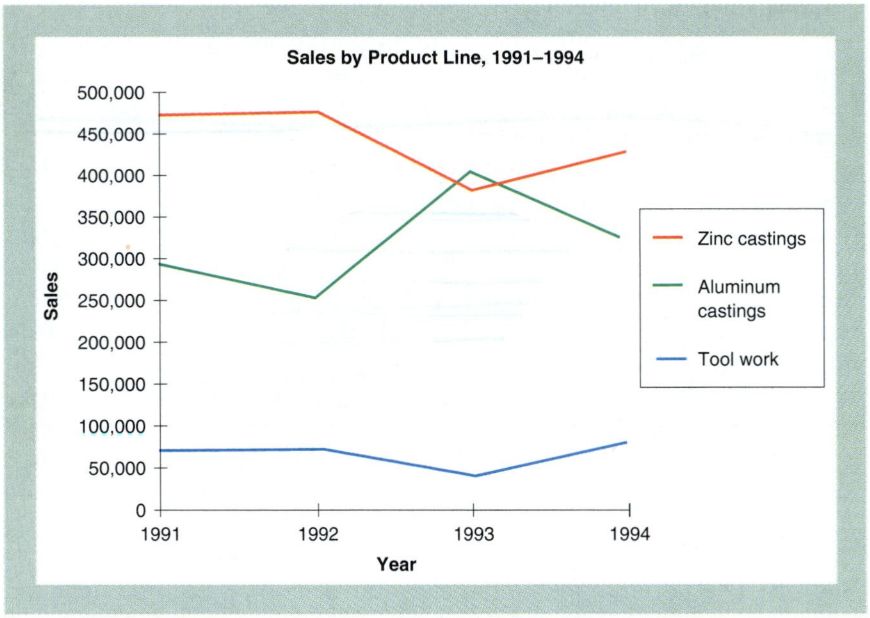

b. **A line graph shows the changes in values over time. Note the components of the graph.**

FIGURE 5-23 **Spreadsheet Graphing**

DEVELOPING SPREADSHEET APPLICATIONS

Before undertaking any project—building a deck, writing a résumé, or preparing a four-course dinner—you need a plan. Without blueprints, outline, or chart of cooking times for each course, you would have difficulty doing any of the three projects effectively. You might muddle through

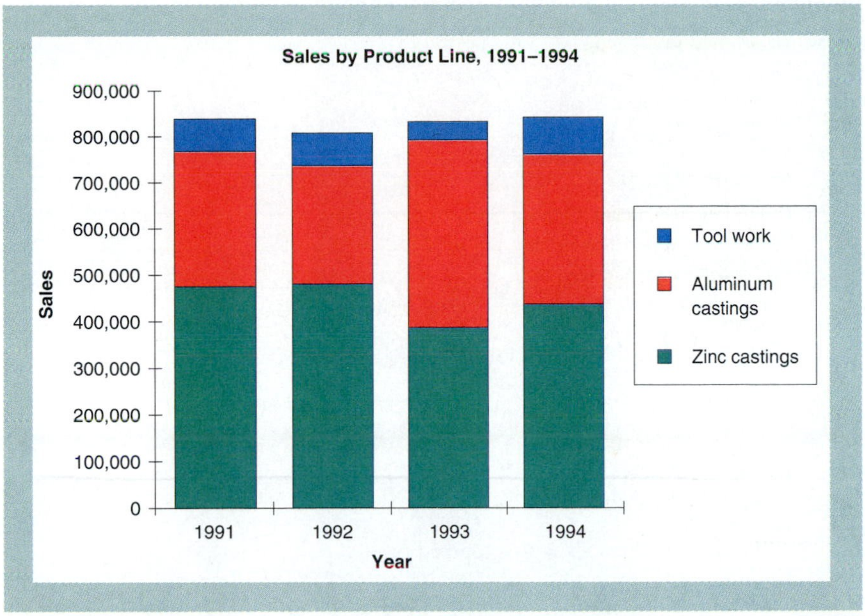

FIGURE 5-24

Bar Graph

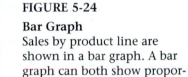

Sales by product line are shown in a bar graph. A bar graph can both show proportions and compare totals.

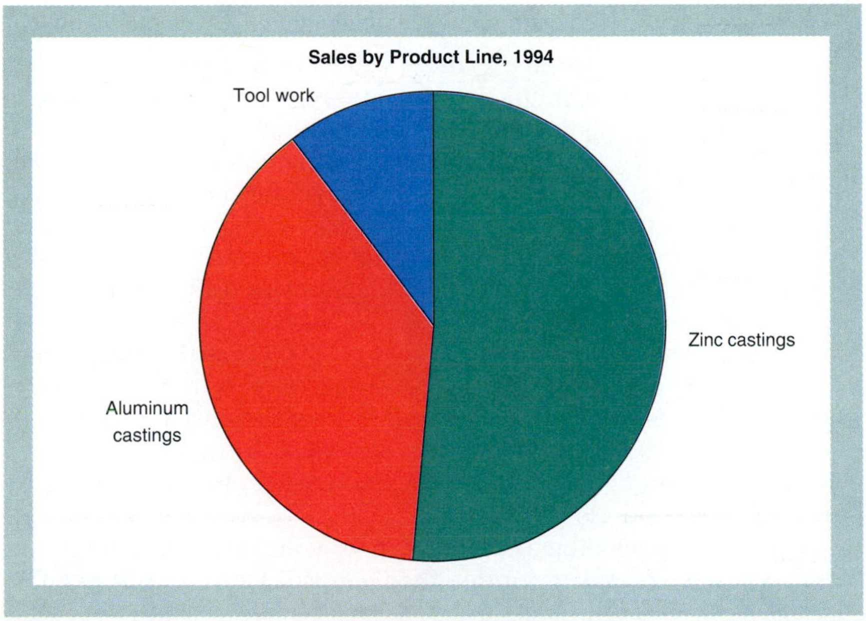

FIGURE 5-25

Pie Graph

Sales by product line for 1992 are shown in a pie graph. The pie graph focuses sharply on the proportions of a single whole thing.

somehow, but the results probably will not be as good as they would be with some careful planning. The same is true for spreadsheet applications. Planning before building is essential. In fact, we can break the process of developing a spreadsheet application into four steps: designing the model, designing the spreadsheet, building the spreadsheet, and testing the spreadsheet. These steps are summarized in Figure 5-26.

- ▶ Designing the model
  - Define problem
  - Identify outputs
  - Identify inputs
  - List assumptions and decisions
  - Document formulas
- ▶ Designing the spreadsheet
  - Develop spreadsheet map
- ▶ Building the spreadsheet
  - Enter labels, headings, and other internal documentation
  - Enter spreadsheet data and formulas
  - Build macros
  - Write external documentation
- ▶ Testing the spreadsheet
  - Develop test cases
  - Calculate results manually
  - Run test cases
  - Compare actual results with expected results
  - Debug

FIGURE 5-26
Steps in Developing a Spreadsheet Application

Designing the Model

During this step, you design the model you will use to solve the problem. The model, based on a definition of the problem, includes formulas, inputs, assumptions, and decisions.

Begin by defining the problem you are trying to solve. Some problems are simple, such as developing your own budget for the school year. Others require research. Consider the construction materials spreadsheet we examined earlier. Suppose the lumberyard charges 6 percent for delivery. Turn back to Figure 5-5 and determine the formula for computing delivery charges.

Did you have enough information to do that correctly? Did you realize that delivery charges are based on the price before sales tax—that is, on the total of the discounted prices? Or did you assume we meant that the delivery charge was 6 percent of the invoice total? The point here is not to trick you. It is simply to emphasize the importance of knowing what you are doing before you do it.

If you are developing a spreadsheet for your own application, over which you have complete control, then you will know most if not all of the answers at the beginning. If you are developing a spreadsheet for someone else or if there are undefined factors, then some investigation is in order.

Also during this step, you need to identify the outputs you want so you can in turn identify the inputs you need. For example, in order to compute an invoice total, you need not only each item's price, but also the number of items the customer bought.

Having identified the data, you can list your assumptions and decisions. Making an **assumption** means giving a value, which you suppose

FIGURE 5-27

A Fundamental Tool Today, businesses expect that new staff members will understand how to make effective use of the spreadsheet tool.

to be accurate, to a variable over which you have no real control. For example, if you were doing sales projections, you might assume that you would increase sales next year by 5 percent. If you were doing a yearly household budget, you might base it on the assumption that you will receive a 3 percent raise in July and that the price of home heating oil will be $1.69 per gallon. Those assumptions may or may not prove to be accurate.

Making a **decision** means giving a value to a variable over which you have complete control. For example, the lumberyard owner may decide to give contractors a 5 percent discount. At any time, the owner can change that to 0 percent, 6 percent, or 10 percent.

Finally, before you ever even load your spreadsheet software, remember to document the formulas you plan to use. Write them in English in algebraic format. For example, the formula for computing the contractor's discount might be written as follows: Contractor's Discount = (Item Price × Number Ordered) × Discount Percentage.

Designing the Spreadsheet

The spreadsheet design involves determining the parts of the actual spreadsheet and how they will be related. For example, many recent spreadsheet programs let the user create a **workspace** consisting of several relatively small, interrelated worksheets to perform a single task. One worksheet might be designed entirely for data entry, another for reporting results, another to contain macros, and so on. Cells on the various worksheets in a workspace are linked, permitting the various spreadsheets to share use of the data.

FIGURE 5-28

Suggested Layout for a Spreadsheet Map
This layout, adapted from one described by Jack Holt in *Cases and Applications in Lotus 1-2-3* (Homewood, IL: Irwin, 1988), suggests how the sections of a large spreadsheet can be conveniently arranged.

<table>
<tr><th colspan="2">Documentation</th><th colspan="2">Macros</th></tr>
<tr><td colspan="2">Independent Variables
(assumptions and decisions)</td><td colspan="2">Scratch Area
(graphs, data tables, etc.)</td></tr>
<tr><td colspan="3">Calculations
(formulas)</td><td>Summary Area</td></tr>
</table>

The more traditional design involves creating a **spreadsheet map**, showing the allocation of various areas of a single large spreadsheet to contain the sections. Figure 5-28 shows one useful basic spreadsheet format using this traditional design.

Whether an application is designed as a workspace of separate spreadsheets or as a series of sections in a single, large spreadsheet, consider the use of a common set of areas: documentation, independent variables, calculations, macros, scratch area, and summary area.

The Documentation Area Documentation for a spreadsheet should include both internal documentation and external documentation. Internal documentation is located within the spreadsheet itself and is entered as labels in cells. External documentation is usually recorded on paper and is often stored in a notebook next to the computer.

Internal documentation should appear on the opening screen, which appears when the spreadsheet or workspace is first loaded. This opening screen is often the home screen. By locating documentation there, you ensure that the first thing you (or any other user) will see is the documentation. It describes the spreadsheet's name and general purpose, author, date of creation, and assumptions or limitations. Documentation should also list the names and functions of any macros used. It must contain a spreadsheet map indicating the locations of the spreadsheet sections (or names of the spreadsheets in a workspace)—for example, where calculations begin, where macros are found, and where assumptions and decisions are located. Documentation can also be placed at the beginning of each part, explaining features of the entries in the section.

External documentation describes the spreadsheet or workspace in more detail than does the internal documentation. Also, it contains a list of the contents of every cell, including a list of all formulas. This is especially valuable documentation. Often you (or a user, an auditor, or someone else) may need to check the validity and accuracy of various formulas. Having a listing of formulas is more desirable than having to load the spreadsheet and examine each cell one by one.

The Independent Variables Area In the **independent variables** area, the variables whose values the user can modify are defined. (For example, in Figure 5-12, the user could vary the starting value of the 12-month certificate of deposit and the interest rate.) Independent variables are defined in this section and then referenced in the formulas in the calculations section.

As an illustration of the use of independent variables, consider the construction materials spreadsheet. In Figure 5-29*a*, the formulas are displayed in the appropriate cells. Notice that, in the Discount column, the numeric constant .05, representing the discount rate, appears in every formula. Similarly, in the Sales Tax column, the 8 percent sales tax rate appears in every formula.

Now consider the alternative design shown in Figure 5-29*b*. In this case, the discount rate and the sales tax rate are defined as independent variables and placed at the top of the table. Now the formulas for computing the discount and the sales tax can refer to those cells instead of using constant numeric values. As a result, when either value needs to be changed, as it inevitably will sooner or later, the change is easy. You only have to modify the values in the Discount and Sales Tax cells. If the sales tax rate changes to $8^1/_2$ percent, you only have to enter *0.085* in the Sales Tax cell.

Without this independent variable entry, you would have to go through the whole spreadsheet, find every use of the tax rate, and change its value. Look again at Figure 5-30*a*, and see how much more difficult this would be. Errors are nearly inevitable when you make changes like this.

The Calculations Area The calculations area contains the formulas that do the main work of the spreadsheet. Whenever possible, avoid hard-coding constant values into formulas (as we did, incorrectly, in Figure 5-29*a*). As a general principle, all constant values that could possibly change in the future should be defined in an independent variables area, and every formula in the calculations area should reference them there by address.

The Macros Area To permit convenient inspection and modification, all macros should be clustered together in one area. In some spreadsheet programs, macros are located on a separate spreadsheet in the workspace. In others, macros are located on the main spreadsheet. On the main spreadsheet, macros are often located at the top of the spreadsheet to the right of the introductory documentation. This makes them easy to find for inspection and modification, and it minimizes the chance that they will be unintentionally interrupted when users insert additional rows.

The Scratch Area A scratch area can be used for temporary values in the spreadsheet—for example, tables to arrange data for graphing, look-up tables, and other working values. Data to be graphed does not always appear in the spreadsheet in the correct form for graphing. By creating a separate graph table, pulling data from its original position, you can optimally position columns and make other changes that result in professional-looking graphs. A look-up table might include a list of part numbers of all construction materials used in a project—for example, with the price of each. To create an item entry, the user would simply enter the part num-

MATERIALS	Units	Type	Cost/Unit	Discount	Discounted Price	Sales Tax	Item Total
LUMBER (Board feet)							
	6,000	2 x 4	1.65	=B4*D4*0.05	=B4*D4-E4	=F4*0.08	=F4+G4
	4,000	2 x 6	2.45	=B5*D5*0.05	=B5*D5-E5	=F5*0.08	=F5+G5
	15,000	3/4" ext plywood	0.95	=B6*D6*0.05	=B6*D6-E6	=F6*0.08	=F6+G6
INSULATION							
	180	Roll 16" R23 Kraft	12.00	=B8*D8*0.05	=B8*D8-E8	=F8*0.08	=F8+G8
	50	Roll 16" R16	8.50	=B9*D9*0.05	=B9*D9-E9	=F9*0.08	=F9+G9
	200	Lb. loose fiberglass	0.28	=B10*D10*0.05	=B10*D10-E10	=F10*0.08	=F10+G10
FASTENERS							
	100	#10d common	3.57	=B12*D12*0.05	=B12*D12-E12	=F12*0.08	=F12+G12
	20	#8d finish	4.41	=B13*D13*0.05	=B13*D13-E13	=F13*0.08	=F13+G13
	50	#6d roofing	6.45	=B14*D14*0.05	=B14*D14-E14	=F14*0.08	=F14+G14
	50	Box #8 wood	3.00	=B15*D15*0.05	=B15*D15-E15	=F15*0.08	=F15+G15
	20	Box #4 wood	2.75	=B16*D16*0.05	=B16*D16-E16	=F16*0.08	=F16+G16
	540	Joist hanger	0.18	=B17*D17*0.05	=B17*D17-E17	=F17*0.08	=F17+G17
						TOTAL COST	=SUM (H4:H17)

Constants

a. Spreadsheet formulas containing numeric constants.

FIGURE 5-29 **Value of a Separate Independent Variables Area**

ber, and the spreadsheet would look up and record its price. Not all spreadsheets include such features. As you create your physical design, provide space for the features that your spreadsheet requires.

The Summary Area The summary area summarizes the results of calculations. For example, if the calculations generate figures for 100 monthly expenses for a four-year period (a large spreadsheet), you can place a summary of expenses and totals in the summary area. When you change any of the data in the calculations, the values in the summary area are automatically recalculated. The summary area is an excellent place to format one or more output reports for printing.

Building the Spreadsheet

During this stage of spreadsheet application development, you actually create the spreadsheet described in your model and design. This is the time to load your electronic spreadsheet program and construct the spread-

Discount rate: 0.05
Sales tax rate: 0.08

MATERIALS	Units	Type	Cost/Unit	Discount	Discounted Price	Sales Tax	Item Total
LUMBER (Board feet)							
	6,000	2 x 4	1.65	=B6*D6*C1	=B6*D6-E6	=F6*C2	=F6+G6
	4,000	2 x 6	2.45	=B7*D7*C1	=B7*D7-E7	=F7*C2	=F7+G7
	15,000	3/4" ext plywood	0.95	=B8*D8*C1	=B8*D8-E8	=F8*C2	=F8+G8
INSULATION							
	180	Roll 16" R23 Kraft	12.00	=B10*D10*C1	=B10*D10-E10	=F10*C2	=F10+G10
	50	Roll 16" R16	8.50	=B11*D11*C1	=B11*D11-E11	=F11*C2	=F11+G11
	200	Lb. loose fiberglass	0.28	=B12*D12*C1	=B12*D12-E12	=F12*C2	=F12+G12
FASTENERS							
	100	#10d common	3.57	=B14*D14*C1	=B14*D14-E14	=F14*C2	=F14+G14
	20	#8d finish	4.41	=B15*D15*C1	=B15*D15-E15	=F15*C2	=F15+G15
	50	#6d roofing	6.45	=B16*D16*C1	=B16*D16-E16	=F16*C2	=F16+G16
	50	Box #8 wood	3.00	=B17*D17*C1	=B17*D17-E17	=F17*C2	=F17+G17
	20	Box #4 wood	2.75	=B18*D18*C1	=B18*D18-E18	=F18*C2	=F18+G18
	540	Joist hanger	0.18	=B19*D19*C1	=B19*D19-E19	=F19*C2	=F19+G19
						TOTAL COST	=SUM (H6:H19)

Independent Variables

b. The constant values have been moved to an independent variables area, where formulas reference them by address. Putting such key values in an independent variables area makes them easy to find and change.

sheet, write internal documentation, build macros, and enter spreadsheet data and formulas.

This stage may take only a few minutes or hours for a simple spreadsheet application. It might take several days for a large and complex application. What is important is not the amount of time you take, but the careful adhering to your design. If you vary from your original design, you should update your documentation accordingly. Also, develop external documentation during this stage.

Testing the Spreadsheet

As a part of your design, create a very simple set of test data to give your formulas an initial test. Then, when the spreadsheet is completed and apparently working, use a more comprehensive set of test data to give you more confidence that it produces correct results.

Your initial test data should include simple values giving clear results that can easily be checked. For example, to check a sum formula, you might use data values that sum to a round number, such as 1,000. In this way, errors will be apparent, and you will be alerted to correct your work immediately.

When the spreadsheet is completed and seems to be working, test it with a comprehensive series of test cases. At the very minimum, for the simplest of spreadsheets, two or three test cases are needed. The general principle is that, if you test using very small values and then very large values, you may be reasonably confident that your formulas will produce equally correct results for the values in between. Thus, one set of test data should contain the smallest values that are likely to be entered into each input cell, and another set should contain the largest. If your spreadsheet includes several interacting parts or formulas that use the IF function, then you should devise additional test data cases to ensure that a reasonable sampling of the processing options is tested.

Comprehensive testing is important. Too often it is overlooked or poorly done, and the result is spreadsheets that produce incorrect results. Testing can be time-consuming, but it almost certainly will take less time if it is done systematically. Use the following five-step process:

1. Develop and document a set of test cases. Write all test cases on paper. Do this before the actual testing. Creating test cases "on the fly," during the actual testing process, leads to errors and incomplete tests.
2. Calculate the results manually. Using a calculator, figure out what results the program should produce with the test data. Write these results down. Do this before you enter any test data into the spreadsheet.
3. Run the application with the test data you created in step 1.
4. Compare the actual results (the ones produced by the application) with the expected results (the ones produced manually in step 2). If any discrepancies exist, investigate the problem and find an explanation.
5. Debug the spreadsheet. **Debugging** means modifying the spreadsheet to remove any bugs, or flaws. When you believe you have the problem resolved, go back to step 3 and try again. Repeat this process until you get the results you expect.

When you are satisfied that your spreadsheet produces correct output, you can begin to use it with "real" data. But be sure to save the test data in the notebook with your documentation. Then, if questions arise about the correctness of your work, you can demonstrate that you tested the data before you began to use the spreadsheet. In addition, if you ever modify the spreadsheet (say, by changing formulas, inserting new columns, or writing a macro), then you can rerun the application with the original test cases, knowing that the original spreadsheet processed them correctly. Having a set of test cases available can be very helpful and timesaving.

Summary

An electronic spreadsheet is a program that enables you to use the power of a personal computer to manipulate data in a spreadsheet format. Its power arises from the fact that you can define formulas so the computer performs all your calculations. And when any data on the spreadsheet changes, all the figures affected by the change are automatically recalculated. It also offers larger size than practical manual spreadsheets and can produce presentation graphics—charts that summarize and visually compare data.

Spreadsheets are used extensively for numerical summaries and for financial modeling. They also can be used for record keeping, though that is not their primary strength. Because it comes from the computer, spreadsheet output is sometimes given more weight than it deserves in decision making.

Key elements of spreadsheet operations that should be understood include spreadsheet screen, process of entering and formatting alphanumeric and numeric data (including formulas), command structure, spreadsheet printing process, macros, templates, consolidation and linking, and presentation graphics.

Developing a spreadsheet application should be done systematically. Appropriate steps are designing the model, designing the spreadsheet, building the spreadsheet, and testing the spreadsheet.

Key Terms

electronic spreadsheet
column
row
cell
address
coordinates
formula
function
automatic recalculation
window
split screen
simulation
financial model
import
home
control panel
cursor
current cell
label
constant
range
display format
justification
range name
condensed print
landscape printing
macro
template
presentation graphics
assumption
decision
workspace
spreadsheet map
independent variable
debugging

Review Questions

1. How long have electronic spreadsheets been commercially available?
2. Describe the physical structure of a spreadsheet.
3. What is a cell?
4. How does a user refer to a specific cell?
5. What is a formula?
6. Describe what a spreadsheet function does.
7. Explain the automatic recalculation feature.
8. Why is the automatic recalculation feature so helpful to users?
9. What is a window?
10. Describe the split-screen feature.
11. Name and explain three applications of electronic spreadsheets.
12. How might an electronic spreadsheet program and a DBMS be used together?
13. Are the numbers on an electronic spreadsheet always correct? Should they always be accepted as true?
14. Differentiate among the three basic types of spreadsheet programs.
15. Define these terms: *home, control panel, cursor, current cell.*
16. Differentiate between alphanumeric cell entries and numeric cell entries.
17. How does the spreadsheet program differentiate between alphanumeric entries and numeric entries?
18. Ordinarily what is displayed in a cell that contains a formula?
19. Write the formula to find the average of the values in cells B17 through B20.
20. Name three display aspects that can be modified by cell formatting commands.
21. Describe the commands used in spreadsheets.
22. What is a range name?
23. Define condensed print and landscape printing.
24. What is a macro?
25. Describe the purpose of a template.
26. Define consolidation and linking. What are these techniques used for?
27. What kind of information is conveyed with a line graph? A bar graph? A pie graph?
28. To show the portion of each tax dollar spent on medical expenses versus other types of expenditures, what type of presentation graph would you use?
29. Describe the process of developing a spreadsheet application.
30. Differentiate between designing the model and designing the spreadsheet.
31. What is an assumption? What is a decision?
32. What is a spreadsheet map?
33. Describe internal documentation and external documentation.
34. Describe the process of testing a spreadsheet application.

Discussion Questions

A. It has been said that the electronic spreadsheet changed the way Americans do business. Do you agree or disagree? Give several reasons for your answer.

B. Name the five most important reasons for the popularity of the electronic spreadsheet program. If possible, compare your answers to those of other students in your class. After discussion, see if you can agree on a single list of five reasons that represent your group's combined thinking.

C. It has been said that electronic spreadsheets made microcomputers popular. It has also been said that personal computers made electronic spreadsheets possible. Both have enjoyed enormous popularity in the past ten years. Why do you suppose they both "came of age" at the same time?

D. Drawing on your knowledge of business, your past business experiences, or your own personal business activities, describe the following: three specific numeric summary applications of spreadsheets other than those described in this chapter, three financial modeling applications, and three record-keeping applications. Take several sentences to give a clear picture of the usefulness of each application.

E. Briefly describe three applications for spreadsheet templates, other than checkbook register and departmental budgeting. For each, what major elements would be included in the template?

F. As a way of summarizing the differences between the uses of the various types of graphs, describe at least six applications of graphs other than those discussed in the chapter. For each, select the best type of graph for the application and explain the reasons for your selection. If possible, share your conclusions with other members of your class and see whether your group can agree on a set of choices and reasons.

G. Design on paper a small spreadsheet for some particular purpose. (What are the elements that should be included in such a description?) If possible, develop your program using a graphics-based spreadsheet program such as Excel. Now, if possible, use a character-based program, such as Lotus 1-2-3, Release 2.2, to develop it. Compare the results. How easy or how difficult was each to learn? How easy or how difficult was each to use?

H. Suppose you were given an electronic spreadsheet program as a gift. Describe the first application you would develop for it. Be specific. If you have access to a spreadsheet program, develop that application.

I. Design a spreadsheet application to track your personal income and school-related expenses for the next two years. Follow the steps for spreadsheet application development described in this chapter. If you have access to an electronic spreadsheet program, implement and test the application.

MINICASE

International Spreadsheets

If your work spans the globe, you can use Microsoft Excel versions 3.0 and 4.0 for Windows to easily exchange data with users in different countries. To help break through the business barriers between countries, Microsoft designed Microsoft Excel to automatically deal with differences in date, number, and currency formats, built-in named ranges, find-and-replace operations, and macros.

Microsoft Excel reads the date, number, and currency settings individually from the international Control Panel of Windows so you can choose any combination that best suits your needs. In addition, Microsoft Excel retains currency formats already entered in a worksheet to prevent the currency confusion that can happen when you use other spreadsheet applications to convert worksheets. While retaining previously entered currency formats, Microsoft Excel does convert thousands separators and decimal points.

International macro sheets in Microsoft Excel

Microsoft Excel versions 3.0 and 4.0 have an international macro sheet format for transferring macros between countries. You can run international macros without having to convert files to another language version of Microsoft Excel. Put simply, we've taught foreign language versions of Microsoft Excel to understand English functions.

Creating international macros in the United States

You can create a new international macro by selecting the Int'l Macro option from the New command on the File menu. You can also save a standard macro created in Microsoft Excel 2.x, 3.0, or 4.0 as an international macro by using the Save As command on the File menu. If necessary, you can translate quoted text strings.
Note: The Int'l Macro option appears in the New dialog box only if you select a non-U.S. country setting in the Windows Control Panel.

Creating international macros outside the United States

When you create a new international macro, make sure that all functions and formulas are in English with U.S. country settings. This international macro will run without modification in different language versions of Microsoft Excel. You can also save an existing macro created in a non-English version of Microsoft Excel as an international macro by using the Save As command on the File menu. Microsoft Excel converts functions and formulas to English, with U.S. country settings. You must manually convert text arguments within certain functions for the macro to run with other language versions of Microsoft Excel.

If you're working with an international macro, Microsoft Excel displays and uses U.S. defaults in dialog boxes. If you switch to any other worksheet, Microsoft Excel displays local language defaults.

Questions

1. Summarize the capabilities described in this advertisement. Describe a task that you think would require these capabilities.
2. Suppose you receive spreadsheets that produce projections of your company's product sales in Europe. Assume you receive a separate spreadsheet for France, Germany, England, Spain, and Italy. Also assume that projections for each spreadsheet are expressed in both units and local currencies. Your boss asks you to produce a report summarizing total European sales. Describe the major tasks you would need to accomplish to create such a report.
3. What features and functions are described in the above ad that you think would be helpful in producing the report in question 2? Assume that all of the spreadsheets you receive are in Excel format. How would your answer change if some of the spreadsheets were in Lotus 1-2-3 format, some in Quattro Pro format,.and some were in Excel format?
4. Describe the advantages that would occur if all of the offices in your company were to use the same spreadsheet product. Describe the disadvantages. Suppose your boss asks you to recommend a spreadsheet for use by all divisions of the company in all locations. Describe the factors that you would need to consider.

Excerpted from Microsoft's *View* (May 1992): p. 3.

CHAPTER 6

Personal Database Applications

Jerry is responsible for the Southern California–Arizona sales district for a manufacturer of laboratory instruments. As a sales representative, he calls on potential customers, provides product information and technical support, accepts orders, and helps customers remain satisfied with his company's products and services. He is paid a commission on company sales in his district.

Several months ago, his company gave each representative a battery-powered portable computer with programs for product pricing and order entry. Since each product came in many versions and configurations, pricing and order entry were difficult and had been sources of problems in the past.

As Jerry considered additional uses for his computer, the most important one seemed to be getting control of his customer files, which were spread all over his home office—two bulging file drawers plus stacks of notes and papers on the desk, chair, and floor.

The reason was simple: His most important resource was the time he had available to call on customers. To maximize his commission, he needed to schedule customer calls efficiently. For example, if he made a four-day trip from home to Phoenix, he needed to call on all the most important Phoenix customers. He did not want to remember a week later that he missed one customer and then have to travel back.

In addition, he needed to manage the notes he made after calls. At follow-up calls on each customer, he needed to answer questions, check on concerns, and remember personal things about the contact person that might help make conversation. In the past, his notes had often disappeared—they had been misfiled or had sat in piles waiting to be filed. The experience of walking into a contact's office with no memory of past conversations was all too common.

CHAPTER OUTLINE

EXAMPLE: TRACKING CUSTOMERS

Jerry was faced with a business problem: how to maximize the use of his time in calling on customers. If his time had not been limited, he could have called on every customer frequently.

His new computer came with a word processing program, an electronic spreadsheet program, and a personal **database management system (DBMS)**, a program that manipulates data in databases. After briefly considering the spreadsheet program as a solution to his problem, Jerry decided to use the DBMS. Although he was already very familiar with the spreadsheet program, he remembered warnings he had read (such as those later in this chapter) about the very limited list-management facilities of spreadsheets. He figured the extra time it took to learn to use a DBMS would pay off in better results.

Jerry recognized that typing in data on more than 400 active customers in his district would be a very large job. Unless the DBMS made the data more useful in some ways that added directly to his income, he felt that he should spend his time on other activities that would.

The value he hoped to get from the DBMS arose from its ability to provide reports that would be difficult or excessively time-consuming to produce by hand. To create these reports, Jerry would have to use selection and sorting operations to produce a particular subset of the data ordered in a particular way. For example, if Jerry could get one report showing Phoenix customers by volume with the highest-volume customers at the top, and another report arranged by the amount of time since his last call, then he could quickly and confidently schedule calls for his next trip to Phoenix.

After jotting down ideas over a few days' time, Jerry arrived at a tentative set of goals for the project. To plan an efficient schedule of calls, he

FIGURE 6-1
Checking the Numbers
With his laptop computer, Jerry can provide accurate estimates no matter where the sales meeting takes place.

wanted to produce lists of customers in particular areas (represented by groups of zip codes). These lists would be ranked by potential purchase vol ume (represented by dollar volume of purchases last year) and by date of his last call. Since the computer was portable, he would have it with him on calls. Therefore, he decided to include customer notes so he could quickly check them before walking into the contact's office.

Based on these goals, Jerry spent a weekend developing a simple data model, creating a database, and testing it with about a dozen records of sample data. Figure 6-2*a* shows the structure of Jerry's database.

Jerry decided to hire a temporary clerical worker to enter the remaining data. As a result, he did not have to enter all the data himself, but cleaning up his files and pulling together all the material from the piles in his office was still a major task. He also found that he had to verify the worker's data entry more carefully than his own—in addition to typographical errors, she sometimes made mistakes because she misunderstood information in Jerry's files. It was several weeks later when the full database was ready for use.

Almost immediately the first challenge arose. At a regional sales meeting, the company announced an important new series of products in its spectrum analyzer line and asked all sales reps to make calls on companies who had made purchases in that product line in the past. Brochures were to be delivered, and information about the products, presented. In his office, it took Jerry less than 20 minutes to identify all the companies who had purchased that product line in the past, and he began scheduling calls almost immediately.

After a few months of experience with the new system, Jerry identified the following advantages. First, his call records showed that he was making about 15 percent more calls per week because his computer-aided planning let him minimize travel time between calls, concentrating a day's

CUSTOMER
Company_name
Contact_person
Contact_address
Contact_city
Contact_state
Contact_zip
Contact_location (building, office number, etc.)
Sales_volume (last year's volume in thousands of dollars)
Date_of_last_call
Product_line (code representing one of nine company lines)
Contact_notes

a.

COMPANY
Company_name
Company_address
Company_city
Company_state
Company_zip
Sales_vol

CONTACT
Contact_name
Contact_address
Contact_city
Contact_state
Contact_zip
Contact_location
Prod_line
Last_call
Notes

b.

FIGURE 6-2

A Customer Database
Jerry's customer database began as a single table (a). Later, he added a second table to make the database more useful (b).

calls in one area. Second, he was able to ensure that he regularly called on all high-volume customers. Finally, his notes from previous calls were nearly always available for review just before each call. Since his system had been implemented, he had not had to walk into a customer's office once with no memory of the previous call.

THE BENEFITS OF PERSONAL DATABASE INFORMATION SYSTEMS

Personal DBMSs are used by people who need to keep track of something. Consequently, the types of problems solved by a personal DBMS involve record keeping of one sort or another. Because personal DBMSs are relatively inexpensive and easy to use, many people purchase them to keep track of just a few simple files. On the other hand, because personal DBMSs are versatile and powerful, other people use them to address complex applications involving dozens of interrelated tables containing thousands of rows and hundreds of columns. Beyond just creating databases, DBMS support helps users manipulate data in a number of ways.

Record Keeping with a Single Table

Taking advantage of its user-friendly definition and manipulation functions, some people use a DBMS to maintain just a single table. Examples include Jerry's customer list in the example above; a club's mailing list; a caterer's recipes; and a personal library of books, videocassettes, audiotapes, or compact disks. Although using a DBMS rather than a simpler list-management program for such record keeping might seem like overkill, for the person who already knows how to use a DBMS, it may be simpler to use that program than to learn a separate list manager program.

Record Keeping with Related Tables

Unlike the applications just described, which involved only one table, some personal DBMS applications involve several tables of related data. For example, suppose Jerry discovers that, in some customer companies, he needs to call on more than one contact person. For example, one contact person may be responsible for ordering certain products, and another, for ordering other products. In this case, Jerry may redesign his database by creating two tables: a table of companies and a table of contact persons. They are two different entities, yet they are related. The tables might look like those shown in Figure 6-2*b*.

Questions such as the following can be answered by consulting only one of the two tables:

- What is the total volume of sales to all companies in the territory last year?

- How many companies in this territory purchase more than half-a-million-dollars' worth of goods from us annually?
- To prepare a mailing list for special promotional literature, what are the names and addresses of all the contact persons primarily interested in the spectrum analyzer product line?
- Which companies have addresses with 85705 zip codes?

In other instances, however, both tables (or more, if they exist) are needed:

- Which contact persons primarily interested in the spectrum analyzer product line work for companies with purchase volumes greater than $100,000 annually?
- What are the names and telephone numbers of contact persons in companies located in Phoenix?
- What are the names and sales volumes of companies with more than one contact person?

In such a situation, a database application would be very effective. Once developed and tested, the application enables the user to address those problems efficiently.

Manipulating the Data

When data is stored in a database, users need to manipulate it in a variety of ways. For example, they need to add and delete data, obtain printed listings of data, sort the data, select subsets of data, and get answers to questions like those listed above. The DBMS provides facilities to do all these things.

THE COMPONENTS OF A PERSONAL DATABASE INFORMATION SYSTEM

A personal database information system has five components: database, DBMS, application program, set of forms for manipulating the data, and user (see Figure 6-3). The database contains the data, the relationships among the data, and a description of how the data is stored. The DBMS provides basic resources to define and manipulate database data. The application defines particular manipulations of the data in ways specified by the user's design. The forms specify data entry screens, report formats, and on-screen menus, and they provide a way of asking questions about the data. The user is responsible for defining the data to be stored and the needs to be served by the system. We will consider each component in turn.

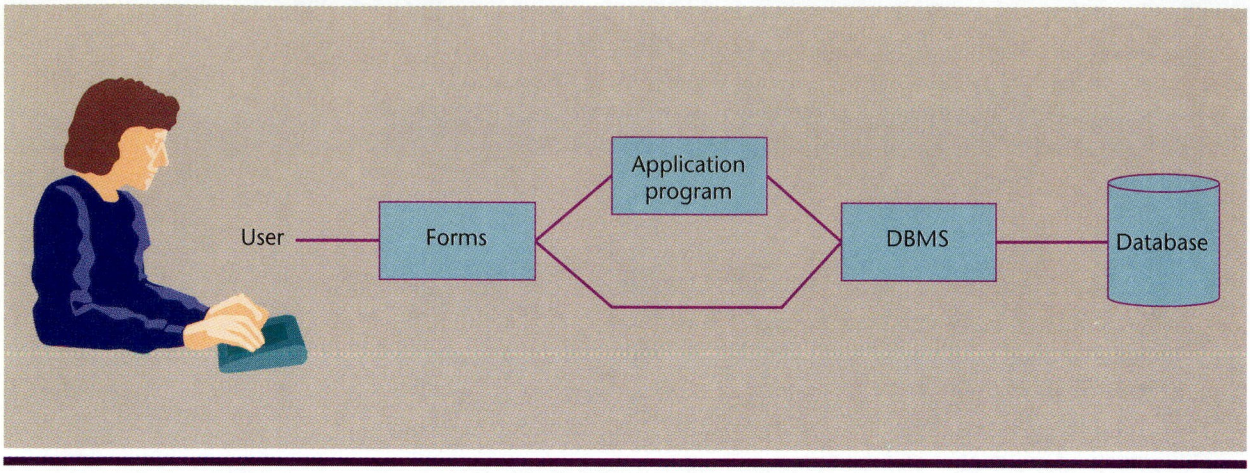

FIGURE 6-3 **Components of a Personal Database Information System**

What Is a Database?

A **database** is a self-describing collection of integrated records. Unlike data files, whose physical structures must be known by the programmers who write code to process them, a database contains its own description, which can be read by the DBMS. The net result is that less effort needs to be spent on writing code, so that more effort can be spent on solving business problems. In addition, a data file normally consists of a series of records that share the same structure. In a database, some records will share the same structure, but others may share a different structure. There may be many sets of records, each with different structures. In addition to storing the data records themselves, the database also stores information about the relationships among the data. This is what we mean when we say that the database is integrated. Let's consider an example.

Imagine a small retailer who needs to keep track of customers, salespeople, and sales. He might have one file cabinet filled with customer records, another file cabinet filled with sales personnel records, and a third file cabinet filled with sales receipts (see Figure 6-4). Each customer's record contains the same kind of data: account number, name, address, telephone number, and account balance. Similarly, appropriate details are stored about each salesperson and each sale. Notice that the sales receipt shown in Figure 6-4 contains both the name of the customer who made the purchase (Johnson, Inc.) and the name of the salesperson who closed the deal (Katz).

Figure 6-5 shows the same data stored in tables. The CUSTOMER table contains columns for account number, name, address, telephone number, and balance. Likewise, the SALESPERSON and SALE tables contain columns for appropriate details. A column corresponds to a field, as defined in Chapter 2. Each row in the CUSTOMER table describes a customer; each row in the SALESPERSON table describes a salesperson; and so on. Thus, a row corresponds to a record, and a table roughly corresponds to a file.

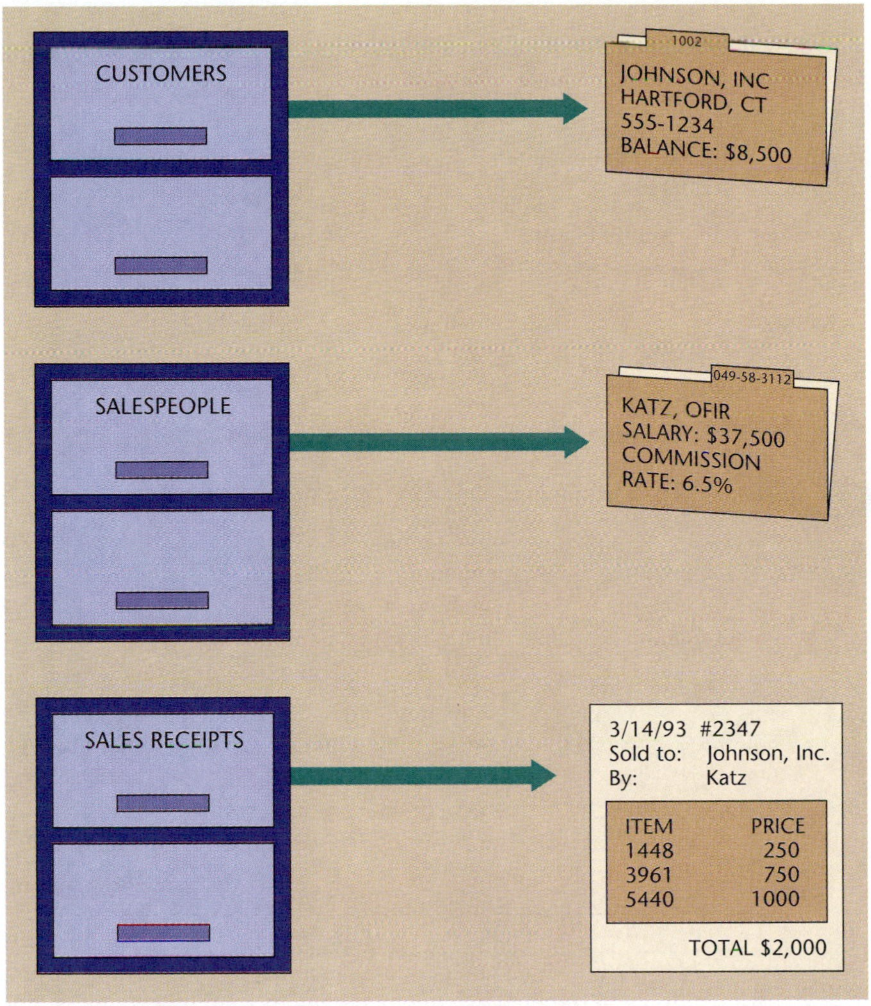

FIGURE 6-4
Data in File Folders Used by a Retailer

In the CUSTOMER table, the Account Number field has a unique value for each customer. In the SALESPERSON table, the Social Security Number field has a unique value for each salesperson. Such identifying fields are called **key fields**.

Notice that no matter how the retailer stores his data—in file cabinets or in computerized tables—the data is essentially the same. In either case, he is keeping track of three related things: customers, salespeople, and sales. Look at the diagram in Figure 6-6. Each rectangle represents an entity that is important to the retailer. A line between two rectangles means that the two entities are related. For example, a sale occurs when a customer purchases something. Therefore, the customer and the sale are related.

By storing his data in a database, the retailer can employ powerful DBMS software to retrieve and manipulate the data. He can answer questions such as the following:

CUSTOMER

Account Number	Name	Address	Phone Number	Balance
1002	Johnson, Inc.	Hartford, CT	555-1234	$8,500

SALESPERSON

Social Security Number	Name	Salary	Commission Rate
049-58-3112	Katz, Ofir	$37,500	6.5

SALE

Sale Number	Date	Amount	Customer Account Number	Salesperson Social Security Number
2347	03/14/93	$2,000	1002	049-58-3112

FIGURE 6-5
The Retailer's Data in Table Form

- Which customers made purchases on August 1?
- What did Akim Associates buy this month?
- Did Bob Asbury sell anything to customers in Springfield last week?

Databases are often far more complex than the example we have been discussing. And many DBMSs are very complex and very powerful. But to the user, a DBMS appears to be simple and straightforward—it just manipulates a collection of related tables. And if it is designed properly, a database application such as the one described at the beginning of this chapter is easy to use.

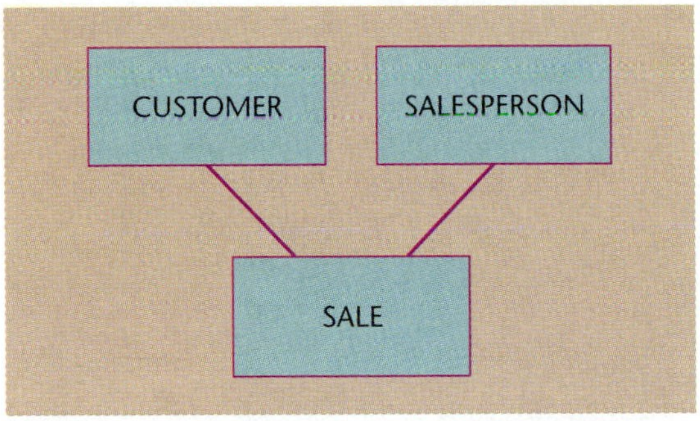

FIGURE 6-6
Entity Relationships

What Is a DBMS?

A DBMS is a program (or set of programs) that develops and uses databases and database applications. A DBMS provides the user with three sets of tools. First, it provides a means of defining the database itself. This is done with a **data definition language (DDL)**. Second, a DBMS provides a means of accessing (storing, retrieving, and changing) database data. This is done via the **data manipulation language (DML)**. Third, the more user-friendly DBMSs also provide easy-to-use tools to define the database and database application components. These components include menus, reports, and data entry forms. Widely used personal DBMSs are Paradox, dBase IV, R-Base, Double Helix, and Oracle.

Most personal DBMSs include application-development tools. Consequently, you do not have to learn DDL or DML. Instead, you can load your personal DBMS into your computer and use the application-development tools that are provided. Unknown to you, the development software constructs the appropriate DDL or DML commands, while you define your database and application interfaces by filling in forms on the screen. In other words, the software does the hard work for you.

One special type of personal DBMS (which was mentioned earlier in this chapter) should properly be termed a **list manager**. Its main purpose is to automate the storage and retrieval of data in a single table. Widely used list managers are Q&A, PC-File, and Filemaker Pro.

Enforcing Constraints Many DBMSs can enforce **constraints** on database data. A constraint is a limitation to permit only certain data to be stored. For example, a salesperson keeping track of customers and sales might establish the constraint that any sale added to his table must be for one of his customers. Thus, if his customers' account numbers are 12, 45, 64, 99, and 104, the database application will prevent him from entering a sale for customer number 401. The benefit of constraint enforcement is that the DBMS automatically checks the data as it is entered. The salesperson will discover immediately that he has typed 401 rather than 104, and he can correct it right away.

Consider again (from the beginning of this chapter) the database that Jerry designed to keep track of customers. For each customer, Jerry included the name of the contact person—the individual in that company on whom he called. In building his customer database, Jerry might have considered placing a constraint on the data so that every contact person would have to be associated with a company. Before he had done this, however, he would have had to consider whether any circumstance might arise in which a contact person should not be associated with a company. What do you think he should have done?

What Is a Database Application?

You may often need to process database data in a way that built-in DBMS functions—such as adding, editing, deleting, and sorting data—cannot handle. DBMSs are designed to make the storage and retrieval of data easy. And they provide features that make simple report writing and data maintenance straightforward. However, some business problems are not easily solved with the data-retrieval features of a DBMS. These problems require further programming. In such cases you may need to develop a **database application program**.

For example, suppose the retailer wants his application to do the following: (1) compute salespersons' paychecks; (2) automatically deposit the paychecks in the salespersons' bank accounts; (3) write a summary report; and (4) record all the transactions on disk. Some of the data required to compute paychecks is found in the database (for example, salary and commission rate are part of the SALESPERSON table, and total sales for each salesperson can be derived from the SALE table). But other details used in the computations, such as deductions, withholding tax rates, federal insurance rates, and so forth, are found elsewhere. In addition, the retailer's

FIGURE 6-7

Retail Database Application In a retail store, a database application can maintain data on sales, customers, and salespersons. It can produce a variety of useful information.

DBMS does not have communications abilities for transferring the funds to the bank accounts; it cannot do all the necessary calculations; and it cannot write the resulting data to disk. (It could write a report to disk, but this is not a report.) Thus, an application program is needed to extract data from the database, do the calculations, and issue the required output.

Such database applications are as complex to develop as are computer programs for any other purpose, and they are normally designed by professional systems developers or consultants and written by professional programmers. To use such an application, the user runs it and chooses from a predefined list of options to carry out tasks supported by the application. The user does not need to know what the structure of the database is, how the application works, or how to write program code. The user does not even have to know how to operate the DBMS.

Consider the example database in Figure 6-8. The retailer who owns this database might need to perform the following business functions:

CUSTOMER

Account Number	Name	Address	Phone Number	Balance
1002	Johnson, Inc.	Hartford, CT	555-1234	$8,500
1009	Akim Assoc.	Wethersfield, CT	555-6901	$7,000
1028	Dane, M.	Springfield, MA	555-1977	$5,200
2402	Annino, E.	Clinton, CT	555-0652	$4,900

SALESPERSON

Social Security Number	Name	Salary	Commission Rate
049-58-3112	Katz, Ofir	$37,500	6.5
286-00-0552	Asbury, Bob	$42,900	7.2
111-22-3333	Trask, Judy	$38,000	6.9

SALE

Sale Number	Date	Amount	Customer Account Number	Salesperson Social Security Number
2347	03/14/93	$2,000	1002	049-58-3112
2348	03/14/93	$2,500	1028	111-22-3333
2349	03/14/93	$6,000	1009	049-58-3112

FIGURE 6-8

Customers, Salespersons, and Sales

- Adding new customers, salespeople, and sales
- Changing data about customers, salespeople, and sales
- Deleting customers, salespeople, and sales
- Extracting information from the database to answer questions
- Printing reports containing data extracted from the tables
- Issuing salespeople's paychecks

These functions are provided by the database application program.

(4)

What Are Database Forms?

Most DBMSs include facilities for creating data entry screens, report forms, query forms, and menus. These forms can be used by a database application program, or they can be used when the user directly interacts with the DBMS to manipulate the data. For example, to add a new customer to the database, the retailer can run his database application program and select the Add Customer function. In response, the application program will display the appropriate data entry form. Alternatively, the retailer may directly interact with the DBMS (without using the application program) by entering DBMS commands to select the CUSTOMER table and add a row, using the same data entry form.

Data Entry Forms **Data entry forms** are custom-developed video displays used to enter and change the data in a particular database. In Figure 6-9 you can see a data entry form for entering a sales receipt. A video form can resemble the hard copy paper forms of the business and thus facilitate interaction with the database. Some of the data in Figure 6-9 is entered by the user (for example, sale number and customer account number). Some of it (such as customer name) is looked up by the DBMS and displayed on the computer screen. Look back at the CUSTOMER table in Figure 6-8. Once the user enters the account number, the DBMS can automatically retrieve the customer name. And some of the data on the form is computed and displayed (for example, the total).

This form can be used to display and possibly change sales data that is already stored in the table. Suppose a clerk mistakenly entered Ofir Katz's Social Security number for a sale instead of Bob Asbury's. By bringing up the sales record in this form, the retailer could change the "Sold by" entry.

Reports A **report form** is a hard copy output of database data. It is by far the most common way of displaying database data. Reports can contain data from one or several tables. Well-designed reports make the output information much easier to use, so take the time to design useful and readable reports. A report should be attractively formatted with report and page headings, date, page numbers, column headings, summary lines, and totals. Figure 6-10 shows an example report form.

Queries A **query** is a question about the data. This question is answered

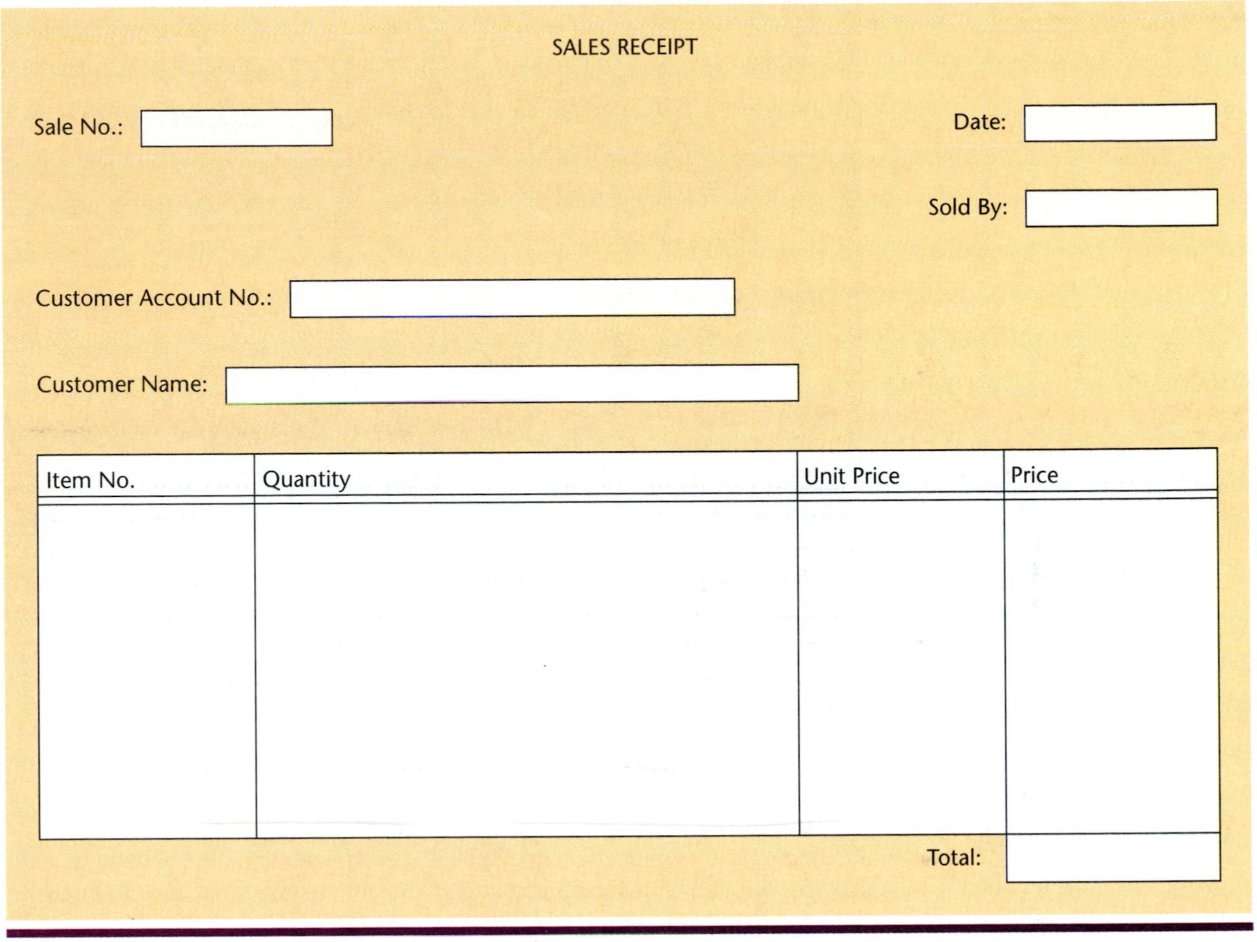

FIGURE 6-9
Data Entry Form for Sales Receipt

by selecting data that meets certain criteria. The answer may be in the form of a summary, such as a count of customers whose purchases totaled more than $1,000 last year or the total value of purchases sold by Ofir Katz last month. Or, the answer may consist of a list of data, such as the names and addresses of customers with current account balances over $1,000.

The DBMS includes a **query language**, which is a general-purpose language for obtaining data from the database. To phrase a query, you must understand how your database data is linked together (that is, how you can use data from one table to look up data in another table). For instance, using the data in Figure 6-8, answer the following questions:

1. To which customers did Judy Trask make sales?
2. With which salesperson(s) did Johnson, Inc., do business?
3. Did any salespeople make sales in Springfield, Massachusetts? If so, who?

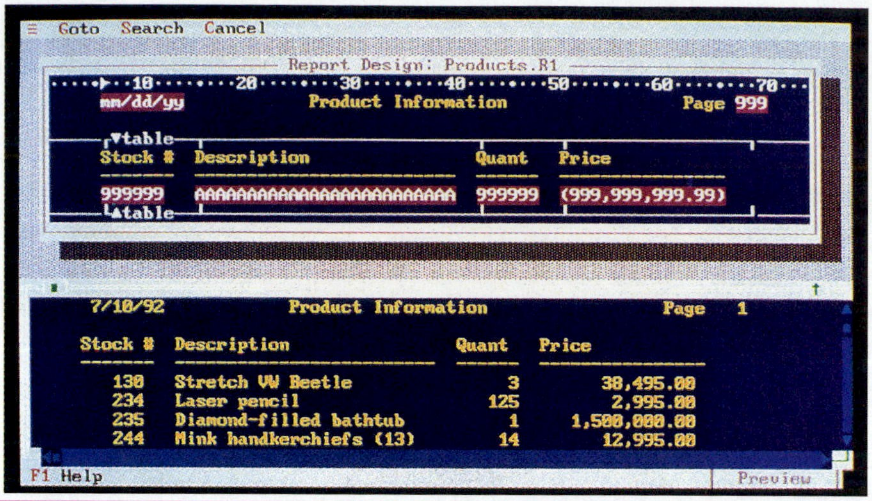

FIGURE 6-10
Report Form

4. How much money did Ofir Katz make in commissions on these sales?

Your answers should have been: (1) M. Dane and ~~E. Annino~~; (2) Ofir Katz and ~~Bob Asbury~~; (3) yes, Judy Trask; and (4) $520. If these were not your answers, keep working on the questions until you figure out how to use the data to answer them.

The important aspect of this exercise was to show you how to find the desired data by going from one table to another. For instance, to figure out how much money Ofir Katz made in commissions, look up Ofir's row in the SALESPERSON table and determine his Social Security number and commission rate. Then look in the SALE table for all the sales containing his Social Security number. (There are two.) Next, sum the amounts for the two sales (the total is $8,000) and multiply the sum by Ofir's commission rate (6.5%), which is found in the SALESPERSON table. The answer is $520.

Imagine how difficult that task would have been if all the data were stored on paper in file cabinets. The beauty of storing such data in a database and using a personal DBMS to access it is that these questions (and many others) can be answered quickly and easily with just a few keystrokes because the data is stored with the relationships maintained. Of course, in the exercise you maneuvered your own way through the tables. If you used an actual DBMS to answer, say, question 2 above, you would enter a query language instruction such as the following:

```
SELECT NAME
FROM SALESPERSON
WHERE CUSTOMER-ACCOUNT-NUMBER = '1002'
  AND
SOCIAL-SECURITY-NUMBER.SALESPERSON =
SALESPERSON-SOCIAL-SECURITY-NUMBER.SALE
```

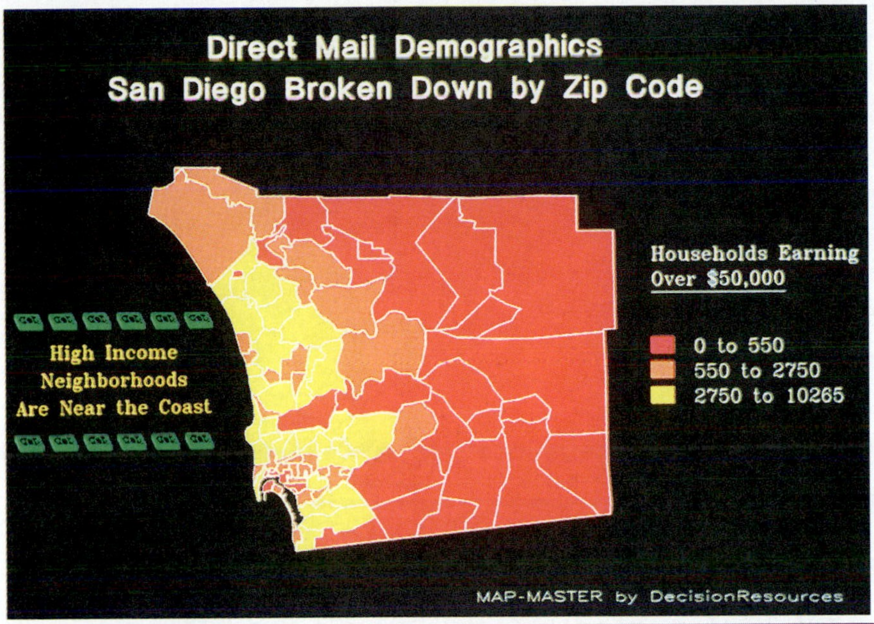

FIGURE 6-11
Specialized Database Output
Database output can be in graphics form, such as this map, which displays database data about households in a market area.

The DBMS's response to the query would be as follows:

```
Katz, Ofir
Asbury, Bob
```

This query is written in SQL, the standard query language for DBMSs. It is used by programmers to write application programs.

Ad hoc queries are questions about the data that arise from time to time—questions that were not specifically envisioned when the database and its application were designed. For example, Jerry must call on a customer in Prescott tomorrow, and, in case he finishes the appointment early, he may have time to call on other customers in the Prescott area. He can use an ad hoc query to get a list of those customers.

Ad hoc queries can be entered using SQL, and some advanced users learn SQL well enough to use it effectively. But most personal DBMSs provide tools that make ad hoc queries easier than remembering the rules of SQL. One common approach is **query by example (QBE)**. Using QBE, the DBMS displays on the screen forms that show table and row structure of the database. The user specifies the fields to be retrieved and the retrieval criteria simply by selecting from the display. Then the QBE facility translates that information into the query language statements needed to complete the task. Figure 6-12 shows a QBE screen.

Menu Menus are lists of actions with which the user can tell the computer to perform specific application functions. Sometimes choosing an option on one menu causes the application to display another menu, and so forth, for several levels. An example of a menu for the retailer appears

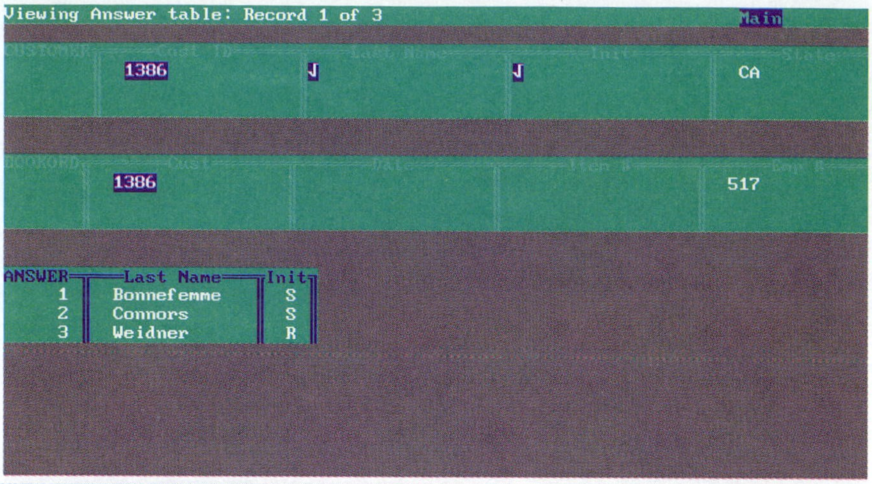

FIGURE 6-12
Query by Example
By making entries into a query-by-example form, the user of this database has requested the names of all California customers whose orders were accepted by employee number 517. To answer the request, the DBMS must relate data in two tables, CUSTOMER and BOOKORD. The result is placed in a third table named ANSWER.

in Figure 6-13. As you can see, selecting the Sale option from the original menu causes the Sale menu to be displayed. Menus are usually used with an application program.

What Is the User's Role?

The user has a two-part role in a personal database information system. First, the user is ultimately responsible to define the problem that the system must solve and the requirements that the system must meet. The user may call on the services of a professional systems analyst or consultant, but the user takes final responsibility. Second, the user is responsible for the operation of the system: entering data, requesting output, and so on.

For very simple systems, the user may also take the role of developer. If a system can produce the required results without an application program, then an experienced user may develop it personally. However, when programming is required, most users employ a programmer or a consultant to get the development job done correctly and efficiently.

Choosing Between Spreadsheet Application and Database Application

Many people are unclear about the appropriate uses of spreadsheet and database applications. In fact, spreadsheets and DBMSs are quite different programs, and they are intended to meet two separate needs.

Spreadsheet programs make repetitive calculations on interrelated variables. Some spreadsheet programs offer a very basic set of commands for querying data within the rows and columns. These facilities encourage unknowing users to attempt to perform DBMS functions with a spreadsheet. This is unfortunate. The facilities are crude and cumbersome and usually serve to create more problems for the user than they solve.

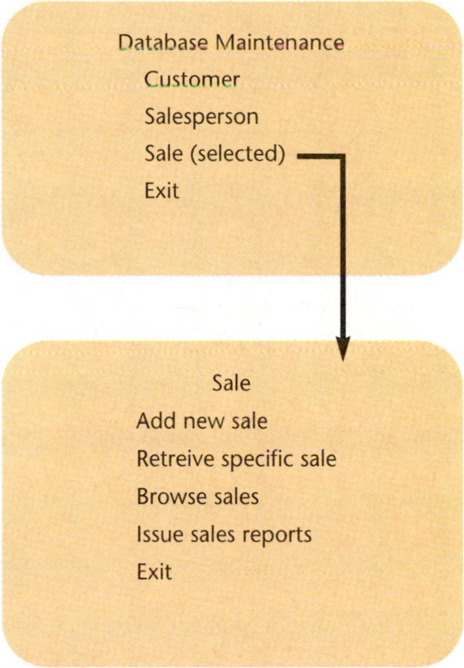

FIGURE 6-13
Menus for a Retail Application

DBMSs are designed to keep track of facts and figures about entities such as employees and schedules. DBMSs manage tables of data, and they provide a means for creating, changing, deleting, and displaying values in those tables. Rows in database tables are not related to one another by formula as they are in a spreadsheet. Rather, they are related by data-item value. For example, an EMPLOYEE table row and a SCHEDULE table row are related if the value of EmpName in EMPLOYEE matches the value of EmpName in SCHEDULE.

Some DBMSs offer formula-calculation capabilities that are similar to those available in spreadsheet programs. With these facilities, users sometimes attempt to do spreadsheet work with a DBMS. This, too, is a mistake. The facilities available are generally not robust enough. In any case, it will take longer and be more cumbersome to attempt spreadsheet analysis with the DBMS.

Finally, an important difference exists in the way that spreadsheets and DBMSs handle data. A spreadsheet product assumes that the computer's RAM is large enough to hold the user's spreadsheet. The user is thus restricted to that amount of data. A DBMS, on the other hand, does not make this assumption. Most DBMSs assume that databases may involve millions of characters of data, and so they use both active memory and magnetic disk during their processing. This means, in general, that a DBMS can process, at any one time, far more data than can a spreadsheet program.

Sometimes a user may need to process the same data both in spreadsheet fashion and in DBMS fashion. For example, a financial analyst may

INCREASING YOUR PERSONAL PRODUCTIVITY

Box 6.1

Buying Smart: Curing Dataphobia

If the idea of managing a data base gives you the heebie-jeebies, you'll be glad to know that several of these personal data bases are genuinely easy to use. But to find a package that's useful and easy, you must consider each program's data input skills, the flexibility of its forms and views, and its querying and report capabilities, as well as its performance and technical support.

Ease of Use Are the menus well organized, with data input, querying, and reporting functions clearly and logically arranged? How's the help? If you're desperate, several programs include prewritten applications, like address books.

Data Input These programs all support text, number, date, logic and calculated fields. Variable-length memo fields let you add notes to your records without limiting their size ahead of time. Once you've designed your data base, you'll want to be sure the right data gets into it. Lookup tables let you define lists of possible entries for each field, while rules governing data input let you limit a field's entries. Unique fields prevent you from duplicating key information. If you want to use data from another application, most of these programs import ASCII, DBF, and 1-2-3 files.

Forms and Views Once you've input the data, you're going to want to look at it, which is what form and table views are for.

The *form view* is where you input and edit data; it looks something like a paper form. A *forms painter* customizes the form view by rearranging fields and adding lines and boxes. Most programs let you look up information in other files when entering.

A *table view* looks like a spreadsheet and lets you see many records at once. Some programs let you customize the table view by changing the order and width of columns; good ones let you edit data in the table.

Queries and Reports *Querying* is a way of searching for and displaying groups of records. *Query by form* (QBF) is the simplest: A form pops up, and you type in the values you want to search for in the appropriate fields. Unfortunately, QBF won't let you add fields not already in the data base (such as calculations) or query data files that aren't already linked. For these more complicated queries, you need *query by example* (QBE). QBE uses a table instead of a form and lets you link files and add fields.

While queries select records, *reports* summarize information, usually in printed forms. Most programs have *quick-report writers*, which create basic, spreadsheetlike reports. With *band-oriented report writers* you can design more complex reports by dividing the screen into horizontal *bands* for the likes of column headings, details, and subtotals. Some programs have a query and/or report languages that let you further customize your output. *Cross-tab reports* let you summarize several fields at a time in a matrix.

Performance If you're sorting thousands of sales records by three criteria and totaling several fields, you'll appreciate a program's speed.

Service and Support No matter how easy a program is to use, the time will probably come when you'll want to call for help. Unfortunately, many vendors are using 900 numbers these days, which can cost you $2 or $3 a minute.

spend many weeks developing a budget using a spreadsheet program. Then, once the budget is completed and approved, she may choose to store the spreadsheet data in database form, using the DBMS, which allows very efficient searching and retrieval. Most DBMSs and spreadsheet programs exchange data.

In summary, learn to use both spreadsheet programs and DBMSs for their intended purposes. When your work requires both types of processing, exchange the data between the programs. Trying to use a spreadsheet for a DBMS job or a DBMS for a spreadsheet job will create frustration and inefficiency.

DEVELOPING PERSONAL DATABASE APPLICATIONS

Before describing the development of a personal database information system, we must first explain how to build and use a **data model**, which is a statement of data requirements for the database and its applications. Building a data model is the first step in developing a personal database information system. The remaining steps are designing the tables, building the database, testing the database, designing the application, building the application, and testing the application.

The techniques discussed here are used both for the personal database systems described in this chapter and for the large shared database systems described in Chapter 10. Users can employ the following basic guidelines to develop small, simple systems. These are, however, only the bare essentials of a rich, powerful set of techniques that would require an entire college database course to fully explore. You may want to take such a course at a later point in your studies.

Building a Data Model

To develop a database, we must first determine its contents. Since a database application is used to track things that are important to the user, we must find out what those important things are. We must also decide what facts the user wants to record about those things. There are two general approaches for making such determinations: top-down data modeling and bottom-up data modeling.

Top-Down Data Modeling The **top-down data modeling** technique proceeds from the general to the specific, or from the top, down. Using this technique, we consider the user's environment and figure out the things, or **entities**, that are important to the user. An entity is a person, place, thing, or event such as a customer, a warehouse, a piece of equipment, or an order. Once we have determined the entities, we then determine what characteristics, or **properties**, of those entities are important to the user. For example, properties of the customer entity that might be used in a database are customer number, customer name, and customer phone number.

Using top-down modeling, we identify the entities and their properties, and then we assess the **relationships** among those entities. We might determine, for example, that a customer entity is related to an order entity, since customers place orders. More specifically, we might determine that each customer is potentially related to many orders.

Once we have determined an initial set of entities, properties, and relationships, we document those findings using an **entity-relationship**

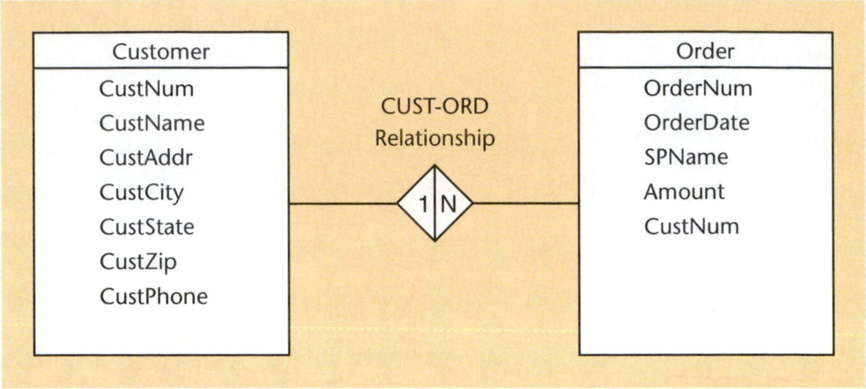

FIGURE 6-14
Example E-R Diagram

CUSTOMER

CustNum	CustName	CustAddr	CustCity	CustState	CustZip	CustPhone
100	Ajax	124 113th	Los Angeles	CA	98004	332-5578
200	Beemis	34 Elm	Culver City	CA	98055	221-4455
300	Xypher	2245 99th	Torrance	CA	98334	213-4456

ORDER

OrderNum	OrderDate	SPName	Amount	CustNum
1000	05/05/93	Jones	$345.88	100
1010	05/05/93	Parks	$122.45	300
1030	05/06/93	Jones	$224.56	100
1040	05/07/93	Jones	$335.44	100

FIGURE 6-15
Example Tables for the E-R Diagram in Figure 6-14

(E-R) diagram. An E-R diagram for customer and order entities is shown in Figure 6-14. In this figure, the entities are listed in rectangles with properties listed below the entity name. Relationships are shown in diamonds. The relationship 1:N inside the diamond means that one customer entity is related to potentially many order entities. The name of the relationship is shown above the diamond.

Once we have the E-R diagram, we transform it into a set of tables—the CUSTOMER and ORDER tables—to be stored in the database. Tables for the E-R diagram in Figure 6-14 are listed in Figure 6-15. We will describe the process for obtaining the tables below.

Bottom-Up Data Modeling The **bottom-up data modeling** technique proceeds from the specific to the general, or from the bottom, up. With this technique, we obtain specific examples from the users and the clien-

CLUB LISTING

Club	Office	Phone	Faculty Advisor
Aeronauts	520 Engineering	7884	R. O. VanDeever
Astronomy	034 Science	2823	J. Hubble
Lacrosse	421 Business	2240	I. J. Short

CLUB MEMBER DATA FORM

Name: Wilson, Kathy D.	Student ID: 425-34-0923
Club: Lacrosse	Class: Junior
Advisor: I. J. Short	Phone: 9556
Address: 242 Rundler Hall Campus	Date Joined: 02/19/90

FIGURE 6-16
Example Form and Report for the Club Database

Clubs/Members
Office
Phone
Faculty advisor
Member name
Student ID
Class
Address
Phone
Club
Advisor
Date joined

a. List of data items.

Data Items about Clubs	Data Items about Members
Club name	Member name
Office	Student ID
Phone	Class
Faculty advisor	Address
	Phone
	Date joined

b. Data items grouped by theme.

FIGURE 6-17 Grouping Data Items

tele about what they need. We gather documents, such as reports and forms that they currently use (or want to have), and analyze those documents in order to determine what the content of the database should be.

Consider the example form and report shown in Figure 6-16. There are several ways of analyzing these documents to do bottom-up data modeling. The simplest and most appropriate method for personal database applications is to list all the data items that appear in these two reports. Such a list is shown in Figure 6-17*a*.

To determine which tables should exist in the database, we examine this list and group together data items that appear to be related to one another by a common theme. The data items in Figure 6-17*a* have two themes: clubs and members. We group the data items around these themes, as shown in Figure 6-17*b*. Also observe in this list that two different names exist for the same data item. The names *faculty advisor* and *advisor* represent the same data item, so we represent that item by a single entry to avoid confusion.

At this point, we transform the list of items into an E-R diagram and proceed as described above. Figure 6-18 shows an E-R diagram for the data in Figure 6-17. The E-R diagram is then transformed into tables. As you will learn in the next section, the E-R diagram in Figure 6-18 would be transformed into the following tables that contain the listed data items:

```
CLUB   (ClubName, Office, ClubPhone, Advisor)
MEMBER (MembName, StudID, Class, Address,
        MembPhone, DateJoined)
```

Sometimes you can use both top-down data modeling and bottom-up data modeling. Proceed from the top and move down until you run out of ideas. Then gather forms and reports and proceed from the bottom and move up. Integrate the designs from the two approaches. For a more extensive discussion of these two processes, see David M. Kroenke's *Database Processing*, 4th edition (New York: Macmillan, 1992).

Creating the Database Design

Two tasks must be accomplished in order to transform an E-R diagram into a database design. First, the tables must be designed, then the relationships among the tables must be represented.

Table Design When developing a database design from an E-R model, we create a table for each entity in the E-R diagram. To minimize duplicated data, every table in a database should have a single theme. After creating a table for each entity, we check the tables to see if they do contain just one theme.

FIGURE 6-18
CLUB-MEMB E-R Diagram

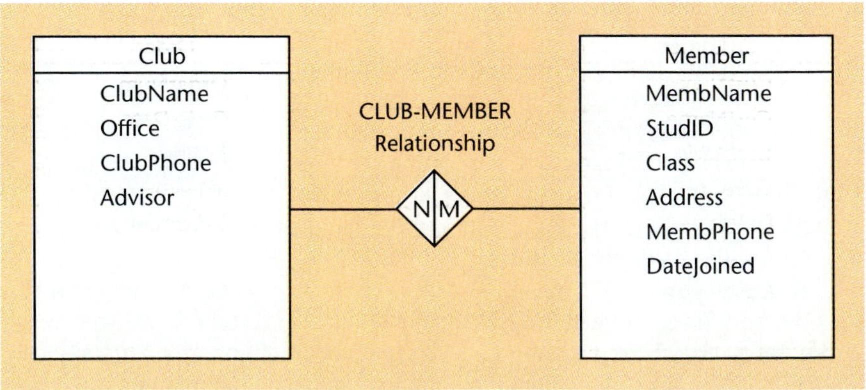

If the entities were constructed by grouping data items, using the bottom-up process, it is likely that each table we create will have only a single theme because such themes were used to group the data items in the first place. Still, it is important to check.

If the entities were developed using the top-down process, then it is possible that some of the resulting tables will have more than one theme. Consider Figure 6-19, which shows a different version of the E-R diagram in Figure 6-14. In Figure 6-19, the Order column contains data about the order, but it also contains additional data about the salesperson's number (SPNum) and commission percentage (SPComPer) for the order. Now, if we create a single table from the order entity, it will have the following format:

```
ORDER  (OrderNum, OrderDate, SPNum,
        SPName, SPComPer, Amount, CustNum)
```

This table contains two themes. There is a theme about orders, but there is also a theme about a salesperson and his or her commission rate. To represent the order entity properly, two tables are required, as shown in Figure 6-20. Observe that the two tables are linked by the common item SPNum.

A *key*, as we have seen, is a column (or group of columns) that identifies one particular row in a table and no other. Since no two rows may have the same key, the key uniquely identifies a row. The key of the ORDER table above is OrderNum since a value of OrderNum will determine a unique row in the ORDER table. The key of SALESPERSON in Figure 6-20 is SPNum.

Sometimes, when documenting table structure, the key of the table is underlined. Thus, the structure of the two tables in Figure 6-20 would be written as follows:

ORDER (<u>OrderNum</u>, OrderDate, SPNum, Amount, CustNum)

SALESPERSON (<u>SPNum</u>, SPName, SPComPer)

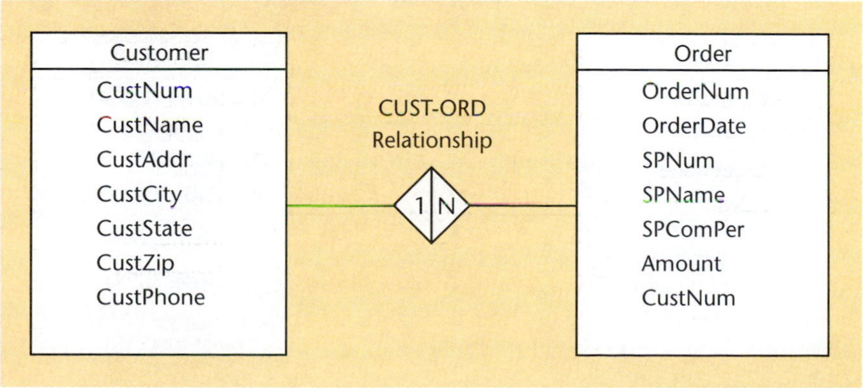

FIGURE 6-19
Modified CUST-ORD E-R Diagram

ORDER				
OrderNum	OrderDate	SPNum	Amount	CustNum
1000	05/05/93	10	$345.88	100
1010	05/05/93	20	$122.45	300
1030	05/06/93	10	$224.56	100
1040	05/07/93	10	$335.44	100

SALESPERSON		
SPNum	SPName	SPComPer
10	Jones	0.12
20	Parks	0.10

FIGURE 6-20
Two Tables Required for the Order Entity in Figure 6-19

For these tables, the column SPNum in ORDER is called a **foreign key**. It is given this name because SPNum is the key of SALESPERSON. SPNum, when it is contained in ORDER, is the key of a **foreign table**. It is used to relate records in the two tables—in this case to identify the salesperson who sold a particular order. We will use this terminology below.

Relationship Representation E-R diagrams show both entities and relationships. We define tables to represent the entities as just described. Once those tables have been defined, however, we must then modify them to represent relationships. For example, in Figure 6-19, the CUST-ORD relationship must be represented in the CUSTOMER and ORDER tables. The way in which relationships are represented depends on the type of relationship.

In general, there are three types of relationships between two entities. They are (1) **1:1** (one-to-one) **relationships**; (2) **1:N** (one-to-many) **relationships**; and (3) **N:M** (many-to-many) **relationships**. These relationship types are sometimes called the relationship's **cardinality**.

Figure 6-21 shows an example of each of these types of cardinality. In Figure 6-21*a*, one employee entity corresponds to one company car entity. This means that an employee is assigned, at most, one company car and that a company car is assigned to, at most, one employee. In Figure 6-21*b*, one salesperson entity corresponds to many order entities. This means that one salesperson can relate to many orders but that an order is placed by only one salesperson. In Figure 6-21*c*, one club entity relates to many member entities, and one member entity relates to many club entities. This means that a person can be a member of several clubs and that a club can have several members. Each of these types is represented differently in a database design.

In the following discussion, we assume that each entity is represented by a single table. For the entities in Figure 6-21, then, there are the corresponding tables: EMPLOYEE, COMPANY CAR, SALESPERSON, ORDER, CLUB, and MEMBER.

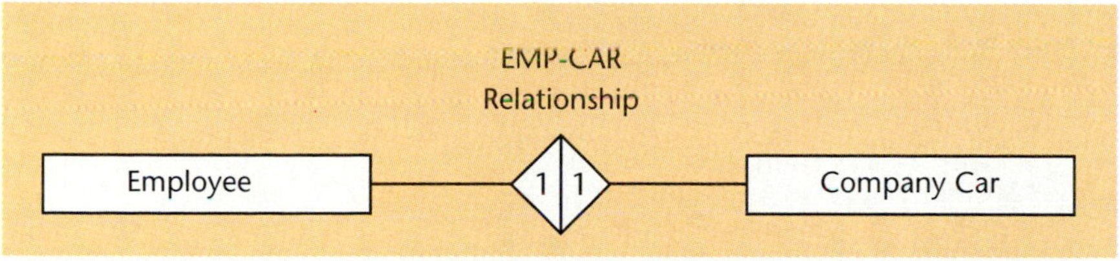

a. **1:1 (one to one)**

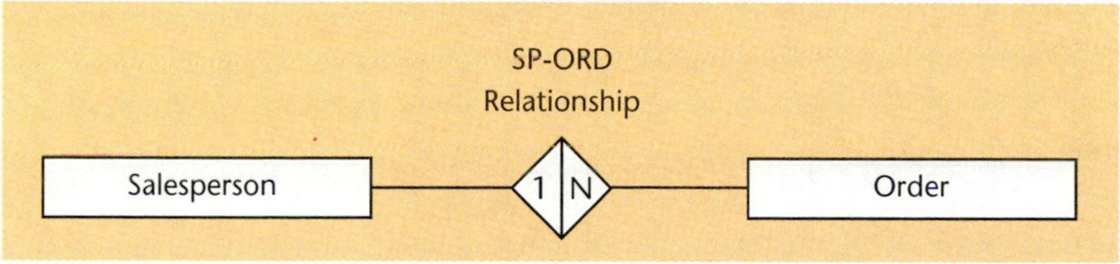

b. **1:N (one to many)**

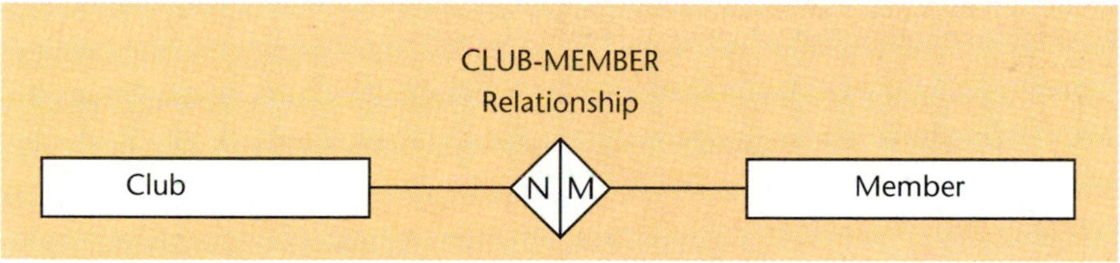

c. **N:M (many to many)**

FIGURE 6-21
Three Types of Relationships

1:1 Relationships To represent 1:1 (one-to-one) relationships, we place the key of one of the tables into the other table. Assume that the following two tables represent the entities in Figure 6-21*a*:

```
EMPLOYEE     (EmpNum, EmpName, EmpPhone)
COMPANY CAR  (LicenseNum, Type, Color, Year)
```

To represent the relationship between the rows of these tables, we can place either the key of EMPLOYEE into COMPANY CAR or the key of COMPANY CAR into EMPLOYEE. Either of the following two constructions will work:

```
EMPLOYEE    (EmpNum, EmpName, EmpPhone, LicenseNum)
COMPANY CAR (LicenseNum, Type, Color, Year)
```

or

```
EMPLOYEE     (EmpNum, EmpName, EmpPhone)
COMPANY CAR  (LicenseNum, Type, Color, Year, EmpNum)
```

FIGURE 6-22
1:N Relationship
This is an example of a 1:N relationship.

Consider the first example. If we have an employee and want to know which car he or she is assigned, we can look up the employee's row in the EMPLOYEE table and obtain LicenseNum. With this number, we can look up the correct row in COMPANY CAR. Similarly, if we have a car's license number and want data for the employee who is assigned that car, we can look up the EMPLOYEE row that has the given value of LicenseNum. Analogous processes work for the second alternative.

1:N Relationships Consider the 1:N (one-to-many) relationship between salesperson and order in Figure 6-21*b*. Assume that the following tables represent these entities:

```
SALESPERSON  (SPNum, SPName, SPComPer)
ORDER        (OrderNum, OrderDate, Amount)
```

We have two choices. We can place the key of SALESPERSON into ORDER, or we can place the key of ORDER into SALESPERSON. Unlike 1:1 relationships, only one of these alternatives will work. To see why, consider the data in Figure 6-23. Suppose we try to place the key of ORDER into SALESPERSON. As shown at the bottom of the figure, salesperson 10 has placed three orders. If we try to put the key of ORDER into her row in SALESPERSON, we have a problem: There is only enough space for one value in each cell of the table. We cannot place just OrderNum 1000 into the cell or just OrderNum 1030 or 1040 into the cell. We need to place all three there. Hence, we cannot put the key of ORDER into SALESPERSON.

Consider the second alternative: Place the key of SALESPERSON into ORDER. Since each row in ORDER corresponds to only one row in SALESPERSON, this alternative will work. This results in the tables that we used

ORDER

OrderNum	OrderDate	Amount	CustNum
1000	05/05/93	$345.88	100
1010	05/05/93	$122.45	300
1030	05/06/93	$224.56	100
1040	05/07/93	$335.44	100

SALESPERSON

SPNum	SPName	SPComPer
10	Jones	0.12
20	Parks	0.10

Relationship facts:

Orders 1000, 1030, and 1040 were sold by Jones (SPNum 10)

Order 1010 was sold by Parks (SPNum 20)

FIGURE 6-23
Sample ORDER and SALESPERSON Data

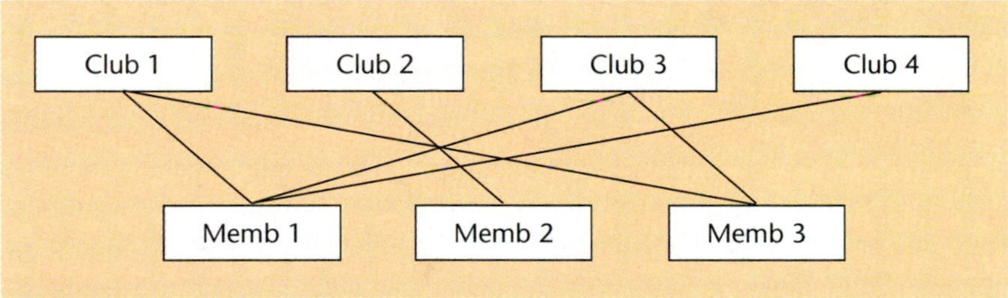

FIGURE 6-24
Example CLUB and MEMBER Relationships

in the example in Figure 6-20. The SPNum column is contained within ORDER.

In general, for a 1:N relationship, we place the key of the table from the "one" side of the relationship into the key of the table on the "many" side of the relationship. Thus, the key of SALESPERSON (SPNum, from the "one" side of the relationship) goes into ORDER (on the "many" side).

N:M Relationships Consider the N:M (many-to-many) relationship between club and member in Figure 6-21*c*. To understand the meaning of an N:M relationship, consider the sample relationships shown in Figure 6-24. Each line in this figure represents a relationship between a club and a member. According to this figure, the club Club1 includes members Memb1 and Memb3. Similarly Memb1 belongs to Club1, Club3, and Club4.

Assume that the following tables represent the club and member entities:

```
CLUB   (ClubName, other data)
MEMBER (MembName, other data)
```

Box 6.2

INCREASING YOUR PERSONAL PRODUCTIVITY

Mapping Database Information

Database management software teams up with graphics software to form the Geographical Information Systems (GIS). GIS began as software for displaying and analyzing geographical data on mainframes and microcomputers. It has since been adapted for the more expensive lines of microcomputers, making it available for a wider variety of applications.

What distinguishes GIS from products is its links between maps and databases. When a user creates and stores a map on the system, the program treats the information in the map as data for the database.

For example, users at Indianapolis Water Company have stored a high-resolution map on the system. The map shows details as fine as fire hydrants and manholes, as well as buildings, property lines, and streets. According to Larry Stout, a civil engineer with Indianapolis Water, "We'll be able to say, 'Show me a picture of all the 12-inch water mains that we installed in 1982,' and just those lines will show up (on the map produced by the system)." The system would search the database to find which water mains fit the designated criteria, then would use the data to create a map.

As in Stout's example, the software enables users to create graphic displays of data from the database. Besides data retrieved from maps stored on the system, the data might also consist of demographic information.

Indianapolis Water's GIS system is installed on a network of personal computers. Such hardware arrangements are particularly attractive because they cost less than mainframes and minicomputers. Furthermore, cartographic data in digitized form—available from the Census Bureau and the U.S. Geological Survey—are more economical than ever. The low cost is especially attractive to organizations that wish to create a GIS by combining geographic information with internal data such as customer lists.

We will not show nonkey data here, since it is not needed to show relationships. Example data for these tables is shown in Figure 6-25.

For N:M relationships, placing the key of one table into the other will not work. To see why, consider Figure 6-26. Here we have attempted to place the key of MEMBER into CLUB. For the example data shown in Figure 6-24, Club1 includes 2 members—Memb1 and Memb3. In Figure 6-26, we cannot place both members in the MembName column, since only one value is allowed per cell. For the same reason, we cannot place the key of CLUB in MEMBER.

To represent an N:M relationship, we must create a third table, as shown in Figure 6-27. The rows of this new table, called CLUB-MEMB, represent each line in Figure 6-24. The first row—Club1, Memb1—represents the first line in Figure 6-24. Other rows represent the other lines.

Now we can determine who belongs to a club by looking up the club's key in the CLUB-MEMB table. For example, to find the members of Club3, we look up that value in CLUB-MEMB and find member names (in the MembName column) Memb1 and Memb3. Similarly, to find the clubs that

CLUB

ClubName	Other Club Data
Club1	....
Club2	....
Club3	....
Club4	....

MEMBER

MembName	Other Member Data
Memb1	....
Memb2	....
Memb3	....

FIGURE 6-25

CLUB and MEMBER Tables

CLUB

ClubName	MembName	Other Club Data
Club1	MEMB1 but ???	....
Club2		....
Club3		....
Club4		....

MEMBER

MembName	Other Member Data
Memb1	....
Memb2	....
Memb3	....

FIGURE 6-26

N:M Relationship—An Incorrect Approach
In this N:M relationship, placing the key of the MEMBER table into the CLUB table does not work.

CLUB

ClubName	Other Club Data
Club1	....
Club2	....
Club3	....
Club4	....

MEMBER

MembName	Other Member Data
Memb1	....
Memb2	....
Memb3	....

CLUB-MEMB

ClubName	MembName
Club1	Memb1
Club1	Memb3
Club2	Memb2
Club3	Memb1
Club3	Memb3
Club4	Memb1

FIGURE 6-27

CLUB, MEMBER, and CLUB-MEMB tables

FIGURE 6-28

Creating the Database Design

Building the data model and creating the database design should be completed using paper and pencil or word processor before you load the DBMS.

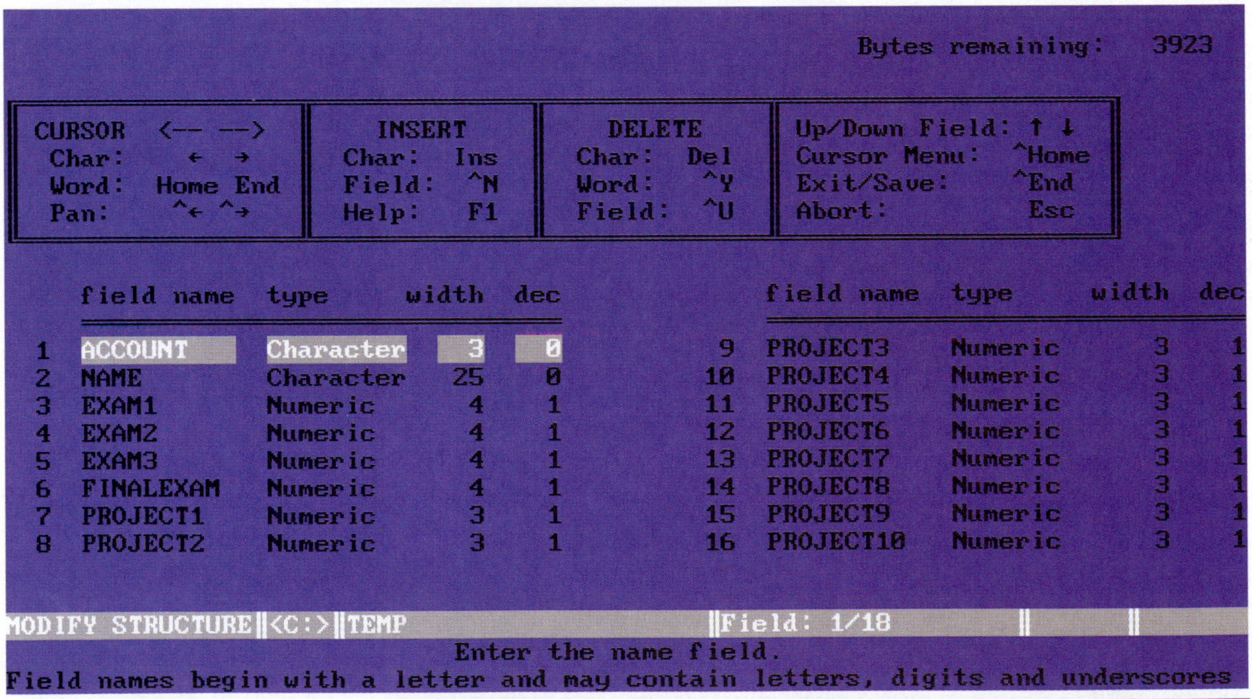

Bytes remaining: 3923
CURSOR <-- -->
Char: ← →
Word: Home End
Pan: ^← ^→
INSERT
Char: Ins
Field: ^N
Help: F1
DELETE
Char: Del
Word: ^Y
Field: ^U
Up/Down Field: ↑ ↓
Cursor Menu: ^Home
Exit/Save: ^End
Abort: Esc
field name type width dec
1 ACCOUNT Character 3 0
2 NAME Character 25 0
3 EXAM1 Numeric 4 1
4 EXAM2 Numeric 4 1
5 EXAM3 Numeric 4 1
6 FINALEXAM Numeric 4 1
7 PROJECT1 Numeric 3 1
8 PROJECT2 Numeric 3 1
field name type width dec
9 PROJECT3 Numeric 3 1
10 PROJECT4 Numeric 3 1
11 PROJECT5 Numeric 3 1
12 PROJECT6 Numeric 3 1
13 PROJECT7 Numeric 3 1
14 PROJECT8 Numeric 3 1
15 PROJECT9 Numeric 3 1
16 PROJECT10 Numeric 3 1
MODIFY STRUCTURE <C:> TEMP Field: 1/18
Enter the name field.
Field names begin with a letter and may contain letters, digits and underscores

FIGURE 6-29 **Defining a Database Table**

a given member belongs to, we look up the member's name in CLUB-MEMB and find the names of the clubs that he or she belongs to. Thus, to find the clubs that Memb3 belongs to, we look up that value in CLUB-MEMB and find club names (in the ClubNames column) Club1 and Club3.

Building the Database

With tables designed, load the DBMS into your personal computer and activate the database definition feature. Notice that the design was done without the benefit of computer technology. It was mostly thinking and writing notes.

The tools for building databases differ among DBMSs, but, in general, you will create tables one at a time until the database is complete. For each table, you will be asked for a table name, then for each column's name, data type, and length. Figure 6-29 shows how the computer screen might appear. Most DBMSs limit the length of table and column names, so abbreviations are often used (such as CustNum for customer number). Consequently, it would be wise to build a glossary of column names on a piece of paper as you go along. That way, you can remember exactly how you spelled each abbreviation.

Testing the Database

When you finish defining the structure of the database (that is what all the table definitions are), then enter a few records into each table. Do not enter all your data before you have tested your application. With just a few records in each table, browse the tables to be sure everything is stored as it should be. (You might want to postpone this step until you develop at least parts of your database application. Then you will have data entry forms and reports to make the testing process a little easier.)

Designing the Application

With the structure of the database tables complete, move on to designing the application. In this step, use paper and pencil to decide on the format of your menus, data entry forms, and reports.

Note that the application described here is too complex for a beginner to develop. If you require an application that includes all these elements, then you definitely need professional help in developing it. However, if you understand the elements and the basic techniques, you can assist the professional by describing your requirements more accurately. That is the goal of this section.

Designing menus means sketching a tree. The **main menu** is the first menu the user will see when loading the application. This menu offers the first set of processing options. The menu tree illustrated in Figure 6-30 is similar to the menu system we saw in Figure 6-13.

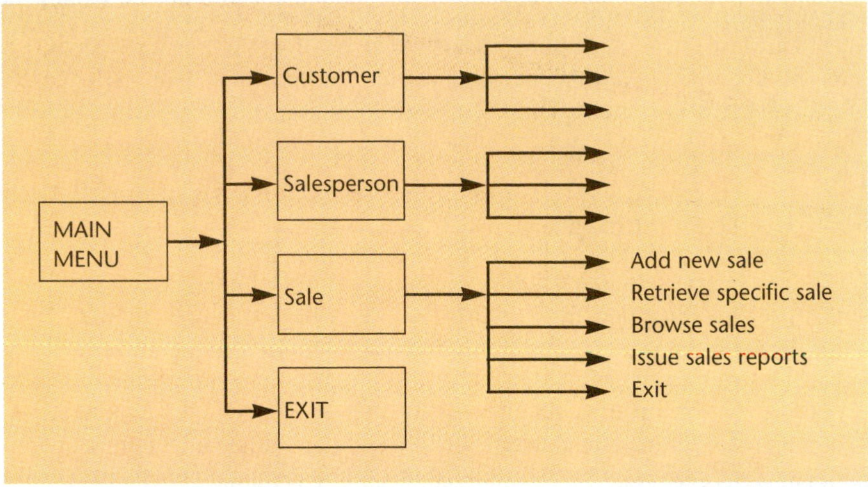

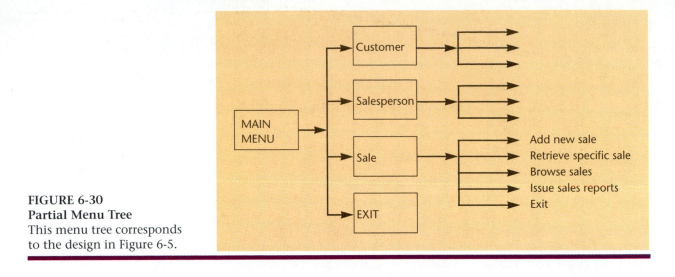

FIGURE 6-30
Partial Menu Tree
This menu tree corresponds to the design in Figure 6-5.

Next, we decide exactly what each menu option is supposed to do. In some cases, the action is to display another menu. In other cases, it will assist you in adding a record to a table, deleting a record, changing data, sorting data, selecting data, printing a report, and so forth. Write the actions next to the appropriate menu selections on the menu design form.

Designing data entry forms means choosing the form layout (the location of the prompts and the field-entry areas) as well as the actual prompts. For example, what do you want the user to see on the computer screen when he or she is supposed to add a new customer to the database? This can be sketched on paper, then used in the next step to build the actual form.

Finally, you need to design your output reports. You may already have completed this step (or at least started it) in the process of modeling the data. If, during that step, you considered your output needs, then at least some of your report designs may already exist. Add to them any other reports your application will issue. In designing reports, consider three sections: (1) the columns of information themselves, (2) the heading information, and (3) the summary information.

First consider the columns of information in the body of the report: What columns are needed? In what order? How wide should each column be to contain the required information? Will the total width of all columns fit within the width of the printout page?

Then consider what information the heading should contain: report title, date, column headings, and other information. Determine exact phrasing for each, bearing in mind that each element must fit in the space provided for it.

Finally, consider the summary information. For example, in a report of sales by salespersons, do you want a subtotal after each salesperson's sales? A subtotal after each day's sales by a salesperson? A subtotal after each department's sales? Do you want a grand total of all sales shown in the report? Do you want any other columns totaled? Each item is an example of the kind of summary information you may specify.

Building the Application

At this point, load the DBMS once again and, this time, use the application definition feature. Using the designs you developed, build all menus, data entry forms, and report formats.

An example of a data entry form for the CUSTOMER table is shown in Figure 6-31. Notice that the words used as prompts on the data entry form are not necessarily the same as the column names for the CUSTOMER table, as shown in Figure 6-29. As you define a data entry form, indicate the prompt (such as Account Number), the screen location where the data will be entered, and the names of the table and the column that the data will be stored in (such as CUSTOMER CustNum).

If your DBMS enforces constraints (not all do), then you need to describe them here. For instance, if no CustNum value could be less than 0500, then that rule would be stated in the data entry form for the CUSTOMER table. Thereafter, when this data entry form is used, an attempted entry of a number less than 0500 in the CustNum field will be rejected by the DBMS.

With all data entry forms defined, you might next define your reports. In defining a report, you need to name the report and define its layout. The layout includes constants—such as report title and column headings—and variables. Variables are either extracted from the database or derived arithmetically from numbers in the database. Your glossary of table names and their composition will come in handy here, because you need to use the variable names you used when defining the tables. Now is not the time to wonder, Did I name it "CustNum" or "CustNo"? In defining

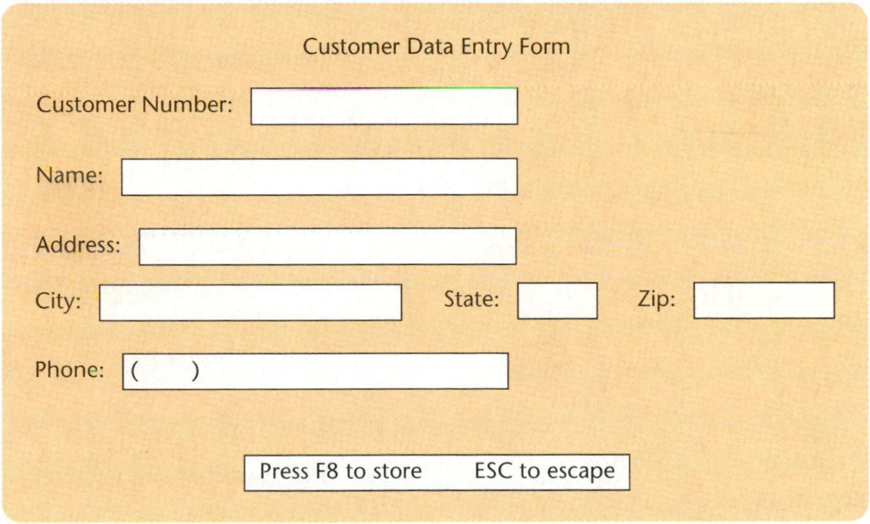

FIGURE 6-31
Data Entry Form for CUSTOMER Table

reports, some DBMSs let you pick from a list of correct table and column names, which simplifies this process.

The remaining step in building the application is to define the menus. When defining a menu, name it, then specify the list of menu options. For each option, specify the action to be taken: Perhaps display a data entry form, issue a report, invoke another menu, or exit. If you follow the design for your menus, this step can go very quickly.

Testing the Application

The final step is to test the application. Load the application—the main menu should be displayed on the computer screen. Choose the option you need in order to add data to your tables. Then, using the data entry forms, enter a few records of data into each table. Attempt to add data that violates your established constraints, just to be sure it is rejected correctly.

Next, try each report. Are the results what you expected? Are all totals correct? Is the right data being displayed? Are any records left out that were supposed to be there? Attempt to add, change, and delete entries in every table. Can you perform all these functions? If anything is not correct, make notes of the problem and continue testing. When testing is completed (or when errors force you to suspend testing), load the DBMS again and use the data definition function to fix the problem areas noted. Then load the application and test it again. Do this until you eliminate all the bugs you can find.

When you are satisfied that your application produces the anticipated results, install the system by loading all the data into the appropriate tables. Now you can use your personal database application.

Summary

Businesspeople use personal database information systems for simple record keeping, for complex record keeping involving multiple tables and large data volumes, and for data manipulation.

The components of a personal database information system are a database, a DBMS, an application program, a set of forms for manipulating the data, and a user. Appropriate applications for database processing and for spreadsheet processing are distinct, though some data may be processed by both types of programs at different times.

The process of developing a personal database information system involves building a data model, transforming the data model into a database design, building the database, testing the database, designing the application, building the application, and testing the application.

Key Terms

database management system (DBMS)
database
key field
data definition language (DDL)
data manipulation language (DML)
list manager

constraints
database application program
data entry form
report form
query
query language
ad hoc query
query by example (QBE)
menu
data model
top-down data modeling
entity
property
relationship
entity-relationship (E-R) diagram
bottom-up data modeling
foreign key
foreign table
1:1 relationship
1:N relationship
N:M relationship
cardinality
main menu

Review Questions

1. List three kinds of uses for personal database information systems.
2. Describe what we mean by ad hoc questions.
3. Name three elements of a personal database information system.
4. Explain each part of the definition of database.
5. Differentiate among a database, a database application, and a DBMS.
6. What are the components of a database application?
7. Describe the purposes of a query language and a query by example.
8. How can a database application enforce constraints?
9. In a database application, what is an application program?
10. Define DBMS, DDL, and DML.
11. Differentiate between a DBMS and a list manager.
12. What are the distinguishing characteristics of an appropriate database application, as compared to an appropriate application for a spreadsheet program?
13. List the seven steps in building a personal database information system.
14. Differentiate between top-down data modeling and bottom-up data modeling.
15. The elements of a data model are entities, properties, and relationships. Describe what each means.
16. What is an E-R diagram?
17. Name and define the three relationships shown in E-R diagrams.
18. Describe the form that would be appropriate for a database application menu design, a data entry form design, and an output report design.
19. What are the three sections of an output report that should be designed?
20. Differentiate between designing a data entry form and building a data entry form. For each, what kind of action does the developer perform?
21. Describe at least four activities that are included in testing a personal database application.

Discussion Questions

A. Consider a college instructor's student grade database for a course that has three exams and 15 projects and assignments. Make an E-R diagram for this database with two entities: student and grade. Imagine the attributes and relationships as accurately as you can. As an alternative, consider the fields that would be needed to create this database as a single table. Which do you think would be preferable? Defend your answer.

B. Suppose that a teacher implements the student grade database you designed in response to the previous question. Describe at least six situations in which the instructor may need to process an ad hoc query in this database.

C. For a small retailer, compare the costs and benefits of storing data about customers, salespeople, and sales in file folders (in a file cabinet) as opposed to in a computer. List all the costs and benefits of manual processing using the file cabinet and all the costs and benefits of computerized processing using the computer. In your analysis, which is more beneficial? Can you visualize any circumstances in which the other method (the one you did not select) would be more cost-beneficial?

D. Summarize the differences between appropriate uses for spreadsheets and appropriate uses for personal DBMSs. Phrase your answer as decision criteria for your own future use in choosing either a spreadsheet or a database as a program for particular applications.

E. Draw an E-R diagram for a simplified college student registration system. Consider the following five entities: student, course, instructor, classroom, and department. Students register in courses that have course names, course numbers, and other attributes. Courses meet in classrooms that have building names, room numbers, seating capacities, and other attributes. Courses have instructors who have names, Social Security numbers, office addresses, office hours, and other attributes. Instructors are members of departments that have department names, department chairperson names, and other attributes. Imagine additional attributes and relationships as accurately as you can. Be prepared to defend the choices you made in creating your diagram.

F. In considering the student registration system in the previous question, describe the process of top-down data modeling that you would use in analyzing that situation, then describe the process of bottom-up data modeling that you would use. Specifically, what actions characterize top-down modeling, and what other actions characterize bottom-up modeling?

G. From your own daily experiences, give at least five examples of the following kinds of relationships: 1:1, 1:N, and N:M.

MINICASE

Artist Tracks Customers with Database Application

Beth Farrell paints murals on the walls of homes and businesses in the Pacific Northwest. After studying fine arts at the Cornish Art Institute in Seattle, she began by painting furniture and other decorative jobs. Over a five-year period she gained a solid reputation for her work and now paints about thirty or so murals or other wall treatments a year.

"All of my business is by word of mouth," she says. "I'm lucky in that I've never needed to advertise." She is also active in the design community and is invited each year to paint in one or two homes in the Street of Dreams, a Pacific Northwest event in which major architects, contractors, and decorators build example homes and invite the public to tour them.

"Usually, when someone calls, they'll say something like, 'I'm a friend of the Forsythe's and I like their bathroom mural. Can you do something similar for me?' That's great, but the problem is that I've painted maybe 500 jobs so far, and I often don't remember what I did," says Farrell. She says another problem is that when customers call, they usually know about what their friends paid and they expect a similar price. "My fees range from $500 for a very small job to $5000 or more for a mural, so it varies a lot."

In order to respond to these calls more effectively, she uses a database application that contains records of her customers and the jobs she's performed for them. "I key in the customer's last name, and the system lists the jobs I've painted for that customer, along with the prices I charged. I also use the computer to record prices of jobs that I've bid," she says.

"Another problem is that I need to keep track of who referred customers to me. Sometimes, there's an agreement on a referral fee, and I want to be clear about the amount involved before I give a bid to the customer."

Farrell used to keep all of this data on three-by-five-inch cards. With that system, however, she wasn't able to look up customer data fast enough. "Art is very personal," she says. "People expect me to remember what I've painted for them. But, their job may be one of fifty I've done in their area, and I just can't remember each job off the top of my head. So, I get their data on the computer while we're on the telephone. It jogs my memory, and then I can be much more personal."

She also uses the database system to print invoices. "Most of the time, people pay right away, but now and then I need to send a second, reminder bill. It's nice to have the computer print it for me," she says.

Farrell's system was developed by an independent consultant who was recommended by one of her clients. "The only real problem I had was in explaining how simple my business is. He kept wanting to add things I don't need." She didn't want to do accounting, nor did she want to keep track of materials or time spent on a job. "I just want to keep track of referrals, customers, and jobs. I probably would never enter all that other data, anyway."

The total cost of the system was $3,700, which included a used computer, software, and the consultant's time. "It was a little rocky at the start, but after two or three bugs were fixed, it's been fine."

Questions

1. Summarize the major benefits that Farrell receives from her database application.
2. Farrell does not use the computer system to track time or materials, nor does she use it for accounting. All of that work is done manually. Why do you suppose she chooses to do this? What advantages would she receive by using computer systems for this work? What disadvantages?
3. Farrel's system is a DOS-based, character-oriented application. In a few years, it will be technically obsolete. Does that matter to her? Should she attempt to keep up with newer technology? What advantages would there be? What disadvantages?
4. Draw an Entity-Relationship diagram that you think would represent Farrell's business. Your diagram should include data for customers, jobs, and people who make referrals. Assume a customer is referred by only one person. Explain how you would represent the entities and relationships with tables.

Interview by the authors, June 9, 1992.

C H A P T E R 7

Developing Personal Information Systems

This is the first of two chapters about systems development. This chapter describes the development of personal information systems for single users. It describes a development method using prototyping. Chapter 11, the second chapter on systems development, describes the classical systems development life cycle approach to the development of shared systems.

To understand the need for a methodical approach to information systems development as described in this chapter, it is important to see what can go wrong when such an approach is not followed. For that purpose, meet Earl, owner of Earl's Calligraphy, a successful mail order source of calligraphy supplies: ink pens, points, specialized papers, and dyes. Earl is an intelligent, resourceful businessperson who was just recently beginning to learn about computers. As you will see, when he started, he knew much less than you do about computers, and he was about to get a fast education through hard experience.

A careful buyer all his life, Earl was baffled by the gray box sitting on his desk. The salesman had promised an end to his record-keeping woes if he bought this system. He had told Earl that this was one of the most versatile printers for the money and that this integrated software would let him do not only spreadsheets and word processing, but also graphics and DTP. Unfortunately, the system never delivered on those promises. Earl never became comfortable with the DOS commands that he needed in order to keep track of his programs and data files. The system was so slow that it seemed like he spent more time waiting than anything else. The "database" system did not allow any queries with multiple conditions (such as, Who are the customers in the Southwest with yearly purchases over $1,000?). And though the graphics looked great on the screen, they were muddy and blurred when printed.

Earl was just beginning to realize that he had made a mistake. He paid over $8,000 of his hard-earned cash for what he believed would be a first-class solution to many of his business problems. Instead, the system was turning into a first-class headache. Although he was angry at himself for letting this happen, at this point he simply needed a way to make the best of this very bad investment.

THE SYSTEMS DEVELOPMENT PROCESS

Earl's lament could be repeated by thousands of disappointed consumers across the country. Most people, when they feel they are ready for a computer, take their checkbook down to the local computer store, talk to a salesperson for a little while, maybe try some software and computers on display, and, in a few hours or days, buy a "system." After living with their purchases for a while, these customers, like Earl, all too often discover the shortcomings of the system and complain about the computer, the software, or the vendor. One part of the problem is that many people do not know what to expect. Another part of the problem is that people simply do not realize that they need to determine systematically (1) whether they actually need a personal information system, (2) what present and future needs a personal information system might help address, and (3) what the best configuration is for their specific needs. A system that your sister, the lawyer, thinks is great might be a poor investment for your jewelry store.

In the previous three chapters you learned about applications using certain types of computer software. Those chapters presumed that you had a system (hardware, software, etc.) in place. In this chapter you will learn an approach that you can use to develop a personal information system, including all five of its components: hardware, programs, data, procedures, and people.

Systems analysts use classical systems development to develop large, complex systems. This process involves five stages. The first stage involves defining the problem, determining the feasibility of using computer technology to solve that problem, and developing a plan for the project. The second stage involves developing a list of specific requirements—things the system must be able to do, such as produce a report or do a calculation. The third stage involves evaluating the requirements—reconsidering each requirement in light of the cost of satisfying it. As a result, you eliminate some requirements and firmly establish the rest. In addition, you define the technology to be used—describe, in principle, how the system will be implemented. The fourth stage involves designing each of the five system components in detail. The fifth stage involves acquiring, integrating, testing, and installing the system components. This plan is called the **systems development life cycle (SDLC)**. It will be described in detail in Chapter 11.

Prototyping

Prototyping is a modification of the classical SDLC plan. In SDLC, the requirements are defined as a paper-and-pencil exercise before the design

FIGURE 7-1
Developing a Personal Information System
Developing personal information systems to meet your needs is a critical skill in business.

stage. By contrast, a system's requirements are developed in prototyping by building a working version, or prototype, of the application. When you can see the system working, it is often easy to discover useful changes or additions. Using the same prototyping techniques, those ideas can be quickly added, and the system can be tested again. This process is sometimes called *stepwise refinement*—you repeat the process, refining your prototype step by step, until you feel that it completely meets your needs. Then you implement the final version.

This strategy is only practical when prototypes can be quickly developed—which means developed by some method other than traditional programming. Fortunately for most personal applications, the software you are using—electronic spreadsheet, database, or word processing system—makes it possible to prototype quickly. As a result, the easiest way to determine the requirements is to use the application itself. For example, suppose you have the job of developing a small spreadsheet application. The easiest way to determine the requirements is not to write them in words, but rather to develop an example spreadsheet using electronic spreadsheet software, show the results to potential system clientele to invite comments, then revise the system.

A Systems Development Plan for Personal Systems

A plan for developing a personal information system through prototyping consists of the five stages shown in Figure 7-2.

First, define the problem. As you will see, the goal here is to be certain that you correctly understand the problem and that a computer-based information system is a feasible alternative. You are also creating a working plan in this stage, which shows the steps in the project and a completion schedule.

Second, classify the problem solution. Determine the type and size of the application and any constraints.

Third, use this information in creating the system platform. This platform consists of hardware and programs that will be used in prototyping the system, along with data, procedures, and people involved in the prototype. You will use the platform, first, to build the prototype, then, as the basis for the operational system.

Fourth, with the systems development platform in place, create the application design. As we have seen, this is an iterative process in which you create an initial set of requirements and use them to develop a working system. Use that system experimentally and consider improvements and additional requirements that might be added. Then develop a second version and experiment with it. Repeat the process until you are satisfied with the results. When you have reached this point, the system is designed.

Fifth, implement the design—that is, put it to use. Because you used prototyping to develop the design, it is already largely implemented. The final result, or last prototype, is documented and put to use.

1. **Define Problem**
   - Define problem
   - Assess feasibility
   - Create a project plan
2. **Classify Solution**
   - Determine application type
   - Determine application size
   - Determine constraints
3. **Create System Platform**
   - Select programs
   - Select and install hardware
   - Install programs
   - Learn to use hardware and programs
   - Identify sources of help
4. **Design Application**
   - Develop initial design
   - Create prototype
   - Redesign
5. **Implement System**
   - Produce results
   - Document system

FIGURE 7-2

Stages in Developing Personal Information System with Prototyping

The remainder of this chapter summarizes and illustrates each of the above stages.

DEFINING THE PROBLEM

Figure 7-3 summarizes the tasks you need to accomplish during the problem definition stage. First, define the problem. This sounds easy—even obvious. But when a problem is not well defined, putting together a system is like shooting in the dark. When you know the nature of the problem, then you can decide between alternative ways of proceeding to a goal. The goal, of course, is to solve the problem.

When defining a problem, it is tempting to be vague and to use phrases like "poor quality," "dissatisfied customers," or "error-prone data entry." Be specific in setting a goal that technology will help you reach. What is your target? How will you know when you have hit it? How will you measure your success? Phrases like "increase sales by 20 percent," "reduce travel costs by 15 percent," or "reduce customer complaints to no more than 1 in 20" are much clearer and therefore more useful in helping you find a solution.

Since the problem is a perceived difference between *what is* and *what ought to be*, it is often useful to state both aspects in common terms. This clarifies the difference, which is the problem. For example, a small company might state its problem like this: Our current sales are averaging $14,300 per month. We believe our sales could be about $17,000 per month. Thus, the problem is to increase our sales by $2,700 per month.

Problem Definition at Earl's Calligraphy

In this section, we will consider two scenarios involving Earl. One describes what happened. The other describes what might have happened if Earl had known about the five-stage development process.

What Happened One day Earl decided what his problem was: He needed a computer. He had read in some magazines that entrepreneurs like himself used them for everything from budgeting to proposal writing to solar house design. If he had a computer, then maybe he could spend his time more productively and increase his calligraphy supplies business. He talked to his brother-in-law, whose architectural firm had dozens of computers. Impressed with the firm's extensive use of computers and convinced that this was the right thing to do, Earl went to one of the computer retailers in town to select a computer.

What Could Have Happened Earl studied his sales figures and operating costs for the past three years. He was doing fairly well financially, but he thought business could be better. On examining his sales data, he noticed that most of his business came from mail orders. Sales increased sig-

- **Define Problem**
  A distinction between what is and what should be
- **Assess Feasibility**
  Cost
  Schedule
  Technical
- **Create a Project Plan**
  Completion dates
  Costs

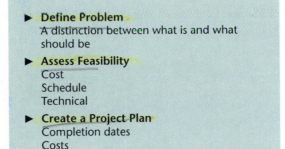

FIGURE 7-3
Major Tasks in the Problem Definition Stage

nificantly each time he issued a new catalog, and he was mailing catalogs five times a year. He estimated how much sales would increase if he doubled that to ten times per year, but was very concerned about production cost. Each catalog was expensive to produce.

In addition, Earl felt he could depend on a loyal customer base only so much. Doubling the number of catalogs per year probably would not double sales. He estimated that he needed to increase his customer base by 20 percent. Earl jotted these notes:

Problem: Need to increase sales.
Solution: Issue mail order catalog ten times per year (increase of 100 percent).
Problem: Catalog production costs too high.
Solution: Do not know. Need to study production costs to see where they can be reduced. Goal is to reduce production cost by 10 percent.
Problem: Current customer base cannot support desired growth.
Solution: Increase customer base by 20 percent.

With a clearer understanding of his problems, Earl thought he would pay a visit to a few computer retailers within the next few days.

Assessing Feasibility

Feasibility measures the likelihood that you can solve your problem with existing technology and within your own financial and time constraints. During this step, you need to consider cost feasibility, schedule feasibility, and technical feasibility.

Cost Feasibility The first aspect is **cost feasibility**. Here you must decide if an information system is likely to provide a cost-effective solution to the problem. If production costs for a catalog are \$0.75 and Earl issues 20,000 of them five times per year, then his catalog costs are \$75,000 per year. If he develops a system that reduces his per-catalog cost to \$0.68 (a 10 percent reduction), then he will spend only \$68,000 on catalogs, or \$7,000 less. Earl wanted the system to pay for itself in three years or less. Assuming that catalog costs were Earl's only problem, then a system costing

Problem Definition	30 Apr
Solution Classification	
Determine type	
Determine size	
Determine constraints	7 May
System Platform Creation	
Select and install hardware	
Select and install programs	
Learn to use hardware and programs	
Identify sources of help	15 Jun
Costs: Hardware	
Programs	
Initial payment to consultant	
Application Design	
Prototype	
Mailing list system	
Purchase tracking system	
Management reporting system	
Catalog production system	15 Jul
Costs: Consultant's fees	
Implementation	
Develop procedures	
Document system	1 Aug

FIGURE 7-4
Plan for System Development at Earl's Calligraphy

$21,000 or less (ignoring interest he would pay to finance his purchase) would be cost feasible.

Schedule Feasibility **Schedule feasibility** concerns whether the system will be available in time. For example, if Earl needs a system to report annual earnings to the state by January 31, then the system is not schedule feasible if it is not available until February 15. In reality, Earl would like to have the system available as soon as possible, but he has no reason to require it on a particular date. Thus, schedule feasibility is not a problem.

Technical Feasibility **Technical feasibility** concerns whether the system can be developed with the available technology and technical skills. After discussion with knowledgeable friends, Earl realized that he did not have all the computer skills that he would need for the solution. Therefore, he decided that his project should include assistance from a consultant. With a consultant's help, the project is technically feasible.

Creating a Development Project Plan

After the problem is defined and the feasibility assessed, the last step is to build a development plan. A development plan identifies each step, estimates the time each step will take, and often indicates how much money is needed and at what points. A plan will help you with your own scheduling and budgeting processes (see Figure 7-4).

CLASSIFYING THE SOLUTION

Once the problem has been defined, the next step (as described in Figure 7-5) is to classify the solution. This step produces the information necessary for creating the system platform. It also serves to establish guidelines for the development activity.

Determining Application Type

The first task is to determine the application type that will solve the problem. Consider the categories listed in Figure 7-6. These categories include analysis, tracking and monitoring, communication, and integrated applications. The problem statement should help you determine which type of system is appropriate.

In Earl's case, his problems involved tracking and monitoring customers and producing catalogs. Maintaining a customer list is an obvious application for a database program. This list could be used not only for producing a catalog mailing list, but also for keeping track of how long it has been since each customer placed an order and which customers were placing first-time orders. The database could also be used to track the various items to be listed in his catalog, which would allow easy additions and deletions as necessary.

Catalog production could be done either with a word processing system or with a DTP system. When Earl saw how much a DTP program would improve his catalog from its current typed form, he decided to use DTP software. In his catalog production system, he would need to combine item listings from the database with graphics from a graphics program, adding text (such as ordering information) from a word processing program.

- ▶ **Determine application type**
- ▶ **Determine application size**
- ▶ **Determine constraints**

FIGURE 7-5
Classifying the Solution

- ▶ **Analysis**
  Spreadsheet
- ▶ **Tracking and Monitoring**
  Database
- ▶ **Communication**
  Word processing
  Graphics
  Desktop Publishing
- ▶ **Integrated**
  Combination of two or more applications

FIGURE 7-6
Personal Information Systems Application Types

Finally, in analyzing sales and customer information, Earl may want to use a spreadsheet program to produce tables and graphs. Therefore, Earl's application involved database management applications, graphics applications, word processing applications, DTP applications, and electronic spreadsheet applications.

Determining Application Size

The next task is to determine the size of the application. Major considerations are the amount of data to be stored and the volume and frequency of input and output. When developing size estimates, it is also important to estimate application growth. The size estimates that you develop here will be used later to determine specifications for the system platform.

One of the first questions Earl was asked when he entered the computer store was, How much data do you have? Since he was unprepared and was not following the process you are learning here, he did not know the answer, and he was not in a good position to select a platform. He said he thought he had about 8,000 customers. What more should Earl have been able to say about his data?

He should have known the following: (1) amount of data (number of customers, number of items in his catalog, and size of his mailing list); (2) frequency with which data is added or changed (for example, how many sales are processed per day, how many new customers are added to the mailing list, how many people ask to be removed from the mailing list, how often products are added or discontinued, and how often item prices change); and (3) frequency with which reports are produced. (In this case, Earl knew his catalogs came out five times per year. But he also needed to define how often he wanted his new reports to be issued: daily? weekly? monthly?)

In developing this information, Earl should have reviewed his current documents. Examining his current mail order catalog and mailing list labels, for example, would provide information about amounts of data to be stored and processed. In addition, he should have reviewed his problem statement, which included increasing his customer base by 20 percent. Thus, he might want a monthly report like the one in Figure 7-7 to help him track his company's progress toward its goal. He might also want graphical output, such as the line graph in Figure 7-8.

Using this information, Earl could have developed the estimates shown in Figure 7-9.

FIGURE 7-7
Sample Customer Base Report for Earl's Calligraphy

CUSTOMER BASE REPORT

	Jan	Feb	Mar	Apr	Total
Number of Sales	250	200	280	250	980
New Customers	50	45	63	62	220
% New Customers	20	22.5	22.5	24.8	22.4
% Change	—	+2.5	0	+2.3	—

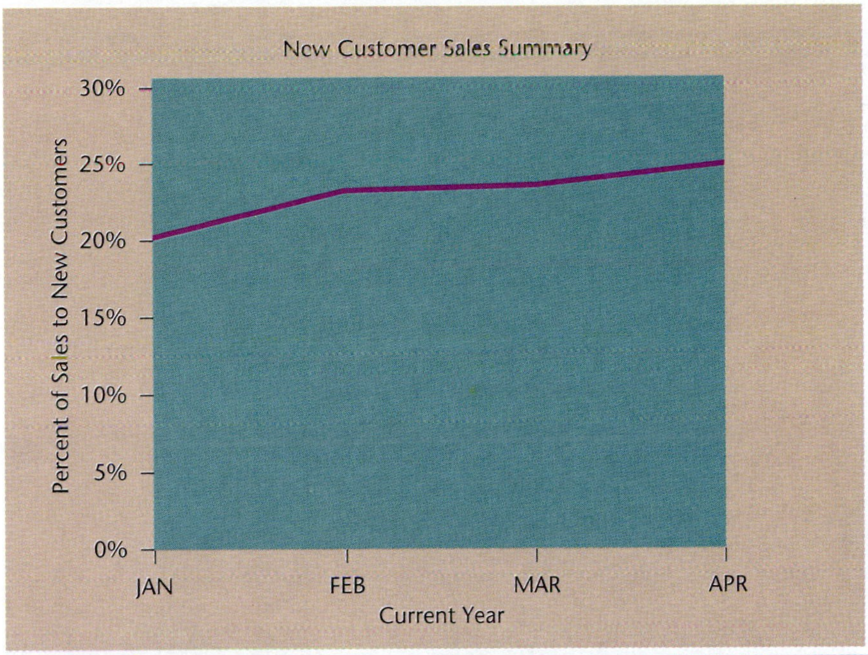

FIGURE 7-8
Example of Graph to Be Issued by Earl's System

FIGURE 7-9
Estimates of System Size for Earl's Calligraphy

- **Data storage requirements**
  Mailing list
  20,000 at 170 bytes each = 3.4 MB of mailing list data
  Active customers
  8,000 at 200 byptes each = 1.6 MB of active customer data
  Purchases
  250 per month for 3 years = 9,000 purchase records
  30 bytes each = 270,000 bytes of purchase data
  Total storage for current data = 5.27 MB
- **Data update requirements**
  Annual increase is
  300 new active customers at 200 byptes each = 60,000 bytes
  10,000 new names on mailing list at 170 bytes each = 1.7 MB
  600 new purchases at 30 bytes each = 9,000 bytes
  400 purchases over three years old deleted each year at 30 bytes each = –1,200 bytes
  Total projected annual growth is 1.7678 MB
- **Report generation requirements**
  Catalog produced 10 times per year
  Customer base reports produced monthly

INCREASING YOUR PERSONAL PRODUCTIVITY

Box 7.1

Insurance Giant Adds New Life to Its Laptops

Metropolitan Life Insurance Co. has come up with a surefire way to extend the life of its laptops. The company's field agents frequently run out of disk space on their laptops, most of which are equipped with 40M to 80M byte hard drives. Met Life's solution: data-compression software.

The decision to install data-compression software, rather than buy new laptops or larger disk drives for the 132,000 laptops used by field agents in the United States, will translate into big savings for the insurance giant, company officials said.

Early Snafus

First introduced in the late 1980s, much early data-compression software delivered 2-1 compression ratios but often degraded system speed. A marked improvement in performance of data-compression software (made possible by faster algorithms) is what finally convinced Met Life to take the plunge, after two years of in-house testing.

Although the company's machines run DOS, which takes up just 2M bytes of disk space, the advance of operating systems such as Windows and OS/2 is likely to spur more corporate interest in compression software, industry analysts said. OS/2, for instance, can take up to 28M bytes of disk space.

Still, Met Life is part of a rare corporate breed instituting such solutions to stave off hardware purchases. If you look at the average large corporate site, you'll find a few people using data-compression software, but they haven't standardized. Most companies leave it up to the users to deal with issues like that, unless there are big requests from MIS.

So far data compression software has been installed in more than 1,000 Met Life laptops. It is also being considered for use on desktop computers as well.

Determining Constraints

In addition to knowing what you want the system to do, you often need to define conditions or situations that will **constrain**, or limit, the system.

First, hardware constraints might exist. If you already own a computer, for example, then your project may be cost feasible only if you can use that computer. If you are developing a personal information system for use within a larger company, the company might have policies governing the make and model of personal computers used.

Second, software constraints might exist. For example, you might already know how to use one database management program or a word processor. In such a case, your project may be schedule feasible only if you use those programs. Within a company context, you may be constrained by company standards governing the software that can be used.

Hardware and software often impose constraints on one another. For example, the effective use of GUI software such as Windows may require a high-powered processor, a graphic display adapter and monitor, a large amount of main memory and disk storage space, and a mouse, none of which may be needed for character-oriented software. Similarly, the effective use of a sophisticated DTP program may require a laser printer, which may not be required with a word processing program. Thus, deciding on software limits your choices of hardware, and vice versa.

Finally, additional constraints may arise from the people component, such as limitations in your abilities as developer and operator—or your preferences. If you lack both programming experience and inclination to learn to program, then solutions requiring programming are not acceptable. If you strongly prefer programs that run under a GUI, then this may become a constraint for the selection of your platform.

Constraints for Earl's Calligraphy System

In the "ideal" scenario we are again considering here, Earl did not yet own a computer. Therefore, he faced no hardware or software constraints. His mailing labels were being produced by a local service company, and Earl was told he could get the mailing list from the company in whatever format his new system required. His only constraints, then, had to do with the amount of data and the anticipated increase, as described in Figure 7-9.

CREATING THE SYSTEM PLATFORM

This stage involves selecting and assembling a system platform that can be used in prototyping, and that, eventually, can serve as the basis of the operational system. The platform is an information system, so it has each of the five components that we have discussed before (see Figure 7-10). We will consider each in turn.

Selecting Programs

Generally, you should select the application programs first. The programs you select may constrain the type and amount of hardware that you need. For example, some products are available only on the Macintosh; others work only with Windows system software. Some products require more memory or disk space than others.

- ▶ Select programs
- ▶ Select and install hardware
- ▶ Install programs
- ▶ Learn to use hardware and programs
- ▶ Identify sources of help

FIGURE 7-10
Steps in Creating the System Platform

In the previous stage of system development, the solution was classified. This classification will indicate the type of application programs you need to use. You may already own a program of that type and know how to use it. If the program meets your needs, you may want to use it. Otherwise, approach knowledgeable associates, consultants, computer retailers, and other sources for advice to learn about products of that type.

In general, unless you have substantial expertise in an area, it is best to choose an established, mainstream product. The major products all have useful aftermarket support, including authorized training centers, effective customer support, large pool of experienced consultants, and so forth. Unless you are a seasoned user, stay on the beaten path.

Once you have determined the application program(s) you need, select the system software. You will need at least an operating system and possibly Windows. Unless the application you purchase indicates otherwise, select the most recent version of the system software. A reputable vendor can help with this.

Selecting and Installing Hardware

Before you select your hardware, review "How to Select Your Own Personal Computer System" in Chapter 3. In general, buy at least two to three times as much disk storage as you think you will need. Storage is not that expensive, and, if you are like most people, you will find applications for your computer that you cannot anticipate at the time you purchase it. Further, as vendors bring out new products, the need for disk storage continues to rise.

The dealer may offer to set the system up at your location and to install software for an additional fee. You may want to have this done. How-

FIGURE 7-11
Selecting Programs
In some software stores, you can experiment with programs before you buy.

ever, if you can systematically follow directions, step by step, then you will probably be able to install hardware and software yourself.

Installing Programs

After the hardware is installed, the programs are next. Even when a system is delivered in boxes for you to assemble, the dealer typically has formatted the hard disk and installed the operating system. If not, then these tasks should be your first steps.

The documentation that comes with the operating system should include a detailed, step-by-step description of the installation process. An installation program may do most of the work, based on your answers to questions, and the questions should be explained in the documentation. The operating system must be completely working before any application software can be installed. The operating system provides an environment for the other software, so if it does not function properly, then the results from your system will be unpredictable, at best.

The next step is to install the application software. Software publishers generally provide helpful, accurate installation instructions. Sometimes the vendor will include a READ ME file on the installation disk. This file might contain modifications to the printed documentation, so read it first.

Many commercial programs have installation utilities that automate much of the installation process. Questions regarding the hardware in use will often be asked. Examples include type of display; type of printer; number, type, and size of disk storage units; and miscellaneous facts such as the country of use (for proper interpretation of keyboard and display of special characters and currency symbol). When you acquire your system hardware, complete (or have the computer retailer complete) a chart like the one in Figure 7-12. Even if you do not understand every entry, you will have on one page the data you need to respond to software installation prompts. Keep the form in your documentation notebook, and change it whenever you update your system.

Learning to Use Hardware and Programs

The next system component consists of procedures. At this stage of the project, you need to learn how to use the application programs. You can take classes in the use of applications, but such classes are often not necessary. Vendors of major products today provide, as part of the product, computer-based training (CBT) tutorials for learning how to use the product. Before enrolling in a class, spend time with the tutorial. You may find that this provides you with sufficient training.

Also, all contemporary application products have sophisticated help facilities. Vendors put substantial resources into such facilities. Take time to learn how to use your product's help functions. Many products provide **context-sensitive help**. When you use the Help command in these programs, it provides help messages that are directly related to whatever you are doing at the moment.

Software Installation Checklist

Computer:

_________ XT (8088 or 8086) _________ AT (80286) _________ 80386 _________ 80486

Memory Capacity:

___________K Ram

Expanded Memory ___________ (K or Megabytes)

Extended Memory ___________ (K or Megabytes)

Monitor:

Color ______ Yes ______ No

Type ___________ Monochrome/Text only ___________ EGA

___________ Monochrome/Graphics ___________ VGA (Monochrome or Gray Scale)

___________ CGA ___________ VGA (Color)

___________ Multisync

Communication Ports:

Number of Serial Ports ___________

Connected to:

COM1 ___________ COM3 ___________

COM2 ___________ COM4 ___________

Number of Parallel Ports______

Connected to:

LPT1 ___________ LPT3 ___________

LPT2 ___________ LPT4 ___________

Printers:

Manufacturer ____

Model ____

Type ___________ 9 Pin Dot Matrix ___________ Laser Printer

___________ 24 Pin Dot Matrix ___________ Other (inkjet, thermal)

Connected to Communications Port ______________________

(COM 1, 2, 3 or 4 for Serial Printer, LPT 1, 2, 3, or 4 for Parallel Printer)

Emulates the following printers:

1. ____________________ 3. ____________________

2. ____________________ 4. ____________________

Disk Drives:

Hard Disk(s):

Manufacturer ______________________________

Model(s) ______________________________

Capacity__________________________ megabytes

Floppy Disk Drives:

Enter number of drives at each capacity:

5¼" 360 K _____ 3½" 720 K _____

5¼" 1.2 MB _____ 3½" 1.44 MB _____

Mouse:

Manufacturer:

Type ___________ Bus ___________ Serial Port

If Serial Mouse:

Connected to Serial Port ____________________

(COM 1,2,3 or 4)

Emulates the following model(s):

___________ Mouse Systems ___________ Microsoft Mouse

Modem:

Manufacturer ______________________________

Model ______________________________

Maximum Baud Rate ____________________ (2400/1200/300)

Connected to Communications (Serial) Port:

__________________________ (COM1/COM2/COM3/COM4)

Reprinted from *PC Today*, September 1989, p. 91.

FIGURE 7-12 Software Installation Checklist

Identifying Sources of Help

The last component of the system platform is people. You are most likely the developer. In addition, however, you will probably need access to experts. Before starting, it is wise to identify people who can help you.

In a company, one source of help is other employees within your department. They may be knowledgeable about your application type. Your company's MIS department may also have experts available as internal consultants, and for specific problems about products, you can contact the vendor's customer support line. Articles about innovative ways to use products often appear in popular magazines such as *PC World*, *Mac World*, and *PC Magazine*. Finally, you can hire a consultant to assist you in the development of your application, as Earl did.

Selecting a Platform for Earl's Calligraphy

Here's what Earl should have done in selecting a platform. In the ideal scenario, Earl had not already purchased a computer, so he was free to consider all alternatives. After discussing his requirements with a computer store salesperson (recommended to him by a friend), and after trying out several computers and software packages on display, Earl and the salesperson narrowed his platform alternatives to two, as Figure 7-14 shows. The two were very similar, except that the first was based on an IBM-compatible computer and the second was based on an Apple Macintosh computer. Each alternative included the same categories of software. In fact, word processor and electronic spreadsheets in both systems were marketed under the same names. The salesperson checked to be sure that the programs could share data if necessary. She also double-checked the entire configuration to make certain that the hardware would support the programs.

The system alternatives both use GUIs, so Earl was not worried about having to memorize a lot of complicated commands. He finally selected the IBM-compatible alternative. He found the DTP features of both systems impressive and was sure he could become proficient (with hard work) fairly quickly. But the IBM-compatible alternative was more cost-effective, and he was especially impressed with its DBMS, which had useful features not available in the Macintosh DBMS. The query capabilities were such that, once he had gotten his system established, Earl would be able to produce special mailings targeted at certain groups of customers. In addition, the salesperson assured him that the system would be highly expandable as his needs grew.

If he had already purchased a computer and some programs, as we originally envisioned, this story would have been quite different. The computer hardware, configured for DOS, would have required a significant, and expensive, upgrade to support Windows and DTP effectively. He would have needed mouse, more memory, more disk storage, and upgraded display.

In addition, he would almost certainly have lost much of the investment he had made in buying and learning to use software. To meet his requirements, he needed full-featured word processing, database, and DTP

FIGURE 7-13

Helpful Publications

These publications and others can be helpful in selecting platform programs and hardware.

programs, rather than the partially-featured modules found in his integrated program. It would have been difficult to abandon the integrated program and begin learning three or four new, complicated programs instead. But if he had stayed with the integrated program, he would have been hampered in his work month after month.

In the ideal scenario, however, Earl placed his order. Three days later, he went back to the store and picked up several large boxes containing his platform hardware and software. His dealer offered to deliver the system and set up the hardware for an additional fee, but Earl felt that setting up the system would help him become familiar with it. He found that the directions included with each unit were sufficient, since he took his time

Alternative 1

Software:	Word processor, DBMS, electronic spreadsheet, DTP, graphics, DOS operating system, Windows
Hardware:	33 MHz, 386 IBM:compatible computer with 6MB main memory, 80 MB hard disk, VGA display adapter with monitor, keyboard, mouse, and laser printer

Alternative 2

Software:	Word processor, DBMS, electronic spreadsheet, DTP, graphics, System 7 operating system
Hardware:	Apple Macintosh II with 6MB main memory, 80MB hard disk, high-resolution color display, keyboard, mouse, and laser printer.

FIGURE 7-14
Platform Alternatives for Earl's Calligraphy

and methodically followed each step. The salesperson offered to help him by phone if he ran into any problems, but this did not turn out to be necessary.

Installing the software took several days of Earl's spare time, spread over about three weeks. Even though Earl had prepared a systems specification sheet like the one shown in Figure 7-12, he had to guess at the answers to some of the questions asked in the installation of two packages. In one case, the software did not work correctly after installation, so Earl telephoned the free *technical support line* listed in the instruction manual and received the help he needed.

Learning to use each package took longer than Earl expected. Since he still had a business to run, he could spend only spare time on the learning, and each package's tutorial program required several hours. Although both the dealer and a local college offered courses in each package, Earl decided to learn by doing—he simply began prototyping his system. By working slowly and allowing plenty of time to stop and check the reference manual periodically, Earl tackled each package in turn. He found the spreadsheet, database, and graphics programs fairly easy to use. The word processor, because it had many useful commands, took somewhat longer to become comfortable with. The DTP package was much more difficult, and Earl finally enrolled in a course that successfully got him started. Friends with computer experience provided invaluable help throughout the learning process.

DESIGNING THE APPLICATION WITH PROTOTYPES

As we have seen, the process of prototyping is a repetitive process in which you start with an initial rough guess at a design, create a system to that design, experiment with the system to see its strengths and weaknesses, refine the design, create a new, improved system, and so on (see Figure 7-15). Approach prototyping with an inquisitive and experimental spirit.

- ▶ Develop initial design
- ▶ Create prototype
- ▶ Redesign

FIGURE 7-15

Designing the Application with Prototyping

If others will be involved with the system—for example, as consumers of its output—then show them the prototype's output and ask for suggestions. If others will ever use the system, let them try out the prototype and offer comments. If expert help is available, get that person's advice too.

For simple, easily modified systems, the first or second prototype may be fairly usable. Yet, you may continue changing the system—tinkering with it—for the rest of its useful life. For more complex systems, where changes are time-consuming and might introduce possible error, plan each prototyping episode to get the most value for your time. In such a case, consider drawing up specifications for the changes you intend to make in the revised prototype, for how you intend to test it, and for the kinds of feedback you intend to get— exactly what do you want to find out in creating this prototype? Putting a plan onto paper increases the chance that your work will produce useful results.

A potential problem with prototyping is that it can be difficult to know when to finish and to declare the system complete. As a businessperson, your time is costly, so you should declare the system complete as soon as it is providing acceptable results. Exactly what that means depends very much on the type of system you are preparing. If your system provides quantitative results, the answers should be completely correct and in usable form. If your system is used to communicate to customers or others, then you should declare your system completed when further changes do not seem likely to improve its communication effectiveness. Before you begin the prototyping process, it is a good idea to think about how you are going to know when the system is complete.

Prototyping the Application at Earl's Calligraphy

As we have seen, Earl decided to combine the program-learning process with the initial prototyping process. When he had finished the tutorials for each program, he began using the program to develop parts of the applications he needed. For example, his practice with the database program involved developing the database application that he wanted. As a result of taking this approach, he often found himself trying to use techniques that he did not completely understand, but he also found that experimenting with the techniques led to deeper understanding. Since these were the techniques he needed for his applications, he was willing to tolerate the mild frustration of having to look up nearly every step in the manual as he went along.

Earl could have brought in his consultant right from the beginning and let him build the initial prototypes. However, he needed to learn the packages anyway. What better way to learn than by prototyping? He knew that, when he got stuck, as he inevitably would, he could call in the consultant. The consulting fees would be well spent at that point.

Earl's prototyping involved three areas: designing and creating the database, designing the spreadsheet report, and designing the catalog production system.

The Database Application Since it seems central to the remaining applications, Earl (once again, in the ideal scenario) began his prototype by

FIGURE 7-16
Evaluating the Prototype
If your system's output will be used by other people, ask them to help evaluate your prototype output.

developing the database application. Reviewing the problem definition that he had developed at the beginning of the project, Earl determined that his database should (1) maintain a mailing list; (2) track customers' order histories so he could determine for each order whether the buyer was a new customer; and (3) maintain a list of catalog items with descriptions and prices. As you can see in Figure 7-17, Earl first built his database with three tables: one for customer data, one for order data, and one for catalog item data. Orders are linked to customers by including the customer's number in the ORDER table. Each order can include up to four separate items.

Since it was available on diskette, Earl loaded the entire inventory list into his ITEM table for testing. (Before he did this, he carefully made a copy of the diskette and set the original aside, just in case a glitch in the prototype's performance should damage the data.) To provide test data, he manually entered about a dozen ORDER records and CUSTOMER records. In the dozen orders that he pulled out at random to use as test data, two included more than the four items that he allowed in the ORDER table. Therefore, they could not be entered. This was a problem!

Earl considered several solutions, but none seemed ideal. Therefore, he decided to seek help from his consultant. The consultant suggested that he replace the one ORDER table with two tables: an ORDER table and an ORDER/ITEM table. Figure 7-18 shows the result. After creating these tables and reentering the test data, he found he could get the results he wanted. Therefore, he began the long task of entering the remaining catalog item and order records to permit full-scale testing.

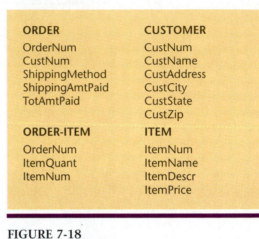

ORDER	CUSTOMER
OrderNum	CustNum
CustNum	CustName
Item1Quan	CustAddress
Item1Name	CustCity
Item1UnitPrice	CustState
Item2Quan	CustZip
Item2Name	**ITEM**
Item2UnitPrice	ItemNum
Item3Quan	ItemName
Item3Name	ItemDescr
Item3UnitPrice	ItemPrice
Item4Quan	
Item4Name	
Item4UnitPrice	
ShippingMethod	
TotAmtPaid	

FIGURE 7-17
Earl's Database—First Try

ORDER	CUSTOMER
OrderNum	CustNum
CustNum	CustName
ShippingMethod	CustAddress
ShippingAmtPaid	CustCity
TotAmtPaid	CustState
	CustZip
ORDER-ITEM	**ITEM**
OrderNum	ItemNum
ItemQuant	ItemName
ItemNum	ItemDescr
	ItemPrice

FIGURE 7-18
Earl's Database—Improved Version

At his request, the consultant also helped him create a preliminary design on paper of the data entry screens, the report formats, and the menu structure of his application. Earl and his consultant agreed that he would try to build the screens and reports that they designed, and that the consultant would build the menus and write the brief programs that would be required.

As he began experimenting with his partially developed system, Earl thought of a completely new use for it. If he could summarize each customer's purchasing history, then he could create direct mail advertisements to pinpoint the needs of specific customers. For example, customers who had bought mostly specialized papers could receive ads targeting that need, and so on. He tried adding this feature to his design, but found that he needed help. His consultant suggested that he first complete the system as it was originally planned and that he meanwhile make a list of possible future enhancements. Then, when the basic system was complete, he could reconsider the items on his list. Additions would make his application more complex, but by then, his experience with computers would also have increased.

The Spreadsheet Report The second area of prototyping Earl's system involved the development of a spreadsheet template for the planned management report. Initially, Earl decided to manually copy the few data values from the database output into the electronic spreadsheet. In an evening's work, he developed a template for the report he wanted, much like the one in Figure 7-7. Since the report is entirely for his own use, he decided to stick with the first prototype. Two items were added to his list of future enhancements. These items enabled the spreadsheet to read database output directly and included several graphs.

Catalog Production The final area of prototyping, which has been delayed while Earl learned to use the DTP program, involved reducing catalog publication costs through DTP techniques. Earl's first try at a DTP version of the catalog did not look terrific, even to him. The people he showed it to did not much like it, either. He decided to produce the current catalog by the old method and to work further on the design.

In his spare time, Earl pored over the design pointers in the documentation that came with his DTP program and further experimented with the catalog. In addition, a customer representative at his printing company helped him locate a design consultant who provided useful suggestions for improvement. The resulting design was much more impressive.

It was at this point that Earl decided to use this design, with DTP, to produce the next catalog. He hoped to gain additional experience with his DTP package as he produced the next two or three versions of the catalog, improving each one as he went along. Then he planned to hire the consultant to review the design again. In this way, he believed, he could get the most return for the consultant's cost.

IMPLEMENTING THE SYSTEM

As you have seen, by the time a system has been repeatedly prototyped, its hardware, software, data, and people components are usually nearly complete. Often, its procedures component has not yet been developed, and it has not been well documented. If this is the case, then you should attend to these areas during the implementation stage.

The result of implementation should be a mature system that is free of error, that is reasonably comfortable for its user(s) to operate, and that produces useful results. If the final prototype fails to measure up to this standard in any way, then continue prototyping until it does.

Often, the point at which prototyping ends and implementation begins is rather fuzzy. Some simple systems essentially remain prototypes forever, as their user/developers continue to experiment and improve them. For more complicated systems in which changes are difficult and time-consuming, you may prefer to do all the experimenting during one period and then to live fairly permanently with the system in the form in which it emerges from that period.

Developing and Testing Procedures

The first task in implementation is developing and testing procedures. The nature of the procedures to be developed depends, to some extent, on the type of system. For a database system, typical procedures involve updating the data in response to changes, producing required outputs, and regularly backing up the system. Other types of systems may need other procedures.

One procedure that should always be developed for every type of system is regular backup. If the system is used irregularly, a backup should be included as part of each use. Otherwise, a backup should be scheduled fairly frequently—for example, once a week. In backing up a system, the idea is to ensure that a second copy (usually on diskettes or tape) of all system programs and data exists. Your procedure should be devised to ensure this. As long as system programs are not changed, a single backup can continue to serve. Data files that change over time, however, should be frequently backed up.

Testing of your procedures is important for two reasons. First, you may not be the only one who ever uses the system. Consider Earl's case again. As his company grows, he undoubtedly will hire some help, perhaps to do some of the record-keeping chores. The procedures must work correctly, and they must be documented clearly and accurately. Second, your procedures may contain mistakes. Until all the processes have been worked through, there is always the possibility that, for example, you will try to use data that is not yet entered, that the product will not work quite the way you expect it to, or that it will take you much longer to do something than you anticipated.

Documenting the System

In documenting a personal information system, concentrate on documenting each of the system components. Hardware documentation should include all the printed documentation that was provided when you purchased the components, along with all receipts, order forms, and the like. Included should be records showing purchase date(s), prices, exact model numbers, and configurations of each unit. If you assembled or configured any parts, then your notes should be included. All this information will be invaluable when questions arise later, after your memory has faded.

Program documentation should include all the printed documentation that was provided with the platform programs, along with descriptions, sample printouts, and other records that would let you reconstruct or modify your final system, should it become necessary. Printouts of your operating system's start-up configuration, such as copies of your CONFIG.SYS and AUTOEXEC.BAT files, are particularly useful as changes are made over time. Lists of the operating system add-ons, support programs, and utility programs that are necessary or useful in support of the system should be compiled, in case the system must ever be reconstructed.

Data documentation should include record descriptions of all data files, table and column descriptions for all databases, and printouts showing cell contents for all spreadsheets.

Procedures documentation is particularly important. Do not depend on your memory—write the procedures down. They should detail every step required to perform each function. You can compile them by writing down everything you do as you actually perform the function, then adding the things the user needs to know to make sense of the instructions. Before you finalize such procedures, ask a potential user to follow

Box 7.2

INCREASING YOUR PERSONAL PRODUCTIVITY

Ergonomics of Computing

Key Elements of a Well-Designed Work Station

- Adjustable chair with good mid- and upper-back support
- Adjustable bilevel terminal table
- Padded and detachable wrist rest
- Copy holder
- Adequate knee clearance
- Adequate work space
- Footrest
- Printer noise shields (if printers are adjacent to work areas)
- Good lighting, including task lighting when needed
- Antiglare shields (or properly shielded windows to prevent glare on monitors)
- Thin, detachable keyboard

them while you watch and take notes. Then go back and polish the parts that need to be clarified.

People documentation lists names, addresses, and telephone numbers of people you have identified as helpful during the development process. Computer store salespersons, consultants, vendor technical service clerks, knowledgeable friends, and others should be listed. The next time you need help may be 18 months away, and it will be difficult to remember or to dig out these names and phone numbers at that time. Making a list and keeping it current is good insurance.

Implementation at Earl's Calligraphy

Earl needed to establish procedures for several activities: maintaining the database, producing the catalog, printing mailing labels, and backing up his files.

To maintain the database, for example, Earl needed to decide when to delete a customer from the mailing list. He decided to do that whenever a customer requested it or when a customer had not placed an order in 24 months. He also established a procedure for eliminating duplicate (or near-duplicate) mailing labels.

To produce a catalog, Earl established procedures for producing camera-ready copy (including page size, margins, overall design, typefaces, type size, borders, placement of photos and drawings, and other standards); for matching photos and drawings to page locations; and for delivering copy to the printer.

Earl needed mailing labels when the catalogs arrived from the printer, and he scheduled their printing accordingly. Furthermore, he needed to add customers to and delete customers from the mailing list before he printed labels.

Finally, Earl decided that he would back up his database once each week (on Friday) and that he would keep three week's worth of backups at his home. In addition, Earl purchased a customer service agreement from the vendors of his word processing program and his DTP program. This arrangement, though it cost a few hundred dollars more, would allow him to call the vendors' customer service engineers and get immediate answers to any problems he encountered.

Earl wrote all these procedures in a notebook that he kept near the computer. When he needs it, his documentation is readily available.

Epilogue

Within four months, Earl's system was satisfying the requirements he had established at the beginning of the system development process. He was doing his own catalog page layouts, as planned. His goal had been to decrease catalog production costs by 10 percent, but after four issues, Earl discovered that his new system had enabled him to slash costs nearly in half.

Earl also increased his mailing list by purchasing some other lists and merging them with his own. Sales increased accordingly.

The discovery that surprised Earl the most was that his customer base was exceedingly loyal. Repeat customers constituted over 90 percent of his sales. He had grossly underestimated this figure in the past, but now he had the facts before him. Such knowledge would be very useful when planning marketing strategies.

Summary

Prototyping is a modification of the classical SDLC methodology. With prototyping, instead of defining system requirements ahead of time on paper, the developer defines requirements by building a working prototype of the system, or part of it, and, by stepwise refinement, improving the prototype until it is satisfactory.

A systems development plan using prototyping involves five stages. First, the problem is defined, and the feasibility of solving the problem through a personal information system is assessed. Second, the solution is classified by determining application type and size and system constraints. Third, the system platform, consisting of all five system components, is selected and implemented. Fourth, the system is prototyped, and the prototype is refined until the system is satisfactory. Fifth, the system is implemented by developing procedures and documentation.

Key Terms

systems development life cycle (SDLC)
prototyping
cost feasibility
schedule feasibility
technical feasibility
constraint
context-sensitive help

Review Questions

1. Name the five stages of classical SDLC.
2. How is prototyping different from classical SDLC?
3. Explain the meaning of "stepwise refinement," as it is used in connection with systems development by prototyping.
4. Prototyping personal information systems is only practical when one condition is met. What is that condition?
5. What are the five stages of developing a personal information system through prototyping?
6. In prototyping, list the tasks to be accomplished during the problem definition stage.
7. What is a problem?
8. Name three kinds of feasibility.
9. Describe a development project plan.
10. In prototyping, what tasks are involved in classifying the solution?
11. Name three factors that should be included in a description of application size.
12. List the components of a system platform.
13. Describe the order in which the elements of the system platform should be selected.
14. Name at least three resources that you may call on for assistance in installing programs on a computer.
15. List four sources of expert assistance in developing a system platform.
16. In prototyping, describe the process of designing the application.
17. Who should be consulted when a prototype has been developed?
18. In prototyping, how should you decide when to declare the system complete?
19. In prototyping, what tasks make up the implementation stage?
20. Describe the documentation that should be assembled for each of the five components of a personal information system.

Discussion Questions

A. In the case of Earl's Calligraphy, summarize the costs and benefits of system development by the "bad" scenario and system development by the "ideal" scenario. That is, in the "bad" scenario, what investments (time, money, and so on) did Earl make, and what return did he receive on his investment? Also answer these questions for the "ideal" scenario.

B. Do you agree that following a specific methodology in developing a system such as Earl's is worthwhile, say, in comparison to just sitting down and working it out logically? Defend your answer.

C. A wide variety of constraints may limit each of the five components of a system. Many of these may be so obvious that, in real situations, they go without saying. For each of the five components of a typical personal information system such as Earl's, list at least five constraints that may commonly limit that component. If possible, combine your list with those of other members of your class.

D. How is creating a system platform—the third stage in the prototyping systems development process—different from just going to a computer store and buying a computer, as Earl originally did? Describe the differences in detail.

E. Do you think it makes sense to select programs first, then to select hardware? Or should we select hardware first, then select programs that run on that hardware? Defend your answer.

F. Summarize what we mean by prototyping in the development of personal information systems. That is, exactly what do we do in the prototyping stage of the process? Describe prototyping in some detail.

MINICASE

Product Evaluation Backup Software

The following information is excerpted from the June 1, 1992, issue of *Infoworld,* a weekly computer industry newspaper. *Infoworld,* like many personal computer publications, regularly reviews and rates products. Read the following abbreviated review and product comparison, and use it to answer the questions that follow.

For recovering data, scores of products are available—antivirus programs, unerasing and unformatting utilities, and special programs designed to repair or recover damaged data files from specific types of applications.

Where data is concerned, however, nothing beats an ounce of prevention. The first line of defense is backing it up. In this comparison we look at six software backup programs. . . .

Each product is scored by *Infoworld* on a variety of factors as shown in the Report Card below.

Infoworld describes the testing that they perform on each criteria. Two of the criteria are described as follows:

Reliability: We graded reliability on the software's capability to back up and restore data intact. We loaded a small test subdirectory with just

REPORT CARD INFO WORLD

Backup Software

	(InfoWorld weighting)	**Central Point Backup for DOS** Version 7.1	**Central Point Backup for Windows** Version 7.2	**Fastback Plus for DOS** Version 3.04	**Fastback Plus for Windows** Version 1.01	**Norton Backup for DOS** Version 2.0	**Norton Backup for Windows** Version 1.2
List price		$129	$129	$189	$189	$129	$149
Performance							
Reliability	(200)	Very Good	Very Good	Satisfactory	Very Good	Excellent	Excellent
Speed	(150)	Excellent	Very Good	Very Good	Very Good	Excellent	Excellent
Documentation	(75)	Very Good	Very Good	Very Good	Very Good	Very Good	Very Good
Ease of learning	(100)	Excellent	Excellent	Very Good	Good	Very Good	Very Good
Ease of use	(150)	Good	Good	Very Good	Good	Very Good	Very Good
Support							
Support policies	(50)	Very Good	Very Good	Excellent	Excellent	Very Good	Very Good
Technical support	(75)	Very Good	Very Good	Very Good	Very Good	Satisfactory	Satisfactory
Value	(200)	Excellent	Excellent	Good	Good	Excellent	Excellent
Final scores		**8.4**	**8.0**	**6.8**	**7.0**	**8.6**	**8.6**

enough data to ensure that all of the backups would fill one disk. For each product we backed up the same data to a set of 1.2 megabyte 5¼ inch and 720K 3½ inch floppy disks . . . . We double checked the backups with the program's Compare function, restored the files to the second hard drive, and compared them once again to the original files using DOS Comp. We achieved successful backups with all six packages.

After this, we used an engineer's scale and the tip of a knife blade to scratch the first disk of each backup set to simulate real-world damage. In order to see how well each program could recover different areas of damage, we tested each program with two variations of the scratch. . . . We then attempted to restore the files to the second hard drive again and compared the recovered files to the originals. To earn a satisfactory score, a program had to accurately recover the majority of files from a damaged area and report the files and data it failed to recover. . . . We award an excellent score to products that fully recover data and are capable of printing a separate report.

Speed: We score speed based on a curve. The fastest product earns an excellent score; the other products earn excellent or lower scores depending on how far behind the leader they finish.

Questions

1. Describe, in your own words, the purpose of the products evaluated in this article.
2. Compare and contrast the differences in the evaluation between the Central Point product for DOS and the Norton Backup product for DOS. Describe a circumstance in which, according to this review, Central Point's product would be better than Norton's. Describe a situation in which, according to this review, Norton's would be better than Central Point's.
3. Suppose that you are asked to give an opinion on which of these products should be used by all of the employees in your department. Are you content to rely only on the opinions expressed in this article? If not, describe other sources of information that you would check before developing your opinion.
4. Assume you are asked to help a co-worker who has developed large desktop publishing and word processing files, but who never backs up those files. Explain how you would use the systems development process described in this chapter to create a backup system for this person.

Excerpted from Tom Bigley, "Backup Software," *Infoworld* (June 1, 1992): pp. 59–61.

P A R T   T H R E E

SHARED INFORMATION SYSTEMS

The personal information systems you studied in Part Two play an important role in business. But despite the proliferation of personal information systems, most of the computing done worldwide is accomplished by larger, more complex, and more expensive shared systems—systems in which many people share access to the data. In such systems, as few as three or four users—or as many as thousands—can access the same database or use the same computer resources concurrently. In Part Three you will learn what problems are raised by shared access and how they are addressed.

Chapter 8 is a foundation for the remaining chapters in this part. It presents the types and functions of shared systems and describes their components.

Data communications is an essential feature of nearly all shared systems. Chapter 9 focuses on the techniques of data communications and the ways that people use data communications in shared systems.

Shared databases are a common component of shared information systems, and are used in the most important systems in typical organizations. Chapter 10 describes the structure and uses of shared databases.

As a future end user, you need to know what shared information systems are and what you can gain from them. And you need to know what your role will be when your company or organization develops a shared system. A shared system is developed in a multistage process, just as a personal information system is. The entire process is more complex, however, as you will learn in Chapter 11.

As you study Part Three, think about how you as a user fit into the larger scheme of things. What role will you play if you take a job at a bank, an insurance company, a manufacturer, an accounting firm, or a school? How will you use teleprocessing or a LAN? How will you use a shared database? What are the kinds of business decisions for which you will need computer-generated information?

CHAPTER 8

Introduction to Shared Information Systems

This chapter introduces shared information systems. We first discuss the benefits of shared systems and then discuss their components. In this chapter we will discuss just the data, procedures, and people components. The hardware and program components are more complicated and will be discussed in the next chapter.

The personal information systems you studied in the last five chapters provide important services and benefits to individual businesspeople. However, the strongest benefit of these systems is also their greatest liability: They are personal systems. Some kinds of data can be processed in a single-user system, but other important data must be shared, such as companywide budgets, inventories, operating plans, and billing systems. Entering and processing such data involves the coordinated activity of many people. For such purposes, shared information systems are needed.

Shared information systems are more complex than personal information systems. Simply the fact that a shared information system involves multiple users makes it more complicated. For example, you might think that customer order entry is a fairly straightforward process—just entering the customer's name and a description of the items ordered into a computer. In fact, a large company's order entry system is very complicated indeed. Consider the order entry system at Jenner-Kline Corporation, a large manufacturer of industrial test equipment.

CHAPTER OUTLINE

EXAMPLE: ORDER ENTRY AND PROCESSING

Most customer orders come to Jenner-Kline Corporation by telephone. A customer representative with a telephone headset sits at a computer terminal, takes the calls, and begins entering data. Processing an order involves determining the answers to a series of questions, as implied by Figure 8-1. The first questions are, Who is placing the order? and Is Jenner-Kline currently accepting orders on credit from this customer? To answer these questions, the customer representative enters the customer's name at the keyboard. This triggers the order entry system to access customer payment history data that is used by the company's accounts receivable system. If the data shows a record of prompt payment, then order entry can continue. Otherwise, the customer representative must ask the customer to arrange for cash payment.

The next question is, Where should the merchandise be shipped? A typical Jenner-Kline customer is a large corporation that may have many branches. Different orders from that corporation may have different shipping addresses. Shipping address data will be used by the company's computerized shipping system. It will be printed on the warehouse packing slip that will be used in assembling and shipping the order.

The next question is complicated: Can Jenner-Kline ship the needed merchandise in time to meet the customer's requirements? To answer the question, the customer representative enters the first item ordered: part number, quantity, item name, and date needed. This triggers the order entry system to access the company's finished goods inventory data about products that are in the warehouse ready to ship. If a sufficient quantity of the item is available in the warehouse and is not committed to another order, then the system OKs the item and moves on to the next item.

If this is not the case, however, then the order entry system must check production scheduling data to determine whether the item is scheduled for production in time for shipment. If it is, then the system OKs the item and moves on to the next item. If it is not, then the next question is asked: Can the item now be scheduled for production in time to meet the customer's requirements? To answer this question, the order entry system transmits a request to the production scheduling system.

To schedule production, the company must commit raw materials, workers, and production machines. To determine whether raw materials will be available, the production scheduling system must first determine what raw materials are needed. This data is available in the database used by production scheduling. Then the system must check the raw materials inventory to see whether these materials are available and not committed to some other scheduled production. If some raw materials are unavailable, then the system checks whether the materials have been ordered for delivery in time.

If raw materials are available or are on order, then the system must check whether workers and machines are available to produce the goods. If they are available, then the system schedules production; commits raw materials, workers, and machines to the production process; and OKs the order for shipment. If they are not available, the system places a backorder to be scheduled for production and shipment as near as possible to the date when the customer needs the goods.

All this processing takes place in a tiny fraction of a second, and the result simply pops up next to the item listing on the customer representative's screen as "OK" or "Backordered." The representative communicates the result to the customer and moves on to the next item.

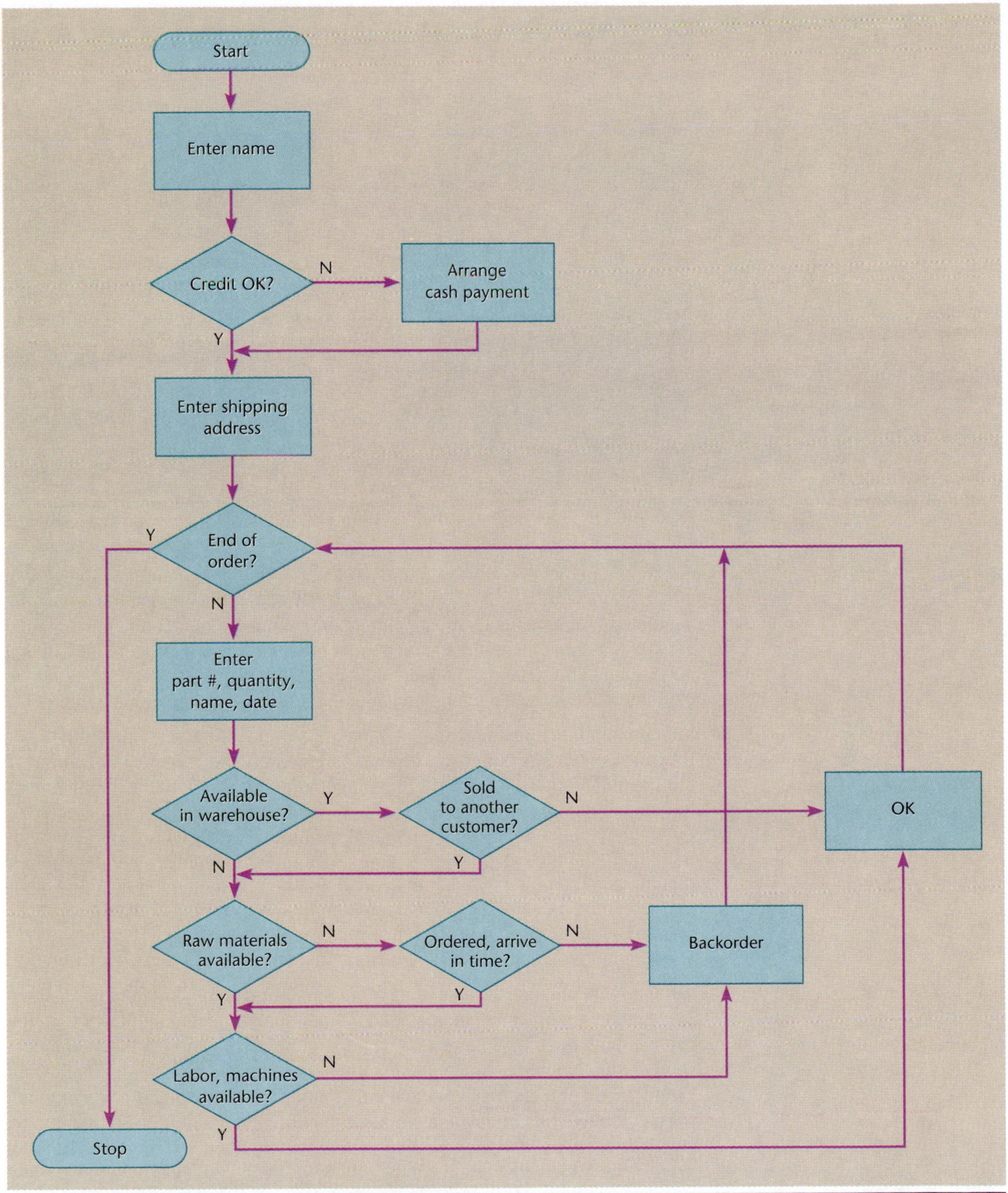

FIGURE 8-1 **Order Entry Processing**
This flowchart is a simplified version of the order entry process at Jenner-Kline Corporation.

FIGURE 8-2
Customer Representative
This customer representative is entering data to the order entry system.

This description gives you a taste of order entry processing at Jenner-Kline. The system in all its detail is considerably more complicated than we have space to describe here. For just one example, Jenner-Kline has three production plants: one at the headquarters in Tulsa, one in Mexico, and one in Taiwan. To schedule production, all three production factors must be available at the same plant: raw materials, workers, and machines. Inventories and production schedules for each plant are maintained on computers at the plant, and each plant must be checked in turn for each item ordered. Therefore, processing an order often involves repeated communication among computers many thousands of miles apart.

Jenner-Kline's order entry system and many of its other processing systems are closely interrelated. Figure 8-3 shows some of the interrelationships. Each system had to be designed with the other systems' needs in mind, which made the design much more complicated.

The order entry system and the other systems that interact with it were designed to meet a set of important corporate needs. The key benefits are improved customer service and reduced costs. Customer service is improved because the customer can be given firm shipping dates for each item ordered and because the production planning module makes the manufacturing process faster and more flexible in responding to customer needs. The cost savings arise through accurate planning. For example, inventory costs are reduced because the company knows exactly what raw materials will be needed on each day and therefore does not have to maintain large reserve stocks in case they might be needed. Labor and machine costs are reduced because both workers and machines can be scheduled to work steadily and efficiently. These systems are required to maintain Jenner-Kline's competitive position in its marketplace.

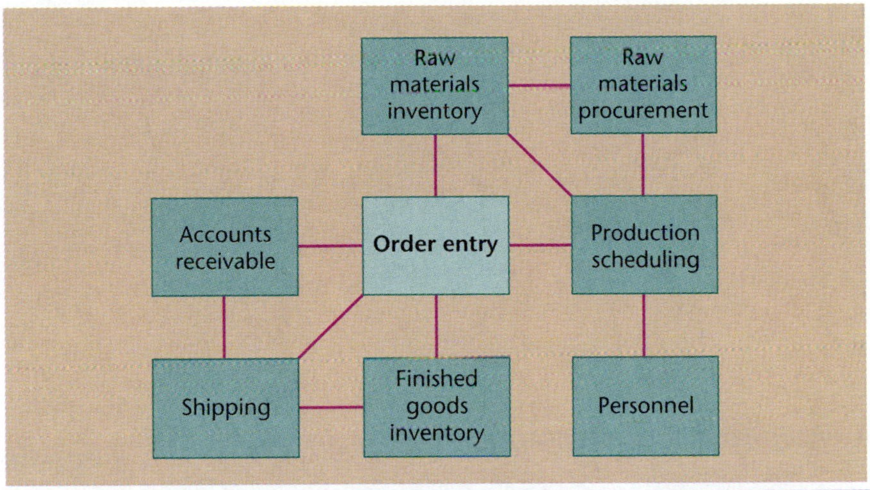

FIGURE 8-3
Interrelated Systems
The order entry system is closely related to several other companywide processing systems.

HOW SHARED INFORMATION SYSTEMS BENEFIT ORGANIZATIONS

Shared information systems have one key feature: They have more than a single user. Shared information systems serve four fundamental purposes: to share hardware, to share programs, to share data, and to facilitate human communication. This section briefly describes each purpose.

Sharing Expensive Hardware

Hardware-sharing systems let multiple users share access to expensive hardware devices that they could not justify for their own applications alone. For example, eight members of a department occasionally create publications and other graphics output. No one application that they use could justify the expense of a $10,000 high-resolution laser printer. However, if all their applications can share the printer, those applications can also share the expense. Expensive printers, plotters, scanners, and other input/output (I/O) hardware are often shared this way. In addition, fast, large-capacity disks can also be shared.

Figure 8-4 shows two ways that hardware can be shared. The system in Figure 8-4a is primitive: Users copy data onto floppy diskettes and physically carry it to the PC with attached plotter, printer, or other device. This is sometimes called **sneaker-net** (that is, put on your sneakers, grab the diskette, and run down the hall). Figure 8-4b shows a more sophisticated system using a **local area network (LAN)**—a group of microcomputers and other hardware devices interconnected by a high-speed data communications link.

Another form of hardware sharing was common before the advent of personal computers and is still used in some companies. In this form, the

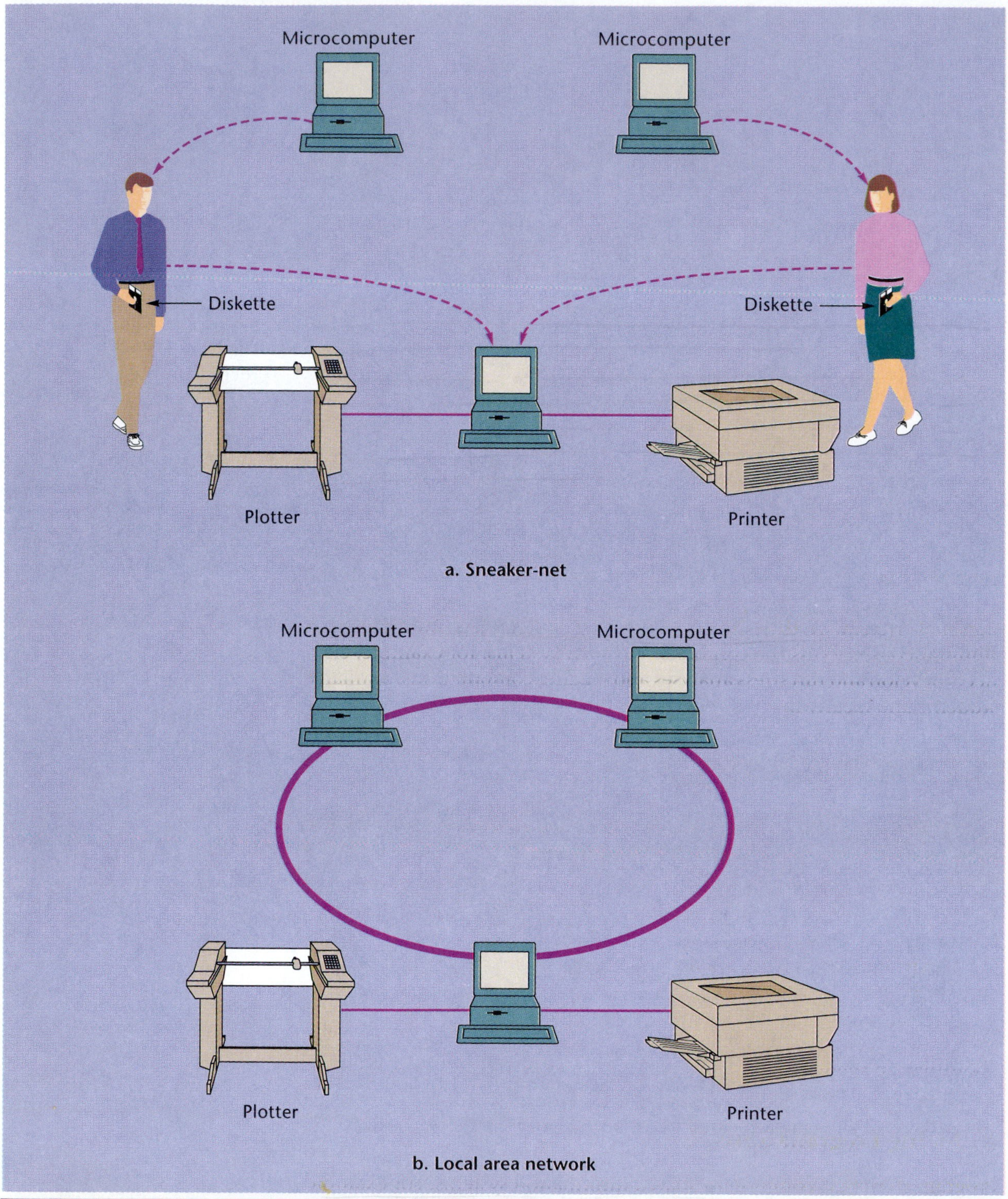

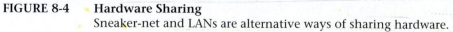

FIGURE 8-4 **Hardware Sharing**
Sneaker-net and LANs are alternative ways of sharing hardware.

FIGURE 8-5

Timesharing System
This minicomputer is the hub of a timesharing system. Along with the terminals in this room, about two dozen additional terminals are located throughout the building, and another dozen are at remote locations.

processing power of a minicomputer or a mainframe computer is shared among users sitting at separate terminals, each of whom uses it as a personal system. A **timesharing** operating system lets multiple users simultaneously access the computer. On such systems, for example, engineers develop and run stress analyses and loading computations. Similarly, students and faculty in colleges use the system to learn programming and do statistical manipulations.

When personal computers were introduced, many simpler timesharing applications were shifted to PCs, and timesharing gave users access to more computer power than a personal computer provides. For intensive computation, such as large engineering or statistical analyses, the power of a minicomputer or a mainframe computer is often needed. More recently, however, the power of microcomputers has increased to exceed that of many larger computers, and even many of these computation-intensive applications are being shifted to PCs.

Hardware-sharing systems are, in many ways, the simplest type of shared computer system. Multiple uses of hardware must be coordinated, just as shared use of a copying machine is coordinated. But this is often easy to do, and some shared hardware devices can automatically do the coordination themselves.

Reducing Program Costs

Program sharing is common in shared information systems. For example, one computer with a large, fast hard disk may store the programs used on all the computers in a LAN. This saves storage space, since all users load the program into their computers' memories from the same disk copy. It

FIGURE 8-6
Program Sharing on a LAN
Program sharing is often via a LAN.

also usually saves money, since most vendors charge less for the single network version of their programs than for the many individual copies that would otherwise be required. In addition, when new versions of programs become available, installing the updated program on the single computer is much easier than installing it separately on each of the dozen or more computers in the LAN.

Some vendors require that each company pay a license fee for every computer in a LAN that carries their programs. Others require only that a fee be paid for the number of users who will simultaneously run the program. In that case, a company can provide very inexpensive program access to employees who use the program only occasionally. System software can limit the number of simultaneous users to meet the terms of the agreement.

Shared Access to Data

Data sharing is another common reason for shared systems. Data-sharing systems are the oldest and most common form of shared system. Until recently, the term *shared-data system* usually referred to database processing, and databases still represent the bulk of such systems. However, with new technology emerging, other shared-data systems are coming to the forefront. We will consider shared-text, spreadsheet, and database applications.

Text Applications Text-sharing systems allow users to share access to text data. Text files often include not only words and sentences, but also

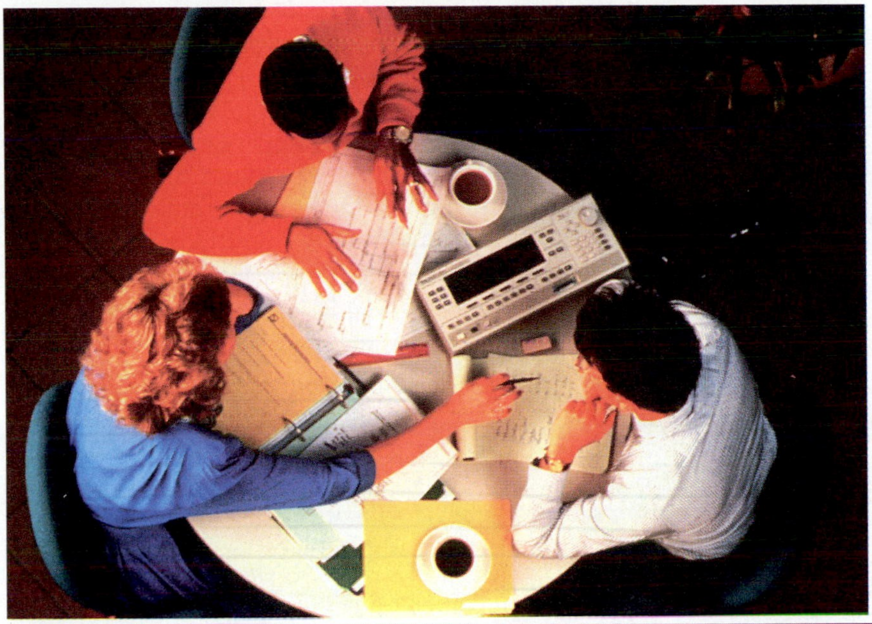

FIGURE 8-7
Sharing a Spreadsheet
One person developed the template of this spreadsheet, and several others added data to it.

formatting specifications such as type fonts, underlining, boldface, and italics. In addition, in this context the term *text* is broadened to include graphics, drawings, illustrations, and other forms of image data.

For example, staff members in a department may share the task of developing and presenting a major report. Each section, when completed by its author, may be circulated for review and comment to the others. Sections may include text, graphs, pictures, and even full-motion video and sound for the presentation. Reviewers see not only the document, but also the comments of prior reviewers.

Spreadsheet Applications Some groups of people share spreadsheet data. A group of budget analysts, for example, might share the fundamental format (the template) for the corporate budget. One copy of the spreadsheet is filled with budget figures for each department in the company. Then the results are integrated into a company-level spreadsheet.

Shared spreadsheets can be implemented in several ways. For one, a spreadsheet program can reside on multiple microcomputers connected via a LAN. For another, a single spreadsheet program can reside on a mainframe computer or a minicomputer, and multiple users can access shared data through a timesharing system. For a third alternative, personal computer spreadsheet programs can transfer data to and from a shared mainframe or minicomputer spreadsheet.

Database Applications Shared database systems are probably the most widely used shared systems today. The general-purpose databases of most large corporations fall into this category. These systems store accounting and inventory information and support sales and order processing, production and operations, and many other companywide functions. In addition, many department-level applications may involve shared databases separate from the companywide database. For example, an engineering department may maintain a database to show which engineering drawings pertain to each model of the company's various products. Similarly, to aid in solving current problems, a quality assurance department may maintain a database of past quality problems and their solutions.

Electronic Mail

Some shared systems exist to facilitate human communication. **Electronic mail (E-mail)** is the most common example. The purpose of E-mail systems is to provide a means for creating, editing, and distributing messages electronically. With E-mail, each person connected to the system is allocated a **mailbox** and a set of programs for creating, transmitting, and reading mail. The mailbox is simply a file into which the E-mail system deposits electronic correspondence.

Figure 8-8 shows a schematic of a typical E-mail application. This system consists of a group of microcomputers connected via communications lines in a LAN. E-mail can also be accessed through a timesharing system. For the system in Figure 8-8, each computer has a mailbox on a centralized disk where the E-mail system deposits mail. Periodically, the microcomputer users examine their mailboxes (via the LAN) to see if they have mail.

Figure 8-9 shows a screen that is used to create mail. You enter the recipient's electronic address and type in your message. The recipient can be an individual or a distribution list, which is a file containing the names of a group of recipients, such as all employees in a department or all members of a project team.

Technology is developing rapidly in the field of shared communication systems, and during your career new forms will probably evolve. Group conferencing and group decision support, for example, are now being developed, and other forms are in the experimental stage.

The hardware and program components of shared information systems are discussed in the next chapter. This chapter considers the data, procedures, and people components.

DATA COMPONENT

The most important issue related to the data in shared information systems concerns where the data is located. On the one hand, the data may all be stored in a single computer where every user accesses it. On the other hand, the data may be **partitioned**—split into pieces that are stored on various computers—or **replicated**—copied, with parts that are stored on two or more computers.

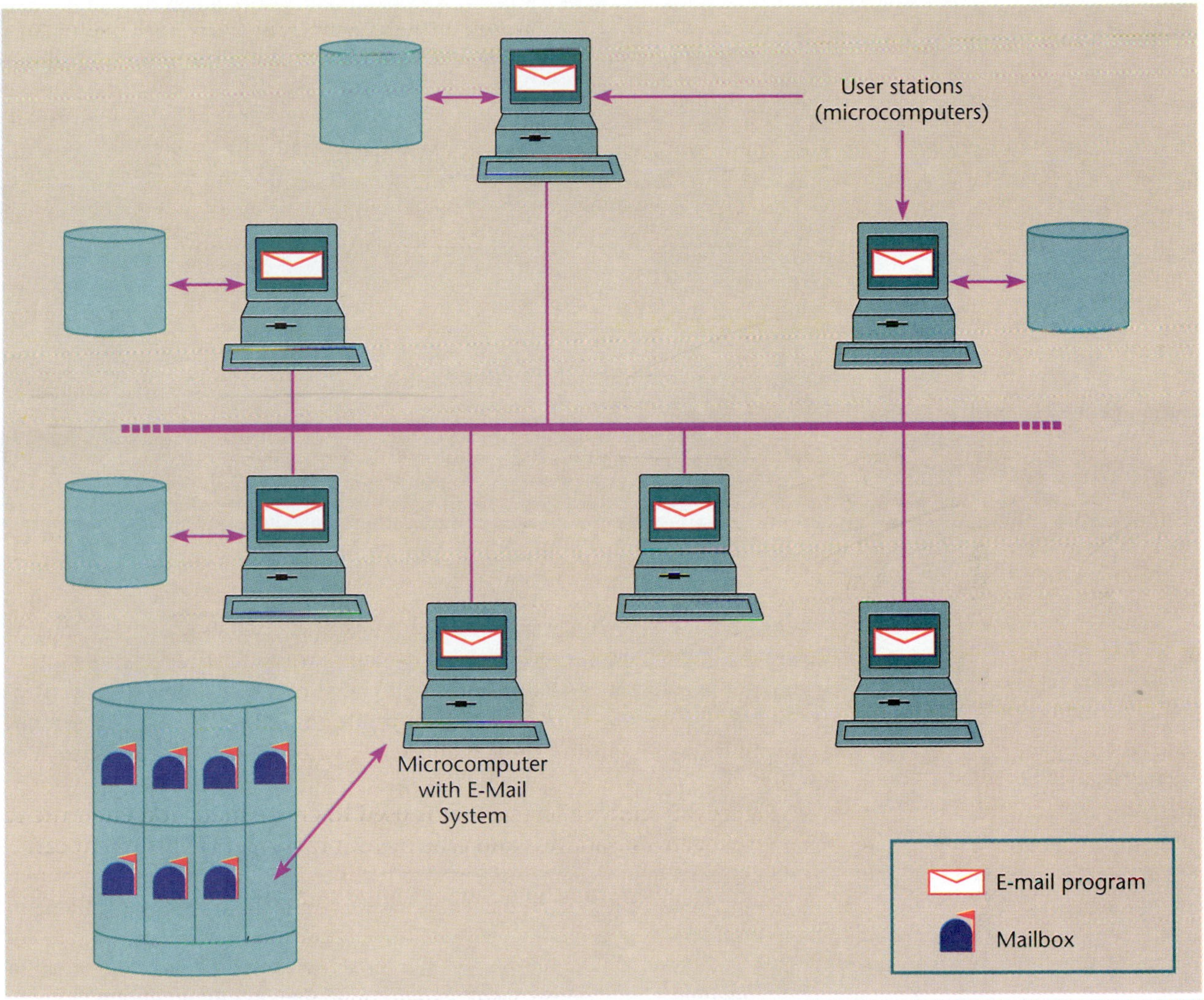

FIGURE 8-8

E-Mail System

The E-mail system program runs on a computer, and its hard disk stores mailboxes for each user. Programs on user computers can request mailbox contents, display incoming messages, and create outgoing messages.

Partitioning the Data

A typical reason for partitioning data is to locate each set of data near its major group of users. For example, a large hotel chain could process all data on a single, centralized computer at headquarters, but it could alternatively place a computer in each hotel for processing the data related to that hotel's operations. A centralized system typically costs less than several processing centers in a partitioned system; it is easier for top management to control; and it offers less risk of unauthorized access (see Figure 8-10).

However, a partitioned system has important advantages, too. An information system on a computer in a hotel is likely to be more flexible in meeting that hotel manager's information needs. Its staff reports directly to the manager, who decides pay raises and promotions. Therefore, the

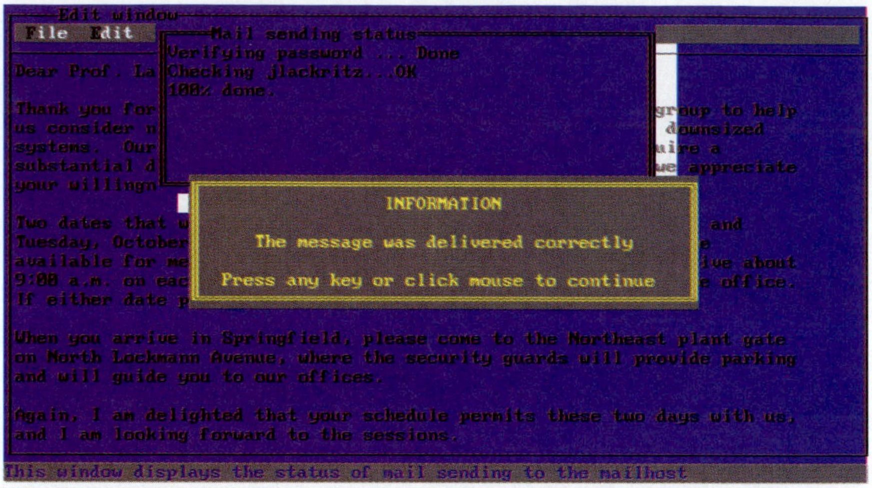

FIGURE 8-9

E-Mail Screen

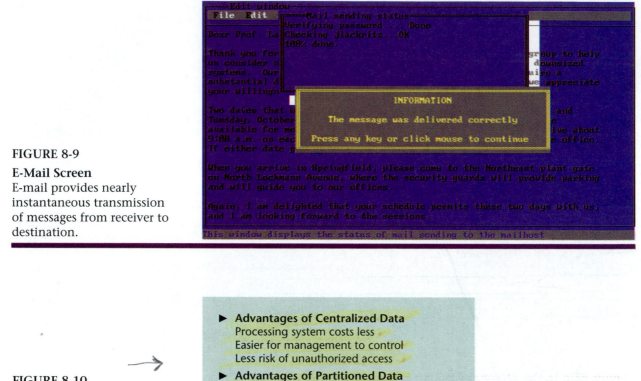

E-mail provides nearly instantaneous transmission of messages from receiver to destination.

FIGURE 8-10

Centralized and Partitioned Data

- **Advantages of Centralized Data**
  - Processing system costs less
  - Easier for management to control
  - Less risk of unauthorized access
- **Advantages of Partitioned Data**
  - Flexibility in meeting local needs
  - Local management feels data ownership

manager can expect developers to be very responsive in meeting local needs.

At the same time, the manager, who is receiving useful output from the system, has a personal interest in making sure that data entry is done quickly and accurately. The manager feels a personal ownership of the data. When the data processing center is two thousand miles away, the manager is only one among many seeking the attention of developers, and output probably only partly meets the manager's specific needs. In such a case, timely and accurate data entry may receive a much lower priority, partly because the manager feels (correctly) that someone else owns the data. In some cases, the improvement in data accuracy alone is sufficient reason to partition the data.

When data is partitioned, procedures must be established to give data access to users in all parts of the organization. In the hotel chain, for example, users at headquarters need regular access to summary data such as room occupancy rates, maintenance costs, and labor costs. Under special circumstances, headquarters personnel may need access to very specific data, such as the name of the current occupant of room 423, the exact

Box 8.1

INCREASING YOUR PERSONAL PRODUCTIVITY

Togetherness in the Realm of "Virtual Reality"

Entering a computer-generated world known as virtual reality (VR) is a thrill. Using goggles and gloves, you can explore in 3-D color and manipulate objects. But there's been no way to share the experience.

Now, Japan's NEC Corp. has designed a prototype that brings up to five people together in a simulated environment—so engineers in different places, for example, could work on a common design problem. Instead of bulky headgear required by most U.S. VR systems, NEC uses goggles that convert a computer-screen image to three dimensions. And when participants wear gloves linked to workstations in a high-speed network, their hand motions are mirrored by hand-like icons on the screen.

Crunching the data for these moving images strains today's workstations, so the objects are just crude animations. But within three years, NEC predicts, more powerful computers will enable teams in Europe, America, and Japan to share "virtual workbenches" to design cars and aircraft.

amount paid to the plumber who last repaired the toilet in room 719, or the amount of federal tax withheld from Jennifer Weldon's March 23 paycheck. Occasionally, personnel in one hotel may need to access data stored in another. For example, they may need to assist a guest by reserving a room in another hotel of the chain and therefore must access reservation data stored on that hotel's computer. Thus, the owners of various parts of partitioned data must agree to maintain the data in such a way as to provide these kinds of access.

Replicating the Data

The salespeople at Jenner-Kline Corporation (described at the beginning of this chapter) travel extensively to meet with their customers. Ideally, before they make a sales presentation, they would like to know the customer's purchasing habits, payment history, and even personal data such as the names of the customer's spouse and children. All of this data is stored in the company's order-processing database, but, on a practical level, the salespeople cannot take that massive database with them.

To meet this need, each salesperson has been allocated a laptop computer. Before leaving on a trip, a salesperson extracts selected customer data and stores it on the computer. Then, on the road, the salesperson accesses this downloaded data to obtain customer information.

Handling the data in this manner creates two potential problems. First, the salespeople have downloaded data that is current only at the moment when they extract it. Two milliseconds later, massive changes may be made to the data they just extracted, but they will not see these changes until the next time they download the data. This limitation is usually not a problem because the salespeople do not need up-to-the-minute data. They can meet their needs by remembering that the data was current as of Monday morning, when it was downloaded. If this were not so—if the salespeople needed the most current data—then replicating this data would not be feasible.

The second potential problem of replicated data arises if the salespeople are permitted to update values in their data and then return the updated values to the company database. This will effectively bypass the company's carefully designed data entry procedures and avoid the extensive protections against erroneous data that those procedures provide. Instead, if a salesperson believes data is incorrect, he or she must use a different system to correct the data, one designed to make data changes. Then, the next time the data is downloaded, it will be correct.

PROCEDURES COMPONENT

As we saw earlier in this book, information systems commonly include four categories of procedures: user procedures for normal processing and for failure recovery, and operations procedures for these same two situations. Procedures not only must be developed, they also must be clearly and completely documented. The documentation makes procedures usable.

We will consider the four categories of procedures in turn. Then we will consider two areas of special procedural requirements for controlled sharing in shared-data information systems: concurrency control and EDP controls.

User Procedures for Normal Processing

Users need to know how to access the processing system and how to do their work (see Figure 8-11). In addition, they need to know what constraints exist on their activities. For example, if they cannot change downloaded data and then return it to the company database, they must know what they should do instead when changes are needed. Documentation of such a constraint should explain why the constraint is needed.

Finally, users need procedures for security and control. When users share a system, they also share responsibility to protect the data against mistakes in processing, inadvertent losses, and intentional malfeasance. The basic EDP controls are described later in this chapter.

Operations Procedures for Normal Processing

Operators need instructions for starting and running the system, maintaining the various hardware devices and file systems, and regularly back-

- Initiating access to processing system
- Accomplishing work
- Understanding constraints on processing
- Maintaining security and control

FIGURE 8-11
User Procedures for Normal Processing

- Starting and running hardware and programs
- Maintaining backup
- Monitoring and tuning system
- Periodically maintaining hardware, programs, data
- Maintaining security and control
- Maintaining activity log and other record keeping

FIGURE 8-12
Operations Procedures for Normal Processing

- Detecting failures and correcting errors
- Maintaining business operations during failure
- Implementing postrecovery measures

FIGURE 8-13
User Procedures for Failure Recovery

ing up the data (see Figure 8-12). In addition, the communications hardware and programs used in shared systems have adjustable features that are set depending on the work to be done. The adjustment is sometimes called **tuning** the system. Most systems produce performance statistics to facilitate such tuning. Operations personnel need procedures to obtain and interpret such statistics as well as procedures for making specific adjustments.

Finally, operations personnel need control and security procedures. These procedures specify when the system can be used, who can access it, and so forth. Most data communications systems maintain a log of activity that must be examined periodically for unauthorized or suspicious activity.

User Procedures for Failure Recovery

Users need procedures for detecting failures and correcting errors (see Figure 8-13). They also need to know what to do when the system has failed. For example, in an order entry system, customers will continue to place telephone orders even though the system that processes the customer database has failed. How should the representatives proceed? What orders should they accept? What data should they gather? What restrictions should they place on their activities? Finally, users need to know what steps are needed to resume normal activity when the system returns to service.

FIGURE 8-14
Operations Procedures for Failure Recovery

- Detecting failures
- Determining steps to take in case of failure
- Initiating recovery activities
- Maintaining failure logs and other record keeping

Operations Procedures for Failure Recovery

Operators also need to know how to detect that failure has occurred and how to recover if it has (see Figure 8-14). Whom should the operator call for assistance? What users need to be contacted? What files may need to be recovered from backups? What work may need to be reprocessed? Such procedures must be carefully thought out and tested well in advance.

Finally, operations personnel need a standard procedure and a format for keeping records of failure and recovery activities. These records serve several purposes, including that of documentation for complaints to vendors and even for potential litigation.

Coordinating Data Access in Shared Systems

A key challenge of shared information systems is to coordinate access to shared resources in ways that meet users' diverse needs and prevent users from interfering with each other's work. **Controlled sharing** implements reasonable controls over access to data and prevents one person's work from interfering with another's. Much of the complexity of shared systems arises from this need for coordination.

Concurrent processing occurs when two or more users access the same data at the same time. For example, in a typical shared order entry system, many customer representatives are concurrently entering orders into the same database.

The nature of the required coordination in concurrent processing depends, in large degree, on the amount of data allocated to a particular user. **Granularity** refers to the size of the units of data that are shared. For example, the granularity of a shared word processing system could be a document. If so, an entire document may be checked out to an individual and no one else may be permitted to access that document until the person is finished with it. Alternatively, the level of granularity might be major sections within a document. In this case, only a portion of a document is checked out to a particular user.

The level of granularity influences the throughput of the shared system. The larger the level of granularity, the greater the chance that there will be delays due to contention for access to the data, but the easier it is to administer the system. On the other hand, the smaller the level of granularity, the less chance there is of contention, but the greater the cost of administering the shared resources.

	DATA			
User A	W_1	W_2	W_3	User B
1. Read count for Warehouse 1 (4)	4	10	7	2. Read count for Warehouse 2 (10)
	4	7	7	3. Decrement count by 3 (7)
				4. Write count for Warehouse 2 (7)
5. Read count for Warehouse 2 (7)				6. Read count for Warehouse 1 (4)
7. Read count for Warehouse 3 (7)				8. Add 3 to Warehouse 1 count (7)
9. Total 18 (should be 21)	7	7	7	10. Write count for Warehouse 1 (7)

FIGURE 8-15

Inconsistent Read Problem User A attempts to get a total of refrigerators in all three warehouses while User B is transferring three refrigerators from Warehouse 1 to Warehouse 3. Follow the steps in order and see how User A gets the wrong total of refrigerators.

Typically, database applications share data at the record (or table row) level of granularity. Applications such as word processors and spreadsheets usually share data at the file level of granularity.

Record-Level Sharing Two users can share access to the same record in three different ways: (1) read/read, where two users concurrently read the same record without updating it; (2) read/update, where one user reads the record while a second user updates it; and (3) update/update, where both users update the record.

No problems will arise in the read/read case. Both users can concurrently read the same record without interfering with each other. The read/update case may or may not raise a problem, however, depending on the needs of the applications. No problem will occur as long as users who are reading understand and accept the likelihood that the data they are viewing may be changed as they are viewing it.

For example, in an order entry system, suppose that one user is producing a summary report about the number of sales by each salesperson during the current week while the order processing is continuing. Salespeople are making sales and updating data at the same time that the report is being generated. In this case, the user of the summary report must realize that the report is based on changing data.

However, awareness of potential errors does not always guarantee no problems. If the user needs an exact report of the number of orders at a particular point in time, then concurrent changes may be a serious problem. For example, if the report is used to compute bonuses for salespersons, then it must be based on consistent data.

Here is another example involving read/update concurrency. User A, in Figure 8-15, wants to count the number of a certain product—say, Model 51B Refrigerators, in Warehouses 1, 2, and 3. User B, concurrently, is transferring three such refrigerators from Warehouse 1 to Warehouse 2. Because of the order in which the reads and writes are processed by the file server, User A concludes there are three fewer refrigerators in

User A (Remove 3 units from inventory)	DATA W_1	W_2	W_3	User B (Remove 2 units from inventory)
1. Read count for Warehouse 1 (4)	4	10	7	2. Read count for Warehouse 1 (4)
3. Decrement by 3 (1)				
5. Write count for Warehouse 1 (1)	1	10	7	4. Decrement by 2 (2)
	2	10	7	6. Write count for Warehouse 1 (2)

FIGURE 8-16 Lost Update Problem
Follow the steps in order and see how User A's update is lost through a problem in concurrent processing.

inventory than there actually are. This is sometimes called the **inconsistent read problem**. Before discussing means of preventing this problem, we will consider the final type of concurrency.

Update/update concurrency occurs when two users attempt to update the same data concurrently. Such concurrency is always a problem. Figure 8-16 shows an example of the **lost update problem** in which two users read and change the same data. Changes made by the first user are lost due to an update made by the second user.

In general the solution to problem situations involving concurrent access is for each user to lock data that is read with the intent to update. A **lock** prevents any other program from using the data until the lock is released. Thus, in both Figure 8-15 and Figure 8-16, reads for updates must be preceded by lock requests and followed by release requests. Locks prevent the inconsistent read problem because the reading user cannot obtain the data until the update is complete. Similarly, locks prevent lost updates.

Locking solves one problem but introduces another. Suppose two users are running application programs to process orders, as in Figure 8-17. Both are processing orders for diamond necklaces and plush black velvet boxes. Suppose User A's program obtains a lock on the record for diamond necklaces while User B's program obtains a lock on the record for velvet boxes. Now suppose that User A requests the record for plush black velvet boxes. User A cannot lock that record because User B already has it locked. So User A must wait. Next, User B requests the record for diamond necklaces. User B cannot lock that record because User A has it locked. User B must wait as well. This situation, called **deadlock**, or **deadly embrace**, can be overcome only by canceling one of the transactions and starting it over.

This circumstance occurs rarely, but it does occur. It becomes apparent to the user only because the system will issue a message like, "System contention error," and then ask the user to start the order over.

The locking and unlocking of data is done by the application program or by the DBMS. Users are never asked (or trusted to remember) to place locks before accessing data. You should know, however, that such locks are being placed, and that on rare occasions users may be required to restart transactions.

DATA			
User A	**Necklace**	**Box**	**User B**
1. Access necklace record for update	Lock		
		Lock	2. Access box record for update
3. Request box record for update			
			4. Request necklace record for update
(Awaiting access)			(Awaiting access)

FIGURE 8-17

Deadlock Problem

User A and User B are each processing orders for a diamond necklace and a plush black velvet box. Follow the steps in order and see how User A and User B have each blocked the other from completing their processing.

CONTENTS			
Action	**User A Memory**	**User B Memory**	**Disk Storage**
User A calls up document for edit	Original document		Original document
User B calls up document for edit	User A edited version of document	Original document	Original document
User A saves edited document	User A edited version of document	User B edited version of document	User A edited version of document
User B saves edited document	(Other work)	User B edited version of document	User B edited version of document

FIGURE 8-18

Lost Update Problem with Documents

User A's editing changes to the document are lost.

File-Level Sharing The second major type of concurrent data sharing is at the file level of granularity. This type of data sharing occurs in information systems in which **monolithic files** such as word processing documents, spreadsheets, publications, and graphic images are shared across the department. These files are called monolithic because they are not structured into records as databases are. Such files must normally be processed as one unit.

For example, when members of a project group share in the preparation of a report, the coordination usually involves a combination of programs and procedures. Programs that support group word processing normally include features to check out documents, such as report sections, to a single user at a time. This avoids the lost update problem with documents (as shown in Figure 8-18). While one user is working on the document, other users are prevented from accessing it. In some cases, a distinction may be made between full access and read-only access. Under read-only access, a user may view the document but may not change it. A shared version of a program may permit only one full-access user at a time but any number of read-only user accesses.

Not all programs support limited access, though as more programs become available in shared (or "network") versions, this capability will be increasingly available.

Program-supported limited access is typically supplemented by agreed procedures. For example, each section of the report may be assigned to one author, who is the only person permitted to change it. Others may offer suggestions, but all agree that only one specific person may actually make changes.

PREVENTING COMPUTER CRIME: COMPUTER AUDITING AND CONTROLS

The term **EDP controls** originated with accountants and auditors. (*EDP* is an accounting term that stands for "electronic data processing," which refers to the processing systems that enter and maintain data in the company's central accounting database.) EDP controls are features of any of the five components of a business computer system that reduce the likelihood of unauthorized activity. The basic categories of EDP controls that users must understand are management controls, organizational structure controls, data center resource controls, and input/processing/output controls. (Two additional categories of EDP controls—data administration controls and systems development controls—are of concern mainly to information systems professionals and will not be considered here.)

Example: Detecting Computer Crime

Modern Record Distributing Company (MODREC) was a spinoff company. It had been a rock music division of a large, traditional record manufacturer. The separate company was created to support MODREC's sales of more than $5 million annually.

MODREC's first president was the son of a parent company's director. He was promoted to his position through influence rather than ability. Consequently, MODREC's sales began to slip, personnel morale fell, and MODREC lost many opportunities in the marketplace.

MODREC's small data processing department was managed by the chief accountant. The accountant meant well, but he was uneducated about data processing.

When Harold Johnson applied for the systems analysis/programming job, the chief accountant was delighted. At 25, Harold was young for the position, but he had an impressive background. He had had major responsibility in the development of three different computer systems in his prior position. He left that position because he believed the major challenges were over, and he wanted something new. He was highly motivated and willing to spend many hours solving difficult problems. Furthermore,

INCREASING YOUR PERSONAL PRODUCTIVITY

Box 8.2

A Computer Virus: What It Is and How It Spreads

Creation: A programmer writes a tiny bit of computer code, which can attach itself to other programs and alter them or destroy data kept on a computer disk. The virus also can reproduce by copying itself to other programs stored on the same disk.

Distribution: Most often, the virus is attached to a piece of normal software. The virus spreads as the owner exchanges software with other computer enthusiasts via electronic bulletin boards or by trading floppy disks.

Infection: The more its host program is swapped, the more the virus replicates itself, until it becomes pervasive. But no one is aware of the infection, because the virus has been designed to remain dormant—perhaps for months.

Attack: At a predetermined time, the virus activates itself. It takes its cue from the internal clock/calendar that computers use to time-stamp their work. The virus seizes control of the computer and works its mischief.

Prevention: Do your utmost to protect the security of your system, especially when exchanging software or otherwise communicating with the outside world. Consider the use of an antivirus program (or Vaccine), which attempts to foil viruses by keeping them out of your system and preventing them from replicating if they do get in.

he was courageous and would stand up to anybody when his ideas were disputed. He was also creative and adventurous, and he enjoyed challenges. In short, he had all the skills and traits needed to be a superior systems developer.

In his first year, Harold made many contributions to the company's data processing function. There was a vast improvement in the level of service. Salespeople were given better information about their customers. The time required to deliver an order was cut in half, and sales went up. Further, the accounting systems were improved, and the chief accountant had better information than ever.

Unfortunately, Harold began to feel discontented. Nobody paid attention to him. He felt that no one recognized the contributions he had made. He probably would have gone to another company, but after a year MODREC gave him a substantial pay increase, and he earned more than he could get elsewhere.

As he worked with the accounting systems, Harold began to notice MODREC's large profits. These profits were possible, in spite of ineffective management, because MODREC's products had a very high markup. Harold concluded that MODREC was "ripping off" its customers.

One day Harold mentioned this to Joan Everest, the manager of a neighborhood record store that ordered from MODREC. "Harold," said

Joan, almost in jest, "why don't you reprogram one of those computers to offer special discounts to my store? Perhaps I could share the savings with you."

Harold was never quite the same. He was bored at work, and the technical challenge of programming such ``special discounts" excited him. Additionally, he was angry with the way MODREC had treated him, and he believed that it was unfair for the company to make so much profit. Joan needed the financial help, and MODREC could easily afford to lose $40,000 to $50,000 per year. In some ways Harold felt he was playing Robin Hood—stealing from the rich and giving to the poor.

Once Harold decided to cooperate with Joan, the technical aspects of his task were easy. He changed the pricing program to look for Joan's customer number and to reduce her prices by 85 percent. He was the only one to see the special copy of the program. The unchanged version was kept in the program documentation library for appearances.

Harold Johnson is a typical computer criminal. To see how he was caught, we must consider EDP controls.

Management Controls

Harold Johnson was dissatisfied with the management at MODREC. He felt underappreciated. Because his boss was only the chief accountant, Harold was buried in the finance department. Consequently, neither he nor anyone else in data processing had access to top management.

The members of top management did not have access either to Harold or to data processing operations. They knew little of what he was doing, and they had only a limited idea of how data processing operated. They allocated considerable money on data processing, but they did not know how the money was spent. In short, there was a large gulf between top-level management and data processing operations.

Over the years, professionals have learned that a management situation like the one at MODREC is an invitation to trouble. Senior managers of a company should take an active part in the management of the data processing function. They do not have to run machines or mount tapes. However, they should recognize the importance of data processing to the company, and they should set the direction for, and be actively involved in, data processing plans. In other words, **management controls** (summarized in Figure 8-19) need to exist.

Senior managers can handle data processing in several ways. First, they can demonstrate an appreciation for and an interest in the data processing function. Occasional visits to the computer staff, recognition of them in the company newsletter, and references to data processing operations in the year-end report are examples of showing interest.

Senior managers can recognize the data processing function in another significant way as well. They can place that function high in the organizational structure. Instead of burying data processing somewhere in accounting or finance, where none of the senior managers ever sees or

- Senior management demonstrates knowledge and support of data processing.
- Data processing is placed at high organizational level.
- Senior management communicates the importance of controls to the entire organization.
- Data processing steering committee takes active role in data processing.
- Management requests and reviews periodic operations reports.

FIGURE 8-19
Management Controls

hears of it, they can make it a department on a par with other business departments.

Next, senior managers can understand the company's vulnerability to computer crime. Once they do, they can communicate the importance of controls to the entire organization. As we will see, controls on the data processing function involve more than just the data processing department. To encourage other departments to cooperate, management needs to be very positive about the need for controls.

Another responsibility for management is to form a steering committee to control data processing development efforts. The committee receives reports about project status and makes go/no-go decisions, as appropriate.

Finally, management can take a role in data processing by requesting and paying attention to periodic operations reports. Management should know how well the computing resources are being used, how happy or unhappy the users are with the data processing function, and what the major data processing problems are. These reports increase the amount of communication between data processing and senior management.

Organizational Controls

Harold Johnson had free access to the computer and all of its resources. When Harold needed a tape file to determine Joan's account number, he walked into the tape library and got it. When he wanted to obtain the pricing program, he instructed the computer to print a copy of it. After he made the changes, Harold put the changed program into the standard program library. No one checked Harold's authority to do these things.

Organizational controls concern the organizational structure of the company. We have already mentioned that data processing should be organizationally on a par with other functions of the company. Figure 8-20 shows alternative organizational plans that meet this need. In addition, the company should be structured so that authorization and duties are separate.

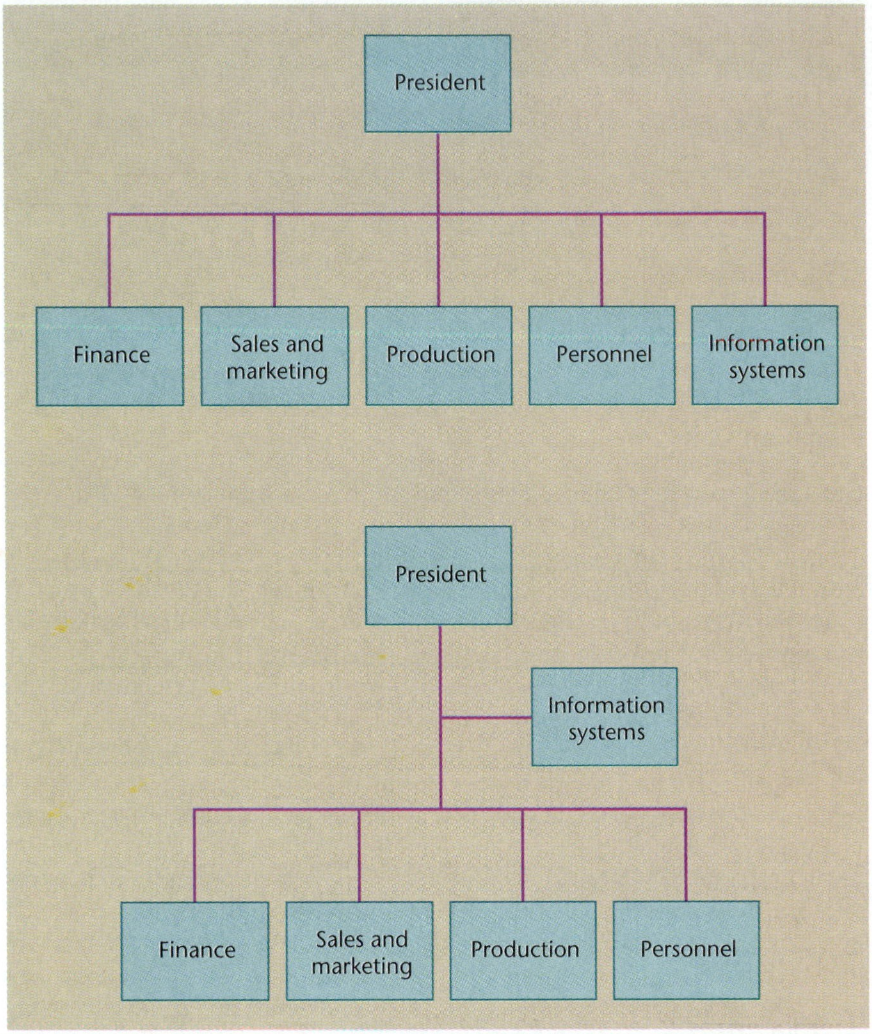

FIGURE 8-20
Organizational Controls
These two organizational structures each recognize the information systems department.

The MODREC case is a good example of what can happen when no separation exists. Data processing employees had unlimited access to the computer. MODREC should have at least two categories of data processing personnel: development and operations. The development group should develop new programs in accordance with requirements. The operations group should control the equipment and the production program library containing the programs in day-to-day use. Only the development programmers should develop program changes, and only the operations department should put these changes into the production library. Thus, the two groups should provide checks and balances on each other. Further, making changes to the program library would require a supervisor's authorization. In general, the more people and the more levels of management that are involved in authorizing and performing duties, the less susceptible the system is to unauthorized activity.

FIGURE 8-21

Data Center

Controls are needed to limit access to the data center and to schedule data center activities.

- Access to data center is controlled.
- Operating procedures are documented and monitored.
- Program libraries are secure.
- Backup and failure recovery procedures exist.
- Protection from natural hazards exist.
- Documented emergency procedures exist.

FIGURE 8-22

Data Center Resource Controls

Data Center Resource Controls

After Harold Johnson changed the pricing program to give Joan special discounts, he wanted to test it. After all, he did not want to make a mistake and give the discounts to the wrong customer. However, to test the change, he needed to mount the customer and price files onto the tape drives. To avoid suspicion, Harold stayed at work after hours the next week. Since none of the managers paid any attention to data processing, they did not ask Harold what he was doing. Harold took his time, and after three short nights, he had fully tested his program. Not only was he sure it would work, he was also sure no one could trace the changes to him.

Data center resource controls should also be implemented (see Figure 8-22). Processing should be controlled by schedules, and records of use should be reviewed. Therefore, access to the computer must be controlled. Only authorized personnel should be allowed in the computer room. This restriction not only protects the equipment from damage, but also helps to ensure that outputs are delivered only to the right people. Program libraries should be stored in a secure area.

Computer operations should be controlled as well. Procedures and job schedules should be documented and followed. A supervisor should examine records of operations to ensure that the procedures are followed. It should be very difficult for operators to deviate from the established schedule and procedures.

In addition to protecting computing resources during normal operations, plans and procedures should exist to recover from failures. Recovery procedures should be well documented, and the staff should be trained in their use. In addition, the company should also have a disaster-recovery plan that explains what to do in case of fire, flood, earthquake, or other disaster.

Input, Processing, and Output Controls

Harold Johnson did not have to modify program inputs. He found a way to provide special discounts by changing the processing. This process changed the outputs. If anyone had ever examined the invoices generated by the pricing program, that person would have seen that something was amiss. Luckily for Harold, MODREC did not have a policy of examining outputs.

Input, processing, and output controls should be used, as summarized in Figure 8-23. First, the authorized form of input data should be documented. The operations personnel should be trained not to accept unauthorized input data. Second, data processing personnel should be trained not to make changes to input data. Such changes should be made by the system users. Where appropriate, control totals should be used. For example, when the users send the weekly payroll to data processing, they should calculate (independently) the sum of the hours worked or a similar total. The payroll program should be written to calculate the total number of hours worked and to print this total on a summary report. The report should be examined by the payroll department after the payroll run

FIGURE 8-23
Input/Processing/Output Controls

Category	Type of Control
Input	Documentation of authorized input format
	Separation of duties and authorities
	Verification of control totals
	On-line system input controls
Processing	Documented operating procedures
	Reviews of processing logs
	Adequate program testing
Output	Documented output procedures
	Control over disposition of output
	Users trained to examine output

to ensure that the manually prepared total and the computer-generated total match.

Processing controls involve processing all data according to prescribed schedules, documenting the processing, and monitoring the records to be sure that deviations from schedules are not caused by unauthorized activity. In addition, processing controls include adequate program testing to reduce the likelihood of unapproved changes.

Finally, the output of all data processing activities should be controlled. Procedures for disseminating output should be documented and followed. Output should be given only to authorized users, and these users should examine the output for completeness and accuracy. If some individual had been given the responsibility to examine the records of invoice processing, Harold Johnson's crime probably would have been detected fairly quickly.

In fact, Harold Johnson and Joan Everest were able to continue their crime for 18 months. During that period, they obtained $150,000 worth of records for $22,500. The crime would have gone on longer, except for a change of management at MODREC.

A new president was hired, and he expected better performance from the entire company. As part of his improvement program, he required the sales force to increase sales. When one of the new sales managers reviewed the performance of the region containing Joan's store, he detected something suspicious. It seemed that the volume of sales should have netted larger income. He examined the sales invoices for the past year and saw what had been going on. He contacted the new president, and the game was up.

MODREC threatened to sue for damages, but a settlement was made out of court. Harold and Joan paid MODREC $50,000, and Joan turned over a sizable part of her record inventory. In addition, criminal action was taken. Since both Harold and Joan were first-time criminals, they received light sentences. They each spent 60 days in jail and were fined $5,000.

PEOPLE COMPONENT

The final component of shared information systems is people. As in other information systems, people take the roles of user, operator, client, and developer. In shared systems, the roles of user, client, and developer are similar to those discussed previously, but the role of operator needs further discussion. In addition, a new role appears: data administrator.

Computer Operator

In personal systems, the user is also the operator. With shared data systems, however, this is often not true. There are too many activities for users to perform on their own. So people need to be identified as system operators.

If the system is used only within a department, some departmental employees are given special training to operate the LAN (or centralized computer) and associated equipment such as file servers. These people are trained in the procedures listed in Figure 8-12 and Figure 8-14. They know how to start and stop the system, how to respond to routine problems, and whom to call in case of nonroutine problems or failures.

Systems that cross several departments are usually operated by professionals in the MIS department. These people will be trained in procedures and operations. Unlike a departmental user/operator, an MIS department operator normally does operations on a full-time basis.

Data Administrator

The users of shared data have a variety of different needs, objectives, and goals. Because of this, they sometimes have different ideas about how the data should be processed. Also, from time to time, two users may want to take actions that are inconsistent with each other or to make conflicting changes to the system. This situation gives rise to the need for a new function, data administration, and a new job title, **data administrator**.

The functions of the data administrator are to guard and protect the data. Without a data administrator, shared data has no owner other than the community of users. Consequently, no one will accept the personal responsibility to protect the data. When a problem occurs, members of the community may accuse one another. "I thought *you* were going to make the backup!" and so forth. The data administrator ensures that backup and recovery procedures exist and that they are followed.

Additionally, this person or group provides a focus for discussions about structure, use, and meaning of the data. The administrator is a focal point for questions, problems, and concerns. For example, at Jenner-Kline Corporation, the customer support department proposed that each product's item number be changed to include the release number, which indicates exactly which engineering drawings apply to that individual unit. Such a change would help customer support provide help to customers, since it would indicate the exact configuration of the unit that the customer is using.

The sales department objected strenuously. Sales would have to go back and reprint several million dollars worth of sales literature and retrain salespersons to cope with the new numbering system. In addition, customers familiar with the old system would be confused. Finally, salespersons and order entry personnel would be asked to spend time entering the new, longer item numbers, and they would receive no direct benefit from the change.

In resolving this problem, the data administrator had no direct authority to impose a solution. Instead, the parties to the dispute were offered a forum in which they could consider the costs and benefits of the change to all parts of the company and arrive at an equitable agreement. The data administrator's role in that discussion was entirely persuasive. A good data administrator works effectively in this setting.

FIGURE 8-24

Data Administration
When conflicts arise, the data administrator's role is to facilitate discussion and seek a mutually acceptable solution.

Without an administrator, issues about care, control, and processing of the data often go unaddressed. Assigning a person to these tasks increases the usefulness and reliability of the data.

For departmental data, data administration can be a part-time job. For data that is shared by several departments, data administration is probably a full-time job. And, as mentioned, for data shared by the entire organization, data administration may involve a sizable staff.

Summary

Some of the data processed by organizations needs to be shared among more than a single user. Shared information systems meet this need. Shared systems are more complex than personal systems.

Shared information systems let users share access to hardware; programs; data (including text, spreadsheets, and databases); and communications systems such as E-mail.

The new key hardware and program components of shared information systems comprise their data communications function. The most important issue relating to data concerns the location of the data—whether it is partitioned and whether it is replicated. In addition to the expected categories of procedures—user procedures for normal processing, operations procedures for normal processing, user procedures for failure recovery, and operations procedures for failure recovery—shared systems need procedures both for controlled sharing of concurrently processed data and for EDP controls to reduce the likelihood of unauthorized activity. In addition to the roles for people that are found in all systems, shared information systems involve the roles of operator and data administrator.

Key Terms

shared information system
sneaker-net
local area network (LAN)
timesharing
electronic mail (E-mail)
mailbox
partitioned data
replicated data
tuning
controlled sharing
concurrent processing
granularity
inconsistent read problem
lost update problem
lock
deadlock
deadly embrace
monolithic file
EDP controls
management controls
organizational controls
data center resource controls
input, processing, and output controls
data administrator

Review Questions

1. Name the strongest benefit and at the same time the strongest liability of personal information systems.
2. What is the key feature of shared information systems?
3. Name the four fundamental purposes of shared information systems.
4. Describe at least two specific examples of hardware sharing.
5. Differentiate between the operation of sneaker-net and the operation of a LAN.
6. How is a LAN different from a timesharing system?
7. Why are applications being shifted from timesharing systems to PCs today?
8. Which type of shared information system is the simplest?
9. Name two advantages of sharing programs over providing individual copies of programs for each user.
10. Describe the method typically used for sharing programs.
11. What is the most common form of shared information system?
12. Name three types of shared data systems. Which type is most widely used today?
13. Describe the process of creating and transmitting an E-mail message.
14. Name two new communication sharing systems that are now being developed.
15. What is the key component of hardware and programs in shared information systems?
16. Differentiate between partitioned data and replicated data.
17. Name three disadvantages and two advantages of partitioning data.
18. Describe the two problems that are created by replicating data. How can each be solved?

19. What are the four categories of procedures that are expected in all information systems?
20. Name the two additional categories of procedures (beyond the four that you named in response to the previous question) that are needed in shared information systems.
21. Give three examples of user procedures for normal processing.
22. Give three examples of operations procedures for normal processing.
23. Give three examples of user procedures for failure recovery.
24. Give three examples of operations procedures for failure recovery.
25. Why is controlled sharing needed?
26. Give at least three examples of granularity in shared data systems.
27. Describe two consequences of larger granularity and two consequences of smaller granularity.
28. Name the three ways in which users can share access to the same record. What problems can arise in each case?
29. Describe each step leading to the inconsistent read problem.
30. Describe each step leading to the lost update problem.
31. How does a lock help to solve the problems of record sharing?
32. Describe each step leading to a deadlock, or deadly embrace.
33. Name typical program features and the procedures used in file sharing.
34. What are EDP controls?
35. Name the four categories of EDP controls that are relevant to users.
36. Describe four steps that senior management should take to control shared information systems.
37. What are the two major purposes of organizational controls?
38. Name five steps that should be taken to implement data center resource controls.
39. Describe the steps that should be taken to implement input controls, processing controls, and output controls.
40. Explain the background and training needed in a person typically selected as operator of a department-level information system and of an information system that crosses several departments.
41. Describe the basic duties of a data administrator.
42. What benefits does a company receive from a data administrator?

Discussion Questions

A. Interview your school's business information systems manager to obtain a description of the school's student registration system. Compare that system to the Jenner-Kline order entry system described at the beginning of this chapter. Describe at least five main similarities and five main differences. Estimate the complexity of the registration system as compared to the order entry system.

B. Based on the knowledge you have gained from this book up to now, compare a LAN and a timesharing system as ways of providing computer power to workers. What factors should be considered in such a comparison? How do the LAN and the timesharing system rate on each factor?

What situations favor use of the LAN, and what situations favor use of timesharing?

C. Find an article describing a specific computer crime against a company, and consider the kinds of controls that the company could have implemented to prevent or quickly detect that crime. In your own words, describe the crime, the possible motivations of the criminal, and at least five specific controls that the company should implement in the future.

D. Summarize the advantages and disadvantages of partitioning data and replicating data, as compared to maintaining a single central data store. What factors should be considered in such a comparison? Describe at least three situations that favor partitioning, three that favor replicating, and three that favor a centralized data store with no partitioning or replicating.

E. List the five most important EDP controls that apply to each component of a business information system: hardware, programs, data, procedures, people.

MINICASE

Networked PCs Become a Crime-Fighting Tool in New York

When the New York City School Construction Authority (SCA) decided to protect its $5 billion annual budget against corruption three years ago, it was fortunate enough to pick Nicholas Nagorny to head its technology efforts.

As MIS director for the Office of the Inspector General of the New York City SCA, Nagorny has set up an enterprisewide LAN architecture that allows law enforcement investigators and analysts to prevent illegal use of taxpayer funds. . . .

"Our office's job is to keep the process of constructing schools in New York City clean," says Nagorny, who serves 65 employees at the Inspector General's office dedicated to this task.

Its main weapon: information.

The Office of the Inspector General is new; it was formed only three years ago. And in just two years, Nagorny has put a computer on every employee's desk.

A Novell network with two 486 EISA PC file servers supports 65 users, who use the network to access a broad range of public and private databases, electronic bulletin boards, and other on-line data sources, such as Dun & Bradstreet, Nexis, and Lexis.

Analysts and investigators, instead of pounding the pavement, now burn up electronic networks in their search for unsavory business practices.

"From the beginning, I was determined to create an electronic community where the computer was a tool for everyone—not just secretaries and administrative help," Nagorny says. There are tremendous cost savings to having everyone—including senior managers—completely trained on PC applications. . . . "If a worker has to go down the hall to a special computer in order to get financial data on a New York City vendor, utilization of the resource goes way down," Nagorny says. Getting the PC skill level of his users up to speed was a challenge, however.

"NYC detectives for 20 years have been enamored of the Rolodex, and it was only in the late 1980s that some of them began using typewriters," Nagorny says. "Now I'm asking them to become experts in Lotus, which is quite a big step for them."

Nagorny arrived at his current position after a

career in law enforcement investigation. After receiving his bachelor's degree in history and education—and after a brief stint as a seventh-grade teacher in New York City—Nagorny took a job as an analyst with the FBI in 1980. In 1982, he was asked to organize a crime information system, and he spent the next seven years learning about PC hardware and software and applying the concepts to his job.

Questions

1. Describe what you think appears to be the primary reason for connecting the users to a local area network.
2. Nagorny uses the term *electronic community*. Describe what you think he must mean by this term.
3. According to this article, Nagorny has faced a challenge in getting the users "up to speed." What kinds of challenges do you suppose he faced? Describe two or three key elements of the strategy that you would use in a similar situation.
4. Describe Nagorny's background. In the future, do you think it will be more or less common for people to have a similar career progression? What steps can you take while you're in college to prepare yourself for this possibility?

C H A P T E R 9

Data Communications for Shared Systems

CHAPTER OUTLINE

Example: An Electronic Workday Morning

Data Communications Fundamentals

Teleprocessing Systems

Distributed Systems

Hybrid Systems

Wide Area Networks

International Data Communications

Summary

Key Terms

Review Questions

Discussion Questions

As you saw in Chapter 8, an important component of most shared systems is the communication of data. For example, users entering data at terminals must be connected to the mainframe computer that processes the data. Or, mail users at microcomputers must have a communications channel for the flow of mail. Similarly, large manufacturers need inventory data both from major suppliers and from major customers to allow them to plan effectively. Data communications is vital to shared systems.

EXAMPLE: AN ELECTRONIC WORKDAY MORNING

It was a typical morning in the sales department. When Susan arrived at 9 A.M., she immediately began thinking about her section of the major departmental report being written this week. She sat down, switched on her PC, and checked her E-mail before turning to the report.

Opening a mail window on her PC screen, she found 14 messages. Three were from her boss, and she selected those to read first. One message complimented her on her contributions to last Friday's new product presentation. The other two contained ideas and suggestions for her report section. She printed copies of those for reference.

Six additional E-mail messages were from district sales directors, and each requested a change in the sales volume projection for a major customer. Quarterly, the sales department created projections of sales volume for each of the company's top 100 corporate customers. Then, as salespeople developed new information about these customers—new product announcements, government contract awards, and so on—they relayed the information to their district sales managers. If the information might significantly affect sales to that customer, district sales managers passed the information on to the corporate sales office and requested adjustment of the sales projection for the customer. Susan coordinated requests for all sales districts in the western United States.

Susan inspected each request for change and verified that it met the guidelines. Then she ran the projection-adjustment application, which created a second window on her PC screen for data entry. She entered data about the six changes, one after the other. After each entry, the projection-adjustment application logged into the company's central computer and requested processing of a sales-projection–adjustment transaction. The result of each transaction was an update in the sales projection data in the sales and marketing database. Typical time required to log in, upload the transaction data, and receive confirmation of the transaction processing averaged .2 second per transaction.

Of the remaining five E-mail messages, one was a company policy notice distributed to all employees, two were departmental notices, and one announced a department meeting the following week. She made note of each.

The final message was a reply from Janet Worgern in the finance department providing projected operating figures that Susan needed for her report section. She saved this message on disk, and prepared to work on the report. Since her requests for information from the production and marketing research departments had not been answered, instead of closing the E-mail window on her screen, she reduced it to a small box and left it active in background. As she worked, it would immediately show each arriving message and its source.

Then Susan ran her word processor, which was loaded into her computer's memory through a LAN, and called up the draft report section, which she had begun and stored in the LAN's storage system the day before. The first task on the report project this morning was to download some data from the company's sales and marketing database. To do this, she opened a window for the database query application (loaded from LAN storage), entered her query, and submitted it to the central computer for processing. While she waited for the download, she reviewed yesterday's draft of her section and improved several phrasings.

When the download was complete, Susan created a spreadsheet window on her screen (loading the spreadsheet from LAN storage), transferred the downloaded data into the spreadsheet, and analyzed the data. Fortunately, her analysis showed trends that supported the points she wanted to make. Therefore, she created the detailed summary that she needed. To be sure the trends were communicated clearly, she reworked the summary three times. The result, she felt, was completely clear. She used the spreadsheet's graphing capability to create two graphs to illustrate important points. Then she transferred the summary and the two graphs from the spreadsheet to her word processor, saved the spreadsheet to LAN storage, and closed the spreadsheet window on her screen.

At about 10 A.M., Susan's mailbox showed new mail from Gerald Leedom in the production department. It was the production figures she had requested. She transferred the figures to the word processing window, where she added them to her report. Ten minutes later, a message from Leeta Reynolds in marketing research provided the final set of figures.

Susan was working on the report when, at exactly 11 A.M., a window automatically popped up on her screen to indicate that her daily automatic download of world currency exchange rates from London was completed. She switched to that window, printed a copy of the results, and transferred the downloaded data to the E-mail window for transmission to the list of recipients whom she daily served with this information.

It was a typical morning for Susan. Sitting in her office, concentrating most of her attention on her current report-writing project, she received and used information from a wide variety of sources. Through E-mail, she exchanged information with people throughout her company. Through a LAN, she shared programs, documents, and other data with workers in her department. Through communication with her company's central computer, she submitted transactions to update company data and accessed information that she needed to do her job. And through an international data communications network, she downloaded vital currency exchange information from a foreign capital.

DATA COMMUNICATIONS FUNDAMENTALS

During the morning, Susan accessed several kinds of shared information systems. This chapter considers three shared system architectures: teleprocessing, distributed, and hybrid. In a **teleprocessing**, or **centralized system**, all computing is done by a central computer, and the devices connected to it function only as simple I/O devices (see Figure 9-1). In a **distributed system**, multiple computers share the processing and are connected by a LAN (see Figure 9-2). A **hybrid system** contains a central processing computer along with additional processing computers (see Figure 9-3). The central processing computer typically processes the data shared by the entire organization. It is supported by additional processing computers that process data for departments or workgroups. The additional processing computers are often connected to each other and to the central processing computer through LANs. Figure 9-4 summarizes the characteristics, control philosophies, and primary applications of the three types of shared system architectures. This chapter will consider each architecture in turn.

However, before we can consider specific architectures, we must understand the fundamental technology on which such systems are built. The key technology involves the widely used communications media and their applications.

Comunications Media

A communications medium is the physical system used to transport the data from one place to another. The transmission rate of a medium is measured in **bits per second (bps)**. Thousands of bits per second are expressed in Kbps (or "kilo" bps); millions of bits per second, as Mbps (or "mega"

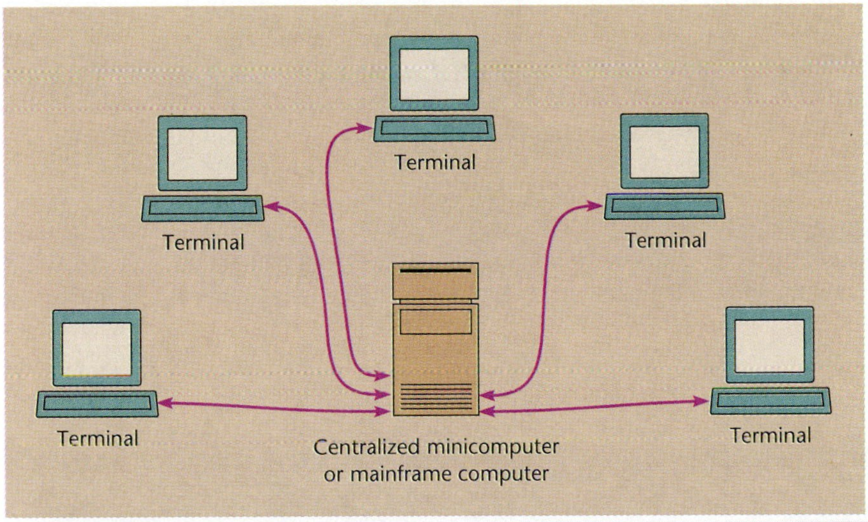

FIGURE 9-1

Teleprocessing Architecture
In teleprocessing, or centralized, architecture, terminals are connected by communications lines to a centralized computer that does all the processing.

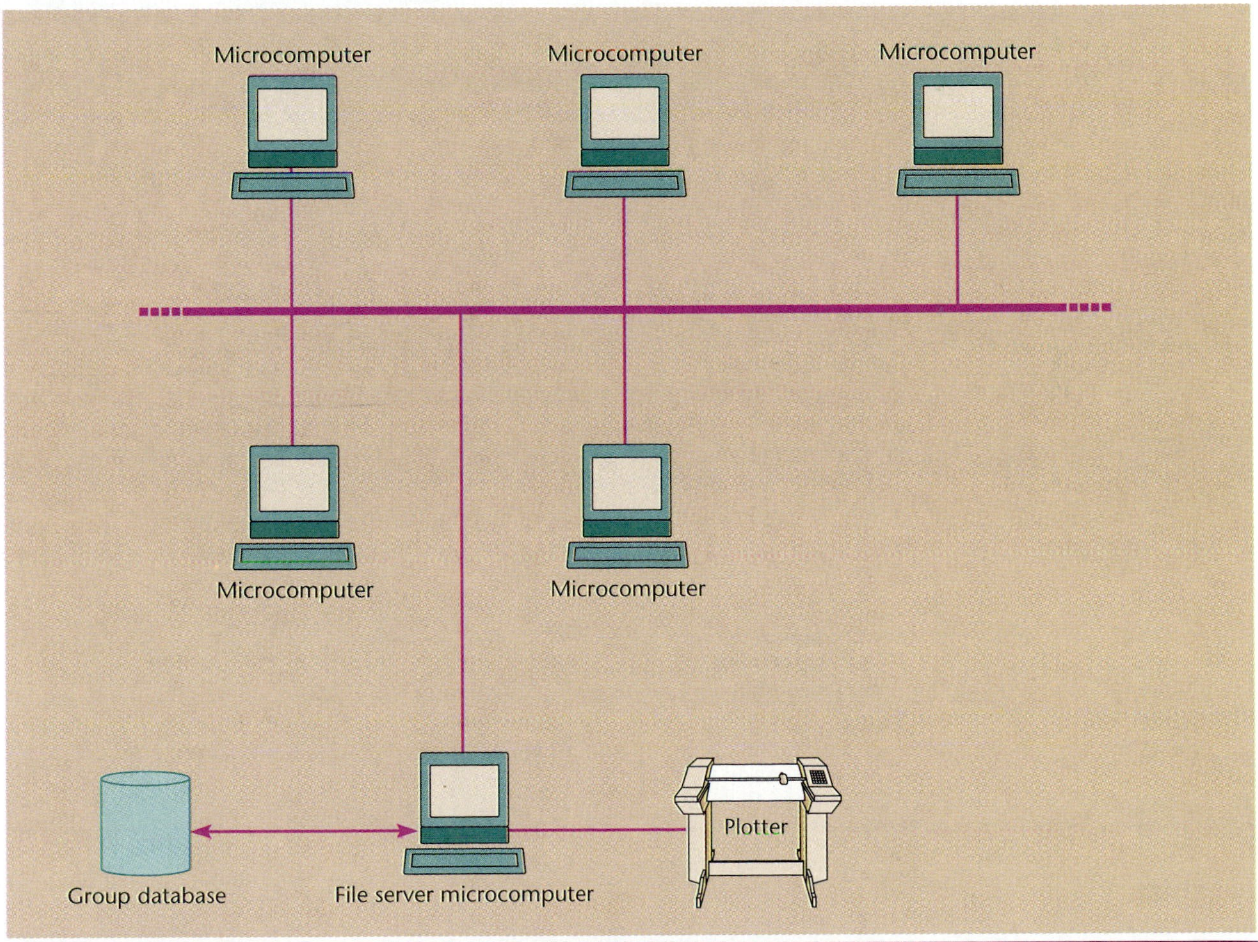

FIGURE 9-2 **Distributed Processing Systems**
In this LAN-based system, microcomputers share access to data on a file server and use of a plotter.

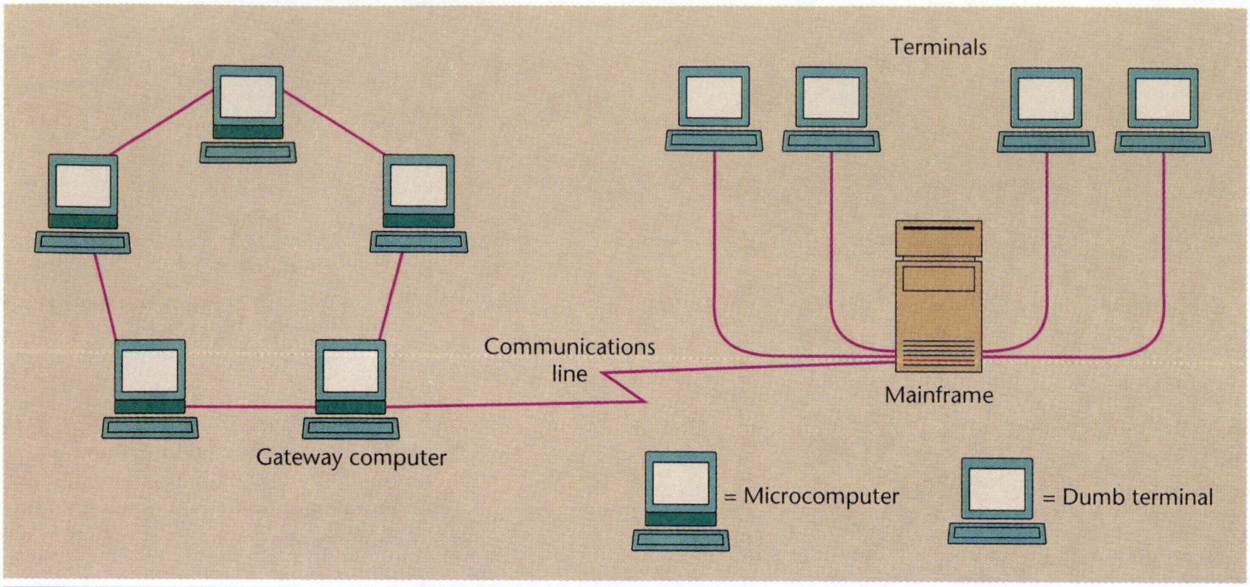

FIGURE 9-3 **Hybrid System Architecture**
The hybrid system architecture combines features of teleprocessing systems and distributed systems. In a hybrid system, both terminals and LANs communicate with a central processing computer.

	Characteristics	Control Philosophy	Primary Application
Teleprocessing	Intelligence centralized on a single computer Dumb terminals or micros that emulate dumb terminals	Centralized control of all activities	Organizational processing systems; some workgroup processing systems
Distributed	Independent micros communicate via LAN or other medium File server provides librarian and disk management	Independent processing on micros Central control of data when residing on file server	Workgroup information systems
Hybrid	Mixture of micro LANs and mainframe or minicomputers	Hybrid control	Organizational information systems

FIGURE 9-4 **Shared System Architectures**

Medium	Rates
Twisted pair	
Switched lines	9,600 bps; 19,200 bps
Leased lines	56 Kbps; 80 Kbps
Coaxial cable	1 Mbps; 2 Mbps; 10 Mbps; 50 Mbps
Optical fiber	1 Gbps
Microwave	45 Mbps
Satellite	50 Mbps

FIGURE 9-5

Typical Transmission Rates of Data Communications Media

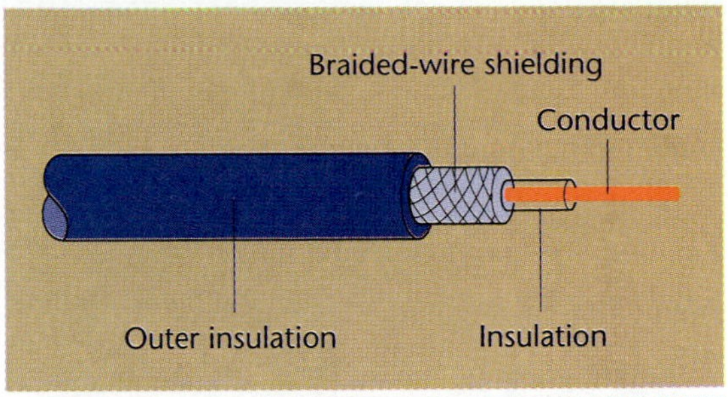

FIGURE 9-6

Coaxial Cable
Coaxial cable uses a single wire to conduct signals. The wire is covered by insulation and contained in a tube of braided wire mesh, which protects it from outside interference.

bps); and billions of bits per second as Gbps (or "giga" bps). Media are divided into two groups: high-speed media and low-speed media. Figure 9-5 compares the speeds of commonly used data communications media.

High-Speed Media The high-speed media are coaxial cable, optical fibers, microwaves, and satellite transmission.

The most common high-speed medium today is **coaxial cable**. As Figure 9-6 shows, it consists of a conductor wire surrounded by insulation, then by a layer of wire braid to shield it from interference from outside electronic signals such as radio waves. As signals travel through coaxial cable, like other media, they slowly weaken until they finally become difficult to detect. After several miles in a typical cable, a **repeater**, a small electronic device, is needed to amplify the signals.

The most common high-speed medium in the future is likely to be **optical fiber** (see Figure 9-7). These tiny glass fibers, which are usually bundled into a cable, carry signals by means of light pulses generated by lasers. Each fiber, smaller than a human hair, can carry up to 1 Gbs—(1 billion bits per second). A cable of these fibers has almost unimaginable data capacity. Optical fiber channels require repeaters, but these are spaced at much longer intervals than with coaxial cable. Thus, the cost of optical fiber channels is about the same as coaxial cable for distances long enough to require repeaters in the coaxial cable.

Microwaves are radio signals similar to those used in UHF television broadcasting—TV channels 14 and above in the United States. Microwaves travel in straight lines, so they do not bend around the curvature of the earth. As a result, transmission of microwaves for long distances requires that repeating stations be provided about every 30 to 50 miles along the transmission route (see Figure 9-8). Microwave transmission provides rates up to 45 Mbps.

FIGURE 9-7
Optical Fiber
Optical fibers smaller than a human hair carry signals consisting of pulses of light.

FIGURE 9-8
Microwave Repeater
Since microwaves do not bend with the curvature of the earth, repeater stations must be located every 35 to 50 miles along the transmission route.

Satellite transmission uses communications satellites located directly above the equator 22,300 miles in space (see Figure 9-9). At that height, a satellite revolves around the earth at exactly the same rate as the earth's rotation, so the satellite appears to hang above a fixed point on the equator. Such an orbit is called **geosynchronous**. An antenna on the earth's surface pointed at the satellite will remain pointed at it indefinitely, so both transmitting circuits and receiving circuits can be focused very sharply. The satellite contains repeater circuitry, so when it receives signals

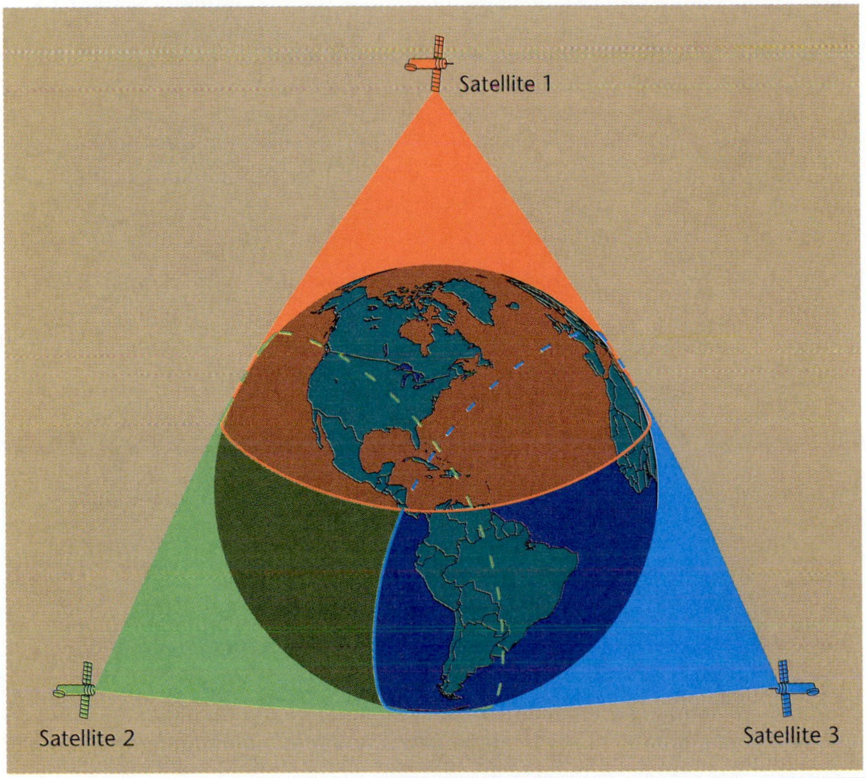

FIGURE 9-9

Communications Satellites in Space Communications satellites in geosynchronous orbit appear to hang motionless in the sky. As few as three satellites can serve the entire surface of the earth.

beamed up from an earth station, it retransmits them on another channel. Earth stations in other locations receive and distribute the signals to their intended recipients.

Consider a 1000-mile data communications link. To use coaxial cable, a company would have to contract with every landowner over the 1000 miles and install underground conduit, cable, and repeaters. To use microwave transmission with repeater stations every 30 miles, the company would have to erect 33 repeater stations (1000 miles divided by 30 miles per repeater). This would require purchasing or leasing 33 plots of land, erecting 33 repeater stations, running heavy-duty electrical supply lines to each, and equipping each with microwave electronics systems. To provide satellite transmission, the company would have to buy and launch a space satellite and build the required earth stations (see Figure 9-10).

Because of the cost, companies that need long-distance data communications channels seldom provide their own. Rather, they lease the partial use of channels maintained by **common carriers**, companies that provide data communications facilities for a fee. The channels are called **leased lines**. By sharing expensive resources—right-of-way for coaxial cable, repeater stations for microwaves, and space satellite—among many customers, common carriers can afford to invest in these costly communications channels.

FIGURE 9-10
Launching a Communications Satellite
Part of the cost of satellite communications is launching the satellite into space in a geosynchronous orbit.

Low-Speed Media The most common low-speed medium is telephone wire. In a telephone system, a separate pair of wires connects each telephone to a switching device in the telephone company's office. En route to the office, pairs of wires are bundled into tightly packed cables. To keep the signals on the various pairs from interfering electronically, the wires of each pair are twisted about each other—thus, the name **twisted pair** for the medium.

The major advantage of the twisted pair medium is that it is used in the worldwide telephone network, which can be accessed for data communications simply by dialing a telephone. Such a channel is called a **switched line**. The connection between sender and receiver is made through the telephone switching system.

The cost of creating a low-speed link between two points by switched line is low. A short-term link for communicating a small amount of data between any two places in the world can be created by hooking computers at each end to telephone lines and dialing the phone. For example, the cost to transmit a brief electronic document to virtually anywhere in the world is only a few dollars. At the same time, the cost per transmitted bit of switched lines is relatively high. Therefore, if the connection must be made frequently and large amounts of data must be communicated, then high-speed media may be more cost-effective.

In addition to its use in telephone systems, twisted pair is also used as the communications medium in some LANs, where the greater channel capacity of coaxial cable is not required. Twisted pair is less expensive than coaxial cable.

Box 9.1

INCREASING YOUR PERSONAL PRODUCTIVITY

Telecommuting and Corporate Culture

Only a few companies have adopted formal telecommuting programs for their employees. That's too bad, because real benefits are there for the takers. And given the state of technology, it's a wonder more places haven't jumped into it.

Setting up remote computing is a cinch. The recipe is uncomplicated. Just add a modem, phone line, and software to a "host" PC. There's a vast array of mature products on the market, such as: Microcom's Carbon Copy, Symantec's PC Anywhere. or Ocean Isle Software's Reach Out. Or, for hostless access to an Ethernet LAN, check out Shiva's NetModem/E. Then, provide personnel with complimentary gear for the other end. Voilà, it's done.

The software and hardware work so well that frequently the whole process can be set up, tested, and installed in less than a day. So much for technology. Now comes the hard part: getting remote communications through the corporate culture. It seems that more folks stumble on implementing "change" rather than the technology itself.

First, there are corporate and employee security concerns. But the fact is that a number of the remote-access products have implemented good security within the products. Some have come a long way with special keys, encryption techniques, and dial-back features.

Then there's the reliability objection. Early remote-access products didn't always work so well—back then there were plenty of glitches—from faulty file transfers to software that would drift off into never-never land and hang up. It's different today. Most of he packages work with a variety of hardware combinations, modems, and error-checking transfer protocols. Although it's difficult to guarantee 100 percent up time, some users are seeing near-perfect responses from their equipment.

Finally, some people abstain because they are concerned about how much time it will take to maintain remote users. Frankly the concerns are often bigger than the problem. Once the hardware and software is set up, users generally find it takes less than 3 or 4 hours a month to maintain these systems. That includes time for checking security, adding and deleting users passwords, and troubleshooting.

The Rise of Telecommuting

The number of U.S. telecommuters rose from 2.5 million in 1988 to 5.5 million in 1991. The number is expected to jump to 11.2 million by 1995.

Six Steps to a Successful Telecommuting Program

1. **Select the Right Employees for Telecommuting.** Telecommuters should be self-motivated and organized and their jobs should require minimal supervision.
2. **Trust Telecommuters.** Manage by objectives and results instead of by observation.
3. **Set Specific Ground Rules.** A detailed, written agreement accepted by the telecommuter and the supervisor helps assure that all goes smoothly.
4. **Invest Time Up Front.** Be prepared to spend extra time at the outset in administering, evaluating, and reporting results to senior management.
5. **Keep Telecommuters Visible.** Part-time arrangements and regular staff meetings assure that those working away from the office don't get "lost."
6. **Start with a Pilot Program.** Research carefully, and look to other areas of the company—especially the sales department—for ideas.

Media Applications

In addition to the types of communications media, we must consider the ways in which these media are used to transmit signals. Here are some examples:

- A medium can be primarily equipped to handle voice signals, or it can be equipped to handle the digital signals of computers.
- Data can be transmitted in single characters or in blocks of characters.
- Several architectures can be used in interconnecting the devices.
- Methods can be used to detect and correct errors in the transmitted data.

Analog and Digital Signals As Figure 9-11a illustrates, when **digital signals** are transmitted, the electrical voltage is always one of two values. One value, such as +5 volts, may represent a 1, and the other value, such as 0 volts, may represent a 0. The signals inside a computer representing 1s and 0s are digital signals.

On the other hand, **analog signals** are complexly changing voltages representing the varied frequencies and intensities that characterize speech and music. The line in Figure 9-11b represents variations in electrical voltage that could be used to drive a loudspeaker to recreate the sound of a voice. The signals carried by telephone lines are analog signals.

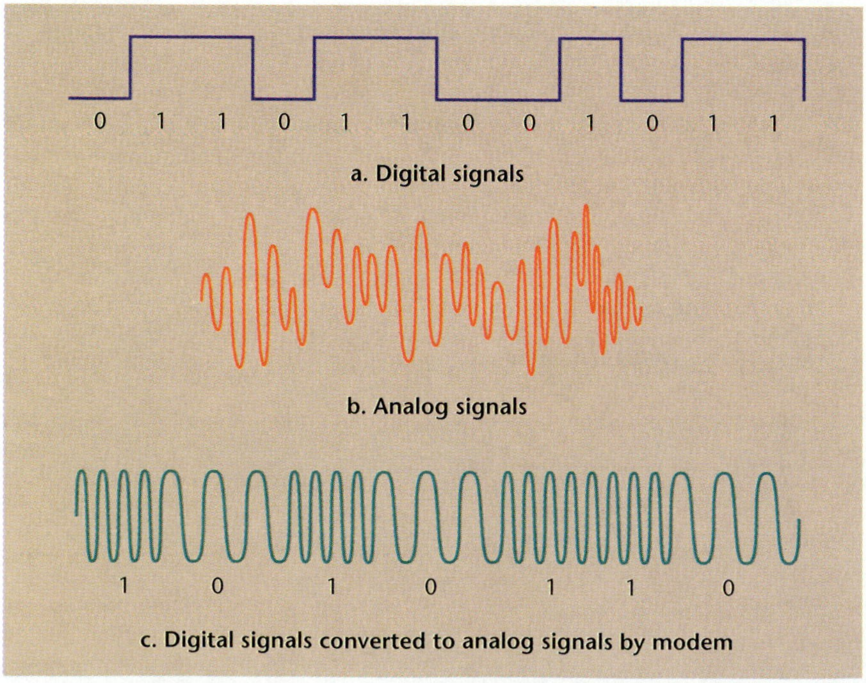

FIGURE 9-11

Digital versus Analog Signals

Digital signals (*a*) are created by a voltage that is either on or off. Analog signals (*b*) vary in voltage in complex forms to represent the sound of voice or music. To transmit digital signals through a channel equipped for analog signals, the digital signals must be converted to analog signals by a modem. The resulting wave form (*c*) consists of a tone representing a 1 and another tone representing a 0.

The various media can be used to transmit either digital signals or analog signals. However, the equipment used in switching systems, repeater devices, and other circuits is optimized to handle only one or the other. Because most telephone equipment was designed for analog signals, its equipment handles digital signals only poorly. Therefore, digital signals must be converted by a modem to analog signals so they can be handled by telephone lines. As Figure 9-11c shows, a modem creates one audio tone to represent a 0 and another, to represent a 1. The resulting tones are transmitted through the telephone lines.

When channels are equipped to handle digital signals, as fiber optic channels typically are, then analog signals must be converted to digital signals for transmission. A device called a **codec** performs this conversion, as Figure 9-12 illustrates. A codec produces a series of numbers, which are transmitted as binary numbers through the channel. At the other end, the numbers are converted back to a varying electrical voltage, which can be used to drive a loudspeaker. This technology is also used in compact disk audio recording. The data on the disk is a series of numbers representing an analog audio signal.

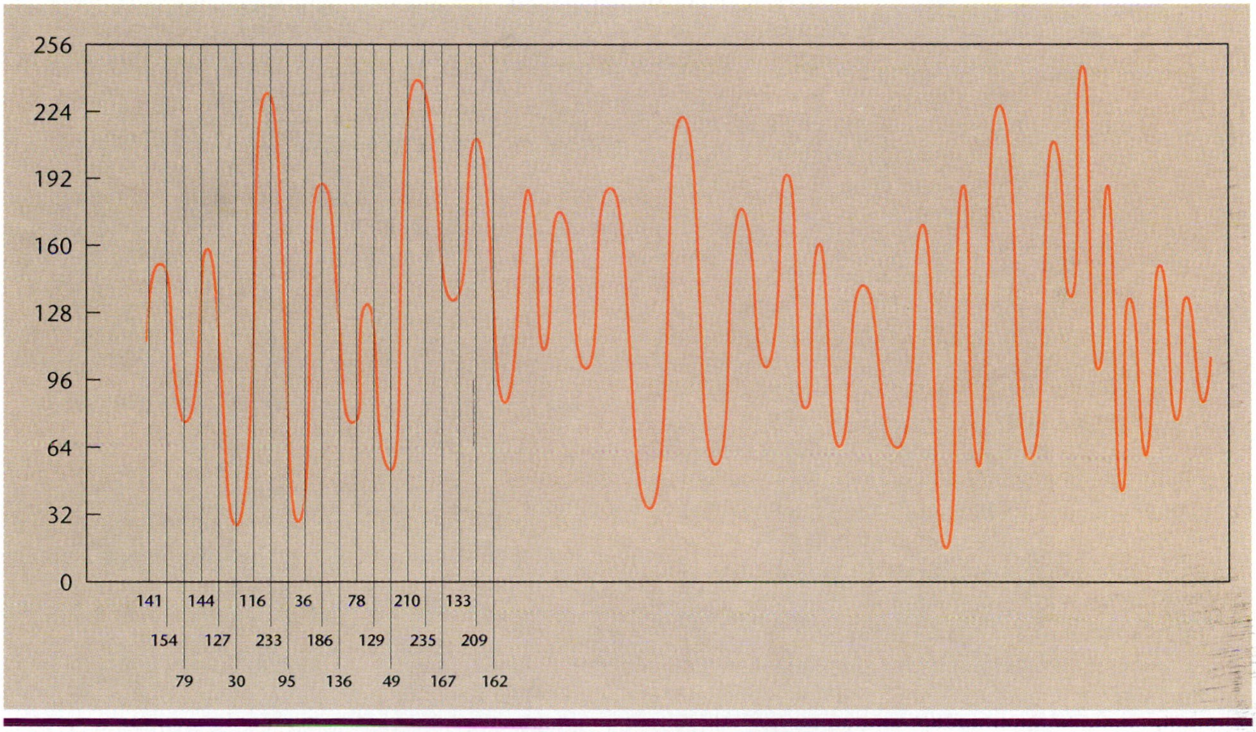

FIGURE 9-12 Converting Analog Signals to Digital Signals
A codec converts voice signals for transmission on a digital channel by measuring the instantaneous voltage of the analog signal many thousands of times per second and recording each value as a binary number. The binary numbers are transmitted through the channel. At the other end, the numbers are used to recreate the analog signal.

INCREASING YOUR PERSONAL PRODUCTIVITY

Box 9.2

The Ten Deadly Network Sins

We've all heard the horror stories of a network gone wrong. PC World asked Patrick Corrigan, managing director of the San Francisco–based network consulting and training firm The Corrigan Group, to discuss the most frequently encountered networking mistakes.

1. **The "I'll do it myself" installation.** Networks are "complicated stuff," says Corrigan, and too many companies install their own LANs, without sufficient experience or knowledge, or professional help.
2. **The "bargain basement" approach.** Shopping for the cheapest hardware and operating system may ease the initial pain of investing in networking technology, but will cost you when you run into the inevitable incompatibilities. Make sure you buy from reputable hardware and software vendors committed to supplying adequate support.
3. **Using an untested reseller or system integrater.** "Too many people are orphaned by a dealer, VAR [value-added reseller], or consultant when things don't go right," says Corrigan. To save yourself from that fate, he suggests getting references, particularly from companies that have implemented a LAN in a similar environment.
4. **Poor planning and design.** Most networks just happen, says Corrigan. But as the network gets bigger and takes on a more critical role, the lack of planning becomes all too evident. Corrigan suggests that issues such as user account information, directory structures, and deciding who has access to different types of data should be hammered out when the network is installed—with an eye toward future growth.
5. **Unrealistic expectations.** Most organizations install a network expecting it to be a quick and easy process. Neither is ever true, says Corrigan, adding that the payoff might be months—or years—away.
6. **Assuming everything will work when the last wires are connected.** Rarely is this the case, says Corrigan, even if you've got a professional network installer handling the project. The lesson? Don't move your strategic applications over too quickly. Assume you'll have a shakedown period while all the bugs get worked out.
7. **Networks maintain themselves, right?** One of the most serious mistakes a company can make is assuming that anyone can manage the LAN, says Corrigan. Every network—regardless or its size—requires the ongoing attention of a trained network administrator. Backups application installation and maintenance, management of user accounts, and hardware and software compatibility are just a few of the issues the network manager will have to deal with almost daily.
8. **Lack of user training.** Many companies don't recognize the need to train users how to work effectively in a networked environment. Instead, users are simply given a password and shown how to log on to the network. Says Corrigan, users need to be schooled in issues such as dealing with shared peripherals and shared applications.
9. **Improper backup.** A major source of trouble for networks of any size, says Corrigan, is a failure to follow proper backup procedures. Intermediate backups should be done regularly—nightly ideally—and with proper redundancy, says Corrigan. Full backups should be done as often as possible.
10. **Disaster recovery? We'll think about that tomorrow.** Every company, says Corrigan, needs a comprehensive disaster recovery plan, but it's particularly critical when your business depends on the smooth operation of the network. Key issues include the impact of the system going down, the amount of time required to get the network back up and running, and designating an individual or individuals who'll be responsible for implementing the recovery plan.

Digital transmission provides more accurate output than does analog transmission, with fewer errors such as static or hiss in the resulting signal. In addition, digital transmission permits higher transmission rates, allowing more signals to share the use of a given channel. Finally, digital transmission allows improved security, since its signals can more easily be encrypted—translated into unintelligible form—to prevent unwanted interception.

Asynchronous and Synchronous Transmission In some data communications, each character is transmitted as a separate action. In others, blocks of data are transmitted as a unit. When each character is transmitted separately, the system uses **asynchronous** transmission. This mode is most common in low-speed communications links. When a block of data is transmitted as a unit, the system uses **synchronous** transmission. This mode is most common in high-speed links.

Network Architectures Several patterns, or architectures, can be used in interconnecting **nodes**, which are computers, terminals, and other devices that communicate data. These patterns include **hierarchical architecture**, **star architecture**, **ring architecture**, and **bus architecture**.

Hierarchical architecture (see Figure 9-13a) is often used to connect a company's central computer with several departmental computers. Both the central computer and the departmental computers communicate with terminals and other devices. Star architecture (see Figure 9-13b) is typically used to connect a central computer to its terminals. Both hierarchical architecture and star architecture depend on high reliability in the central computer, since the central computer is a required participant in most communications.

In the ring architecture (see Figure 9-13c) and the bus architecture (see Figure 9-13d), the nodes must be computers, or at least have some processing power, since each node participates actively in the communications process. If one or more nodes is out of service, communications can usually continue by simply bypassing that node.

Error Detection and Correction Because many factors can cause errors in data transmission, data communications involves a higher probability of error than do other aspects of computing. Therefore, some method of detecting errors is commonly used in data communications systems. The simplest widely used method is called **parity**. In this system, an additional bit is added to each byte of data. Under odd parity, the added bit is selected so each byte plus parity bit includes an odd number of 1s. Thus, if the data byte is 10110101, which has five 1s (an odd number), the parity bit would be 0. If the data byte is 10000001, the parity bit would be 1. (Even parity works in the same way, except that the number of 1s including the parity bit is always made even.) Hardware systems to add parity bits to outgoing data and to check parity bits on incoming data are simple and fast, so parity is widely used. (It is even used in the main memory of IBM Personal Computers and clones.) Parity checking has about a 50-50 chance of detecting a single error in data transmission due to line noise.

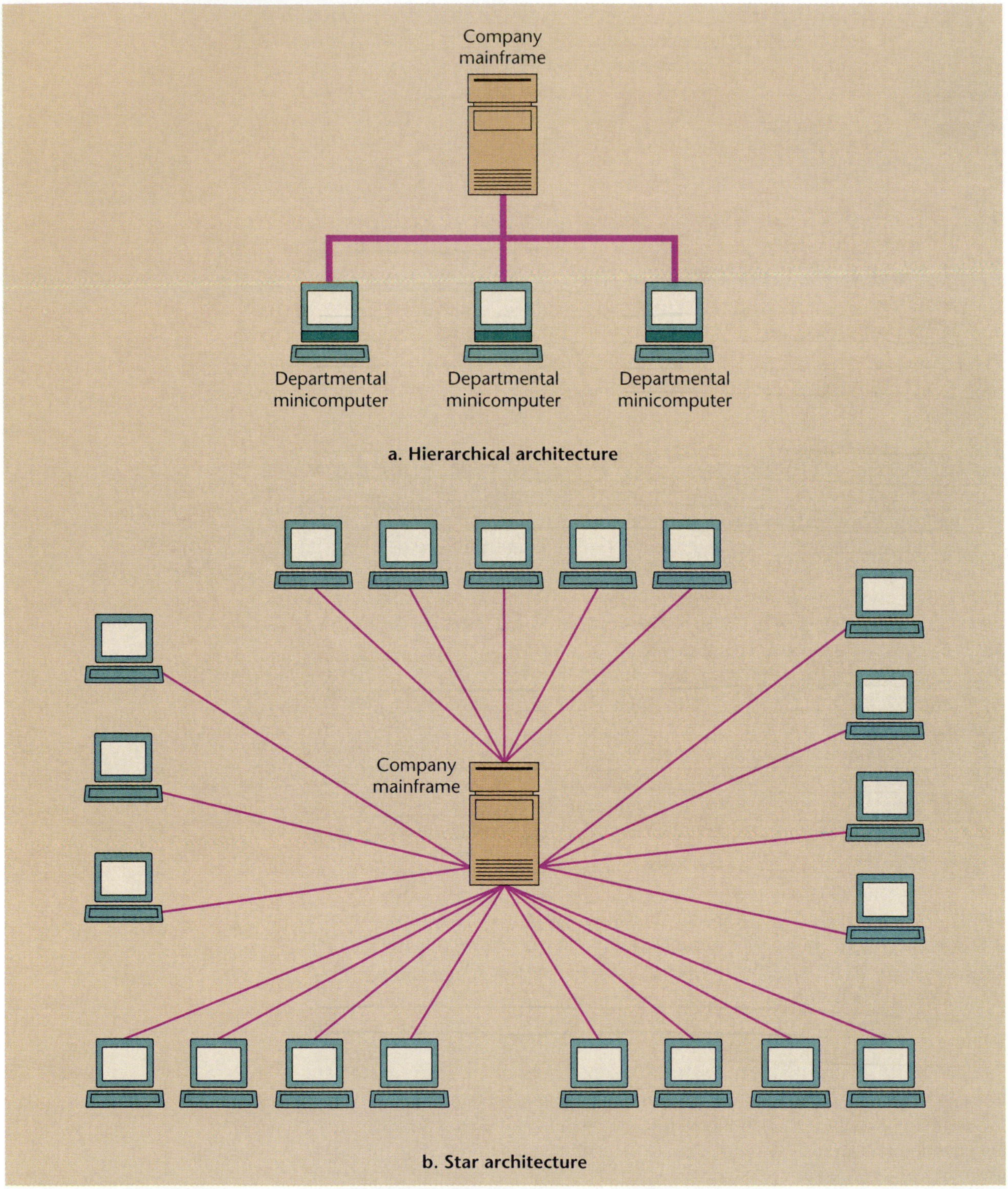

FIGURE 9-13

Network Architectures for Data Communications

The widely used network architectures are hierarchical, star, ring, and bus.

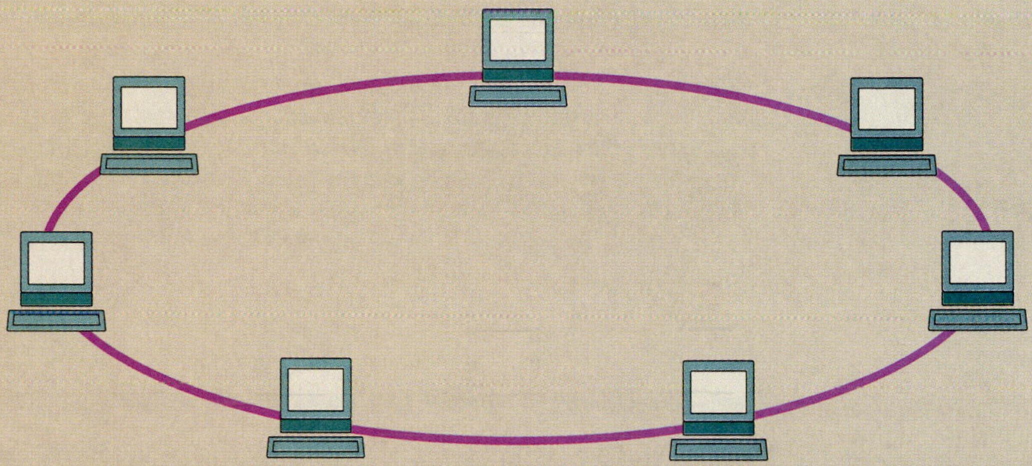

c. Ring architecture

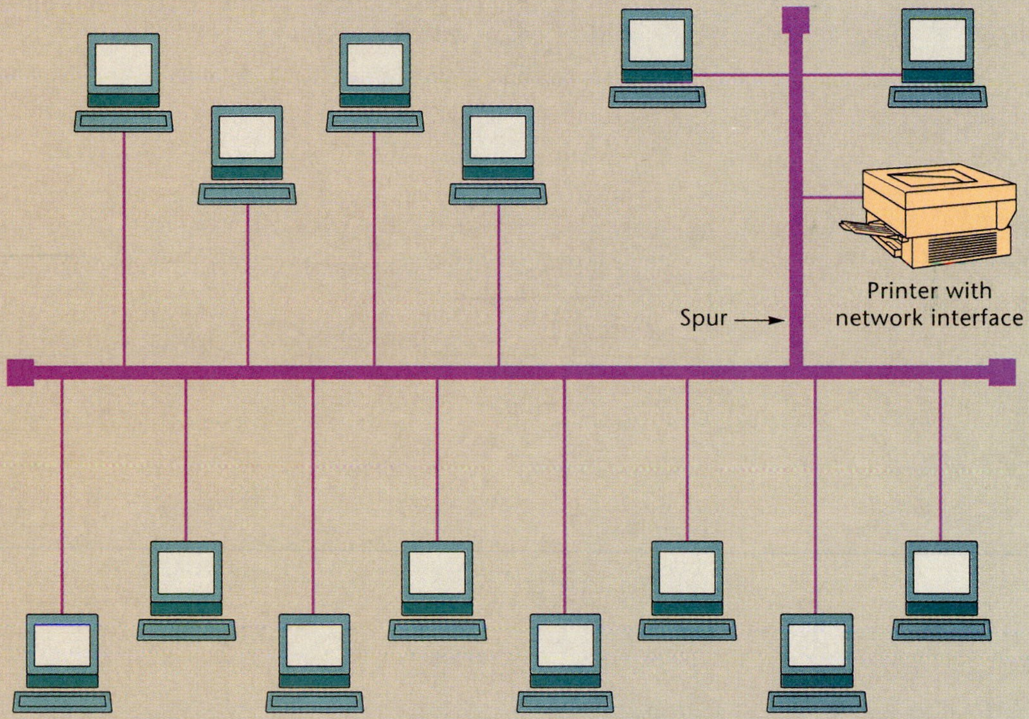

d. Bus architecture

A more complicated error-detection scheme, called the **Cyclic Redundancy Check (CRC)** can detect more than 99 percent of transmission errors, allowing the system to retransmit the block of data or to make some other correction. CRC systems require computation of a check sum for each series of data bytes, so their use involves a cost in computer power.

Some error-detection systems also permit the correction of the error. For example, a system called **Hamming codes** adds data to each block that permits both the detection and the correction of a wide variety of errors. Use of these codes slows data transmission somewhat, since the added codes increase the volume of the data.

Data Communications Protocols

Before any data communications session, the operators of each device must agree on a set of rules for the session. Consider the following examples:

- Whether ASCII or EBCDIC code will be used to represent data.
- How data is to be displayed on the screen—for example, what code is to be used for "newline."
- What codes are to indicate such events as "end of message."
- What electrical signals are to represent 0 and 1.
- How to determine when one device may send data.
- What type of plug is used to attach the device to the communications system.
- Whether asynchronous mode or synchronous mode is used.

An agreement about every aspect of a communications session is called a **protocol**. It is a very complex set of rules for data communications. In fact, standard network protocols are clustered into seven separate "layers" of rules, as Figure 9-14 shows.

Although in theory a company could devise any possible combination of elements in a protocol, in actuality a few widely used protocols form the basis for most data communications. The remainder of this chapter describes data communications systems that use widely accepted protocols.

TELEPROCESSING SYSTEMS

Teleprocessing systems involve a central computer, which does all the processing, and a set of I/O devices called **terminals**. Users at terminals input data for processing by the central computer.

1. **The application layer** contains rules about how an application program requests data transmission and supplies the data to be transmitted in the proper record format.
2. **The presentation layer** contains rules about how the data is to be displayed on the screen, how it may be encrypted or compressed for efficient transmission, and whether it is translated between ASCII code and EBCDIC code.
3. **The session layer** contains rules about how a communication session between two devices is established, what special signals are used to indicate the progress of the dialogue, and how a session is to be reestablished if the connection fails.
4. **The transport layer** contains rules about how the address of the recipient is to be expressed, how large volumes of data are to be broken up into blocks for transmission, and how blocks are to be reassembled into the complete message.
5. **The network layer** contains rules about how to determine the routing of messages from sender to receiver and how to maintain records of messages transmitted.
6. **The data link layer** contains rules about resolving competing requests for the use of the channel, defining the beginning and end of data blocks, and detecting and correcting errors.
7. **The physical layer** contains rules about the shape of connectors to be used, the speed and direction of transmission, and how the bits are to be represented electrically (or by light pulses, or whatever).

FIGURE 9-14
The Seven Layers of Network Protocols

The term *teleprocessing* means that processing is conducted somewhere away from the user (the prefix *tele* means "at a distance"). That is, I/O is performed remotely from the computer. Users' terminals are connected to the computer via communications lines.

The hardware components of a typical teleprocessing system are terminals, line-sharing devices, channel, front-end processor, and host (see Figure 9-15). These hardware components are supported by a system program in the host, which is called a communications control program. This section will discuss each of these components, and it will identify the characteristics of teleprocessing systems.

Terminals

With teleprocessing, all application processing occurs on the centralized computer. Therefore, little processing power is required in the terminals, which can be devices called **dumb terminals** that have keyboards and screens, but no CPUs. As an alternative, microcomputers can be used as terminals, since many users already have PCs on their desks.

If a dumb terminal is used, the connection to the communications line is built into the terminal. If a microcomputer is used, a communications card must be installed in one of the PC's expansion slots.

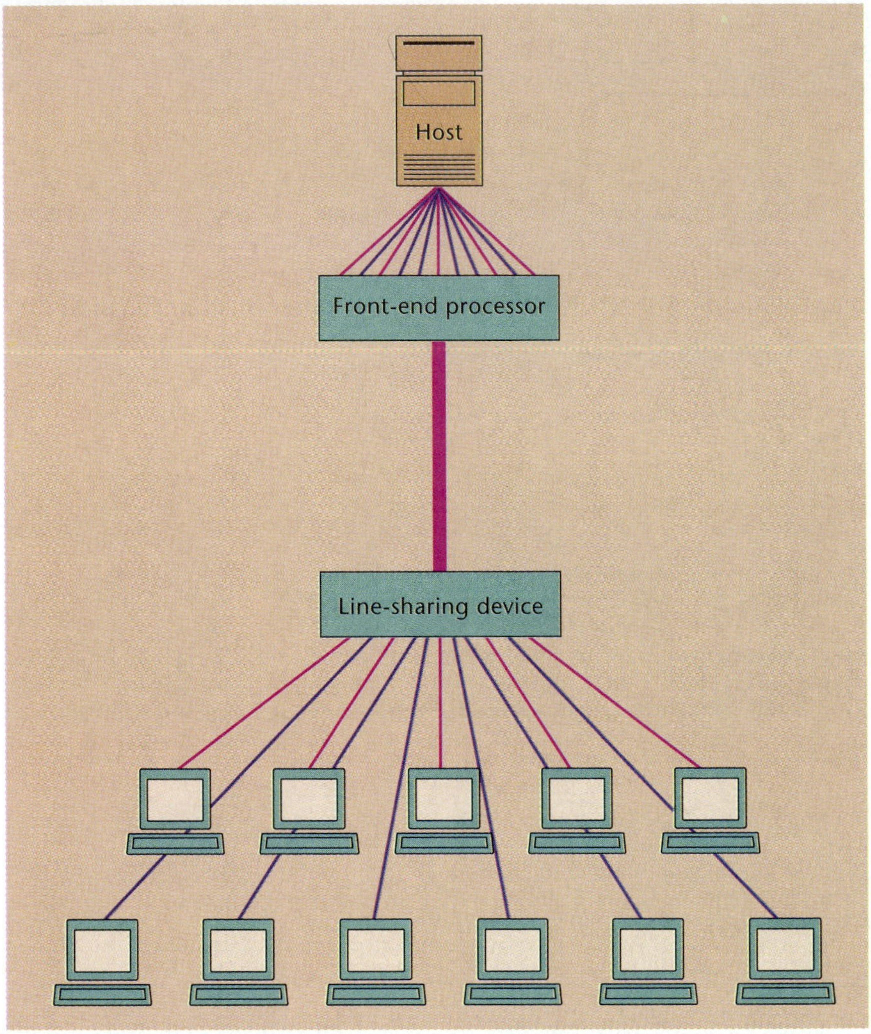

FIGURE 9-15

Components of a Teleprocessing System Teleprocessing system components include host, front-end processor, channel, line-sharing device, and terminals.

In the future, dumb terminals are likely to fade from use, since they cost nearly as much as microcomputers. As they are replaced, the intelligence of the micro is used to manage more and more sophisticated user interfaces. GUIs such as those on the Macintosh and in Microsoft Windows are becoming the norm, as are color monitors.

Line-Sharing Devices

Even a short communications line is a major cost element in a teleprocessing system. If lines must be leased to connect separated sites, a single month's line cost can easily exceed the entire cost of the terminal it supports. In addition, the data capacity of the line is typically many times greater than the rate at which humans can enter data. Therefore, if several terminals are to be connected at a remote location, they may share the use of a single communications line.

Terminals must be considered low-speed devices because they are operated by humans who can enter data and read output only at a slow speed. An extremely fast typist can enter data at a sustained rate of about 100 bps, equivalent to about 100 words per minute, and a good reader can read displayed output at a sustained rate of about 1.2 Kbps, equivalent to just over 1000 words per minute. The line capacity of even a low-speed data communications line is at least several times this transmission rate.

The most common line-sharing device is called a **multiplexer**, which takes the outputs of several low-speed terminals and packs them together onto a single, higher-speed line. At the other end of the line must be a corresponding device to unpack the various streams of data and distribute them as though they arrived by separate channels. That device is a front-end processor.

Channel

The communications channels that link terminals to the host may include any of the communications media described earlier. Terminals in the room next to the computer may be connected by a simple system of direct wiring. At more usual distances ranging from a few hundred feet to many miles, standard data communications media are used.

Front-End Processor

At the host end of the communications line, the situation is much more complicated. Data may be arriving simultaneously on dozens of shared lines, representing up to several hundred terminals of all types. For example, some may be dumb terminals; others may be microcomputers. Some may be directly connected; others may be connected through shared communication lines. Still others may be communicating through LANs. Some may require color display information; others may not. Some may use one set of signals to locate words at a particular place on the screen; others may use completely different signals.

A **front-end processor**, or **communications controller**, a special-purpose computer, handles all the data communications for the host computer. It sorts out which data originated at which terminal on multiplexed lines, takes care of providing correct signals to display output correctly on each type of terminal, and performs a wide variety of similar communications tasks for the host. As a result, the host can simply treat each device as though it were the same, leaving the front-end processor to provide for the differences. A front-end processor can also sense when terminals fail and monitor host response time. This information can be passed to the host for network performance analysis.

Host

The earliest teleprocessing systems used mainframes as the central processing computers. As minicomputers gained prominence, they were used as well. Today, microcomputers have more power than the mainframes of ten years ago, and they can also be used as central computers in teleprocessing systems, but this is not commonly done. The reason has little to do with the raw processing power of microcomputers. Rather, it has to do with the capabilities other than raw power that minicomputers and mainframes provide. Key capabilities are circuitry to control huge storage capacities and circuitry to control high-volume data communications.

For example, in one metropolitan area's local telephone company office, a large room—covering perhaps a quarter of an acre—is packed to capacity with long rows of hard disk drives. Each of these units, about the size of an office file cabinet, contains many gigabytes (billions of bytes) of storage. The system based in this room records all the telephone calls made by customers to locations that are outside their free calling area but inside the area served by this telephone company. Such calls must be listed individually on each customer's monthly bill, so each call must be separately recorded: starting time, ending time, destination telephone number, destination location, amount billed. The amount of storage required is staggering! To maintain control of this volume of data, the system's computer must contain sophisticated, expensive electronics to optimize its interface with disk storage systems. Minicomputers and mainframes provide such capabilities. Microcomputers do not.

Similarly, mainframes and minicomputers contain special expensive electronics to optimize data communications. To communicate effectively with a hundred terminals, as many mainframes can do, a computer must be designed for this purpose. To communicate half-a-billion bits per second with other mainframes requires similar special circuitry.

Thus, there is still a role for mainframes and minicomputers in applications that require optimized disk access and high-speed data communications. At the same time, many former mainframe applications that do not require these capabilities are being **downsized**, or shifted to smaller computers.

Communications Control Program

Communications control programs (CCPs) are system programs that handle the various data communications tasks required in teleprocessing systems: sorting out transaction data arriving simultaneously from up to several hundred terminals at many locations, allocating each transaction to the program that should process it, and maintaining queues of transaction data to be processed in case several transactions for the same program arrive simultaneously. Handling these functions without error is so complicated that the majority of MIS departments allocate their most technically accomplished programmers to the tasks of maintaining and, occasionally, modifying these programs.

With mainframe computers, the CCP is an add-on product purchased separately from the operating system. With minicomputers, the CCP is

- **Interactive applications loaded continuously**
  - Order entry
  - Inventory
  - Customer credit history
  - Production monitoring
  - Accounts receivable transaction entry
- **Interactive applications loaded on demand**
  - Production planning
  - Billing transaction entry
  - Payroll transaction entry
- **Batch applications queued for processing**
  - Weekly production summary reporting
  - Hourly wage payroll processing
  - Weekly labor cost summary reporting
  - Production plan daily update
  - Weekly sales summary reporting
  - Accounts receivable aging reporting

FIGURE 9-16
Examples of Typical Jobs in a Teleprocessing Computer

built into the operating system. This difference arose because, historically, teleprocessing was an add-on to the batch processing typical of early mainframes. Minicomputers were designed from the start to do teleprocessing, so their operating systems included this capability.

Characteristics of Teleprocessing Systems

Since all processing occurs at one site, those who manage the single computer can maintain tight control over processing. They can carefully manage accesses and changes to data, determine the order of processing, and provide extensive security.

Teleprocessing systems are most commonly used to process data shared by people in many parts of the organization, such as data about companywide budgets, inventories, orders, and operating plans (see Figure 9-16). These large systems, often called enterprise systems, are usually operated by professionals within the company's MIS department. At one time, teleprocessing systems were also used to process data shared by people in single departments, such as data about advertising media and marketing simulations. Today, such systems are gradually being replaced by distributed or hybrid architectures.

DISTRIBUTED SYSTEMS

In distributed information systems, multiple independent processing computers are connected to each other via communications lines. LANs are the most common form of distributed system in business today, and this discussion is devoted primarily to them. In describing distributed system architecture as it is used today, we will consider client-server processing, LAN protocols, components of a LAN, and private branch exchange as an alternative type of distributed system. Finally, we will consider the characteristics of today's LANs.

Client-Server Processing

In microcomputer LANs, one or more workstations are usually more powerful computers equipped with very large disk storage systems. These units, called **servers**, provide shared storage for the other computers in the LAN, called **clients**. Some servers, called **dedicated servers**, are used entirely in their capacity as servers. Others may also be used as workstations.

The client-server model is used to describe not only the sharing of disk storage but also the sharing of other resources. For example, **print servers** are computers equipped with expensive or specialized printers to be shared with LAN clients. Print servers commonly provide **spooling** software, which accepts and stores output data as fast as it is received and feeds it to a printer at the much slower speed that the printer can accept. Spooling software commonly can accept data for printing simultaneously from several applications, keep track of which data belongs to which application, and send completed print jobs to the printer one after the other.

A **mail server** provides E-mail mailboxes for LAN clients. A typical mail server has specialized hardware and software for efficient transmission and reception of mail messages. Specialized **database servers** share database processing with workstations in the LAN. Database servers are described further in Chapter 10.

LAN Protocols

A LAN is used to communicate between nodes in a limited geographical area, usually less than a mile. It provides high-speed data transfer with high reliability. Two major types of LANs are in widespread use—Ethernet LANs and token ring LANs. They are distinguished both by their architecture and by the method they use to determine which node has the right to transmit messages at a given time.

Ethernet LANs The most widely used LAN protocol is **Ethernet**, a protocol developed jointly by a group of companies that markets various LAN products. Ethernet uses the bus architecture. The nodes can be computers or other devices, such as printers, that include Ethernet adapter cards and circuitry to manage arriving messages.

There are two ways of using a bus. The first way, through **broadband transmission**, is to divide the bus into a series of smaller-capacity subchannels by giving each subchannel its own frequency—like the frequencies of broadcasting stations on the radio dial. The second way to use a bus, through **baseband transmission**, is to let every node contend for the full LAN transmission capacity, so nodes transmit messages consecutively and more rapidly than in a broadband system. Ethernet uses baseband transmission.

Each node in an Ethernet LAN "listens" to the bus all the time. Transmitted messages include a destination address. If a message arrives that is addressed to a particular node, that node receives it. Otherwise, the node ignores it.

To determine which node has the right to transmit, Ethernet uses **Carrier Sense Multiple Access with Collision Detection (CSMA/CD)**. Under this system, when a node needs to transmit a message, it first "listens" to the bus to see whether another node is transmitting. This is called *sensing* the carrier. The *carrier* is the signal that carries the message. If the system senses the carrier, it waits until the bus is clear, then it transmits. As it transmits, it also monitors. If the signal on the LAN is different from what it is transmitting, then another node must also have begun transmitting at the same time, garbling the message (a *collision*). When a collision is detected, each node stops, waits a randomly determined amount of time (a few thousandths of a second—different for each node), then begins the process again by "listening" for the carrier.

Token Ring LANs The second most widely used LAN protocol is the **token ring**, developed and marketed by IBM Corporation. This protocol uses the ring architecture, with messages moving in one direction around the ring, so each node always transmits to the same "next" node in the ring.

When no node has a message to transmit, then the nodes pass a symbolic **token** around the ring by transmitting its symbol code from one node to the next. When a node has data to transmit, it waits to receive the token, adds its data (with address) after the token, and transmits. If the

FIGURE 9-17
LAN
A LAN links PCs and other devices for shared processing.

token arrives with data already attached, the node receives the data and checks to see whether it is the intended recipient. If it is not, it retransmits the token, the newly arrived data, and its own message to the next station. The standard message block is large enough to accommodate messages from several nodes to several receivers as the block travels around the ring.

The token ring protocol is designed to ignore a failed node. Therefore, if a node fails, the system automatically bypasses it and the remaining nodes function normally.

Components of a LAN

The components of a LAN are network interface cards, channel hardware, workstations, internetwork links, and LAN operating system programs.

Network Interface Card The **network interface card** is a hardware device that plugs into a slot on the motherboard of a microcomputer. Its job is to create the hardware link between the network and the microcomputer, so it includes connectors to plug the microcomputer into the network. It monitors the channel and transmits data into the channel for the workstation. In addition, it creates an address for the workstation, and it monitors incoming messages for this address.

Channel Hardware The LAN channel itself may be coaxial cable, twisted pair, or optical fiber. Because coaxial cable is expensive, its use is decreasing compared to twisted pair. Although optical fiber is new technology and is also expensive, its much greater channel capacity is leading to a growth in its use.

Along with the channel medium, hardware includes bus terminators (special circuitry required at the end of a bus), repeaters (located about every 1,500 feet in typical LANs), and connectors to plug nodes into the LAN.

Workstation The standard LAN workstations are microcomputers equipped with network interface cards. In addition, LANs can be used for interconnecting mainframe computers and minicomputers.

In some LANs, each workstation provides storage for part of the shared data, with no node singled out to provide the majority of the storage. Such LANs are called **peer-to-peer LANs**. This system is often used in the very smallest and the very largest of LANs. More often, LANs use a client-server system to provide shared storage and other resources.

Links Between Networks As we have seen, LANs are often interconnected, and they are often attached to teleprocessing systems, so LAN workstation users can input teleprocessing data. A **bridge** is a workstation that serves as a connecter between two LANs of the same kind. A **gateway** interconnects either two different types of LANs or a single LAN to another type of communications network. The function of the gateway is to reconcile the protocol differences between the two systems.

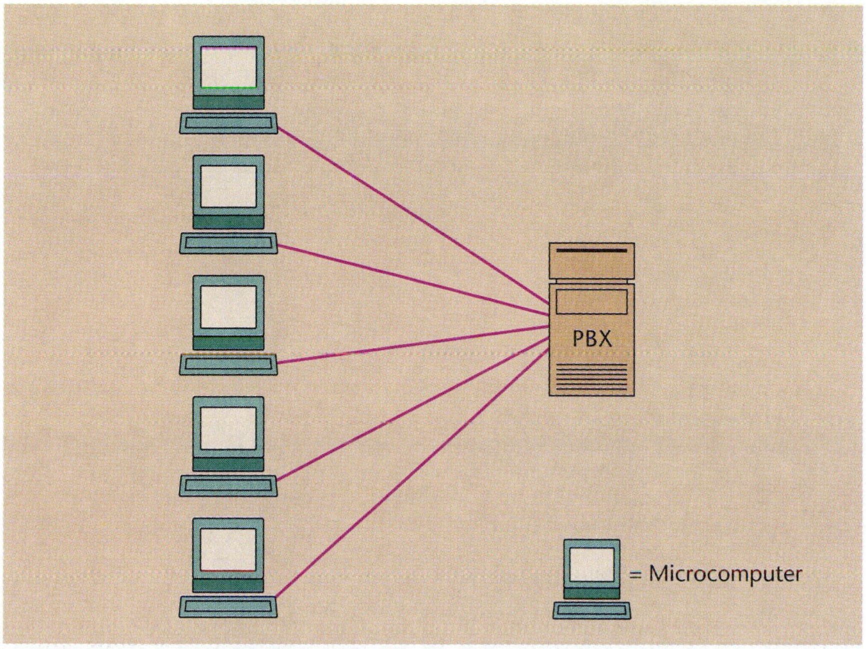

FIGURE 9-18
PBX Network
Using the company telephone system to carry data, the PBX is capable of providing some of the functions of a LAN.

LAN Operating System A **LAN operating system (LAN-OS)** is commonly added onto the standard operating system—such as DOS—of a workstation, though newer microcomputer operating systems such as OS/2 and System 7 provide many functions of a LAN-OS. The LAN-OS provides **transparent access** to the LAN, oversees node-to-node communications, adds security routines to limit user access to certain data, and keeps the sharing orderly. Transparent access means that the user accesses LAN resources as though they were part of the user's own computer. For example, a DOS user whose internal hard disk is drive C: may access a LAN hard disk by designating it drive G:, as though the disk were inside the user's computer.

Specialized LAN-OS functions relate specifically to the operation of a file server. These include controlling concurrent access to programs to support software license agreements, preventing the copying of shared programs by users at workstations, supporting network management by adding and deleting users and establishing security levels, and providing communications links to other systems.

The PBX Alternative

An alternative to the LAN in connecting computers within a local area is the **private branch exchange (PBX)**, as depicted in Figure 9-18. A PBX is a private telephone system used within a single company. Since today's PBXs allow for the transmission of data as well as voice signals, they provide a means for microcomputers to communicate. Theoretically, a PBX

FIGURE 9-19
LAN Management Procedures

- **Procedures for normal operations**
  - Connecting and disconnecting workstations
  - Adding and deleting users; establishing user security levels
  - Installing, modifying, and updating applications
  - Managing shared printing envrionment
  - Backing up files
  - Monitoring and evaluating performance; proposing modifications
  - Maintaining documentation and procedures
- **Procedures for failure recovery**
  - Diagnosing and correcting medium problems, such as faulty connections
  - Determining when a failure has occurred
  - Identifying causes of failures; making corrections
  - Restarting the LAN after failure

could provide data communications capacity equivalent to a LAN, but in practice that capacity has not yet been achieved. Therefore, PBX systems are currently used only for low-volume applications such as E-mail.

Characteristics of Distributed Information Systems

Distributed networks, unlike teleprocessing systems, distribute control and processing throughout the network. Since each microcomputer uses its own microprocessor, it can process independently of the file server and the other computers. A user on one of the micros can run a spreadsheet application using a file that it received from the server and saved on internal disk storage two or three weeks previously and that now contains outdated data. Since the file server was not accessed, no control over this use of data can be exercised. The advantage of this characteristic is that users have more independence and more control over their own processing. The disadvantage is that correct processing depends entirely on the care and judgment of the users. The data in that two-week-old file may be entirely out of date and untrustworthy, or it may be exactly the data that the user needs. A distributed system relies on the judgment of the user about which processing is needed and which data should be used.

Although a LAN is usually less complex and smaller than a teleprocessing system, its management involves dealing with many of the same problems. As we have seen, the manager of a teleprocessing system must be an experienced information systems professional. Yet the manager of a departmental LAN is normally a department staff member who takes on LAN management as a part-time task. If the right person is available, that person may have the qualities and quickly develop the minimum knowledge needed to perform competently. However, in many offices, such a person may be hard to find.

Figure 9-19 shows examples of LAN management procedures for normal operations and failure recovery. As you can see, these procedures cover a wide range of tasks from technical details to resource management to system planning. When a group of users has come to rely on the successful operation of a LAN to get the work done, these procedures are absolutely essential.

HYBRID SYSTEMS

The third shared system architecture is the hybrid. As you would expect from the name, this architecture is a combination of teleprocessing and distributed architectures. Figure 9-20 shows a typical system in a large company, with central company mainframe, departmental minicomputers, terminals, and LANs of various types. Bridges and gateways interconnect the systems. The processing systems in most large corporations take this form.

The hybrid architecture entails hybrid forms of control. For example, the mainframe in Figure 9-20 controls all of its interactions with terminals and minicomputers. However, the mainframe does not control any of the message passing that occurs between PCs via the LANs.

WIDE AREA NETWORKS

A **wide area network (WAN)** is a network that provides data communications services between companies or between separated divisions of the same company. A WAN is owned and operated by a common carrier.

In a teleprocessing system, a company may lease a point-to-point communications line from a common carrier. However, in the case of a WAN, the company buys network services, a much more comprehensive type of support. Instead of simply connecting two particular points, a WAN provides a communications pathway to all other members of that network. Some WANS even provide pathways into other networks, giving a company access to worldwide high-speed data communications.

In addition to data communications service, WANs typically also provide the ability to convert data from one protocol to another. For example, suppose the preferred protocol for communication with the company's mainframe computer in Toledo is synchronous mode using EBCDIC code at 2 Mbps. And suppose the preferred protocol for the minicomputer in that company's branch office in Atlanta is asynchronous mode using ASCII code at 56 Kbps. The WAN can accept data from the

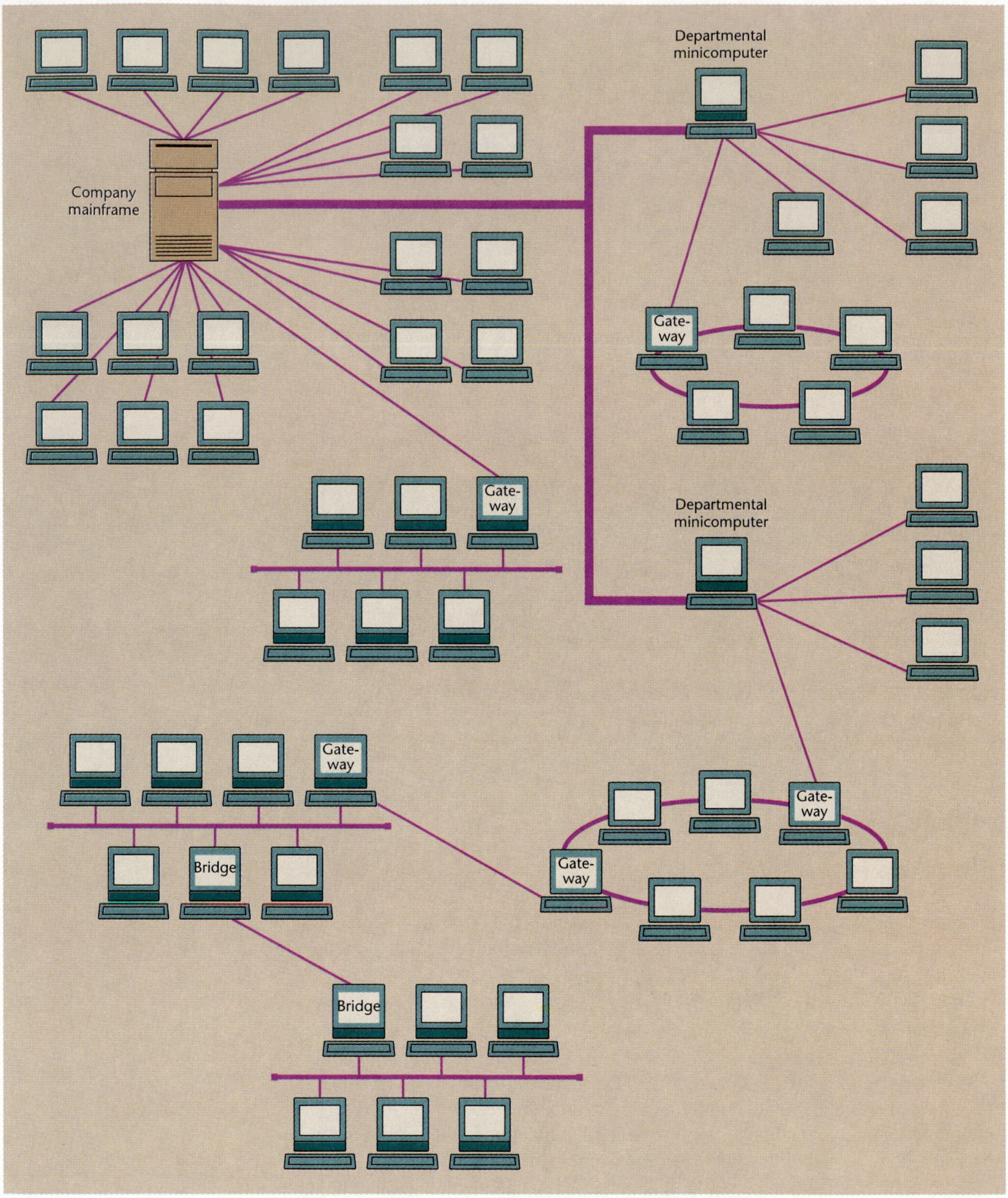

FIGURE 9-20

A Large Company's Interconnected Networks

In a large company, the central mainframe, with its star network of data entry terminals, may also be the center of a hierarchical network of departmental minicomputers. At the same time, LANs in ring and bus architectures may be interconnected to permit communication with the company and departmental computers.

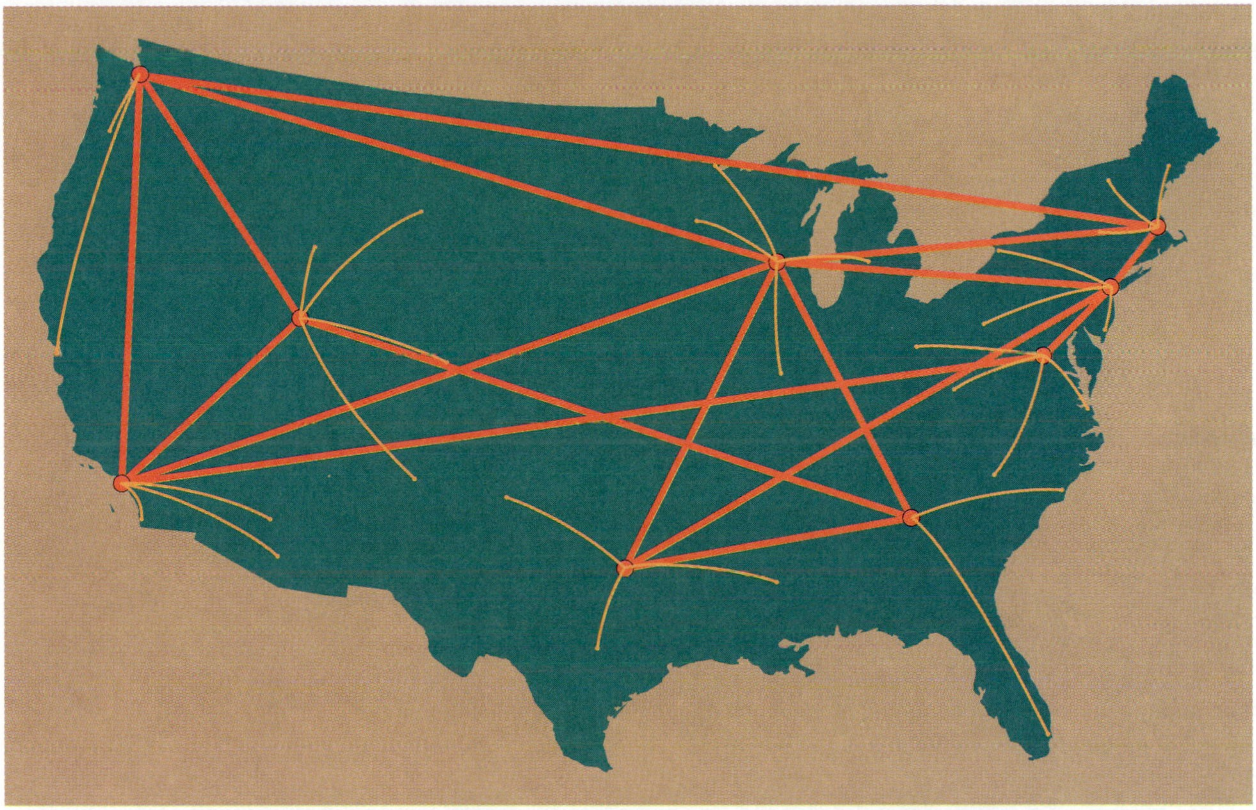

FIGURE 9-21 **WAN**
Major routes on this WAN interconnect major nodes throughout the United States. Minor routes provide service to specific sites near the major nodes.

Toledo computer in its protocol, deliver the data to the Atlanta computer in its protocol, and make the equivalent translation on the return data. This is an important added service.

Most WANs use a **packet-switching** protocol. A message is divided into fixed-size packets, with the appropriate address and an indication of its position in the message—for example, packet number 3 of 15—attached to each packet. Because the load on various pathways through the network, illustrated in Figure 9-21, may vary in a few thousandths of a second, all 15 packets may not be routed identically. In fact, the first packet to be transmitted may not be the first received. But since all packets indicate their position and the total number of packets that should arrive, storage space can immediately be reserved for the whole message.

When any one packet arrives, the receiving node anticipates arrival of the remaining packets in the message. After an interval, if some packets have not arrived, the receiving node sends a request for retransmission of the missing packets, repeating the request at intervals, if necessary, until all the packets arrive. All this is happening at a rate of millions of bits per

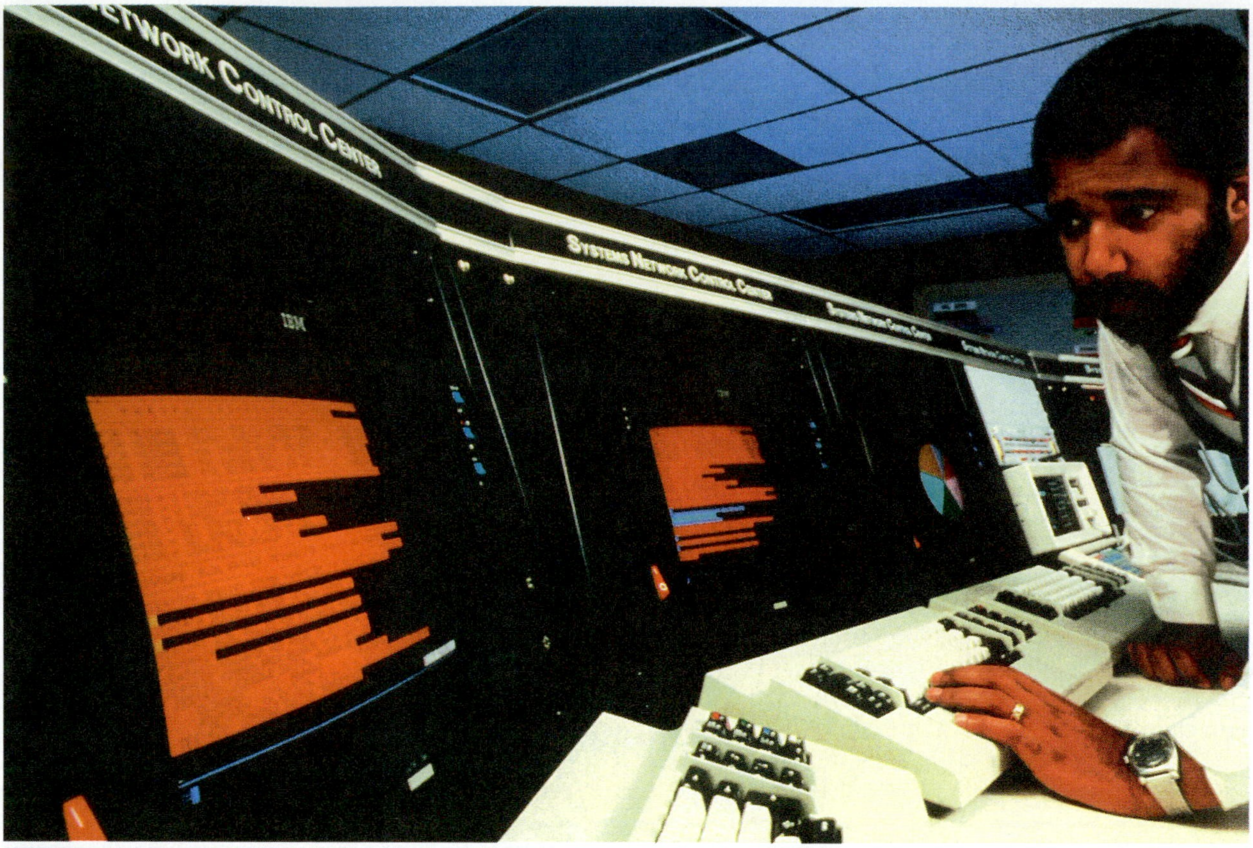

FIGURE 9-22

WAN Control Center
A WAN is managed from a data communications network control center.

second, and to humans, the results appear instantaneous. If you were sitting at a terminal in Atlanta entering transactions into a processing system in Toledo, you would not normally be aware of any delay in the response because of the intervening WAN.

An advantage of the WAN in comparison to leased point-to-point lines is its flexibility. Once the start-up costs have been paid, the cost of a WAN is directly related to actual services provided. Reduced usage results in reduced costs. In addition, if a new office is opened in Denver, it must only establish communications with the WAN's Denver node to become fully accessible by anyone in the network.

INTERNATIONAL DATA COMMUNICATIONS

Among multinational corporations, additional concerns about data communications arise from the problems associated with **transborder data flow**—sharing data across national boundaries. International data sharing raises an important new set of business factors. Consider the following examples:

- Currency exchange fluctuations may change the cost-effectiveness of a data center in one country as compared to another.
- Local differences in time zones, working hours, and holidays affect the timing of data needs.
- Language differences affect not only interpersonal communication, but also language requirements for data entry screens, output reports, and system documentation.
- The use of locally manufactured equipment may be required that is not consistent with equipment used elsewhere in the company.
- Stringent privacy regulations may restrict the transmission of data about individuals across national borders.

Although the common carriers that provide data communications service in the United States are private companies, in most other countries they are operated by government-owned **postal, telephone, and telegraph (PTT)** monopolies. That is, the only data communications providers are government agencies. In some cases, the requirements of PTT agencies are designed to support infant national computer industries by requiring the use of locally manufactured equipment in any system that is connected to data communications services.

FIGURE 9-23

International Trading
Because major markets and traders throughout the world are interconnected through data communications networks, stock trading occurs 24 hours a day.

Privacy

Another important factor in transborder data flow is the stringent regulations that have been established in some countries to protect individual privacy. Within many countries, access to databases containing information about individuals, such as payroll and performance data, is closely regulated to prevent the data's use for purposes other than those specifically authorized. Such countries prohibit the transmission of personal data to destinations outside their national borders, where they lose the ability to regulate its use.

Three main strategies have been adopted by multinational corporations to respond to these challenges. The first strategy is to educate corporate executives about the special factors that apply to international information systems. Thus, the planning of corporate information systems can take these factors into account. The second strategy is to increase local processing of data within foreign countries to reduce the volume of raw data that must cross borders. Reducing the volume of data to be communicated reduces the company's vulnerability to changes in PTT fees and regulations. The third strategy, which is closely related, is to process personal data within the country where it originated (for example, by processing payroll data and producing paychecks there), to avoid problems with privacy regulations. In this way, data is processed locally where privacy regulations can be enforced, and only summary information not identifiable to any individual is transmitted across the national border.

Summary

Data communications uses high-speed media (coaxial cable, optical fiber, microwaves, and satellite transmission) and low-speed media (twisted pair). Long-distance, high-speed lines are leased from common carriers. Low-speed telephone lines are used primarily because they are already in place where data may need to be communicated and can be activated by dialing a telephone. Communications media may be used to carry analog or digital signals. They may be used for asynchronous or synchronous transmission. Nodes may be connected in hierarchical, star, ring, or bus architecture. Error detection and correction codes may be added to data messages. Protocols are complex sets of rules governing data communications links and specifying many aspects of the linkage.

The hardware components of teleprocessing systems are terminals, line-sharing devices, channels, front-end processors, and hosts. These are supported by a CCP in the host. Teleprocessing systems are characterized by strong central control over processing.

Distributed systems used in business today are primarily LANs. Client-server processing is common. The widely used LAN protocols are Ethernet and token ring. The components of a LAN are network interface cards, channels, workstations, links between networks, and LAN-OSs. The PBX is a potential alternative to the LAN, but it is not widely used today. Distributed systems decentralize both processing and control throughout the network. Although LAN management involves many of the same problems as teleprocessing system management, it is often allocated as a part-time task to a user department staff member.

Hybrid systems combine features of teleprocessing and distributed systems. They usually involve an interconnected central computer and a series of LANs. Processing of organizationwide data on the central computer is centrally controlled, and processing of departmental or workgroup data on the LANs is locally controlled.

A WAN provides links between companies or between locations of the same company. WANs provide protocol conversion in addition to point-to-point data transmission. WANs typically use packet-switching protocols. An advantage of a WAN is its flexibility to accommodate changing communication needs.

When data is shared across national borders, additional factors must be considered. Data communications services in most countries are provided by governmental PTT agencies, whose policies often support national goals. National privacy laws may restrict data transmission across borders. Corporate information systems policy makers must be educated about these factors. The resulting systems often process data locally to reduce transborder data flow and eliminate problems with privacy regulations.

Key Terms

teleprocessing system
centralized system
distributed system
hybrid system
bits per second (bps)
coaxial cable
repeater
optical fiber
microwaves
satellite transmission
geosynchronous
common carrier
leased line
twisted pair
switched line
digital signal
analog signal
codec
asynchronous
synchronous
node
hierarchical architecture
star architecture
ring architecture
bus architecture
parity
Cyclic Redundancy Check (CRC)
Hamming code
protocol
terminal
dumb terminal
multiplexer
front-end processor
communications controller
downsize
communications control program (CCP)
server
client
dedicated server
print server
spooling
mail server
database server
Ethernet

broadband transmission
baseband transmission
Carrier Sense Multiple Access with Collision Detection (CSMA/CD)
token ring protocol
token
network interface card
peer-to-peer LAN
bridge
gateway
LAN operating system (LAN-OS)
transparent access
private branch exchange (PBX)
wide area network (WAN)
packet switching
transborder data flow
postal, telephone, and telegraph (PTT)

Review Questions

1. Differentiate among teleprocessing architecture, distributed architecture, and hybrid architecture.
2. Name four units that are used in measuring the transmission rates of data communications media.
3. What are the four high-speed data communications media?
4. Describe the function of a repeater.
5. Compare the cost of coaxial cable and optical fiber media.
6. Why are repeaters required in microwave transmission?
7. Why is a geosynchronous orbit useful?
8. Describe the costs associated with developing a long-distance data communications channel using coaxial cable, microwave transmission, and satellite transmission.
9. What is a common carrier?
10. Describe twisted pair medium.
11. Differentiate between switched lines and leased lines. Describe the transmission rates of each.
12. Describe the common uses of high-speed media and low-speed media.
13. Since it is slower, why would anyone use a low-speed medium?
14. Differentiate between analog signals and digital signals.
15. Contrast the operation of a modem and a codec.
16. Describe the four commonly used network architectures.
17. Name three methods of error detection or correction.
18. What is a protocol?
19. Name at least six topics that might be covered by a protocol.
20. Identify the six hardware components of a typical teleprocessing system.
21. What devices can be used as terminals in teleprocessing systems?
22. Name a line-sharing device, and describe what it does.
23. Identify at least three things that a front-end processor does.
24. Why are microcomputers seldom used as hosts in teleprocessing systems?
25. What is downsizing?
26. Explain what a CCP does.
27. Describe the typical teleprocessing system manager.
28. What is client-server processing?

29. List the key features of the Ethernet protocol.
30. Differentiate between broadband use and baseband use of a bus.
31. List the key features of the token ring protocol.
32. Name and describe five components of a LAN.
33. What is a peer-to-peer LAN?
34. Differentiate between a bridge and a gateway.
35. How could a PBX serve as an alternative to a LAN?
36. Describe the typical LAN manager.
37. Explain the components of a hybrid system.
38. What is a WAN?
39. How is a WAN different from the point-to-point leased line that may be used in a teleprocessing system?
40. Describe the operation of a packet-switching network.
41. Name five factors that are important in transborder data flow.
42. How do privacy laws affect transborder data flow?
43. Name three strategies used by multinational corporations to respond to the challenges of international data communications.

Discussion Questions

A. In your own words, prepare an executive summary of teleprocessing systems and distributed systems. What is the structure of each? How is each used? Identify three specific applications in which you believe a teleprocessing system would be more appropriate, and three in which you believe a distributed system would be more appropriate.

B. A large hotel chain is reconsidering its information systems. A key question is whether the reservations and guest registration system should be a teleprocessing system or a distributed system. Identify the major advantages of each system for this purpose. Indicate which system you would select, and give at least three reasons.

C. If you or a friend have ever used a modem to communicate between a PC and another computer, describe the communication system. What hardware and software components were involved? How was the modem attached to the PC? What medium was used? Were the transmitted signals analog or digital? Was the transmission asynchronous or synchronous? Describe any adjustment or tuning that was required to make the system work correctly.

D. A large corporation would seriously consider using a teleprocessing system for order entry, and it would seriously consider using a distributed system to provide word processing capability to office workers. Summarize the key differences between those applications that make each of those choices seem plausible. Give at least five differences.

E. Consider the assertion that the computer networks in most large corporations consist of hybrid systems. Why do you think this assertion is plausible, or why not? Specifically, why would (or why wouldn't) a combination, rather than a single type of system, be preferred in a large corporation?

F. Explain why a company might spend more than a million dollars for a mainframe computer when it can buy a microcomputer for ten thousand dollars that has about the same raw processing power. Provide sufficient detail to justify spending 100 times as much money.

MINICASE

The "Fed Ex" Mentality: Has all our work really become "extremely urgent"?

Are Americans, as recent Japanese public mutterings have it, lazy workers? Not in the workplaces I visit. If anything, I find people who work too hard, for too long, and who too often take their work home on evenings and weekends. There are Homer Simpsons, no doubt; but many Americans work longer and harder than their parents, certainly longer and harder than most Europeans, and as hard as many Japanese.

Anyone involved in publishing over the last decade can testify to a major change in work patterns. There was a time when lots of lag time had to be built into the system so copy could be sent to the typesetter, photos to the camera department, and so on. At best, those slack times were useful for planning, polishing, and (remember when?) thinking out the next move.

The old excuses are dead. With desktop publishing, it's assumed that all aspects of the job can be done instantly and that deadlines can be held to the last minute for new ads or copy changes. . . .

The symbol of this new rush is the Federal Express package. In many offices, the tempo of work builds to a crisis between five and six o'clock, when the Fed Ex agent comes to pick up packages. On the East Coast, where I live, a second critical point occurs around nine o'clock, the last possible time that you can drop off an overnight package at the airport. "The proofs are in the mail" is no longer an excuse.

Modems and fax machines are Fed Ex's allies. Image-setting can be modemed out in early afternoon and returned the next morning from any service bureau in the United States. Need some last-minute alternations? Fax me within the hour and I'll get them back later today. In theory, everything can be on your desk for your emergency by the next morning, at the latest.

Of course, we all like this sense of instant satisfaction. Anything you need can be delivered by tomorrow morning if you call before five o'clock today. All of this is a great convenience, and it has saved all of our behinds at one time or another. But when it becomes the normal procedure, when "urgent" and "rush" are the only categories of work, things have gotten far out of whack. Too many projects are run this way from start to finish, with the tightest of deadlines, the narrowest of margins, and no room for quiet contemplation or getting ahead of the next deadline. . . .

I see too many talented professionals under the obligation to make these remarkable turnarounds day after day. Just-in-time may make sense in a car assembly plant, but it's hopeless for endeavors where reasoning and creativity have even a little importance. After a while, our heroics don't win us medals, and soon we're noticed only when we fail. Not allowing for mistakes or the inevitable illness creates an appalling load of stress. And with little time for regrouping, planning, or experimenting, the quality of work declines as workers begin to sour on their jobs. . . .

The Fed Ex mentality threatens to keep us so busy dealing with the endless round of deadlines that we forget why we're meeting those deadlines in the first place. While we won't banish this way of thinking entirely (I write this as my deadline for *Aldus Magazine* draws closer), we do have to schedule time for planning and review of past and current work, rather than simply react to the latest crisis or try to beat the clock. When our tools (overnight delivery, faxes, modems) become our bosses, something is seriously wrong.

Questions

1. This article directly addresses urgency in the world of desktop publishing. Is such urgency a factor only in the desktop publishing industry or do you think this same sense pertains to other industries and job categories as well? What other industries do you think are prone to this phenomenon?
2. The author mentions tools of "overnight delivery, faxes, modems." What additional tools and technologies that are described in this chapter could also contribute to the "Fed Ex Mentality?"
3. What do you think are the consequences on individuals of working too hard, too fast, too long? What do you think are the consequences for an organization? What do you think are the consequences for a society?
4. As we develop more communications technology, the world becomes smaller and the pace of life continues to increase. What measures do you think individuals and organizations can take to avoid the consequences described in your answer to question 3?

CHAPTER 10

Shared Database Applications

This is the second chapter in this book about database applications. The first such chapter, Chapter 6, described personal database applications. Rather than repeat material already presented there, here we will focus on the unique characteristics of shared database applications.

EXAMPLE: REGISTERING FOR CLASSES

It was July 8, the day Kevin was scheduled to register for Fall classes. In the preceding days, Kevin had considered his four-year program, consulted the class schedule, and selected the classes he wanted to take (first and second choices). He had carefully worked out a schedule that met his priorities: (1) no early morning classes and (2) no evening classes that would conflict with his work hours.

Kevin prepared to register. Then he picked up the phone and dialed.

"Welcome to registration for Fall term. Please enter your student number, followed by the pound sign," said the computerized registration system's voice output module. Kevin entered his 9-digit student number and pressed the pound (#) key on his telephone keypad. "Your name is Kevin Ryan. K-e-v-i-n R-y-a-n. If any of this information is not correct, please press 8 and the pound sign to exit the system, and then call again to retry.

"To add a class, press 2 and the pound sign now. To drop a class, press 3 and the pound sign. To request help, press 4 and the pound sign. To list your enrolled classes, press 5 and the pound sign. To list all open sections of a course, press 6 and the pound sign. To exit the registration system, press 8 and the pound sign. For help from a staff member, exit the registration system and call registration help at 555-4357."

Kevin pressed 2 and #. "Add a class. Enter the 5-digit schedule code of the class you wish to add and then enter the pound sign." Kevin entered the code. "You have requested English Composition, section 4, which meets on Monday, Wednesday, and Friday mornings from 11:00 to 11:50. You have successfully added that class."

In a few minutes, Kevin completed registration for a full schedule of Fall classes. Then he asked the system to review the list to be sure his handwritten listing was correct, and he exited the system.

During the 20 minutes that Kevin spent registering, 62 other students also registered. In three weeks of registration, nearly all of the 32,762 students who attend the university completed registration. During that period, on average, a student completed registration every 13 seconds, and nearly 100,000 successful course enrollment transactions were processed.

The registration system at Kevin's university was a computerized database processing system using touch-tone input and voice output. Computerized registration systems are relatively new. When Kevin's grandfather attended the same university in 1952, registration was done by a manual system. Faculty members sat at tables in the gymnasium, and students went from table to table to sign in—literally—to courses.

In businesses at that time, manual systems were used for payrolls and other accounting systems. When computerized systems appeared, their designers capitalized on people's knowledge of successful manual systems. Since today's complex systems have evolved from those simpler ones, it is useful to trace their evolution. In this chapter, we will briefly consider manual file processing, batch file processing, and on-line file processing. Then we will turn our attention to shared database processing.

MANUAL FILE PROCESSING

Until the early computerized data processing systems were developed, most data processing systems used **manual file processing** methods. Indeed, when we talk about file processing, the terminology comes from the processing methods in which clerks wrote data in the blanks on printed forms stored in manila file folders in office filing cabinets. In fact, many early computerized file processing methods were developed directly from standard manual procedures.

Consider an hourly wage payroll done manually. A clerk picks up a time card, reads off the name, and goes to the bank of file cabinets to locate the master folder for that employee. Folders are filed alphabetically, so the clerk must locate the drawer that includes this section of the alphabet, then track down the file for this employee. The clerk pulls out the file, leaving a place marker in its position, and takes the folder to a desk. Making entries on a line in the payroll worksheet form in the master file folder, the clerk fills in hours worked, pay rate, gross pay, deductions, and net pay. A mechanical adding machine on the desk helps with the arithmetic. The clerk fills in the blanks on the check stub for the employee's in-

FIGURE 10-1
Manual File Processing
File processing terminology arose from data on paper forms in file folders stored in file cabinets.

formation and uses a check-writing machine to type the paycheck. Then the clerk carries the folder back to the file cabinet, opens the drawer, replaces the file in the correct place, and picks up another time card.

This process, called a **file update**, is part of a larger system called a **transaction processing system (TPS)**. TPSs are used to create and maintain a company's accounting records. In addition to the file update, a payroll TPS includes procedures for adding new employees, deleting records of persons no longer currently employed, gathering the data to be processed, improving the accuracy of the data, and producing and distributing information based on the data.

If human clerks were infallible, then the manual file update would have the disadvantages of only being slow and inflexible. The system is inflexible because, if the company needs to change the data it collects, it must print all new forms, and clerks must copy all the old data onto the new forms, a prohibitively large job.

But humans are not infallible. Clerks sometimes mistakenly select the wrong file folder. They make arithmetic errors. They sometimes copy data incorrectly. And despite taking great care, they replace file folders in the wrong place so often that one clerk in a group typically has the task of going through the drawers in the file cabinets, one by one, and realphabetizing the folders. In a large file system, a clerk may do this continuously from beginning to end of the files, then, upon finishing, immediately go back to the beginning and start again. What a dreary job!

During the first half of this century, manual file processing was mechanized. It used punched card equipment combined with mechanical adding machines, which are much more elementary than electronic computers. These were called **unit record** devices. Although mechanization eliminated much of the human handling of data and thus improved the accuracy of the results, the processing methods remained much the same.

COMPUTERIZED FILE PROCESSING

When computers began to do business file processing in the 1960s, systems designers took advantage of many years of company experience with manual file processing. Designing systems that imitated manual methods helped to assure that their designs met all the requirements of the task. The result was the computerized batch processing system.

As computers improved and business information systems continued to evolve, on-line processing systems gradually replaced batch systems. This section describes batch and on-line file processing systems. In diagramming the architecture of these systems, we use a time-honored set of system flowchart symbols shown in Figure 10-2.

Batch File Processing

In a **batch file processing** system, data is collected for a period and then processed together (as a *batch*). For instance, in a payroll system, as time cards are collected, they are given to **data entry clerks** at keyboards. These clerks enter the data onto recorded media—magnetic tape or punched cards in the early days, magnetic disk recently. A flowchart for the batch processing of a file appears in Figure 10-3.

Unfortunately, data entry clerks share a limitation with all other human beings: They cannot do precise work with perfect accuracy. The most proficient data entry clerks average about 1 percent error—that is, about 1 of every 100 keystrokes is incorrect. To put it another way, if a time card entry is 37 characters long (25 for name, 9 for employee number, and 3 for hours worked), then a very good data entry clerk will make 1 error in almost every 3 time cards, on average.

Error Detection and Correction Accuracy in accounting data is very important. Therefore, a TPS includes an edit program to detect and correct certain kinds of errors.

The methods used in error detection for each data item depend on the type of data. For example, a Social Security number should be exactly nine digits, all numeric. A name should include only alphabetic characters and perhaps periods, apostrophes, and a hyphen. We use a **validity check** to ensure that the data is of the correct length and type—numeric or alphabetic. Many data items can be checked for this kind of mechanical correctness.

A second method of error detection checks that the data is within an accepted range. For example, in most companies, the computer is not permitted to process a time card showing more than, say, 55 hours of work in a week. Although an employee may work this much, it is not very likely. (Notice that 55 hours is over 9 hours a day for 6 days!) That time card is probably incorrect, so a human being must verify the hours and either correct the error or take personal responsibility for issuing a check. This is called a **reasonableness check**.

Symbol	Name	Comments
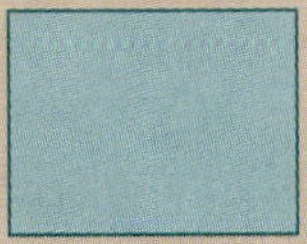	Computer program	Program runs on a computer, which is usually not shown
	User workstation	Keyboard and screen Can be terminal or microcomputer connected to computer
	Direct access storage device (DASD)	Data repository Data can be read or written in any order
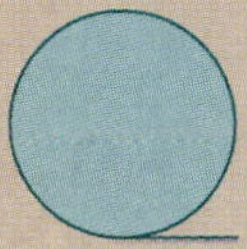	Tape—sequential access device	Data repository Data must be read and written sequentially
	Document	Report or form
	Telecommunications link	Telephone line or similar connection
	Manual process	Activity performed off-line by a person such as key-to-disk operator
	Data input	Keying performed by user or data entry clerk
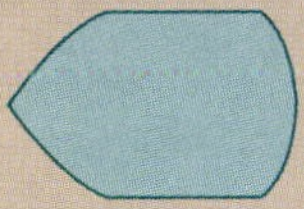	Screen display	Output to display screen

FIGURE 10-2
Symbols Used in System Flowcharts

A third method of error detection checks whether the data agrees with other existing data. For example, a zip code can be checked to determine whether it is consistent with the data on city and state. A mail order auto parts company can check the part numbers on a customer's order to determine whether those parts fit the make and model of car listed. This is called a **consistency check**.

Not all errors can be detected even by the most careful checking. If a job applicant erroneously writes the number 23 in the "Age" line on a form, when the correct value is 32, computerized checking cannot detect

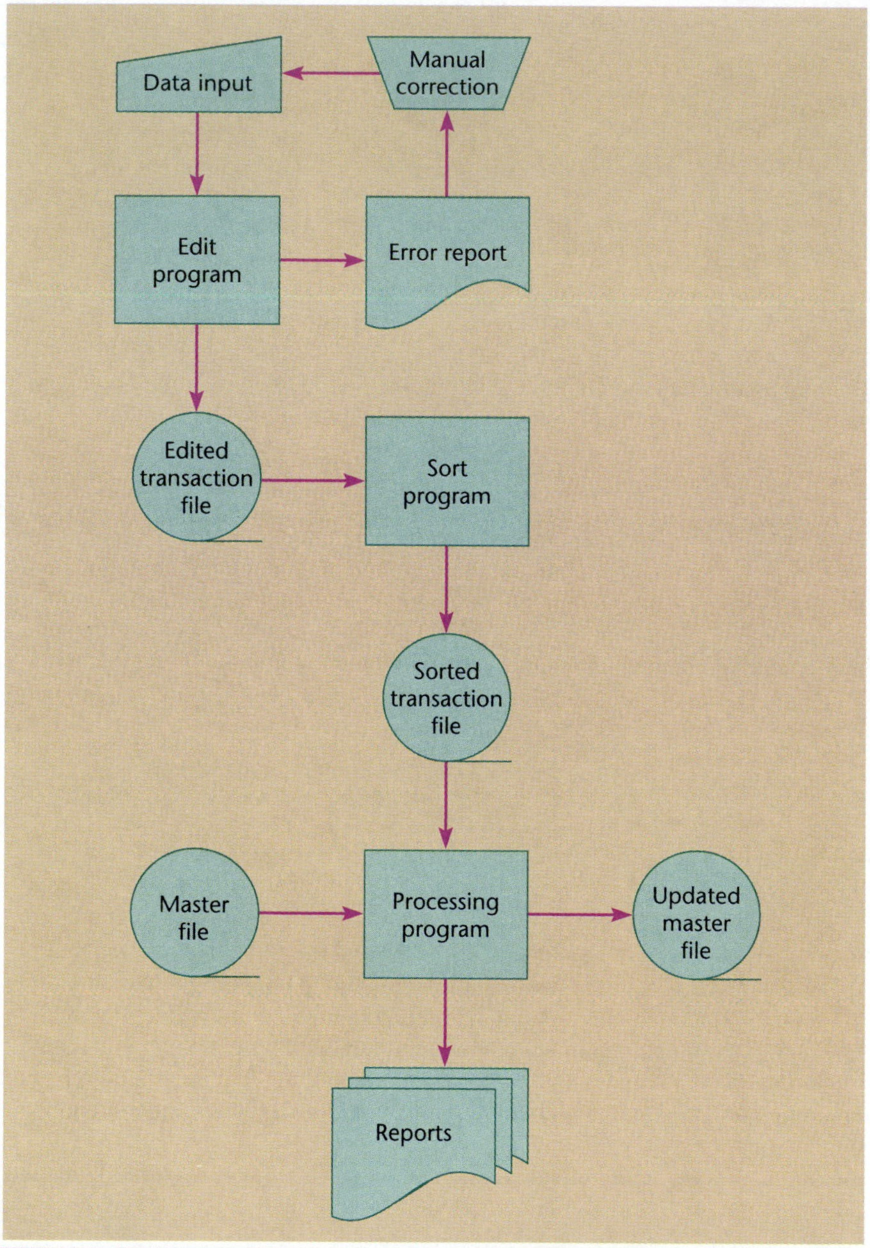

FIGURE 10-3
Architecture of a Batch File Processing System

that error. However, systems should be designed to detect as many errors as can be caught cost-effectively.

Data records that fail the editing tests are rejected—placed into a separate file, which is processed manually. The kind of processing used depends on the type of data and the nature of the problem. For example, when a time card shows 55 hours of work in a week, a clerk may contact the employee's department and verify the correct number of hours. If 55 is correct, the clerk may issue a paycheck manually. If it is not correct, the clerk enters corrected data and processes the record again. Procedures to handle rejected records must be planned as a part of the TPS design.

Processing the Data The result of all this checking and hand correcting is an edited **transaction file**, shown in the system flowchart in Figure 10-3 as a data tape. The next step is to sort the transaction file records into the same order as those in the **master file**. Records in the master file contain the company's permanent data about each employee—the employee's name, address, employee number, department, pay rate, total pay for the year to date, total tax withheld for the year to date, and other totals.

The processing program uses the transactions—the recorded and sorted time cards—to update records in the master file. The processing program copies each master file record over to a new copy of the master file. As it copies, it processes and updates the records of employees who worked last week—those for whom there is a time card. Records for those who did not work are simply copied over without change. As it processes, the program compiles values for various payroll reports, and, of course, it produces paychecks. This process is called a **sequential file update**.

Characteristics of Batch Processing Batch processing makes extremely cost-effective use of computer resources. It uses inexpensive sequential access to files, which can be stored on inexpensive tape, and it makes very efficient use of the CPU. Back in the days when $3 million mainframes had less power than today's microcomputers, the cost of processing each transaction was very high, even with such a system.

In addition, batch processing automatically creates backups of its important master files. Last week's master file, along with this week's transaction file, can be used to recreate this week's master file if it should be lost or damaged.

Finally, batch processing works very effectively in operations that are naturally periodic, like payroll. Processing a wage payroll weekly makes sense, since paychecks will be distributed weekly anyway.

On the other hand, the data in a batch processing system is not always current. For example, in an inventory system, people need up-to-date information, not information that was correct yesterday morning, when the batch run was made. Currency is valuable. Therefore, as computer costs came down in the 1970s, companies began switching over to on-line systems.

On-Line File Processing

As you can see in Figure 10-5, **on-line file processing** systems involve fewer steps than do batch systems. A user or a clerk enters data at the keyboard when it becomes available. It is immediately edited—checked for validity, reasonableness, and consistency. If errors are identified, the system notifies the user right then and asks for corrections. When the data is correct, the master file record is accessed, updated, and rewritten immediately. The master file looks much like a batch system master file, except that it is

FIGURE 10-4

IBM 360

This computer was considered powerful when it was introduced in 1964, but it had less power than today's PCs. For cost-effectiveness, it was used for batch processing.

a direct access file that is updated immediately when each transaction is entered.

Characteristics of On-Line Processing Programs for on-line processing are larger, more complicated, and more expensive than those in batch systems, since editing and processing must be combined into one program. In addition, the processing program must remain available all day every day, in case a user has data to enter. Finally, on-line processing requires direct access disk storage. Disk storage costs many times more than tape storage, which is sequential. All these things are true, yet they make very little difference. Hardware costs have come down so dramatically that neither batch hardware nor on-line hardware costs very much, compared to the company's overall data processing budget.

On-line processing does not automatically create a backup of the master file, as sequential processing does. In fact, every change involves physically erasing old values and writing new values in the same place on the disk. This is a serious problem because it creates a risk of data loss. As a result, companies must spend substantial effort in providing alternative means of restoring master file data in case of damage.

On-line processing has one important advantage: Its master files are up-to-date. Many vital systems absolutely require current data. For exam-

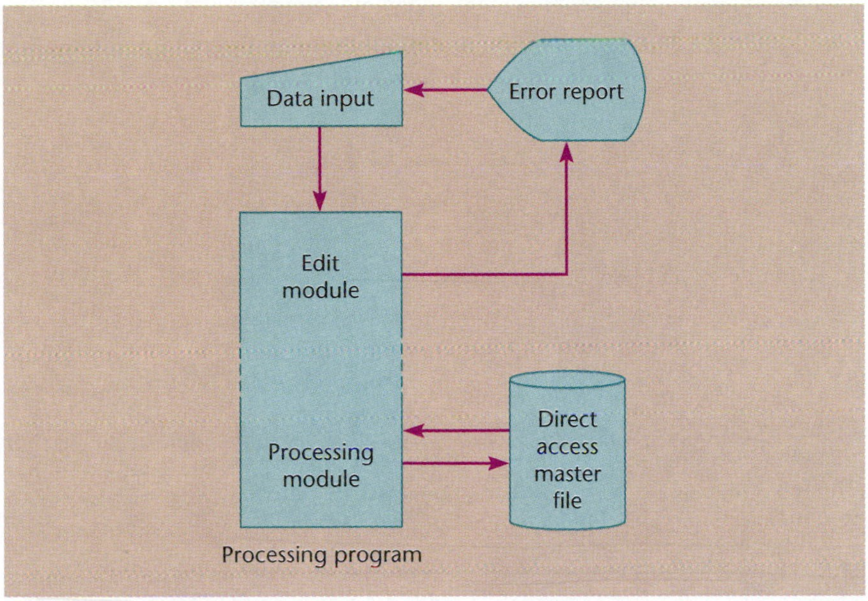

FIGURE 10-5
Architecture of an On-Line File Processing System

ple, airline reservation systems and production monitoring systems cannot work without current data. Other systems may not absolutely require current data, but most work better with it. For example, companies did order entry back in the batch processing days, and they managed to make it work. However, order entry works much better when you can tell the customer, based on absolutely current data, that you have goods to ship. Because of this advantage, most TPSs in most companies today are on-line systems.

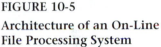

DATABASE PROCESSING

In **database processing**, a new component, the DBMS, has been added. The DBMS is a set of programs for manipulating a database. Whereas file processing programs access the stored data directly, database applications access the stored data only through the DBMS. This is an important difference because it gives the system developer a way to coordinate the activities of multiple users. Figure 10-6 shows the structure of a database processing application, which is similar in many ways to that of on-line file processing.

What Is a Database?

A database, as we saw earlier, is a self-describing collection of integrated records. Self-describing means that, in addition to the data, the database also includes a description of its own structure.

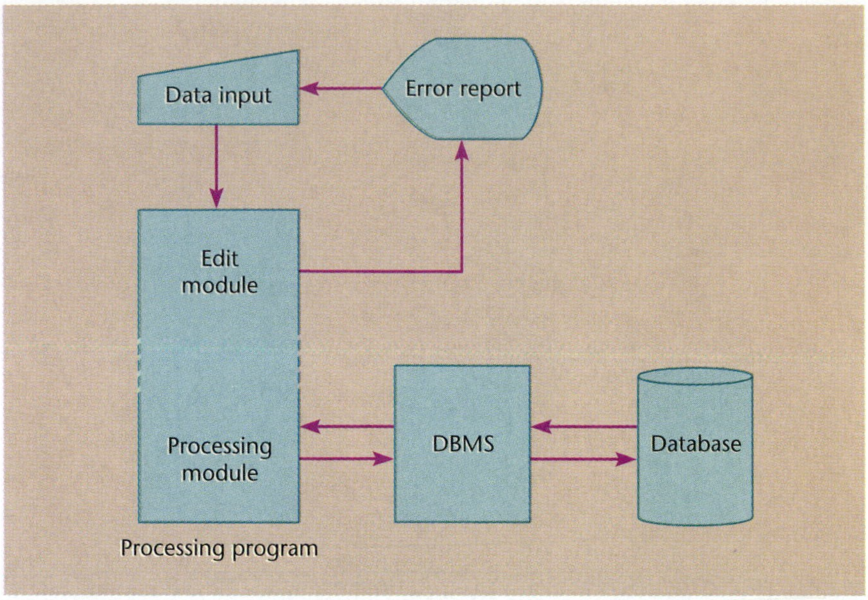

FIGURE 10-6
Architecture of a Database Processing System

When we say that a database contains integrated records, we mean that the database contains not only the data itself, but also descriptions of the relationships among the data. For example, when a student has been hospitalized, the health service may need the telephone numbers of all the student's professors. A database is able to store the connections among course registrations, course instructors, instructors' offices, and office telephone numbers to be able to retrieve the needed data.

What Is a Database Management System?

The primary program component in database processing is the DBMS. The functions of a DBMS are listed in Figure 10-7. The DBMS stores and retrieves data on behalf of application programs. In addition, the DBMS lets users enter queries directly, without the need for an application program. The DBMS calls on the operating system to perform the physical read and write operations on the disk. The DBMS also provides utility programs to facilitate the creation and maintenance of database application components such as menus, forms, and reports.

Finally, the DBMS supports database administration. When people share a database, conflicting needs, goals, and objectives often cause coordination problems. The DBMS provides tools that include the following safeguards:

- Requiring that the user enter a secret password to access the database
- Limiting specific users access to particular data

- Stores and retrieves data at the request of application programs.
- Provides query or query/update facility.
- Provides utilities to define and update database structure.
- Provides utilities to create and maintain application components (menus, forms, reports).
- Provides utilities to support database administration.

FIGURE 10-7
Functions of a DBMS

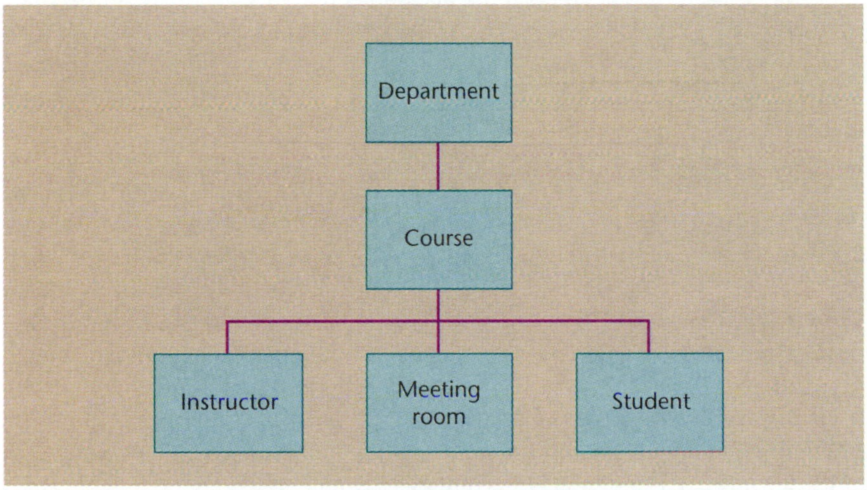

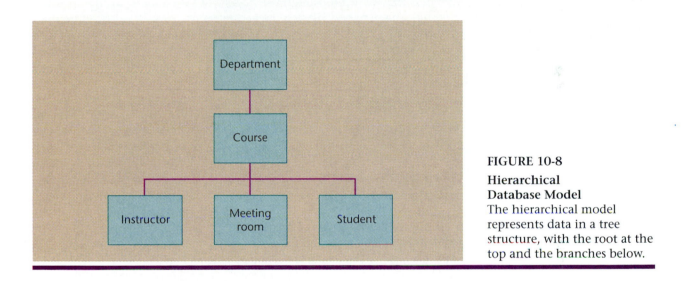

FIGURE 10-8
Hierarchical Database Model
The hierarchical model represents data in a tree structure, with the root at the top and the branches below.

- Providing the ability to lock records or other units when necessary
- Keeping records of all user access in a log

The technical design of a DBMS depends on the database model that it supports.

Database Models Over the history of business computing, three **database models**, or designs for DBMSs, have been widely used. These are the hierarchical model, the network model, and the relational model.

The earliest database model still in use is the **hierarchical model**. As Figure 10-8 shows, this model required that data be organized into a hierarchical structure, similar to an organizational diagram. Each data element may correspond to many elements below it on the hierarchy, but each element corresponds to only one element above it. Thus, the hierarchical model is useful for representing 1:1 relationships and 1:N relationships, but it does not readily represent N:M relationships. For example, it can represent the fact that a course has one instructor (1:1), meets in one classroom (1:N), and has many students (1:N), but it cannot straightforwardly represent the fact that each course may enroll many students *and* each student may enroll in several courses (N:M). The hierarchical DBMS is the smallest and simplest in structure, but because of its limitations, it is the most difficult to use.

The second database model to come into widespread use in business information systems was the **network model**. This model can more easily represent N:M relationships and thus can represent both the links between a course and many students and the links between a student and several courses (see Figure 10-9). However, the network model can only access data through links that are planned in advance. Its ability to answer ad hoc queries is limited, even though the necessary data may be available in the database. The network DBMS is larger and more complex in structure than the hierarchical DBMS, but it is considerably easier to use.

The database model most widely used today is the **relational model**, in which data is organized into tables as described earlier in this book (see Figure 10-10). The relational model represents 1:1 and 1:N relationships easily, and it represents N:M relationships by linking tables. Its DBMS is the largest and most complex in structure of the three, but it is the easiest to use. It handles both planned and unplanned ad hoc queries readily. The database examples in this book assume the use of a relational database.

Centralized Database Processing Figure 10-11 shows the programs required to support a database in a centralized teleprocessing environment. The categories of programs are the same whether they support a single- or multiple-application database. The difference is in the number and type of application programs required. In a single-application system, only one application program is required, or a few closely related ones.

The CCP controls and coordinates the communications traffic within the processing computer. As part of this function, the CCP routes transactions to appropriate application programs. Application programs process transactions and update data in response to user input. For example, a purchasing application program that processes purchases of raw materials

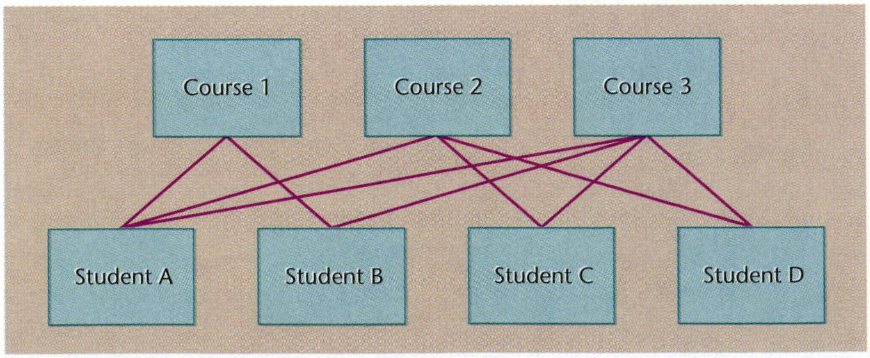

FIGURE 10-9

Network Database Model
The network model represents relationships among data values by links created as a part of the database design.

STUDENT

Student ID	Student Name	Student Address	Date First Admitted	Current Status	Probation	Major Code
049944586	Ring, T.	Santa Fe, NM	01/93	A	N	0734
182773948	Lane, A.	Taos, NM	09/93	A	N	9281
283774827	Briggs, B.	Tucson, AZ	01/92	I	A	0552

COURSE

Course ID	Course Department	Course Number	Course Name
05992	Math	119	Introduction to Statistics
06173	Biology	101	Principles of Biology
09374	English	100	Composition
10345	Business	130	Information Systems

INSTRUCTOR

Instructor ID	Instructor Name	Instructor Address	Instructor Office	Instructor Department	Instructor Status	Instructor Rank
183746394	Levi, A.	Taos, NM	LH 441	English	F	F
283774629	Lee, M.	Sands, NM	SS 919	Biology	P	I
294573826	Ray, V.	Taos, NM	BA 214	Business	F	F

COURSE OFFERING

Year	Semester Code	Course ID	Meeting Time	Meeting Room	Instructor ID	Maximum Enrollment
94	F	06173	MWF 1300	SS90	283774629	28
94	F	05992	TTh 0900	HH 130	394883746	22
94	F	06173	TTh 1000	SS 55	283774629	35
94	F	10345	MWF 0900	BA 230	294573826	24

COURSE ENROLLMENT

Year	Semester Code	Course ID	Student ID	Grade	Student Evaluation
94	F	05992	049944586		
94	F	10345	049944586		
94	F	10345	283774827		

FIGURE 10-10 **Relational Database Model**
A relational database represents data in tables. The data in the various tables is related by common data elements. Thus, when a course is offered in a particular semester, a record is added to the COURSE OFFERING table. Similarly, when a student enrolls in a course, a record is added to the COURSE ENROLLMENT table.

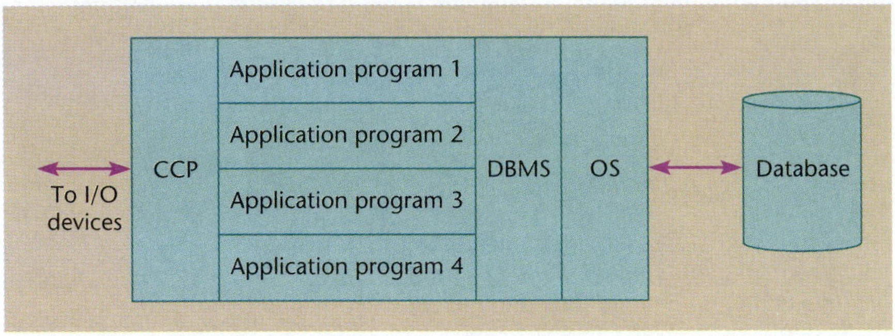

FIGURE 10-11 **Programs Required for Database Processing in a Teleprocessing Environment**
In a teleprocessing environment, the CCP controls communications to terminals and allocates transactions to applications. The DBMS performs data access through the operating system (labeled OS) on request from applications.

updates raw material inventory records according to the transactions. Application programs call on the DBMS to gain access to the database.

DBMS products used in teleprocessing environments typically cost considerably more than those for microcomputers. DBMS software for a personal computer might cost from $500 to $5,000. The licensing fee for a minicomputer DBMS may be $10,000 or more. The fee for a mainframe computer may exceed $100,000. These fees do not mean there is that much more complexity and logic involved. Rather, they reflect the smaller numbers of units that can be sold (there are fewer mainframes than minicomputers, for example), and they also reflect the greater utility that can be obtained by supporting more users. A single DBMS on a mainframe often supports hundreds of users.

Client-Server Processing In a distributed client-server system using a LAN, the DBMS is divided into two parts (see Figure 10-12). One part, the user–application program interface, $DBMS_{Client}$, resides in the memory of the client computer. It displays data entry forms, reports, and menus if requested; it accepts commands from the user or application program; and it checks the commands for errors or inconsistencies. Then it translates the commands into the special form required by the second part of the DBMS and commands the operating system to transmit them to the server.

The second part of the DBMS, the operating system interface, $DBMS_{Server}$, resides in the memory of the server. This portion formats read and write requests, sends the requests to the operating system for physical processing, packs and unpacks data for storage, and so forth.

In Figure 10-13, computers A, C, and D have $DBMS_{Client}$ in their memories, since those computers are processing database application programs. Computer E, the database server, has $DBMS_{Server}$ in its memory, since this computer is managing the data. Computers B and F are not currently accessing the database, so they do not need to have $DBMS_{Client}$ resident in

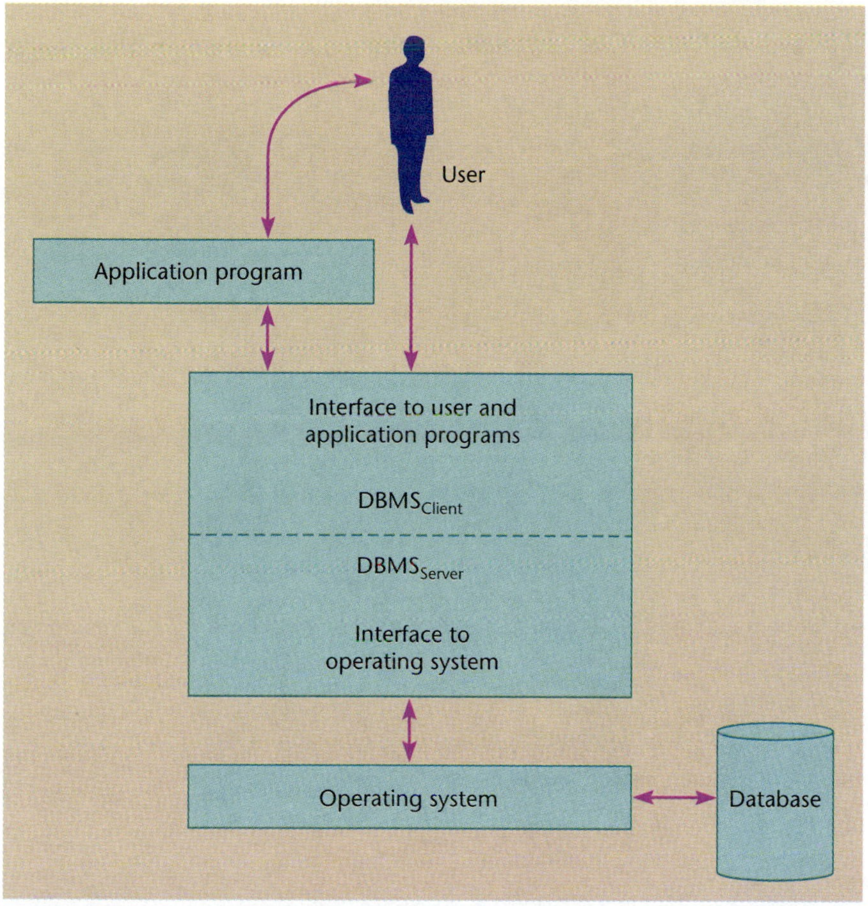

FIGURE 10-12

Programs Required for Database Processing in a Distributed Client-Server Environment

In a client-server environment, the DBMS is divided into two parts. The first part, $DBMS_{Client}$, serves as interface to user and application program. The second part, $DBMS_{Server}$, performs data access through the operating system in response to commands from $DBMS_{Client}$.

their memories. Any computer in the LAN may load $DBMS_{Client}$ into memory when it is needed.

To understand this arrangement, suppose the application program on computer C in Figure 10-13 needs the names and addresses of all customers in the zip code 98117 area. The application program sends a command to the $DBMS_{Client}$ on computer C to obtain this data. The $DBMS_{Client}$ checks this command for accuracy and so on, and, if it is valid, formats a request for the $DBMS_{Server}$ on the file server. It passes this request to the operating system (labeled OS) on computer C, which in turn passes the request to the LAN-OS on computer C. The LAN-OS formats the message for transmission to the LAN-OS on computer E and sends it over the network.

When computer E receives the request, its LAN-OS passes the request to its OS, which in turn passes the request to its $DBMS_{Server}$. Computer E's $DBMS_{Server}$ determines where the needed data is located on the disk and commands the operating system to read that data. The read is done and the operating system hands the data back to the $DBMS_{Server}$ on computer E. The data is then formatted and transmitted through the LAN-OS back to

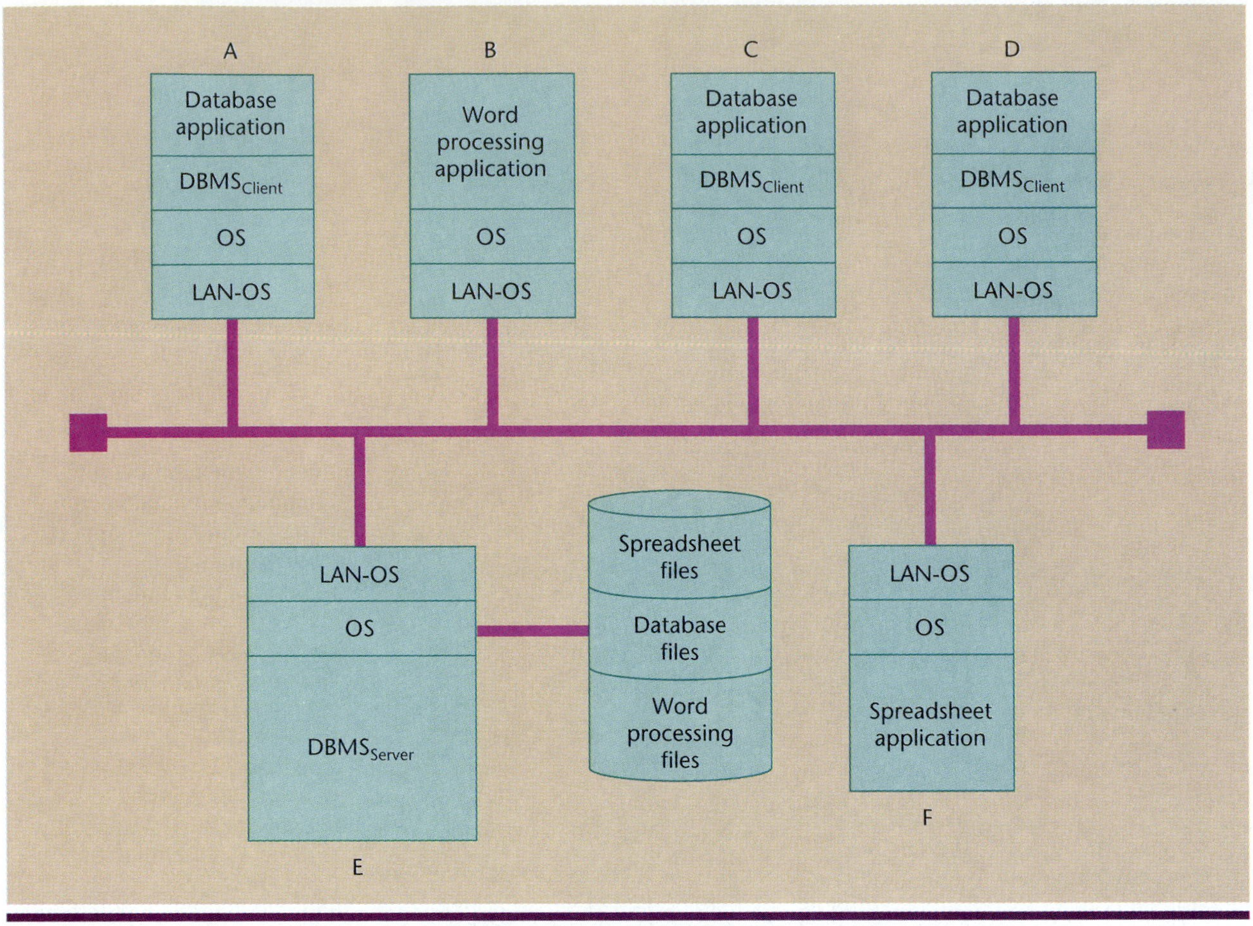

FIGURE 10-13 **Location of DBMS Programs in a LAN Environment**
In a LAN environment, one part of the database ($DBMS_{Client}$) is located in the memory of the client computer and the other part ($DBMS_{Server}$), in the memory of the server.

computer C, where it is delivered to the application program that requested it.

The most important purpose of splitting the DBMS is to move as much work as possible to the users' PCs. Users' systems can all process simultaneously, rather than perform tasks one after the other, as the server does. This makes the system as a whole much faster. The goal is to achieve as much simultaneous processing as possible.

Another reason for splitting the DBMS is to coordinate various user requests to access the database. When the same database is accessed by separate users with single-user DBMS software (rather than the client-server DBMS described here), applications are oblivious to one another, and the accesses are uncoordinated. The result is almost certain to be data loss. A shared DBMS handles the coordination to avoid these problems.

INCREASING YOUR PERSONAL PRODUCTIVITY

Box 10.1

Doing Your Off-Site Back-up the High-Tech Way

At a secret location in Portland, Oregon, neither flood nor fire nor volcanic eruption at nearby Mount St. Helens in Washington is likely to threaten data in the care of DataSafe, Inc. Guards patrol outside its bunkerlike storage facility and view every inch of the interior via closed-circuit television. The walls are double concrete block filled with a "bank mix" of concrete; the ceiling is thick concrete; and the doors are steel reinforced with titanium. The building also features an anti-magnetic shield, a four-hour-rated fire vault and an elaborate alarm system. "The Fire Department couldn't get through the doors without the Jaws of Life," owner Jerry Barnett said proudly. In case a blaze breaks out, firefighters have secreted a key in a special lockbox.

Welcome to the world of serious data security. There are several options for off-site data archiving, the most common of which is trucking tapes or disks once a week to a safe location. One of the easiest ways to ensure the safety of your files, though, is subscribing to an automatic archiving service that backs up data over phone lines on a daily or weekly basis and stores it in a super-safe facility, such as DataSafe's. DataSafe counts several of the Northwest's largest companies as clients, and similar services are growing rapidly in every region as companies respond to disaster recovery needs and perceived dangers from corporate espionage or sabotage.

Most use a similar process to get and store data. At DataSafe, a subsidiary called American ComNet uses its proprietary software, Autovault, to pull data from remote IBM PCs and compatibles and mainframes, and store it on digital audio tape. Macs will be added to the mix at some point, Barnett said, noting that clients can send important Mac data to an office mainframe or networked PC to make it available for remote archiving. Autovault is installed on each computer to be backed up. At a time the client selects, Autovault wakes up the computer, puts any new data through an encryption-and-compression process, then uploads it to American ComNet's storage system via a dial-out-only phone connection. American ComNet employees can't access the client's computer system or the archived data—cracking the encryption system requires a two-part "key," of which Barnett holds half. "We can't even decompress it on this end; that [technology] is held at our bank," he said.

In the case of a few damaged files, a subscriber can simply call American ComNet and recover lost data using a password. Barnett will send employees out to restore entire systems.

Such automatic off-site backup services cost $25 per month and up, depending on the archiving company and the amount of data stored. That's slightly less expensive than storing boxes of files at a traditional off-site facility, and for many companies it's a drop in the bucket compared with the cost of losing important files.

Characteristics of Database Processing

In comparison to file processing systems, database systems offer important advantages: data integration, improved data integrity, program/data independence, and data compatibility.

Data Integration A database system stores not only the data, but also the relationships among data values. By contrast, an organization's various file processing systems use files that store only data.

FIGURE 10-14

Master Files in a College Course Registration System

Student Master File

Student name
Student ID code
Student address
Date first admitted
Class level code
- 1 - Freshman
- 2 - Sophomore
- 3 - Junior
- 4 - Senior
- 5 - Graduate student

Current status
- A - Active
- I - Inactive
- G - Graduated

Probation
- N - None
- A - Academic probation
- D - Disciplinary probation

Major code
Date admitted to major
Units earned to date
Grade point average
Courses
- (repeats for each course taken)
- Course ID code
- Course department
- Course number
- Semester code
- Year
- Grade
  - A–F - Grade (with + or –)
  - I - Incomplete
  - W - Withdrawal (no grade)
  - C - Currently enrolled (not completed)

Course Master File

Current semester code
Current year
Course ID code
Department
Course number
Course name
Meeting time
Meeting room
Instructor ID code
Instructor name
Instructor address
Instructor department
Maximum enrollment
Current enrollment
Students
- (repeats for each student enrolled)
- Student name
- Student ID code
- Student address

Instructor Master File

Instructor ID code
Instructor name
Instructor address
Instructor office
Instructor office hours
Instructor department
Instructor status code
- F - Full time
- P - Part time
- I - Inactive
- S - On sabbatical
- L - On leave

Instructor rank
- F - Full professor
- C - Associate professor
- S - Assistant professor
- I - Instructor
- L - Lecturer
- G - Graduate teaching assistant

Courses
- (repeats for each course taught)
- Semester code
- Year
- Course ID code
- Course department
- Course number
- Average of grades given
- Average of student evaluations

For example, Figure 10-14 shows some of the separate master files used by a university in its student records system, its course registration system, and its faculty register system. Each of these file processing systems is maintained and operated separately. At that university, Professor Leonard Smalley is retiring after 35 years of service. In celebration, the faculty wants to invite former students to write letters to be assembled into a scrapbook. They ask the information systems department to list names of students who earned A or B in Professor Smalley's courses.

This apparently simple request will be extremely expensive to process because it cannot be answered by the data in one source. A programmer must write a program to extract a list of Professor Smalley's courses from the instructor master file. Then the program must search through every record in the student master file to determine whether the student took one of Professor Smalley's courses and earned an A or a B. In this example, the contents of two files must be coordinated. Think how complicated it would be to coordinate data among three files—or ten! In fact, when the faculty finds out how much the list will cost, they will almost certainly abandon this worthwhile project.

In a database system, all the data is stored in a single database, which includes information about relationships, and all access to the data is handled by the DBMS. An application can ask the DBMS to access student records, faculty records, or both. If data from two applications must be combined, as it must be to produce the list of Professor Smalley's former students, the DBMS will perform the necessary operations to combine it. Thus the programmer is no longer responsible for the details of these complex tasks.

Figure 10-15 shows a college database corresponding to the set of master files in Figure 10-14. In the database, the STUDENT table provides all of the data about students. When an application needs a student's address, the DBMS supplies it from this table. The INSTRUCTOR and COURSE tables work in the same way.

Two tables in Figure 10-15 represent relationships: COURSE OFFERING and COURSE ENROLLMENT. These tables create relationships between data in other tables. For example, the COURSE OFFERING table contains information about a specific offering of a course: year and semester, instructor, meeting time, meeting room, and maximum enrollment. Note that information about the course, such as its name and department, is not included in the COURSE OFFERING table. If these values are needed, the DBMS can retrieve them by using the course ID code, which serves to connect the COURSE OFFERING table to the COURSE table. In the COURSE table, course ID code is identified as a key. Similarly, data about the instructor is in the INSTRUCTOR table, where the DBMS can retrieve it using the instructor ID code as the key.

When the college decides to offer a particular course, a new record is added to the COURSE OFFERING table describing that course. Since historical data about course offerings is needed, COURSE OFFERING table records are maintained in the table indefinitely. For example, when a student applies for graduation, COURSE OFFERING data may be needed to determine the name of the student's English composition instructor, should a question arise.

When a student registers for a course, a new record is added to the COURSE ENROLLMENT table to show year and semester, course ID code, and student ID code. In addition, space is provided to record the student's grade and the student's evaluation of the course. That data is added in separate transactions when it becomes available.

Improved Data Integrity When a database is used, each data value is stored in only one place. As a result, updating that value requires only locating it and changing it. By contrast, in the set of file processing systems used in a typical organization, many data values are stored repeatedly.

Student

Student ID code
Student name
Student address
Date first admitted
Current status
  A - Active
  I - Inactive
  G - Graduated
Probation
  N - None
  A - Academic probation
  D - Disciplinary probation
Major code

Course

Course ID code
Course department
Course number
Course name

Instructor

Instructor ID code
Instructor name
Instructor address
Instructor office
Instructor department
Instructor status code
  F - Full time
  P - Part time
  I - Inactive
  S - On sabbatical
  L - On leave
Instructor rank
  F - Full professor
  C - Associate professor
  S - Assistant professor
  I - Instructor
  L - Lecturer
  G - Graduate teaching assistant

Course Offering

Year
Semester code
Course ID code
Meeting time
Meeting room
Instructor ID code
Maximum enrollment

Course Enrollment

Year
Semester code
Course ID code
Student ID code
Grade
  A–F - Grade (with + or –)
  I - Incomplete
  W - Withdrawal
Student evaluation of course

FIGURE 10-15
A College Database

When a value must be updated, the problem arises of finding every instance of the value and making sure all are changed.

For example, in the university's master files, listed in Figure 10-14, an instructor's address is stored both in the instructor master file and the course master file. Student addresses are duplicated in the student master file and the course master file, where they appear repeatedly (and are needed to send a grade report at semester end). This duplication creates a problem of **data integrity**.

Collected data has integrity if the data is consistent. Duplicated data items must agree with each other. Poor data integrity often develops in file processing systems. For example, if a student changes addresses, then all the files containing that data need to be updated. The danger is that all files may *not* be updated, causing discrepancies among the files. If the data does not agree, which is correct?

With database processing, duplicate data is minimal. Instead of duplicating data for each application that uses it, the data is stored in one place. Whenever it is needed, the DBMS can retrieve it from that place. And when

FIGURE 10-16
Programming an Application
The programmer's task is made simpler and less error-prone by program/data independence.

it is modified, only one update need be performed. Data integrity is dramatically improved because there is less opportunity for discrepancies between multiple copies of the same data item.

Another type of data duplication arises with **calculated values**. For example, the grade point average in the student master file in Figure 10-14 is calculated from the grades earned by the student in each course taken. In a certain sense, this value is duplicated data, since it depends directly on other values recorded in the file. If an instructor discovers an error and changes a student's grade in a course, then the student's grade point average must also be recalculated and changed.

Ideally, such a value should be recalculated each time it is needed, ensuring that it is calculated using current data. However, in file processing systems, such values are often recalculated and stored in the file when changes are made. This is done because systems designers cannot depend on being able to recalculate the values every time they are needed. Recalculation of such values requires the action of a program, and users may access the file without using a program capable of doing the recalculation. In database processing systems, data is always accessed by the DBMS, which is capable of doing this kind of recalculation. Therefore, in the college database, calculated values such as grade point average, average of grades given in a course, and average of student evaluations of a course are not stored. Rather, they are recalculated by the DBMS with current data each time they are needed.

Program/Data Independence In a database processing system, application programs request data from the DBMS by specifying a *logical* description of the data needed. For example, "Get me the instructor of CIS

3060, section 3, for Fall 1993." By contrast, an application program in a file processing system must include a *physical* description of the data needed: "Get the data in the tenth field of the 493rd record of the course master file."

If the course master file (Figure 10-14) is reorganized so the Instructor Name field is no longer the tenth field, every reference to this field in every application must be found and adjusted. By contrast, if the database (Figure 10-15) is reorganized in a way that changes the position of the Instructor Name field in the INSTRUCTOR table, no change is required in applications that access this data. This is called **program/data independence**.

Data Compatibility Since all data is stored in the same database, problems of data incompatibility are reduced considerably. The various processing systems that use database data can share data because all the data shares the same format. The output produced by the DBMS may not be directly compatible with completely separate programs such as word processors or spreadsheet programs. However, all the output is in a single format, and conversion must only be capable of handling that format. Many word processors and spreadsheet programs can convert data from common database output formats.

The detailed structure of data files in file processing systems may vary, depending on which programming language or application program created them. If some files are created and processed by programs in the COBOL language and others by programs in the C language, then both may have to be converted to a common structure before they can be processed by a program in the BASIC language or by a microcomputer database program. This incompatibility increases the difficulties raised by the other problems.

SHARED DATABASE PROCESSING SYSTEMS

The four categories of database processing systems are shown in Figure 10-17. Of these, personal database systems were considered in Chapter 6. Most support only one application.

Shared database processing systems are the topic of this chapter. Shared single-application systems are commonly used by small groups of workers to maintain the data for a specific project or activity. For example, a single department may maintain an inventory of office equipment. Similarly, a laboratory may maintain a log of test results.

Shared multiple-application database processing systems are commonly shared by an entire organization and frequently maintain accounting data. For example, a college may use such a system to maintain student, instructor, course, and billing data. Applications may include course registration, student records, instructor records, and student billing.

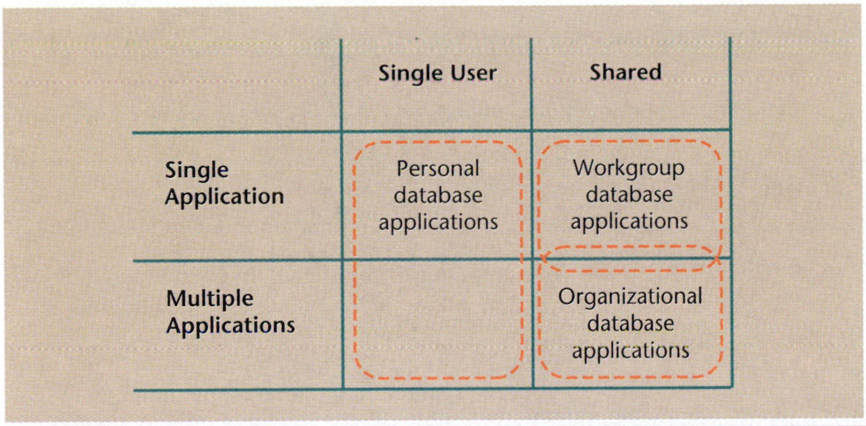

FIGURE 10-17
Categories of Database Processing Systems

Transitions Between Types of Systems

The shift from single-user systems to shared systems is a major one. When we let multiple users access the same data, we encounter a host of problems. Businesspeople are often surprised at the difficulty of this transition. For example, a small business or department may be operating a single-user database application. As business expands, insufficient time is available on the single computer to enter all of the data. So a second computer is installed and connected (usually via a LAN) to the same database.

At this point, difficulties immediately become apparent, because a number of significant (and expensive) changes must be made in the DBMS, the application programs, and the procedures, to support the multiple users. If these changes are not made, loss and corruption of data is virtually certain. Since the managers seldom know about the need for these changes, chaos often does occur.

A similar situation occurs when the transition is made from a single-application shared database to a multiple-application shared database. Here, problems occur because different users view the data differently. For example, a user of one application may want to delete data in a way that is unacceptable to a user of a different application. In the college database described in Figure 10-15, users of the student registration system wanted to delete COURSE OFFERING table data at the end of each semester. However, users of the grade record system needed continued access to that data for periods up to seven or more years until all the students enrolled in a course had departed. Thus, during the transition from a single-user to a shared system, users need to adapt their practices to the needs of a wider community.

Multiple-Application Databases

Multiple-application databases integrate data from different departments in a company. They allow all employees to share the same data values. The

Box 10.2

INCREASING YOUR PERSONAL PRODUCTIVITY

Errors Are Greatest Threat to Data Security

When it comes to computer security, many corporations focus on protecting themselves from outsiders rather than insiders—whether malicious or ignorant. Both fiction and media coverage tends to reinforce this view; neither the movie *War Games* nor the nonfiction book *The Cuckoo's Egg* would have been as interesting if the villain were an assistant clerk. Furthermore, in all probability the crime wasn't a crime at all but an accident, such as the mistyping of a log-in sequence, security experts say.

Consequently, corporations spend a lot of money and effort buying expensive security software and setting up elaborate systems, when their time might be better spent making use of the security systems already in place, educating their employees, and ensuring that backups are performed regularly.

Often we only hear about the one case with the crazed hacker—you don't hear about the 10 cases with the fumble-fingered "sysadmin" who hit the button at the wrong time.

Types of Problems

Whether your network includes PCs, Macintoshes, Unix workstations, minicomputers, or mainframes, security problems tend to fall into the same few broad categories. Moreover, a few preventive measures will take care of a majority of potential security problems. The major challenge is to make administrators and users aware of the potential problems and inform them of the tools available to solve them.

The two greatest steps an organization can take to improve security are to perform regular backups and to implement system passwords, security consultants say. And regular backups help with the everyday, small occurrences.

The other step is passwords. But what makes a good password? Something difficult to guess. Enforcing good password choice is a real big win because that's where most people get in. Programs are available to system administrators as well as hackers—that run through a password file looking for obvious ones. Best off would be for users to avoid using any standard words at all—because some "password cracker" programs simply use the computer's power to check every word in the system dictionary.

On some systems, such as more recent Unix systems, "shadow password" files are included that keep the password data separated from the user data. The method puts an encrypted password into a file with restricted access.

Some experts recommend that users change their passwords frequently and even run a program that forces them to change their passwords every few months.

goal is to increase consistency in business operations. For example, the price quoted at the time of sale should be the same as the price on the invoice, even though the order entry and billing systems may be separate applications.

To increase the likelihood of consistent behavior, businesses choose to develop a single database that supports multiple applications rather than multiple databases that each support a single application. The chief advantage of a multiapplication database is that data values are recorded once, and all operations throughout the company are based on that data. Thus, multiapplication databases increase the likelihood of appropriate and consistent responses. Or, as one analyst put it, "A single database makes it possible for all of us to read from the same sheet of music."

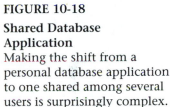

FIGURE 10-18
Shared Database Application
Making the shift from a personal database application to one shared among several users is surprisingly complex.

In a typical company, salespeople, purchasers, production workers, and accounts receivable personnel all have interactions with the customer, and, to produce appropriate and consistent behavior, each department must refer to (and maintain) data about its interactions with the customer. Also, when appropriate, each department would like other departments to know about significant interactions with the customer after they have occurred.

Data Views

A description of all the data contained in a database is called a **schema**. However, most individual applications do not access all the data in the schema. Even though various applications share data, they seldom need to share exactly the same data. Usually, one application will need some data items used by another application, plus other data items. A grouping of data items used by a particular application is called a **sub-schema**, or **view**.

For example, Figure 10-19 calls for two different views of customer data. Figure 10-19a shows what customer data is required by salespeople. This data helps sales personnel to decide which customers to call on and when. Figure 10-19b shows what customer data is required by the accounts receivable department. This data helps receivables clerks determine a customer's creditworthiness. The organizational information system used for order processing must be able to support both views.

Company Name: ____________________

Contact: ____________________

Phone: ____________________

Last Order Date: ___/___/___ Last Order Amount: $__________

Credit Status: __________ Last Contact Date: ___/___/___

a. Salesperson customer contact report

Company Name: __________ Credit Status: __________

Contact: __________ Phone: __________

Date	Order	Payment	Balance
Oct. 10 '94	100		100
Oct. 18 '94	200		300
Nov. 8 '94		100	200
Nov. 20 '94		200	0
Dec. 11 '94	350		350
Dec. 14 '94	400		750
Dec. 29 '94		350	

b. Accounts receivable customer payment report

FIGURE 10-19

Different Views of Data Salespeople and workers in accounts receivable need access to some of the same data elements, along with some different data elements.

Examine Figure 10-19 more carefully. Company name, contact, phone, and credit status are shared by both departments. The other data items shown are used by one department but not the other. Furthermore, each customer may have many orders and many payments.

Figure 10-20 shows the structure of a database to support the views in Figure 10-19. Each rectangle represents a table of data. The CUSTOMER table has one row for each customer; the ORDER table has one row for each order; and the PAYMENT table has one row for each payment. The columns of the tables contain the data required for the views shown in Figure 10-19. The forks on the lines between the tables indicate that a row in CUSTOMER can correspond to many rows in ORDER and that a row in CUSTOMER can correspond to many rows in PAYMENT.

This database is a simple example. Constructing a database to support many different views of many different departments often involves con-

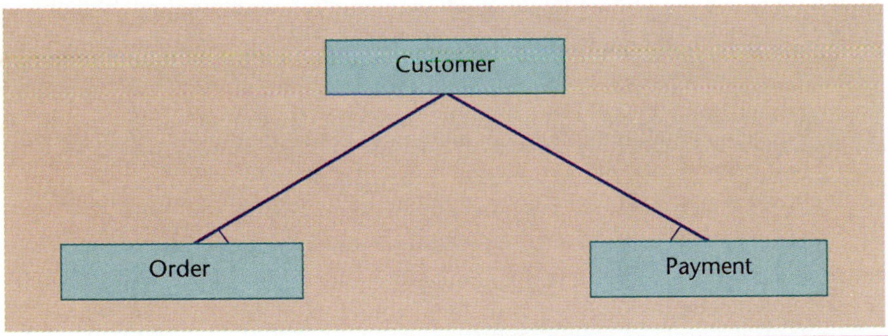

FIGURE 10-20
Structure of Customer Data in a Database
The database consists of three tables.

Department	Views
Sales	Orders by salesperson Orders by region Orders by customer
Operations	Orders processed Orders to be processed Back orders
Warehouse	Picking slips Item locations Item use
Accounting	Receivables by customer Receivables by date Invoice

FIGURE 10-21
Examples of Data Views in a Large Corporation

siderably more work. For example, Figure 10-21 shows a more realistic listing of the data views that would be used in a large corporation.

The important point is that the data you process may be stored in a manner and format that is considerably different from what you see. Since this is so, restrictions that do not appear to make sense may be placed on your activities, at least based on the data you see. If that seems to be happening, ask for an explanation from your organization's MIS department.

Summary

The first computerized processing systems imitated manual file processing methods. Manual TPSs were slow, inflexible, and error-prone. Computerized batch processing used data in a transaction file, after error detection, to update a master file. Batch processing used computer resources efficiently, but its reports were not completely current. As computer hardware improved, on-line file processing was widely used. It can provide completely current data.

Database processing stores integrated data in a database, accessed by a DBMS. Widely used database models have been hierarchical, network, and relational. The structure of a DBMS differs, depending on whether it must perform centralized database processing or client-server processing. Database processing provides data integration, improved data integrity, program/data independence, and data compatibility.

The shift from single-user database applications to shared database applications raises many new problems. Similarly, the shift from single-application database processing systems to multiple-application systems raises significant problems. Multiple-application databases are used to increase consistency in a company's use of data. Different applications use different views of the data.

Key Terms

manual file processing
file update
transaction processing system (TPS)
unit record
batch file processing
data entry clerk
validity check
reasonableness check
consistency check
transaction file
master file
sequential file update
on-line file processing
database processing
database model
hierarchical model
network model
relational model
data integrity
calculated value
program/data independence
schema
subschema
view

Review Questions

1. Describe a manual file processing system.
2. Name the components of a typical TPS.
3. Explain the disadvantages of a manual file processing system.
4. What are unit record devices, and how were they used?
5. When did computers begin to do business file processing?
6. Name the most important limitation of human data entry clerks.
7. Describe three checks used to detect errors in input data.
8. In a batch processing system, what should happen to records that do not pass all the error checks?
9. Differentiate between the contents of a transaction file and the contents of a master file.
10. Describe a sequential file update.
11. Name four important characteristics of batch file processing.
12. Describe on-line file processing.
13. Name three important characteristics of on-line file processing.

14. Name the most important difference between a database processing application and an on-line file processing application.
15. What is a database?
16. List the functions of a DBMS.
17. Name the three database models.
18. What is the most important limitation of the hierarchical database model?
19. What is the most important limitation of the network database model?
20. Describe the method of data storage used in the relational database model.
21. Explain the configuration of program used for database processing in a centralized teleprocessing environment.
22. Explain the configuration of program used for database processing in a distributed client-server environment.
23. What are the two purposes of splitting the DBMS into two parts in a distributed environment?
24. Name four characteristics of database processing.
25. In a file system, a data value may be repeated in several places. What problem does this raise?
26. Explain why a calculated data value should be considered an example of data duplication.
27. Differentiate between the physical description needed to retrieve data in a file processing system and the logical description needed to retrieve data in a database processing system.
28. What is program/data independence?
29. Describe a typical, shared single-application database processing system.
30. Describe a typical, shared multiple-application database processing system.
31. Why is the shift from a single-user database processing system to a shared system a source of problems?
32. What problems are raised in the transition from a shared single-application database processing system to a multiple-application system?
33. Name the most important advantage of a multiple-application shared database processing system.
34. Differentiate among schema, subschema, and view.

Discussion Questions

A. Describe the student registration system used at your college. If possible, determine whether it is processed as a batch file system, an on-line file system, or a database system. If it is a database system, determine whether it is a single-application system or a multiple-application system. How many course enrollment transactions does it process in what period?

B. Consider the changes that would be required in standard business practices if businesses could only use manual file processing. For example, would this change limit the practical size of companies? Would tax codes need to be changed? What current jobs would be eliminated? What categories of employees would be in high demand? What changes would be required in multinational corporations?

C. Prepare an executive summary of computerized data processing methods: batch processing, on-line processing, and database processing. Indicate the strengths and weaknesses of each. Give examples of applications well suited to each. How should a manager select which processing method to use for a particular application?

D. Design a data file for storing information about students in your class. What information should be included? For each data element in the file, describe as many specific error-detection checks as possible that would be applicable to that item. For example, a name field should consist only of alphabetical characters and spaces plus certain punctuation marks: hyphen and apostrophe (also period, if abbreviations are allowed, and comma, if names are last-name-first). As you devise error-detection checks, also develop data entry rules. For example, are periods and commas to be used in names? Are hyphens in Social Security numbers included or excluded? Are city, state, and zip code three fields or one combined field?

E. For centralized database processing and for client-server processing, trace the sequence of commands that pass from system to system in response to a transaction entered by a user. Show the results in a block diagram for each system.

F. Based on your knowledge of college operations and on your imagination, list at least ten data views that may be based on the data in your college's student records database.

MINICASE

Eastman Kodak's DB2 Access Using PC-Based Oracle Tools

In today's business environment, enterprisewide data access is crucial. But traditionally, applications were designed and written for the hardware platform and environment of which a particular IS department had experience. As a result, applications now run on multiple hardware platforms, in many different languages, and use a multitude of database managers. Not only do they fail to communicate effectively (if at all), but processing isn't efficient.

Increasingly, we find the need to integrate heterogeneous computers, operating systems, networks, and DBMSs. The differences must be transparent to users. Distributed technology is evolving to allow fragmentation of databases in the design phase; these fragments can then be put on the most appropriate machine. Tools and applications can be run on a different machine than the database manager, thus delivering appropriate hardware for the job.

Eastman Kodak has several DB2 databases on the IBM mainframe that many users need to access from their PCs. The databases contain corporate financial data that users typically extract, print, and rekey into Lotus 1-2-3 worksheets or departmental spreadsheets. Transferring this data manually is not only a waste of time and resources, but is highly error-prone. As a solution, I wanted to integrate the PC's capabilities with the power of the mainframe; to do so, I had to evaluate the use of a PC to support access to DB2 databases via PC tools.

Oracle's distributed architecture was chosen for this project. We looked at how the PC Oracle tools could access mainframe DB2 databases, join DB2 and Oracle databases, and move data between Oracle and DB2. . . .

Working with two different DBMSs add complexity to the environment. To understand Oracle's distributed architecture and my research, let's take a moment to consider the important distinction between distributed processing and distributed database.

Distributed processing enables an application to run on a machine different from that of the database and the DBMS. This configuration is typically called client/server architecture. The database resides on the server platform, and is managed there by the DBMS. The server must have a multiuser operating system and should be a larger computer. The client platform carries the application programs and tools, so it doesn't need the database or DBMS (unless a local database exists). The client is usually a PC.

Distributed database spreads your data among multiple machines on a network—the database may consist of multiple DBMSs. Physically, many databases can logically appear as one. The DBA can set up the databases so the location of data is transparent to the application designers and users.

Data distribution provides facilities for storing data in the most optimal locations. Data distribution reduces network traffic and provides local control of local data and central control of central data. Together, distributed processing and distributed database form a distributed environment.

My company used Oracle's distributed architecture to create our distributed environment. This architecture lets you write applications that can run on remote machines. In addition, databases spread across the network can appear as a single, logical database. Existing data becomes more accessible and presentable. . . .

[However], the technology for a truly distributed environment isn't yet supported. While distributed queries are supported and perform as expected, I'd be cautious about using applications that require data distribution alternatives and distributed updates until the technology catches up.

This is an exciting time in database technology. Distributed environments are the wave of the future. Oracles' distributed environment is headed the right way, but all of the pieces aren't yet available. . . . It's thrilling to join databases from different DBMSs, and the potential savings are great, but the holes in the technology have to be addressed before it becomes popular.

Questions

1. According to this article, why is it necessary to link data from two different databases?
2. Explain the differences in the author's use of the terms *distributed application, distributed database,* and *distributed environment.*
3. Do you think the author recommends distributed databases? What limitations does she impose on their use?
4. This article addresses some of the technical issues involved in distributed databases. Consider the potential organizational and management issues. Suppose, for instance, that the marketing department wants access to shipping data maintained by the operations department and access to billing data maintained by the accounts receivable department. What nontechnical problems do you foresee in such a situation?

CHAPTER 11

Developing Shared Information Systems

CHAPTER OUTLINE

Shared systems are very complex. As a result, developing them is risky. Organizations have found through experience that better systems result when users are involved, especially in the early stages of a systems development project. Thus, during the course of your career, it is quite likely that you will be personally involved in the development of shared business information systems.

By covering the following topics, this chapter gives you the background that you will need to work effectively on a systems development project team:

- Systems development life cycle
- Dataflow diagrams
- Prototyping
- Computer-aided software engineering

DEALING WITH COMPLEXITY

Developing new shared information systems is an extremely complex activity. Some experts believe it is one of the most complex tasks undertaken by humans. There are two main reasons to believe this. First, the systems selected for computerization are among the most complicated systems in an organization. Their complexity is one of the reasons for selecting them.

Second, computerizing a system makes it more complex. Computerization requires that we reduce a process to sets of tiny steps, sequence each set of steps correctly, and then determine which of the sets of steps to apply in every possible situation.

FIGURE 11-1

User Representatives Bright, energetic, young businesspeople who have spent enough time in their departments to understand its activities and procedures are often selected as user representatives on systems development project teams.

By contrast, when we teach a new procedure to a person, we expect the person to understand much larger steps. In addition, we expect the person to recognize unusual situations and to seek special instructions when they arise.

However, with a computerized system we cannot wait until situations arise to consider how to handle them. Rather, we must anticipate every possible situation in advance during systems development. For example, we must anticipate every possible type of error, determine how the computer is to recognize each, and specify exactly how the processing of each should be performed.

Because of this extreme complexity, the risk of failure in systems development is high. Therefore, it is essential for the project team to follow working methods that increase the chance of developing a successful system. Those methods are embodied in the five-stage systems development process described in this chapter.

There are many successful variants on these methods. The ones described here are not necessarily the only good ones. They are simply ones that work effectively. If you become involved in a systems development project, you should satisfy yourself that a carefully considered methodology is used.

SYSTEMS DEVELOPMENT LIFE CYCLE

The process used to develop a shared information system is similar to the process used with personal systems. With personal systems, prototyping is used to develop system requirements and design, and the system platform is defined early in the process.

With shared systems, prototyping can still be used, but the systems tend to be so complex that prototyping can seldom serve as the only method of developing requirements. In addition, when systems become as large as typical shared systems, prototypes often become expensive to construct and evaluate. With shared systems, platform options are more complex, so the platform is defined later in the process.

Thus, the development of shared systems follows the more formal plan described in this chapter. The five stages of the **systems development life cycle** for shared systems are as follows:

- Problem definition
- Requirements definition
- Evaluation of alternatives
- Design
- Implementation and maintenance

In the first three stages, the users and the systems analyst do most of the work. In the last two stages, the systems analyst may be assisted by other computer professionals—such as system designers and programmers—and the users become primarily overseers of the development activities. We will consider each stage in order.

Problem Definition Stage

Three major tasks form the problem definition stage: defining the problem, assessing the feasibility of developing a system to solve it, and building a plan for developing the system. The problem definition stage is summarized in Figure 11-2.

Defining the Problem Problems are harder to define in shared information system settings than in personal system settings. There are two reasons for this. First, a problem is a perceived difference between what is and what ought to be. Since there are many people in a shared setting, there will be several, perhaps many, different perceptions of the problem. Unless the developer is very lucky, a system designed to solve one perceived problem will not solve the other perceived problems. Thus, when the developer has finished and is waiting for applause, the main response may be strong criticism instead.

Therefore, the developer of a shared system must seek a definition of the problem that is understood and accepted by the majority of users, especially by the influential people in the user community. This means that the problem definition will need to be documented, presented to key people for feedback, and, if necessary, adjusted. If this is not done, the entire development effort is probably directed toward the wrong goal.

The second reason why problem definition for shared systems is more difficult and time consuming is that the systems themselves are more complicated. The systems involve more people, more activities, and greater volume and variety of data.

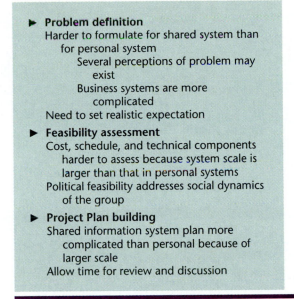

- **Problem definition**
  Harder to formulate for shared system than for personal system
    Several perceptions of problem may exist
    Business systems are more complicated
  Need to set realistic expectation
- **Feasibility assessment**
  Cost, schedule, and technical components harder to assess because system scale is larger than that in personal systems
  Political feasibility addresses social dynamics of the group
- **Project Plan building**
  Shared information system plan more complicated than personal because of larger scale
  Allow time for review and discussion

FIGURE 11-2
Problem Definition Stage

Dataflow diagrams (DFDs) are useful tools for expressing the fundamental nature of a business system in a way that can be readily understood. They can express both what is and what should be. Figure 11-3 shows an example DFD. DFDs will be discussed later in this chapter.

Assessing Feasibility The second major task in the definition stage is assessing whether it is feasible to solve the problem by building a new system. In Chapter 7 we discussed three dimensions of feasibility: cost, schedule, and technical feasibility. These dimensions also apply to shared information systems development. An additional factor, political feasibility, is new to shared systems.

Cost, schedule, and technical feasibility may be more difficult to assess for shared systems than for personal systems, because the scale of the system is larger. There are more cost factors to consider, more people and activities to schedule, and more technological factors to evaluate.

In a shared information system, the assessment of **political feasibility** should address the informal social dynamics of the group or groups involved. For example, if a new system in one department requires state-of-the-art equipment for its users, then comparable users in other departments may need to be accommodated with upgraded equipment, even though their systems do not require it.

If a system is considered in a positive light, people will try to make it work. If it is considered in a negative light, people may not care to make it work, and it may be ineffective no matter how well designed. Therefore, it is important that users perceive the system as positive.

Group expectations, habits, and practices often influence users' response to the new system. The developer should pay attention to such factors and work with them. If the resulting system conflicts with group expectations about what it should do or how it should work, the expectations eventually prevail.

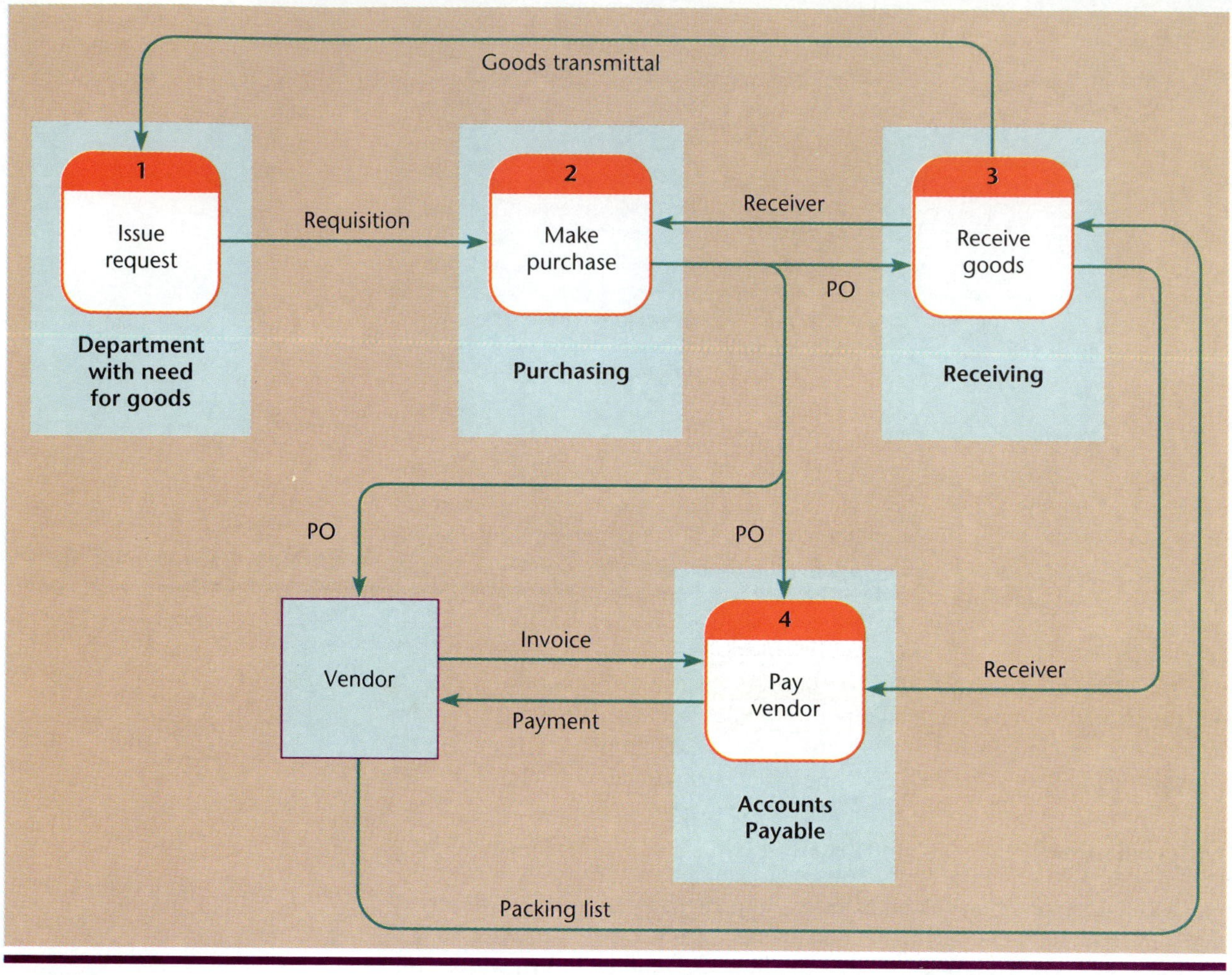

FIGURE 11-3

Dataflow Diagram
This diagram documents the processes and the dataflows involved in one company's purchasing function.

Another factor in political feasibility is the support of upper management. If users' bosses are telling them that a system is vital and must succeed, users will usually work to make it effective. If bosses do not appear to care much about the system, then users may have little incentive to make it effective. Since completed systems commonly require an initial period of adjustment before they work well, upper management support is especially vital in the initial period.

However, do not assume that a system supported and judged politically feasible by management is necessarily politically feasible to employees. Often management does not understand the dynamics of the user group or share its point of view. The best way to assess political feasibility among group members is to discuss it with them.

Building a Project Plan The third task in the definition stage is to build a project plan. The plan should indicate steps involved, scheduled completion dates for each step, and costs associated with each step.

- **Output**
  Assess what information people need to do their jobs
  Use various reports from the same data to serve different needs
- **Input**
  Work backward from output requirements to identify required inputs
  Review existing forms for possible inputs
- **System size**
  Estimate storage volume and input and output volumes
  Estimate concurrent processing requirements
- **Constraints**
  Identify constraints on hardware, programs, data, procedures, and people
- **Documentation**
  Foster user understanding, acceptance, and support of requirements
  Schedule time for review and discussion

FIGURE 11-4
Requirements Definition Stage

The work is not different from that for personal information systems. It is just more complicated. More people will be involved, and more activities will need coordinating. This means that having a project plan is all the more important.

The management of a large, complicated project is difficult. How can a manager know, for example, whether the project is half completed when half the time has passed or half the money has been spent? To rationalize project management, project milestones should be established. These are times when specified tasks should be completed. The minimum milestones should be the completion of each stage of the development process. In complex projects, additional intermediate milestones may be needed.

For each milestone, **deliverables** should be specified: evidence that the required tasks have been completed. Deliverables usually consist of documentation.

In the project plan, time will be needed at each stage for review, discussion, and possible rework. To be successful, a system must be understood, accepted, and supported. This means that key people are given a chance to comment on and influence the development of the system. Such activity takes time.

Requirements Definition Stage

The purpose of the requirements definition stage is to identify what the system is supposed to do in detail. The requirements definition stage is summarized in Figure 11-4.

INCREASING YOUR PERSONAL PRODUCTIVITY

Box 11.1

Characteristics of a Successful Systems Analyst

Current research in systems analysis and design suggests that a systems analyst should demonstrate:

logical ability
thoroughness
ability to observe
resourcefulness
imagination
oral ability
abstract reasoning
emotional balance
interest in analysis
writing ability
curiosity
decisiveness
empathy
mature judgment
practicality
ability to work with others
dislike of inefficiency
initiative
integrity
intelligence
interest in technology
interest in staff work
numerical ability
open-mindedness
selling ability
intuition

And be well versed in:

organizational theory
law
the art of interviewing
project management
economics
user training
the art of expression
information analysis
software engineering
programming
databases

Apparently, the education of such a person is going to take time, possibly a lifetime. Possibly even more than a lifetime.

In identifying requirements, it is particularly useful to review the methods currently used to accomplish the purposes of this system. Looking at the current methods helps to ensure that all necessary system outputs are identified, and it also helps identify unexpected aspects of system operation—side benefits of the current methods that may be valuable.

Because the main office building was overcrowded, for example, one small manufacturing company temporarily located its order entry clerks in a corner of the warehouse. Clerks and warehouse workers shared coffee breaks. Three years later, when order entry was moved to more pleasant surroundings, inventory difficulties surfaced. Frequent parts shortages began causing production delays, and the company missed deadlines with important customers. Investigation revealed that order clerks had been alerting the warehouse manager, over coffee, when large orders were received, so he could press suppliers for immediate delivery of required parts. When the two groups no longer shared coffee, this communication channel had to be established in another way.

On large development projects, a project team is created for requirements definition consisting of user representatives, management representative, and systems analyst. User representatives contribute expertise in their specific domains and take responsibility for completeness and accuracy of the result. The systems analyst coaches the user representatives in the working methods to be applied and provides technical support. The management representative communicates with upper management and coordinates management support when necessary.

Determining Output Requirements The project team determines output requirements by assessing what information people need to do their jobs. Each user does a different job and must have appropriate information to make decisions. A word processing operator, for example, might have to decide, "Can I finish this document and have it printed by four o'clock?" To decide, the operator may want a system that shows what other work needs to be done, what jobs are in the print queue, and what other jobs in process will soon be in the print queue.

The shift supervisor, on the other hand, often needs to review employee performance. Thus, the same system must show how much work has been done per shift by each operator.

The word processing department manager, meanwhile, needs to determine next year's budget. Thus, the system must summarize the work done this quarter and compare it with prior quarters.

In developing output requirements, the various system users need to be identified and interviewed. Further, their specific requirements in terms of menus, output displays, and reports need to be documented. Prototypes are especially useful, as you will see later in this chapter.

Determining Input Requirements The basic method of developing input requirements is to work backward from the output requirements. To produce a particular output, what input data is logically required? Most input data items can be identified in this way, but not all.

To identify the remainder of the input requirements, the project team takes advantage of the organization's standard forms—computer data entry screens and printed paper forms. These forms are a rich source of requirements for input data.

Consider the form in Figure 11-5. It is completed when an attorney leaves work to be done by the law firm's word processing department. Whoever designed this form thought that each of the data items was important. Unless the form was poorly designed, each data item in the form was needed somewhere in the department at some time in the past. With the form in hand, the project team can investigate the current need for each item. Some items may be redundant or no longer needed, and these can be eliminated. Those that remain are added to the list of inputs.

Standard forms can also be used to check the completeness of output requirements. If the department collects data on an input that does not show up on any of the output requirements, then that omission might indicate that (1) some outputs were missed, (2) the input is not actually needed, or (3) data is needed by another system.

Sources of input documents and forms can be identified in several ways. DFDs are most commonly used for this purpose. They are discussed later in this chapter.

Estimating System Size All of the considerations for estimating the system size or **processing scale** of a personal information system also pertain

Word Processing Work Request

Job #: ____________

Date: ____________ Requested by: ____________

Time: ____________ Phone: ____________

Related job numbers: ____________

Date needed by: ____________ Completed: ____________

Description: ____________

Operator: ____________ Supervisor approval: ____________

Special equipment: ____________

Number of pages: ____________ Number of copies: ____________

FIGURE 11-5

Example of Printed Form
This form is used by an attorney requesting work by the firm's word processing department.

to shared information systems. These include the amount of data to be stored and the volume and frequency of input and output.

In addition, since these systems involve multiple users, estimates of the degree of **concurrent work load** also need to be made—that is, estimates of how many users will be simultaneously using the system. Ask questions like these: How many concurrent users will there be? How long will their sessions last? Over which hours of the day? On which days of the week? What will be the average number of concurrent users? The maximum number?

Identifying Constraints The constraints on hardware, programs, data, procedures, and people described for personal information systems also pertain to shared information systems. Shared systems may have additional constraints.

Restrictions on duties and authorities are an example. In a department that produces negotiable instruments (like checks), usually one person authorizes payments while another person produces checks. If a single employee was allowed to both authorize payments and generate checks, a control weakness would exist. (The employee could authorize and write checks to fictitious people and cash them.) Thus, to strengthen control, duties and authorities are separated.

- ▶ **Descriptive**
  Background, context, and processing environment
  Specific requirements
  Constraints on system
  Constraints on procurement process
  Needs, not specific products or configurations (expect the vendor to propose specific products)
  General description of evaluation criteria (how you will judge proposals)
  Response dates
  Single contact person for questions
- ▶ **Clearly written**
- ▶ **Complete**

FIGURE 11-6
Characteristics of a Good RFP

When such procedural restrictions are in place, the shared information system must support (or at least not counteract) them. Consequently, such constraints need to be made part of the requirements.

Documenting and Reviewing Requirements To be successful, a shared information system must have the understanding, acceptance, and support of the user group. To gain these things, influential members of the user community must participate in requirements development. If such users are involved in requirements specification, then the requirements will be more accurate and the users will be more committed to the project.

Once the requirements have been determined, they must be documented and reviewed. The particular form of the requirements documentation varies from project to project. Usually, the requirements are presented as text descriptions; DFDs; prototype forms, reports, and menus; and any other descriptions or examples that illuminate the users' needs. The project team's deliverable, to management at the end of the requirements definition stage is the documentation of system requirements.

If the project will involve products or services from an outside vendor, and this is often the case, then the approved and accepted requirements for that part are put in the form of a **request for proposal (RFP).** The purpose of the RFP is to provide information that the vendor will use in proposing a solution to your problem: which of the vendor's products or services you should purchase and what the cost will be.

The RFP describes the project's background; specific requirements (output, input, scale, and constraints); schedule; selection criteria; and other information that will be helpful to a vendor in preparing a proposal. Depending on the size and nature of the project, it may be appropriate to have the corporation's legal counsel review the RFP. The characteristics of a good RFP are summarized in Figure 11-6.

Alternatives Evaluation Stage

In this stage, the project team reviews requirements and considers the possible ways in which all the requirements can be met. For example, information processing could be manual processing, on-line file processing, or database processing. The architecture could be teleprocessing or distributed processing. The platform may involve mainframe, departmental minicomputers, or networked microcomputers. The alternatives evaluation stage is summarized in Figure 11-7.

The job of generating all possible alternatives and evaluating them must be shared between users and computer professionals. Each has a perspective that contributes to the solution. Computer professionals see the technical capabilities and limitations of potential systems, and users see the applicability of alternative solutions to the business problem being solved.

The alternatives evaluation stage is a transition stage between the stages in which users play the primary role—problem definition and requirements definition—and the stages in which computer professionals play the primary role—design and implementation. Most users are not equipped to play a substantial role in designing and implementing a shared information system. Instead, they provide guidance and direction and approve the initiation of work and the disbursement of funds.

When developing a shared information system, you will most likely employ a professional or a group to design and implement your system. This group might be employees of the MIS department of your own corporation, or it might be an outside contractor, or both. This is one of the key alternatives to be determined in the alternatives evaluation stage, and it has significant effects on the remaining stages.

Using In-House Personnel If your project is developed in-house, then a development team of users and MIS professionals designs and implements the system. (This may be a continuation of the project team formed in the requirements stage, with added technical specialists.) The users on

FIGURE 11-7
Alternatives Evaluation Stage

- **In-House development**
  Form development team
  Assess alternative approaches and architectures
  Select one alternative
- **Outside Vendor development**
  Identify qualified vendors
  Describe needs
  Request proposals (RFPs)
  Evaluate proposals
  Select a vendor
  Negotiate and sign contract

this team serve as experts in the domain of the application. They clarify requirements and test various components of the system as the development proceeds. Users, who are the ultimate beneficiaries of the system, are responsible for its development. When problems arise that might compromise the resulting system, users need to bring these problems to the attention of the professional developers.

During the evaluation stage, the development team assesses various approaches and architectures for the potential system. They then evaluate the alternatives and select one. Normally, the deliverable documentation consists of a presentation of the decision process and a brief specification of each of the five components of the information system selected.

Using Outside Vendors If your project is being developed by an outside vendor, then the developer has three major tasks. First, the project team must locate qualified vendors, describe your needs, and ask for a proposal. This is usually done via an RFP. Second, once the responses are in hand, the team must evaluate them and select one. Finally, the team must negotiate and sign a contract. Normally this involves professional legal assistance.

When working with outside vendors, it is a good idea to build review dates into your contract. It is even better to tie vendor payments to the successful completion of these reviews. During these reviews, you can verify that the project is on track and on schedule.

Design Stage

Beginning in the design stage, your role as user member of the project team is to become the consumer of someone else's expertise. Your responsibility in the design and implementation stages is managerial—to oversee the creation of detailed technical specifications for a system to meet your requirements. The design stage is summarized in Figure 11-8.

- **Manage as technical project**
  - Assess people
  - Follow intuition
  - Get help when necessary
- **Understand procedures component**
  - Check for completeness and feasibility
  - Ensure appropriateness of data entry and conversion procedures area
- **Understand people component**
  - Review draft of new or altered job descriptions
  - Prepare for personnel training
- **Develop system installation plan**

FIGURE 11-8
Considerations for the Design Stage

Thus, user representatives do not develop the design. In fact, there are aspects of hardware, program, and data design that you need not even understand. But it is crucial that your system designer understand them. Therefore, you should manage this activity as you manage the activity of any other technical effort. Assess individuals and their competency. When you suspect problems are developing, follow your intuition, getting help from someone who understands the technical details, if necessary.

As a representative of the user community, you should review and approve the design of the user interface. This includes menus, data entry forms, report layouts, and command sequences. While some of these components will have been established during requirements definition, it is important to verify that the developer has understood and incorporated these requirements. Any new elements of the user interface should receive thorough review.

As a user, you should understand the design of the system components for procedures and people. It should be clear to you from the design how procedures will be established and maintained. You should be given a draft of the user job descriptions and an outline of user procedures. Review them to ensure that they are complete and realistic. Take corrective action if they are not.

You should also participate actively in developing a personnel training plan. The training plan should be developed cooperatively by user representatives and technical specialists. Both contribute necessary expertise.

Finally, during the design stage, the project team should develop a system installation plan. User representatives and technical specialists share responsibility for this plan. System installation is a risky time, because shared systems are so complex that unexpected problems are likely to arise. It is quite possible that the system may not initially work correctly—or it may work correctly but too slowly to be usable. As a result, it is prudent to consider installation strategies very carefully, especially for systems that are vital to the company's day-to-day operations.

The four major installation methods are listed in Figure 11-9. **Plunge installation** means completely abandoning the old system and immediately putting the new system in place. This is a very dangerous approach, because virtually no backup exists when problems are encountered. The plunge approach is the most risky one and generally should be avoided for important systems. On the other hand, it is the least expensive approach, and it should be considered in cases where temporary system failure would be no great loss.

- Plunge
- Parallel
- Piecemeal
- Pilot

FIGURE 11-9

Four Approaches to System Installation

Parallel installation, on the other hand, is the safest approach, but the most expensive. In parallel installation, you run the new system in parallel with the old one until the new system proves itself effective and reliable. For example, in shifting its capital assets management system from batch processing to on-line database processing, a department may continue the batch system alongside the new on-line system. Since data entry must be done twice, the parallel operation will be fairly expensive. However, if the new system turns out to have problems, the company can continue to rely on the old system while corrections are made.

Piecemeal installation, sometimes called phased installation, occurs when one portion of the system is installed at a time. If that portion functions properly, then other pieces are added until the entire system is installed. For example, in shifting its major systems over to database processing, a company might first shift the main order entry and accounting systems, then shift the inventory and production planning systems, and so on.

Pilot installation means implementing the entire system, but in only one part of an organization. For example, if a company consists of four branch operations, it could install the entire system in just one branch, then another, and so on. If problems are encountered in a branch, vulnerability is limited to that one branch.

Many installation plans involve a combination of approaches. For example, a company might begin by installing only the accounts receivable portion of a larger system for a single group of users in the St. Louis office, while continuing to operate the existing system for all users, including the group of users in St. Louis. Such a plan combines elements of piecemeal, pilot, and parallel installation method. Such a strategy may provide useful system testing with reasonable safety at acceptable costs.

Since most shared systems are vital to a company's operations, you should generally avoid the plunge approach for these systems. Instead, investigate the pilot, piecemeal, and parallel strategies. In a shared setting, the parallel method is probably the most frequently used. The basic installation events should be decided by the end of the design stage.

The deliverable at the end of the design stage should be documentation of the technical design for the system.

Implementation and Maintenance Stage

In the implementation and maintenance stage, each of the five components is separately obtained, installed, and tested. Then the system is integrated and tested. Finally, you convert to the new system. As a user representative, you are primarily a manager of others' activities again during the implementation stage. See Figure 11-10.

Hardware is obtained, installed, and tested first, followed by programs. Manage this activity to keep it on schedule. If delays develop, do not allow test procedures to be abbreviated to make up for lost time. It is better to be behind schedule than to accept defective components that will cause operational problems after your department has become dependent on the system.

During implementation, data is entered and verified. Here again, manage this activity to keep it on schedule. Do not let verification procedures be abbreviated.

Procedures are documented during this stage. As the documentation is created, review the procedures yourself and review them with key members of the group you represent. Ensure that the procedures are realistic and that you have scheduled sufficient training for users to learn the procedures.

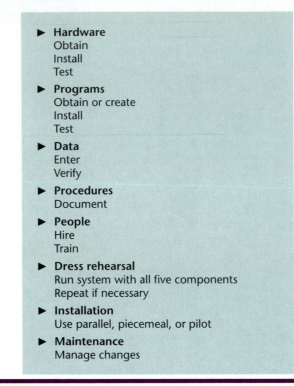

- **Hardware**
  Obtain
  Install
  Test
- **Programs**
  Obtain or create
  Install
  Test
- **Data**
  Enter
  Verify
- **Procedures**
  Document
- **People**
  Hire
  Train
- **Dress rehearsal**
  Run system with all five components
  Repeat if necessary
- **Installation**
  Use parallel, piecemeal, or pilot
- **Maintenance**
  Manage changes

FIGURE 11-10
Implementation and Maintenance Stage

Finally, hire and train new employees, if required, and provide adequate training for existing employees. If the quality of the training is not adequate, take corrective action. Training is an area in which plans often fall short of fully meeting the need. When training is insufficient, problems arise after installation, when they are more difficult to solve.

When each of the five components has been installed and tested, the system is ready for a dress rehearsal. As a user representative, you should take responsibility for maintaining the rehearsal schedule and spending the time to give the system a thorough trial. After evaluating the results of the rehearsal, make the decision either to implement the system or to rework some components. When you are satisfied with the results of the dress rehearsal(s), you can initiate your installation plan.

The deliverables for the implementation and maintenance stage are the various packages of documentation for the finished system. Included should be documentation for users and computer operators, along with a description of the system for upper management.

Following installation, the system must be managed as it is used over its lifetime. This process is called **system maintenance**. Its most important component is to manage the changes that must be made as systems requirements change over time. Because a system's environment changes, new data must be stored and retrieved, new reports are needed, and new computations must be made.

However, each change in the system introduces the likelihood of new errors. Therefore, each time a system is changed, it must be retested to en-

FIGURE 11-11

Adequate Training Is Vital
An important aspect of implementation is training employees in the use of the new system.

sure its integrity. Such testing is extremely expensive. Therefore, when small changes are needed, they are often delayed until enough changes have collected to make such testing worthwhile. This process of planned maintenance, called **staged maintenance**, extends the life of systems by helping to ensure that crippling errors do not creep in over time as the result of frequent untested changes.

DFDs

Shared information systems are more complicated than personal information systems because they involve the interaction of many people who work in complex relationships with one another. This complexity makes it difficult to define the problem to be solved and to develop the system's requirements. DFDs are tools that can be used to document the business activity and the interaction among employees. Obviously these diagrams do not make the system any less complex. They do, however, provide a means for developers to deal with the complexity.

Using DFDs to Document Systems

The purpose of a DFD is to represent the flow of data among functions and people. A DFD is a snapshot of the data movement in a system.

Since the flow of data is not something we normally think very much about, DFDs help us focus on the aspects of the business that pertain to

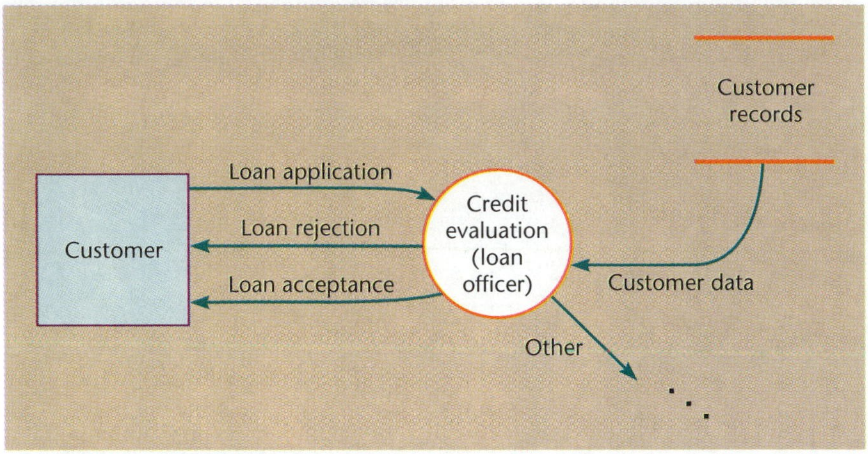

FIGURE 11-12
Portion of a DFD
This portion of the diagram documents the procedure of producing forms entitled Loan Rejection and Loan Acceptance. A DFD does not document how these forms are selected or why they are produced. It only documents dataflows.

dataflow. They work, as much as anything, by *excluding* from our attention all the factors that are not directly concerned with dataflow. They do this by giving us symbols that can only diagram dataflows—symbols for other factors simply are not provided.

DFDs do not show logic. They are unlike flowcharts and other tools used for documenting program logic. For example, consider the portion of a DFD shown for a credit union in Figure 11-12. Among other things, this diagram indicates that two forms are produced by a process labeled Credit Evaluation. One form is labeled Loan Acceptance, and the second is labeled Loan Rejection. The DFD indicates that both items flow out of the process and go to a Customer. But the DFD does not show the conditions under which either form is sent. That is not the purpose of the DFD.

Dataflow Symbols

Figure 11-13 is an example DFD. This diagram shows the flow of data in the customer support department of a software publisher (such as Microsoft or Lotus). Four types of symbols are used in this diagram: rectangles, circles or rounded squares, arrows, and open-ended rectangles. They are summarized in Figure 11-14.

Rectangles represent external entities—offices, departments, companies, or people that are *external* to the system being modeled. Such entities are called sources and sinks. A **source** is an external entity that produces a dataflow. A **sink** is an external entity that absorbs a dataflow.

The second symbol type is a circle (sometimes called **bubble**) or a rounded square representing a process. Process symbols represent entities—such as offices, departments, processes, or people—that are *internal* to the system being modeled. Processes often transform data from one form to another. In those cases, they are labeled with the name of the process.

The third symbol is a labeled arrow, representing a dataflow. In the upper-left-hand corner of Figure 11-13, there is an arrow labeled Registra-

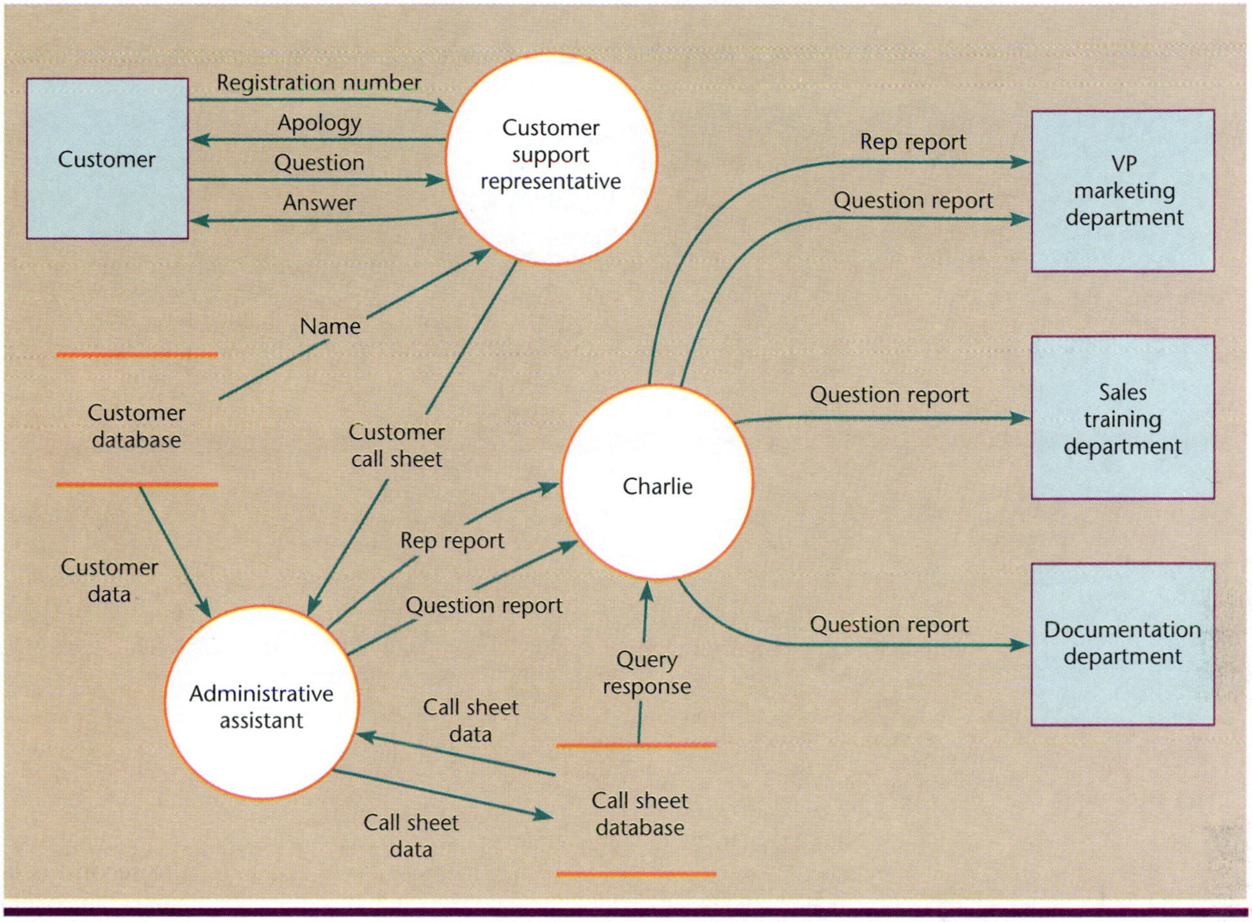

FIGURE 11-13

DFD of Customer Support Department

This DFD documents the dataflows between entities within the customer support department: customer support representatives, administrative assistant, and Charlie. It also documents dataflows between the department and four outside entities: customers, vice president of marketing department, sales training department, and documentation department.

tion Number. The arrow emerges from the Customer rectangle and flows into the Customer Support Representative bubble. The arrow means that a data item, the registration number, is provided by the customer to the customer support representative. The medium of the flow is not shown. This number could be provided verbally over the telephone, in writing on a request form, or in another way. In general, no transfer media are shown in DFDs.

Sometimes dataflows are forms or documents. The dataflow going from the circle labeled Charlie to the rectangle labeled VP Marketing Department represents a report. At times we even show the flow of physical entities such as shipments on DFDs. Strictly speaking, such physical items do not belong on DFDs. However, we include them when their presence adds to the clarity and communicative value of the diagram.

The final symbol type is an open-ended rectangle (sometimes simply a pair of horizontal lines with a file name between them). This symbol represents a data store, or **file**—that is, an entity in which data is stored. All the processes that move data into and out of a file may not appear in a single DFD. As a result, a file may appear to be read-only or write-only.

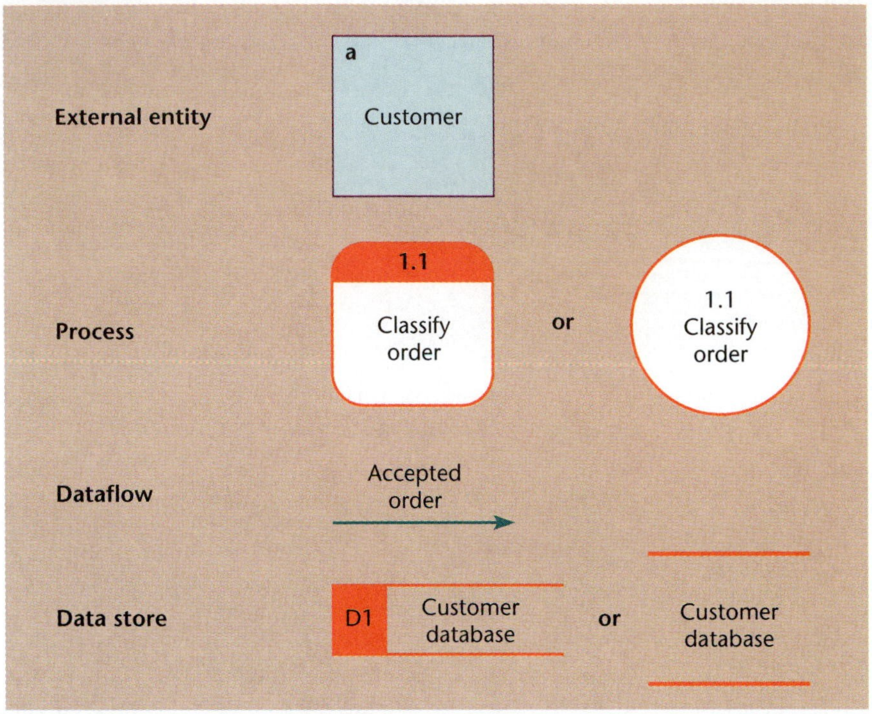

FIGURE 11-14
Fundamental Dataflow Symbols

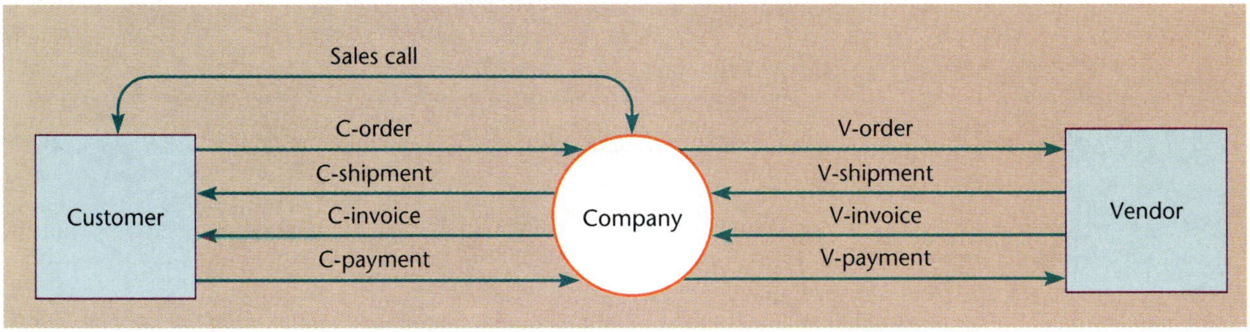

FIGURE 11-15
Level 0 DFD
This diagram summarizes the data relationships between a landscape design firm and its customers and vendors.

For example, in Figure 11-13, the only dataflows relating to the file named Customer Database are out of the file. From this single diagram it appears that data is being spontaneously generated. In fact, the process that writes to the file is shown in another DFD.

Levels of DFDs

A DFD is an explanation. In explaining something orally, you sometimes give a condensed or high-level summary and other times give a long, detailed discussion. In DFDs, you frequently do the same thing. For example, Figure 11-15 shows a very high-level chart of a landscape design company's

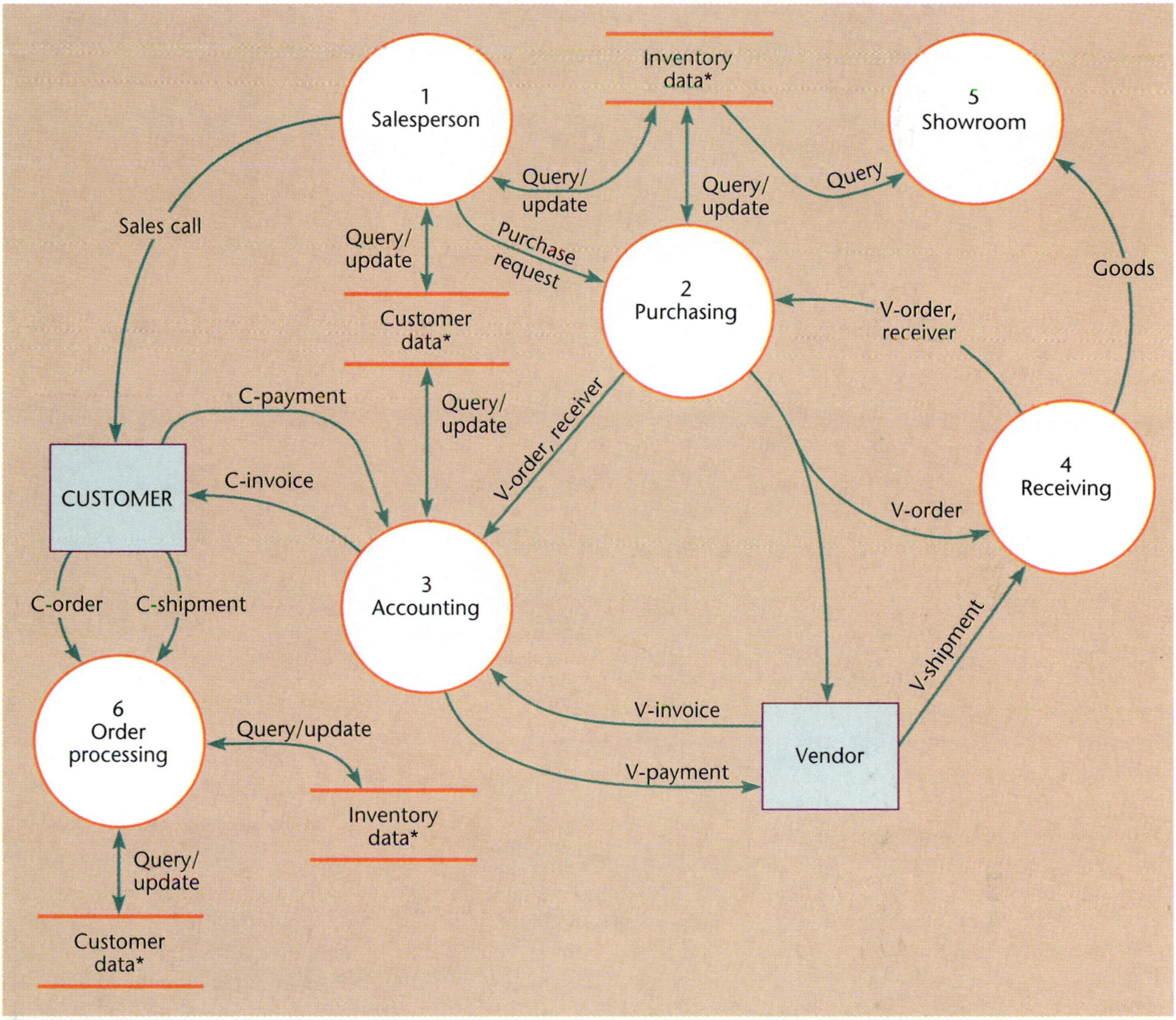

FIGURE 11-16

Level 1 DFD

This DFD expands the Company bubble in the level 0 diagram in Figure 11-15. It shows dataflows among the following processes: Salesperson, Purchasing, Accounting, Receiving, Showroom, and Order Processing. It also includes external entities Customer and Vendor that appeared in the level 0 diagram.

operations. The chart depicts the relationship of the company to its customers and its vendors. Since this diagram depicts the dataflow at the highest level, it is labeled level 0.

We will now expand the Company bubble and show departments within the company. This next diagram will be called a level 1 DFD, since it shows the dataflow at the next level of detail. The process of "exploding" a bubble in this way is called **leveling**—establishing multiple levels of diagrams, each expanding on the amount of detail provided in the one above.

Figure 11-16 is a level 1 diagram showing the dataflows among the processes involved in the purchasing function in the company: Salesperson, Purchasing, Accounting, Receiving, Showroom, and Order Processing. It also includes Customer and Vendor, external entities from level 0.

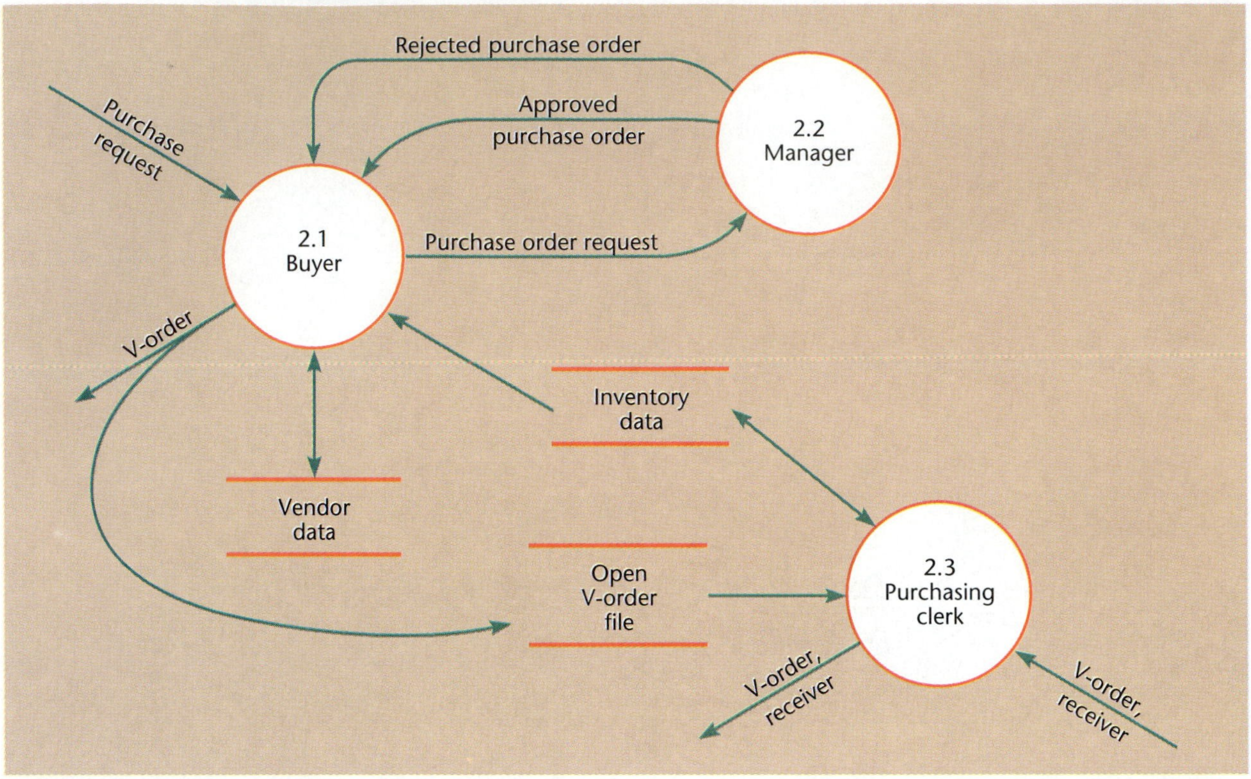

FIGURE 11-17

Level 2 DFD

This level 2 diagram expands the Purchasing bubble in Figure 11-16. It shows dataflows among three processes: Buyer, Manager, and Purchasing Clerk. It reveals two new files that do not appear in higher-level diagrams: Vendor Data and Open V-Order File. It also shows dataflows to and from other processes that appear only at higher levels.

Figure 11-17 shows a level 2 diagram that expands the Purchasing bubble in Figure 11-16. In Figure 11-16, Purchasing is labeled as process 2. In Figure 11-17, the bubbles within Purchasing are labeled 2.1, 2.2, and so forth. This numbering system is carried down to the lowest-level diagram. Thus, in a level 3 diagram expanding the buyer process, the bubbles would be labeled 2.1.1, 2.1.2, and so on.

Two files appear in Figure 11-17 that have not appeared before. These files exist entirely within the Purchasing bubble, and they are not visible until that bubble is expanded. If a file were to be used by, say, both Purchasing and Receiving, then it would have been documented between those two bubbles in Figure 11-16.

Data Dictionary Although we have chosen names for dataflows in these diagrams that suggest the meaning of the data items, this is often not enough. In Figure 11-17, for example, what exactly is a purchase order request?

DFDs are given meaning when they are accompanied by a description of the dataflows. Such a description is sometimes called a **data dictionary**. This dictionary is a file or a database that documents data requirements and explains, in detail, the meaning of each dataflow.

PROTOTYPING

Prototyping was introduced in Chapter 7, where it formed the heart of the development process for personal information systems. Prototyping is also used in developing shared information systems, though it seldom plays as central a role as in personal systems.

The word *prototype* means a sample, a pattern, an example, or the first thing of its kind. As applied to systems development, it is a simulation, a demonstration, a piece of a system, or the first instance of a system. Usually prototypes are limited to hardware, programs, and data.

Types of Prototypes

The simplest type of prototype is a **simulated**, or **slide-show, prototype** (see Figure 11-18). This type is most often used for prototypes of user interfaces. With it, dummies of menus, data entry forms, or reports are constructed. The user then uses the keyboard as he or she would with the actual system. Behind the scenes, a program reads files of predrawn screens and data to simulate what would happen with the actual system.

The advantage of simulated prototypes is that they are quick to develop. They also can provide a realistic-feeling impression of what the user interface is like. Usually, however, this type of prototype is restricted to a canned script, or only minor variations from a canned script. This means that users cannot perform realistic tests with varied data against such a prototype.

When, as a business professional, you use or review a prototype, be certain to ask what type it is. If it is a simulation or a slide-show prototype, keep in mind that none of the actual work in building the system has been done and that the prototype only indicates the nature of the idea.

A second type of prototype is the **proof-of-concept prototype** to demonstrate the technical feasibility of an idea or approach. Such prototypes are developed when there is substantial risk that the proposed design will not work. Building the prototype reduces the dollars and other resources that must be placed at risk.

Proof-of-concept prototypes typically have a very rough user interface (unless, of course, the user interface is the concept being proved). Little time is spent developing program instructions to accept data or return results. Instead, the programming activity is focused on the particular aspect of the problem whose feasibility is unknown. The results should be evaluated by competent information systems professionals.

The remaining types of prototype, the **partial-function prototype** and the **pilot prototype**, are closely related. In a partial-function prototype, a part of the actual system is *partially* developed and tested. Such prototypes are constructed to demonstrate a key feature of the system. Elements not included are often the user interface and routines to detect and

- ► Simulation, or slide-show, prototype
- ► Proof-of-concept prototype
- ► Partial-function prototype
- ► Pilot prototype

FIGURE 11-18
Types of Prototypes

FIGURE 11-19

Testing a Prototype
A prototype is being tested in an IBM software usability laboratory.

handle errors in data or processing. In the pilot prototype, a part of the operational system is *fully* developed. All the features and functions, the entire user interface, all error processing, and all other aspects of that part of the system are developed.

The assumption behind partial-function and pilot prototypes is that the prototype will become part of the actual system. Thus, the programs, even though they only partly implement a part of the system, are written with the same care and control as the operational system. Such prototypes take longer and cost more to develop than either simulations or proof-of-concept prototypes, but the work invested saves work later.

Avoiding Prototyping Risks

While there are substantial advantages to building a prototype, there is a risk that the users may not understand what has been accomplished and what remains to be done. Rapidly developed prototypes may seem like nearly completed systems to users, who wonder why the remaining development is so expensive and time-consuming. A complete system must not only process all of the features and functions, but must also handle exceptions and errors. It must also run fast enough to meet its concurrent processing requirements. Prototypes seldom include these capabilities.

In addition, prototypes typically focus on the user interface, which is demanding, but not usually technically difficult. As a result, a prototype may not solve what turns out to be the most critical and difficult technical problems.

Therefore, reviewers must be fully informed about the nature of the prototypes they are reviewing and their limitations. Otherwise, prototypes may make the system appear far easier to develop than it is.

Box 11.2

INCREASING YOUR PERSONAL PRODUCTIVITY

A Properly Planned Interview Can Be an Analyst's Best Tool

While the methods of obtaining useful information from the user vary greatly, the personal interview will bring the best results and best understanding, if conducted properly.

An important key to excellent interviewing skills is the ability of the analyst to prepare to deal with the different personalities and attitudes of people being interviewed. If the analyst can modify personal style to complement the personality of the interviewee, then a channel of communication will be established that will allow ideas to be effectively communicated and the needed information to be obtained.

Studies indicate that verbal messages convey 7%, intonations convey 38%, and body language conveys 55% of the total message. Body language is the key factor, and the alert and well-informed analyst and interviewer should take advantage of this fact during the interview.

Listening has specific goals as they relate to the interviewee as an employee:

1. To raise the level of employee motivation.
2. To increase the readiness of subordinates to accept change.
3. To improve the quality of all managerial decisions.
4. To develop teamwork and morale.

Active listening is characterized by a nonjudgmental attempt on one person's part to allow the other person to explore a problem. Use of body language that encourages openness and acceptance should motivate the employee to participate in the interview more fully, and this should be the interviewer's goal in obtaining information. As with other attitudes, openness encourages similar feelings.

COMPUTER-AIDED SOFTWARE ENGINEERING

Computer-aided software engineering (CASE) is a methodology and set of tools to facilitate the development of information systems. CASE uses information systems to build information systems.

A CASE system includes a **CASE product**, a software package containing CASE programs, which are called **CASE tools**. However, as many companies have learned, purchasing a CASE product and using the tools does not, by itself, improve systems development. The successful use of CASE requires not only programs but also trained people following well-designed procedures, called **CASE methodology**. This is an extension of the systems development methodology described earlier in this chapter.

CASE Methodologies

In CASE methodology, the organization first decides which information systems it needs. Then, since it needs more systems than it has time or

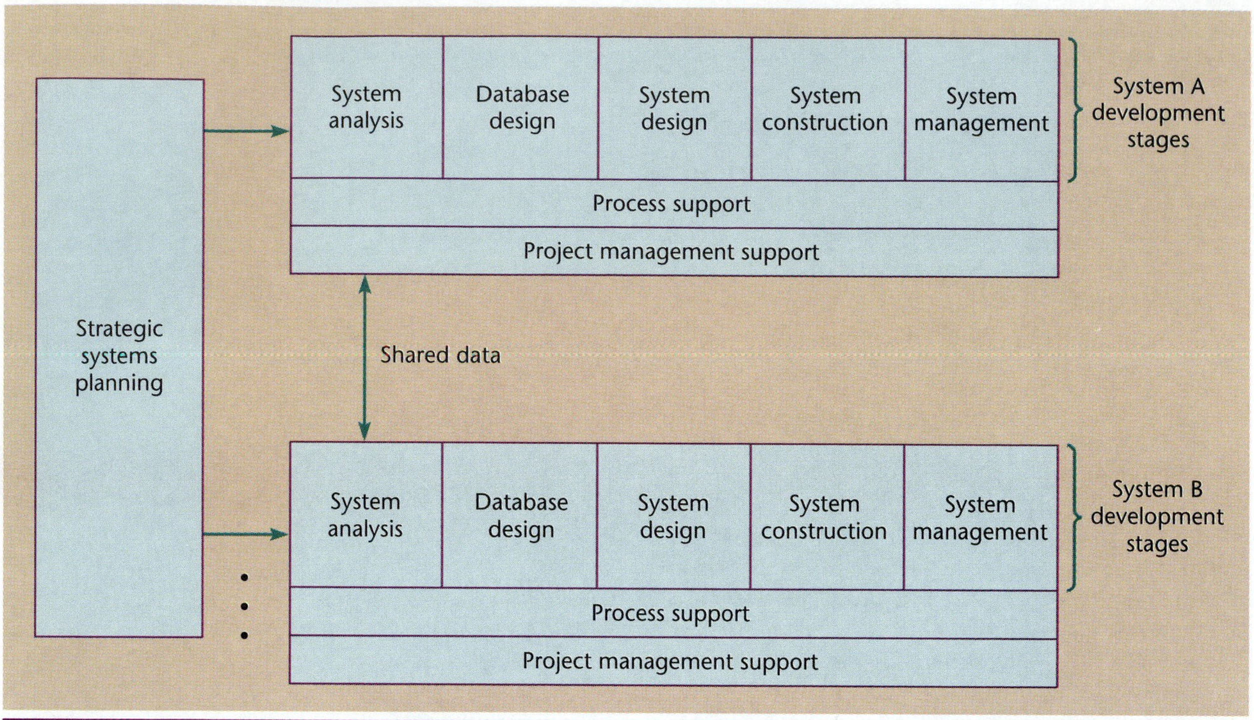

FIGURE 11-20

CASE Methodology
In strategic planning, the organization decides which systems to develop. Each system's stages of development are supported by process support and project management support aided by CASE tools. Because systems are interrelated (that is, they share data and I/O), sharing of data among development teams is important.

money to develop immediately, it sets priorities. Prioritizing is complicated by the fact that the systems are heavily interrelated. They feed inputs and outputs to one another. For example, a database created by one system may provide required input to another.

Next, a development process is followed for each system on the list, according to the established priorities. The development process includes five stages: system analysis, database design, system design, system construction, and system management. In Figure 11-20 two systems are being developed, A and B.

In the first stage of the development process, a *system analysis* is performed: requirements are developed, including DFDs and data dictionaries. With some CASE tools, requirements developed for one system can be used as input to others. This is useful when an office or a department is common to both systems. In this situation, DFDs and data dictionary that have been developed for one system can be used as a starting point for the analysis of a second.

The next stage is *database design*. In this stage, data in the data dictionary is used to develop a design of the database.

System design is the next stage. CASE tools specialize in supporting and documenting the design of programs, user interfaces, forms, and reports, but generally not hardware specifications, procedures, or job descriptions. Therefore, designers must document these components separately.

The next stage is *system construction*—that is, the creation of programs, user interfaces, forms, and reports. A long-term goal of CASE technology is to automatically produce programs directly from their specifications, eliminating a separate step of programming by human programmers. This would substantially reduce the cost of system development. However, automatic code generation has proven an extremely difficult technology to develop. Today, this goal is only partly achieved, even in the most advanced CASE systems.

The last stage is *system management.* During this stage the system is monitored, and changes are made to it in a controlled fashion. Versions of programs and other system components are managed so that configuration of the system is always known and under control.

The process described here is similar to the systems development life cycle described earlier, but it emphasizes different aspects of the development effort. With large, organizationwide systems, much more time must be placed on the coordination of the new system with the existing systems. In addition, since such systems are typically far more complicated than personal or departmental systems, this methodology places greater emphasis on design activities. And, since the systems are larger, it also places more emphasis on system management.

Although the methodology provides for these differences, it is consistent with the five-stage systems development life cycle concept. The definition stage occurs during strategic systems planning; the requirements and evaluation stages occur during system analysis; the design stage occurs during database and system design; and the implementation stage occurs during system construction and management.

CASE Products

The goal of CASE is to use computer technology to facilitate the development of information systems by improving human productivity for each of the activities in Figure 11-20.

Figure 11-21 shows the general architecture of a CASE product, which is a collection of CASE tools plus a database of systems development data. The database, shared among all of the tools, is often called the **CASE encyclopedia**. The advantage of sharing the database is that the results from one stage of development are automatically available to tools in a subsequent stage.

There are CASE tools for each activity shown in Figure 11-20. For example, tools to facilitate the creation of DFDs are typically graphical, using mouse input. They provide a standard set of symbols that can be placed and moved about the screen, and they allow the input of both text and drawings. Using them, DFDs can be developed with far greater ease and productivity than when they are drawn by hand. In addition, these tools provide automatic validation checking. For example, they ensure that, as a dataflow process is expanded to another level, no inputs or outputs are left out or added. They also create the new system's data dictionary.

Some packages provide programs to construct a database design from data descriptions recorded in the encyclopedia, though today these are only partially successful. Others produce large sections of source code that application programmers then move into the programs they write. This

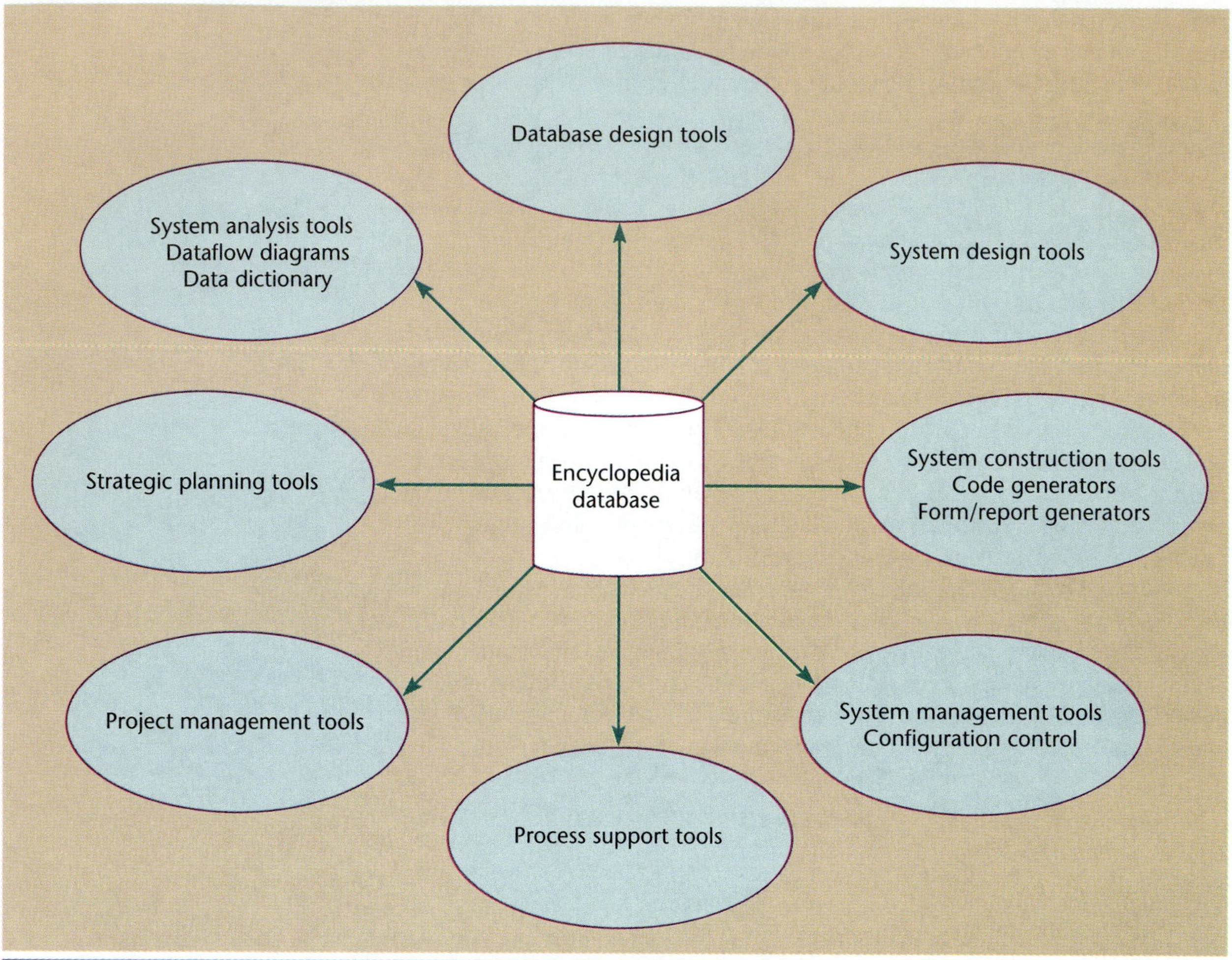

FIGURE 11-21
Architecture of a CASE Product
A variety of specialized tools all draw upon a common database of information about the application.

saves considerable time and eliminates the need for much of the programming work that is boring and repetitive. Today, CASE systems do not satisfactorily generate whole programs, ready to run.

Most packages provide tools to facilitate the design of programs, menus, forms, and reports. These tools can access the data dictionary to make it easy for the human designer. For example, the human need only specify the name of a table when designing a report, and the systems design tool can obtain the names of all columns of that table and guide the designer through the process of locating the columns on the form.

Summary

Designing new shared information systems is very complicated. Therefore, a methodology called the systems development life cycle is used. The stages are problem definition, requirements definition, alternatives evaluation, design, and implementation and maintenance. A project team, which includes user representatives, does most of the work in the first three stages and oversees the work of others in the last two.

The problem definition stage includes defining the problem, assessing the feasibility of developing a system to solve it, and building a plan for developing the system. Feasibility assessment includes estimates of cost, schedule, technical, and political feasibility. The project plan should include milestones and deliverables.

The requirements definition stage includes determining output requirements, determining input requirements, estimating system size, and determining constraints.

The alternatives evaluation stage involves considering all the possible ways in which the requirements can be met and selecting the best. Development may be with in-house personnel or outside vendors.

In the design stage, user representatives largely oversee the work of others in creating a detailed technical design for the new system. The design should include an installation plan. Common approaches to installation are plunge installation, parallel installation, piecemeal installation, and pilot installation.

Implementation and maintenance involves creating the system, installing it, and maintaining it.

DFDs are used in documenting systems. Symbols used in DFDs represent external sources and sinks, processing steps, dataflows, and data stores. DFDs can include various levels of detail. DFDs are often accompanied by a data dictionary.

The types of prototypes used with shared systems development projects are simulated, or slide-show, prototypes, proof-of-concept prototypes, partial-function prototypes, and pilot prototypes. Care is needed to explain what a prototype represents to avoid creating unrealistic expectations in the minds of those who see it.

CASE is a methodology and a set of tools to facilitate the development of information systems. CASE methodology is an adaptation of the systems development life cycle. It includes system analysis, database design, system design, system construction, and system management. CASE products are software packages of CASE tools. A CASE encyclopedia is a database shared among the tools.

Key Terms

systems development life cycle
dataflow diagram (DFD)
political feasibility
deliverable
processing scale
concurrent work load
request for proposal (RFP)
plunge installation
parallel installation
piecemeal installation
pilot installation
system maintenance
staged maintenance
source
sink
bubble
file
leveling

data dictionary
simulated prototype
slide-show prototype
proof-of-concept prototype
partial-function prototype
pilot prototype
computer-aided software engineering (CASE)
CASE product
CASE tool
CASE methodology
CASE encyclopedia

Review Questions

1. Who should define the requirements for a new shared information system?
2. Describe the membership of the project team for a new shared information system.
3. Why does computerizing a system make it more complex?
4. Name the five stages in the systems development life cycle.
5. What are the three major tasks in the problem definition stage?
6. Name four kinds of feasibility.
7. Why are milestones used in a system development project? What are deliverables?
8. What is the purpose of the requirements definition stage?
9. Why is it useful to investigate the current system or method of achieving the new system's projected goals?
10. What are the roles of user representatives, systems analyst, and management representative on a shared systems development project team?
11. How are output requirements determined?
12. How are input requirements determined?
13. Name four factors that should be considered in estimating system size.
14. What is the project team's deliverable at the end of the requirements definition stage?
15. Describe the contents of an RFP.
16. What is the purpose of the alternatives evaluation stage?
17. What is the role of user representatives and computer professionals in the alternatives evaluation stage?
18. Differentiate between in-house development and development by outside vendors.
19. If in-house development is selected, what is the project team's deliverable at the end of the alternatives evaluation stage?
20. What are the responsibilities of the project team if development by outside vendors is selected?
21. Describe the responsibilities of user representatives on the project team during the design stage.
22. Name and describe each of the four major installation methods.
23. Describe how installation methods can be combined.
24. What is the deliverable at the end of the design stage?

25. Describe activities related to each of the five components of the information system that are performed during the implementation and maintenance stage.
26. Explain the purpose of a dress rehearsal, and describe the responsibilities of the user representative with respect to a dress rehearsal.
27. Explain the purpose of staged maintenance.
28. What do DFDs do?
29. Name four types of symbols used in DFDs, and describe the usage of each.
30. Explain the use of source, sink, bubble, and file in DFDs.
31. Describe the process of leveling in DFDs.
32. What is a data dictionary in relationship to DFDs?
33. Identify four types of prototypes used in the development of shared information systems.
34. Differentiate between the partial-function prototype and the pilot prototype.
35. What risks are associated with the use of prototypes in developing shared information systems? How can the pitfalls be avoided?
36. Describe the use of CASE in the development of shared information systems.
37. Differentiate among the CASE product, the CASE tool, the CASE methodology, and the CASE encyclopedia.
38. Describe the purpose of each of the five stages of CASE methodology.

Discussion Questions

A. In most college courses, the instructor must assign a grade to each student. Suppose you are participating in the project team to design a system for that purpose. Propose a definition of the problem that would provide a useful focus for the project. Hint: What criteria are applied and by whom, in judging the quality of the grades assigned?

B. Assess the feasibility of developing an information system for use by a college instructor in assigning grades to students in courses. Consider the information you would need to assess the cost, schedule, technical, and political feasibility of such a system. When you have determined what you need to know, interview your instructor, then report your results.

C. For a manager who will be responsible for a shared system development project, summarize the deliverables that the manager should expect to receive from the project team at the end of each stage. What content should be included in each? What criteria should the manager use to assess the quality of the work performed by the team in each stage?

D. Determine output requirements, input requirements, system size, and constraints for an information system for use by a college instructor in assigning grades to students in courses. When you have determined what you need to know, interview your instructor, then report your results.

E. The systems development life cycle is a fairly complicated set of working methods for developing new shared systems. Do you think that a methodology of this complexity is really necessary to create real shared systems? All the work to be done by the project team and others during these stages is costly. Do you think that using the systems development life cycle is likely to be cost-effective, as compared to simpler, more direct approaches? Support your answers with detailed reasons.

F. Create a DFD for an information system for use by a college instructor in assigning grades to students in courses. Consider external sources and sinks, processes, dataflows, and files. For example, the college registrar is usually an external source who provides a list of students who must receive grades. What other external sources of data should be considered? Who receives data from such a system—that is, what are the external sinks? What data-storage entities (files) are used? Where, in the system, does processing take place?

MINICASE

IS Professionals Combine Talents to Create Their Own Niche

Dave Gusman knows that IS workers in the 1990s have to be as customer-driven as any salesperson who meets with clients face to face.

As a systems officer for Cleveland-based Society Bank, Gusman and his colleagues are practicing what many IS consultants are merely beginning to preach.

"When you think about what our bank offers as a product, it's not really a savings or checking account—although from the consumer side that is certainly the delivery vehicle—but the handling of financial information," Gusman says.

For example, when a customer deposits money in an account, that in essence is an information transaction. A record is created that instructs the bank to move money from one place to another.

"Just as an actual mechanical assembly line is critical to Ford, General Motors, or Chrysler, our information technology function is important to us," Busman says. And he does his part to ensure that this new age assembly line doesn't break down.

As the manager in charge of Society Banks' IS telecommunications research and development function, Gusman has been involved since 1988 in the organization's implementation of its "intelligent workstation" architecture.

Among other duties, Gusman is responsible for communicating to the rest of the bank about emerging technologies and the potential impact on the bank's overall IS and business strategies.

Since 1988, the PC has been the cornerstone of the bank's enterprise computing architecture. At that time, the IS department wrote an office systems strategy that in retrospect turned out to be right on target, Gusman says.

Society Bank is also ahead of its time in another area: By dividing up its IS staff into departments based on function, and not platform, it has already started down a path that other IS organizations are just beginning to envision.

The bank recognized early on the need to link the PC environment to mainframe operations. So Society Bank created a division that performs all end-user support activities for micro and mainframe services. The group provides traditional help-desk functions.

Another department focuses on business process re-engineering, or the redesign of computer applications according to work-flow patterns. Still another department of IS, called the Branch of the Future, focuses on using technology to find new ways that customers can interact with their financial institution. A separate department is dedicated to knowledge-based systems; and finally, there is an imaging department involved in imaging research.

Questions

1. Consider the assertion that a customer deposit is an information transaction. What do you think that statement means? How is an information

system at a bank like an assembly line at an auto manufacturer?

2. Describe two ways that the author claims Society Bank is ahead of its time. Do you think those ways translate into a competitive advantage for the bank? If so, explain how. If not, why not?
3. Explain how Society Bank has divided its IS staff by function, not platform. What advantages do you think accrue to the bank because of this division?
4. This article contains an error. Business process re-engineering is not "the redesign of computer applications according to work-flow patterns." Rather, it is the redesign of work-flow patterns so that work is combined with technology to gain the best advantage for the organization. Explain the difference between these two meanings. Are they significant? Do you think it is unusual for such errors to occur in the press?
5. Compare *Infoworld* with this textbook. Which is more likely to contain errors? Which is more likely to be current? When they disagree, which do you believe? Why? In question 4, which meaning of business process re-engineering do you think is correct? Why? What conclusions do you reach from your answers to question 4 and this question?

P A R T   F O U R

MANAGEMENT INFORMATION SYSTEMS

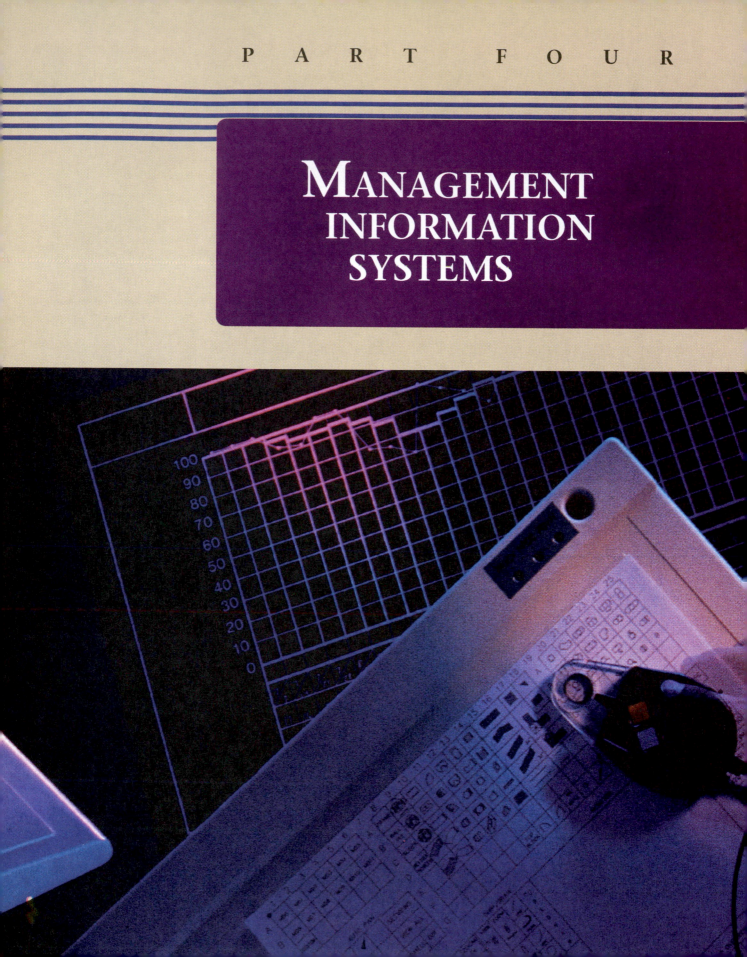

Throughout this book, you have studied basic concepts of information systems—personal information systems and how they are developed, and shared information systems and how they are developed. This material has given you an understanding of the many specific types of business information systems: what they are, how they work, what they do, and how they are developed.

Having mastered those concepts, you are ready to turn to the whole-organization level and consider how an organization's entire set of business information systems, personal and shared, fit into the operation of the organization. Although this part contains only a single chapter, in many ways it is the most important chapter in the book because it ties together nearly all the preceding material.

As you study this part of the text, you must assume the view of someone who is concerned with the entire organization—president, chief executive officer (CEO), or other senior manager. Although you may find it challenging to press your imagination this far, doing so will give you the right perspective for the material in Part Four.

C H A P T E R 12

Management Information Systems for Competitive Advantage

CHAPTER OUTLINE

This chapter presents concepts that tie together the material you have studied throughout this book. Its focus is the role of information systems in a business organization. First, we will define the term *management information system*. Then we will consider the elements of a large company's MIS, describing each element. Although you are already familiar with many of these elements, we will be especially concerned with how they fit together into a unified, whole MIS.

Next, we will see how an MIS gives competitive advantage to an organization. Information systems are expensive, and we should be able to describe how they repay their cost to the organization. An MIS improves an organization's internal effectiveness, and it also improves its products.

In addition, we will consider organization and management of an MIS department. We will examine typical components in large organizations and in small ones.

Finally, we will consider trends in information systems. Although it has proven difficult to make accurate predictions about the future of a field like information systems that is based on such rapidly changing technology, current trends help us to know what kinds of changes to anticipate.

WHAT IS AN MIS?

The term *management information system* (MIS) refers to *the development and use of effective information systems in organizations*. Although the word *management* appears in the name, MIS is not limited to management kinds of applications. It also includes all of the other people in an organization and the structure and design of the organization as well. A better term would be *organizational information system*, but the term *management information system* has become established and accepted.

When people use the term *MIS*, they are often referring to the sum of all the company's information systems. On the other hand, when they talk about a *business information system*, they are often referring to a particular individual system. Thus, the term *MIS* is often concerned with organizationwide issues, and the term *business information system* is concerned with particular-system issues.

ELEMENTS OF AN MIS

An MIS includes five major elements: transaction processing systems, management reporting systems, decision support systems, communication support systems, and executive support systems. This section examines each system type in turn.

Transaction Processing Systems

Transaction processing systems (TPSs) are the organization's basic accounting and record-keeping systems. Examples include ticket reservation systems, order entry systems, check processing systems, accounts payable systems, inventory systems, and payroll systems. All these systems help a company conduct its operations and keep track of its activities. Figure 12-1 lists the important characteristics of TPSs.

TPSs are the oldest type of information system. They were first developed in the 1950s in the accounting departments of major corporations. They have been the workhorses of the information systems industry for the last 30 years.

TPS Architecture TPSs have three major architectures: batch file processing architecture, on-line file processing architecture, and database

- Supports day-to-day operations
- Processes high volume of data
- Needs high performance (because of large amount of data)
- Has relatively simple processing logic
- Requires high degree of accuracy
- Processes data repetitively
- Supports many users
- Is vulnerable to unauthorized or criminal activity

FIGURE 12-1
Characteristics of TPSs

FIGURE 12-2
TPS Data Entry
Transaction data for a TPS is being entered through a terminal.

processing architecture. All three were described in Chapter 10. Figure 12-3 illustrates the common elements of the TPS architectures. TPS inputs consist of transaction data. Processing consists of checking the data and updating the database or master file. TPS outputs consist of updated master data, operational results, and various types of reports.

TPS Outputs The outputs obtained from a TPS are of three main types. The first type consists of updated master data. From the MIS (or whole-organization) point of view, this is the most important result. Master data may be stored in a series of separate master files or in one or more databases.

The second type of output consists of operational results, such as a paycheck from a payroll program, a customer bill from an accounts receivable program, or a warehouse packing list from an order-processing system. These may be the direct results of a transaction, such as a paycheck, or they may be instructions for operating the business, such as job orders in a manufacturing plant or stock buy and sell orders in a brokerage house.

The third type of result from a TPS consists of operational and summary reports. These reports result directly from the processing of transactions. One type, called a **detail report**, includes information about each

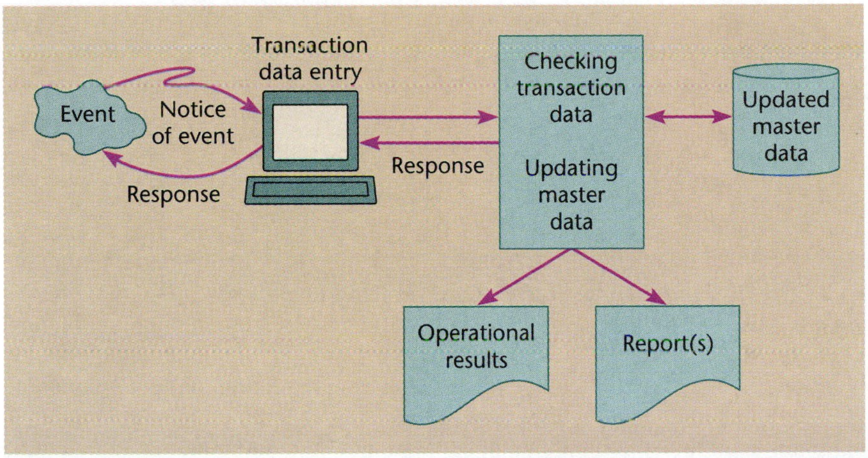

FIGURE 12-3

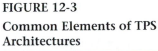

Common Elements of TPS Architectures

FIGURE 12-4

TPS Outputs
A major TPS output is comprised of reports to support operational and management control.

transaction processed. In a payroll processing system, such a report would go to the payroll inquiry desk, where employees can come and raise questions about their paychecks. The report contains an entry for each paycheck, showing hours, pay rate, gross pay, withholding for taxes and other purposes, deductions, and all other values involved in the computation of a paycheck.

Another type of TPS report is a **summary report**, showing totals and averages. A typical payroll produces several summary reports. One report, intended for crew supervisors, shows labor cost by crew. Another report, intended for plant managers, shows labor cost by plant. Yet another report, for top management, shows total labor costs for the entire company.

Sales for the Week of August 8				
SALESPERSON	HOURS WORKED	NUMBER OF SALES	DOLLAR SALES	DOLLAR SALES/HOUR
Jane Adams	40	486	$10,692	$267
Mark Baker	40	654	$16,350	$409
Michelle Johnson	20	392	$10,192	$510
Bill McIntyre	40	441	$10,143	$254

FIGURE 12-5 **Example of a Management Reporting System Report for Ticket Sales Activity**

A third type of TPS report is an **exception report**, showing results that fall outside predefined boundaries. In a production tracking system, for example, such a report would show crews who failed to make their production quotas or who exceeded the acceptable amount of overtime. A crew would be listed only when its values fell outside the predefined boundaries.

Management Reporting Systems

Management reporting systems, as the name implies, produce reports to support business management. Management reporting system reports are not concerned with day-to-day operations (the province of TPSs) but rather with the management of resources involved in operations. Such resources include labor, money, materials, equipment, and the like.

In a ticket reservations system, for example, a TPS is used to take orders and print tickets. It reports the number and value of tickets sold. A management reporting system is used to measure and report the performance of each agent who sells tickets. Such a system keeps track of the number and dollar amount of sales by each agent and regularly produces reports about agent effectiveness. An example report of this type is shown in Figure 12-5. This report is used by the sales office manager to track agent performance, identify problems, and reward exceptional sales activity.

Management reporting systems are sometimes called MISs. Thus, the term *MIS* has two very different meanings. The first meaning is broad and encompassing and refers to the general application of information systems in business. The second, much narrower meaning, is a synonym for management reporting system. In this book, we use the term *MIS* in its broad meaning, and we substitute the term *management reporting system* for its narrower meaning.

Management Reporting System Architecture Usually, management reporting system applications process data that is generated by a TPS or by some other internal information source. Figure 12-6 shows a typical management reporting system architecture. The user submits a request for a report to a management reporting system program. The program processes

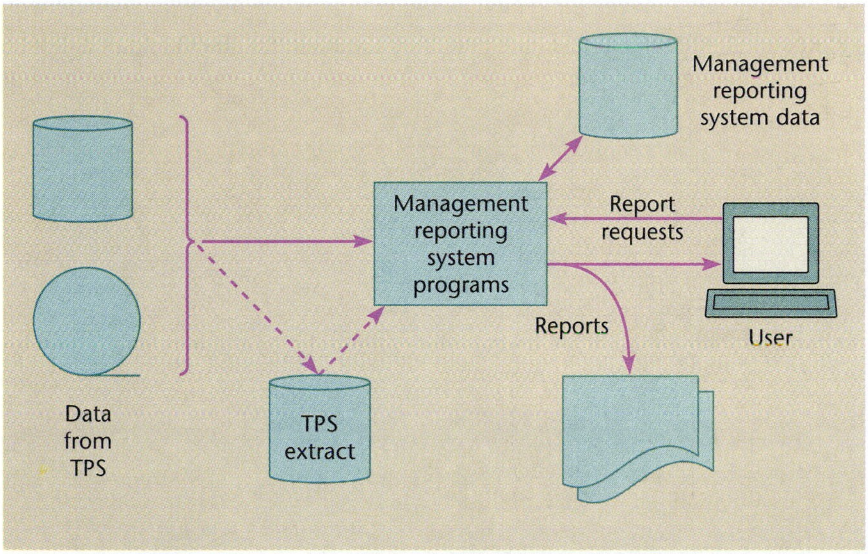

FIGURE 12-6

Architecture of a Generic Management Reporting System Application
Data created by the action of one or more TPSs is processed to produce reports that provide information for decision making.

the TPS data by aggregating and reformatting it to produce a report. The report is either printed or displayed on the user's workstation.

Reports may be automatically generated. For example, the management reporting programs may be written to produce a certain series of reports on Monday mornings, at the close of every business day, or at the end of some other period. Sometimes the management reporting application programs are written to look for exceptional conditions in the data and to produce reports if those conditions occur. A ticket agency, for example, might have a management reporting application that prints an exception report listing artist, date, and location of any concert that is not at least one-third sold out three weeks prior to the event.

In some cases, the management reporting application does not access the operational TPS data directly. Instead, an extract of the TPS data is made, and the management reporting application processes the extract. This is done for a variety of reasons—to provide security for the TPS data, to transfer data across computers when the TPS and the management reporting system operate on different machines, or to consolidate data to make the management reporting processing more efficient.

Example: Evaluating Labor Effectiveness Figure 12-7 shows the architecture of a management reporting system used for tracking labor effectiveness. Observe that this system is a special case of the general architecture shown in Figure 12-6. Data is extracted from the payroll TPS. This system, which resides on a mainframe computer, transmits data to the management reporting system application, which resides on a microcomputer. The management reporting system application processes the extracted payroll data, along with budget data that is part of the management

INCREASING YOUR PERSONAL PRODUCTIVITY

Box 12.1

EIS Moves to the Desktop

A new crop of Windows-based products allows you to view, analyze, and report on vital business data existing in a variety of formats, from IBM's DB2 in the mainframe's data bank, to Oracle on the department's file server, to Lotus 1-2-3 on your PC's hard disk. These products are called executive information systems.

An analogy to an EIS would be the Sunday newspaper section that focuses on the events of the past week. This section pulls together stories from a variety of sources, makes them understandable, and provides underlying news analysis. An EIS provides similar benefits to company managers at all levels by providing software tools that retrieve company data from many sources (mainframe, minicomputer, LAN servers, and local PCs) and present this data clearly. Unlike the static newspaper, however, EISes let you scan the data headlines, selectively "drill down" (in hypertext fashion) on a headline to see more information, combine this data with other data, and make more informed decisions based on data that is constantly being updated.

Originally intended to replace inch-thick paper reports, EISes were first designed as specialized mainframe applications, with costs starting at $100,000. But the explosive growth of PC LANs has radically altered the EIS landscape. The new realities of the marketplace have challenged the efforts of traditional EIS suppliers to keep pace. Today's EIS has specific capabilities: It can

- perform data retrieval across a wide range of platforms and data formats;
- analyze data in a variety of ways;
- graphically present the information;
- create ad hoc reports; and
- contain customized application-development tools to build an application that automatically performs routine tasks.

Getting Started

Deciding to go to EISes is not a sudden decision for most companies. Instead, it is a growing corporate-wide understanding that managers need specialized data quickly and presented in a clear, easily adjustable format. For example, a sales manager wants to be able to see data by channel and by product. Unwilling to wade through the swamp of printed reports, the manager wants to get to the bottom line as quickly as possible. In a competitive business environment, it's imperative to be able to quickly identify key business trends, data relationships, and exceptions to your plan.

Once the need is identified, other fundamental requirements for the success of an EIS include

- identifying who has a thorough familiarity with the company's data assets;
- gaining the interest, attention, and creativity of the organization that will use the system;
- management's committing to the project's success as well as to its ongoing maintenance; and
- devoting programmers to design and create the user-specific application.

reporting system, and produces reports for management regarding labor and labor effectiveness.

Figure 12-8 shows an example of the extracted data that is inputted to the management reporting system. For the sake of brevity, just a few records are shown. In a real application, there might be hundreds or thousands of such records. The data includes each employee's payroll data for the week—job code, project number, pay, and vacation and sick days taken.

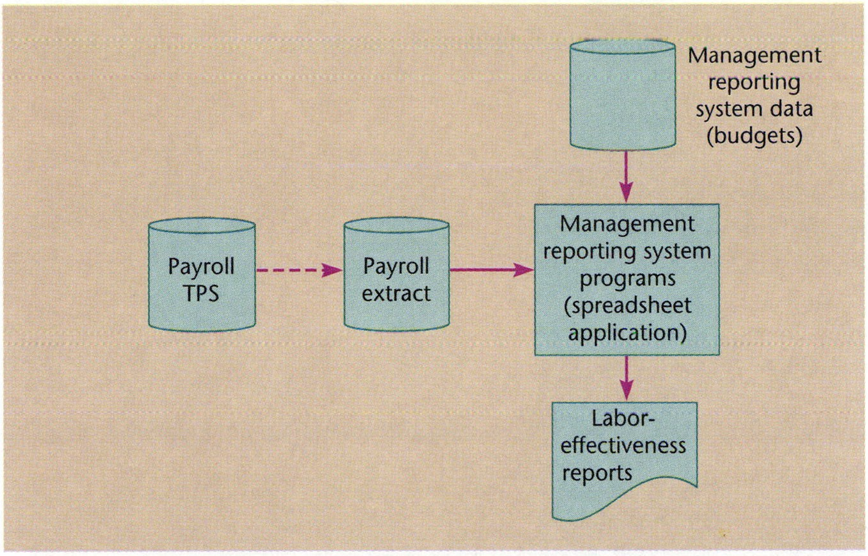

FIGURE 12-7

Architecture of Labor-Effectiveness Management Reporting System

In this system, a mainframe program extracts data from a payroll TPS and transmits it to a microcomputer, where it is combined in a spreadsheet with budgets stored in the management reporting system. The result is comprised of labor-effectiveness reports.

Hourly Payroll Data
Week of April 23, 1994

Emp#	Dept	JobCode	Project#	TotPay	VacDays	SickDays
100	Acct	1010	P1200	$1,459	0	0
200	Acct	1010	P2000	$2,099	0	2
250	Marketing	2070	P1200	$2,889	2	1
300	Marketing	2070	P1200	$3,257	0	2
400	Marketing	1010	P2000	$3,321	0	3
450	Marketing	2100	P2000	$2,765	2	0
500	Sales	2100	P1200	$2,340	0	0
550	Sales	2100	P1200	$3,550	1	0

FIGURE 12-8 Example of Payroll Data Extracted from the Payroll TPS

The management reporting system produces several standard reports, as shown in Figure 12-9. First (see Figure 12-9a) is a summary report that shows total and average payroll and total and average vacation and sick days taken. The second report (see Figure 12-9b) analyzes the data by department, job code, and project. In the third report (see Figure 12-9c), actual hourly payroll data is compared to budgeted data for each project.

A general manager of the company would find this data useful. The summary report indicates that, on average, each employee took one day

Hourly Payroll Summary Week of April 23, 1994	
Total hourly payroll	$21,680
Average paycheck	$2,710
Total vacation days	5
Average vacation days	0.625
Total sick days	8
Average sick days	1

a. Summary report

Hourly Payroll Statistics
by Department

Dept	TotPay	AvgPay	TotVac	AvgVac	TotSick	AvgSick
Acct	$3,558	$1,779	0	0	2	1
Marketing	$12,232	$3,058	4	1	6	1.5
Sales	$5,890	$2,945	1	0.5	0	0

Hourly Payroll Statistics
by Job Code

JobCode	AvgPay	AvgVac	AvgSick
1010	$2,293	1.00	1.67
2070	$3,073	1.00	1.50
2100	$2,885	1.00	0.00

Hourly Payroll Statistics
by Project

Project#	TotPay	AvgPay	AvgVac	AvgSick
P1200	$13,495	$2,699	0.60	0.60
P2000	$8,185	$2,728	0.67	1.67

b. Payroll statistics by department, job code, and project

FIGURE 12-9

Labor-Effectiveness Reports Produced by a Management Reporting System

of sick leave last week. The manager is concerned about this high rate of absenteeism and so examines the more detailed reports to see whether there is an explanation. The report showing payroll data by department indicates that an unusually high number of sick leave days was taken by employees in the marketing department. Looking further, the highest number of sick days was taken by employees with job code 1010 and on project number P2000. Using this information, the manager can then follow up to determine what factors have caused this situation.

Hourly Payroll Project Labor Dollars: Budget vs. Actual Week of April 23, 1994	Project P1200	Project P2000	Total
Week			
Budget	$12,000	$9,000	$21,000
Actual	$13,495	$8,185	$21,680
Month			
Budget	$48,000	$36,000	$84,000
Actual	$55,987	$33,787	$89,774
Year			
Budget	$107,800	$36,000	$143,800
Actual	$127,800	$33,787	$161,587

c. Labor costs: budget versus actual

Decision Support Systems

Decision support systems (DSSs) are interactive (on-line), computer-based facilities for assisting human decision making. DSSs support the solution of problems that are less structured than those of a management reporting system or a TPS. In fact, DSSs in many ways are not formalized, closed systems, but rather are a set of facilities for helping people make decisions. Often, DSSs are created to solve particular problems on an ad hoc processing basis. Thus, a DSS could be used to study unique, unstructured, and possibly one-of-a-kind problems or opportunities.

For example, suppose a strike by the musicians' union forces the cancellation of opera performances. The management of the opera association wants to know the impact on revenue of each performance cancellation and turns to its ticket agency for information. A DSS could be used to process the ticket agency's data to produce this information.

Actually, the term *decision support facility* would be more accurate than *decision support system*. A DSS is not a structured, finished system as is a TPS or a management reporting system. Rather, it is a collection of data and processing tools used creatively to manipulate data to answer unknown and often unexpected questions. Also, the users of a DSS often do not have the assistance of professional information systems personnel. Instead, they employ the tools on their own.

DSSs involve models of business activity. DSS models often are complex and dynamic. The DSS user frequently changes the models to adapt them to changing understandings and needs. For example, the ticket agency may have a series of equations that predicts ticket sales on the basis of type of performance, day of the week, time of the year, and so forth. As the musicians' strike progresses, the DSS users may add to or otherwise modify these equations to produce information that is important for negotiating a resolution to the strike. These models become part of the DSS stored data.

DSS Architecture Figure 12-10 shows the architecture of a DSS. Data from the organization's TPS and management reporting applications is inputted to the DSS programs, along with data from external sources, such as independent data utilities. The DSS may store and later reprocess its own model data as well. The user interacts with the DSS on-line, making requests, creating or adjusting models, manipulating data, and so forth. DSS program output can be text, structured reports, or graphics.

A variety of programs support the DSS, including spreadsheet programs, DBMSs, word processing packages, graphics generators, statistical packages, and other special-purpose programs.

DSS Types We will consider four different types of DSS in this section: financial-modeling applications, database query applications, expert system applications, and group DDSs.

Financial-Modeling Applications Probably the most common type of DSS involves the use of **financial models** and other types of business models. The applications most frequently involve the use of electronic spreadsheets. In these applications, TPS, management reporting system, and external data is input to spreadsheet models. Such models are composed of a series of equations that relate outputs to values of input data.

For example, one company has a model containing equations that predict sales based on number of salespeople, dollars spent on advertising,

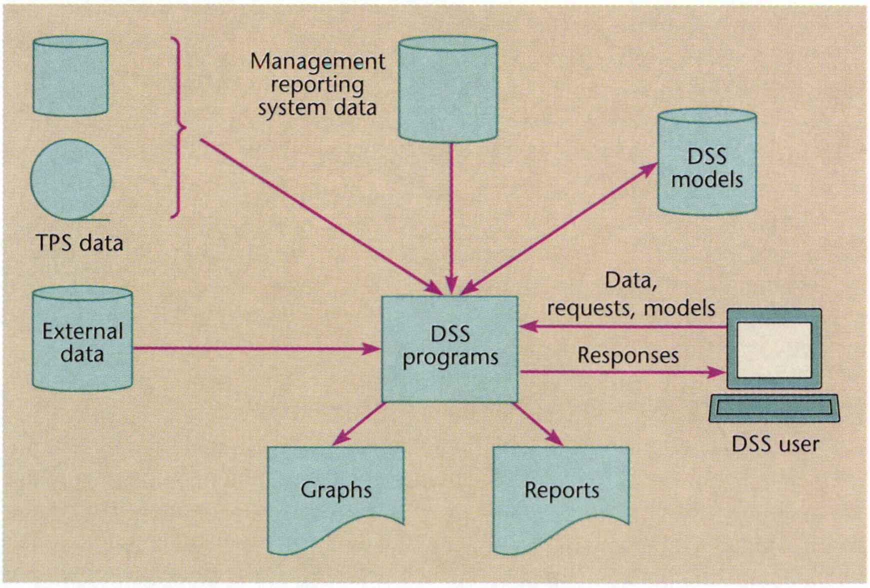

FIGURE 12-10

Architecture of a Generic DSS Application
DSS programs draw data from TPS data, management reporting system data, DSS models, and external sources. They process interactively in response to entries from a user. They produce screen and printed reports and graphs.

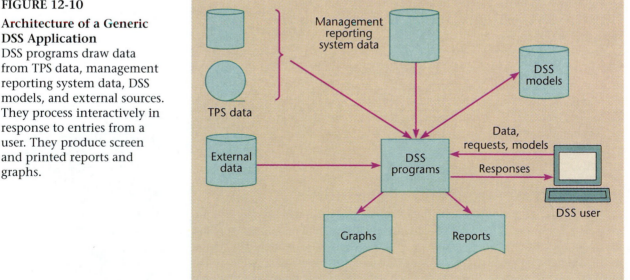

Number of Salespeople	Advertising Budget (Millions of $)	Assumed Market Size	Projected Sales (Millions of $)
50	1.3	100,000	22
50	1.7	100,000	27
75	1.7	200,000	35
75	2.0	200,000	38
100	2.0	300,000	41
100	2.5	300,000	49

FIGURE 12-11
Results from a What-If Analysis

and size of the market. These equations were developed by analyzing TPS data from past periods. Using the equations, the decision makers vary the inputs (number of salespeople, dollars spent on advertising, and assumed size of market) and obtain various sales projections. Figure 12-11 shows several examples. Such an analysis is sometimes called a what-if analysis because it shows what is expected to occur if different courses of action are taken.

Database Queries **Database query applications** involve the ad hoc querying of databases. These databases may contain TPS data, management reporting system data, external data, or some combination thereof. The decision maker processes the data using a query language. A standard query language used with DBMSs on systems of all sizes is SQL, or structured query language.

Expert Systems An **expert system** is a computer-based system in which knowledge about some problem domain is represented in data and is processed systematically to make a diagnosis, make a recommendation, create a design, or produce some similar output. Figure 12-12 lists some kinds of activities that are addressed by expert systems.

An expert system has a limited scope of expertise. For example, expert systems might give advice on certain problems in processing an insurance claim or give advice on problems that arise in the installation of a certain computer software package.

For example, a steel manufacturer has developed an expert system to diagnose potential causes of imperfections in molten steel. In the production of high-quality steel, materials must be carefully blended at certain temperatures for specific periods of time. Sometimes the process goes awry. Often, when this occurs, the batch can be saved if the appropriate corrective action is taken in time. This company's expert system lets production workers enter data that describes the problem, and the expert system identifies possible causes and suggests courses of action.

- Procedures
- Diagnoses
- Monitoring
- Configuration and design
- Scheduling and planning

FIGURE 12-12
Types of Problems Addressed by Expert Systems

Group Decision Support Systems **Group decision support systems (GDSSs)** let people process, produce, and interpret information together as a group. These systems are an extension of the group conferencing systems described earlier. If the group meets in a single location, members sitting at

FIGURE 12-13
GDSS Facility
The University of Arizona's Decision Planning Lab is an example of a GDSS. (Courtesy of Karl Eller, Graduate School of Management, College of Business and Public Administration, The University of Arizona. Photo by Steven Meckler.)

PCs in the room can observe group proceedings on a shared central display screen while creating information privately on their own PCs (see Figure 12-13). If members are geographically dispersed, their computers are connected via communications lines.

Example: Controlling Quality Suppose a quality control analyst is attempting to determine the cause of a large number of rejected products. Assume the analyst is able to obtain two tables of data from TPSs. Sample data is shown in Figure 12-14. The analyst is uncertain about the cause of the high number of rejects. First she wonders whether it might be due to an overzealous inspector. Using a DBMS, she issues a query. The result is shown in Figure 12-15a. The analyst decides that differences among inspectors do not appear significant.

Next, she considers the possibility that there was a problem with one or more production batches. To study that, she issues another, similar query command that produces the data shown in Figure 12-15b. Examining this data, the analyst decides that some batches seem to have much higher reject percentages than others.

She now decides to determine when and where the batches with the highest reject rates were produced. She issues a third query and obtains the results shown in Figure 12-15c. At this point, the analyst has determined that batches produced at a particular plant (building A) on a particular day (04/23/94) have been the source of most of the problem.

PROD-QUAL TABLE

Product#	Batch#	Inspector	Reject%
100	1000	Jones	2.30
101	1500	Jones	15.70
102	2000	Parks	3.05
104	1500	Smith	15.00
105	1500	Parks	17.50
106	1000	Parks	3.40
107	2000	Smith	2.20
108	1700	Jones	12.40

BATCH-PROD TABLE

Batch#	Date	PlantLocation
1500	04/23/94	Bldg A
1000	04/23/94	Bldg B
1700	04/23/94	Bldg A
2000	04/25/94	Bldg B

FIGURE 12-14
Example Quality Control Data

FIGURE 12-15
Results from Database Query

Inspector	Average Reject %
Jones	10.13
Smith	8.60
Parks	7.98

a. Average reject percentage by inspector

Batch#	Average Reject %
1000	2.85
1500	16.07
1700	12.40
2000	2.63

b. Average reject percentage by batch number

Batch#	Date	PlantLocation	Reject%
1000	04/23/94	Bldg B	2.85
1500	04/23/94	Bldg A	16.07
1700	04/23/94	Bldg A	12.40
2000	04/25/94	Bldg B	2.63

c. Batch, date, and location reject percentages

The DSS played a supporting role in identifying the source of this problem. The DSS did not solve the problem, but it provided a facility to identify the source of the problem.

Communication Support Systems

Communication support systems use computers to assist in human communication throughout the organization. The systems are used by people engaged in all kinds of communication activities throughout the organization. Communication support systems are not a single system, but rather a set of capabilities that an organization provides to most users. Communication support systems are often, but not always, provided on PCs. The widely used communication support systems are word processing, graphics, DTP, E-mail, and electronic conferencing systems.

Word Processing The first communication support systems were word processing systems used by secretaries and typists to automate traditional clerical tasks. Two decades ago, each manager was typically supported by a secretary and several clerical workers whose primary task was the production of correspondence, reports, and other documents. Recently, more powerful hardware and software has made it possible for businesspeople to produce their own correspondence with little or no human clerical assistance. Today, instead of secretaries, managers typically have administrative assistants who are specialists in business problems rather than in communication.

Graphics Managers in many companies also produce their own slides and graphs for presentations. Projected slides or transparencies like the one in Figure 12-16 are now nearly universally used during oral presenta-

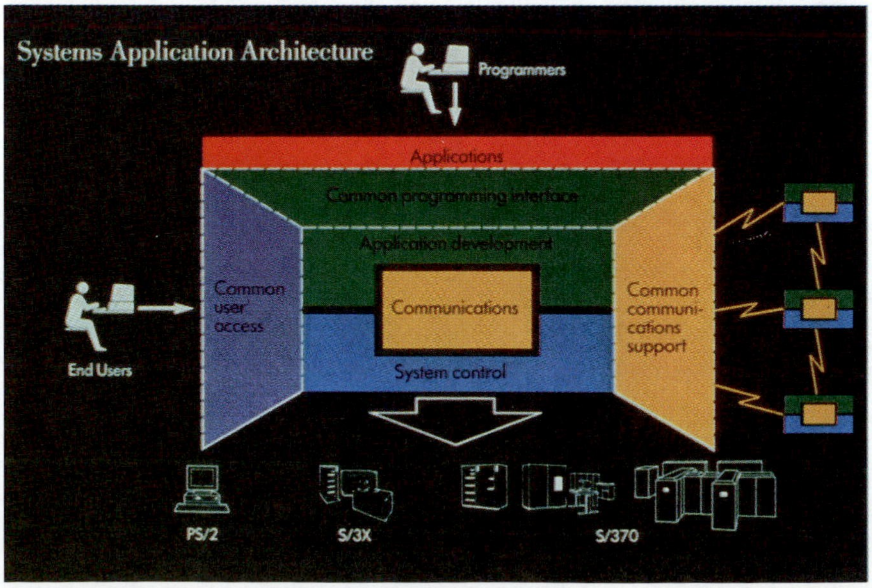

FIGURE 12-16
Slide for a Presentation
Slides like this one can be created using presentation graphics applications and printed in color on transparency masters for projection during presentations. Such technology is no longer prohibitively expensive.

tions. Slides focus audience attention and increase communication effectiveness. A few years ago, each slide would have been developed by a graphic artist at great expense—or it would have been crudely hand-drawn in crayon on a large, paper flip chart. Today, presentation graphics applications let the user develop professional-looking materials easily and quickly. For example, word charts like the one in Figure 12-17 can be created by an experienced user in only minutes.

Desktop Publishing Similarly, some managers produce newsletters, leaflets, and brochures by DTP. However, because DTP programs and the associated graphic techniques are time-consuming to learn, DTP programs are often used by specialists with graphics knowledge. Managers who need DTP services prepare text and art, and the specialists use these in creating publications. With DTP and other computer support, specialists can work more efficiently than they could previously.

E-Mail E-mail has replaced telephoning for many purposes. Many telephone messages involve a single, simple question with a simple answer. For example, "Johnson-Wells has made an offer of $34,800 on the Alexandria project. I think that is the best we'll get. Should I accept it?" To ask a busy executive this question by telephone could take 30 to 40 minutes of a subordinate's time: dialing, finding that the executive is in a meeting, leaving a message to return the call, missing the return call because the subordinate is in a meeting, calling back, and so on. (This is called *telephone tag.*) When the two finally connect, they do not just ask the question and get an answer. They feel more comfortable visiting and chatting a bit. So the call may take three or four minutes. E-mail is much more efficient.

E-mail lets you draft the message when you have time, and it is then available whenever the executive has time to answer it. Since a tradition

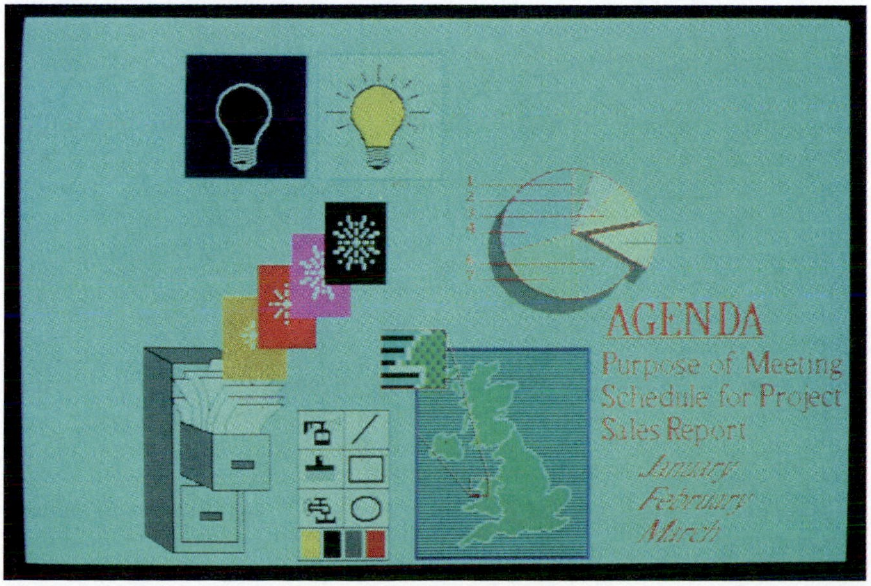

FIGURE 12-17

Word Chart

Word charts display a series of concepts or topics, like the agenda for this meeting or the key points in a presentation.

of answering E-mail at least twice a day usually quickly arises, turnaround time is typically less than four hours. E-mail messages are usually short, simple, and right to the point, so they do not take very long to draft.

Electronic Conferencing The **electronic conference** is a specialized kind of file sharing. In group conferencing systems, which have already been described, participants meet with computer support at the same time. By contrast, in electronic conferencing, members need not participate at the same time. Participants post messages on the agreed topic, much like E-mail, except that the messages are shared by all participants. Rather than sit down together in a room, participants read the common file of messages two or three times a day when they each have time. One person may post a message suggesting an idea. Others may respond over the next few hours, each seeing the accumulated messages that arrived before. When issues need not be resolved immediately, electronic conferencing can be as effective as many face-to-face meetings.

Public electronic conference systems are called **electronic bulletin boards**. To participate, people dial in by modem, read the accumulated messages on the topics they select, leave messages, and so on. Bulletin boards often offer free programs and data files for downloading.

Some bulletin board–like systems are national or international in scope. For example, Prodigy, CompuServe, and America Online offer conferencing systems called **forums**, nationwide E-mail service, and access to information resources such as airline reservations systems and electronic encyclopedias. Some charge a flat monthly fee. Others charge for individual services.

Students with university E-mail access often can use international E-mail systems such as the Internet and Bitnet. These systems provide E-mail, electronic conferencing, and access to shared files to users throughout the world. Users of these systems have traditionally been computer enthusiasts, so their user interface is often fairly technical.

Executive Support Systems

Executive support systems (ESSs), sometimes called **executive information systems (EISs)**, support the information needs of senior executives. ESSs present highly summarized data. They usually produce reports in standard formats, and they often involve graphics. In many cases, the most expensive color monitors with the highest resolution and clarity are used, as are the best plotters and color printers. For example, the executive may select from menu choices by double-clicking: Stock Price, Sales, Revenues, Production, and so on. The result may be a large, color wall-screen display with several graphs showing absolutely current figures for the chosen subject.

ESS Architecture Figure 12-19 shows the generic architecture of an ESS application. The ESS accepts data from all the other types of information systems. It also accepts inputs from those who support the executive, such as administrative assistants. As you can see, the primary goal of an ESS is

FIGURE 12-18
ESS
This ESS provides the current status of the organization's key variables.

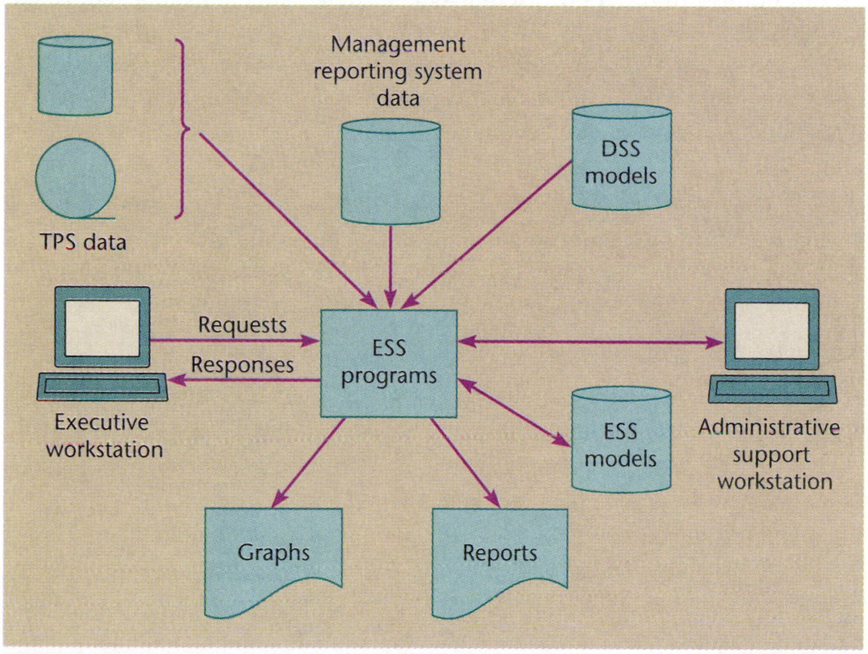

FIGURE 12-19
Architecture of a Generic ESS Application
In response to requests from the user, an ESS program gathers data from a variety of sources for presentation.

to obtain data from a variety of sources, integrate and aggregate the data, and display the resulting information in an easy-to-use, comprehensible, attractive format.

ESSs are the newest of the system types. To date, they have had limited acceptance, partly because most executives started their careers before the widespread use of computer-based information systems. They did not study information systems in college, and they are reluctant users. Many, in fact, still consider using a keyboard to be secretarial work. Furthermore, most executives have a staff of assistants who can produce written reports when information is needed.

This situation is changing, and, during your career, computer-experienced business professionals will rise to senior executive positions. They will expect useful support from computer-based systems.

The five elements of an MIS share a common purpose: to make the organization more competitive. As you read the next section, consider how an MIS can give a competitive advantage.

MIS FOR COMPETITIVE ADVANTAGE

MIS, as you recall, is the development and use of effective information systems in organizations. A large organization, such as IBM or General Motors, includes literally thousands of information systems of all kinds. To understand all the benefits of MISs, we must simplify by categorizing them.

Goals of MIS

Figure 12-20 shows the kinds of benefits that an organization should expect from an MIS. Strategic planning is the long-term planning done by an organization's upper management. It includes defining the organization's goals, designing the organization itself to meet those goals, determining major lines of products or services, and so on. Strategic planning involves a time span of years and decades. An MIS supports strategic planning.

Management control provides resources to meet the organization's goals: money, people, machines, and so on. Management control plans budgets with time spans of a month, a quarter, and a year. An MIS supports management control.

Operational control deals with the day-to-day problems of operating the business. Its key issues are getting today's work done, collecting and paying out money, and planning tomorrow's work. Its time spans are hours and days. An MIS supports operational control.

Types of Problems

An MIS deals with three types of problems: structured, unstructured, and semistructured. A **structured problem** can be solved by a known method using fully available data. For example, the method of computing an employee's paycheck can be specified as a series of mathematical operations on data that is available.

FIGURE 12-20
Benefits Expected from an MIS

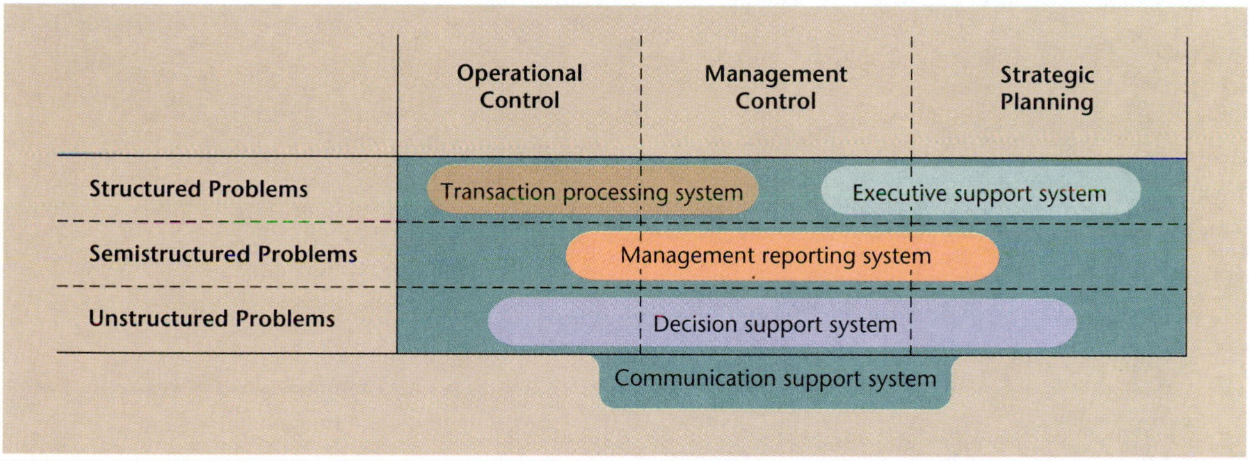

FIGURE 12-21
Uses of the Elements of an MIS

An **unstructured problem** is one in which the method of arriving at a solution is not known in advance and the applicable data is not all available. For example, the problem of determining the effects of governmental regulations on a company's business five years in the future is unstructured. Various sources of data must be identified on an ad hoc basis, and experts probably will disagree on the appropriate calculations to solve the problem.

Semistructured problems have characteristics of both structured problems and unstructured problems. That is, some aspects of semistructured problems can be solved by known methods using available data and other aspects cannot. Determining the cause of quality problems in a manufacturing plant is an example. Figure 12-21 shows how the major components of an MIS support strategic planning, management control, and operational control to solve structured, unstructured, and semistructured problems.

Strategic planning, management control, and operational control are internal applications of MIS support. An MIS also benefits the organization externally, by improving its products. It provides both improved product quality and improved product delivery.

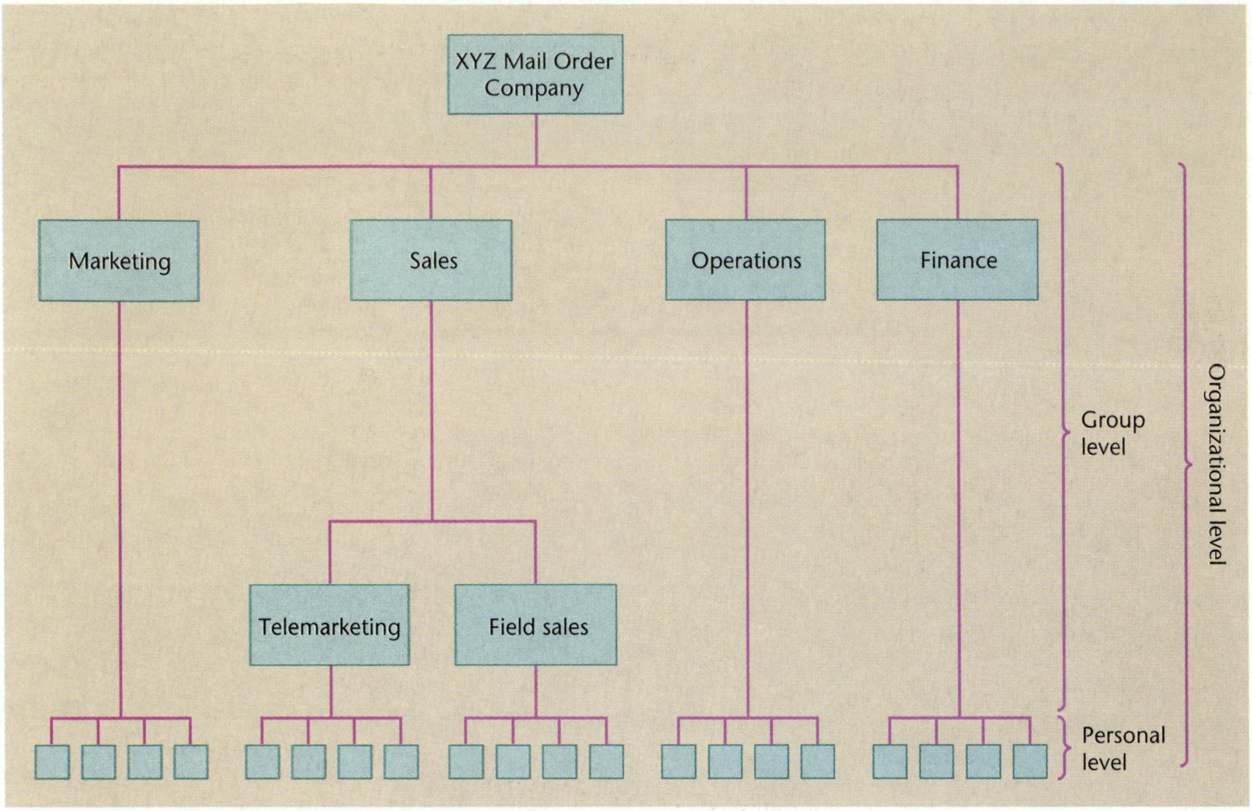

FIGURE 12-22
Three Levels of Information Systems

Levels of Information Systems

Figure 12-22 shows a portion of an organizational chart for XYZ mail order company, with four major departments: marketing, sales, operations, and finance. It is divided into three levels: organizational, group, and personal.

Organizational Systems The XYZ revenue generation system operates at the organizational level to track and report on every activity that affects the company's finances. As a result, all departments use this system (see Figure 12-23a).

Group Systems Look again at Figure 12-22. Within the sales department, the telemarketing group operates at the group level. This group calls prospective customers on a rotating basis and tries to contact every active customer at least once per quarter. The actions of telemarketing representatives need to be coordinated. While the group does not want to miss any customers, neither does it want to duplicate calls. Furthermore, some calls require follow-up. The telemarketing group does not want to drop the ball even if the particular representative who promised to follow up is not working at the appointed time.

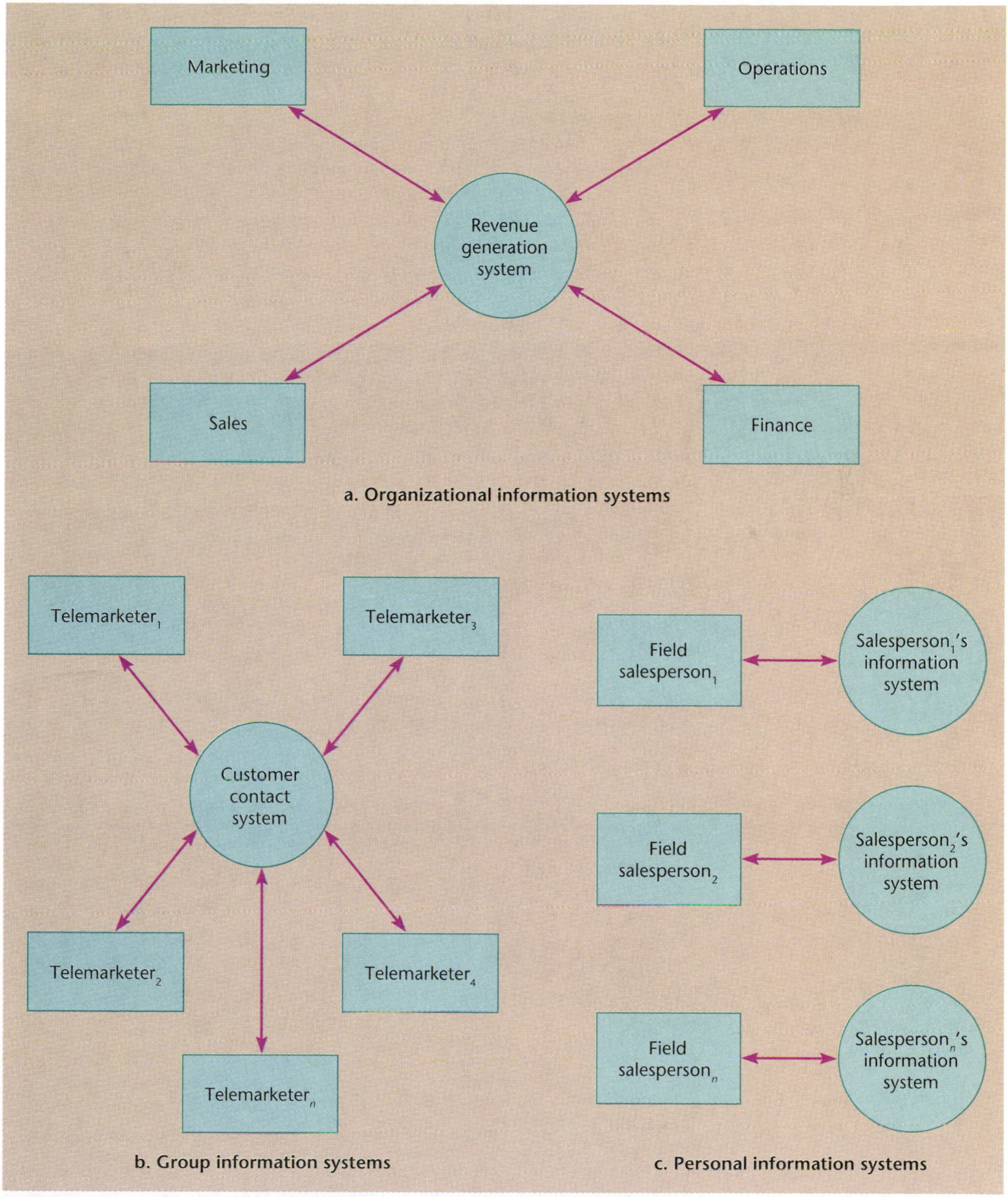

FIGURE 12-23 Systems in XYZ Mail Order Company

To meet these needs, the telemarketing group has developed a group information system (see Figure 12-23b). This system maintains a file of customers and assigns customers to representatives on a rotating basis. It also keeps track of the need for follow-up calls and assigns these calls to representatives.

Just as the organizational system coordinates the activities of the individual departments, so, too, does the group system coordinate the activities of the individual sales representatives within the department.

Personal Systems In addition to the telemarketing group, the XYZ company employs a field sales force (Figure 12-22). Field salespeople are each assigned a particular territory, and they operate independently. Salespeople are paid on commission. They want the highest productivity, making the most sales in the shortest time.

Salespeople can use personal information systems to gain higher productivity. Each salesperson can have his or her own system: The systems do not interface with one another (see Figure 12-23c). For example, a salesperson could use a mail merge word processing system to generate personalized form letters and to prequalify customers. Or, the salesperson could keep track of sales calls and resulting sales to determine which customers are the most responsive. Or, the salesperson could use an information system to identify potential contacts, and so forth. These are all uses of personal information systems.

Benefits at Each Level

Figure 12-24 provides a framework for considering the benefits of an MIS at all three levels of the organization. The benefits apply not only to the organization as a whole but also to the other two levels.

FIGURE 12-24

Benefits of MIS at Each Organizational Level

	Level		
	ORGANIZATIONAL	GROUP	PERSONAL
Support for Strategic Planning			
Support for Management Control			
Support for Operational Control			
Improved Product Quality			
Improved Product Delivery			

Consider a department. Departments are groups that must manage and coordinate operations and plan for the future. Information systems can facilitate both activities. Departments also have products. The product of the accounts receivable department, for example, is collections. Information systems can be used to improve the product by identifying who owes what amount, how long they have owed it, and how their current payment pattern differs from their payment history. Information systems also can be used to improve the delivery of the product by providing the information when it is needed to make collection calls.

Now consider the benefits of information systems to individual employees. Individuals do long-term strategic planning, manage resources, and control day-to-day activities, just as organizations and departments do. For example, the salesperson plans sales strategies in the long term. The salesperson manages resources such as transportation, telephone access, and printed sales materials. And the salesperson controls day-to-day operations: selecting specific customers for sales calls, following up sales calls, and so on. The individual also has a product. The salesperson's product consists of sales calls, follow-up calls, and sales letters. Personal information systems can support all these activities.

Thus, the table shown in Figure 12-24 provides a framework for thinking about the role and the potential benefits of information systems at all three levels of organization. Whether you are considering an information system for an individual, for a workgroup (either a group or a department), or for the entire organization, you can use this framework to help you understand and organize the benefits of the potential system. Also, when wondering if an information system is appropriate for a situation, you should consider the types of benefits shown here.

MANAGEMENT OF INFORMATION SYSTEMS

This section considers the management of information systems and the acquisition and use of information technology.

Both system users and information systems professionals have a role in the management of information systems. We will begin by examining the organization of the MIS department, the department that specializes in information systems. Then we will consider the organization of an information center. Finally we will discuss the role of end users in the management of information systems.

MIS Department

The MIS department is responsible for the development, maintenance, and security of the information systems. The organization of the MIS department is important to you for two reasons. First, you may decide on an information systems career. If so, many of the jobs that you might want are

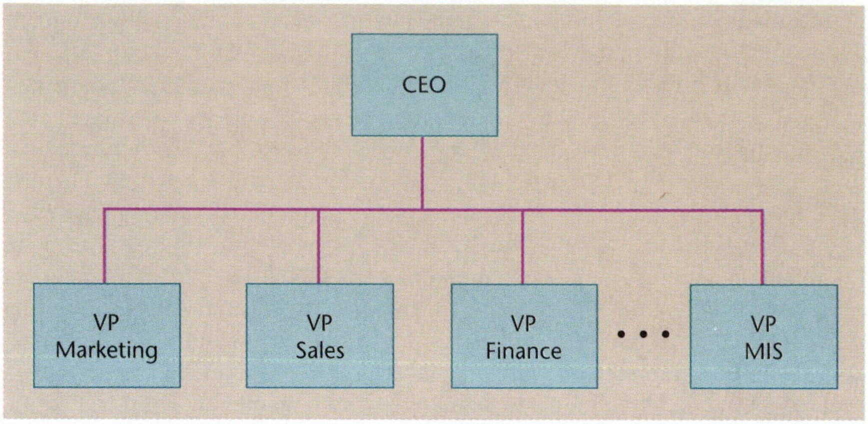

FIGURE 12-25
High-Level Corporate Organization

located in this department. Second, you need to know about the organization of the MIS department so that, as an end user, you can be an effective consumer of that department's services and resources.

Organizational Placement Figure 12-25 shows a high-level organizational chart of a typical corporation. User departments are supported by the MIS (or information services or information technology) department. As shown in this figure, the vice president (VP) of the MIS department reports directly to the CEO. This arrangement reflects the importance of information and information systems in business.

In the past, the MIS department often reported to the VP of the finance department. (Early business computer systems were nearly completely financial.) This structure eventually proved to be unworkable, primarily because organizations need other information systems besides those of concern to the finance department. The organization in Figure 12-25 enables the MIS department to serve the needs of the overall organization as opposed to the needs of the finance, or any other, department alone.

Role of the MIS Department The MIS department is the organization's primary source of information technology and is responsible for ensuring that the organization uses such technology well to accomplish its goals and objectives. That responsibility breaks into two major functions. The first function is to develop, operate, maintain, and manage organizational information systems. The second function is to acquire technology and to help end users apply it appropriately.

Today, the organization of MIS departments recognizes these dual roles. Consider Figure 12-26, which shows the organizational chart of a typical MIS department for a large corporation. This organization has two major divisions. The data processing division develops and operates the organizational information systems. The end user support division helps end users apply computer technology for personal and workgroup information systems. We will consider each of these divisions in turn.

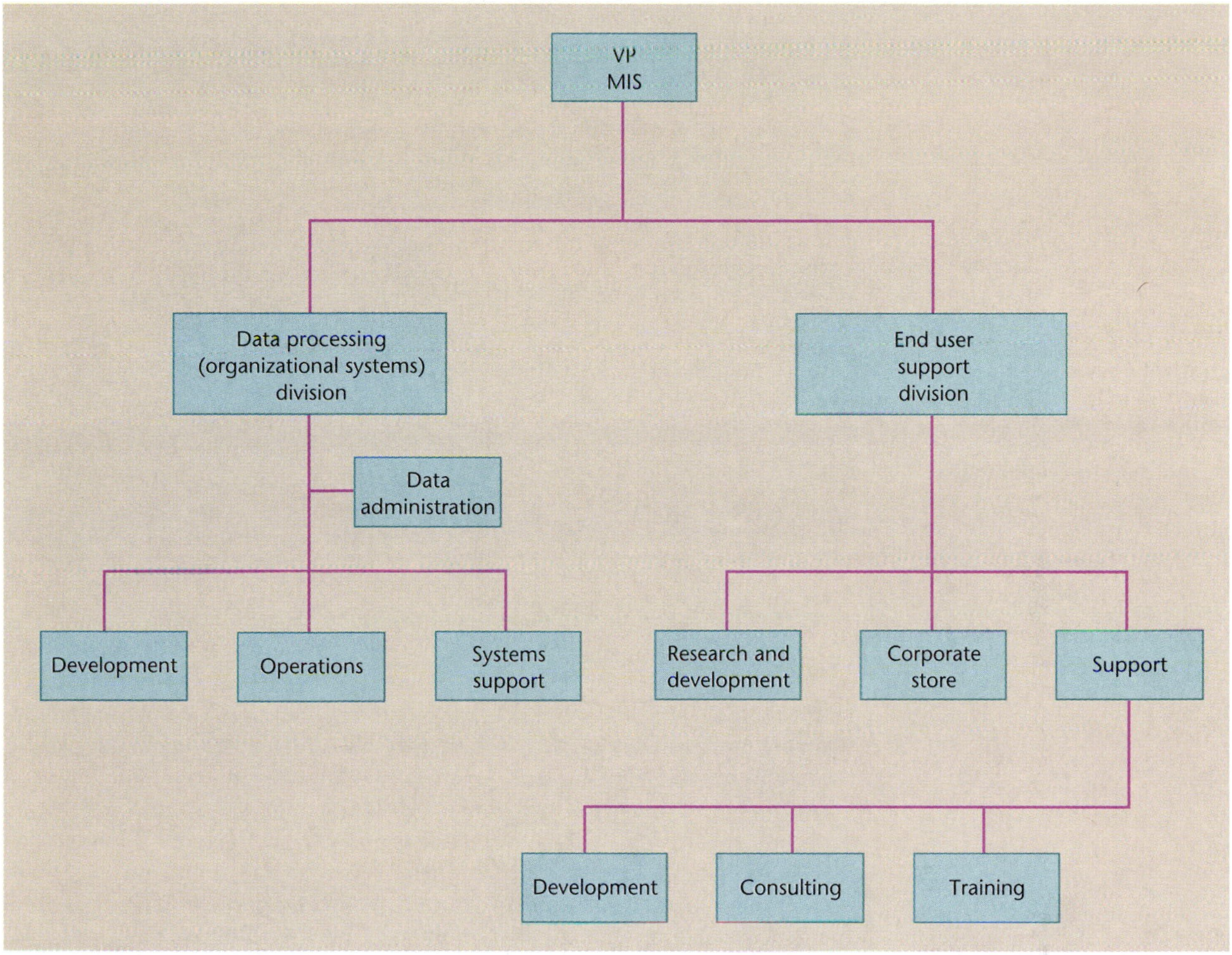

FIGURE 12-26

Organization of a Large Corporate MIS Department

Data Processing Division The **data processing (DP) division**, or as it is sometimes called, the organizational systems division, has the responsibility for developing, operating, and maintaining organizational information systems. As shown in Figure 12-26, this division normally has a development group, an operations group, and a systems support group. Then, too, there is generally a data administration group that provides a staff function to the DP director.

The **development group** consists of systems analysts and programmers who work with users to create organizational information systems. Normally, a senior systems analyst is the leader of a systems development project, though in some cases, a senior end user is the leader.

The systems analysts guide the project through all five of the stages described in Chapter 11. Systems analysts are responsible for ensuring that all five components of an information system are properly developed.

Programming personnel, on the other hand, are concerned only with the program components and possibly with data and hardware as they

FIGURE 12-27
Computer Operations
The operations group includes computer operators, data control clerks, and others.

relate to programs. As you know, application programs can be purchased from a vendor or they can be written in-house. If they are written in-house, there will most likely be a team of from two or three to several dozen programmers creating the programs. Systems analysts and application programmers normally have degrees in information systems.

In addition to creating the system, the development group typically is responsible for maintaining the system. The term maintenance refers to the process of changing the system to meet new requirements, or to make the system do what the users really wanted to begin with. In some organizations, more people and resources are used for system maintenance than for system creation.

The **operations group** runs the computer hardware. This group normally consists of several shifts of computer operators. It may also include a data entry group if the organization requires one, and several data control clerks who control the receipt and disbursement of data to and from the data center. The operations group normally manages the tape or other data library as well, and sometimes it includes a hardware maintenance group.

The **systems support group** consists of highly technical programmers who select, install, tune, and maintain systems software. This software includes operating system, CCP and other teleprocessing software, DBMS, systems utilities, and other programs. Normally, the members of this group are very talented, skillful programmers.

All shared data systems require data administration. For group or departmental systems, administration normally takes place from within the group. For systems that span several departments, this arrangement is unworkable. For these systems, data administration is performed by the MIS department.

INCREASING YOUR PERSONAL PRODUCTIVITY

Box 12.2

MIS Ethics 101: Ethical Issues for the '90s

The following questions take into account the rise of local area networks and electronic-mail privacy factors, software copyright battles, and intellectual property disputes. How would you or your future employer respond to these ethical issues?

1. Does your company have an official, stated ethics policy regarding any of the following technologies or technology issues?
    - Electronic-mail
    - Software licenses
    - Hardware access
    - Intellectual property ownership
    - Software copyrights
    - File access
    - Data ownership
2. Do you believe companies have the right to monitor their employee's electronic mail?
3. Do you believe employees should be notified if their electronic correspondence is being monitored?
4. Do you feel it is right or wrong for managers to have overriding access to their subordinates' files or queues?
5. Do you believe employees should be notified when such access exists?
6. Should IS managers be held accountable for licensing violations by their subordinates?
7. Should IS managers be held responsible for the existence of stolen competitive data?
8. Have you ever had to dismiss or punish (or known of someone who was dismissed or punished) for any of the following infractions?
    - Illegal distribution of software beyond license
    - Illegal acquisition of software
    - Wrongful acquisition of data
    - Violating electronic mail or file privacy
    - Any other illegal or unethical reasons
9. Do you think the creation of a code of ethics for IS professionals is a worthwhile endeavor? Why or why not?

Figure 12-26 shows the **data administration group** as a staff function under the DP director. This group acts as custodian or trustee of the organization's data. Its functions include establishing data conventions and standards, managing the configuration of organizational databases, ensuring that adequate backup and recovery procedures exist and are followed, ensuring that adequate security controls and procedures exist, and performing any other tasks needed to protect the organization's data assets.

Data conventions and standards are required for data consistency. Although there may be many views of data and data may occur in many different systems, the organization needs a standard set of data definitions and formats. Consider, for example, a product number. The organization needs to have one standard set of product numbers with one standard set of meanings. If several different product-numbering schemes are allowed to develop, chaos will result. One department or function will be unable to communicate with another. Sometimes it is not possible to gain consistency. In these cases, the inconsistencies should be defined and documented.

Organizations are dynamic. They change in response to both external and internal stimuli. As they change, it is often necessary to alter the structure of organizational databases. Since such databases are shared, however, this change must be accomplished to minimize the consequences on other systems and applications.

End User Support Division The purpose of the **end user support division** is to help end users employ computer technology to solve their own problems. Whereas the DP division creates, maintains, and operates systems for users, the end user support division helps end users help themselves to create and operate both personal applications and group applications.

You learned in Chapter 7 that end users can develop many of their own personal information systems. It is less likely, however, that they will develop their own departmental or other group systems. For such systems, end users typically obtain the support of an outside consultant or a professional within the MIS department. If the former approach is taken, then the end user support division will often help in selecting such a person or company. If the latter approach is taken, then normally someone from the end user support department provides development expertise and, when necessary, personnel from the development group in the DP division get involved.

End user support divisions are organized in many different ways. The organization shown in Figure 12-26 is one arrangement. You may encounter others. Here, there is a group doing research and development. The function of this group is to keep pace with the rapid growth in technology, products, and services available from the microcomputer and end user support industries. This group typically evaluates new releases and new products and determines whether they offer potential benefits to the company. The group also has a crucial role in setting organizational standards.

Many MIS departments operate their own company microcomputer store. Large companies are often able to negotiate dealer status with many vendors. The advantage of this is that the MIS department is then able to buy products at the same price as dealers can. Large companies might buy as many copies of, say, a spreadsheet program, as a small dealer would. Since this is the case, they want the same price breaks that a dealer gets.

The third group shown in Figure 12-26 is the support group. This group provides consulting and training services to end users. It may also provide a limited amount of development service. For example, an accounts payable department may be able to get along perfectly well with the standard features of a spreadsheet program for all but 5 percent of its work load. For that 5 percent, however, personnel in the department need specialized programs or macros. Rather than involving DP development personnel, many companies use personnel in the end user support group to provide this service. Custom development is generally restricted to a few hours or workdays of labor.

Information Center

The character of DSS applications is considerably different from that of other information systems. Because of this, some companies have a special DSS support organization. This organization is often called an **information center.**

An information center provides facilities to support the development, operation, and maintenance of DSS applications. Such a department may operate its own minicomputer or mainframe computer, or it may support users in acquiring their own hardware resources. Additionally, information centers provide DSS programs and libraries both of models and of other DSS data. Such centers also provide a professional staff.

The staff in an information center is analogous to the staff in an organizational MIS department. There are personnel involved in supporting DSS operations, others for developing and supporting programs, and still others for data administration. There are also consultants who assist users in the utilization of the information center's resources.

MIS Department in Smaller Companies

The organization shown in Figure 12-26 is typical for large corporations. For smaller companies, some of these functions will be combined, as shown in Figure 12-28. For example, in the DP division, the data administration and systems support functions may be performed by one group. For reasons of control, however, it is never a good idea to combine the operations and development groups.

In the end user support division, smaller companies do not operate their own computer store. Further, the research and development group may be combined with the support group. In very small organizations, the functions of the entire end user support division may be performed by the

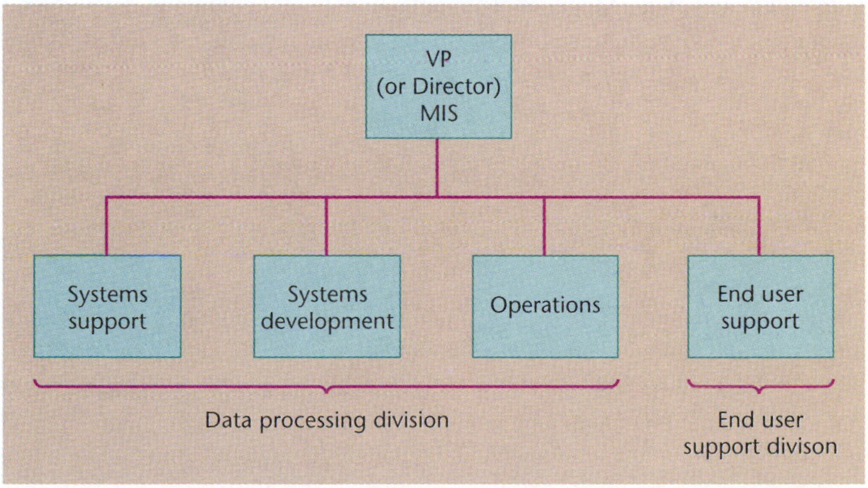

FIGURE 12-28
Organization of an MIS Department in a Smaller Company

development group in the DP division. In this case, the MIS department and the DP division become one and the same.

End User Computing

In addition to the important role of the MIS department, users also play a part in MIS management. Although this text may sometimes imply that users are all alike, that is certainly not so. Users differ in education, experience, job title, job level, and interest in and desire to learn about information technology. Consequently, users differ in the amounts of training, documentation, and other support that they need.

Additionally, users' attitudes about information systems vary considerably. Some users do not care about the role of the information systems, whereas others want to understand how each component relates to the others. Some users want to be taught only how to perform a particular function. Others are constantly searching for unknown features, functions, or capabilities.

Over time, some users get so interested in computer technology that co-workers will come to recognize that person's special skills and knowledge and will bring new, difficult, or anomalous situations to that person's attention. Over time, such a person becomes an informal, internal systems consultant and manager. Some organizations recognize these users by names such as key user, information systems liaison, or power user. Here, we will employ the term *key user*.

A **key user** is a person who holds a job in an end user department—say, accounting—and who, because of an interest in computers and information systems, has gained specialized expertise. This person becomes a local broker of information systems knowledge. Other end users go to this person when they have problems or need help.

With the development of departmental LANs, a key user may become a LAN manager. This is a professional information systems position, even though the person works in a user department. Downsizing and line MIS, described below, will create additional positions for information systems specialists who are employed in user departments. Such positions will become more and more common over the coming decade.

ETHICS

The ethical issues that arise in the use of computers are similar to ethical issues in any business activity. However, the ethical issues in computing are complicated by the fact that computers let people do unethical things faster and more conveniently than otherwise. In addition, computers let people do things that were too difficult or costly to be done manually. Before computers, for example, it was simply impractical to compile and access large databases of information about individuals, so the ethical questions of the right to privacy inherent in such databases did not arise.

An action is unethical if it causes unnecessary harm to another person or has the potential to do so. Some guidelines for ethical behavior are suggested by Ernest Kallman and John Grillo in *Ethical Decision Making and Information Technology: An Introduction with Cases* (McGraw-Hill, Inc., 1993).

1. Is the action consistent with corporate policy? Companies often provide guidelines to individual action in the form of policies.
2. Does the action violate corporate or professional codes of conduct or ethics? Such codes are often quite specific and can be very helpful as guides for individual conduct. For example, Figure 12-29 is a code adopted by a professional organization of computer users and developers.
3. Does the action violate the Golden Rule? Are you treating others the way you would wish them to treat you?
4. Does the action serve the majority rather than a minority or even only yourself? Generally, serving the common good is deemed a more desirable outcome than serving a few people or even one individual.

Key ethical issues in relation to business information systems activities are software piracy, viruses and logic bombs, privacy, employee monitoring, job displacement, and personal use of organizational resources.

Software Piracy

Software piracy is the making of unauthorized copies of a computer program. Companies that develop programs have the right to control the distribution of their product, just as they would if they manufactured computers. It would be unethical to steal a computer, and it is unethical to steal a program by copying it in a way that is not permitted by the company's software license agreement.

In general, you should check the license agreement, provided with the package when it was purchased, before making a copy of the program for any purpose. Acknowledging the practical need to backup data and programs, most developers permit the making of a single copy entirely for backup purposes, but you should verify this for each package. Few companies permit you to make copies for your friends or colleagues to try out, except when the package is distributed as shareware.

Viruses and Logic Bombs

Viruses and logic bombs are the results of unethical actions on the part of skilled programmers. A **virus** is a small piece of program that can attach itself to other programs and change them or destroy data stored on a disk. Viruses spread through computer networks and through the exchange of

PREAMBLE

Commitment to professional conduct is expected of every member (voting members, associate members, and student members) of the Association for Computing Machinery (ACM). This Code identifies several issues professionals are likely to face, and provides guidelines for dealing with them. Section 1 presents fundamental ethical considerations, while Section 2 addresses additional considerations of professional conduct. Statements in Section 3 pertain more specifically to individuals who have a leadership role, whether in the workplace or in a professional organization such as ACM. Guidelines for encouraging compliance with this Code are given in Section 4.

1. General Moral Imperatives

As an ACM member I will. . .

1.1 Contribute to society and human well-being,
1.2 Avoid harm to others,
1.3 Be honest and trustworthy,
1.4 Be fair and take action not to discriminate,
1.5 Honor property rights including copyrights and patents,
1.6 Give proper credit for intellectual property,
1.7 Access computing and communication resources only when authorized to do so,
1.8 Respect the privacy of others,
1.9 Honor confidentiality.

2. More Specific Professional Responsibilities

As an ACM computing professional I will. . .

2.1 Strive to achieve the highest quality in both the process and products of professional work,
2.2 Acquire and maintain professional competence,
2.3 Know and respect existing laws pertaining to professional work,
2.4 Accept and provide appropriate professional review,
2.5 Give comprehensive and thorough evaluations of computer systems and their impacts, with special emphasis on possible risks,
2.6 Honor contracts, agreements, and assigned responsibilities,
2.7 Improve public understanding of computing and its consequences.

3. Organizational Leadership Imperatives

As an ACM member and an organizational leader, I will. . .

3.1 Articulate social responsibilities of members of an organizational unit and encourage full acceptance of those responsibilities,
3.2 Manage personnel and resources to design and build information systems that enhance the quality of working life,
3.3 Acknowledge and support proper and authorized uses of an organization's computing and communication resources,
3.4 Ensure that users and those who will be affected by a system have their needs clearly articulated during the assessment and design of requirements; later the system must be validated to meet requirements.
3.5 Articulate and support policies that protect the dignity of users and others affected by a computing system,
3.6 Create opportunities for members of the organization to learn the principles and limitations of computer systems.

4. Compliance with the Code

As an ACM member, I will. . .

4.1 Uphold and promote the principles of this Code,
4.2 Agree to take appropriate action leading to a remedy if the Code is violated,
4.3 Treat violations of this code as inconsistent with membership in the ACM.

FIGURE 12-29 **ACM Code of Ethics and Professional Conduct**
Draft Revision, February 12, 1992, *Communications of the ACM*, May 1992, 94–95.

disks from one computer to another. A **logic bomb** is a section added to a program to causes the program to malfunction under some circumstances. For example, a programmer may add a small section to a payroll program that checks for the programmer's name in the employee data. If the programmer is no longer listed as an employee, then the data file is corrupted or some other damage is done.

Computer programmers have the potential to cause great harm by unethical actions, such as by creating viruses and logic bombs. As a result, programmers have special responsibilities to consider the ethical implications of their actions.

Privacy

By making it possible to compile and process large databases inexpensively, computer technology lets us use information about individuals in ways that previously were too costly to be practical. For example, computerization makes it possible to maintain national databases of credit information about individuals. In some cases, the information may be incorrect, making it impossible for individuals to purchase homes or automobiles on credit unless the error can be corrected. In addition, it may be possible for unauthorized persons to access the information and use it in harmful ways.

Several ethical issues are involved: Do you have a right to control the use of information about yourself? Do you have a right to be informed, at least, on how information about you is used? Do you have a right to be certain that information about you is correct? In many countries, as we have seen, these rights are supported by law.

Employee Monitoring

Computer networks make it possible to monitor the performance of employees in new ways. For example, supervisors may have access to data about numbers of keystrokes per hour or error rates in great detail for each employee. In addition, supervisors may be able to access the contents of any employee's display screen without the employee's knowledge. However, the fact that these capabilities are technically possible does not make their use necessarily ethical.

Part of the ethical question concerns the employee's knowledge and agreement. Does the employee know about the monitoring and how the results are to be used? Does the employee agree to it?

Job Displacement

One of the results of computerization has been the loss of jobs of those who performed the work now done by computer. This raises the problem of dealing ethically with those who are displaced. For example, many of those displaced may be retrained for other work, and new computer-related jobs may be created. When displacement occurs, organizations should consider the ethical issues raised.

Personal Use of Organizational Resources

An employee who would not consider stealing a company computer for personal use may personally buy and install a computer game on a company PC and play the game during breaks. Is such personal use of company resources unethical? What if the employee is playing the game for an hour or more each day during work time? What if several employees, playing the game together through a network, are degrading the ability of the network to perform at the required level?

Ethical issues such as these do not have clear and definite answers. Different individuals and companies may draw the ethical line in different places. Most would agree, however, that using company computer resources for profit-making personal business activities is not ethical. Similarly, most would agree that personal uses of company computer resources that interfere with company operations is not ethical. Company policies and codes of conduct may offer guidance in the more difficult cases.

TRENDS IN MIS

The basis for MIS is a technology that is changing extremely rapidly. The changes bring advantages, but they also create problems for those who must manage and use technology.

One such change is the increase in the power and usefulness of microcomputers. For most of the history of information systems, the MIS department has held near-exclusive control over all computing resources. When the microcomputer became available, however, that control began to fade. At first, MIS professionals made fun of the primitive and sometimes erratic personal computers. They called them toys. But, over time, as microcomputers and their software matured, end users found that they could accomplish many of their information requirements on their own, without the assistance of the MIS department. Some MIS departments found themselves bypassed by the new technology.

Meanwhile, senior managements began to look more closely at the costs and benefits of their investment in information technology. In many cases, it was not at all clear that the enterprises were obtaining sufficient returns on their investments in information technology.

The emerging independence of end users, along with the increasing scrutiny of costs and benefits, has placed MIS departments under considerable pressure. As a result, in some enterprises, the MIS departments have begun a transformation into much leaner organizations that serve a staff and advisory function. As such, the MIS department is taking less of a direct role in the development of new information systems. Two new development strategies are emerging as a result: outsourcing and line MIS. We will consider each.

The Explosion of Information Technology

MIS is based on technology that is changing explosively. The change is rapid, and it is becoming more rapid with each passing month. In fact, even the *rate* of change is increasing. Because of this technology explosion, computers have become incredibly powerful at the same time that they are decreasing in price. Personal computers of unimaginable power and utility are now available quickly for very little money.

The explosion is happening in all areas of computing. One especially useful area is **source data automation (SDA)**, data input that bypasses the keyboard. SDA is critical because humans operate the keyboard slowly, and they inevitably make errors. To eliminate this bottleneck, technology now permits much data input without keyboarding. The early SDA technologies are mature today: MICR systems in banking and bar-code systems in retail trade. Additional SDA technologies are approaching maturity: optical character recognition, handwriting recognition, and voice recognition.

The benefits of the technology are widely recognized. The many costs and problems it creates are less well known. Hardware becomes obsolete so quickly that it is hard to depreciate it fast enough. MIS personnel need to be constantly retrained on new technologies. Some people cannot adapt to new technologies, methods, and procedures, and they become deadwood in their organizations. Immature products are introduced that cause incredible disruption and stress until their quirks are removed or understood well enough to be overcome or avoided.

These problems are especially troublesome to MIS departments because MIS personnel are constantly having to learn new techniques. As soon as one problem is solved, another one pops up. The knowledge painfully gained to solve one problem is seldom used more than once.

Outsourcing

In response to these factors, many companies are turning to third-party specialists to run their computing equipment and systems in a process called **outsourcing**. Companies such as Andersen Consulting and Electronic Data Systems are offering to operate organizational computers and systems for a fixed price.

Third-party specialists can perform these services for less money because they are able to gain efficiencies of scale. An outsource vendor can negotiate better prices on hardware because it buys the hardware in large volume. Such vendors can train more efficiently because they develop training programs to upgrade the knowledge of hundreds of personnel, not just a few. As outsource vendors learn the quirks of new products, they can apply that knowledge to dozens or even hundreds of installations rather than just to one.

Outsourcing is new, and it is not clear how successful it will be in the long term. Some would say that by outsourcing, management is giving away its responsibility to outsiders. They would say that outsourcing is equivalent to admitting failure. Others say that, because of economies of scale, outsourcing is an appropriate and wise course of action. In any case, it appears that you can expect to see more and more outsourcing, at least in the early years of your career.

Line MIS

The success that end users have had in developing their own personal MIS has given them confidence in their ability to satisfy their own information requirements. This emerging confidence began with simple systems such as a personal word processing application or a single-user spreadsheet analysis. Later, users found that, if they could download enterprise data, they could develop their own personal database applications to format that data in ways that were most meaningful to them.

In part, this movement arose out of necessity. MIS departments were overwhelmed with requests for service, and they were unable to satisfy many user needs. Application backlogs of over two years were commonly reported. Even though many end users did not want to become involved with information technology, they found that they had to do so in order to accomplish their work.

Furthermore, technology helped to make users more self-sufficient. Twenty years ago, all applications were developed using custom programming. Several years of training were required to be able to develop even the most rudimentary applications. As application packages that could be altered and adapted became available, the education and training time required to develop applications were dramatically reduced. One consequence of this has been the rise of **third-party system integrators**: companies that acquire hardware and programs and integrate these into business solutions for end users. These companies also work with their customers to develop the data, procedure, and personnel components of the systems they integrate.

With growth in the end users' confidence, simplifications of development due to changes in technology, and emergence of system integrators, end users have begun to take more responsibility for development and use of their own information systems. This phenomenon is sometimes called **line MIS.**

Traditionally, the MIS department has taken responsibility for creating and maintaining information systems other than personal information systems throughout the organization. Under line MIS, departmental information systems are created and operated by the departments themselves. The MIS department remains responsible for controlling organizationwide data, but it does so mainly by developing standards and procedures for the use of that data.

The rise in line MIS will create new, important career opportunities. Someone who has knowledge of a business area—say, manufacturing—and who also knows information technology could be given important responsibilities and could make substantial contributions to the enterprise.

Changing Role of MIS

If outsourcing and line MIS become prevalent in business organizations, then the role of the MIS department will change dramatically. Instead of directly developing and operating information systems, the MIS department will begin to serve more of a staff function that oversees, advises, and supports the efforts of others.

Few MIS departments currently function in this way. Most are structured as described earlier in this chapter, and most still develop, operate, and maintain organizational MIS. The changes described in this section will mean a dramatic reduction in the number of personnel in the MIS department and in the power and influence of the MIS director. Hence, there is likely to be considerable resistance to this evolution. Still, there are strong economic and technological pressures on organizations to shift to outsourcing and line MIS, and it is likely that the changes described here will come about eventually.

Summary

MIS refers to the development and use of effective information systems in organizations. An MIS includes five major elements: TPSs, management reporting systems, DSSs, communication support systems, and ESSs.

TPSs are the basic accounting and other operational-level information systems. Architectures include batch processing, on-line file processing, and database processing architectures. TPS outputs include detail reports, summary reports, and exception reports.

Management reporting systems produce reports to support decision making at all levels of the organization.

DSSs are computer-based facilities to assist decision makers in solving problems. Often, the problems are relatively unstructured, one-of-a-kind problems. An important component of a DSS is a set of complex dynamic models of business activity. Types of DSS include financial models, database queries, expert systems, and GDSSs.

Communication support systems assist in human communication throughout the organization. The most widely used communication support systems are word processing, graphics, DTP, E-mail, and electronic conferencing systems.

ESSs (or EISs) support the information needs of senior executives. They present highly summarized data in a very attractive form and often involve graphics displays.

An MIS provides many benefits. Internally, it supports strategic planning, management control, and operational control. Externally, it improves the organization's product and provides improved product delivery. It provides these benefits not only at the organizational level, but also at the group and personal levels.

An MIS must be managed both in user departments and in the MIS department. The MIS department is responsible for the development, maintenance, and security of the information systems. The VP of the MIS department often reports directly to the organization's CEO. The MIS department typically includes a DP division and an end user support division. The DP division includes development, operations, systems support, and data administration groups. The end user support division may be organized in several ways. A common pattern includes research and development group, computer store, and support group. An information center supports the use of DSSs. It may be a part of an MIS department, or it may be a staff support function of the CEO. In smaller companies, MIS functions are combined into fewer groups.

In user departments, key users and LAN managers provide important information systems support.

Ethical issues include software piracy, viruses and logic bombs, privacy, employee monitoring, job displacement, and personal use of organizational resources.

The role of MIS in organizations is changing. Explosively accelerating technology provides opportunities, but it also brings problems. Outsourcing is one common response. Line MIS is developing as PCs become more powerful and distributed systems involve users in computer technology. These developments may result in major changes in the role of the MIS department.

Key Terms

transaction processing system (TPS)
detail report
summary report
exception report
management reporting system
decision support system (DSS)
financial model
database query application
expert system
group decision support system (GDSS)
electronic conference
electronic bulletin board
forum
executive support system (ESS)
executive information system (EIS)
structured problem
unstructured problem
semistructured problem
data processing (DP) division
development group
operations group
systems support group
data administration group
end user support division
information center
key user
software piracy
virus
logic bomb
source data automation (SDA)
outsourcing
third-part system integrator
line MIS

Review Questions

1. Define MIS.
2. Why is the term *organizational information systems* not used instead of *MIS*?
3. Differentiate between MISs and business information systems.
4. Name the five elements of an MIS.
5. What is a TPS?
6. Name at least six characteristics of TPSs.
7. List three TPS architectures. What are their common elements?
8. Explain the function of each of the three kinds of TPS reports.
9. What is a management reporting system?
10. Describe the architecture of a management reporting system.
11. What is a DSS?
12. Why might *decision support facility* be a better term than *DSS*?
13. Describe the architecture of a DSS.
14. Explain the function of each of the three types of DSS.
15. What is a communication support system?
16. Name and explain five types of communication support system.
17. Differentiate between group conferencing systems and electronic conferencing systems.
18. What is an ESS?
19. Describe the architecture of an ESS.
20. Explain the five types of benefits provided by an MIS.
21. What are the three levels of information systems?
22. Differentiate among the three types of problems that an MIS deals with.
23. Name two professional information systems positions in user departments.
24. To which organizational officer should the VP of the information systems department report?
25. Describe the functions of the MIS department.
26. Name the two major divisions of a large corporation's MIS department.
27. Describe the functions of each of the four groups in the DP division.
28. Describe the functions of each of three groups often found in the end user support division.
29. Explain the functioning of an information center.
30. How are MIS organizational plans in smaller companies different from those in large corporations?
31. What is an unethical action?
32. Give four guidelines for ethical behavior.
33. Identify five key ethical issues in relation to business information systems activities.
34. Why is source data automation useful?
35. Explain how explosively accelerating technology creates problems for people who work with it.

36. What is outsourcing?
37. What is line MIS?

Discussion Questions

A. Create a single chart showing the architecture of an entire MIS, including all five parts and their architectures. How can you represent the architecture of communication support systems in such a chart?

B. Briefly describe a particular large business organization, then select and describe a specific group or department within that organization and a specific individual or job title. Then give at least one example benefit of MIS of each of the five types at each of the three levels, as in Figure 12-24. For example, give one strategic planning benefit at the organizational level, one strategic planning benefit at the group level, and so on. Use the knowledge you have gained in studying this book, along with your imagination, to identify benefits. Be specific in identifying particular benefits.

C. If a person is interested in information systems and would like to prepare for a position as an information systems specialist in a user department, what preparation do you think would be appropriate? For example, should the person major in information systems or in some other field? Defend your answer.

D. Is it preferable for the director of a corporate MIS department to report to the CEO rather than to another officer of the corporation? Defend your answer by citing benefits to the organization.

E. From your own knowledge, other than the technologies directly mentioned in the book, describe at least five new information-related technologies that are being introduced today or that may be introduced in the near future. If each technology is adopted by a business, how would it fit into the organization's MIS architecture? What changes in the organization, if any, do you think the use of that technology would bring?

MINICASE

Kennametal Finds the Right Tools

Kennametal Inc., a leading producer of metal-working and mining tools, quietly spent the 1980s investing heavily in new technology to reverse a market slide and stave off powerful foreign competitors.

By last year, that strategy had propelled it into the ranks of the nation's 500 largest companies with net income of $21 million and revenues of $618 million. And a more visible sign of success, Kennametal's stylish new $25 million research and development center opened next to the company's headquarters on the rural outskirts of this small city, an hour's drive east of Pittsburgh.

Kennametal's rebound provides a case study of how even companies in stodgy, slow-growing businesses can use information technology to improve their efficiency and provide new services that turn customers into partners.

Today, Kennametal's information management systems have more in common with trend-setters in retailing, banking and transportation than those of most of its peers. The company has also invested

M O D U L E A

History of Information Systems

CHAPTER OUTLINE

The history of computing began several thousand years ago when people started to count on their fingers. In fact, fingers and toes were probably the earliest computational devices. As business and commerce developed, however, a need arose for methods of numerical record keeping and for calculations with numbers greater than 20.

The lines of development that led to modern computers involve two technologies. The first technology is that of data storage and retrieval. The second technology is that of computation.

A variety of methods of data storage and retrieval have been invented. Herders invented the bag of stones (in Latin, *calcula*), with each stone representing one lamb or calf. In agricultural societies, patterns of knots in cords represented amounts of grain. Early writing was used largely to represent business transactions. Money was developed to represent value that could be exchanged for goods.

Progress with the technology of computation began with methods of using written numbers to calculate. An important step was taken when Arabic mathematicians invented a number system including the zero, which increased computational power tremendously.

The **abacus** shown in Figure A-1 is an early machine that was used to assist in computation. Various versions of it were used for centuries by people of many nations and areas of the world. The abacus was used even before numbers were represented in writing. Other computational devices were constructed throughout the centuries. The numerical wheel calculator (see Figure A-2) invented by **Blaise Pascal** was the predecessor of the adding machines and mechanical calculators that were commonly used before the electronic calculator. The slide rule (see Figure A-3) was another type of computational device.

In this part we present two special topics. They may be assigned as supplementary reading, or they may be incorporated into the course itself.

Module A outlines the history of computing, which dates back farther than you might suspect. As you will see, some mistakes made early on are still being made today.

Module B presents a brief introduction to BASIC programming and covers just enough BASIC instructions to get you started. You can use the lessons in Module B to learn BASIC on your own. Having mastered this fundamental material, you might decide to study BASIC further, using one of the many tutorials on the subject.

PART FIVE

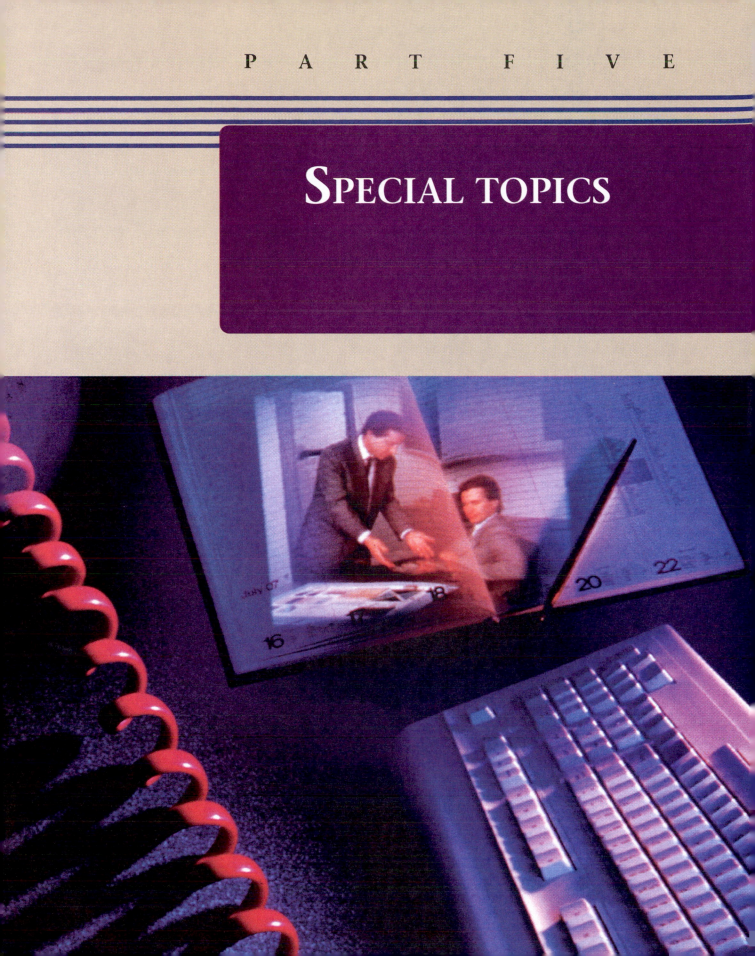

SPECIAL TOPICS

heavily in computer-based manufacturing. The investment in information technology has allowed it to serve customers more quickly and reduce inventories. The computer systems have also been used to offer customers additional services, like tool management support. Just like drug distributors who stock pharmacists' shelves, Kennametal now stocks and manages the tool storage areas for some customers. . . .

One early payoff came when Kennametal was selected by the Saturn project of General Motors over several experienced tool distributors to be its sole supplier of all metal-cutting tooling, including products that Kennametal itself does not make.

Its success at Saturn helped persuade Kennametal to branch out of its traditional manufacturing business, which is plagued by falling demand as tools last longer and more metal components are replaced by plastics. Through a series of acquisitions, Kennametal now distributes a wide range of industrial products from other manufacturers.

Kennametal also used its information systems to force its various European subsidiaries to work more cooperatively. All of them are tied into the data center here through a communications network administered by British Telecom, which Kennametal turned to for help in designing the system and getting it approved by telephone authorities in Europe.

More recently, Kennametal's use of electronic data interface, known as E.D.I. among information managers, has cut the costs of administering transactions with the General Electric Company's aircraft components business in Albuquerque, N.M., by 96 percent. G.E.'s electronic orders for tools go directly to Kennametal's computers, which automatically do the paperwork, issue notices of when the tools will be shipped and send bills. Employees first become a part of the transaction when workers in an Albuquerque warehouse get a printed order to pack and ship the tools. The payoff: Kennametal Albuquerque has annual sales of $861,000 per employee, compared with an average of $254,000 for members of the Industrial Distribution Association.

Questions

1. Summarize the ways in which Kennametal has used information technology to improve its operations.
2. Explain how the use of information technology in the Saturn project caused Kennametal to expand into a new market.
3. Kennametal chose to work with a British communications company for the development of its European communications link. What advantages do you think Kennametal found in contracting with a British company for this work? What disadvantages might have existed?
4. Consider the information system that is in use at Kennametal Albuquerque. How does the integration of information systems between G.E. and Kennametal benefit both companies? What are the risks to G.E. of such an arrangement? What are the risks to Kennametal? What problems does such an arrangement pose for one of Kennametal's competitors? Summarize the ways in which this system provides Kennametal with a competitive advantage.

FIGURE A-1
Abacus

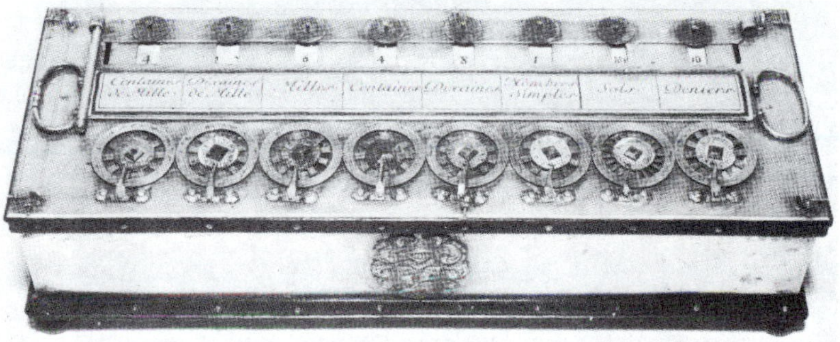

FIGURE A-2
Numerical Wheel Calculator

CHARLES BABBAGE AND HIS MACHINES

Charles Babbage was far ahead of his time. He developed the essential ideas for a computer over 100 years before the first computer was constructed. He was so advanced that practically none of his contemporaries appreciated him. In addition to his contributions to computing, Babbage made contributions to mathematics, optics, underwater navigation, railroads, industrial engineering, mechanics, and other fields.

Many of the mistakes that Babbage made continue to be made today, and so it is worth considering his life's activities in some detail.

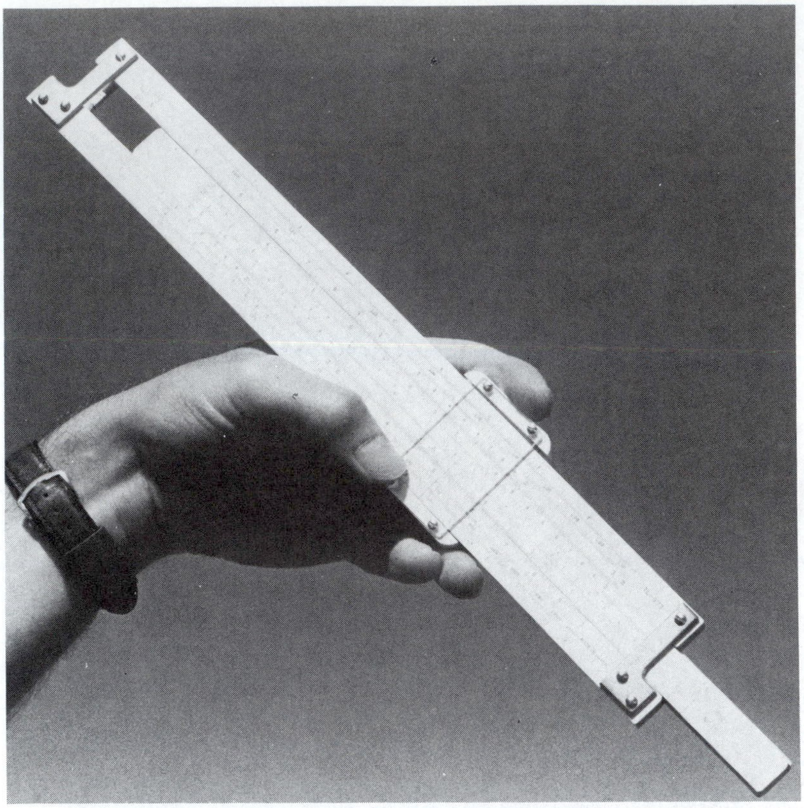

FIGURE A-3
Slide Rule

Babbage's Life

George Washington was still alive when Babbage was born in England in 1792. His father was a wealthy banker who left him a sizable fortune. When Babbage was in his 20s, he and his friend John Herschel were checking data calculated for the Astronomical Society. In frustration, Babbage remarked to Herschel, "I wish to God these calculations had been executed by steam." (Steam engines were common.) In 1822, Babbage proposed the design of a **difference engine** composed of gears and wheels (see Figure A-4). This engine would automatically compute functions of the form

$$y = a + ax + ax^2 + \dots + ax^n$$

In 1823 the British government granted Babbage money to build the difference engine, and the first government-sponsored computer project was on. Like most of those to follow, the project fell behind. By 1833 the government had invested 17,000 pounds ($85,000 at the 1833 rate of exchange), and only part of the difference engine was completed. Meanwhile, Babbage's active mind had been extending the possibilities of automated computing. By 1834 he had developed the idea of an **analytical engine.** The analytical engine would compute any mathematical function. It embodied most of the concepts that early computers did.

FIGURE A-4
Babbage's Difference Engine

In 1834 Babbage asked the government whether it wanted him to finish the difference engine or start on the analytical engine. After eight years of frustrating correspondence, Prime Minister Robert Peel told Babbage that the government was going to abandon the project. This case may have established a record for governmental delay.

The analytical engine had a main memory that Babbage called the *store*. It was to have room for 1,000 variables of 50 digits each. It had an arithmetic-logic unit that he called the *mill*. Programs for the mill were written on punched cards. The engine would drive a typesetter. It had logical capability and could ring a bell or take other action when a variable passed zero or exceeded the capacity of one of the words. All of these operations were to have been implemented mechanically.

People had a hard time understanding the concept. Mathematicians asked Babbage how the engine would use logarithms. He told them that it would not need logarithms because it could compute any function. Some people did not believe this claim, so he showed them how it could be programmed to ask an attendant to supply a logarithm from a library of cards. Furthermore, it would check for the correct logarithm.

Ironically, Babbage got more attention from outside England than from within. He had two automated devices in his home: a clockwork woman who danced and a part of the difference engine. He reported that his English friends would gather about the dancing lady, whereas an American and a Hollander studied the difference engine. In fact, a Swedish printer, George Scheutz, built the only complete version of the difference engine, except for one made recently by IBM. Babbage was delighted and helped Scheutz explain it.

We know about the analytical engine largely from a paper written by an Italian, L. F. Menabrea. This paper was written in French and translated into English by **Ada Augusta, the Countess of Lovelace**, whose contribution to early computing was significant.

Ada Augusta was the only legitimate daughter of the poet Lord Byron. She was an excellent mathematician and understood Babbage's concepts perhaps better than anyone. In 1842, when she translated Menabrea's paper of 20 pages, she added 50 pages of "notes." Babbage wanted to know why she did not write a paper of her own. "I never thought of it," she replied. In fact, she did not sign her translation or her notes, but used the initials A. A. L. instead. Apparently, ladies did not do such things.

However, ladies could go to the racetrack. The Countess loved racing, and it may have been inevitable that she would use the difference engine to determine horse bets. Apparently, it did not work too well. She lost the family jewels at the track. Her mother, Lady Byron, had to buy them back.

The Countess died of cancer at the age of 36, just ten years after reading Menabrea's description. Her death was a big loss to Babbage and perhaps to the world. The programming language Ada is named after Ada Augusta Lovelace.

Babbage was a fascinating person. Charles Darwin reported lively dinner parties at Babbage's home. Another person complained of barely being able to escape from him at 2:00 in the morning. Babbage once said that he would be glad to give up the rest of his life if he could live for three days five hundred years in the future.

Lessons We Can Learn from Babbage

Many of the errors Babbage made have been repeated again and again in the computer industry. For one, Babbage began with vague requirements. "Let's compute numbers by steam," sounds all too much like, "Let's use a computer to do billing." Much more precise statements of requirements are necessary.

Second, it appears that Babbage started implementing his plans before his design was complete. Much work had to be redone. His engineers and draftsmen often complained that they would finish a project only to be told the work was wrong or not needed because the design had been changed. The same complaint has been made by countless programmers since then. Another mistake Babbage made was to add more and more capability to his engines before any of them was complete. As his work progressed, he saw new possibilities, and he tried to incorporate them into his existing projects. If he had completed a project first, then modified it to incorporate the improvement, then at least one version of the outcome would be entirely usable. Then he could have demonstrated his concepts and, perhaps, the government would have continued his funding. Many data processing systems have remained uncompleted for the very same reason.

Work on the difference engine was set back considerably by a crisis over the salary of Babbage's chief engineer, Joseph Clement. Clement quit, and Babbage had little documentation to know exactly what had been done. Further, Clement had the rights to all the tools. Who knows how many systems projects have failed because indispensable programmers quit in the middle of them? Documentation of work in progress is crucial for successful system implementation.

Even Lady Lovelace's losses at the track have a lesson. Systems ought not to be used for purposes for which they were not designed. The computer industry has experienced much inefficiency because systems are applied to problems for which they were not designed.

There was no electronics industry to support Babbage's ideas. All of the concepts had to be implemented in mechanical components, and the tolerances were so fine that they could not be manufactured within the limitations of 19th-century technology. Furthermore, Babbage's plans were grandiose. Building a computer with 1,000 50-decimal-digit numbers was a large task. He might have been more successful if he had completed a smaller computer first, giving him time to build credibility with his government and solidify his funding before starting on a larger one. Many government-sponsored projects fail today because of a lack of technology to support grandiose plans. The lessons we can learn from Babbage are summarized in Figure A-5.

We do not know what impact, if any, Babbage's work had on future development. One pioneer, Howard Aiken, discussed later in this chapter, reported that he worked for three years before discovering Babbage's contributions. We do not know about the others.

Babbage's design was directed toward improving the ability to perform calculations. Another line of development took place in data storage and retrieval. The innovator was Herman Hollerith.

Babbage's Mistakes

- Vague problem definition and requirements
- Implementation started before design was complete
- Requirements added during implementation
- Working documentation not complete
- Dependency on one person
- System used for unintended purposes
- Grandiose plans that exceeded existing technology

FIGURE A-5
Mistakes Babbage Made That Are Still Made Today

HERMAN HOLLERITH

In the late 19th century, the U.S. Census Bureau had a problem. The bureau was supposed to produce a census of the U.S. population every ten years. The census is constitutionally required as the basis for redistricting the Congress. Thus, when tabulation of the 1880 census results took seven-and-a-half years to finish, members of Congress were bringing great pressure to get results. In addition, by the time the census data was processed, much of it was no longer useful. Furthermore, at the rate that the population was growing, the Census Bureau was afraid that the 1890 census could not be tabulated before the 1900 census was due to begin.

In 1879, the bureau hired **Herman Hollerith** to help them with their data storage and retrieval problem. He worked for the Census Bureau for five years and then started his own company. Hollerith designed and managed the construction of several punched-card processing machines (see Figure A-6).

In 1889, the bureau held a contest among Hollerith and two competitors to determine whose system was the fastest. Hollerith's system required only one-tenth of the time needed by his nearest competitor. Using this equipment, the first tabulation of the 1890 census took only six weeks! The final, official results were announced in December 1890.

Hollerith's equipment was an extension of the work of Joseph Marie Jacquard, who designed looms in which punched cards controlled the pattern on woven material. In Jacquard's looms, needles fell through holes in the cards. The needles lifted threads to produce a pattern. This technique had been used in the weaving industry since 1804, and is still seen in some parts of the world today.

Hollerith extended this concept by using the cards to control electrical circuits. Data was punched on cards, which were fed into a machine that moved the cards under a group of pins. If there was a hole in a card, the pin would fall through the hole and touch a pool of mercury. This contact closed a circuit, which could be used to control processing. Apparently, the machine worked so well that the humans became exhausted from feeding cards into it. There is a story that occasionally someone would pour all of the mercury into a nearby spittoon. The machine would stop, and everyone would take a rest.

Hollerith's machine was highly marketable. He sold equipment to railroads and other large companies that had data storage and retrieval problems. This step represented the start of the punched-card industry. Hollerith built up his business and then sold it to the company that later was to become IBM (International Business Machines).

The punched-card industry was the beginning of automated data processing. The machines were called **unit record equipment**, combining punched cards for data storage with mechanical adding machines for simple computation. Companies found that, to use this new technology successfully, they needed to plan and create systems, including hardware, pro-

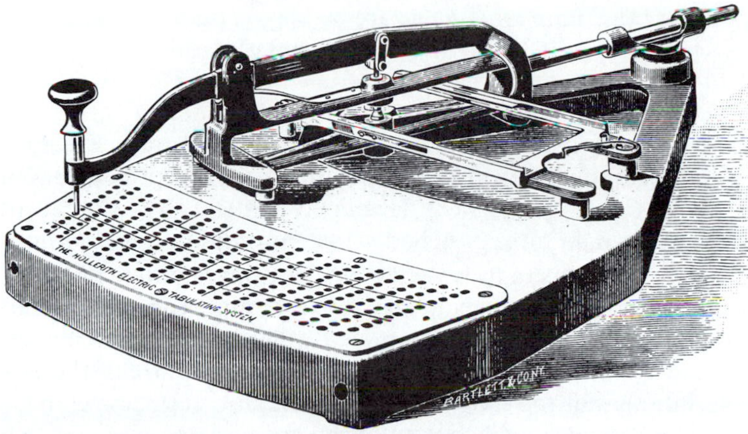

FIGURE A-6
Hollerith's Punched-Card Machines

grams, data, procedures, and trained personnel. The earliest business computer systems were developed around unit record technology and these systems concepts.

As punched-card equipment became more sophisticated, it became possible to change the wiring of the equipment to make it do different things. People who changed the wiring were doing an elementary form of programming. Programming as we know it today did not exist until stored-program computers were developed in the middle of the 20th century. However, the concepts used in business computer systems started evolving with the 1890 census.

In an amusing series of coincidences, the size of the dollar bill in 1890 determined how many characters are displayed on a line of a PC display today. Here is how it happened. Since trays and other equipment were available and were used by banks to handle dollar bills—which were larger then—Hollerith adopted the same size for his punched cards. The cards were stiff enough so that 80 data characters could be punched across a card without danger of tearing out the separation between punches. When terminals with CRT displays were developed in the 1970s, they were often used to display data from punched cards, one card per display line. Thus, they needed to display 80 characters per line. Early microcomputers used the displays originally developed for those terminals, so they also displayed 80 characters per line. Computer displays since then have remained compatible with those early displays. Therefore, the size of the 1890 dollar determined that the standard PC display shows 80 characters per line.

IBM continued to develop punched-card technology for data storage and retrieval over the ensuing 50 years and more. The next major step in the story of computing involves rapid advances in calculation machinery in the mid-20th century.

EARLY COMPUTERS

In 1937, **Howard G. Aiken** proposed the use of electromechanical devices to perform calculations. He was a professor of applied mathematics at Harvard at the time, and the IBM Corporation gave him a grant to pursue his ideas.

In 1944, Aiken and IBM completed an electromechanical calculator called the **Mark I.** This computer had mechanical counters that were manipulated by electrical devices. The Mark I could perform basic arithmetic, and it could be changed to solve different problems (see Figure A-7).

At about that time, the U.S. government signed a contract with the University of Pennsylvania to develop a computer that would aid the military effort during World War II. As a result of this contract, **John W. Mauchly** and **J. Presper Eckert** developed the first all-electronic computer, called the Electronic Numerical Integrator and Calculator, or **ENIAC**. Unlike the Mark I, ENIAC had no mechanical counters. Everything was electronic.

Although Mauchly and Eckert are often given credit for developing the first electronic computer, their work was actually based in part on work that had been done by **John V. Atanasoff**, a professor at Iowa State University. In 1939 he had developed many ideas for an all-electronic computer. In 1942, he and a graduate student, Clifford Berry, completed an electronic computer that could solve systems of linear equations.

ENIAC, the Mauchly-Eckert machine, was used to perform many different calculations. It had 19,000 vacuum tubes, 70,000 resistors, and 500,000 soldered joints (see Figure A-8). The ENIAC could perform 5,000

FIGURE A-7
Mark I Computer

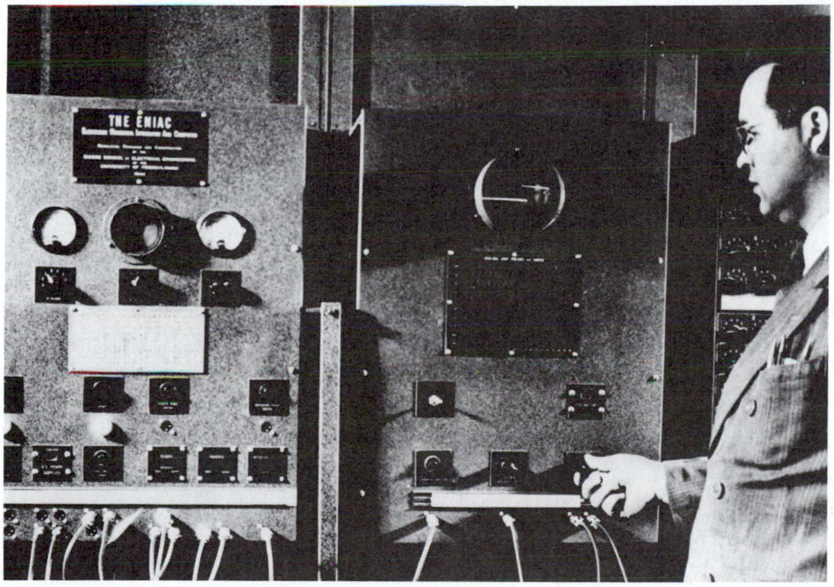

FIGURE A-8
The ENIAC, a First-Generation Computer

additions per second. It used 150,000 watt-hours of power a day—so much that, when it was turned on, the lights in one section of Philadelphia dimmed. Unfortunately, changing its program meant rewiring the machine. Since the program could be changed, it was programmable. However, it was not programmable in the sense that we understand the term today.

In the mid-1940s the mathematician **John von Neumann** joined the Mauchly-Eckert team. Von Neumann proposed a design for a computer that stored programs in its memory. He also developed other concepts that

FIGURE A-9 **UNIVAC I**

were to become the foundation for computer design for 30 years. Two computers evolved from this work: the **EDVAC** (Electrical Discrete Variable Automatic Computer) and the **EDSAC** (Electronic Delay Storage Automatic Calculator). Both machines stored programs. EDSAC was completed in England in 1949, and EDVAC, in the United States in 1950.

At the time, the potential of these machines was not understood. Atanasoff could not get support from Iowa State, where the administration thought that there would be a need for only three or four of these devices throughout the United States. In the late 1940s, members of the ENIAC-EDVAC staff were passed over for promotion to full professor at the Moore School of Engineering. People felt the work was not very important.

The first programmers for the Mark I and the ENIAC were U.S. Navy Rear Admiral **Grace Hopper** and **Adele Goldstine**. Both of these women were talented mathematicians. Their presence undoubtedly helped to establish women's strong position in the computer industry.

John Mauchly and Presper Eckert decided to follow in Hollerith's entrepreneurial footsteps, and in 1946 they formed the Eckert-Mauchly Corporation, which was soon purchased by Remington-Rand Corporation. Remington-Rand's first computer product was **UNIVAC I** (Universal Automatic Computer), the first computer built to sell. The Census Bureau took delivery of the first one in 1951, and it was used continuously until 1963. It now resides in the Smithsonian Institution (see Figure A-9).

Meanwhile, other companies were not idle. IBM continued development on the Mark I computer and eventually developed the Mark II through the Mark IV, as well as other early computers. Burroughs and Sperry Rand (today combined into Unisys), General Electric, Honeywell, Xerox, and RCA were also busy with computer developments.

IBM took an early lead in the application of the new computer technology to business problems. The company developed a series of business-oriented computers and sold them to its punched-card customers. Because IBM had a virtual monopoly on punched cards (for which it had been unsuccessfully sued by the U.S. government in the 1930s), it was in a strong position to capitalize on the new technology.

Furthermore, IBM had an extremely effective marketing philosophy that emphasized solving business problems. It developed products that were useful to businesses and showed businesspeople how to use those products. It provided excellent customer service and good maintenance. The fact that IBM understood this first has much to do with the company's strength in the computer market today.

The computers manufactured in the 1950s are often called **first-generation computers.** Their major components were vacuum tubes. Most of them used magnetic drums as their primary storage devices. Main memory as discussed in this book did not exist at that time.

Because of the number and size of the vacuum tubes, these computers were huge. Furthermore, they generated tremendous amounts of heat, were expensive to run, and experienced frequent failures. A large first-generation computer occupied a room the size of a football field. It contained row upon row of racks of tubes. A staff of a half-dozen people was required just to change the tubes that burned out.

COMPUTERS IN THE 1960s AND 1970s

In the late 1950s and early 1960s, vacuum tubes were replaced by transistors. This development led to **second-generation computers.** These computers were much smaller than vacuum-tube computers, and they were more powerful. A new type of main storage was developed. It was called **core memory** because it used magnetized, doughnut-shaped cores. Even today, some people use the term *core* to mean main memory, but this usage is technically incorrect because main memories today do not contain magnetic core.

The first high-level programming languages were developed during this stage. First-generation computers were programmed in **machine code**, but second-generation computers were programmed in **assembly language** and English-like **high-level languages** such as FORTRAN and ALGOL. Further, primitive operating systems were installed on second-generation machines.

Most of the business computer systems at this stage were designed for accounting. The computer was used to produce checks for payroll and accounts payable and to keep track of inventories. General ledger was also computerized. However, processing was done in batches. Inputs were gathered into groups and processed, and outputs were produced. Applications, such as order entry, that required interaction could not be handled.

FIGURE A-10
A Second-Generation Computer: The IBM 7094

FIGURE A-11
Integrated Circuit on a Silicon Chip

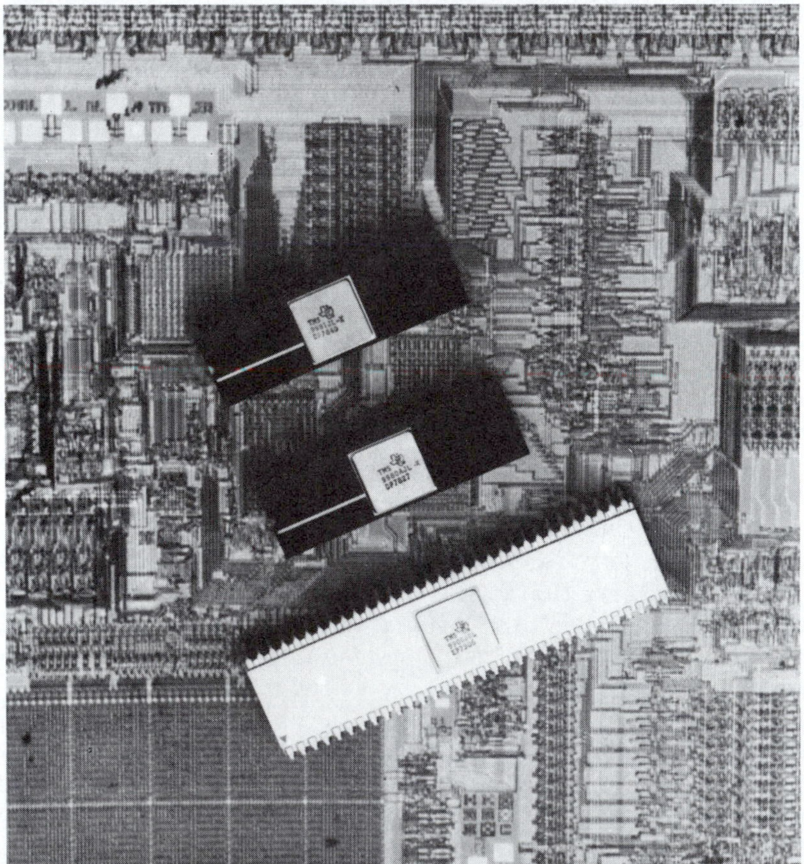

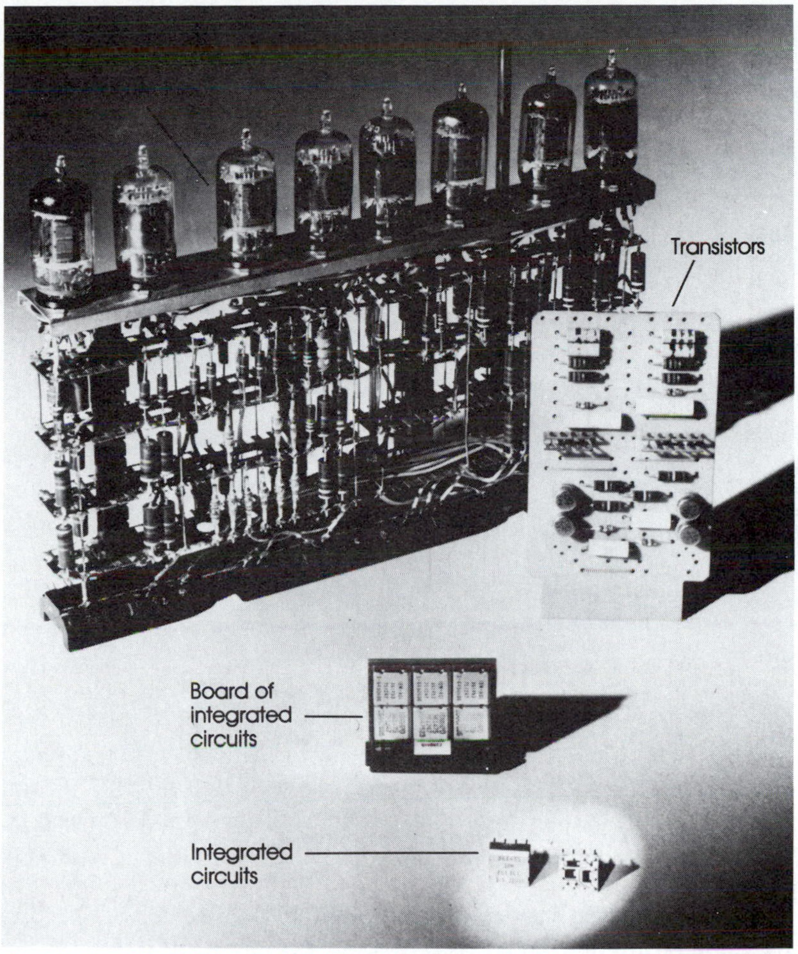

FIGURE A-12
Three Generations of Hardware Components

In the 1960s, the **third-generation computers** became available. In these computers, **integrated circuits** were used instead of transistors. An integrated circuit is a complete electrical circuit including many transistors on a single, small chip of silicon (see Figure A-11). Because of these chips, third-generation computers are smaller, more powerful, and cheaper to manufacture than second-generation computers. Figure A-12 compares the sizes of vacuum tubes, transistors, and integrated circuits.

Vast improvements in programming were also made for third-generation computers. Sophisticated operating systems were developed, allowing many programs to be executed concurrently. Slow input and output operations such as card reading or printing could be performed in the background: One job would be processing while another was being read and the output of a third was being printed. This arrangement eliminated the need for the off-line processing typical of second-generation computers. Figure A-13 shows a typical third-generation computer.

Third-generation computers also supported interactive, **on-line processing.** Users could interact with the computers to perform functions like

FIGURE A-13
A Third-Generation Computer: The Honeywell 6000

entering orders or making on-line airline reservations. Although some on-line processing had been done by earlier, military systems, these applications were very specialized and not economical. The third generation of computers allowed on-line processing to be a standard operation.

Minicomputers appeared in the mid-1960s. Initially, minicomputers were small, special-purpose machines designed for military and space applications. Gradually, however, the capability of these machines has increased to the point that, today, the more powerful minicomputers and the less powerful mainframes have overlapped. Figure A-14 shows a Digital Equipment VAX minicomputer, a very powerful machine that exceeds the capability of many so-called mainframes. Thus, it now is hard to distinguish between the two categories of computers.

THE FOURTH GENERATION

Fourth generation computers, developed in the 1980s, are characterized by **very large-scale integration (VLSI).** With VLSI, millions of transistors and other components—even an entire CPU—can be placed on a single silicon chip. The computer that may have occupied a large room in 1952 is today less than the size of a dime.

VLSI chips can be mass-produced, which means that they can be manufactured and sold in quantities of thousands. Because so many are sold,

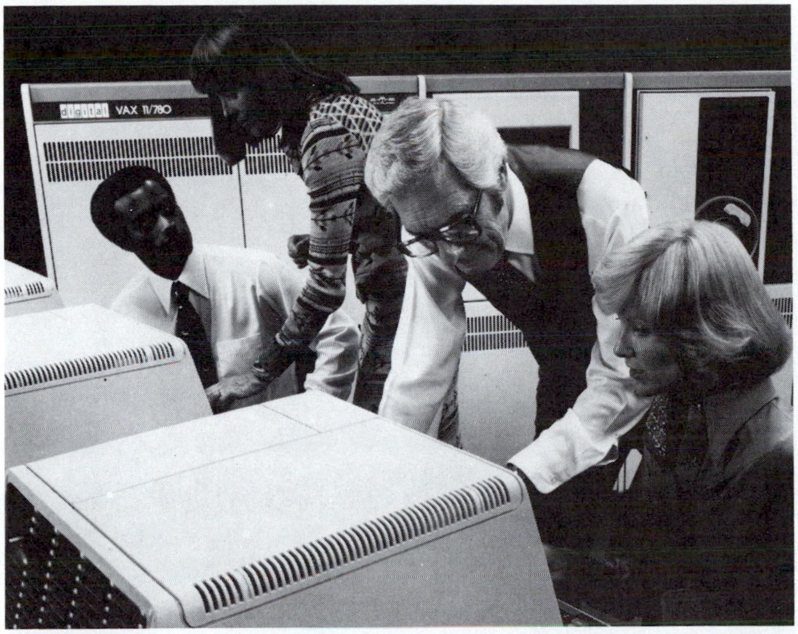

FIGURE A-14
The DEC VAX Minicomputer

the costs of research, development, and tooling are spread over many units. Thus, VLSI chips are extremely cheap. A circuit that might have cost $50,000 ten years ago can now be purchased in quantity for $10 or less. Thus, VLSI technology has caused a tremendous decrease in the price/performance ratio of new computers.

A computer on a chip is called a **microprocessor.** When the chip is installed with electronics to perform input and output processing and other functions, it is called a **microcomputer.**

Microprocessors were designed more or less accidentally. As technology permitted more and more circuitry on the chip, engineers experimented with applications. For example, the Intel 8008, a microprocessor, was originally developed as the controller for a CRT terminal. Although the chip was never used for this purpose, Intel put it in their catalog. To their surprise, it sold very well. The company saw the demand, put a design team together, and a year later introduced the Intel 8080 microprocessor, shown in Figure A-15. This product became very popular, and other manufacturers quickly followed suit. Today there are dozens of microprocessor products to choose from.

All of this development means that computers have become cheaper and cheaper. Some experts believe that the cost of computer processing power will soon be essentially zero. At least, the cost will be negligible compared to that of other components of a business computer system.

These inexpensive microprocessors may well lead to entirely new computer architectures. Since microprocessors are so cheap, it becomes feasible to develop and market **desktop supercomputers** that are banks of many microprocessors. For example, a supercomputer could contain a

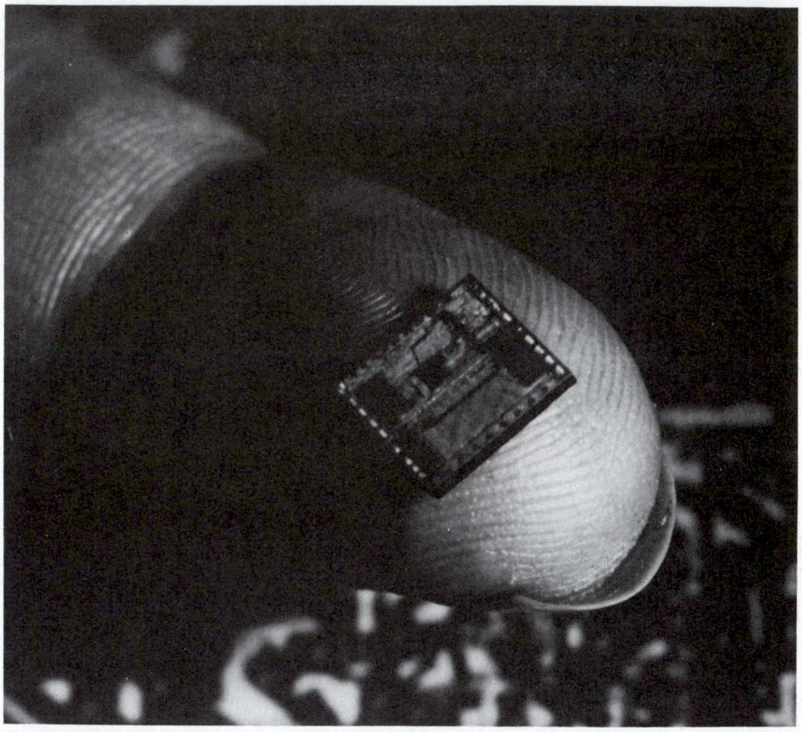

FIGURE A-15
The Intel 8080 Microprocessor

100-by-100 array of microprocessors. The power of such a machine strains the imagination.

The Microcomputer Explosion

In the early 1970s, the cheapest computers cost about $100,000. These were minicomputers that were accessed through terminals. Many people in universities and companies knew how to use them and appreciated their power. Thus, when affordable personal computers became available, there was a tremendous demand for these devices.

The first microcomputer was a kit computer called the Mark-8, which was designed by Ed Roberts in 1974. He followed the Mark-8 with a machine called the Altair, named for the destination of the starship Enterprise on a Star Trek episode. The Altair sold for $397 in 1975. The bank that had financed Roberts's company, MITS, hoped he could sell 200 computers. In April 1976, MITS reported at a meeting of the Homebrew Computer Club, a pioneering microcomputer club, that 4,000 Altairs had been ordered.

The Tandy Corporation began as a leather business in 1927. In 1962 the owner's son suggested buying a chain of mail order electronics stores in Boston called Radio Shack, which was losing $4 million a year. By August 1977 the TRS-80 microcomputer was announced. Within a month the Tandy Corporation had sold 100,000 units.

The Apple computer was developed by Stephen Wozniak and a high school friend named Steve Jobs (pronounced "jobes" with a long "oh"). Wozniak was an electronics experimenter. He knew about the Altair computer, but he could not afford one at the time. So, to get one, he was forced to design his own. In February 1977, the Apple Computer Company opened its doors in Cupertino, California. The Apple II computer was unveiled a few months later, at about the same time as the Radio Shack TRS-80.

IBM entered the microcomputer market on August 12, 1981, with its announcement of the IBM Personal Computer, or IBM PC. The IBM name on the computer helped to legitimize microcomputers as business machines. The IBM PC was built from parts available to the general public, so other manufacturers could duplicate it, and they did. An entire industry has grown up around the IBM PC and "IBM work-alike" computers, called **clones**. More than 60 million have been sold.

Apple went on to develop its Macintosh series of computers, which succeeded largely because it was successfully marketed to major corporations that had traditionally bought computers from IBM. The Macintosh's superior user interface was an important factor in its success. This interface made the computer much more approachable for first-time users.

Special-purpose microcomputers called **workstations** are used primarily by engineers. These computers have high-quality graphics and fast processors. They are used in all types of industries for engineering applications such as design and drawing. Sun, Apollo, and Hewlett-Packard are the leading workstation manufacturers.

Microcomputer Software

As the first microcomputers were introduced, Bill Gates was a Harvard freshman. He and a programmer friend, Paul Allen, learned about the Altair, wrote a BASIC language system for it, and convinced its manufacturer to adopt their system. Allen and Gates subsequently established Microsoft, one of the world's largest software publishers. Today, Microsoft publishes DOS and Windows, along with competitive packages in each major category of microcomputer software. The packages include word processor Word, spreadsheet Excel, and DBMS FoxPro.

The first widely used business application program for microcomputers was VisiCalc, a spreadsheet program designed by Dan Bricklin, a programmer and student at Harvard Business School. The fact that VisiCalc ran on the Apple II computer helped the Apple II to predominate among business purchasers until the IBM Personal Computer was introduced. For several years, VisiCalc was the only spreadsheet program.

The first widely used word processing program was WordStar. In the early days of microcomputers, WordStar commands were so familiar to users that designers of other programs could confidently adopt them, knowing that most users would already know them.

Then, as now, the capabilities of microcomputer hardware was increasing rapidly, and, to remain competitive, software packages needed frequent updates to use new hardware capabilities. Authors of many early successful packages, suddenly wealthy, felt little incentive to update, often letting competitors quickly overtake them. For example, VisiCalc was overtaken by Lotus 1-2-3, a spreadsheet package for the IBM PC, which had a million dollars in sales in its first week on the market and quickly became the standard spreadsheet program for business microcomputers. Similarly, WordStar was overtaken by WordPerfect and other word processing packages.

Today, widely used software packages are typically the products of large companies rather than single authors. These companies often recognize the need for continuous updating to keep their products competitive and include regular updates in their basic strategies.

An exception to this pattern is a type of author-supported software called **shareware**. Hundreds of shareware programs have been freely distributed among friends and through forums and bulletin boards. Users are free to try the programs. If a user continues using a shareware program after a reasonable trial, then the user is obliged to mail a registration fee directly to the author. The fee entitles the user to technical support and program updates. Some shareware authors have incomes of over a million dollars a year.

Summary

Although the history of computation began thousands of years ago, the development of computers is a recent phenomenon. In the early 1800s, Charles Babbage developed many of the design concepts used in today's computers. However, these concepts were not implemented at that time. Many of the mistakes that Babbage made are still being made today.

In the late 1800s, the U.S. Census Bureau hired Herman Hollerith to develop automated ways of tabulating census data. This led to the development of punched-card equipment and the beginning of the punched-card industry.

Computers were developed in the mid-1940s. Early computers were produced through the cooperation of universities, government, and industry. There have been four generations of computers. First-generation computers had vacuum tubes, and main storage was a magnetic drum. These computers were huge and very hard to maintain. Programs were written in machine code.

Computers in the second generation used transistors and had main memory made of magnetic core. They were smaller and still very expensive. High-level languages were developed for programming, and rudimentary operating systems were invented.

The third-generation computers have integrated circuits on silicon chips. These chips are used both for arithmetic-logic unit and for main memory. Third-generation computers are much smaller and cheaper than first- or second-generation computers.

Today computers are in their fourth generation. They have become significantly cheaper and more powerful. In the near future, the cost of a CPU will be insignificant. We may see the development of supercomputers that are banks of microprocessors.

Microcomputers were developed in the mid-1970s. The Apple II computer with VisiCalc, a spreadsheet, was used by many businesspeople. The IBM PC and clones have been very successful as business microcomputers. The Macintosh, with its advanced GUI, is increasingly accepted among businesses.

The microcomputer software industry began with the first microcomputers. Bill Gates developed Microsoft, beginning with a BASIC language system. Early software, often developed by individual programmer entrepreneurs, was often supplanted by packages developed and regularly updated by large software companies. Shareware provides an alternative method of distributing microcomputer software.

Key Terms

abacus
Blaise Pascal
Charles Babbage
difference engine
analytical engine
Ada Augusta Lovelace
Herman Hollerith
unit record equipment
Howard G. Aiken
Mark I
John W. Mauchly
J. Presper Eckert
ENIAC
John V. Atanasoff
John von Neumann
EDVAC
EDSAC
Grace Hopper
Adele Goldstine
UNIVAC I
first-generation computer
second-generation computer
core memory
machine code
assembly language
high-level language
third-generation computer
integrated circuit
on-line processing
minicomputer
fourth-generation computer
very large-scale integrated (VLSI) circuit
microprocessor
microcomputer
desktop supercomputer
clone
workstation
shareware

Review Questions

1. Name the two technologies that developed into modern computers.
2. List four early technologies of data storage and retrieval.
3. List four early technologies of computation.
4. Name the two machines invented by Charles Babbage. What was each designed to do?

5. What was the power source for Charles Babbage's computers?
6. Describe the contribution of Ada Augusta, the Countess of Lovelace, to computing.
7. List four lessons to be learned from Charles Babbage's experience in designing and constructing computers.
8. During which decade did Charles Babbage's work take place?
9. Identify Herman Hollerith.
10. Describe the machine that Herman Hollerith invented.
11. What company of today traces its roots back to Herman Hollerith?
12. Identify unit record equipment.
13. Why do character-oriented displays today display 80 characters in an output line?
14. Identify Howard G. Aiken, John W. Mauchly, J. Presper Eckert, John V. Atanasoff, John von Neumann, Grace Hopper, and Adele Goldstine.
15. Describe the Mark I. When was it constructed?
16. Describe the ENIAC. When was it constructed?
17. Identify EDVAC, EDSAC, and UNIVAC I.
18. What were the major components of first-generation computers? When were they manufactured?
19. What were the major components of second-generation computers? When were they manufactured?
20. What were the major components of first-generation computers? When were they manufactured?
21. Describe the programming methods used with first-generation and second-generation computers.
22. What were the major components of third-generation computers? When were they first manufactured?
23. What progress in programming was made in the third generation of computers?
24. Describe the capabilities of minicomputers.
25. What are the major components of fourth-generation computers? When were they first manufactured?
26. Differentiate between a microprocessor and a microcomputer.
27. Describe the reduction in the price of the cheapest computers during the 1970s.
28. When were the Radio Shack TRS-80, the Apple II, and the IBM PC introduced?
29. What are IBM PC clones?
30. Name an early microcomputer programming language and the company that was founded to market it.
31. Name the first spreadsheet program and the first widely used word processing program.
32. What is shareware?

Discussion Questions

A. What difference do you suppose it would have made in modern history if Charles Babbage's steam-powered computer had been successfully built and used in the 1830s? Would there have been differences, for example, in science, manufacturing, international relations, and warfare?

B. One description of the effects of computerization over the past 40 years goes roughly like this: In the early days, computerization made it possible for organizations to deal with very large numbers of people (as, for example, in a payroll), as long as you treated everyone exactly alike. Today, computerization makes it possible to deal with very large numbers of people and to treat each one as a special case. Do you agree or disagree? Support your conclusions.

C. Do you agree that the innovation of microcomputers should be described as an explosion? Defend your conclusions.

M O D U L E B

BASIC Programming

In the mid-1960s, two college professors developed a programming language that they used to teach the fundamentals of programming to beginners. The language, called **BASIC**, for Beginners' All-purpose Symbolic Instruction Code, has become a very popular one, especially for personal computer users. BASIC was not standardized for a long time, so many versions of the language exist. This means that a BASIC program written for, say, a Hewlett-Packard minicomputer will not work on an IBM PC unless the program is modified. However, the bulk of BASIC is similar enough from one computer system to another for a programmer to make an easy transition. In this text we use Microsoft BASIC, run under DOS.

With the abundance of personal productivity tools such as spreadsheet programs and DBMSs, it is unlikely that, as a user, you will ever need to develop a program in BASIC (or in any other programming language). Still, an understanding of programming—even in a simple language like BASIC—can help you to understand and appreciate the effort that goes into developing application software. And who knows—maybe you will be intrigued enough with programming to consider studying it in more depth. Maybe you simply will find it fun.

To learn BASIC you need to do the exercises and examples here with a computer as you read. You need to have a computer that runs BASIC, a hard disk or a floppy disk containing the DOS operating system, and a blank, formatted floppy disk to store the programs you write. If you do not know how to format a disk, consult with your instructor or a lab assistant.

GETTING STARTED

When you write a program in BASIC, the instructions you write must be translated into machine language by a translator program. Consequently, you need to load a copy of the BASIC translator into your computer's main memory before you write any programs. This is called "loading BASIC."

Loading BASIC

The steps needed to load BASIC vary from one computer to another. If you use Microsoft BASIC (included in the DOS operating system), then follow these steps:

1. Insert the DOS disk into disk drive A.
2. Power on your computer.
3. At the A> prompt, type BASIC or BASICA, and press Return. (BASICA accepts more instructions than BASIC, but you can use either for purposes of this appendix.) The operating system will load the BASIC translator, and you will be ready to begin.

The BASIC prompt—the indication that BASIC is loaded and ready to be used—is OK.

4. Remove the DOS disk from drive A, and insert the blank disk on which you intend to store your programs. Most people do not store programs on a system disk.

If you use another version of BASIC or another computer, write in the box provided here the sequence of instructions your instructor gives you for getting started.

Signing On

BASIC Modes

BASIC can be run in two modes, direct and indirect. In **direct mode**, each BASIC instruction you type is executed by the computer as soon as you press Return. This is sometimes useful. For instance, you might want to use the computer as a calculator. To calculate a 9½ percent sales commission on a sale of $6,732.98, you could type the following instruction, then press Return:

```
PRINT .095 * 6732.98
```

(Note: In this text we use uppercase letters for all commands and statements, but BASIC accepts both uppercase and lowercase letters.) The computer executes the computation and displays the following answer:

```
639.6331
```

More often, you will run BASIC in **indirect mode.** This means that you will write a group of instructions, called a program, and execute them as one entity. To use indirect mode, you assign each instruction a line number between 1 and 99999. Regardless of the order in which you enter instructions, they will be executed in sequence according to their line numbers. (There are some exceptions, because you can change the order of execution with certain BASIC statements such as IF and GOTO—we will discuss these statements later.) Line numbers do not have to be consecutive. Most programmers number their lines in increments of ten, to make inserting instructions easier. Here is an example of BASIC in indirect mode:

```
10 PRINT .095 * 6732.98
20 PRINT "All done."
```

Type those instructions just as you see them, pressing Return at the end of each line. You should press Return after each instruction. We will not explicitly tell you to do so from now on. Notice that the instructions are not executed as soon as you enter them. They are being stored as a program and will not be executed until you give the command to run the program. Now type RUN. This time the computer displays

```
639.6331
All done.
```

BASIC Commands

BASIC commands perform various kinds of program maintenance, such as loading and saving programs. Commands—when not preceded by a line number—are executed as soon as you enter them. The commands you will use most often are LIST, NEW, LLIST, RUN, SAVE, and LOAD. The format notation used in this text appears in Figure B-1.

LIST The LIST command allows you to review a BASIC program by listing all or part of the program on the computer screen. The format of the LIST command is

```
LIST [line number][-line number]
```

If you specify a line number, that line will be listed on the screen. If you do not specify a line number, the entire program will be listed. Two line numbers

[ ]	*Italics*	. . .	CAPS	Punctuation	Spaces
Square brackets indicate that the entry inside is optional.	*Italics* indicate that you must enter the data. For example, RUN *program-name* means you have to enter the name of the program you want to run.	Ellipsis points indicate that an entry may be repeated.	Capital letters indicate parts of a BASIC statement that must be entered exactly as shown.	All punctuation, such as commas, quotation marks, parentheses, and equals signs, must be entered exactly as shown.	Spaces are used to separate words, items in a list, and other entries. Wherever one space is required, several may be entered.

FIGURE B-1 Format Notation for BASIC Statements

separated by a hyphen (-) tell the system to list a **range** of lines, beginning with the first line number and ending with the second one.

If the program to be listed is too long to fit on one screen, it is **scrolled**, like the credits at the end of a movie. Find out from your instructor how to stop the scrolling and restart it, so you can read the program before it whizzes by. Record how to do this in the box provided here.

Controlling Scrolling

If the two-line program that you just typed is still in the computer's memory, type LIST and see what happens. If the program is not in memory, enter those two lines first and then type LIST.

NEW The function of the **NEW** command is to clear the computer's memory when you want to enter a new program. If you do not issue this command, your new program statements may be interspersed with whatever happens to be in the computer's memory at the time you enter the program. The format of the NEW command is

```
NEW
```

Type NEW, then type LIST. There are no program statements remaining in memory, so no listing appears.

LLIST The function of the **LLIST** command is to print your program listing on paper. For lengthy programs, some people prefer to work with printouts, or **hard copy**. As you enter and modify your program, you should occasionally print your program as a backup. The format of the LLIST command is

```
LLIST [line number][-line number]
```

Two line numbers specify a range, just as in the LIST command format.

RUN The function of the **RUN** command is to execute all or part of a program. The formats of the RUN command are

```
RUN [line number]
```

and

```
RUN "program name"
```

Use the first format when you want to run a program that already has been loaded into main memory. When you specify a line number, program execution begins at that line. Type the two-line program into memory once more:

```
10 PRINT .095 * 6732.98
20 PRINT "All done."
```

Now type

```
RUN 20
```

This time, the only output is

```
All done.
```

because the program started running at line 20.

The second format of the RUN command is used when you want to execute a program stored on disk. In some versions of BASIC, the quotation marks are optional. When you specify a program name, the operating system will find that program on disk, load it into the computer's memory, and begin executing it. We will illustrate this format after discussing the SAVE command.

SAVE The function of the **SAVE** command is to store a BASIC program on hard disk or floppy disk. Every saved program needs a unique name. If you are working on a program that you already have saved on disk, then saving it again with the same name will erase the old version of the program, replacing it with the new one. Be careful when saving programs. Most computer systems do not warn you if you are using a program name that already exists—you could inadvertently erase a good program. Keep a handwritten list of the programs you already have saved, and a brief description of each one. The format of the SAVE command is

SAVE "<u>program name</u>"

Program names should not exceed eight characters.

With the two-line sample program in memory, save it on disk:

1. Insert a formatted disk into drive A.
2. At the BASIC prompt (OK) type

```
SAVE "TEXT1"
```

Now that the program is saved, erase it from memory by typing NEW. To be certain it is gone, type RUN. Now run it from disk by typing RUN "TEXT1". The system responds by displaying

```
639.6331
All done.
```

If those are not your results, trace through the steps above again.

LOAD The function of the **LOAD** command is to place into memory a copy of a BASIC program stored on disk. This is useful when you want to work on a program without running it. The format of the LOAD command is

LOAD "<u>program name</u>"

The six BASIC commands you will use frequently are summarized in Figure B-2. Commands are not preceded by a line number, so they are executed immediately. The formats of these commands may be slightly different on your computer system. If so, note the appropriate formats in the margins of this text.

BASIC Statements

BASIC statements are instructions preceded by a line number. They become part of a program. One BASIC statement you have seen already is PRINT. You will learn several more BASIC statements throughout this module. Each of the following lessons introduces one or more BASIC statements. In some instances, you will learn new formats for statements you have already learned.

LESSON 1

In this lesson you will learn about formats for the INPUT, PRINT, and CLS statements and about string and numeric variables. You will also learn how to insert and delete BASIC program statements.

With your computer on and BASIC loaded into memory, type the following program:

```
NEW
10 PRINT "THIS PROGRAM WAS WRITTEN BY"
20 PRINT "CINDY BIRDSONG"
RUN
```

Command	Function	Examples
LIST	Displays program on screen	LIST LIST 20-100
NEW	Clears memory for new program	NEW
LLIST	Prints hard copy of program	LLIST LLIST 20-100
RUN	Executes BASIC program	RUN RUN 100 RUN "Taxes"
SAVE	Stores BASIC program on disk	SAVE "GRADES"
LOAD	Places BASIC program into memory	LOAD "GRADES"

FIGURE B-2
Frequently Used BASIC Commands

The output is

```
THIS PROGRAM WAS WRITTEN BY
CINDY BIRDSONG
```

INPUT

Of course, unless your name happens to be Cindy Birdsong, the program just told a lie. (Actually, the programmer is the malfeasor. Keep that in mind the next time someone tells you "The computer made a mistake." People, not computers, make the mistakes.) To allow you—or anyone using the program—to enter his or her own name, change the program this way:

```
10 INPUT "NAME"; N$
20 PRINT "THIS PROGRAM WAS WRITTEN BY"
30 PRINT N$
RUN
```

The **INPUT** statement displays whatever is in quotation marks as a prompt, then waits until the user types a response and presses Return. In response to the NAME prompt, type your name, then press Return. The program output is

```
THIS PROGRAM WAS WRITTEN BY
your name
```

Notice that your name appears exactly as you typed it, using uppercase and lowercase letters, even typographical errors. When you type input data, BASIC distinguishes between upper- and lowercase letters. It does not distinguish between them when you enter instructions.

Now type RUN again, but enter someone else's name at the NAME prompt. Because you can vary the value, N$ is called a **variable**. Variables contrast with constants. A **constant** is a value that does not change during program execution. Anything enclosed in quotation marks is a constant, as is any number. If you wanted to enter your age in this program, you could do it this way:

```
10 INPUT "NAME, AGE "; N$, A
20 PRINT "THIS PROGRAM WAS WRITTEN BY"
30 PRINT N$
40 PRINT "WHOSE AGE IS"
50 PRINT A
RUN
```

At the first prompt (NAME, AGE), type your name, then a comma, then your age in years. When you press Return, the output is

```
THIS PROGRAM WAS WRITTEN BY
your name
WHOSE AGE IS
your age
```

Numeric and String Variables

BASIC (and computer programs in general) distinguishes between **numeric variables** (ones that contain numeric data) and **string variables** (ones that contain alphanumeric data). In BASIC, the variable name chosen by the programmer identifies the type of data. The strictest standards for variable names are the ones we will use here. They are as follows:

1. All variable names must start with a letter.
2. Variable names can be one letter or one letter followed by a digit.

3. String variables, in addition, must end with a dollar sign.

Using these rules, the following are examples of valid variable names: A, X, A1, X7, P0, A$, and T3$. Notice that A$ and T3$ are string variables. The others are numeric variables. Using the same rules, the following are examples of invalid variable names: 8A, XXY, BB, X12, and AB$.

Many versions of BASIC allow you to use extended variable names, having, say, eight characters (instead of two, as we described above). If you can use extended names, then by all means, do so. Extended names can be more descriptive—for example, TAX, COST, SCORE, NAME$, and BALANCE. Ask your instructor about the rules for variable names for the computer you use.

As you can see from the program on your computer screen, you are expected to input one alphanumeric string (N$), then a number (A). What happens if you enter two strings instead of a string and a number? Try it and find out.

PRINT

You can print more than one entity on the same line by listing the items (constants and variables) separated by semicolons (;). Change the sample program by typing

```
20 PRINT "THIS PROGRAM WAS WRITTEN
   BY"; N$
40 PRINT "WHOSE AGE IS"; A
30
50
RUN
```

Now the output looks like this:

```
THIS PROGRAM WAS WRITTEN BYyour name
WHOSE AGE ISyour age
```

Notice that no space separates your name from the word BY. This happens because BASIC accepts whatever appears between quotation marks just as it appears. Change line 20 by putting a space between the letter Y and the quotation marks. Run the program, and observe the results.

Deleting a Line

Typing a line number with no BASIC statement deletes it from the program. If you had not typed 30 and 50 in the last program, those lines would have remained in the program. Type LIST to look at the current version of the program. It should look like this:

```
LIST
10 INPUT "NAME, AGE"; N$, A
20 PRINT "THIS PROGRAM WAS WRITTEN
   BY "; N$
40 PRINT "WHOSE AGE IS "; A
```

Inserting a Line

Now insert two more lines into the program by using line numbers to indicate where you want them to be:

```
5 CLS
25 PRINT "A BRILLIANT PROGRAMMER"
RUN
```

CLS

This time the program started by clearing the computer screen and positioning the cursor in the upper-left corner, called the **home** position. The BASIC statement that clears the screen this way is **CLS.** You inserted that statement on line 5. Also, you added an editorial comment about yourself on line 25. The program now looks like this:

```
5 CLS
10 INPUT "NAME, AGE"; N$, A
20 PRINT "THIS PROGRAM WAS WRITTEN
   BY "; N$
25 PRINT "A BRILLIANT PROGRAMMER"
30 PRINT "WHOSE AGE IS "; A
```

Now move CLS from statement 5 to statement 15, then run the program:

```
5
15 CLS
RUN
```

This time the input prompt appears on the next line on the screen, but the output is on a clean screen. This is true because, in the new program, you cleared the screen only after you got the input variables. As you can observe, the order in which statements are executed is significant.

Lesson 1 Exercises

1.1 What is a variable? What is the difference between a numeric variable and a string variable?

1.2 Give examples of five valid variable names. Give examples of five invalid variable names. Explain why they are invalid.

1.3 Write a program to input one numeric variable, the wholesale cost of a product; to print the words COST IS; and to print the value of the variable on a second line. The retail price is 150 percent of the wholesale cost. Calculate the retail price and print it with an appropriate heading.

1.4 Do the same as in exercise 1.3, but print the values on the same lines as the words.

1.5 Do the same as in exercise 1.4, but clear the screen before prompting for input.

1.6 Write a program to input one string variable, to print the words WINNER IS, and to print the value of the variable on a second line.

1.7 Do the same as in exercise 1.6, but print the constant and the variable on the same line.

1.8 Write a program to input a salesperson's name and amount of sale, to print the words SALESPERSON AND AMOUNT OF SALE, and to print the variables on a second line.

1.9 Do the same as in exercise 1.8, but print the constant and variables on the same line.

1.10 Do the same as in exercise 1.8, but print only one line containing the word SALESPERSON, then the name of the salesperson, then the word AMOUNT, and then the amount.

LESSON 2

In this lesson you will learn another way to prompt a user, the END statement, the REM statement, how to perform calculations, and the USING option of the PRINT statement.

Prompting for Input

With your computer on and BASIC loaded into memory, enter the following program:

```
10 PRINT "TYPE YOUR NAME"
15 INPUT N$
20 PRINT "THIS PROGRAM WAS WRITTEN
   BY "; N$
99 END
RUN
```

When you run this program, you see that the prompt message is printed on one line, then a question mark appears on the next one where the input is entered. An INPUT statement that does not include a prompt message displays only a question mark. If you use this form of the INPUT statement, always precede it with a PRINT statement that tells the user what to enter.

END

The physical end of a program is the last instruction—the one with the highest line number. Often, but not always, this is also the logical end of the program—that is, the last one executed. If no explicit instruction to stop is given, the program stops when the last physical instruction is executed.

Most programmers prefer to state explicitly when the program should stop. To do this, they use the END statement. Line 99 contains an **END** statement for this sample program. Using a high number such as 99 allows the programmer to insert other lines easily, if needed. The format of the END statement is simply

```
END
```

When the END statement is encountered during program execution, the application program is terminated and control returns to the BASIC system. The END statement can appear anywhere in a program, but by definition it is always the last one executed.

REM

Just as labeled prompts make a program easier for a user to understand, comments within a program make the program itself easier for a programmer to understand. In BASIC, program comments are made with the **REM**—for "remark"—statement. REM statements can be placed anywhere in the program. When the translator program encounters a REM statement, it bypasses it. Therefore, you can write anything in a REM statement and it will be ignored. It will be printed when you LIST or LLIST the program.

In the following example, we use the REM statement to add a program comment that stands out in the listing, making it easy to read. With the program that you last wrote in memory, add these statements:

```
5 REM ********************************
6 REM * THIS IS A VERY SHORT PROGRAM *
7 REM ********************************
```

Now list the program. You get

```
5 REM ********************************
6 REM * THIS IS A VERY SHORT PROGRAM *
7 REM ********************************
10 PRINT "TYPE YOUR NAME"
15 INPUT N$
20 PRINT "THIS PROGRAM WAS WRITTEN
   BY  ";N$
99 END
```

Run the program, and notice that the remarks have no effect on it. Remarks are useful for explaining complex parts of programs, identifying the author, and indicating when a program was updated and by whom, and for other situations in which comments are helpful.

Performing Calculations

BASIC programs often include arithmetic operations. These are accomplished by means of the **LET** statement. The format of the LET statement is

LET <u>variable</u> = <u>expression</u>

Notice that the word LET is optional. You need only the equals sign (=) to indicate a LET statement. For illustrations of the LET statement, clear your computer's memory and enter this program:

```
NEW
10 REM HERE ARE EXAMPLES OF
   LET STATEMENTS
20 INPUT "ENTER ITEM PRICE  ", P
30 X = P * .075
40 PRINT "SEVEN AND ONE-HALF
   PERCENT TAX IS  "; X
50 T = P + X
60 PRINT "TOTAL IS  "; T
99 END
```

This program accepts an item price (P), computes $7^1/_2$ percent sales tax (X), displays the tax, computes the total price (T) for the item, and then displays it. (Notice that $7^1/_2$ percent is written .075. Numeric constants contain no punctuation except a decimal point and minus sign, if necessary.) Run the program several times with different item prices.

The two LET statements are in lines 30 and 50. They could be written as follows:

```
30 LET X = P * .075
50 LET T = P + X
```

As mentioned earlier, the word LET is optional. Although LET statements look like equations, they are not. The equals sign should be read "be made equal to." Thus, line 30 is read "Let X be made equal to P times .075." Line 50 is read "Let T be made equal to P plus X." When a LET statement is executed, the expression to the right of the equals sign is evaluated, and the value is placed in the variable on the left of the equals sign. The expression can be an arithmetic expression, another variable, or a constant. For example, you could set a variable to represent the sales tax rate, R, to 7.5 percent by writing

```
R = .075
```

or

```
LET R = .075
```

Arithmetic Expressions

An arithmetic expression can contain numeric variables, numeric constants, arithmetic operators, and parentheses. The **arithmetic operators** are symbols we use to indicate which operations we want performed on the data. The operations are addition (+), subtraction (–), multiplication (*), division (/), and exponentiation (=T or **). The **operands** in an arithmetic expression must be either numeric constants or numeric variables. The computer cannot perform arithmetic on string

Symbol	Operation
( )	Parentheses
^ or **	Exponentiation
* and /	Multiplication and division
+ and –	Addition and subtraction

FIGURE B-3
Arithmetic Operators Listed in Hierarchy

data. Here are some examples of LET statements that perform calculations:

```
A = B / C
A = B / 10
A = B + C
A = B + 10
A = B * C
A = B / C
A = B + C - 30
A = B * C / D
```

Order of Arithmetic Operations

As you can see, an arithmetic expression can be a combination of operations. When several operations are included, the computer follows a specific order, or **hierarchy**, to perform operations (see Figure B-3). Thus, for example, multiplication and division are done before addition and subtraction. Operations at the same level are performed from left to right. Sometimes you want the expression evaluated in an order different from the standard one. In this case, use parentheses around the part of the expression you want done first. For example, suppose you wanted to find the average of two test grades, T1 and T2. Clear your computer's memory and enter this program:

```
NEW
10 INPUT "TEST SCORES ", T1, T2
20 A = T1 + T2 / 2
30 PRINT "AVERAGE IS "
40 PRINT A
99 END
RUN
```

When prompted, enter the scores 100 and 80. The average, obviously, is 90. But this program says, incorrectly, that it is 140. That is because it first performed the division (T2 / 2 = 40) then added T1 (100) to the result, yielding 140. Now change line 20 this way:

```
20 A = (T1 + T2) / 2
RUN
```

Enter the scores 100 and 80 again. Note that this time the scores are first summed (100 + 80), then the total (180) is divided by 2, yielding the correct result (90). Use parentheses whenever you want to supersede the normal hierarchy of arithmetic operations.

Now change lines 10 and 20 so you can find the average of three test scores, as follows:

```
10 INPUT "ENTER SCORES ", X, Y, Z
20 A = (X + Y + Z) / 3
```

Lines 30, 40, and 99 remain the same. Run the program several times, entering different sets of scores.

PRINT USING

When prompted, enter the scores 65, 85, and 90. Notice that the average is several decimal places long. Sometimes this level of precision is desirable, but in other cases it is not. A teacher, for example, might be satisfied with just one decimal place. In order to round the average to the nearest tenth of a point and print the answer you need to use the **print format** option of the PRINT statement. Change line 40 as follows:

```
40 PRINT USING "##.#"; A
```

Notice that we have added the word USING followed by a print format, which is enclosed in quotation marks. Each number sign (#) indicates a digit position. Digit positions are always printed, except for leading nonsignificant digits. A decimal point, if you need one, may appear anywhere in the format. If all the digits to the left of the decimal point are zeros, then only one zero will print—the rest of the positions will be filled with blanks. If there are more digits to the right of the decimal point than your print format can accommodate, the number will be rounded when it is printed. Figure B-4 contains several examples of formatted numbers.

Now change line 40 in the program using different print formats. Run the program with the same data, and observe the results.

Print Format	Data	Displayed Results
"##.##"	15.78	15.78
"##.##"	.78	ƀ0.78
"##.##"	.786	ƀ0.79
"#,###.##"	2365.86	2,365.86
"#,###.##"	2365.8	2,365.80
"#,###.##"	.892	ƀƀƀƀ0.89

Note: ƀ indicates a blank print position.

FIGURE B-4
Formatted Numeric Data

Lesson 2 Exercises

2.1 What is the purpose of the REM statement?

2.2 What is the difference between a LET statement and an equation?

2.3 In an arithmetic expression, which operation is evaluated first, multiplication or subtraction? Multiplication or addition? Exponentiation or division? Exponentiation or an operation inside parentheses?

2.4 Write a program that accomplishes the following:

- Include your name, the date, and the exercise number in remarks. (Do this for all subsequent exercises in this and all future lessons.)
- Prompt the user to enter the number of cases of soda pop he or she wants to buy.
- Display the price of the pop, figured at $6.99 per case.

2.5 Do the same as in exercise 2.4, but print the answer with only two decimal places.

2.6 Write a program to do the following:

- Prompt the user for the number of people who will be attending a dance.
- Prompt the user for the cost of each ticket to the dance.
- Calculate and display the expected gross proceeds from the dance, using an appropriate print format.

2.7 Do the same as in exercise 2.6, but add the following features:

- Subtract the cost of the disc jockey ($500.00).
- Compute and subtract the cost of refreshments ($1.50 per person).

2.8 The campus student center needs new carpeting, and some student groups are trying to raise money to have it replaced. Write a program to do the following:

- Prompt the user for the dimensions (width and length) of the area to be carpeted.
- Prompt the user for the price per square yard of the carpet.
- Use a fixed price of $2 per square yard for the carpet pad, which is required for installation.
- Compute and display the total cost of installing the new carpet.

2.9 The same campus student center needs to be repainted. Write a program to do the following:

- Prompt the user to enter the number of square feet of wall space to be painted.
- Note that one gallon of paint covers approximately 500 square feet and costs $12.50. (This paint can be purchased in whole gallons only.)
- Compute and display how many gallons of paint will be needed and how much the paint will cost. Note: To round up to a whole gallon, compute the number of gallons needed (it probably will include a fraction); add 0.5 to this answer; print the new answer using this print format: "###".

2.10 The president of the United States is coming to visit the campus, so the students are mobilizing volunteers to paint the student center. They estimate that it takes one student two hours to prepare, paint, and clean up a 500-square-foot area. Write a program to do the following:

- Prompt the user to enter the number of square feet of wall to be painted.
- Compute and display the number of student-hours required to paint the student center.
- Compute and display the number of volunteers that will be needed for the job if each volunteer agrees to work for four hours. Note: you cannot have fractional volunteers, so round this answer up using the same method as described in the previous exercise.

LESSON 3

In this lesson you will be introduced to program design, and you will learn about program loops and the IF and GOTO statements.

The programs you have been studying and writing until now have been relatively simple. Each one consists of several statements, executed from beginning to end, one time through. If you want to execute a program more than once, you have to run it again. Sometimes that is not adequate. Sometimes we want to control execution of a program from within the program.

Loops

Consider the flowcharts in Figure B-5. The flowchart in Figure B-5*a* shows a series of instructions that are carried out just once. The flowchart in Figure B-5*b* shows those same instructions, but in this case they can be repeated if the user wants them to be.

Here is the program that matches the flowchart in Figure B-5*a*:

```
10 REM THESE INSTRUCTIONS ARE
   EXECUTED ONLY
```

FIGURE B-5

Program Logic with and without Loops

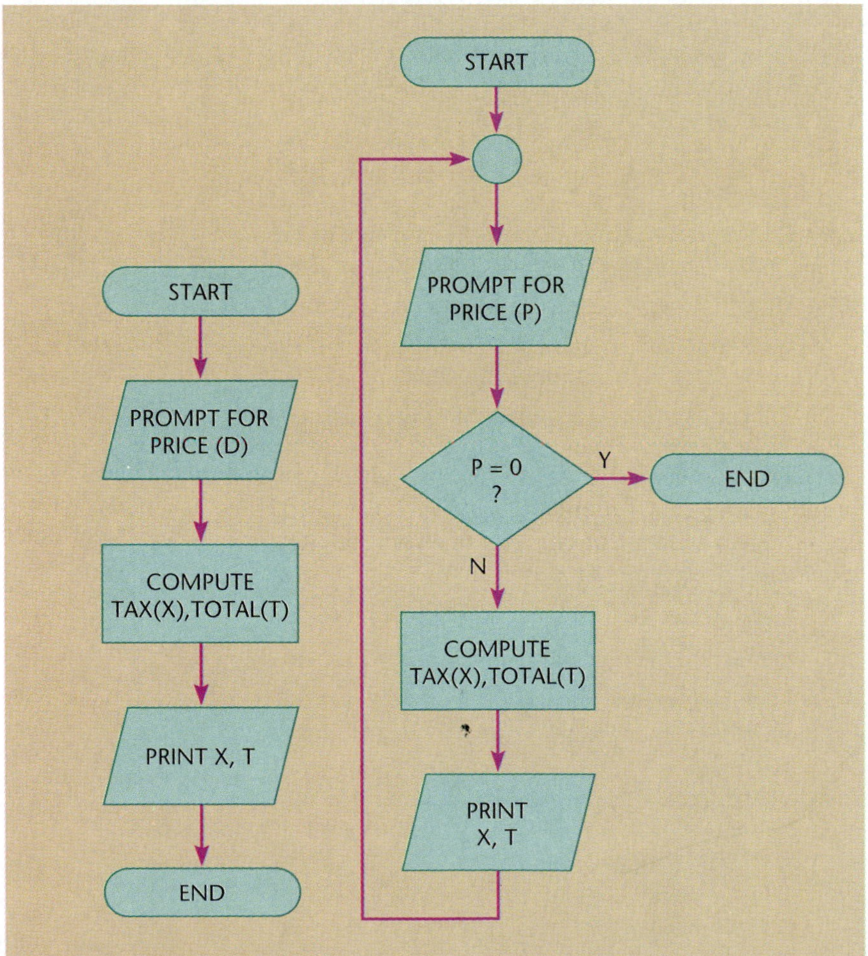

a. Executes one time through

b. Contains a loop

```
20 REM ONCE EACH TIME THE PROGRAM
   IS RUN
30 INPUT "ENTER ITEM PRICE ", P
40 X = P * .075
50 T = P + X
60 PRINT "TAX IS "; X
70 PRINT "TOTAL IS "; T
99 END
```

Here is the program that matches the flowchart in Figure B-5*b*. Modify the existing program so it looks like the following, then run it.

```
10 REM THIS PROGRAM CONTAINS
   A LOOP
30 INPUT "ENTER ITEM PRICE, OR
   0 TO QUIT ", P
35 IF P = 0 THEN END
40 X = P * .075
50 T = P + X
60 PRINT "TAX IS "; X
70 PRINT "TOTAL IS "; T
80 GOTO 30
```

Notice that the program "offers" to be executed again. In fact it will stay in this loop until you enter a price of zero.

Many new things are being introduced to you at once. Let's examine each one individually, starting with program design.

Program Design with Flowcharts

Before writing a complex program, programmers design the logic that the program will follow. **Logic** simply means the sequence of instructions including transfers of control that change the ordinary sequence. Remember, a program ordinarily executes in the order of its line numbers unless you tell it to do otherwise.

Program logic can be illustrated using a variety of techniques. A commonly used technique is the **flowchart**, a graphic diagram that uses symbols to indicate the type of operation being performed. In the flowcharts in Figure B-5, several symbols are used. The oval ⬭ indicates the starting and ending points of the program. A parallelogram ▱ indicates an input or output operation. A rectangle ▭ indicates an operation. A diamond ◇ indicates a condition being tested. And arrows indicate the flow of control from one operation or decision to another—hence the name flowchart. Trace the logic in the flowcharts in Figure B-5, and see if you can easily follow it.

GOTO

Let's turn our attention to the program now in your computer. Two new statements are introduced here, in lines 35 and 80. Let's look first at line 80, which says GOTO 30. The format of the **GOTO** statement is

```
GOTO line number
```

The GOTO statement is an unconditional transfer of control. This means that when a GOTO statement is encountered during program execution, control is transferred immediately to the line number specified and program execution continues there. By transferring control to an instruction that already has been executed, we produce a **loop**. Because of this loop, you do not need to run the program several times to input different data.

The IF statement in line 35 plays an important role. It terminates the loop when the user wants to quit—that is, when the user enters a price of zero. Whenever you put a loop into a program, make sure there is a way to stop the loop. Sometimes programmers make errors in a program that result in an endless loop, one that has no achievable end condition. In that case, some outside intervention is needed, such as holding down Control while you press the *C* key. Find out from your instructor how to interrupt a program during execution, and write the instructions in the box provided here.

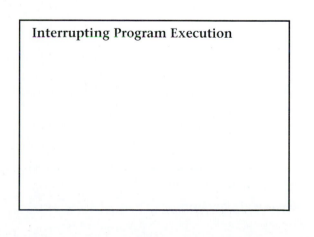

Interrupting Program Execution

Now delete line 35 from the program and run it. Notice that you are in an endless loop: The program has no built-in means of terminating. Interrupt the program following the instructions you wrote in the box above. Then put statement 35 back into the program:

```
35 IF P = 0 THEN END
```

IF ... THEN ... ELSE

The format of the IF statement is

```
IF condition THEN statement(s)
[ELSE statement(s)]
```

The function of the **IF** statement is to make a decision regarding program flow based on the result of a test condition. When an IF statement is encountered during program execution, a condition is tested. If the condition is true, then the statement or statements following the word THEN are executed, but not the ones following the word ELSE. If the condition is false, then the statement or statements following the word ELSE are executed, but not the ones following the word THEN. If the path taken does not include a GOTO, then program execution resumes at the next sequential instruction following the IF statement. The statement(s) following the word THEN (or ELSE) can be any BASIC statement, such as LET, GOTO, END, or even another IF. You will learn about this possibility in Lesson 4.

Notice from the format that the ELSE part of the IF statement is optional. Leaving out the ELSE simply indicates that something will be done only if the condition is true. Nothing special happens when the condition is false. This is sometimes referred to as a null ELSE.

A **condition** is a logical expression composed of variables, constants, and relational operators. **Relational operators** are used to compare two values. Figure B-6 shows the relational operators and their meanings.

Here is an IF statement that gives a bonus of 5 percent to anyone whose salary (S) is more than $30,000, and a bonus of $500 to anyone earning $30,000 or less:

```
IF S > 30000
  THEN B = S * .05
  ELSE B = 500
```

For the sake of readability, the condition and each of the two actions were written on separate lines. *Note that some versions of BASIC do not allow this format. Consequently, the entire IF ... THEN ... ELSE statement must be typed before pressing Return.*

Here is an IF statement that sets the tax rate (X) at 8 percent for sales made in the state (S$) of Connecticut:

```
IF S$ = "CT"
  THEN X = .08
```

Notice that the above IF statement has a null ELSE.

The following IF statement displays an error message if the parent's age (P) is less than or equal to the child's age (C):

```
IF P ≤ C
  THEN PRINT "AGE ERROR. REENTER
  AGES."
```

Now let's examine line 35 of the sample program.

```
35 IF P = 0 THEN END
```

Each time this statement is encountered, P is compared to zero. If it is equal to zero (meaning the user just typed in a "price" of zero), the statement following THEN is executed. In this case, it stops the program (END). If P is not equal to zero (and the user has typed in some other number), then nothing special happens because the statement has a null ELSE. Instead, control passes to the next in-

Operator	Relation Tested	Example
=	Equality	= 30000
< >	Inequality	< > 30000
<	Less than	< 30000
>	Greater than	> 30000
< =	Less than or equal to	< = 30000
> =	Greater than or equal to	> = 30000

FIGURE B-6
Relational Operators

Program Listing

```
REM   ***************************
REM   *   Number Guessing Game   *
REM   *     A QBASIC Program     *
REM   *        by R Hatch        *
REM   *        July 1992         *
REM   ***************************
REM
RANDOMIZE TIMER
TheNumber = INT (100 * RND + 1)
PRINT "I am thinking of a number
      between 1 and 100."
PRINT "You try to guess what
      it is."
PRINT
PRINT "Your guess";
INPUT YourGuess
WHILE YourGuess <> TheNumber
      IF YourGuess < TheNumber THEN
        PRINT "Too low"
      ELSE
        IF YourGuess > TheNumber THEN
          PRINT "Too high"
        END IF
      END IF
      PRINT "Your guess";
      INPUT YourGuess
WEND
PRINT "Correct! You got it!"
END
```

Program Run

```
I am thinking of a number between
  1 and 100.
You try to guess what it is.
Your guess? 50
Too high
Your guess? 25
Too high
Your guess? 12
Too low
Your guess? 18
Too high
Your guess? 15
Too high
Your guess? 13
Correct! You got it!
```

FIGURE B-7

Programming in QBASIC
BASIC has continued to evolve. Although Microsoft BASIC described in this module continues to be the most widely available, current versions of DOS include QBASIC, with additional capabilities. Programs in QBASIC do not require line numbers, use longer variable names, and can include WHILE loops.

struction following the IF statement—in this case, line 40.

Consider another example. Suppose you wanted to determine someone's average grade for an unknown number of tests. You would need to sum all the test scores and divide them by the number of tests. The flowchart for this program appears in Figure B-8. Examine it now. When you are sure you understand it, clear your computer's memory and enter this program:

```
10 REM T IS TEST SCORE
20 REM S IS SUM OF TEST SCORES
30 REM N IS NUMBER OF TESTS
40 REM G IS AVERAGE GRADE
50 REM
100 CLS
110 INPUT "ENTER TEST SCORE  ", T
120 S = S + T
130 N = N + 1
140 INPUT "DO YOU HAVE MORE TESTS
    (Y / N)?  ", A$
150 IF A$ = "Y" THEN GOTO 110
160 G = S / N
170 PRINT "THE AVERAGE IS "
180 PRINT USING "###.#"; G
999 END
```

Run the program using the scores 75, 83, 60, 40, and 99. You should get the answer 71.4. If you do not, carefully compare your program to the one in the text and correct any differences. Note: When the program prompts "DO YOU HAVE MORE TESTS (Y / N)?" only a response of uppercase Y will enable you to enter another score. Lowercase y or any other input causes the program to leave the loop, calculate the average, and stop. As an exercise, can you modify the program so it will accept lowercase y also?

Line 120 means "Add to whatever the accumulated score is so far (S) the value of this test (T), and put the new answer back in S." S is called an **accumulator**.

Line 130 means "Add 1 to the total number of tests so far (N) and put the new answer back in N." N is called a **counter**.

Change the program to allow the user to find the average of another set of scores. (This would be useful to a classroom teacher.) Add these statements:

```
190 INPUT "PRESS Y IF YOU WANT TO
    ENTER ANOTHER SET ", B$
200 IF B$ "Y" THEN GOTO 100
```

Now run the program, entering these test scores: 50, 100. The average you get is 75. When prompted

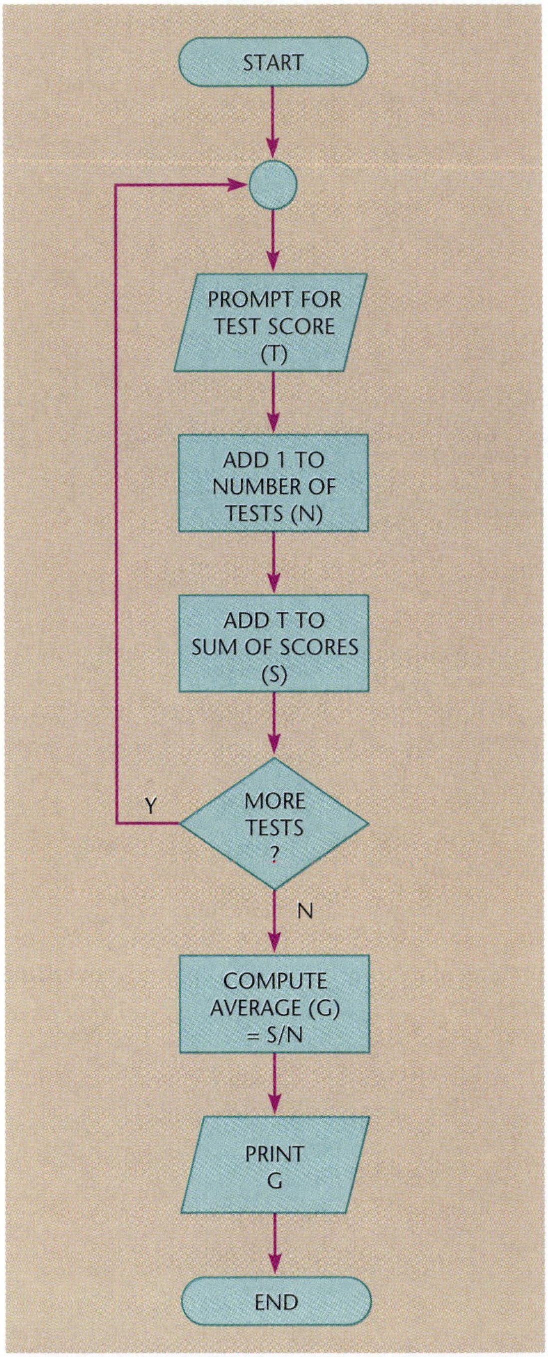

FIGURE B-8
Logic for Program to Find Test Average

to go again, answer Y. (Use an uppercase Y.) This time, enter only one score: 95. The average you should get is 95 (95 / 1 = 95), but the program says the average is 81.7. That obviously is incorrect. How did that happen?

Resetting Accumulators and Counters

Well, 81.7 is the average of 50, 100, and 95. As you recall, 50 and 100 were the test scores you entered for the previous student. When the program was done with those scores, it had a value of 150 in variable S and a value of 2 in variable N. The variables act just like calculators: The first time you use them they have already been set to zero, and if you want to use them again from the beginning, you need to zero them out, or **reinitialize** them. In this program, you can reinitialize by making the following program changes:

```
105 S = 0
107 N = 0
```

Now when you loop back to line 100 to enter the next set of grades, you start off by resetting S and N to zero. With those changes, run the program again with two sets of grades, first with 50 and 100 (giving an average of 75), then with just 95 (this time giving a correct average of 95). If you do not get those results, compare your program with the one in this text and correct any discrepancies.

Lesson 3 Exercises

3.1 What is a loop?

3.2 What is an endless loop? How do you prevent it? How do you stop it if your program goes into one?

3.3 What happens when a GOTO statement is encountered during program execution?

3.4 Write the IF statement that counts the number of people whose age (A) is under 25.

3.5 Write a program to do the following:
- Identify yourself, the date, and the exercise number in remarks, as usual.
- Prompt the user to enter a loan amount.
- Calculate and display the simple interest on the loan (9.9 percent).
- Allow the user to repeat the process.
- Quit when the user enters a loan amount of zero.

3.6 Write a program to do the following:
- Prompt the user to enter his or her net earnings for the past five years.
- Calculate and display the average earnings.
- Allow the user to repeat the process using any method of your choice to stop the loop.

3.7 Do the same as in exercise 3.6, but allow the user to enter any number of years' earnings.

3.8 Write a program to compute batting averages. Note: a batting average is the ratio of the number of hits to the number of times at bat, expressed as an integer. A batter who gets 2 hits out of 4 times at bat has a batting average of 500. A batter who gets 3 hits out of 10 times at bat has a batting average of 333.

3.9 Write a program to count the number of excellent customers, and calculate their average purchase amounts. Include the following:
- Prompt the user to enter a customer name and two purchase amounts.
- If the sum of the purchases is $300 or greater, print the message, "*customer name* IS AN EXCELLENT CUSTOMER."
- When the user has entered all the customer data, compute and display the average purchase amount *for excellent customers only*. Print the number of excellent customers.

3.10 Write a program to calculate employee pay amounts for an undetermined number of employees.
- Prompt the user to enter the number of hours an employee worked and the employee's hourly pay rate.
- Compute regular pay for the first 40 hours.
- Compute overtime pay as time-and-a-half for all hours worked over 40. There may be none.
- Calculate total pay: regular pay plus overtime pay.
- Enable the user to repeat this process. Stop the loop using any method you choose.

LESSON 4

In this lesson you will learn about nested IF statements and the TAB function of the PRINT statement.

Nested IF Statements

Consider this problem: Develop a program to accept sales data, then count the number of sales up to $300.00, the number between $300.01 and

$600.00, and the number over $600. Examine the program logic illustrated in the flowchart in Figure B-9. Trace the logic. One of the conditions (S > 300?) is tested only if the previous one (S > 600?) was false. Here is the program that matches that flowchart. Enter it on your computer and run it.

```
10 REM COUNT SALES
20 REM A IS COUNT OF SALES OVER
   $600.00
30 REM B IS COUNT OF SALES BETWEEN
   $300.01 AND $600.00
40 REM C IS COUNT OF SALES UP TO
   $300.00
100 INPUT "ENTER SALE AMOUNT OR
    ZERO TO STOP ", S
110 IF S = 0 THEN GOTO 140
120 IF S > 600 THEN A = A + 1
    ELSE IF S > 300 THEN
    B = B + 1 ELSE C = C + 1
130 GOTO 100
140 PRINT "OVER $600: "; A;
    "BETWEEN $300.01 AND $600: ";
    B; "UP TO $300: "; C
999 END
```

The **nested IF statement** is in line 120. As stated earlier, BASIC requires that the entire IF statement exist on one line—that is, with a single line number. The IF statement may be longer than one screen line, and BASIC automatically continues it on the next line. But the programmer does not press Return until the end of the entire statement. The structure of the nested IF statement can be seen more clearly if it is written like this:

```
IF S > 600
THEN A = A + 1
ELSE IF S > 300
     THEN B = B + 1
     ELSE C = C + 1
```

With this indentation it is easier to see which THENs and ELSEs go with which IFs. Obviously, nested IFs can get very complex and confusing. Therefore, try to limit yourself to only one or two levels of indentation—that's what we have used in the example.

Consider another example. Excise taxes for electronic equipment manufactured in the country of Circuitoria are levied at different rates. Products are categorized into computer and noncomputer equipment. Excise tax for noncomputer equipment is 15 percent. Computer equipment is further classified into laptop computers and desktop computers. Laptops are hit with an excise tax of 22 percent, and desktops are taxed at the rate of 28 percent. A program to determine the appropriate tax rate and then compute excise tax might be designed as illustrated in Figure B-10. Note that this flowchart contains a nested IF.

Here is the BASIC program that matches the flowchart. With your computer on and memory cleared, enter this program:

```
10 REM CALCULATE EXCISE TAX
100 R = 0
200 INPUT "ENTER PRICE  "; P
210 INPUT "ENTER CATEGORY:
    N, L, OR D  ", C$
220 IF C$ = "N" THEN R = .15
     ELSE IF C$ = "L" THEN R = .22
     ELSE IF C$ = "D" THEN R = .28
     ELSE PRINT "INVALID CATEGORY.  "
250 T P * R
280 PRINT "EXCISE TAX IS "; T
300 INPUT "DO YOU WANT TO GO AGAIN?
    (Y)  ",A$
310 IF A$ "Y" THEN GOTO 100
999 END
```

Notice that in this example we are checking for valid categories (that is, either N, L, or D). In case the user makes a mistake when entering the category (say she enters an R instead of a D), this program will tell her an error was made. Suppose we had written line 220 like this instead:

```
220 IF C$ = "N" THEN R = .15
     ELSE IF C$ = "L" THEN R = .22
     ELSE R = .28
```

What would happen if the user entered an incorrect category such as R or B or &? If you said that the excise tax rate would be set to 28 percent then you have correctly interpreted the IF statement. Programs that accept input data from a user need to perform extensive verification procedures to prevent bad data from entering a system and to give users an opportunity to correct bad data at the beginning. In fact, some estimates indicate that in some programs as much as 80 percent of the instructions exist just to verify the input data and only 20 percent are used for actual processing.

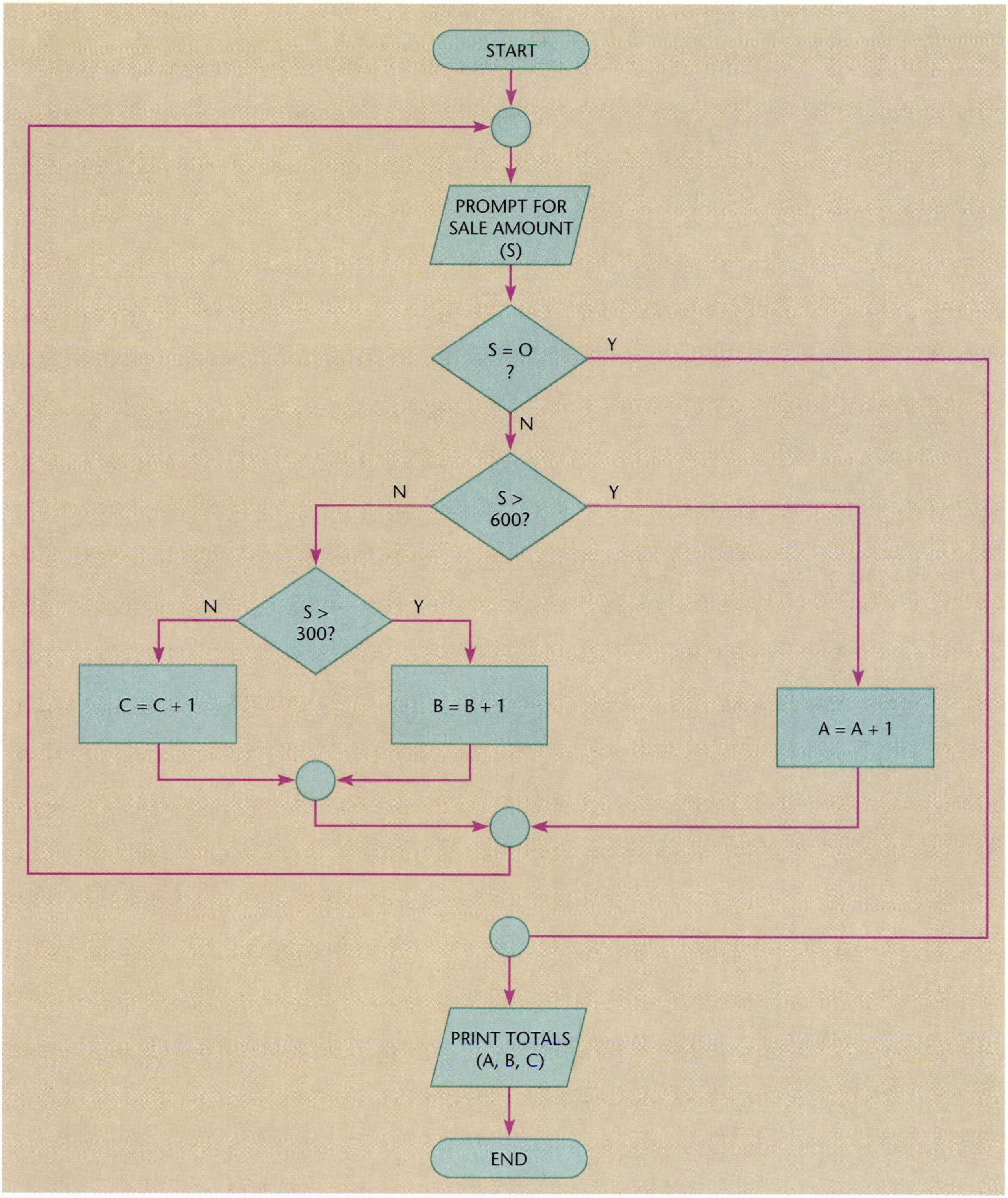

FIGURE B-9
Program Logic with Nested IF Statements

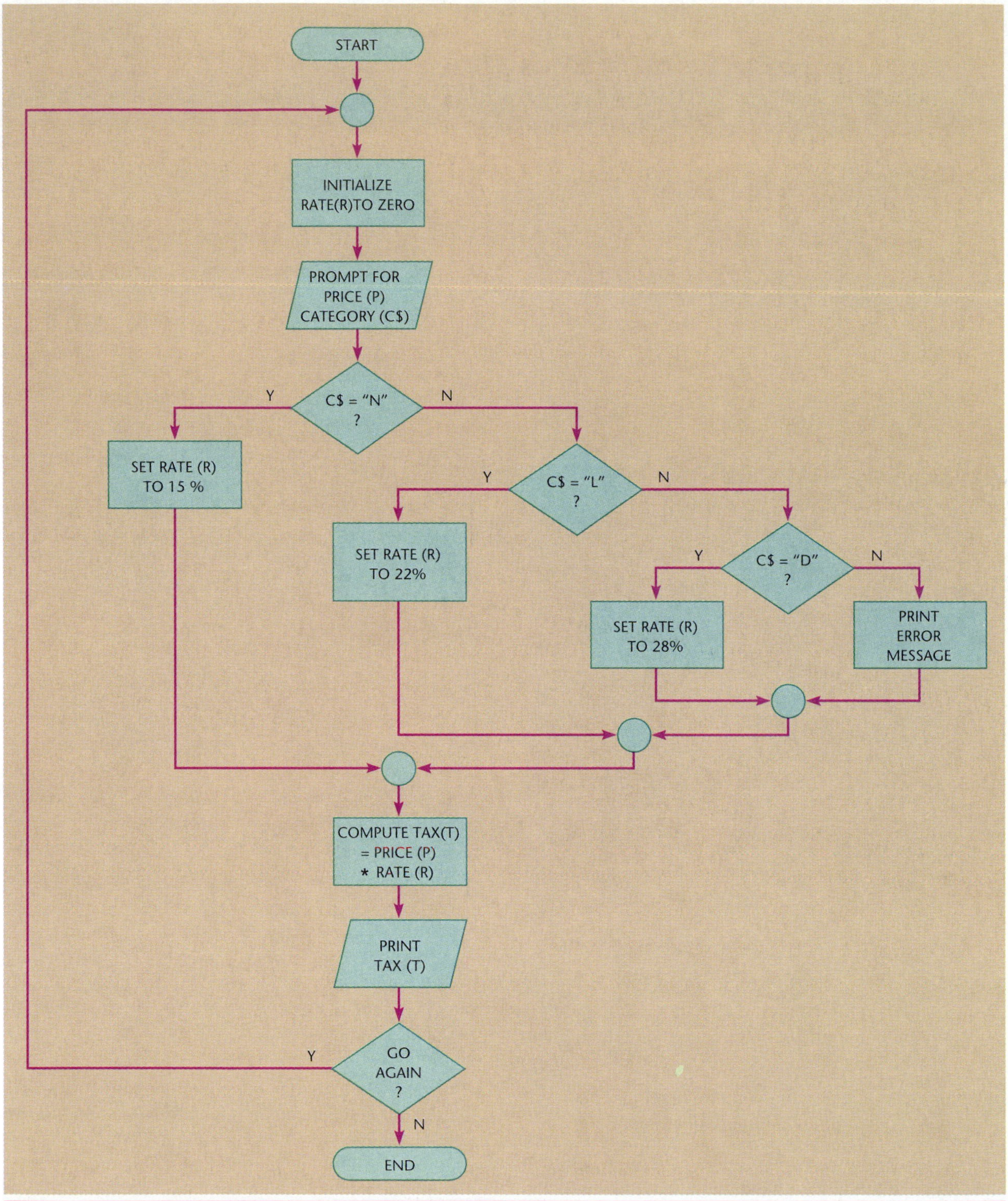

FIGURE B-10
Logic for Program to Determine Excise Tax

PRINT and PRINT TAB

Let's take another look at the first program example in this lesson:

```
10 REM COUNT SALES
20 REM A IS COUNT OF SALES
   OVER $600.00
30 REM B IS COUNT OF SALES BETWEEN
   $300.01 AND $600.00
40 REM C IS COUNT OF SALES UP TO
   $300.00
100 INPUT "ENTER SALE AMOUNT OR
    ZERO TO STOP ", S
110 IF S = 0 THEN GOTO 140
120 IF S > 600 THEN A = A + 1
    ELSE IF S = 300 THEN B = B + 1
    ELSE C = C + 1
130 GOTO 100
140 PRINT "OVER $600:  "; A;
    "BETWEEN $300.01 AND $600:  "; B;
    "UP TO $300: "; C
999 END
```

Previously we were concerned with the nested IF logic in the program. Now let us turn our attention to the output produced by this program. Examine line 140:

```
140 PRINT "OVER $600:  "; A;
    "BETWEEN $300.01 AND $600:  "; B;
    "UP TO $300:  "; C
```

By stringing several items together in the same PRINT statement and separating them by semicolons, we produce output that looks like this:

```
OVER $600: 3 BETWEEN $300.01 AND $600:
     8 UP TO $300: 4
```

Although it may be correct, the presentation of the results is not very easy to read. It can be made more readable by separating items. Their locations on the printed line are specified by means of the **TAB** function of the PRINT statement. So if we wanted to print the word OVER beginning in position 1, the word BETWEEN beginning in position 25, and the word UP beginning in position 50, we would change the PRINT statement as follows:

```
140 PRINT TAB(1) "OVER $600:  "; A;
    TAB(25)
    "BETWEEN $300.01 AND $600:  "; B;
    TAB(50)
    "UP TO $300:  "; C
```

The result is a printed line that is easier to read and interpret. Enter the program with the updated line 140 and try it. Change the TAB positions and see what happens. Put TAB positions in front of the variables, A, B, and C, then print the line and observe the results. Using TAB gives you more control over the design of your output.

Finally, you may want to leave some space on the screen before printing the output line. You leave space by printing blank lines. The format for printing a blank line is simply

```
PRINT
```

Add this line to your program:

```
135 PRINT
```

Now run the program and observe the results. If you want to print multiple blank lines, issue multiple PRINT statements, like this:

```
135 PRINT: PRINT: PRINT
```

BASIC allows you to put more than one statement on one line by using a colon to separate the statements.

Lesson 4 Exercises

4.1 What is a nested IF?

4.2 Write a program to accomplish the following:

- Prompt the user to enter a student's grade level (freshman or sophomore, using whatever codes you choose) and grade point average (a number between 0 and 4.0).
- Count and display the number of freshmen and the number of sophomores who are eligible for tuition rebates. Freshmen with GPA of 3.0 or higher and sophomores with a GPA of 3.2 or higher are eligible.

4.3 Do the same as in exercise 4.2, but add this feature:

- Calculate and display the percentage of freshmen, the percentage of sophomores, and the overall percentage of students eligible for tuition rebates.

4.4 A landscaping company sells live plants, silk flowers, and pottery. Handling charges for live plants are 10 percent of the cost; for silk flowers, 13 percent; and for pottery, 8 percent. Write a program to do the following:

- Prompt the user to enter the price and classification of each item a customer buys.
- Compute the total cost of the customer's order, including the handling charges.
- Display subtotals for items and for handling.
- Display the total cost for the order.

4.5 Employees earn vacation time based on the number of hours they work each week. Anyone who works 50 hours or more earns 1/2 day vacation; between 35 and 49 hours, 1/4 day; between 24 and 34 hours, 1/8 day; and below 24 hours, 0 days. Write a program to do the following:

- Prompt the user to enter the number of hours worked by each employee in a department.
- Compute and display the number of vacation days earned by the entire staff.

4.6 Do the same as in exercise 4.5 but add this feature:

- Compute and display the ratio of vacation hours earned to hours worked. A vacation day is equal to 8 hours.

4.7 A survey is being made of salaries earned by male and female employees. Write a program to do the following:

- Prompt the user to enter details on each employee: gender (F or M); work status (executive, administrator, or clerical); and annual salary.
- When all employee data has been entered, compute and display the following: number of men and women in each work status category, average salary in each category, average salary for each gender in each category, average overall salary for men, and average overall salary for women.

Be sure that your output is clearly labeled and is easy to read and interpret.

LESSON 5

In this lesson you will learn how to make program loops using the FOR and NEXT statements.

FOR and NEXT

Looping, or the repetition of instructions, is common in computer programs. We have seen examples of programs that obtain a set of data, process it, produce outputs, and repeat the procedure for the next set of data—that is, programs in which we issue a GOTO to go back to the input instructions. This procedure is called the input/process/output cycle. Other loops occur in programs also. Besides the GOTO statement, BASIC has another technique for handling loops. In this section you will learn about the FOR and NEXT statements.

To introduce these statements, we will consider a very simple grade school problem. We will write a program to count by 5s from 5 to 25. The flowchart for this program appears in Figure B-11*a*. Also, Figure B-11*b* shows a BASIC program using statements you already know.

Here is another version of this algorithm, or program design, using the **FOR** and **NEXT** statements. Load it into your computer and run it.

```
10 FOR N = 5 TO 25 STEP 5
20 PRINT N
30 NEXT N
40 END
```

The meaning of these statements is as follows. At line 10, set the variable N equal to 5. Process all statements until the statement NEXT N is reached (line 30). When NEXT N is reached, go back to the FOR statement (line 10). Add 5 to N and check to see if N is greater than 25. If it is not, repeat the loop. Continue repeating the loop until the value of N exceeds 25. Then skip over the loop and continue execution at the statement following the NEXT N statement (in this case, line 40).

Thus, the FOR statement sets up a variable that serves as an index over the loop. When the value of the index exceeds some specified amount, the loop is terminated. The format of the FOR statement is

```
FOR index = start TO end
[STEP increment]
```

The index is the name of the variable. The start value is the value to which the index is set the first time the loop is entered. The end value is the value that the index is compared to in order to terminate the loop. The increment is the number added to the index each time. Specifying the increment is optional, and the default is 1 (that is, the increment will be 1 unless a different value is specified).

The format for the NEXT statement is

```
NEXT index
```

When a NEXT statement is encountered during program execution, control is returned to the ap-

FIGURE B-11
Counting by 5s to 25

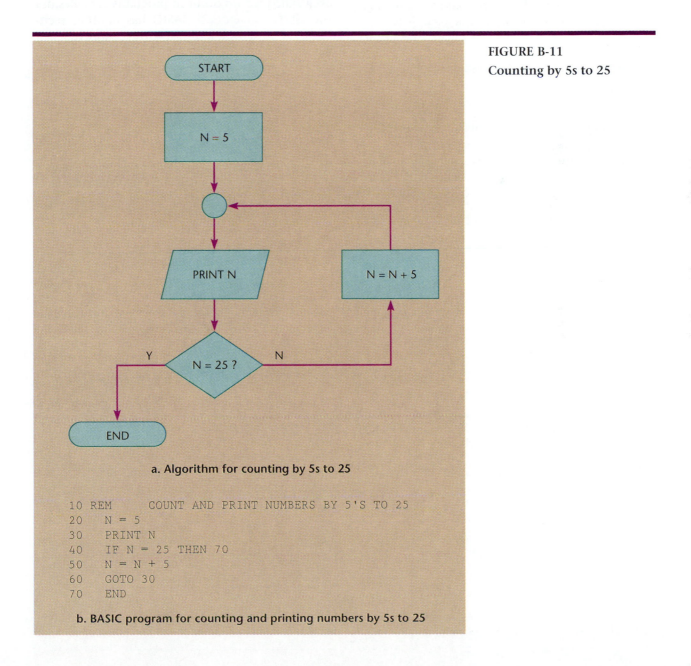

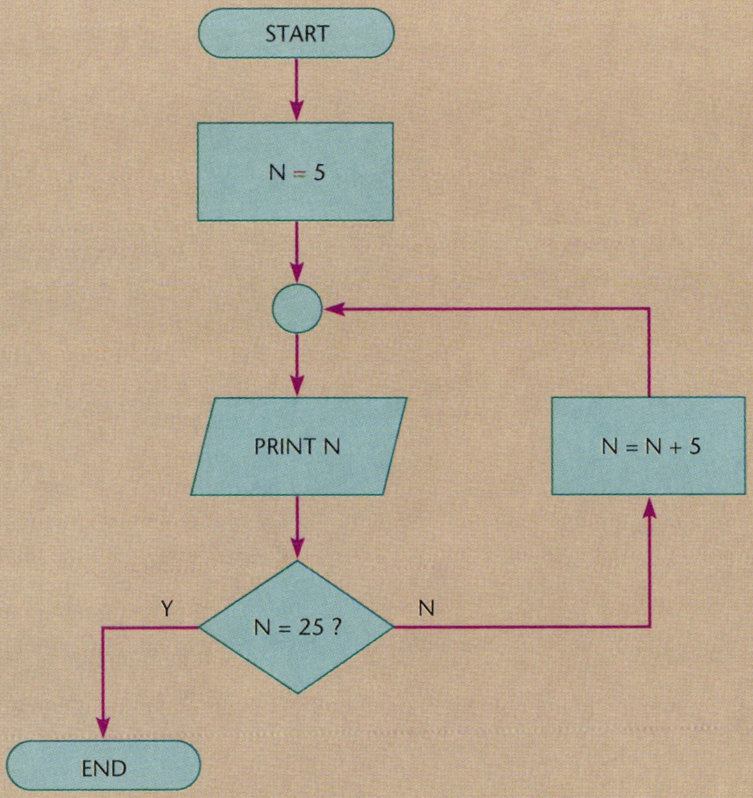

a. Algorithm for counting by 5s to 25

```
10 REM      COUNT AND PRINT NUMBERS BY 5'S TO 25
20   N = 5
30   PRINT N
40   IF N = 25 THEN 70
50   N = N + 5
60   GOTO 30
70   END
```

b. BASIC program for counting and printing numbers by 5s to 25

propriate FOR statement, at which point the index is incremented and tested for the terminal value. FOR and NEXT statements are always used as a pair.

Here is another application for the FOR and NEXT statements. This program prompts the user for exactly five test scores, then computes and displays the average. Enter it into your computer and run it.

```
100 FOR I = 1 TO 5
110 INPUT "ENTER TEST SCORE ", T
120 X = X + T
130 NEXT I
200 A = X / 5
210 PRINT "AVERAGE IS "; A
999 END
```

The next program is a variation of the previous one. In this version, the program prompts the user first to enter the number of tests (N). Then it executes the loop up to N times, and finds the average of N scores.

```
90 INPUT "HOW MANY TEST SCORES? ", N
100 FOR I = 1 TO N
110 INPUT "ENTER TEST SCORE ", T
120 X = X + T
130 NEXT I
200 A = X / N
210 PRINT "AVERAGE IS "; A
999 END
```

One pair (or more) of FOR-NEXT statements can be nested within another pair of FOR-NEXT statements. Consider the problem of producing a multiplication table like the one shown in Figure B-12.

To compute this table we need two variables: one to indicate the column (C) and one to indicate the row (R). To compute the first row, we let R = 1 and let C go from 1 to 5. For each value of C we compute R times C and print the result. To do just that much we would use these BASIC statements:

```
10 R = 1
20 FOR C = 1 TO 5
30 P = R * C
40 PRINT R; " TIMES "; C " EQUALS "; P
50 NEXT C
999 END
```

Enter that program and run it. The results should be:

```
1 TIMES 1 EQUALS 1
1 TIMES 2 EQUALS 2
1 TIMES 3 EQUALS 3
1 TIMES 4 EQUALS 4
1 TIMES 5 EQUALS 5
```

This is the equivalent of the first row of the table. It does not use the same format as the one in Figure B-12, but the values are the same. Printing the second and subsequent rows is done by following

FIGURE B-12
Multiplication Table

		Columns				
		1	2	3	4	5
Rows	1	1	2	3	4	5
	2	2	4	6	8	10
	3	3	6	9	12	15
	4	4	8	12	16	20
	5	5	10	15	20	25

the same order of operation, but this time letting R be equal to 2, 3, and so forth. Change your program by replacing line 10 and adding line 60, as follows:

```
10 FOR R = 1 TO 5
20   FOR C = 1 TO 5
30     P = R * C
40     PRINT R; " TIMES ";
       C " EQUALS "; P
50   NEXT C
60 NEXT R
999 END
```

Notice how we use indentation to make the program logic easier to discern. Now run this program and observe the results. This time, all 25 entries are printed.

Note that the FOR and NEXT statements for variable C are enclosed between the FOR and NEXT statements for variable R. BASIC requires this format. See what happens when you switch the order of the NEXT statements. You should get an error message.

The start value, end value, and step value for an index do not have to be stated as numeric constants. They can also be variables. Consider the following example. A program will begin by asking the user to enter the number (N) of patient weights that will be entered. Then the program will perform its input/process/output loop N times before printing the average weight and stopping. Here is the program:

```
100 INPUT "HOW MANY PATIENTS
    THIS TIME? ", N
110 CLS
200 FOR X = 1 TO N
210 INPUT "ENTER WEIGHT IN
    POUNDS ", W
220 T = T + W
290 NEXT X
400 A = T / N
410 PRINT "AVERAGE WEIGHT IS "; A
999 END
```

Enter and run the program, and observe the results.

Lesson 5 Exercises

5.1 Explain the actions the computer will take for each of the following sets of BASIC statements:

a. 10 FOR J = 1 TO 9 STEP 2
   20 PRINT J
   30 NEXT J

b. 10 FOR J = 1 TO 10 STEP 2
   20 PRINT J
   30 NEXT J

c. 10 FOR J = 1 TO 3
   20 PRINT J
   30 NEXT J

d. 10 FOR J = 1 TO 4
   20 PRINT J
   30 FOR K = 1 TO 3
   40 PRINT K
   50 NEXT J
   60 NEXT K

5.2 Write a BASIC program that will produce a division table for the values 20 through 26 divided by 2, 3, and 4. (Hint: Start by figuring it out manually, so when you print results you will know if they are correct.)

5.3 Write a BASIC program that will prompt the user for the number of shipment weights to be entered. Then accept that many weights, expressed in pounds; convert each weight into its metric equivalent, expressed in kilograms; and print each weight. When all weights have been entered, print the average weight in pounds. Note: One kilogram is equal to approximately 2.2 pounds.

5.4 Write a BASIC program to print a multiplication table that finds the product of 3 times any consecutive numbers the user chooses. Prompt the user for the starting and ending numbers. (Hint: when you run the program, keep the range of numbers small so the table will fit on one screen.)

5.5 Write a program that will calculate and print ten numbers in a series, starting at 1, such that each successive number is the sum of the previous two numbers, like this:

1 2 3 5 8 13

This is known as the Fibonacci sequence. The programming logic for this program appears in Figure B-13. Be certain you understand the logic before you try to write the program.

LESSON 6

In this lesson you will learn how to define and use arrays.

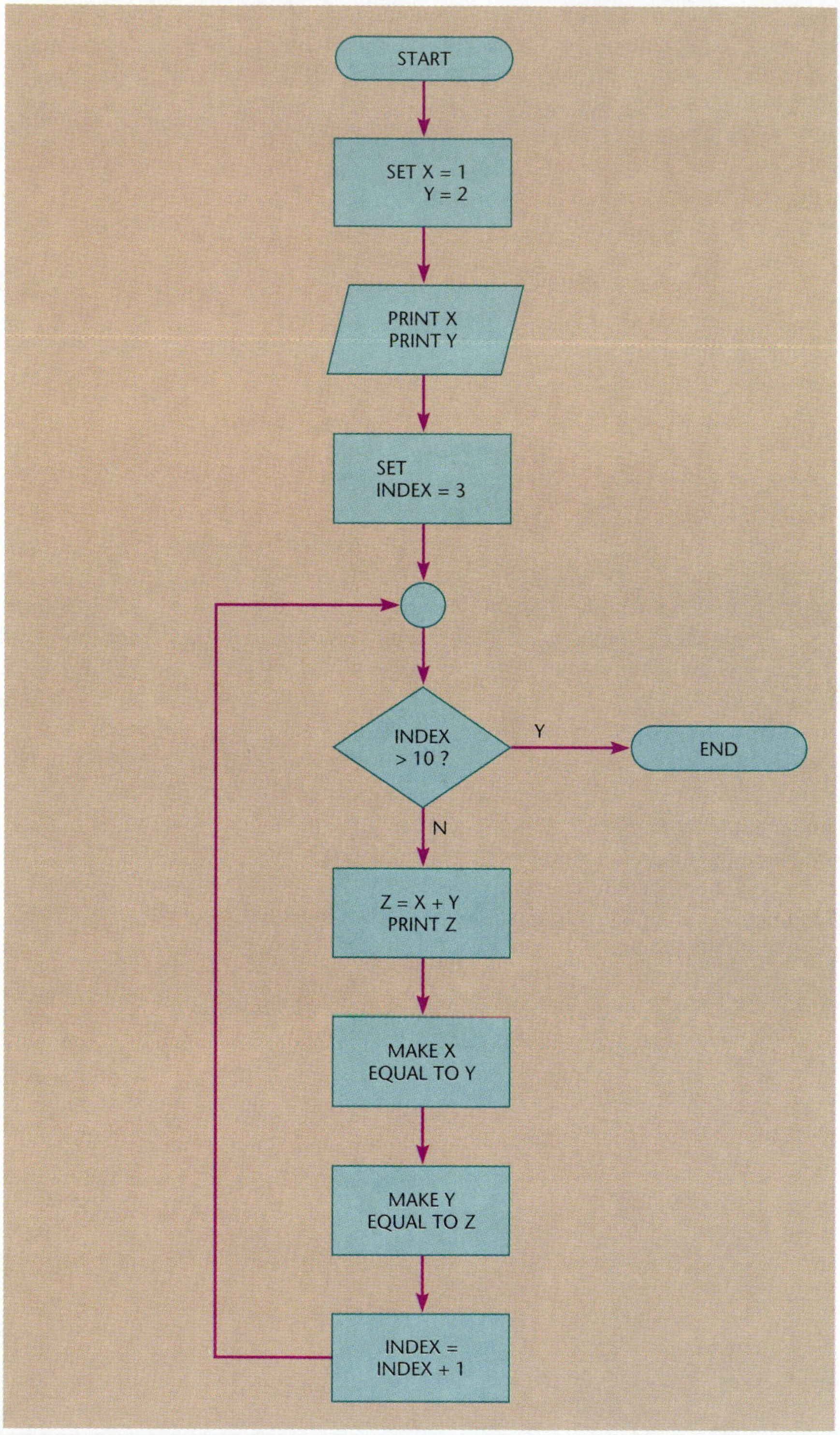

FIGURE B-13
Program Logic for Exercise 5.5

Arrays

An **array** is a table that has rows and columns. People use arrays, or tables, all the time, and they are very useful data structures within programs. Consider, for example, a table you could use to look up shipping and handling charges to add to customer order totals. Each of the six postal zones has a fee associated with it. The table looks like this:

ZONE	FEE
1	10
2	13
3	8
4	16
5	14
6	12

Thus, if a customer lived in zone 2 she would have to pay $13 for shipping and handling. If she lived in zone 6 she would pay $12 for shipping and handling.

In a BASIC program you could determine the shipping and handling fee by writing a series of IF statements, like this:

```
210 IF Z = 1 THEN F = 10: GOTO 400
220 IF Z = 2 THEN F = 13: GOTO 400
230 IF Z = 3 THEN F = 8: GOTO 400
240 IF Z = 4 THEN F = 16: GOTO 400
250 IF Z = 5 THEN F = 14: GOTO 400
260 IF Z = 6 THEN F = 12: GOTO 400
270 PRINT "INVALID ZONE. TRY AGAIN ":
    GOTO 200
400 etc.
```

Notice that the true evaluation of each IF statement causes two statements to be executed. In BASIC you can incorporate more than one statement on a line by separating them with colons (:). Consequently, line 210 reads: If the zone is 1, set the fee to $10 and then skip down to line 400, bypassing all the rest of the IF statements. The other IF statements are interpreted similarly. Now, back to the problem at hand.

The program is an awkward one. What happens if we suddenly expand the business and include 50 more zones? Do we need to write 50 more IF statements? What about a table containing 1,000 entries? Fortunately there is a way to handle tables in BASIC. We will start with some terminology. Because we will be referring to the items in the table we need to give each one of them a name. First, let's call the table T. We also need to name the rows and columns. We can call the first row, row 1; the second row, row 2; and so on. Similarly, we name the columns column 1 and column 2.

Now to identify a particular item, we state the table name, the row name, and the column name. Thus, the value 1 is found at table T, row 1, column 1. The value 8 is found at table T, row 3, column 2. This naming is cumbersome, so we can use shorthand. To reference a particular table location we will put the row and column numbers in parentheses after the table name. So T(1,1) refers to table T, row 1, column 1 (which contains the value 1), and T(3,2) refers to table T, row 3, column 2 (which contains the value 8). The names of the rows and columns are called **subscripts**.

Tables can vary in size. They can have one or many rows and one or many columns. The shipping and handling table we are using for an example has six rows and two columns. The number of rows and columns are called the **dimensions** of the table. The dimensions of the shipping and handling table are 6 by 2.

Before we use a table in BASIC we must define it. This is accomplished by naming the table and giving its dimensions. The system can then reserve space in main memory for all of the values. The BASIC statement used to define a table is **DIM**, which is short for dimension.

DIM

The format of the DIM statement is

```
DIM tablename(subscripts)
```

The subscripts are the numbers that define the maximum value of the dimensions of the array. The rules for creating a table name are the same as for a variable name. To define the shipping and handling table we would code:

```
100 DIM T(6,2)
```

This statement tells the system to reserve enough storage for a table with six rows and two columns.

You can visualize the table as a grid, six rows down and two columns across, whose values are all initialized to zeros. Once the table is defined, we must put data into it.

We could do it with a list of LET statements like this:

```
10 T(1,1) = 1
20 T(1,2) = 10
30 T(2,1) = 2
40 T(2,2) = 13
```

and so forth. But this approach is tedious and would be even worse if the table dimensions were, say, 100 by 100. Also, what if we wanted to input the table values from the user? In this case we might code:

```
10 INPUT "ZONE, FEE "; T(1,1), T(1,2)
20 INPUT "ZONE, FEE "; T(2,1), T(2,2)
30 INPUT "ZONE, FEE "; T(3,1), T(3,2)
```

and so forth. When line 10 is executed, the user is expected to provide two values. The first value will be put into position 1,1 of T, and the second value will be put into position 1,2 of T.

We can employ the FOR-NEXT statements to make the programming easier. Consider this program for defining and filling the shipping and handling table:

```
10 DIM T(6,2)
20 FOR I = 1 TO 6
30 INPUT "ZONE, FEE"; T(I,1), T(I,2)
40 NEXT I
```

The FOR-NEXT loop causes the INPUT instruction to be executed six times. The first time it is executed, I has the value of 1. The second time, I has the value of 2, then 3, then 4, then 5, and finally 6.

This approach has even more appeal when you consider what would happen if the table dimensions were 100,2. Without the FOR-NEXT loop, it would take 100 INPUT statements to fill the table. However, with the FOR-NEXT instructions, it can be filled with just two changes, as follows:

```
10 DIM (100,2)
20 FOR I = 1 TO 100
30 INPUT "ZONE, FEE "; T(I,1), T(I,2)
40 NEXT I
```

Using an Array

Now let's return to the problem of adding the shipping and handling charge to a customer's order total. The logic for this program is shown in Figure B-14. Study it carefully. It may seem a little confusing at first. The program starts by establishing the table: defining it and prompting the user to key in the values.

Next, the user is prompted to enter the customer's subtotal and postal zone. The index (J) is initialized to 1, and the loop begins. First, check to see if the customer's postal zone matches the subscripted table entry. If it does match, add the appropriate shipping and handling fee to the subtotal and print the results.

If the customer's postal zone does not match that table entry, then add 1 to J. At this point, one of two things can be true: Either there are no more entries in the table to search (J > 6), meaning that the user typed in an incorrect postal zone, or the customer's postal zone needs to be compared to the next table entry. Eventually, we will exit from the loop, either because a match was found or because we exhausted all the table entries unsuccessfully.

Now, with your computer on and memory cleared, enter this program:

```
05 REM LINES 10 THROUGH 40
   ESTABLISH THE TABLE
10 DIM T(6,2)
20 FOR I = 1 TO 6
30 INPUT "ENTER ZONE AND FEE
   SEPARATED BY A COMMA  ", T(I,1),
   T(I,2)
40 NEXT I
100 INPUT "ENTER SUBTOTAL AND ZONE,
    SEPARATED BY A COMMA  ", S, Z
120 J = 1
130 IF Z = T(J,1) THEN GOTO 400
140 J = J + 1
150 IF J > 6 THEN PRINT "INVALID
    ZONE. TRY AGAIN.": GOTO 100
160 GOTO 130
400 G = S + T(J,2)
410 PRINT "TOTAL: "; S; "  ";
    T(J,2); "  "; G
500 INPUT "GO AGAIN? ", A$
510 IF A$ = "Y" THEN GOTO 100
999 END
```

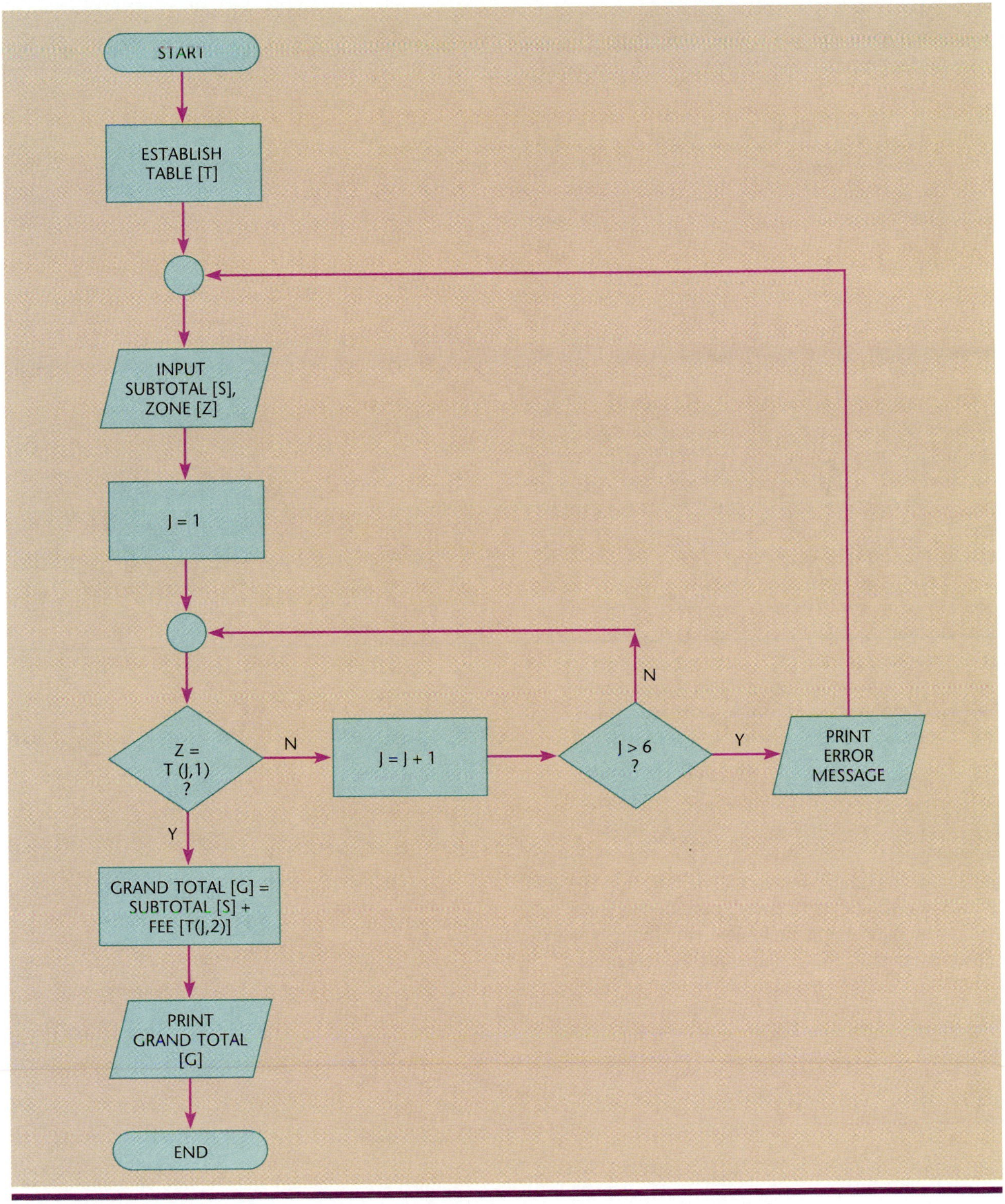

FIGURE B-14
Program Logic for Adding Shipping and Handling Fee to Customer Order Total

Notice that the fee extracted from the table—T(J,2)—is used like any numeric variable. It is an operand in the calculation in line 400. It is printed as output in line 410.

Run the program several times, using both valid and invalid zones. When you have seen how the program works, answer N to the prompt. Then run the program again. Notice that you have to load the table again. In fact, the way the program is right now, the table needs to be loaded by the user every time it is run. In the next section you will learn an easier way to fill the table with data.

READ and DATA Statements

Using the INPUT statement to fill a table may not always be appropriate. It can be time-consuming and error-prone. If a user enters incorrect table data, then the program results will also be incorrect. Building the table values into the program would be better, because then no user intervention is needed to fill the table.

The **READ** statement works similarly to the INPUT statement, except that the program does not look to the keyboard for input. Rather, the program looks through its own instructions for a **DATA** statement. When one is found, values are taken, one at a time. In the following example, values are assigned to variables A, B, and C:

```
40 READ A, B, C
50 DATA 10, 20, 30
```

When line 40 is executed, the value 10 is assigned to A;, 20, to B; and 30, to C. Although DATA and READ statements do not need to be adjacent in a program, organizing them that way makes the program more readable. Consider this program:

```
10 DIM A(3)
20 FOR I = 1 TO 3
30 READ A(I)
40 NEXT I
50 PRINT "THE VALUES OF A ARE  "
60 PRINT A(1), A(2), A(3)
70 DATA 10, 20, 30
99 END
```

READ statements can be executed repetitively. If this is done, however, sufficient data must be provided in one or more DATA statements. In the following program, the READ statement is executed three times. The first two sets of data are taken from the DATA statement in line 50, and the third set is taken from the DATA statement in line 60.

```
10 FOR J = 1 TO 3
20 READ A, B
30 PRINT A, B
40 NEXT J
50 DATA 9, 8, 7, 9
60 DATA 5, 6
99 END
```

Output from the program is as follows:

```
9       8
7       9
5       6
```

Now let's reconsider the program for adding a shipping and handling fee to a customer's order total. In the following version of the program, the table is filled from DATA statements within the program itself. This ensures that no incorrect table data is used.

```
05 REM ** THIS SECTION
   ESTABLISHES THE TABLE**
10 DIM T(6,2)
20 FOR I = 1 TO 6
30 READ T(I,1), T(I,2)
40 NEXT I
50 DATA 1, 10
51 DATA 2, 13
52 DATA 3, 8
53 DATA 4, 16
54 DATA 5, 14
55 DATA 6, 12
90 REM ** THIS SECTION PROCESSES
   CUSTOMER ORDERS **
100 INPUT "ENTER SUBTOTAL AND
    ZONE, SEPARATED BY A
    COMMA  ", S, Z
120 J = 1
130 IF Z = T(J,1) THEN GOTO 400
140 J = J + 1
150 IF J > 6 THEN PRINT
    "INVALID ZONE. TRY AGAIN.":
     GOTO 100
160 GOTO 130
400 G S T(J,2)
410 PRINT "TOTAL:  "; S; "  ";
    T(J,2); "  "; G
```

```
500 INPUT "GO AGAIN? ", A$
510 IF A$ = "Y" THEN GOTO 100
999 END
```

Using READ and DATA Statements

READ and DATA statements are appropriate in situations where the input data does not change very often, such as in the shipping and handling fees in the example above and in income tax tables. Although fees may change occasionally, they remain the same much of the time. Income tax tables change once a year.

READ and DATA statements are inappropriate when input data values change frequently. Consider, for example, a table of currency exchange rates, which can change daily. In that case, it would be better to prompt the user to enter today's rates than to build them into DATA statements. The other option is to teach users how to go into a BASIC program and change DATA statements themselves—but most users are not interested in getting involved in programming. Furthermore, even experienced programmers make mistakes when modifying programs. Making program changes should be avoided whenever possible.

Lesson 6 Exercises

6.1 Explain what the following statements mean:

a. 10 DIM R(50,50)

b. 10 DIM X1(1000)

6.2 Which of the following statements are valid references for question 6.1.a?

a. INPUT R(23,4)

b. T = R(–2,17)

c. Z = R(23,4)

d. Q = R(40,2)

6.3 Which of the following statements are valid references for question 6.1.b?

a. INPUT X1(200)

b. X1 = 75

c. T = X1(–5)

d. INPUT X1(1001)

6.4 What will happen when the following statements are executed?

```
10 READ A, B
20 PRINT A, B
30 END
40 DATA -10, 400
```

6.5 Describe the output produced by the following program:

```
10 FOR J = 1 TO 2
20 READ K, L, M
30 PRINT K, L, M
40 NEXT J
50 DATA 10, 20, 30
60 DATA 40, 50
70 DATA 60
80 END
```

6.6 Write a program to calculate and print a multiplication table. The table should show the product of odd numbers from 1 to 9. Thus, rows and columns of the table are 1, 3, 5, 7, and 9. Use a one-dimensioned array to calculate and print one row of the table at a time.

6.7 For a major cross-country meet, runners are being assigned to starting groups based on their times at an earlier qualifying run. The group assignments are made as follows:

Previous Time	Group Assignment
35 minutes or less	1
36 to 40 minutes	2
41 to 50 minutes	3
51 to 60 minutes	4
Over 60 minutes	5

Develop a program to make the group assignments. Your program should prompt the user to enter runner's name and previous time. It should output runner's name and group assignment.

6.8 Develop a program to compute gross pay and taxes. Input employee name, hourly pay rate, and number of hours worked. Give the employee time-and-a-half for work in excess of 40 hours. Compute taxes on the basis of the table given below.

If Gross Pay Is		
Greater than or Equal to ($)	But Less than ($)	Then Taxes Are
0	200	10% of gross pay
200	600	$20 + 15% of the amount over $200
600	1000	$80 + 20% of the amount over $600

1000	1500	\$160 + 40% of the amount over \$1000
1500 or greater		\$360 + 60% of the amount over \$1500

Your program should output employee name, gross pay, taxes, and net pay. Also calculate and print total payroll, total taxes, and total net pay. Try the following hints:

- Use a table with three columns.
- Use READ and DATA statements to fill the table.
- Test the program for correct results. Show that it works for all possible values.

KEY TERMS

BASIC
direct mode
indirect mode
BASIC command
LIST
range
scroll
NEW
LLIST
hard copy
RUN
SAVE
LOAD
INPUT
variable
constant
numeric variable
string variable
home
CLS
END
REM
LET
arithmetic operator
operand
hierarchy
print format (PRINT USING statement)
logic
flowchart
GOTO
loop
IF
condition
relational operator
accumulator
counter
reinitialize
nested IF statement
TAB
FOR and NEXT
array
subscript
dimensions (of a table)
DIM
READ
DATA

Glossary

Access arm Mechanism on a disk drive that holds read/write heads and moves to access disk tracks.

Ada Programming language developed for the Department of Defense as a standard for all armed services. It is patterned after Pascal, is highly structured, and very complex.

Ad hoc query An unplanned question to be answered by accessing the data in a database.

Aiken, Howard Pioneer in using electromechanical devices to perform calculations; developer of the MARK I computer.

Algorithm A statement of the steps to be followed in solving a problem or performing a process.

Alphanumeric data Another name for textual data.

Alternatives evaluation The third stage of the systems development process in which alternatives for all five components are identified, and one of the alternatives is selected.

American Standard Code for Information Interchange (ASCII) A standard bit pattern using seven bits per byte, traditionally used on smaller computers.

Analog signal Continuous sound signal having a variety of frequencies, like those found in a voice or in music. Contrast with digital signal.

Analytical engine Steam-powered computer designed by Charles Babbage in 1834 that could mechanically compute any function. It had a memory unit and an arithmetic/logic unit. Never built.

Application package A computer program with related manuals, a user's guide, and run instructions.

Application program Program to meet a specific user need—for example, payroll, word processing, inventory, or scheduling.

Arithmetic-logic unit The part of the processing hardware that performs calculations and logical comparisons.

Arithmetic operation Computer processing operations involving adding, subtracting, and other calculations.

Art Any component of a document other than text, including lines, drawings, and photographs.

Artificial intelligence (AI) The use of a computer to perform a task that only humans were previously considered capable of performing.

ASCII *See* American Standard Code for Information Interchange.

Assembler Software that translates assembly language code into machine language.

Assembly language Machine language instructions written mnemonically to aid programmers.

Atanasoff, John V. Pioneer who developed some of the theory behind the first all-electronic computer.

Babbage, Charles Considered by some to be the "father of computing"; designer of analytical and difference engines, steam-powered computers, in the 1820s and 1830s.

Backup procedure Copying data and programs onto an auxiliary disk or other recording medium to protect against loss or damage.

Bar code scanner Machine to read bar codes found on consumer products, used in retail pricing and inventory systems.

Bar graph (graphics) A graph that shows data values as differing lengths of bars.

BASIC *See* Beginner's All-purpose Symbolic Instruction Code.

Batch processing Processing transaction data together in batches to make very efficient use of computer resources.

Baud A term used to describe the speed of a communications line. It measures the number of times a line can change state (as from 1 to 0) in a second. A different and more informative term for business people is bits per second. Line speed in baud is less than or equal to line speed in bits per second.

Beginner's All-purpose Symbolic Instruction Code (BASIC) A programming language developed in the 1960s at Dartmouth College. It is used extensively on microcomputers and in education and small businesses.

Berry, Clifford Graduate student who worked with John V. Atanasoff on the theories for an all-electronic computer.

Binary A number system having two symbols, 0 and 1. Position weights are based on powers of two. Binary is used in computers because zeros and ones are easily represented electronically.

Binary code A pattern of bits used to represent data or instructions in the computer's memory.

Binary digit (bit) The basic building block for computerized data, consisting of a single 0 or 1.

Bit *See* Binary digit.

Bits per second (bps) Measurement of the rate at which data is transmitted over a communications line.

Boot, booting The startup process for a computer or program.

BPS *See* Bits per second.

Bricklin, Dan Designer of the first spreadsheet program named VisiCalc.

Bug An error in a computer program.

Bus architecture A network architecture in which nodes are connected to a single cable that is terminated at each end.

Business information system A collection of computer hardware, programs, data, procedures, and trained personnel that interact to satisfy a specific business information need.

Byte A group of eight bits that can represent one alphanumeric character.

Bytes per inch (bpi) Measure of recording density of magnetic tape. Common tape densities are 800 bpi, 1600 bpi, and 6250 bpi.

C A high-level programming language used for systems and communications programs and most commercial microcomputer programs, such as word processors and spreadsheets.

CAD/CAM *See* Computer-aided design/computer-aided manufacturing.

Carrier sense multiple access with collision detection (CSMA/CD) Protocol used in Ethernet LANs in which each node listens to the carrier (communications signal) continuously. Any node can transmit at any time. If transmissions from two nodes collide, then each stops, waits a brief period, and restarts the transmission.

CASE *See* Computer-aided software engineering.

Cathode ray tube (CRT) A television-like screen used to display computer output.

CD *See* Compact disk.

CD-ROM (Compact disk read-only memory) Laser disk providing very large volume of storage in a compact disk.

Cell (spreadsheet) A location on a spreadsheet at the intersection of a row and a column that holds a single data value.

Central processing unit (CPU) The computer hardware, often on a single chip, that contains the arithmetic-logic unit and control unit.

Character A single letter, digit, or special symbol.

Character-based A display system in which the basic unit of display is 25 rows of 80 display positions, each one of which can display only an ASCII character. A program or operating system that uses a character-based display.

Chip Another name for integrated circuit.

CISC (complex instruction set computer) A computer designed around a large set of complex instructions, in which each instruction may trigger a relatively large task. Contrast with RISC.

Clientele of system The people for whom a system exists; the consumers of the system's services. The clientele of the class enrollment system are students. Clientele for an airline reservation system are airline passengers. Contrast with users.

Clip art Predrawn images supplied on paper or in digital form for use in documents.

Clone A microcomputer designed to work like an IBM PC. A clone can normally run programs intended for the IBM PC.

Coaxial cable High-speed data communications medium consisting of a wire contained inside a shielding of wire mesh to exclude interference from radio signals in the air.

COBOL *See* Common Business-Oriented Language.

Code Program written in a computer programming language.

Codec A device that translates analog (voice) signals to let them be transmitted over a digital data communications line.

Color graphics array (CGA) A relatively inexpensive, low-resolution color display system used in IBM PCs.

COM *See* Computer output microfilm.

Command An instruction to a computer, for example, to run a program or perform a particular operation.

Common Business-Oriented Language (COBOL) A programming language designed in the 1950s to handle business applications. It is the most widely used programming language for business applications on mainframe computers and minicomputers.

Common carrier A company providing data communications services.

Communications channel Medium (such as coaxial cable, microwaves) over which data are transmitted.

Communications support system The portion of an MIS devoted to supporting the interpersonal communications activities of users, usually providing word processing, graphics, E-mail, and other capabilities.

Compact disk A small laser disk primarily used for storing music.

Compatibility The ability of software or peripherals to work on a variety of systems. The ability of data to be processed by two or more different programs.

Compiler A systems program that translates an entire high-level program into machine language so that it can be executed.

Components of a business information system There are five: data, hardware, programs, procedures, personnel.

Computer Equipment used to store and process data according to the steps specified in a program.

Computer-aided design/computer-aided manufacturing (CAD/CAM) The utilization of computers to aid in the design and manufacture of a product.

Computer-aided manufacturing (CAM) Use of computers to control manufacturing equipment.

Computer-aided software engineering (CASE) A methodology and a set of computerized tools to automate the development of applications.

Computer center The physical location of the mainframe computer system, housing the computer hardware, both input and output, and related personnel.

Computer operator Person who starts and runs the computer hardware. In a mainframe computer center, the operator is responsible for the working of the computer and related equipment and is also capable of handling minor equipment emergencies and repairs. In a personal information system, the user also plays the role of operator.

Computer output microfilm (COM) Output data produced as microfilm.

Computer program One of the five components of a business information system. A set of computer instructions designed to control the input, processing, output, and storage performed by a computer. Also known as software.

Computer programmer *See* Programmer.

Concurrent processing The process by which the CPU executes several programs during the same time period, using a system such as time-slicing.

Consolidating spreadsheets Combining the data on two or more spreadsheets into a single spreadsheet, such as combining a series of departmental budgets, each on a spreadsheet, into a corporate budget on another spreadsheet.

Context-sensitive help On-line help provided by a program that displays messages specifically oriented to operations currently being performed by users.

Continuous-tone art Art consisting of complex patterns of dots in many shades, such as paintings and photographs.

Contract programmer Programmer hired by an organization to write a specific program. He/she is not a regular employee of the organization.

Control Procedure that helps reduce illegal or accidental access or changing of data.

Control total Total of some processing value calculated independently of computer processing to verify computer output correctness.

Control unit The part of the CPU that reads and interprets program instructions.

Copy (spreadsheet) The process of duplicating the contents of a cell, row, column, or block of text to another location.

Copy protection Software instructions or device included with some programs to prevent illegal copying.

Core memory An early type of main memory using small ring magnets.

CPU *See* Central processing unit.

Crash Computer failure.

Cray, Seymour Early designer of supercomputers.

CRT *See* Cathode ray tube.

CSMA/CD *See* Carrier sense multiple access with collision detection.

Cursor The flashing box or line on a display that shows where the next character will appear.

Cursor control The use of arrow keys to move the cursor up, down, left, or right through the screen display.

Cut-and-paste A method of moving or copying data in a GUI program in which a block of content is highlighted, its contents moved or copied to a clipboard, and the contents of the clipboard can be inserted (pasted) into another position.

Data One of the five components of a business information system. Raw facts and figures.

Data communications Transmission of data over communications lines.

Data definition language (DDL) A language provided by a DBMS for defining new databases and tables.

Data dictionary A systems development tool that contains the names and structures of all records and files.

Data entry operator A person who enters data into the computer or onto a machine-readable medium.

Data manipulation language (DML) A language provided by a DBMS for manipulating and retrieving data in a database. The most widely used DML is SQL.

Data modeling Designing and documenting the structure of a database to model a particular business process.

Data processing Using computers to process transactions, update master data, and convert data into useful information.

Data storage and retrieval Providing resources to store sets of data and programs and retrieve them in an orderly way.

Database A self-describing collection of integrated records created and accessed through a DBMS.

Database administrator (DBA) The person in charge of designing, implementing, and managing the ongoing operation of a database.

Database management system (DBMS) A program that allows data in a database to be accessed and maintained. It includes a DDL, a DML, and tools to aid in the development of database applications.

Database processing system An information processing system in which data is stored in a single, integrated database.

Dataflow diagram A systems development tool that shows processes, dataflows, and files, and their interfaces.

DBA *See* Database administrator.

DBMS *See* Database management system.

DDL *See* Data definition language.

Deadlock A situation in which two users mutually block the completion of each others' transaction processing, so neither can proceed. To release the deadlock, each processing program must be designed to detect the deadlock, retract the transaction, wait, then reprocess the transaction.

Debugging Finding and eliminating errors in a computer program.

Decimal A number system having ten symbols: 0, 1, 2, 3, 4, 5, 6, 7, 8, and 9. Position weights are based on powers of ten. Humans usually work in decimal.

Decision support system (DSS) The portion of an MIS that provides facilities for answering semistructured ad hoc questions.

Decision symbol Program flowcharting symbol shaped like a diamond indicating a logical decision point.

Default A value that, unless changed by the user, is assumed by a program.

Delete A command used to remove a figure, letter, block of text, or a whole file from disk.

Deliverable A tangible product, usually documentation, scheduled for delivery at the end of a system development stage to verify that the scheduled work was completed.

Design The fourth stage of systems development in which specifications for hardware are developed, program logic is specified, data formats are constructed, procedures are defined, and personnel requirements are determined.

Desktop publishing (DTP) Program to combine text and art into a publication-quality document, such as a brochure, catalog, newsletter, magazine, or book.

Detail report A report based on transaction processing in which an entry appears in the report for each transaction processed.

Development team A group of programmers and systems analysts who work together on the implementation of large projects.

Difference engine A machine designed by Charles Babbage to use a steam engine to compute linear equations.

Digital scanner An input device that scans graphic material and converts it into digital data that can be processed by a graphics program.

Digital signal A signal used in data transmission in which the electricity is instantaneously switched between two values representing 1s and 0s.

Direct access The ability to retrieve and process records immediately from a file regardless of their order without having to read through any intervening records. Also called random access.
Disk A circular platter with concentric tracks that is used as a machine-readable medium.
Disk directory A list on a disk of all the files stored on it. This list is updated and available every time the disk is used.
Disk drive The hardware that spins a disk and positions an access mechanism to locate read/write heads over disk tracks for storing and retrieving data.
Disk Operating System (DOS) A series of systems programs that aid the user in storing, copying, and finding programs on disk, as well as managing the work of the computer.
Disk pack A removable collection of hard disk platters stacked together to allow access and storage of large amounts of data.
Diskette *See* Floppy disk.
Distributed information system A processing system that uses a LAN to interconnect computers for shared access to hardware and data.
DML *See* Data manipulation language.
Documentation Written descriptions of a system, including manuals and a user's guide.
DOS *See* Disk Operating System.
DOS utility One of several programs provided with DOS to perform common disk maintenance functions.
Dot matrix printer An impact printer that forms characters using small dots.
Download Transfer of a program or data from one computer to another. Downloading is commonly from a larger computer to a smaller one.
Downsizing Moving an application from a larger computer to a smaller computer or from a teleprocessing system to a distributed system.
Draw program A program that lets the user manipulate lines and geometric shapes (including very complex shapes) as objects to create charts and drawings.
DSS *See* Decision support system.
Dumb terminal Input/output device containing a keyboard and screen. It has no processing capabilities.
E-mail *See* Electronic mail.
EBCDIC *See* Extended Binary Coded Decimal Interchange Code.
Eckert, J. Presper Codeveloper with John W. Mauchly of the all-electronic computer (ENIAC) and the first commercial computer (UNIVAC I).
Edit To update a text or program by adding, deleting, changing, or moving words, lines, and/or paragraphs.
Editing Programming the computer to check for errors in the input data.
EDP *See* Electronic data processing.
EDP auditor An auditor who specializes in reviewing a company's financial records and procedures that are kept on a computer.
EDP controls Procedures used to reduce the chance of illegal or accidental misuse of any component of a business information system.
Electronic bulletin board A computerized version of a bulletin board that allows users to post messages for others.
Electronic conference A computerized system that lets users simulate a face-to-face conference by sharing access to messages posted by members of the conference.
Electronic data interface (EDI) A system that permits suppliers and buyers to have direct access to portions of each others' databases, including inventory data, to enhance service and deliveries.
Electronic data processing (EDP) An early term for computer processing, used by accountants and auditors.
Electronic mail (E-mail) A system that lets users exchange messages electronically.
Electronic mailbox The personal file or area on disk used to store messages in an electronic mail system.
Electronic Numerical Integrator and Calculator (ENIAC) Built by John Mauchly and J. Presper Eckert, it was the first all-electronic computer.
Electronic spreadsheet A program that allows the user to input rows and columns of data, which can be manipulated and updated through use of spreadsheet functions and commands.
Employee monitoring Using the computer to monitor the work of employees whose jobs relate primarily to computer usage, such as order-entry clerks and airline reservations clerks.
Encryption Encoding data to resist interception by unauthorized persons.
End-user computing Applications where the user is responsible for all aspects of processing: data entry, operations, and using the output.
ENIAC *See* Electronic Numerical Integrator and Calculator.
Entity A person, place, thing, or event about which a business needs to maintain data.
Entity-relationship (E-R) diagram A means of documenting entities and their relationships in data modeling during the development of a database application.
Ergonomics Providing an optimum environment in which work can be completed efficiently and safely.
Error recovery procedure Steps to be taken by people after processing errors occur.
ESS *See* Executive support system.
Ethernet A LAN protocol shared by many vendors using a bus architecture and CSMA/CD.
Exception report A report containing data only about cases that fall outside predefined boundaries, such as accounts where payment is more than 30 days overdue.
Executive support system (ESS) Providing computer support to an organization's top executives. Sometimes called executive information system (EIS).
Expert system A computerized information system that is designed to serve as a substitute for a human consultant in suggesting the most effective course of action within a particular knowledge domain.
Exploded pie chart (graphics) Pie chart in which one piece is separated from the whole for emphasis.
Exponentiation Raising a number to a power or multiplying a number by itself several times; that is, $2^3 = 2 * 2 * 2 = 8$.
Extended Binary Coded Decimal Interchange Code (EBCDIC) A standard code for alphanumeric data traditionally used on mainframe computers.
Facsimile machine Hardware that scans a page, digitizes it, and transmits it by telephone to a remote location, where a copy can be made on paper.
Failure recovery procedure Documented steps to be followed by people when processing failure occurs.
Feasibility evaluation The evaluation of the possibility of satisfying a business need with a computer-based system. Cost, schedule, technical, and political dimensions are considered.
Field A group of characters that represent a single piece of data. A customer's name, address, and phone number are each separate fields.
File A collection of related records; all data about a subject. For example, a

students in a school.

File processing system An information system that maintains a series of separate data files for its various purposes. Contrast with database processing system.

First-generation computers Computers manufactured in the late 1940s and early 1950s using vacuum tubes for processing and memory.

Floating point numbers Numbers represented in a form based on scientific notation. The value of the exponent determines the location of the decimal point; hence the term *floating point*.

Floppy disk A small, flexible disk used to store data.

Floppy disk drive Hardware used to store and retrieve data on a floppy disk. The data is accessed through a window in the disk's cover.

Flowchart A tool used by programmers to document the logic of a program. A flowchart is composed of boxes containing descriptions and arrows indicating flow.

Font A typeface in a particular size and style.

Footer Predefined information to be placed at the bottom of each page of a printout.

Format Facilities to let the user determine font, margins, headers, footers, and other presentation aspects of a final document or spreadsheet.

Formula (spreadsheet) An arithmetic expression entered into a spreadsheet cell. The result appears as the cell's display.

Formula Translator (FORTRAN) A high-level programming language developed for scientific and engineering applications.

Fourth-generation computers Computers with processing hardware characterized by very large scale integrated circuits such as a microprocessor. The current generation.

Fourth-generation language (4GL) Very high-level programming languages that use nonprocedural techniques to help users specify program requirements. Also known as program generators.

Front-end processor A hardware module of a mainframe computer that handles a variety of data communication tasks for the computer, relieving the CPU of those tasks.

Function key One of twelve keys on the typical keyboard used to send special codes for processing by a program.

Gates, Bill Founder of Microsoft Corporation, developer of an early BASIC language system for microcomputers. Currently listed as the richest American.

Geosynchronous orbit The orbit that positions a satellite so it appears motionless above a point on the earth's equator.

Gigabyte A measurement of computer memory or storage capacity equal to one billion bytes.

GIGO (garbage in, garbage out) Rule in data processing that correct output depends on complete and correct input.

Goldstein, Adele Programmer for the ENIAC.

Grammar and style checker Program that detects some kinds of grammatical and stylistic errors in word processing documents.

Graphic display A display in which each screen dot is individually controlled to permit the display of characters in various typefaces, pictures, and other graphics.

Graphics package Application program that allows a user to present data as graphs or charts, and/or do original drawing.

Graphic user interface (GUI) A systems program providing point-and-click command entry. Requires a graphic display and a mouse.

Group decision support system (GDSS) A facility that lets groups of users share access to data and analytical tools in arriving at shared decisions.

Hard copy Output data or information in printed form.

Hard disk A storage system providing rapid direct access to a large volume of data stored in the form of magnetized spots on the surface of one or more inflexible magnetic disks rotating on a common spindle.

Hard disk drive Hardware used to read and write data on a hard disk. The drive accesses hard disks through access arms containing read/write heads.

Hardware One of the five components of a business information system. Computer machinery and associated equipment.

Header Predefined information to be placed at the top of each page of a printout.

Head crash A malfunction of a disk drive, where the read/write head touches the surface of a spinning hard disk and destroys part of the recording medium and its data.

Hexadecimal A number system having 16 symbols: 0, 1, 2, 3, 4, 5, 6, 7, 8, 9, A, B, C, D, E, F. Position weighting is based on powers of 16.

Hierarchical architecture Network architecture in which computers and input/output devices are connected in a hierarchical pattern, like that of a company organization chart.

High-level language A people-oriented programming language, such as COBOL or BASIC, that must be translated into machine language before it can be used by the computer.

High-resolution graphics A way of displaying graphic output using a large number of pixels per screen area that is effective for drawing precise lines and curves.

Hollerith, Herman Inventor who applied punched card technology to census data, thereby starting automated data processing.

Hopper, Grace A mathematician and programmer for the MARK I computer.

Horizontal market program Program designed to meet the general needs of a wide variety of users, such as a word processing or spreadsheet program.

Host Central computer in a teleprocessing system.

Hybrid architecture Network architecture containing a central computer along with one or more LANs and other configurations.

I-beam Distinctive shape of pointer in a GUI system that can be placed between text characters for editing.

IBM personal computer The most widely used type of microcomputer for business applications. Also known as PC.

Icon Pictorial symbol representing data or program function in a GUI system.

Impact printer A printer that produces output by having a hammer strike the paper through an inked ribbon.

Implementation stage The fifth stage of systems development during which the system is constructed, tested, and installed.

Information Knowledge derived by processing data, usually in the form of a printed report or CRT display. Also known as output data.

Information center An organization designed to support end-user computing and provide decision support.

Information system A collection of five components (hardware, programs, data, procedures, and people) that interact to satisfy a business information processing need.

Information utility A company that provides access to information through data communications channels to individuals and companies for a fee.

Ink-jet printer Printer whose mechanism involves small nozzles squirting ink dots to form characters.

Implementation and maintenance The final stage of the systems development process. In this stage the system is constructed, documented, put into operation, and operated over the period of its working life.

Input data Data read into the computer for processing.

Input device Device such as a keyboard that translates data from human-readable form to computer-readable form.

Installation Systems development step involving the set-up and testing of a new system.

Integer Numeric data that does not have a decimal component.

Integrated circuit A complete electrical circuit containing many transistors on a small silicon wafer. Also known as a chip.

Intelligent terminal A microcomputer used as an input/output device in a teleprocessing system.

Interactive Characteristic of hardware or operations involving real-time processing of data and instructions.

Interface A device that converts data signals between different types of equipment.

Jacquard, Joseph Marie Developed use of punched cards to specify weaving patterns on a loom.

Jobs, Steve The man who started the Apple Computer company with Steve Wozniak.

Just-in-time inventory Raw materials arrive in a manufacturing plant just before they are used. This saves inventory and storage costs.

Justification (word processing) To align the right and/or left margins of a document.

K *See* Kilobyte.

Kerning Varying the physical space between letters to make the letters appear to be more evenly spaced, especially in large sizes of proportional typefaces.

Key *See* Key field.

Key field A field in each record of a file that uniquely identifies that record. Also called a key.

Kilobyte (K) A measurement of computer memory equal to 1024 bytes or storage capacity equal to one thousand bytes.

LAN *See* Local area network.

Language translator System program that translates high-level language code into machine language.

Laser disk Very high capacity disk storage, where bit patterns are burned, as small holes, onto the disk surface. Laser disks can store pictures and sound as well as traditional data forms.

Laser printer A nonimpact printer that uses office copier technology to print computer output at relatively high resolution.

Leading Varying the spacing between the lines of type, usually in increments of 1/72 of an inch.

Life cycle Dividing the systems development job into small, organized steps.

Light pen Penlike input hardware that is used to draw directly on a CRT. Its movements are recorded as data.

Line art Art composed of lines and geometric shapes, usually with only a few degrees of shading.

Line graph (graphics) A graphic that uses lines to represent trends in data.

Line MIS The development and operation of shared information systems directly by organizational units other than the MIS department.

Line printer Printer used with mainframe computers and minicomputers that prints an entire line of output in one operation.

Local area network (LAN) A network of computers usually within one building or small area.

Logic bomb A routine placed into a program by a programmer that intentionally causes damage to data or programs under some condition, such as when the programmer is terminated.

Lovelace, Ada Augusta Mathematician who helped explain the theory of Babbage's analytical engine and wrote programs to be performed by it.

Machine language Instructions used by the computer itself. All instructions are reduced to bit patterns. It is not commonly used for application programming. Also called machine code.

Macintosh Apple computer generally considered to have the best-designed GUI available today.

Macro (spreadsheet) A small program built into a spreadsheet that performs a series of instructions. A macro is started by pressing just a few keys.

Magnetic ink character recognition (MICR) Characters used by the banking industry that allow input hardware to read information directly from a check.

Magnetic tape A storage medium for recording data sequentially. Data is recorded as magnetized spots.

Main memory Temporary memory for the data and instructions being processed currently. Programs must be brought into main memory before they can be executed, and data must reside in main memory before it can be processed.

Mainframe computer A large computer used by big businesses and organizations.

Maintenance The updating and reworking of all components of a business information system throughout its lifetime to correct newly discovered errors and accommodate changes in the nature of the data to be processed.

Maintenance programmer A person who modifies programs already in use to correct newly discovered errors and accommodate changes in the nature of the data to be processed.

Management information system (MIS) The collection of all the business information systems used in an organization.

Management reporting system The part of an MIS that produces predefined output reports, usually on a scheduled basis.

Manual file processing The processing of data without the use of computer equipment, usually by writing data values on pages stored in file folders in file cabinets.

MARK I A computer having mechanical counters controlled by electrical devices, developed in 1944.

Mark-sense reader An input device that senses pencil marks on paper and translates these into data values.

Master file Data file containing a company's permanent data records on a particular subject.

Materials requirements planning (MRP) Computer applications in which current inventory and production schedules determine purchase and delivery of additional raw materials.

Mauchly, John W. Codeveloper with J. Presper Eckert of the ENIAC (first all-electronic) and UNIVAC (first commercial) computers.

Megabyte (MB) A measurement of computer memory or storage capacity equal to one million bytes.

Memory *See* Main memory.
Menu A list of available program options that appears on the screen for user selection.
MICR *See* Magnetic ink character recognition.
Microcomputer A small computer, used in homes, schools, and businesses, with processing hardware that is based on a microprocessor.
Microprocessor Processing hardware combining many processing circuits on a small silicon chip. It is the basis for the processing power of the microcomputer.
Microsecond One-millionth of a second; used to measure speed of operations within the computer's processor.
Millions of instructions per second (MIPS) A measurement of processing speed for computers.
Millisecond One-thousandth of a second; used to measure speed of storage systems and other hardware operations.
Minicomputer A medium-sized computer often used in research or to monitor a specific manufacturing process.
MIPS *See* Millions of instructions per second.
MIS *See* Management information system.
Mnemonic A memory aiding device, such as using letters to represent bit patterns, that is the basis of assembler languages.
Model A mathematical simulation or plan representing something requiring a managerial decision.
Modem A device that translates digital (computer) signals to let them be transmitted over voice telephone lines.
Monochrome A screen display limited to one color and black.
Monospace font A typeface in which each character occupies the same amount of space across the line, like typewriter type.
Motherboard A circuit board usually containing a microcomputer's microprocessor, RAM, ROM, clock, and other circuitry.
Mouse Small input device with a rotating ball underneath used to control a pointer on the screen.
MRP *See* Materials requirements planning.
Multiplexer Device that lets several low-speed terminals or other devices share a high-speed channel.
Multitasking Capability of a computer to store and process more than one program during the same period of time.
Nanosecond One-billionth of a second; used to measure speed of operations of main memory.
Network Collection of computers connected by communication lines.
Node A communication station, such as a computer or terminal, within a network.
Nonimpact printer A printer, such as a laser or ink-jet printer, that produces characters through means not involving striking the paper.
Numeric data Data values that contain only digits, decimal point, and sign.
Object oriented Describes an approach to systems design and programming that constructs modules called *objects*, consisting of data and the operations that can be performed on that data.
OCR *See* Optical character recognition.
Online processing Direct input and immediate processing of data in an information system.
Operating system System programs that control the use of the computer's resources, including storage and input/output.
Operations personnel People who start up and operate computer hardware in an information system.
Optical character recognition (OCR) Software that processes digital scanner output or other graphic data to identify sequences of characters contained in the data, for example so the characters can be processed by word processing programs.
Optical disk A form of storage using lasers in data storage and retrieval operations.
Optical fiber Glass fiber data communications medium much finer than a human hair capable of extremely high-speed data communications.
Optical scanner An input device that uses light to read optical marks, bar codes, or marks.
Output Results of computer processing—an image on a CRT, a printed document, or other result.
Output device Hardware used to translate data from computer-readable form to human-readable form, such as printers and screen displays.
Outsourcing Contracting with an outside vendor to provide complete business information systems to a company.
Packet-switching Wide area network protocol in which a message is divided into fixed size parts, or packets, for transmission to a recipient.
Page printer Printer that prints an entire page in a single operation, such as a laser printer.
Paint program (graphics) A program to create and manipulate continuous-tone graphics.
Parallel installation Systems installation method in which the new system is run in parallel with the old one until the new system is shown to be correct and fully operational.
Parallel port Electronic circuitry and a connector usually used for attaching a printer to a microcomputer.
Pascal A high-level, structured programming language developed in the 1970s.
Pascal, Blaise Inventor, in the 1640s, of the first mechanical adding machine.
Password Sequence of data values that must be entered before a system will allow an action to take place, serves as a combination lock on the system.
People One of the five components of a business information system. The key aspect of people is the particular skills that they bring into an information system.
Peripheral device Any online input, output, or storage hardware device used in a computer.
Personal computer A microcomputer system used to meet personal needs.
Phased installation Systems installation in which the system is broken into subsystems, and these subsystems are implemented one at a time.
Pie chart (graphics) A graphic circle divided into slices, each representing a single component's relation to the whole.
Pilot installation Systems implementation in which the using organization is divided into groups, and the system is installed one group at a time.
Pixel One of a matrix of dots that makes up a visual display.
Plotter Output device that draws line art by movement of pen on paper.
Plunge installation Systems implementation in which the old system is abruptly discontinued and the new system replaces it. This is a high-risk implementation method.
Point-and-click A method of selecting computer operations that involves manipulating a mouse to position a pointer on a screen icon and pressing (clicking) the button on the mouse.
Point of sale (POS) terminal A terminal with a cash drawer located at the

point of retail sale and connected to a computer. Replaces cash register.

Port Electronic circuitry and connector on a computer where input or output devices are attached. Also known as an I/O port or input/output port.

POS Point of sale. *See* point of sale terminal.

Presentation graphics Program used to prepare line charts, pie charts, and other images used in business presentations.

Printer Output device that produces hard copy output.

Print server A computer in a LAN that specializes in providing printer access to other computers.

Privacy The right of individuals to control the distribution and use of information about themselves and their actions.

Private branch exchange (PBX) A company's private telephone system, which can be used as an alternative to a LAN for interconnecting computers and other devices.

Problem definition The first stage of systems development. During this stage, the business problem(s) to be solved are identified and documented.

Procedure One of the five components of a business information system. Predefined and documented course of action used by people in a business information system.

Processing The action of a computer on data as it performs calculations or comparisons.

Program One of the five components of a business information system. A set of computer instructions designed to control the input, processing, output, and storage performed by a computer. Also known as software.

Programmer A person who writes instructions for a computer according to set requirements.

Programmer/analyst Person who determines user needs and writes the appropriate programs.

Programming language A particular code for writing instructions for execution by a computer.

Prompt A short indication to the user of the kind of data to be input.

Proportional font A typeface in which various characters occupy different amounts of space across the line.

Protocol Agreed set of rules that two computers follow when communicating with each other.

Prototyping A requirements definition and systems design alternative in which a model, or prototype, of part or all of the system is built and tested.

Public domain software Free programs available to the general public.

Pull-down menu A menu that, when pointed to by keyboard or mouse, expands to show all available options.

Query A question to be answered by accessing database data.

Query by example A method of entering queries by making entries on a form representing the structure of the database to be queried. Entries are translated by the program into corresponding query language commands.

Query language (database) Set of commands provided by a DBMS to store, manipulate, and retrieve data in a database.

RAM *See* Random access memory.

Random access *See* Direct access.

Random access memory (RAM) The technology of today's main memory systems. RAM loses its contents when the power is turned off. Contrast with read-only memory.

Range (spreadsheet) Set of cells to be affected by an operation, specified by the address of cells at opposite corners of the range or by a user-defined symbolic name.

Read-only memory (ROM) Special-purpose memory technology in which the contents of memory are permanently fixed. Loss of power does not affect ROM memory contents. Contrast with random access memory.

Read/write head The mechanism in a tape drive or in a disk drive access arm that reads or writes data.

Record A collection of related fields.

Relational database model Organizes data into tables. Rows are records, and columns represent fields.

Removable hard disk Hard disk module containing an access arm and read/write head in a protective case that can be removed from the drive for transporting data and protecting it from unauthorized access.

Report Program Generator (RPG) A high-level programming language first developed for producing standard reports and now expanded for general business applications.

Report writer (database) A utility program typically provided with a DBMS to define and document predefined report formats for data output.

Request for proposal (RFP) Document describing a problem to be solved and requesting that a vendor propose a set of products and services to solve it and indicate the cost of the proposed solution.

Requirements definition The second stage of the systems development process. During this stage, developers define what the system is supposed to do.

Resolution The sharpness of the image on a display screen, determined by the density of the dots that create the image.

Response time Time elapsed between a user's request and the computer's response.

RFP *See* Request for proposal.

Ring architecture Network architecture in which each node is connected to two other nodes, creating a ring of nodes.

Robotics The use of computers to control machines that move and take physical action.

ROM *See* Read-only memory.

RPG *See* Report Program Generator.

Sans serif typeface Typeface in which character shapes do not include complex curves, flourishes, and cross strokes, giving a clean, contemporary appearance.

Scanner Input device that can translate an image on a page to computerized data that represents the image.

Schema A description of all the data contained in a database.

Scroll Moving a screen window that is capable of showing only a portion of the complete data through a larger text or spreadsheet file. Moving the window down in the file makes the contents of the file slide up on the screen.

SDLC (systems development life cycle) *See* Life cycle.

Search and replace Capability of a word processing program to locate occurrences of a specified phrase and replace each with a specified replacement.

Second-generation computers Computers developed in the late 1950s that used transistors as processing hardware, used core for memory, used an operating system, and were programmed in high-level programming languages.

Sector Subdivision of a track for recording computerized data on a disk.

Semistructured problem A problem in which some parts can be solved by a known procedure using available data and some parts cannot.

Sequential access Retrieving records only in the order in which they physically occur in a file, first to last.

Sequential file A file in which data records are sorted into order by contents of key field and can only be accessed in that order.

Serial port Electronic circuitry and connector often used to attach a modem to a microcomputer.

Serial printer Printer that outputs one character at a time.

Serif typeface Typeface in which character shapes include complex curves, flourishes, and cross strokes, giving a classical, traditional look.

Service technician Person responsible for repairing and installing computer hardware.

Shareware A method of marketing programs in which the program may be copied freely and briefly tested with no charge. If a user continues to use the program beyond a brief test, then the user is obligated to pay a fee to the program author.

Simulation A program that models or mimics a real-life situation through mathematical equations, allowing the user to react without endangering life or property.

Sink A recipient of a dataflow that is outside the system under consideration in a DFD.

Slot Electronic circuitry and connector to plug expansion cards into the motherboard.

Software *See* Program.

Software piracy Copying a program in violation of the license agreement under which the program is used. Many license agreements permit copying purely for backup purposes but not for the purpose of enabling the program to be run on two different computers at the same time.

Sort Program routine that places data into order by a key field identified by the user.

Source An originator of a dataflow that is outside the system under consideration in a DFD.

Source document Form on which data is collected for computer input.

Speech generator Output hardware or program that mimics human speech.

Spelling checker Program module that checks each word in a text against a dictionary—a list of correctly spelled words. Words not found in the dictionary are flagged, and a corrected form may be suggested.

Split screen Display mode in which one part of the screen can display one portion of a document or spreadsheet and another part of the screen can display another portion—or a portion of another document or spread sheet.

Spreadsheet Form in which data values can be entered in rows or columns. *See also* Electronic spreadsheet.

SQL *See* Structured query language.

Star architecture Network architecture in which input/output devices, such as terminals, are connected to a central processing computer. *See also* Teleprocessing system.

Status line (spreadsheet) A line on the screen that indicates the current spreadsheet function.

Stepwise refinement Developing an information system by creating a version that approximately meets the need, evaluating it, improving it, and continuing this cycle until all aspects of the need are completely met.

Storage Devices and media for recording data and programs for long-term retention, often using tape and disk.

String data Programming term for alphanumeric data stored as a sequence of ASCII or EBCDIC character codes.

Structured problem A problem that can be completely solved by known methods using available data.

Structured query language (SQL) The most widely used DML for manipulating and retrieving data in a database.

Subschema A description of the portion of the data in a database that is used by a particular information system.

Summary report Report that summarizes the results of transaction processing, usually in the form of totals, averages, and trends.

Supercomputer A high-speed computer used for matrix manipulations that are common in scientific computations.

Switched line A data communications line that is connected (switched on) by dialing a telephone. The use of standard telephone lines for data communication.

System A collection of elements working together to solve a specific problem.

Systems development life cycle (SDLC) *See* Life cycle.

System programs Class of computer programs that includes operating systems, compilers, utilities, and database management systems.

System test Trying all parts of a business information system under the conditions in which you expect it to work.

Systems analyst A person who works with users to create the five components of new business information systems through the five stages of the systems development life cycle.

Systems programmer A person who installs and tunes systems programs for an organization.

Table A matrix of data organized into rows (fields) and columns (records); used in a database.

Tape A machine-readable medium in which data is stored as magnetic patterns on strips of plastic coated with a metal oxide.

Tape drive Storage device used to access data on tape.

Telecommuting Rather than commuting physically to a workplace, workers remain at or near home and communicate with other workers through communications lines—telephone, computer data communications, facsimile, and other means.

Teleconferencing A conference held between several parties at remote sites through data communications.

Teleprocessing System for shared processing in which all processing is done on a central computer, and users access the processing system through terminals connected to the central computer.

Template The basic design for a spreadsheet or document, with much of the format predefined. A spreadsheet template usually contains labels and formulas, and a user enters data values to activate it. A document template usually contains the formatting specifications, and the user enters text to create a document in the style of the template.

Terminal A device containing at least a keyboard and either a video display or printer that is connected by communication lines to a computer for which it serves as an I/O device. A microcomputer may serve as a terminal if it is under the control of a terminal program.

Testing Searching for errors in systems; verifying that systems do what they are supposed to do.

Text Data consisting of alphanumeric characters organized into words and sentences.

Thesaurus (word processing) Reference source that provides synonyms for a word. An electronic thesaurus is a program that provides this capability.

Third-generation computers Computers developed during the 1960s that uses integrated circuits for processing and memory, usually with multiprogramming and online capabilities.

Time slicing A process by which the CPU allocates small portions of time to each of a set of programs that share memory concurrently.

Touch screen A screen display that also serves as an input device by detecting the screen position of the user's fingertip touch.

Track One of the concentric circles on a disk that stores data.

Transaction A business event about which transaction data is collected for the purpose of updating the organization's master data.

Transaction Processing System (TPS) The portion of an MIS that collects transaction data and processes it to update the organization's master records.

Transborder data flow The transmission of data across national boundaries.

Transistor A small electronic switch that was used in second-generation computers. Integrated circuits, the basic component of today's computers, consist of many transistors on a single chip.

Twisted pair Low-speed data communications medium using telephone wire—fine copper wires twisted about one another to reduce interference from radio waves.

Typeface Family of type fonts based on a single design.

Universal Automatic Computer (UNIVAC I) The first commercial computer, developed in 1950 by John W. Mauchly and J. Presper Eckert.

Unstructured problem Problem in which no aspect can be solved by known methods using available data.

Updating Adding, deleting, or changing records in a disk or tape file.

User Person who interacts directly with a business information system, usually by preparing data for input or directly using the system's output.

User friendly Programs that are self-explanatory and easy to use.

Utility program Operating system programs that perform common functions such as sorting and merging files, copying files, and so on.

Vacuum tube A glass tube containing circuitry, which was the processing basis for first-generation computers.

Vertical market program Program designed to meet the specific needs of a particular type of user or business organization, such as a motorcycle dealership parts inventory control system or a dental office scheduling and billing system.

Video display terminal (VDT) A terminal that provides a video display rather than hard copy output.

View *See* Subschema.

Virtual memory The use of disk storage to supplement memory, permitting a program larger than available memory to be executed.

Virus A program routine capable of writing copies of itself onto storage media and communicating copies of itself through networks with the ultimate goal of infesting as many computers as possible. At some later time, viruses typically act to damage data stored or processed on infected computers.

Voice grade data communications line Low-speed transmission line designed to carry analog signals; telephone line.

Voice output Computer output that mimics the human voice.

Voice recognition device Input hardware that accepts spoken words as data.

Volatile memory Memory whose contents are erased when power is lost; RAM.

von Neumann, John Mathematician who developed the basic design of today's electronic digital computer with the program stored in memory.

Wide area network Network connecting nodes in geographically separated locations, usually operated by a common carrier.

Window A section of the screen devoted to a particular set of output.

Word processing Using computer technology to prepare letters, memos, and other documents.

Word processing program Program to assist a user in writing, editing, formatting, and printing text.

Word size The number of bits of data that can be processed in a single processing step by a processor.

Word wrap (word processing) A document is entered without carriage returns at the end of each line. The word processor senses margins and moves the cursor to the next line when necessary.

Wozniak, Steve Started Apple Computer company with Steve Jobs by building and marketing the Apple computer. Later they formed Apple Corporation.

Write protect A method of locking a disk or tape to prevent write operations on that medium.

WYSIWYG (What You See Is What You Get) Feature of word processing programs, spreadsheet programs, and other software that shows on the screen exactly what will be printed.

Credits

PHOTOS

1-9 Houston Industries, Inc.; **2-2, 2-3, 2-8, 2-11, 2-14, 2-16, 2-17, 2-18, 2-20, 2-21, 2-38, 3-1, 3-3, 3-4, 3-8, 3-10, 3-12, 3-13, 3-14, 4-20, 4-28, 5-4, 5-13, 5-17, 5-27, 6-28, 7-1, 8-5, 9-17, 9-22, 10-4, 10-18, 10-19, 12-16, 12-17** IBM; **2-9** Cray Research, Inc.; **2-10, 2-22, 2-23, 2-40, 3-18, 4-6, 4-30, 4-31, 6-1, 7-16, 8-7, 8-21, 8-24, 9-23, 12-27** Hewlett-Packard; **2-12** Burger King; **2-15** National Semiconductor; **2-26** Federal Bureau of Investigation; **pp. 46–47** Chuck O'Rear; **3-9** Photo Tscherniak/The Computer Museum; **3-2, 3-11, 3-17, 3-19, 3-27, 4-32, 6-22, 8-6** Apple Computer, Inc.; **3-16** Logitech; **3-22** Plus Development Corp.; **3-24a & b** Hayes Microcomputer Products, Inc.; **3-28** Tektronix; **3-32** Corel; **4-1** Adobe Systems, Inc.; **4-21a & b** WordPerfect; **4-23** 3-M; **4-24** ISSCO; **4-27** © 1985 Vibeke Sorensen; **4-28** Autodesk; **4-29** Hitachi, Ltd.; **4-33** Sun Microsystems; **6-7** Circuit City; **6-10** Paradox; **6-11** Decision Resources; **7-11** Computerland Corp; **8-2** Northgate Computer Systems Inc.; **9-7, 9-8, 9-10** AT&T; **12-2** American Airlines; **12-13** © Steven Meckler, University of Arizona.

MINICASES

Chapter 1 (page 24) "High-Tech Rx for Profits," by Ronald Henkoff, *Fortune*, March 23, 1992. Copyright © 1992 Time Inc. All rights reserved.

Chapter 2 (page 69) "McKesson Cuts Costs with Wireless Scanner," by Alice LaPlante, *InfoWorld*, May 25, 1992. Copyright © 1992 by InfoWorld Publishing Corp., a subsidiary of IDG Communications, Inc. Reprinted from *InfoWorld*, 155 Bovet Road, San Mateo, CA 94402. Further reproduction is prohibited.

Chapter 3 (page 113) "Microsoft Nails Some Pirates," by Harriet King, *New York Times*, May 10, 1992. Copyright © 1992 by the New York Times Company. Reprinted by permission.

Chapter 4 (page 152) "Scanning the Past," by David M. Buerge, *Aldus Magazine*, May/June, 1992.

Chapter 5 (page 196) "International Spreadsheets," *View* (Microsoft), May 1992.

Chapter 6 (page 233) "Artist Tracks Customers with Database Application," interview with Beth Farrell.

Chapter 7 (page 260) "Product Evaluation: Back-up Software," by Tom Bigley, *InfoWorld*, June 1, 1992. Copyright © 1992 by InfoWorld Publishing Corp., a subsidiary of IDG Communications, Inc. Reprinted from *InfoWorld*, 155 Bovet Road, San Mateo, CA 94402. Further reproduction is prohibited.

Chapter 8 (page 296) "Networked PCs Become a Crime-Fighting Tool in New York," by Alice LaPlante, *InfoWorld*, May 25, 1992. Copyright © 1992 by InfoWorld Publishing Corp., a subsidiary of IDG Communications, Inc. Reprinted from *InfoWorld*, 155 Bovet Road, San Mateo, CA 94402. Further reproduction is prohibited.

Chapter 9 (page 334) "The 'Fed-Ex' Mentality: Has all our work really become 'extremely urgent'?" by Steve Hannaford, *Aldus Magazine*, May/June, 1992.

Chapter 10 (page 364) "Eastman Kodak's DB2 Access Using PC-Based Oracle Tools," by Karen Hemmenway Schuh, from "Agreeing to Disagree," *Database Programming and Design*, September 1991. Copyright © Database Programming & Design, Vol. 4, No. 9. Reprinted with permission of Miller Freeman Publications Inc.

Chapter 11 (page 396) "IS Professionals Combine Talents to Create Their Own Niche," by Alice LaPlante, *InfoWorld*, June 1, 1992. Copyright © 1992 by InfoWorld Publishing Corp., a subsidiary of IDG Communications, Inc. Reprinted from *InfoWorld*, 155 Bovet Road, San Mateo, CA 94402. Further reproduction is prohibited.

Chapter 12 (page 440) "Kennametal Finds the Right Tools," by Barnaby J. Feder, *New York Times*, May 6, 1992. Copyright © 1992 by The New York Times Company. Reprinted by permission.

INCREASING YOUR PERSONAL PRODUCTIVITY

Box 1.1 (page 10) *InfoWorld*, May 25, 1992; **Box 1.2** (page 16) *Time*, May 18, 1992; **Box 2.1** (page 34) *PC World*, April 1992; **Box 3.1** (page 82) *INC.*, May 1991; **Box 3.2** (page 94) *InfoWorld*, June 8, 1992; **Box 4.1** (page 132) *PC World*, April 1992; **Box 4.2** (page 141) Arnold, *Computers in Society: Impact* (McGraw-Hill, 1991); **Box 5.1** (page 171) *Personal Computing*; **Box 5.2** (page 182) *PC Magazine*, September 27, 1988; **Box 6.1** (page 214) *PC World*, July 1992; **Box 6.2** (page 224) *InfoWorld*, January 22, 1990; **Box 7.1** (page 244) *PC Week*, April 27, 1992; **Box 7.2** (page 257) *PC World*, April 1991; **Box 8.1** (page 227) *Business Week*, January 27, 1992; **Box 8.2** (page 285) Grauer, *Microcomputer Applications, 2nd Ed.* (McGraw-Hill, 1991); **Box 9.1** (page 307) *InfoWorld*, February 1992; **Box 9.2** (page 310) *PC World*, March 1991; **Box 10.1** (page 351) *MacWEEK*, April 27, 1992; **Box 10.2** (page 358) *InfoWorld*, September 9, 1991; **Box 11.1** (page 372) *Communications of the ACM*, June 1987; **Box 11.2** (page 389) *DPMA*; **Box 12.1** (page 406) *Byte*, June 1992; **Box 12.2** (page 427) *InformationWeek*, June 8, 1992.

Index